Sir Philip Magnus-Allcroft, M.A., F.R.S.L., was
educated at Westminster School and Wadham
College, Oxford. After a period as a Civil Servant,
he served during the Second World War as a
Major in the Royal Artillery and the Intelligence
Corps in Iceland and Italy. In 1943 he married
Jewell Allcroft.

Sir Philip and Lady Magnus-Allcroft live in
Shropshire, in a Victorian Elizabethan house
with splendid views. It is close to the famous
thirteenth-century Stokesay Castle which they
also own and open to the public.

Sir Philip is a J.P. for Shropshire, and has been
Chairman of the Planning and Records Committees of the Shropshire County Council. His well-
known books include *Edmund Burke – A Prophet
of the Eighteenth Century*, *Gladstone: a Biography*, and *Kitchener – Portrait of an Imperialist*.

Sir Philip Magnus-Allcroft was awarded the
C.B.E. in 1971.

KING
EDWARD
THE
SEVENTH

Philip Magnus

Penguin Books

Penguin Books Ltd, Harmondsworth,
Middlesex, England
Penguin Books, 625 Madison Avenue,
New York, New York 10022, U.S.A.
Penguin Books Australia Ltd, Ringwood,
Victoria, Australia
Penguin Books Canada Limited, 2801 John Street,
Markham, Ontario, Canada L3R 1B4
Penguin Books (N.Z.) Ltd, 182–190 Wairau Road,
Auckland 10, New Zealand

First published in Great Britain by
John Murray 1964
First published in the United States of America by
E. P. Dutton 1964
Published in Penguin Books in Great Britain 1967
Reprinted 1975 (twice)
Published in Penguin Books in the United States of America 1979

Printed in the United States of America by
Offset Paperback Mfrs., Inc., Dallas, Pennsylvania
Set in Linotype Georgian

To My Wife

Contents

Illustrations

[1] *By gracious permission of Her Majesty The Queen*

[2] *Gernsheim Collection*

[3] *Radio Times Hulton Picture Library*

Author's Note

THE nine troubled years of the reign of Edward VII were no mere pendant to the long Victorian Age. The land's surface glowed with a splendour which suggested serenity, but seismic faults had developed below, and the Edwardian Age is characterized by a rapidly accelerating process of economic, social and political disturbance. The nations of Europe were convulsed by urgent and sometimes insoluble problems which drove King Edward in depressed moods to toy with thoughts of abdication, and which plunged the entire world later into an epoch of revolutionary upheaval.

Untrained in affairs of State at his accession, King Edward displayed an iron resolve to do his duty. Interested primarily in foreign policy and the armed services, his influence was exerted most effectively and forcefully in the Royal Navy; but he loved to be consulted about the widest possible range of official, social and other detail. His papers in consequence are remarkably varied as well as voluminous; and by gracious permission of Her Majesty the Queen, I was accorded unrestricted access to all relevant material in the Royal Archives when I undertook this work.

So much of that material is illuminating that it may seem invidious to particularize, but nine categories of documents at Windsor have been especially helpful:

(1) Papers dealing with the education of King Edward when Prince of Wales.

(2) The early correspondence of the Prince of Wales with his parents.

(3) Queen Victoria's diary.

(4) Typed extracts from the correspondence, owned by Prince Wolfgang of Hesse, between Queen Victoria and her eldest child, the German Empress Frederick.

(5) King Edward's diary written entirely in his own hand since boyhood. A few volumes are missing, perhaps as a consequence of the fire at Sandringham on 1 November 1891. Used partly as an

engagement book and partly as a record of such dull regular factual
items as game bags and horse-race results, the diary lists other
matters also with very rare and brief comment. Those matters consist of deaths, unusual incidents and houses and places visited, as
well as lists of names of people whom he met at dinner in England and abroad, and of the principal individuals whom he received,
or upon whom he called, on the great majority of all the crowded
days of a uniquely gregarious social life.

(6) King Edward's letters to his son Prince George, who became,
successively, Duke of York, Prince of Wales, and King George V.
The father doted upon that son, and their happy relationship, which
resembled that of brothers, was the most satisfying personal experience of King Edward's life.

(7) Official and personal correspondence with ministers during the
reign.

(8) Cabinet documents, reports and memoranda.

(9) Reports sent daily to King Edward, while the House of Commons was in session, by the Prime Minister, or Leader of that House.

I am indebted to a number of owners of collections of unpublished papers for their kindness in according me unrestricted
access to all relevant material in their archives. I express gratitude, accordingly, to Sir William Dyke Acland (Acland Papers);
Lady Phyllis Benton (Paget Papers); Mr Mark Bonham Carter
and The Keeper of Western Manuscripts, Bodleian Library,
Oxford (Asquith Papers); Lord Cadogan (Cadogan Papers);
Lady Crewe (Crewe Papers); the Duke of Devonshire (Chatsworth Papers); Lord Esher (Esher Papers); the late Lord Hardinge of Penshurst (Hardinge Papers); Prince Wolfgang of
Hesse (correspondence between Queen Victoria and the Empress Frederick); Brigadier A. W. P. Llewellen Palmer (Lincolnshire Papers); Mrs M. H. Prance (Gibbs Papers); Lord Salisbury
(Salisbury Papers); and the Council of the Royal College of
Surgeons (account by Sir Frederick Treves of the operation
which he performed on King Edward in 1902).

The 'Reference Notes' at the end of this volume will guide
readers to all material from which I have quoted, or upon which
I have drawn, in the Royal Archives and in other collections
of unpublished papers, as well as in published works. I have not
considered that it would be helpful to include a bibliography of
published works. Aspects of Edward VII, as Prince of Wales
and as King, are described in an immense number of books of
many kinds; and three which I have found epecially interesting
are:

(1) The monumental two-volume official biography (1925–7) by Sir Sidney Lee. This work, which is packed with information, was completed by Mr S. F. Markham.

(2) *Henry Ponsonby. His Life from his Letters* (1942) by his son, Arthur Ponsonby (Lord Ponsonby of Shulbrede). In the continuing absence of any official biography of Queen Victoria, this portrait of her private secretary provides also, I think, the best sketch of the personality of the Sovereign whose example King Edward did his utmost to follow, so far as his different temperament and the changing circumstances would allow.

(3) *Recollections of Three Reigns* (1951) by Sir Frederick Ponsonby (Lord Sysonby). This indiscreet volume of memoirs by King Edward's assistant private secretary provides a vivid sketch of the personality of Edward VII.

I have shrunk from the idea of compiling a list of names of the very large number of other people to whom I am indebted for kindness, guidance and much useful information. I abandoned the attempt because the full list appeared pretentious to me, and because I could see no satisfactory way of overcoming that difficulty; but I have thanked everyone personally and hope that present silence will not be construed as ingratitude. I cannot refrain, nevertheless, from recording a warm sense of obligation to Mr H. R. Creswick, librarian of Cambridge University; Helen, Lady Hardinge of Penshurst; Sir Shane Leslie; Dr John Mason, librarian of Christ Church, Oxford; Sir Owen Morshead; Sir Harold Nicolson; the late Lady Nicolson (Victoria Sackville-West); Miss Enid Price-Hill; and Sir Anthony Wagner for his help on the genealogical tables.

I express finally gratitude for special kindness to Mr Robert Blake, who read my typescript and who advised me most generously; Mr Robert Mackworth-Young, librarian at Windsor Castle, with whom it has been a delight to work and to converse; Mr John Murray, my old friend and publisher, whom no demand or difficulty has ever appeared to ruffle; and Mrs G. M. Thorne, my patient typist, whose efficiency is matched only by her unfailing cheerfulness.

P.M.

Stokesay Court
Onibury, Shropshire

1

Educational Experiment

1841–56

WHEN resuming her diary (2 December 1841), Queen Victoria recorded[1] that her sufferings on the morning of 9 November had been 'very severe, and I don't know what I should have done but for the great comfort and support my beloved Albert was to me during the whole time. At last, at 12 m. to 11, I gave birth to a fine large Boy. . . . It was taken to the Ministers for them to see.' A daughter, Victoria, the Princess Royal, had been born a year earlier, but the infant Prince became heir automatically to his mother's throne.

British sovereigns before Victoria were expected not merely to reign but to rule; and the degree of authority which they exercised depended upon personal factors. It had varied with every king and with every administration, but the growing volume and complexity of business caused a remarkable transfer of initiative from Windsor to Downing Street during the reign of George III. It remained true, nevertheless, that whenever the sovereign failed to decide policy, or to choose ministers to carry it out, the fault lay in himself – in some infirmity of mind or character – and not in the spirit of the constitution or the temper of his subjects.

By 1841 that spirit and temper had changed. The industrial revolution reinforcing the effects of the American and French revolutions had released a great body of doctrines and objectives which competed for the support of an increasingly aroused and informed public opinion. Parliament could not reflect that new democratic opinion effectively and continuously without the aid of disciplined Parties, which became securely based, after a series of extensions of the franchise (1832, 1867, 1884), upon a numerous electorate thinking and voting for the first time in British history in nation-wide political terms.

Party leaders contending about political issues could fill the office of prime minister in turn, but a king who sought to continue to control the executive would have been placed in an untenable position by the revised rules of the game. He would have been compelled either to incur the risk and odium of leading a Party himself, or to jettison principle, pass freely from one side to the other, 'and in turn captain opposite teams'.[2] That dilemma was insoluble unless a republic were established, or unless the sovereign withdrew from the political arena.

During the early years of her reign, Queen Victoria used to complain[3] that 'she could hardly avoid feeling guilty of dishonesty in giving her confidence suddenly to persons who had been acting in opposition to those to whom she had hitherto given it'; and she consulted her confidential adviser, Christian von Stockmar. He advised[4] the Queen's husband, Prince Albert (27 December 1845), that 'in reference to the Crown, the secret is simply this. Since 1830 the executive power has been entirely in the hands of the Ministry.'

An unwritten constitution depends for its smooth working upon good feeling and good sense. Conventions must never be defined so precisely as to be made incapable of further development; and a few days before her son was born Lord Melbourne advised[5] Queen Victoria that the 'Ministerial' part of the constitution, 'the work of conducting the executive government, has rested so much on practice, on usage, on understanding, that there is no publication to which reference can be made for the explanation or description of it. It is to be sought in debates, in protests, in letters, in memoirs, and wherever it can be picked up.'

Where so much flexibility existed, Prince Albert, upon whom the title of Prince Consort was conferred in 1857, proceeded to harness the Queen's magnificent sense of duty, and his own, to the task of exalting the personal power and influence of the Monarchy as a cautionary department of State, in compensation for positions which had been lost.

Believing that that was the best means of preventing the Crown from being submerged beneath the rising democratic tide, he informed[6] Stockmar (6 January 1846) that 'the exaltation of Royalty is possible only through the personal character of the Sovereign. When a person enjoys complete confidence, we desire for him more power and influence in the conduct of affairs. But confidence is of slow growth.'

For that reason the Prince Consort devised for his eldest son an educational plan of unparalleled rigour which made no allowance for human weakness. It was intended to prepare the future sovereign for survival in a harsh democratic climate; but, contrary to expectation, that climate proved to be warm and genial. Eager to make every possible allowance for human nature, the new British democracy accepted, casually and characteristically, as authoritative, an amateur's definition of the altered relationship between the sovereign and the executive. It occurred in Walter Bagehot's popular account of *The English Constitution* (1867): 'To state the matter shortly, the Sovereign has, under a constitutional monarchy such as ours, three rights – the right to be consulted, the right to encourage, the right to warn. And a king of great sense and sagacity would want no others.'

Queen Victoria and her son fought in turn against those limitations; but the Crown was transformed, nevertheless, into a human symbol of authority which its wearer cannot exercise personally, and which, as an article of faith, defies rational analysis. As such it has satisfied a psychological need; and that pattern of sovereignty to which the infant Prince was heir has adapted itself continuously to all changes in the British social climate.

The Prince was born into a family of almost wholly German ancestry which formed part of a European royal caste; and, like the gold standard in the economic field, that caste was believed to afford a guarantee of political and social stability. For many years after the overthrow of the great Napoleon, the European upper class equated stability with the principle of legitimacy; but most members of European royal families suffered from an occupational handicap.

Screened from the world by attendant clouds of ladies and
gentlemen who edited the impressions which they received,
their personalities often failed to become fully adult.

Queen Victoria's eldest son was endowed with so robust a
personality that he was exceptionally successful in bursting
early through a screen which was unusually strong and thick.
Created Prince of Wales on 4 December, he was christened,
Albert Edward, by the Archbishop of Canterbury, William
Howley, in St George's Chapel, Windsor, on 25 January 1842.
Handel's Hallelujah Chorus was played on the organ; the
great Duke of Wellington carried the Sword of State; and
the costly presents distributed by King Frederick William
IV of Prussia, who ruled, as a despot, the least important of
the five European Great Powers, proved the immense satis-
faction which he felt at being invited, as a godparent, to
Windsor.

Every detail of that impressive ceremony was arranged by
Prince Albert, who had been born, like the Queen, in 1819.
He was the younger son of Duke Ernest of Saxe-Coburg-
Gotha, who reigned over a territory which was about the
size of the English county of Staffordshire. Duke Ernest's
sister, the Duchess of Kent, was Queen Victoria's mother, so
that the Prince of Wales's parents were first cousins; and
Prince Albert's mother, the Duchess of Coburg, had been
divorced by her husband in March, 1826.

The Duchess, who married her lover, Alexander von Han-
stein (Count von Polzig-Baiersdorf), a few months later, had
died prematurely in 1831; and half a century later rumours
were circulated, for the first time, that her younger son,
Prince Albert, had been the offspring of an earlier liaison
which his mother was alleged, on no evidence, to have
formed with a chamberlain of Jewish extraction, Baron von
Meyern, at the Court of Coburg. There is no truth behind
these stories, and the unlucky Duchess, in whose memory
Queen Victoria named her sixth child, Princess Louise, appears to have remained consistently faithful to her neglectful
and promiscuous husband before, as well as for some years
after, the birth of Prince Albert.

Queen Victoria and Prince Albert were preoccupied, even

before they started a nursery, with the problem of their children's education; and they placed unlimited confidence in the guidance of their intimate counsellor and friend, Baron von Stockmar, who had been born in Coburg in 1787. After being trained as a doctor, Stockmar had devoted his life to serving the interests of the Coburg family; and he played a great part in negotiating the successful establishment of Prince Leopold of Coburg (Duke Ernest's younger brother) upon the newly created throne of Belgium in 1831.

Thereafter Stockmar extended his interest and protection to King Leopold's very handsome nephew, Prince Albert, whom he accompanied on a year's tour of Italy. He was unmarried and somewhat pedantic but upright, capable and loyal; and his devotion to Prince Albert won Queen Victoria's undying gratitude. 'Nowhere in the records of history has Royalty been served with a devotion so purely noble and unselfish as that of this remarkable man to the Queen and the Prince', wrote [7] Sir Theodore Martin in *The Life of the Prince Consort*, which was published in 1875 with the Queen's active cooperation; and after playing a great part in bringing Queen Victoria and Prince Albert together, and in arranging their marriage, the Baron was allotted a permanent suite of rooms at Buckingham Palace.

Flitting constantly between London, Brussels and Coburg, Stockmar's influence was unchallenged in the British royal nurseries, which grew to include four princes and five princesses between 1840 and 1857, and he was much the strongest influence in shaping the pattern of the Prince of Wales's youth. Starting from the exalted premise that the best hope of saving Europe, from the dangers threatening it in a democratic age, was a new race of enlightened princes, Stockmar attributed to defective education all the glaring errors committed by the sons of George III. He warned [8] Queen Victoria that those errors had 'contributed more than any other circumstance to weaken the respect and influence of Royalty in this country'; and the treadmill devised for the future King Edward VII was a vicarious atonement for the wickedness of George IV.

Queen Victoria, who had been brought up among adults

by her widowed mother, recorded [9] (29 July 1845) that she had been 'extremely crushed and kept under, and hardly dared say a word'; and Prince Albert, who was once described [10] succinctly by his grandson King George V as 'an intellectual', had been bred to a life of studious contemplation by a relentless mechanical time-table in the sham Gothic castle of Rosenau and at Bonn University. Both parents were so much impressed by the corrupting influence of British frivolity that any idea of sending their children to school would have been unthinkable.

Many eminent men were consulted about the education of the Prince of Wales, after Stockmar had warned [11] the Queen and Prince Albert that they were too young to direct it and that it was their 'sacred duty' to follow the advice of more experienced persons; and the Bishop of Oxford, Samuel Wilberforce, suggested [12] that 'the great object in view is to make him the most perfect man'. Other replies were equally platitudinous, and Lord Melbourne sounded the only astringent note. He wrote [13] (1 December 1841) to the Queen: 'Be not over solicitous about education. It may be able to do much, but it does not do as much as is expected from it. It may mould and direct the character, but it rarely alters it.'

That worldly advice went unheeded, and the Prince of Wales was made the unhappy subject of a proud educational experiment which was superbly characteristic of its age. An attempt was made to mould him, in isolation from his contemporaries, into a moral and intellectual paragon. 'Reason' illuminated by 'the lights of science', and 'a sound morality' founded upon 'the deductions of philosophy' and not upon 'mere religious belief', were the goals at which Stockmar aimed; and he elaborated those themes for the enlightenment of the royal parents in a series of nebulous memoranda [14] composed between 1842 and 1848.

Stockmar asked that the tutor to the Prince of Wales should not be a clergyman, but a man of scientific leanings attuned to 'the spirit of the age'. It would be his duty to ensure that the Prince of Wales, as the future 'executive Governor of the State', became 'the repository of all the moral and intellectual qualities by which it is held together and under the guidance of which it advances in the great path of civilization'. Stockmar concluded that the Prince of Wales's education should 'in no wise tend to make him a demagogue, but a man of calm, profound, comprehensive understanding, with a deep conviction of the indispensable necessity of practical morality to the welfare of the Sovereign and People'.

Henry Birch, aged thirty, who had been captain of the school at Eton and a master there for four years, after taking four university prizes at King's College, Cambridge, was selected in April 1849, at the end of a year's anxious search, to serve, at an annual salary of eight hundred pounds, as principal tutor to the Prince of Wales. The Prince was lifted from the nursery at the age of seven and a half and handed over to a team of tutors headed by Birch; and a call, which Birch experienced soon afterwards to take Holy Orders, embarrassed Stockmar. The Queen suggested [15] (26 November 1849) that it would not matter, if he promised not to be 'aggressive', and if he promised also to attend Presbyterian services in Scotland and to continue to participate in 'innocent amusements' – shooting, dancing and theatricals. Prince Albert insisted,[16] however, that entry into the Church should be deferred, in case Birch was tempted to attach greater importance to what he might consider that he owed to his cloth than to what the royal parents and Stockmar might consider best for the Prince of Wales's education.

Pretty and delicately featured, the Prince of Wales had been taught English, French and German previously by three mistresses who reported progress daily through the governess, Lady Lyttelton, to Prince Albert. In that way, although he never rid himself of a German burr when pronouncing the letter 'r', the boy had been brought up successfully to be trilingual.

Although suffering in the nursery from unfavourable comparison with his precocious eldest sister 'Vicky', the Princess Royal, who was her father's favourite, the Prince of Wales, who was called 'Bertie' in his family, had been quite happy. 'There is much good in him', Queen Victoria

noted [17] in her diary on his ninth birthday. 'He has such
affectionate feeling – great truthfulness and great simplicity
of character.' Influenced by Prince Albert, she made resolution to initiate her heir as early as possible into affairs of
State; and she recorded [18] (12 December 1847):

> We talked of Vicky and Bertie, Albert saying the latter ought
> to be accustomed early to work with and for us, to have great
> confidence shewn him, that he should early be initiated into
> the affairs of State. How true this is! So wise and right; and the
> more confidence we shew him the better it will be for himself,
> for us, and for the country.

That resolution was never implemented, and storm-clouds
gathered early around the head of the young Prince of
Wales. Every week-day, including Saturday, was divided
into five hourly or half-hourly periods, during which Birch
taught Calculating, Geography and English; while other
masters, who were expert in their fields and who reported
daily through Birch to Prince Albert, taught Religion,
German, French, Handwriting, Drawing and Music. Lessons were never discontinued entirely for more than a few
days at a time, and the Prince of Wales enjoyed shorter
holidays, and worked under more intense pressure, than any
schoolboy in the land. Family birthdays were, however,
treated invariably as holidays, and some relaxation of pressure occurred whenever a movement of the Court from
London or from Windsor caused some subject or subjects
to be dropped temporarily, owing to the difficulty of securing
the daily attendance of one or more specialist masters.

Three years later (25 February 1852), after he had taken
Holy Orders and resigned his appointment, Birch summarized [19] his impressions of the Prince of Wales for Prince
Albert. He had at first found his pupil to be 'extremely dis-
obedient, impertinent to his masters and unwilling to submit to discipline'. The boy had been extraordinarily selfish
and unable even to 'play at any game for five minutes, or
attempt anything new or difficult, without losing his temper'.
He could not endure chaff or interference of any kind, 'but
I thought it better, notwithstanding his sensitivenesss, to
laugh at him ... and to treat him as I know that boys would

have treated him at an English public school, and as I was treated myself'.

Although 'severe punishment' had had to be inflicted from time to time, Birch's plan had appeared to answer well, 'and for the last year and a half I saw *numerous* traits of a very amiable and affectionate disposition'. It had, however, been 'almost impossible to follow out any thoroughly systematic plan of management or thoroughly regular course of study' because 'the Prince of Wales was so different on different days'. The Prince had continued periodically to display symptoms of dumb insolence or mental collapse, during which he had declined to answer questions to which he knew the answers perfectly well; but he had 'always evinced a most forgiving disposition after I had had occasion to complain of him to his parents, or to punish him. He has a very keen perception of right and wrong, a very good memory, very singular powers of observation.'

Birch recorded his 'deliberate opinion' that many of the Prince of Wales's 'peculiarities arise from want of contact with boys of his own age, and from his being continually in the society of older persons, and from his finding himself the centre round which everything seems to move. ... He has no standard by which to measure his own powers. His brother [Prince Alfred] is much too young and too yielding, and nothing that a tutor can say, or even a parent, has such influence as intercourse with sensible boys of the same age, or a little older, unconsciously teaching by example. I always found that boys' characters at Eton were formed as much by contact with others as by the precepts of their tutors.'

Under a glare of expectant watchfulness directed from all angles at his every thought, word and act, the young Prince was in fact being starved of the encouragement and comradeship which his nature craved, as well as of the indispensable lubricant of competition. Birch concluded, nevertheless, that there was every reason to hope 'that the Prince of Wales will eventually turn out a *good* and, in my humble opinion, a *great* man'.

Birch left Windsor Castle on 21 January 1852, six days

after his successor, Frederick Waymouth Gibbs, had arrived.
Gibbs noted in his diary [20] (21 January) that 'the Prince of
Wales thought it necessary to make a sort of apology in his
walk for his sorrow: "You cannot wonder if we are somewhat dull to-day. We are sorry Mr Birch is gone. It is
very natural, is it not?" The Prince is conscious of owing a
great deal to Mr Birch and really loves and respects
him.'

Gibbs, who was aged twenty-nine, had accepted six
months earlier Prince Albert's offer that he should succeed
Birch as tutor to the Prince of Wales and Prince Alfred
at an annual salary of one thousand pounds, 'with any addition to that sum which Baron Stockmar may decide to be
just and reasonable'. Gibbs's mother had become hopelessly
insane, and his father, a dissenter, who had suffered financial
ruin, lived on a small allowance from rich relations. For
those reasons their only surviving child had been brought
up since his seventh year by Mrs Gibbs's old friend, Sir
James Stephen, who was Professor of Modern History at
Cambridge University, of which Prince Albert was Chancellor.

Baptized formally into the Church of England on his
nineteenth birthday, Gibbs had done well at Cambridge,
where he became a Fellow of Trinity College before being
called to the Bar. Sir James Stephen informed [21] Prince
Albert (22 June 1851) that Gibbs's 'family collectively may
be described as belonging to that section of the middle
ranks of English Society which supplies the City of London
with the majority of its Brokers, Westminster Hall with
the majority of Barristers, and Oxford and Cambridge with
the majority of successful students'. Prince Albert approved
warmly of that class, and Gibbs, who was really hated by
the Prince of Wales, held his new post for seven years before
retiring, as a Companion of the Bath and with an annual
pension of eight hundred pounds, to a very moderate
practice on the Northern Circuit.*

Serving 'in exact obedience and subordination' to Prince

* He was made a Queen's Counsel in 1880 and died unmarried in
1898.

Albert, Gibbs extended the Prince of Wales's lessons immediately to include six and, at one time, seven hourly periods between eight o'clock in the morning and seven o'clock in the evening on six days a week. He was ordered to ensure that the Prince of Wales and Prince Alfred were tired out physically at the end of every day by means of riding, drill and gymnastics; and on 26 January 1852, the Queen called his attention [22] in all innocence to two symptoms of acute exhaustion in the Prince of Wales for which she was at a loss to account:

She spoke a good deal about the Princes and bade me notice two peculiarities in the Prince of Wales. First, at times he hangs his head and looks at his feet, and invariably within a day or two has one of his fits of nervous and unmanageable temper. Secondly, riding hard, or after he has become fatigued, has been invariably followed by outbursts of temper.

The Queen added that the Prince of Wales 'had been injured by being with the Princess Royal, who was very clever and a child far above her age. She puts him down by a word or a look, and their mutual affection had been, she feared, impaired by this state of things.'

Gibbs reserved his opinion at that time: and three of his assistants protested vigorously that the Prince of Wales was being driven too hard. They were powerless, however, against the adamantine opposition of Prince Albert and Baron Stockmar. Gerald Wellesley,* the domestic chaplain, who was responsible for the Princes' religious instruction, warned [23] Gibbs (5 February 1852) that Prince Albert's system had overtaxed the strength of the young Prince of Wales, and that 'the great object is to instruct him without overworking him'. But Gibbs noted with relish that Prince Albert had described the chaplain ironically as 'quite a Wellesley', and that although 'respected and liked by everyone', Wellesley was neither clever nor learned. 'I have no doubt', he confided smugly to his diary, 'we shall get on exceedingly well together'.

* Gerald Valerian Wellesley, subsequently Dean of Windsor, 1809–82.

Dr Voisin, the French master, also warned [24] Gibbs that Prince Albert's system was faulty because it asked too much of a mere stripling: 'You will wear him out early. ... Make him climb trees! Run! Leap! Row! Ride! ... In many things savages are much better educated than we are.' The Frenchman thought that, left to himself, the Prince would be a splendid boy: 'He has the moral sentiments in a high degree – for instance, such a love of truth that he is ready to be a witness against himself. His account of any incident is not biased by his personal interest in it.'

The most cogent indictment of the system was addressed directly to Prince Albert (19 January 1852) by his librarian, Dr Becker, who taught German, in a long document [25] which began by stating that 'the main features in the Prince of Wales's character are a profound religious feeling, a great straightforwardness, and a sense of truth to such an extent as I scarcely ever witnessed in a child of his age'. Dr Becker then warned the royal father that his son's periodic outbursts of blind destructive rage, which dismayed his family and tutors, were a natural reaction to a system of education which placed too great and continuous a strain upon a young mind and body, and which caused at times a nervous condition of total prostration and collapse. 'This weakness is in frequent cases increased to such an extent as to produce a total incapacity. A mental pursuit for about five minutes may sometimes be possible in such a case, but after this an exhaustion ensues, in consequence of which any attempt towards making an impression is just as unsuccessful as with a sleeping person. Neither kindness nor severity can succeed in such a case.'

Dr Becker explained that he had done his duty, nevertheless, by experimenting conscientiously with methods of kindness as well as with methods of severity at times when the Prince of Wales had been reduced to the state described. As a result he had to report that, although kindness had elicited no response, severity had invariably caused gusts of elemental fury in which 'he takes everything that is at hand and throws it with the greatest violence against the wall or window, without thinking the least of the consequences of what he is doing; or he stands in the corner stamping his legs and screaming in the most dreadful manner'.

Dr Becker added that after consultation with Birch, and with 'the Prince's different masters', he was personally satisfied that those outbursts of blind passion were not caused by 'obstinate perversity' but by an uncontrollable and spontaneous nervous reaction to pressures exerted at times when the Prince of Wales was mentally and physically exhausted. 'To anyone who knows the functions performed by the nerves in the human body, it is quite superfluous to demonstrate that these outbreaks of passion, especially with so tender a child as the Prince of Wales in his moments of greatest mental exhaustion, must be *destructive* to the child.'

Dr Becker said that 'a great deal of good would be done by altogether stopping the instruction for a sufficiently long period whenever such a state of weakness occurs'. But in deference, presumably, to the stern views of Prince Albert, who never spared himself, Becker added rather weakly: 'Still, I don't think it is *necessary* to do so. All that is required is to make the instruction interesting and then to afford it in convenient intervals of time. . . . I lay the greatest stress on *this* point. ... After every exertion of *at most* one hour, a short interruption of, perhaps, a quarter of an hour ought to be made to give rest to the brain.'

In a number of palpably conscientious and sincere paragraphs which make, nevertheless, a most disagreeable impression, Dr Becker outlined his methods of bringing the Prince of Wales to a condition of 'repentance that arises from conscientiousness' after his passionate fits had exhausted themselves and left him limp and prostrate. Becker then humbly begged the Queen and Prince 'to pay particular attention to this important point. *Encouragement* of every kind is what the child wants to a high degree. ... The expression of too high expectations which he finds himself not able to meet discourages him instantly and makes him unhappy.' He concluded by imploring the royal parents to desist from employing irony or mockery when they had occasion to correct the Prince of Wales.

Gibbs very quickly established his position in the royal

household because he believed wholeheartedly in the value
of the experiment which he was conducting. Devoid of
imagination and humour, he led a dedicated life; and although he sought and received constant advice from the
Court physician, Sir James Clark, and from the fashionable
phrenologist, Dr George Combe, child psychology was in its
infancy at that period. The method in vogue was that of
phrenology, which claimed to be a science capable of assess-
ing its subjects' abilities and personalities by means of an
external examination of the bumps in their skulls. Dr
Combe examined the Prince of Wales's skull periodically,
and the reports[26] which he made to Prince Albert were
divided into dozens of separate headings – adhesiveness,
amativeness, combativeness, concentrativeness, conscientiousness, destructiveness, secretiveness, self-esteem, etc.,
etc. The continuous enlargement of a number of 'moral and
intellectual' bumps encouraged the hope that the Prince of
Wales's 'higher powers of control' would improve; and, although troubled about dangers inherent in the presence of
some less satisfactory protuberances, Gibbs derived comfort
from Combe's assurance that 'it is a fundamental principle in phrenology that no organs are, in themselves, bad'.

Nothing was left untried which love or conscience, science
or ingenuity could devise, and Gibbs's tireless efforts to make
Prince Albert's system work sufficiently won the complete
confidence of the royal parents. Gibbs agreed[27] with the
Queen that 'the temper of the Prince of Wales should be
put down very decidedly'; and she told[28] Stockmar that
the new tutor was in every way more satisfactory and agreeable than Birch had been. Gibbs agreed[29] also with Prince
Albert that it would be necessary to box the ears of the
Prince of Wales, or to rap his knuckles sharply with a stick,
whenever bad outbursts of temper occurred. Stockmar told[30]
Gibbs in strict confidence that the Prince of Wales was 'an
exaggerated copy of his mother', but that 'you must make
it the business of your life to do the best you can. And if
you cannot make anything of the eldest you must try with
the younger one.' He added that he had told the Queen
as well as Prince Albert 'that they must be able to answer

to their consciences for having done everything that could be suggested; and you will have no difficulty with them. You shall have all my influence to help you as long as I live.'

Gibbs was proud of the conscientious way in which he carried out his duties; and five years after taking up his appointment he sent [31] (28 January 1856) to the King of Sardinia (Victor Emanuel II), who had asked for it, a roseate summary of his methods. He said that the Princes rose early and spent two or three hours every day in the open air. They greatly enjoyed gardening and bathing in summer, and skating in winter, and the Prince of Wales was a most beautiful and graceful dancer; but 'dancing being thought rather effeminate, and insufficient to develop a manly frame, they go through a regular course of military exercises under the instruction of a Sergeant'.

Six hours a day were devoted to study on six days a week, and the periods were divided 'so as not to exact more than two hours' continuous application at a time'. Both Princes learnt Latin, acted in French and German plays, and had their reading directed deliberately to the masterpieces of the English, German and French literatures. They received daily instruction 'in Arithmetic and in the first principals of Algebra and Geometry'; but their instruction in the two latter subjects had been adapted to meet the specific needs of a princely education.

Gibbs explained that 'the difficulty in the education of a prince, especially of the heir to the Throne, is that he is forced early into life, and that too much is expected of him'. For that reason no attempt was being made to carry the Prince of Wales 'through the strictly logical Course of Mathematics followed in the Schools'; but – to take one example only – Algebra and Geometry were being studied with direct reference to 'their applications to Gunnery, Fortifications and the Mechanical Arts'. The objects were to make the Prince of Wales trace for himself the detailed relationship between all the various modern 'Arts and Manufactures' in the kingdom, and their underlying 'scientific bases'; and to build up in his mind, 'by the double exercise of reasoning and observation', a great reserve of 'extensive and accurate knowledge'.

Warming to his theme, Gibbs added that the Prince of Wales was also being made to 'study regularly Chemistry and its kindred sciences, with the Arts dependent upon them'; and that the King must not suppose that more ordinary subjects were being neglected in any way. The Prince of Wales was constantly required to compose essays on ancient and modern historical problems; and to write them sometimes in German and French, as well as in English. He prepared maps to illustrate his reading, and was studying the principles of 'Social Economy'; he was also studying Music and Drawing because both arts were indispensable adjuncts to a princely education.

Gibbs concluded: 'Her Majesty and His Royal Highness Prince Albert take their parts in the daily education of the Princes. They have laid before them at the end of every day a report on the conduct of the Princes and their employment from hour to hour. This has been found a very happy arrangement because it enables Her Majesty and His Royal Highness always to know the exact state of the education of the Princes, and it inspires the Princes with the wish to deserve the approbation of their Father and Mother.'

ii

1856–7

The only aspect of Prince Albert's educational system against which Gibbs attempted to fight was the rigorous isolation imposed upon the Prince of Wales. Excessive anxiety caused the Queen and her husband to draw an arbitrary distinction between companions and friends, and to hold that the latter were a luxury which princes were bound to deny themselves. They warned their children often that they were no better than other children, while hesitating even to admit companions to Buckingham Palace and Windsor Castle because they considered that ingenuous youth would seek inevitably to convert companionship into friendship, and friendship into an impermissible relationship of equality.

While admitting that danger, Gibbs pleaded boldly for companionship, arguing that it would be of great educational value; and, as a result of his efforts, a few carefully selected companions were allowed from the summer of 1852 onwards to come to Buckingham Palace or up the hill from Eton to Windsor Castle, in order to play or ride with the royal children. Charles Wynne-Carrington,* who was selected to be a companion to Prince Alfred, but who began in that way a lifelong friendship with the Prince of Wales, wrote [32] many years later:

Mr Gibbs, the tutor, seemed kindly enough to the Princes, but both were very strictly treated and brought up. Prince Alfred was the favourite but I always liked the Prince of Wales far the best. He had such an open generous disposition and the kindest heart imaginable. He was a very plucky boy and always ready for fun which often got him into scrapes. He was afraid of his father who seemed a proud, shy, standoffish man, not calculated to make friends easily with children. I was frightened to death of him. . . .

Prince Albert, who was always in the offing if not actually present upon such occasions, took his sons to Eton sometimes in order to visit their schoolboy acquaintances. The Prince of Wales was invited to attend meetings of 'Pop', but those visits were dismal failures because the Princes' upbringing had not fitted them to take their places with ease and grace or even, it unhappily appeared, with common politeness in that close-knit schoolboy world. They were aggressive and rude because they lacked self-confidence, and Dr Hawtrey, the Provost of Eton, found it necessary to speak seriously to Gibbs about 'the behaviour of the Princes to their Eton contemporaries'.

In consulting Stockmar (2 March 1853) about that trouble, Gibbs admitted [33] that the Prince of Wales 'had a pleasure in giving pain to others and that it was an "ultimate fact"

* Marquess of Lincolnshire, K.G., P.C., G.C.M.G. (1843–1928).

in his character borne out by the observation of all who knew him'. Stockmar replied,[34] unhelpfully, that the madness of George III was evidently reappearing in his great-grandson, the Prince of Wales; and he said that he based that opinion upon early medical experience. He added that George IV and the Dukes of Kent and Cumberland had taken 'the greatest of pleasure in making mischief – in giving pain to people and in setting them one against another'.

The Prince of Wales displayed an exemplary capacity in later life for preventing mischief, and for making happy everyone by whom he was surrounded; but his youthful personality was badly frustrated. The acceptance and approbation which he craved appeared to depend upon his ability to justify his exalted rank by excelling in every field; and his efforts to excel assumed crudely self-assertive forms because he knew no others. He had not at that time acquired the experience and finesse which other boys acquire through daily intercourse with one another, and which his few companions had imbibed without effort in the democratic atmosphere of a great public school.

Surrounded by adults who thought and acted constantly on his behalf, the Prince of Wales had little stimulus to exercise his own judgement and to develop a balanced and generous outlook. He asserted himself in childish ways, and acknowledged freely in later life that he had been intolerant and suspicious during his youth and too eager to take advantage of his position.[35] Gibbs reported[36] to the Queen (May 1854) that the Prince's 'impulses' were not 'kindly. They lead him to speak rudely and unamiably to his companions ... and in consequence his playfulness ... constantly degenerates into roughness and rudeness. The impulse to oppose is very strong, and Mr Gibbs ... thinks that the Prince is conscious of not being so amiable as ... he desires to be, or so forward as is expected for his age; and that in consequence he looks out for reproof and fancies advice even conveys a reproof beyond its mere words.'

Those faults were all corrected by the Prince of Wales himself after he had torn down with impatient hands the barriers created by excessive anxiety in order to preserve him from possible contamination. As he grew older, and better fitted in consequence to support the pressures to which he was being subjected, the nervous symptoms which had alarmed his family and Stockmar died away; but Gibbs's occasional efforts to relax those pressures were sternly repulsed. At Balmoral, for example, in September 1854, Gibbs attributed [37] the more than usually unsatisfactory conduct of the Prince of Wales to the fact that his father 'early in our visit ... said, in the presence of the Princes, that it must not be supposed that our stay there was to be taken as a holiday; that the Princes had had mistaken notions about this; but that henceforth work must be done diligently. This forced me to contend for work more than I had wished to do on so short a visit. I told the Queen that I thought we had made a mistake.'

Gibbs had asked for deerstalking and for more 'outdoor work such as taking the heights of hills'; but it was useless to appeal to the Queen against her husband's sense of duty. It is true that the Queen did, very occasionally, complain about her husband's harshness; and she wrote [38] for example (5 October 1861) to her daughter, who had then become Crown Princess of Prussia: 'You say no one is perfect but Papa; but he has his faults, too. He is often very trying in his hastiness and over-love of business, and I think you would find it trying if Fritz was as hasty and harsh (momentarily and unintentionally as it is) as he can be !'

That letter, nevertheless, expressed only a passing mood; and the Queen was as inflexibly resolved as her husband was to prepare the Prince of Wales for an administrative role which had ceased already to be constitutional. She conceived it to be her duty to transmit unimpaired to her heir the former authority of the Crown; and it appeared necessary, accordingly, that the Prince of Wales should be induced to display, like his father, qualities of intellect, thoroughness, initiative and drive at least equal to those possessed by an average Cabinet Minister. The Queen knew that it was not flattery but the truth when Lord John Russell told her that

her husband was 'an informal but potent member of all
Cabinets'; when Lord Clarendon said that 'his knowledge
and information are astonishing and there is not a department of the Government regarding all the details and management of which he is not much better informed and more
capable than the Minister at the head of it'; or when Lord
Granville agreed with Lord Clarendon that, in foreign affairs
particularly, Prince Albert 'had kept the Government out of
innumerable scrapes' and had written 'some of the ablest
papers' they had ever read.[39]

That immensely comfortable assurance, and the knowledge that her husband was working tirelessly, selflessly and
ceaselessly on her behalf, relieved the Queen from all sense
of insufficiency and filled her days with an exultant surge of
thankfulness and pride. She was determined that such sacrifice should not be made in vain, and she wrote constantly in
that sense to the Prince of Wales. On 26 August 1857, for
example, she told [40] him:

> You may well join us in thanking God for joining to us all
> your dearest, perfect Father. ... *None* of you can *ever* be proud
> enough of being the *child* of S U C H a Father who has not his
> *equal* in this world – so great, so good, so faultless. Try, all of
> you to follow in his footsteps and don't be discouraged, for to
> be *really* in everything like him *none* of you, I am sure, will
> ever be. Try, therefore, to be like him in *some* points, and you
> will have *acquired a great deal*.

No detail, however small, was overlooked by Prince
Albert, who undermined his health by taking upon his
shoulders, in addition to all his public activities, the day-to-
day task of supervising in detail and reading through the
Prince of Wales's essays, exercises and lessons. He even
insisted that the elements of housekeeping and the art of
bricklaying should be taught in a miniature Swiss cottage
built in the grounds of Osborne House, the royal residence
on the Isle of Wight. He invited the most eminent contemporary scientists to meet the young Prince of Wales from
time to time and to take a hand in the tasks of stretching
his mind and inducing him to use it; and it must have

appeared almost intolerable that so large an expenditure of effort and spirit should reap so indifferent a reward.

The Prince of Wales was introduced by his father to shooting, foxhunting, fishing and deerstalking, as well as to racing at Ascot. He was shown all the principal sights of London and was present on such stirring occasions as the opening of the Great Exhibition in Hyde Park, the funeral of the Duke of Wellington, inspection of troops before they departed to fight in the Crimea, naval reviews off Spithead, and the first distribution by the Queen of Victoria Crosses in Hyde Park which he attended in a kilt on a pony. He was made to keep a daily diary which was constantly inspected, and which proves that he was never unoccupied for a moment; and he was frequently admonished, but in vain, to make that diary, as well as the letters which he wrote, more reflective and elegant, and less factual and jejune. Typical entries,[41] selected almost at random, run:

16 April 1855. Arrival of Emperor and Empress of the French. The Emperor is a short person. He has very long moustachios but short hair, fair. The Empress is very pretty.

1 July 1856. In the morning I went with Mr Gibbs into the Athenaeum Club and to the French exhibition of pictures.

9 May 1857. Walked about the town of Leeds which is very dirty, and the inhabitants low people.

Good use was made of the Drama in the education of the Prince of Wales, and Price Albert invoked the aid of Charles Kean, the best known actor-manager of the day. Kean, an old Etonian, was invited to co-operate with Sir Charles Phipps, Keeper of the Queen's Privy Purse, in arranging that plays by Shakespeare and others should be performed at Windsor before being staged at the Princess's Theatre, which Kean managed. Other companies were later invited to make similar arrangements, and many managers, actors and authors were delighted to watch the theatre grow more fashionable and respectable and to see their productions advertised and hall-marked. The Prince of Wales was taken frequently to the theatre and opera as well as to pantomimes and circuses, and he retained a very great love of the theatre until the end of his life.

Drawing as well as acting amused the Prince of Wales, who displayed proficiency with the brush. Some spirited examples of his work survive, and a drawing which he made of a knight in armour realized 55 guineas in May 1855, at an auction in aid of a Patriotic Fund formed to help the dependants of soldiers fighting in the Crimea. On that occasion a battlefield scene by the Princess Royal was sold for 250 guineas, and three drawings by Prince Alfred and by the Princesses Alice and Helena realized 30 guineas each.

On 31 March 1854, Gibbs sent a closely reasoned paper [42] to the Queen which urged that foreign travel should be made an annual feature of the Prince of Wales's education. Gibbs argued that travel 'would remedy in some degree the disadvantages he labours under from want of companions. He is behind his contemporaries in those qualities which are brought out by intercourse with other boys, and in self-reliance resulting from being thrown on one's own resources. The latter cannot in any case be acquired at home....' He suggested that, as a doctor would have to be included in the Prince of Wales's suite, a young man should be hand-picked who would be an agreeable companion as well as an expert in natural science, and who could be trusted to 'forward the great object to be kept constantly in view – leading him by every kind of means to use his mind'.

In begging the Queen respectfully not to allow herself 'to be disappointed if the plan should not produce the exact advantages that might be hoped from it', Gibbs ventured to assert, almost bluntly, that 'the Prince is a boy, and it is very difficult for older people to say what he should observe and admire'. That advice bore no immediate fruit, but two modest steps were taken to develop a sense of responsibility. On his fifteenth birthday (9 November 1856) the Prince was authorized to choose his own food, 'in accordance with what the physicians say is good for you'; and to choose his own ties, hats and similar trifles, but without any fixed allowance to pay for them. For all his personal expenditure he remained for another year dependent entirely upon his parents.

Three months before those minimal privileges were accorded, the Prince of Wales accompanied his parents and the Princess Royal on a week's State visit to Napoleon III's Court at Paris (20–27 August 1856). Attired in a kilt, his good looks took French hearts by storm, and he was most reluctant to return home. The Prince begged the Empress Eugénie to ask his mother to let him stay for a few days more in Paris, but the Empress replied that his parents would not be able to do without their children in England. 'Not do without us!' the boy retorted.[43] 'Don't fancy that! They don't want us, and there are six more of us at home!'

The young Prince's shrewd appreciation of his parents' attitude may appear to have been justified, in part, on the evidence of a very frank letter which Queen Victoria wrote [44] from Balmoral a few weeks later (6 October 1856) to the Queen of Persia:

Even here, when Albert is often away all day long, I find no especial pleasure or compensation in the company of the elder children ... and only very occasionally do I find the rather intimate intercourse with them either easy or agreeable. You will not understand this, but it is caused by various factors.

Firstly, I only feel properly à mon aise and quite happy when Albert is with me; secondly, I am used to carrying on my many affairs quite alone; and then I have grown up all alóne, accustomed to the society of adult (and never with younger) people – lastly I cannot get used to the fact that Vicky is almost grown up. To me she still seems the same child, who had to be kept in order and therefore must not become too intimate. Here are my sincere feelings in contrast to yours.

The Prince of Wales's nature was extremely affectionate. He reverenced and was devoted always to both his parents, although resentful of their severity. On the day of his return from Paris, he was despatched to Osborne, with his entire staff of tutors, in order to compensate for recent dissipation by some weeks of undistracted hard work; and Queen Victoria noted [45] (27 August) in her diary: 'We took leave of poor Bertie, who was pale and trembling for some time before, and much affected, poor dear child, at the prospect of this first long separation, for he feels very deeply. Though it is sad, I am sure it will be for his own good.'

Unlike the Queen, the Prince Consort tried to treat his children as equals; and they were able to penetrate his stiffness and reserve because they realized instinctively not only that he loved them but that he enjoyed and needed their company. All, except the Princess Royal, were afraid of him, but in a very interesting conversation with Lord Clarendon in December 1858, Prince Albert expressed [46] 'something like regret or doubt' at what he termed the 'aggressive' system that the Queen had followed. He explained that 'he had always been embarrassed by the alarm which he felt lest the Q's mind should be excited by any opposition to her will; and that, in regard to the children, the disagreeable office of punishment had always fallen on him'.

The Prince of Wales, who craved throughout life for comradeship as well as for sympathetic affection, was unconsoled at being despatched incognito during the autumn of 1856 on a walking tour in Dorset with Gibbs and another even older man. A brighter prospect dawned in 1857, however, after an appeal by Lord Granville to Prince Albert.

Four boys of his own age were hand-picked by the Headmaster of Eton to accompany the Prince of Wales and three tutors on a walking tour of the Lake District in May 1857; and to go abroad, later, with the Prince if all went well. The four companions were William Gladstone*, George Cadogan†, Frederick Stanley‡ and Charles Wood§; and, on a hint from Prince Albert, the Rev. Charles Tarver, who had joined the Prince of Wales's staff two years earlier as Latin tutor and personal chaplain, made his pupil compose a preliminary essay on 'Friends and Flatterers'. The Prince wrote [47] that the nature of a friend is to 'tell you of your faults' and that of a flatterer to 'lead you into any imaginable vice'; and Tarver reported [48] to Prince Albert that although 'the composition was not fully worked up ... the judgement shown was .. rightminded'.

* William Henry Gladstone, M.P. and eldest son of the future Prime Minister, W. E. Gladstone (1840–91).
† 5th Earl Cadogan, K.G., P.C. (1840–1915).
‡ 16th Earl of Derby, K.G., P.C., G.C.B., G.C.V.O. (1841–1908).
§ 2nd Viscount Halifax (1839–1934).

Since all went well, the Prince of Wales was despatched on 26 July 1857, 'for the purposes of study' to Königswinter near Bonn on the Rhine; and his father begged [49] him a month later (24 August), 'on the journeys and in the absence of lessons', to 'write to us a little more at length and give us your impressions of things, and not the mere bare facts'. Excursions were made into Switzerland and France; and the Prince of Wales was escorted by his father's private secretary, General Charles Grey (who subsequently became private secretary to the Queen); by his father's equerry, Colonel Henry Ponsonby (who became the Queen's private secretary after Grey's death); as well as by Gibbs, Tarver and a naval doctor, George Armstrong.

Ponsonby's description [50] of the Prince of Wales as 'one of the nicest boys I ever saw, and very lively and pleasant', was endorsed by all who met him; and the only incident which caused a moment's uneasiness occurred on the first evening after the arrival at Königswinter. The Prince of Wales dined slightly too well, kissed a pretty young girl and was suitably admonished; and that salutary experience in the life of any young man was discreetly handled by Grey and Ponsonby. William Gladstone described the incident in a letter to his mother who broke the news to her husband, the Chancellor of the Exchequer; and the Chancellor, replying (4 August) to his wife's letter, wrote [51] ponderously about 'this little squalid debauch'. He described it as 'indeed a paltry affair' which, nevertheless, 'makes one feel what we should, I think, have suspected, viz – that the Prince of Wales has not been educated up to his position. This sort of unworthy little indulgence is the compensation. Kept in childhood beyond his time, he is allowed to make that childhood what it should never be in a Prince, or anyone else, namely wanton.... I am glad that Willy's soul loathes the tuft-hunting.'

On that tour the Prince of Wales experienced gaiety and comradeship for the first time outside the circle of his family, and for that reason a notebook entitled 'Wit and Whoppers' [52] into which his high spirits overflowed is of some slight interest. It had to be inspected, like his diary, by his

father after he returned home. On one occasion, when Cadogan was consuming an eel pie, Ponsonby suggested that it
would make him *eel*. Grey said that Armstrong would be
able to cure him, and Tarver, whom the Prince liked far
better than he liked Gibbs, made the young men roar with
laughter by saying that Armstrong would have to put himself first into an *eel*-eemosynary mood. On another occasion,
after inspecting the synagogue at Frankfurt, the young men
parted from Tarver, whom they called 'Bishop', with the
words, 'Adieu! A Jew! Bishop!' 'Oh, no!' Tarver retorted.
'Can't you see that I'm a Christian bishop!'; and when a
fire broke out in a house in Bonn, all four boys raced to see
the 'bonfire', and to lend a hand, if possible.

The highlight of that tour was a dinner on 16 August
given by Prince Metternich in his castle at Johannisberg at
Niederwald. The eminent Austrian upholder and survivor
of the old absolutist and dynastic European order, who was
then in his eighty-fifth year, was charmed by the slim and
handsome Prince of Wales. He ordered some incomparable
hock to be brought from his famous cellars, and exerted
himself to talk with unabated force and fire as he drew
upon his personal recollections of the inner diplomatic
history of the past three-quarters of a century for the entertainment of his silent and politely bored young guest, who
confided his impressions to the diary[53] which his father
was longing to read: 'He is a very nice old gentleman and
very like the late Duke of Wellington.'

2

The New Land

ON returning home the Prince of Wales was given an annual allowance of one hundred pounds, and was authorized to choose his own clothes, for which his parents would continue to pay. 'We do not wish', the Queen wrote[1] (26 October 1857), 'to control your own tastes and fancies, which, on the contrary, we wish you to indulge and develop, but we do *expect* that you will never wear anything *extravagant* or *slang*, not because we don't like it, but because it would prove a want of self-respect and be an offence against decency, leading – as it has often done in others – to an indifference to what is morally wrong.'

The Prince of Wales implored his parents to allow him to join the Army. His younger brother, Prince Albert, had set his heart upon the Navy; his brother-in-law, Prince Frederick (Fritz) of Prussia, who married the Princess Royal in London on 25 January 1858, was a soldier; and the attention of Englishmen everywhere was focused, for once, upon India, where the great Sepoy Mutiny was being broken in a series of epic battles, marches and sieges. 'Bertie, who was very sensible and amiable,' Queen Victoria noted[2] (7 January 1858) in her diary, '.. spoke of his anxiety to travel and see other countrys and objects of interest, and of his wish NOT to enter the Navy, which I had told him had never been intended, and of his equally great wish to serve in the Army, which, as a profession, I said he could not, though he might learn in it.'

The Queen and Prince Albert held that, although it would be appropriate for their younger sons to serve professionally in the Navy or Army, the heir to the throne, who had still an immense amount to learn, belonged to the whole nation. He could never be allowed to display avoidable partiality; but he was promised an opportunity to pass a military examination later; and the Queen noted [3] on his sixteenth birthday: 'May God bless him, and help him and us through the difficult task of education. It is such an anxiety to us.'

The ceremony of the Prince of Wales's confirmation by the Archbishop of Canterbury, John Sumner, took place shortly afterwards (1 April 1858) in St George's Chapel, Windsor, in the presence of Government and Opposition leaders. The Prince had passed a rigorous examination by the Dean of Windsor, Gerald Wellesley, on the previous day; and an unclouded and humble religious faith remained with him always and was an immense source of strength.

Thereafter the Prince was sent to live with Gibbs and Tarver at White Lodge in Richmond Park, which had been refitted for his reception, and Prince Albert informed [4] Stockmar (2 April) that his son would be kept 'away from the world' for some months. The objects were to enable him to prepare for a military examination, while undergoing an intensive process of mental and social polishing.

The Prince Consort explained to Stockmar that he had appointed 'three very distinguished young men of from twenty-three to twenty-six years of age who are to occupy, in monthly rotation, a kind of equerry's place about him, and from whose more intimate intercourse I anticipate no small benefit to Bertie'. Two, Major Christopher Teesdale and Major Loyd-Lindsay,* had won Victoria Crosses in the Crimea; and the third, Lord Valletort,† had been 'much on the Continent, is a thoroughly good, moral and accomplished man, draws well and plays, and never was at a public school, but passed his youth in attendance on his invalid father.'

In a confidential memorandum [5] the Prince Consort asked the three paragons to help make the Prince of Wales not merely a gentleman but 'the first gentleman in the country'

* Afterwards 1st Lord Wantage, V.C., K.C.B. (1832–1901).
† 4th Earl of Mount Edgcumbe, P.C., G.C.V.O. (1833–1917).

in respect of 'outward deportment and manners', which he discussed under three heads:

1. *Appearance, Deportment and Dress*

... A gentleman does not indulge in careless self-indulgent lounging ways, such as lolling in armchairs or on sofas, slouching in his gait, or placing himself in unbecoming attitudes with his hands in his pockets. ... He will borrow nothing from the fashions of the groom or the gamekeeper, and whilst avoiding the frivolity and foolish vanity of dandyism, will take care that his clothes are of the best quality. ...

2. *Manners and Conduct towards Others*

The manners and conduct of a gentleman towards others are founded on the basis of kindness, consideration and the absence of selfishness. [A Prince must always be scrupulously courteous, attentive, punctual and on guard against the temptation to use harsh, rude or bantering expressions.] Anything approaching to a *practical joke* [would be impermissible].

3. *The Power to Acquit Himself Creditably in Conversation, or whatever May Be the Occupation of Society*

[Gossip, cards, billiards were to be regarded as useless; but] some knowledge of those studies and pursuits which adorn society and make it interesting [was essential. The Prince of Wales must be induced] by persevering example ... to devote some of his leisure time to music, to the fine arts, either drawing or looking over drawings, engravings, etc., to hearing poetry, amusing books or good plays read aloud; in short to anything that whilst it amuses may gently exercise the mind. ...

The Queen and her husband were impatient to form the character of the Prince of Wales before he came of age and, therefore, independent in November 1862. 'I feel very sad about him', the Queen wrote[6] (31 March 1858) to Princess Frederick William. 'He is so idle and weak. God grant that he may take things more to heart and be more serious for the future and get more power. The heart is good, warm and affectionate.'

The characters of the Queen and Prince Albert had developed early as a result of continuous exposure to the external stresses of life; but their son, who was isolated from challenging contacts, was denied the apprenticeship in self-reliance which other boys of all social classes enjoyed. He was deprived of light and air through continuous association in a hot-house atmosphere with older men whose strongly integrated characters and personalities stifled, for a time, the normal development of his; and he became adept, in consequence, at taking on the colour of his surroundings, while evading the necessity for thought.

The Prince of Wales was desperately bored at White Lodge, where he dwelt in monastic seclusion, ploughing through St Simon's Memoirs and the novels of Walter Scott, and giving dinners from time to time to famous men, including Lord John Russell and Professor Richard Owen. Occasionally he noted[7] in his diary the receipt of a 'very jolly letter' from Lady Churchill, one of the Queen's ladies-in-waiting who sympathized warmly with him, but that correspondence was quickly stopped. Lady Churchill, who was happily married and who became the Queen's most intimate friend, was twice severely scolded in 1859 for showing too much interest in the Prince of Wales.

The Prince was thankful when Gibbs, on 10 November 1858, resigned his post as tutor at last; and Queen Victoria wrote[8] (17 November) to Princess Frederick William : 'Poor Mr Gibbs certainly failed during the last 2 years entirely, incredibly, and did Bertie no good.' He was replaced by Colonel the Hon. Robert Bruce, a kindly, conscientious and dapper Grenadier Guardsman who had served as military secretary to the Governor-General of Canada when his brother, Lord Elgin (who brought the frieze of the Parthenon from Athens to London), held that post. Gazetted formally as the Prince of Wales's 'Governor', Bruce reported to the Queen and Prince Albert as frequently and as fully as Gibbs had done; but in a letter[9] (9 November) from his parents, on his seventeenth birthday, the Prince was informed that he would be answerable in future not to his governor but to himself and his parents.

The Prince's annual income was increased to five hundred pounds; and he was exhorted to free himself 'from the thraldom of abject dependence' upon servants. He must learn, above all, to follow Christ's precept 'that you should love your neighbour as yourself, and do unto men as you would they should do unto you'; and he must become 'a good man and a thorough gentleman'. 'Life is composed of duties, and in the due, punctual and cheerful performance of them, the true Christian, true soldier and true gentleman is recognized.'

The Prince of Wales was so much pleased and moved by that letter that he carried it to Gerald Wellesley, the Dean of Windsor, and burst into floods of tears [10]; but he was much less pleased at being gazetted a lieutenant-colonel (unattached) in the Army without any examination. He had wanted to start at the bottom of the ladder; and he told friends in later life that he had loathed [11] being forced to report himself to the Duke of Cambridge in a rank for which he was totally unfitted. It was meant kindly, but his parents forced the pace through fear that all they had achieved in restoring the prestige of the monarchy would be lost if the Queen were to die prematurely; and Queen Victoria wrote [12] (9 April 1859) to her daughter in Germany:

Oh dear, what would happen if I were to die next winter! One trembles to think of it. It is too awful a contemplation. His journal is worse, a great deal, than Affie's [Prince Alfred's] letters. And all from laziness! Still, we must hope for improvement in essentials; but the greatest improvement, I fear, will never make him fit for his position. His only safety – and the country's – is his implicit reliance in everything on dearest Papa, that perfection of human beings!

On 20 November 1858, the Prince of Wales, who had been created a Knight of the Garter and who was accompanied by Bruce and Teesdale, was allowed to pay a three weeks' visit to Berlin, where his sister was awaiting the birth of her first child, the future Emperor William II. The Prince Consort warned [13] his daughter (17 November):

You will find Bertie grown up and improved. Do not miss any opportunity of urging him to hard work. Our united efforts must be directed to this end. Unfortunately, he takes no interest in anything but clothes, and again clothes. Even when out shooting he is more occupied with his trousers than with the game!

I am particularly anxious that he should have mental occupation in Berlin. Perhaps you could let him share in some of yours, lectures, etc. . . .

The Prince of Wales was not formed to be an intellectual, and his interest in clothes constituted merely an immature attempt at self-assertion. He had developed an insinuating charm which produced a gratifying effect, and his visit to Berlin, which was normally a dull place at that time of year, was a brilliant success. Many balls were given specially for him, and he danced with extraordinary grace. He cemented also, on that visit, a lasting friendship with his brother-in-law, the future Emperor Frederick III.

Queen Victoria and her husband corresponded constantly with their daughter, through whom they were doing their utmost to inject liberal thought into Prussia, and many letters referred to the Prince of Wales. Queen Victoria described him[14] (27 November and 4 December) as 'a very dull companion' in comparison with his younger brothers, who were 'all so amusing and communicative'; but Princess Frederick William thought otherwise, and her father wrote[15] (1 December): 'Bertie has remarkable social talent. He is lively, quick and sharp when his mind is set on anything, which is seldom. . . . But usually his intellect is of no more use than a pistol packed in the bottom of a trunk if one were attacked in the robber-infested Apennines.'

After the Prince of Wales had returned home, his mother complained[16] to her daughter (22 December) that, although never tired of relating his experiences, he spoke only of 'parties, theatres, what people said, etc. Of the finer works of art, etc., he says nothing, unless asked.' The Queen could not help comparing her son unfavourably with his father, who wrote[17] also (22 December) to his daughter: 'His manners have improved very much, and the best school for him is the external stress of life. . . . You would hardly believe it, but whilst he behaved so well and showed such tact under the restraint imposed by society, he tormented his new valet more than ever in every possible way, pouring wax on his livery, throwing water on his linen, rapping him on the nose, tearing his ties, and other *gentilesses*.'

A fortnight after his return from Berlin, the Prince of Wales was despatched (10 January 1859) to Rome, to study art, archaeology and current affairs. He was told that he would be sent thereafter successively to Oxford and Cambridge, and that he would be given opportunities for military training and for foreign travel during vacations. That general plan was adopted by the Prince Consort after consultation with Cabinet Ministers, the President of the Royal Academy, the Director of the British Museum, a group of Oxford and Cambridge professors, and John Ruskin; and the Prince of Wales expressed gratitude and approval.

Accompanied by his governor and by Mrs Bruce, as well as by an equerry, a chaplain, a doctor and a tutor, the Prince reached Rome after a leisurely journey on 3 February, and was received at a ten minutes' audience by Pope Pius IX on 7 February. An Italian master and an archaeologist were attached temporarily to his suite in Rome, as well as a Royal Academician, John Gibson; and although a very strenuous timetable, devised in detail by the Prince Consort, was put into immediate effect, Bruce succeeded in controlling without disgusting the Prince of Wales. He restricted him as far as possible to non-political society, going out of his way to cultivate such men as Robert Browning, Frederick Leighton and the American historian, J. L. Motley; and all accounts agree that the young Prince, with his curly hair, fresh and pure complexion, charming manners and boyish ways made a delightful impression.

The Prince Consort could not help comparing his son's letters from Rome unfavourably with those which he received from his daughter in Berlin. He asked his son repeatedly for arguments, reflections and a conversational style, but had to rest content with such replies [18] as (10 March): 'I am very sorry that you were not pleased with my Journal as I took pains with it, but I see the justice of your remarks and will try to profit by them.' The Queen explained [19] (27 April) to Princess Frederick William that, in dislike of clever books and professors, 'Bertie ... is my caricature. That is the misfortune, and, in a man, this is so much worse. You are quite your dear, beloved Papa's child.'

At the end of April, 1859, plans for a tour of North Italy and Switzerland by the Prince of Wales were disjointed by war. King Victor Emanuel, who ruled Piedmont from Turin, succeeded in goading the Emperor Francis Joseph of Austria (who ruled his great Hapsburg inheritance until his death in 1916) into a declaration of war; and the French Emperor, Napoleon III, marched to the aid of his Italian ally. The Prince of Wales embarked (2 May) at Civita Vecchia in the warship *Scourge*, which had been ordered to transport him to Gibraltar, and the Pope told him at a farewell audience that he feared a revolutionary outbreak in Rome.

After noting [20] in his journal that he had enjoyed 'plenty of larking' at Gibraltar, the Prince cruised along the south coast of Spain. He made long excursions inland and stayed a few days in Lisbon with his attractive cousin, King Pedro V, whose father, a Coburg, had married the late Queen of Portugal. Returning home in the last week of June, he was despatched immediately with Bruce and Tarver to the Palace of Holyroodhouse in Edinburgh to undergo three months' cramming in preparation for his entry into Oxford.

The Prince's future law and history tutor at Oxford, Herbert Fisher, was sent to stay at Holyroodhouse; and on 3 September the Prince Consort described [21] to Stockmar 'an educational conference' which he had held at Edinburgh on 30 August 'with all the persons who are taking part in the education of the Prince of Wales':

They all speak highly of him and he seems to have shown zeal and goodwill. Dr Lyon Playfair * is giving him lectures on chemistry in relation to manufactures, and at the close of each special course he visits the appropriate manufactory with him, so as to explain its practical application. Dr Schmitz (the Rector of the High School of Edinburgh, a German) gives him lectures on Roman history. Italian, German and French are advanced at the same time; and three or four days a week the Prince of Wales exercises with the 16th Hussars, who are stationed in the City.

The Prince of Wales, who quite liked Playfair, never

* 1st Lord Playfair, P.C., G.C.B. (1818–98).

wholly forgot some smattering of his lectures on the composition of iron, and Queen Victoria wrote [22] (2 September) to
Princess Frederick William : 'Bertie has been doing better at
Edinburgh than he ever did before.' He resented, however,
not being allowed to accept invitations to shoot in the vici-
nity; and he talked with sly amusement in later life about
the solemn dinners which he was made to give to the leading citizens of the Scottish capital. Even the most serious-
minded professors must have had difficulty at times in
suppressing a smile at the piquant contrast between the
portly, grey-haired guests and the faintly epicene beauty of
their illustrious seventeen-year-old host; and the Queen
told [23] her son (7 September) that he might be able to hold
his own better if he would learn to part his hair in a less
'effeminate and girlish' way, and if he would give up wearing
slippers and 'loose long jackets' which she characterized as
'slang'.

The educational conference at Edinburgh, and rumours
about protracted negotiations between the Prince Consort
and the Vice-Chancellor of Oxford, stirred public interest;
and some verses entitled 'A Prince at High Pressure' which
began :

> Thou dear little Wales, sure the saddest of tales
> Is the tale of the studies with which they are cramming thee

appeared (24 September) in *Punch*. In middle age the Prince
of Wales considered that his father had made a great mistake in not allowing him to reside in college at Oxford like
an ordinary undergraduate, and in insisting that he should
live in a hired independent establishment, Frewin Hall, off
Cornmarket Street, with his governor, Bruce, who had been
promoted major-general, and with an equerry, Major Teesdale, V.C. The Prince resented that arrangement intensely;
but he was spared the incubus of a resident personal physician after the Regius Professor of Medicine, Henry Acland,
had agreed to accept responsibility for his health.

It would have been possible, even at that period, for a
more liberal policy to have been adopted; but neither the
Queen's nerves nor her husband's could have withstood the

anxiety of seeing their son thrust suddenly, without pre-paration, into intimate contact with his contemporaries at a time when the throne had recently been re-established upon a pedestal, and when distinctions of rank were silhouetted with extraordinary clarity in the light, as it were, of a setting sun. The Prince Consort had been most reluctant to allow his son to be associated with any particular college, and had only consented to his admission into Christ Church after the Vice-Chancellor had explained respectfully that the college system was fundamental and could not be set aside. The royal father then warned [24] the Dean of Christ Church, Henry Liddell, that it would be necessary for his son 'to remain entirely master (or for his governor to remain so for him) of the choice of society which he might en-counter'.

The heir to the throne entered into residence, accordingly (17 October) at Frewin Hall, where selected professors de-livered special courses of lectures to him and to six other undergraduates of Christ Church who were handpicked to be his companions. The Prince, who attended as well some ordinary lectures, wore always a special gown and cap with a gold tuft which all undergraduate noblemen wore at that time; and whenever he attended service in the cathedral, walked into a lecture-room, or strolled into the hall of the Union Society to hear, but never, of course, to take part in a debate, everyone rose automatically and remained standing until he was seated. They would have found it unnatural to do otherwise, and any rebel would have risked having his rooms wrecked and being thrown fully-clothed into the river.

In inviting his old tutor, Gibbs, (25 October) to stay for a few days, the Prince said [25] that his first impressions of Oxford were 'very favourable'; but the Prince Consort, who came frequently to Frewin Hall, expressed [26] to Bruce as early as 27 October his 'terrible anxiety' lest precious time might be wasted by social and recreational claims:

The only use of Oxford is that it is a place for *study*, a refuge from the world and its claims. ... You are aware of the prin-ciples which we have laid down after anxious reflection and much communication with the different Ministers of the day, who look, as we do, upon the Prince's life as a *public matter*, not unconnected with the present and prospective welfare of the nation and the State. In whatever decisions you may communicate to the Prince, he will recognize, therefore, the result of these determinations, and he will easily comprehend that his position and life *must* be different from that of the other undergraduates; that his belonging to a particular college even, which could not be avoided, has another significance from what it bears in other young men's lives. He belongs to the whole University and not to Christ Church in particular, as the Prince of Wales will always belong to the whole nation. ...

At the end of each of the four terms which he kept with some unavoidable interruptions, the Prince underwent a specially conducted examination; and his father warned him repeatedly that it was impossible to exaggerate the importance of doing well. He did not do badly, but his father probably resented a leading article in *The Times*, on the occasion of his son's eighteenth birthday, which stated that 'He may be great without the possession of extraordinary talents, and famous without dazzling exploits.'

Because his father required him to give dinners frequently, as an educational exercise, to heads of houses, professors, and selected fellow-undergraduates, the Prince of Wales employed a first-class chef at Frewin Hall; and his parents were quick to complain that he was putting on weight and losing his good looks. Prince Albert rebuked [27] his son (7 February 1860) for a growing love of rich, indigestible dishes which 'an experienced and prudent liver will carefully avoid'; the Queen wrote [28] also (22 January) to castigate a number of alleged faults, and Prince Albert explained [29] succinctly (4 January) to Princess Frederick William that 'Bertie's propensity is indescribable laziness. I never in my life met such a thorough and cunning lazybones.' He admitted the existence of many other rich and lazy youths in England, 'but it does grieve me when it is my own son, and when one considers that he might be called upon at any moment to take over the reins of government in a country where the sun never sets. ...'

To his parents' surprise, the Prince of Wales appeared to work fairly hard at Oxford, and the Prince Consort informed [30] his daughter in Germany that although her brother preferred 'good food' to 'mental effort', 'I must not only censure him. He is very good-natured and does what he *has to do* very well. The Dean of Christ Church was quite satisfied with the result of his last examination....'

The Prince of Wales enjoyed hunting, and the Queen implored him not to break his neck. He played rackets and tennis, but did not begin to make friends easily until his visit to America that summer had established his self-confidence. His German relatives, nevertheless, were impressed by his increased maturity when he visited them (6–24 April) during the Easter vacation; and old Stockmar, whom he was ordered to visit in Coburg, wrote to congratulate the Prince Consort very warmly indeed upon the great improvement in his son. The Prince replied [31] (27 April): 'That you see so many signs of improvement in the young gentleman is a great joy to us; for parents who watch their son with anxiety, and set their hopes for him high, are in some measure incapable of forming a clear estimate, and are at the same time apt to be impatient if their wishes are not fulfilled.'

During the Long Vacation the windows of the conservatory in which the Prince of Wales had dwelt hitherto were thrown open to an intoxicating current of air. He was sent to tour Canada and was charged with the specific duties of opening a railway bridge over the St Lawrence river at Montreal and of laying the foundation stone of the Federal Parliament building at Ottawa. He was instructed also to visit Washington, in response to an invitation which the Queen accepted on his behalf from President James Buchanan, whom she and the Prince Consort had known and liked in London when he was United States Minister.

It would be hard to exaggerate the success of that journey or the impact which it made upon the Prince of Wales, who left Plymouth on 10 July 1860. His suite consisted of the Duke of Newcastle (Secretary of State for the Colonies, who had been harassed by domestic trouble); Lord St Germans (Lord Steward of the Queen's Household); General

Bruce, Colonel Grey and Major Teesdale (governor and equerries); and Henry Acland (Regius Professor of Medicine at Oxford and Physician to the Prince of Wales). They travelled in the battleship *Hero* (91 guns), which was escorted by the frigate *Ariadne* (26 guns) – the two fastest as well as the most powerful and beautiful warships of their classes at that time in the world.

The Prince disembarked in Newfoundland on 24 July at St John's, which was then a dull and remote fishing station, and the tour really started on 30 July at Halifax, which was so wildly excited that offices and stores were closed for two days, and even newspapers failed to appear. The Lieutenant-Governor, Lord Mulgrave, told the Prince that although the best land in his province could still be bought for a dollar an acre, tickets for a ball (at which the Prince danced until 4 a.m.) had changed hands for fantastic sums.

Thereafter every city, with one exception, attempted to surpass the welcome which others had accorded; and on 18 August, in pouring rain which dogged him all the way, the Prince disembarked at Quebec, and went to stay for five nights with Sir Edmund Head, Governor-General of the two – as yet unfederated – Canadas. John Macdonald and George Cartier, Prime Ministers of Upper and Lower Canada, as well as the principal Canadian ministers had been presented six days earlier off the mouth of the St Lawrence; and John Rose, Commissioner of Public Works, who arranged every detail of the Canadian tour, was added to the Prince's suite.

That suite was enlarged further at Quebec to include Lord Lyons, British Minister in Washington; and the Prince conferred knighthoods (21 August) on the Speakers of both Houses of the Lower Canadian Parliament (Sir Narcisse Belleau and Sir Henry Smith). He visited the Heights of Abraham, attended balls and fulfilled public engagements; and one of the many speeches which Newcastle drafted for him caused trouble.

In thanking the French-speaking University of Laval for a loyal address and an honorary degree, the Prince addressed the Roman Catholic bishops as 'Gentlemen', although the authorities had asked that their status should be recognized by some such title as 'My Lords', which would have provoked Protestant resentment in Upper Canada. The Prime Minister felt impelled, reluctantly, to demand an explanation, and, in his published reply, Newcastle maintained his ground. He did so, however, in such polished and conciliatory language that a powerful extremist body of militantly Protestant Orangemen were offended in turn. Their headquarters were in Toronto, and their numerous masonic lodges met annually in many Canadian cities in order to celebrate the defeat of James II by William of Orange (William III) at the Battle of the Boyne in 1690. They were always eager to exploit anti-Papist fanaticism for Party and personal ends, and they ridiculed what they called the flowery pomposity of Newcastle's letter. They denounced him for having allowed the Prince of Wales to visit, and to describe as a cathedral, the new Roman Catholic 'chapel' at St John's, Newfoundland, and became bent upon insult and revenge.

At Montreal, which he reached on a specially chartered steamer, the Prince received a tumultuous acclaim. He opened the Victoria railway bridge on 25 August, fulfilled a number of other engagements, and attended two balls, one of which (27 August) was long remembered as having marked an epoch in extravagance. A gigantic circular ballroom had been constructed at the foot of Mount Royal on land over which cattle had grazed five weeks before. Many circles of columns were festooned with flowers; fountains spurted champagne and claret, and an artificial lake was fringed by specially transplanted trees. The Prince danced until '5 a.m. without sitting out once, while Bruce and St Germans caused amusement by falling asleep at intervals on the royal dais.

On 1 September at Ottawa, then a village, the Prince laid the foundation stone of the Federal Parliament building, which was almost totally destroyed by fire in 1916. Thereafter, as he steamed up the St Lawrence, Orangemen prepared to manifest their resentment at the courtesies which he had exchanged with the Roman Catholics of Quebec.

They organized processions and erected Orange arches, modelled on the historic arched gate-way of Londonderry, across roads along which he would have to drive. They decorated those arches with their colours and with virulently anti-Papist slogans.

The issue was tried at Kingston, Ontario, on 4 September, where an embarrassing situation arose. The Mayor read to his Corporation letters from the Duke of Newcastle and Sir Edmund Head requesting that the Prince's visit should not be made the occasion for an anti-Roman Catholic demonstration; but the place swarmed with Orangemen, and the Corporation resolved that processions should be held and that the Orange arches should be left standing.

The Prince's steamer was greeted on arrival by a royal salute, but two thousand Orangemen waving banners and shouting slogans were assembled on the quay. The Duke of Newcastle went ashore in order to rebuke the Mayor and to warn him that the Prince would not countenance an Orange procession, and that he would depart without landing unless the demonstrators were made to disperse, and unless all arches were immediately taken down.

The Mayor asked that the steamer should remain overnight in order to allow time for heads and tempers to cool. He undertook to come aboard next morning with a loyal address from his Corporation, and he called a joint meeting of that Corporation and of the chiefs of the local masonic lodge. Much liquor was consumed and much hot air talked about the need for educating the Prince of Wales; and in the small hours of the morning a drunken resolution was carried that the Prince should be invited either to land and be decorated with the Orange colours, or to go to hell and take his flunkeys with him.

That resolution was conveyed to Newcastle in more guarded language next morning, while a deputation from the local Presbyterian Church was coming aboard amid jeers and catcalls in order to present an address of welcome. The Mayor stayed away but sent a message which stated that he felt sure that a loyal address from his Corporation would be forthcoming if the Prince would consent to land and take part in an Orange procession. Newcastle at once despatched a letter couched in the strongest terms to the Mayor of Kingston, and as soon as the Presbyterians went ashore the Prince's steamer departed amid a storm of hisses and groans.

News of the events at Kingston caused a surge of anger throughout Canada and a very strong reaction in the Orange lodges themselves. The lodge at Belleville, which was the Prince's next scheduled stopping place, voted almost unanimously that all processions should be cancelled and that all arches should be taken down; and popular indignation reached boiling point when a strong contingent of Orangemen from Kingston used force in a successful effort to prevent that resolution from being carried out, so that the Prince again declined to land. Cameron Hilyard, Grand Master of the Orange lodges, who was a solicitor in Toronto, had his windows smashed by a mob; but he had been horrified by the insults offered to the Prince of Wales and did his utmost to calm his followers. Newcastle obtained from the Mayor of Toronto a promise that all arches would be taken down, and the Prince was received with thunderous applause from a crowd estimated at fifty thousand when he reached the capital of Upper Canada by special train on the afternoon of 7 September.

As the Prince drove to Government House, which had been refitted at great expense for his reception, his carriage passed under a single Orange arch which had been left standing owing to fanatical resistance by a few hotheads. On reaching Government House, Newcastle, whose nerves were jangling, sent immediately for the Mayor whom he castigated, in language which was deeply resented, for having broken his word and entrapped the Prince of Wales. The Mayor, who had brought with him some leading members of his Corporation, retorted that he had done his best and that the Duke's attitude was arrogant and unsuitable. He declined to apologize, and Newcastle said that invitations which had been issued to the Mayor and Corporation to attend the Prince's levée on the following morning would, in consequence, be cancelled.

After abstaining from the levée, the Mayor and Corporation tendered an apology during the afternoon; and although a wave of sympathy carried the Prince's personal popularity to extraordinary heights, Newcastle, who was held in some quarters to have been tactless and overbearing, was hustled in the street when he went with St Germans to make sure that the offending arch had been taken down. The incident was closed on 11 September when the Prince held a special levée for the penitent Mayor and Corporation of Toronto, as well as for a deputation which had come from Kingston in order to tender profound apologies. The Prince told its members that all painful feelings were for ever removed and that he would tell the Queen that he was convinced of their sincerity. He was thanked by the Mayor in a voice half choked by sobs. It was noticed, nevertheless, that, as the deputation withdrew, the Mayor of Kingston ignored the outstretched hand of the Duke of Newcastle.

From the suspension bridge at Niagara on 15 September the Prince watched the French acrobat Blondin cross the Falls from the American side on a tight-rope, wheeling a man in a barrow. When the Prince rode over to Blondin's enclosure in order to give him a purse of gold, the acrobat, a short, sallow-complexioned man with sunken cheeks and rippling muscles, offered to wheel the Prince back to the American side. The Prince accepted with boyish and fearless eagerness, but was prevented, and Blondin returned alone and on stilts to the American side.

On 18 September the Prince inaugurated a monument to Sir Isaac Brock, a hero of the deplorable war of 1812. After capturing Detroit and accepting the surrender of an American army, Brock had fought another battle on Queenstown Heights and had fallen in the moment of victory. The Prince, who chatted individually with a number of survivors, performed his last engagement on Canadian soil on 20 September, when he opened at Hamilton the annual Agricultural Exhibition.

Later that day the Prince went to Windsor on the United States border, where the Governor-General, Sir Edmund Head, with all the principal Canadian ministers had assembled to say good-bye. John Rose, to whom the Prince had become warmly attached, surrendered responsibility for the detailed arrangements of the remainder of the tour to Lord Lyons, and the Prince crossed the river to Detroit where he was welcomed by about thirty thousand Americans.

In the United States, where the menace of civil war was already evident, the Prince travelled as Lord Renfrew and in the character of a student; but that fiction was disregarded by the people. He stayed usually at hotels, which were often larger and more comfortable than comparable establishments in England at that time, and he noticed that he was expected to shake a very much larger number of hands than he had done in Canada.

Another difference which amused the Prince was the sensationalism of the American press. Many articles published about him were vulgar by Canadian as well as by British standards; and the corpulence, melancholy air and involuntary pomposity of Newcastle, the cane, gleaming boots and jaunty air of St Germans and the high domed forehead of the Regius Professor of Medicine, Henry Acland, were constant subjects of facetious comment. The warmth and friendliness of the Prince's welcome were apparent, nevertheless, on the first day, and his bubbling high spirits and inexhaustible vitality worked like a charm. The stern front which Newcastle had presented to the Canadian Orangemen was rewarded in the United States, where the Irish Roman Catholics displayed gratitude by cheering the Prince instead of demonstrating hostility; and Newcastle informed [32] the Queen (23 September) that 'this practical school' was doing the Prince 'much good', and that 'the development of mind and habit of thought is very perceptible'.

The United States Government placed special trains at the Prince's disposal, and he travelled everywhere in a luxuriously appointed director's car. He had an excellent reception in Chicago, and went afterwards to shoot prairie fowl, quail, plover and a few cranes on the soft, rich, breezy meadows round the village of Dwight. He liked always to elicit factual information, and was interested to learn that the price of land in Dwight had risen during the past five years from ninety cents to a hundred dollars an acre.

After visiting St Louis, Cincinnati, Pittsburgh and Baltimore, the Prince reached Washington on 3 October at 4 p.m. He was greeted on the platform by the Secretary of State, General Cass, who took him to the White House in the President's carriage. Newcastle, St Germans and Acland stayed also at the White House while the other members of the suite, including Bruce, went with Lord Lyons to the British Legation.

President James Buchanan, a venerable and handsome old gentleman who had met the Prince as a child at Buckingham Palace, welcomed his guest in a fatherly way. His niece, Miss Harriet Lane, whom the Prince described[33] (7 October) in a letter to the Queen as 'a particularly nice person, and very pretty', acted as hostess; and the Prince gave the President letters which he had been charged to deliver, as well as large portraits of the Queen and the Prince Consort which had been specially painted by Winterhalter.

That evening the President dined as usual at six-thirty, and the Prince met the members of the American Cabinet and their wives. He was taken, next morning, by the President to a reception followed by a luncheon at the Capitol, and was sent on a sightseeing tour during the afternoon. That evening foreign envoys were invited to meet the Prince of Wales at dinner, while the city was illuminated by fireworks.

On 5 October the President took the Prince up the Potomac in a large revenue cutter to visit George Washington's house and simple grave at Mount Vernon, and he organized dancing on deck, during the return journey, after the Prince had planted a chestnut sapling* near the grave. That sym-

---

* During the summer of 1890 the Prince of Wales was told by Sir Julian (Lord) Pauncefote, British Minister in Washington, who was on leave in England, that the chestnut sapling had died a few years after being planted. The Prince gave Pauncefote an English oak sapling to plant in its place, and Pauncefote executed that commission at a charming ceremony very soon after his return to Washington. That oak appeared to be in good condition when I saw it in January 1960.

bolic act by George III's great-grandson at America's national shrine made a profound impression; but the Prince told [34] his father (7 October) that although 'Mt Vernon is a much revered spot by the Americans ... the house is, unfortunately, in very bad repair and rapidly falling into decay.'

The President wrote warmly to Queen Victoria after his guest had left Washington. The Prince reached Philadelphia on 9 October and enjoyed strolling with Bruce about the streets. He thought it the most attractive city which he had seen in North America, and was delighted to find that intense local excitement about an important election to the office of Governor of the State of Pennsylvania saved him from being mobbed.

Nevertheless, when the Prince attended the opera at Philadelphia the audience rose spontaneously to sing *God Save the Queen*. The Prince told his hosts how grateful he felt, and was persuaded to visit a model prison of which the city was rather proud. While touring it, he entered the cell of the notorious ex-Judge Vandersmith, who had been sentenced for corruption and forgery, and asked the convict if he would care to converse: 'Talk away, Prince. There's time enough. I'm here for twenty years!'

The Prince reached New York on 11 October, and General Bruce, who was wedded normally to understatement, wrote [35] (14 October) to Sir Charles Phipps:

The reception at New York has thrown all its predecessors into the shade. I despair of its ever being understood in England. ... Believe me, however, that exaggeration is impossible. ...

This is the culminating point of our expedition, and, ... with the exception of the Orange difficulty, the affair has been one continual triumph. No doubt the primary cause has been the veneration in which the Queen is held ... but it is also true that, finding that sentiment in operation, the Prince of Wales has so comported himself as to turn it to the fullest account and to gain for himself no small share of interest and attraction. He has undergone no slight trial, and his patience, temper and good breeding have been severely taxed. There is no doubt that he has created everywhere a most favourable impression.

The Prince was driven down Broadway in a barouche, specially built for the occasion, beside the Mayor, Fernando Wood, amid an ocean-roar of cheering. As he bowed his acknowledgments from a balcony of his suite at the Fifth Avenue Hotel, the Prince told the Mayor that his rooms were far more comfortable than the ones which he used at Buckingham Palace and Windsor Castle.

The great social event of that visit to New York was a ball on 12 October at the Academy of Music, for which some three thousand tickets had been issued to those considered socially eligible. That degree of exclusiveness aroused a tidal wave of envy and frustration which the organizers took insufficient steps to control, with the result that two thousand additional guests forced a passage through the barriers into the ballroom. That crowd was too great, and shortly before the Prince arrived at 10.30 p.m., to the accompaniment of a fanfare of trumpets, a hollow cracking sound was heard as the centre of the floor gave way and sank three feet very abruptly.

No one was hurt, and an army of carpenters worked noisily with extreme efficiency for two hours. Dancing began at 12.30 a.m., and the Prince was vexed to find that he was expected almost all the time to partner elderly matrons blazing with diamonds instead of pretty young girls of his own age for whom few young men possessed a keener eye.

On 15 October the Commander-in-Chief – the aged General Winfield Scott, who was one of the best-loved men in America – took the Prince to West Point where the cadets were paraded for his inspection. The General told Lord Lyons that he had found his guest 'enchanting'; and, after crowding as much sightseeing as possible into four days, the Prince left for Boston where he met Longfellow, Emerson and Oliver Wendell Holmes, and where he was given what he regarded as his most enjoyable ball in North America.

After a visit to Bunker's Hill, and to Harvard where he complained privately that he had been rushed, the Prince embarked on 20 October at Portland, in the *Hero*. He was seen off by the Governor of the State of Maine as well as by both Canadian Prime Ministers and by most of the mem-

bers of their Cabinets, including John Rose. The voyage
home lasted twenty-six days owing to gales and mountainous
seas, and relief was felt in England when the Prince reached
Plymouth at last on 15 November 1860. He went at once to
Windsor where he was congratulated warmly by his parents,
and Queen Victoria noted [36] that he looked radiant and well
and that he had become 'extremely talkative'.

Everyone agreed that the tour had been immensely beneficial to the Prince of Wales. He had discovered his *métier*,
but some grumpy old Whigs loved to depreciate the value of
royal visits, which had grown frequent in Europe during the
previous twenty years, and to ignore the part played by sentiment in politics. The Foreign Secretary, Lord John Russell, was included among such spillers of cold water, and
Lord Palmerston rejected obstinately the Queen's request
that Bruce should be made a K.C.B. The Prime Minister
argued that Bruce's services to the royal family had been
rendered in a private capacity which it would be inappro-
priate to recognize by a public honour; but Newcastle was
made a Knight of the Garter.

The Prince Consort regretted the storms which had delayed the *Hero* until half the Christmas term at Oxford was
spent; and the Prince of Wales was despatched, accordingly,
only three days after reaching Windsor, to resume his
undergraduate studies with his parents' rare commendation
ringing in his ears. While his son was still in Canada the
Prince Consort had written [37] quizzically (14 September)
to Stockmar: 'Bertie is generally pronounced "the most perfect production of nature"'; but the Queen wrote [38] proudly
(31 October) to her daughter in Germany while the Prince
was still being tossed on the Atlantic: 'He was immensely
popular everywhere and really deserves the highest praise,
which should be given him all the more as he was never
spared any reproof.'

3

Romance

AMERICA had spelt freedom to the Prince of Wales, who experienced difficulty in readjusting himself to undergraduate life. After reviewing, for example, the Oxford University Volunteers immediately before Christmas, as their Honorary Colonel, he remarked that allowance had to be made for such young troops; and the Queen and her husband complained to Bruce that their son was seen constantly with a cigar in his mouth, and that at times he appeared gauche and childish.

In a memorandum[1] (10 March 1861) for the Prince Consort, Bruce attributed 'occasional solecisms in good breeding which have attracted the notice of Her Majesty and Your Royal Highness' to the fact that the Prince had 'never experienced to their full extent those checks and restraints, and those practical lessons in what is due to others, and ourselves, which belong to the ordinary social intercourse of equals'. To the same cause he attributed 'a certain intolerance' and a tendency 'to form hasty and mistaken judgements', as well as 'a love of excitement' which carried him 'almost unconsciously into the company of the idle and the frivolous'.

After leaving Christ Church, Oxford, the Prince of Wales entered Trinity College, Cambridge, on 18 January 1861. He lived four miles out of the town in a large country house, Madingley Hall, and enlisted the sympathy of William Whewell, the Master of Trinity, by expressing forcibly his disgust at his father's refusal to allow him to live in college. Risking Prince Albert's displeasure, the Master allotted a set of rooms in college for very exceptional and occasional use by the Prince of Wales, who rode into town each morning on horseback, or drove in a smart phaeton.

The Prince made more friends at Cambridge than he had been able to do at Oxford, where he had lacked self-confidence, and he was especially fond of Charles Carrington, who hunted the 'Drag' for which another Trinity undergraduate, Nathaniel (Natty) Rothschild,* provided most of the money. The Prince became quite fond also of the Regius Professor of Modern History, Charles Kingsley, whose lectures he attended and whom he entertained frequently; but his heart was set upon a period of army attachment with the Guards, for which he never ceased to plead.

General Bruce was fearful of the risks entailed in acceding to that wish. Many rich Guards officers thought it as natural to keep women as it was to keep hunters during the springtime of a happy privileged life; but the Prince Consort decided, after a conference with Bruce at Cambridge on 13 March 1861, that the Prince of Wales should be subjected to a ten weeks' course of infantry training, under the strictest discipline which could be devised, at the Curragh Camp near Dublin during the summer vacation. A comprehensive memorandum [2] was drawn up and signed immediately by the Prince Consort, who sent it to be initialled by the Duke of Cambridge (Commander-in-Chief) and Sir George Brown (G.O.C., Ireland), as well as by the Prince of Wales.

On the military side, the Prince Consort directed that his son should wear a Staff colonel's uniform and be attached to the 1st Battalion, Grenadier Guards; and that he should 'learn the duties of every grade from ensign upwards' without being 'detained longer at any one than would be necessary for his thoroughly mastering it'. In that way he should contrive to earn promotion every fortnight, and should, 'with some exertion, arrive in the ten weeks before him, at the command of a battalion', and be made competent also 'to manœuvre a Brigade in the Field'.

On the social side of that ambitious plan, Sir George Brown was instructed that camp life was to be treated as 'a school of social as well as military instruction for the Prince

* 1st Lord Rothschild, G.C.V.O. (1840–1915).

of Wales', whose relations with other officers would have to be placed upon 'a becoming and satisfactory footing, having regard to his position both as a Prince of the Blood and Heir to the Throne, as well as a Field Officer in the Army'. The Prince Consort asked, accordingly, that his son should occupy a brigadier's quarters, adjacent immediately to those of the G.O.C. in the centre of the camp†; that he should give dinner parties twice weekly to senior officers; that he should dine twice weekly in his Regimental Mess and once a week as the guest of honour of other regiments in strict rotation; and that he should dine quietly in his own quarters and read or write on two evenings a week, one of which should always be Sunday.

That prospect delighted the Prince of Wales, who was irked by the excessive display which he considered that his mother had made of her grief when his grandmother, the Duchess of Kent, died on 16 March. Rebuked[3] (13 April) by Queen Victoria for selfishness and heartlessness, he replied[4] (16 April) that, 'stunned' by the sudden blow, he had not liked to intrude while his sisters 'were sympathizing with you so warmly and affectionately, not because I had not the same feelings as they had, but because I thought I would be in your way and that they would be a greater support to you'. He added that he had ordered 'some more paper with rather deeper black edges, as you wished'; and Bruce reported,[5] in a covering letter, that 'the sobering and softening effects which the loss has produced are already manifest, to a careful observer'.

An early marriage was regarded by his parents, as well as by Bruce, as the best panacea for the character of the Prince of Wales, and public opinion insisted that he must marry within the royal caste. The Prince of Wales declared uncompromisingly that he would marry only for love, and his father was dismayed by the dearth of attractive young Protestant princesses when he started to compile lists of eligible names.

Princess Frederick William of Prussia, who became Crown

† Sir George Brown surrendered his own quarters to the Prince of Wales, and thus moved into a brigadier's hut adjacent to them.

Princess in July 1861, and who will hereafter be so described, did her utmost to help her parents to find a suitable bride for her brother; and the nineteen-year-old Elizabeth of Wied (Carmen Sylva), who became Queen of Rumania, appeared at one time to be a promising discovery. The Prince of Wales refused, however, to look a second time at photographs which probably failed to do justice to her charms, and Queen Victoria and her husband were compelled, reluctantly, to consider the claims of an obscure but very beautiful schoolgirl in Copenhagen.

Knowledge of the existence of Princess Alexandra Caroline Marie Charlotte Louise Julie of Schleswig-Holstein-Sonderburg-Glucksburg had been concealed carefully from the Prince of Wales because his parents were prejudiced against her mother's family, and because a Danish marriage appeared inconvenient on diplomatic grounds. Princess Alexandra's father, Prince Christian, had been recognized by the interested Great Powers as the heir of the reigning King Frederick VII of Denmark, who was a drunken and divorced debauchee and who was also the last of his line.

Prince Christian, a man of high character who lived on his pay as an officer in the Danish Guards, was poor but well liked and greatly respected. He had married a first cousin of the King of Denmark – Princess Louise, daughter of the Landgrave William of Hesse-Cassel.

Queen Victoria and her husband disliked almost everything which they knew or heard about the Hesse-Cassel family. It was alleged to have become addicted to a fast and frivolous life in the eighteenth-century castle of Rumpenheim (destroyed during the Second World War) on the Main, near Frankfurt. Bequeathed by Princess Christian's grandfather to his six children jointly in 1837, with the expressed wish that they should assemble there and amuse themselves as often as possible, Rumpenheim became a centre of anti-Prussian sentiment and intrigue. It was reputed also to be a scene of gossip, lounging, gambling and unseemly practical jokes which offended the earnest spirit of the age.

Prince and Princess Christian enjoyed many holidays at

Rumpenheim, but a diplomatic objection existed also to any possible marriage between their daughter and the Prince of Wales. A bitter dispute, envenomed by the rising tide of nationalist passion and complicated by legal arguments of an almost incredible complexity, had raged for years between Prussia and Denmark over possession of the Duchies of Schleswig and Holstein which had been ruled by the kings of Denmark in a personal union for centuries.

German nationalists burned with eagerness to seize both duchies and to construct a canal through them between the North and Baltic Seas, and trouble was certain to break out afresh whenever Prince Christian succeeded to the Danish throne. Queen Victoria and her husband sympathized warmly with the Germans on the Schleswig-Holstein problem, and a marriage between their eldest son and Prince Christian's daughter might, therefore, give a false impression to the world.

News that the Emperor Alexander II of Russia had obtained photographs of Princess Alix of Schleswig-Holstein-Sonderburg-Glucksburg, and that he had shown them to his son and heir, reached Windsor at the moment when the Prince of Wales returned from the United States. That formidable competition, in so restricted a field, impelled Queen Victoria to obtain similar photographs through Walburga (Wally) von Hohenthal (a former lady-in-waiting to Crown Princess Frederick), who had married the British minister in Copenhagen, Augustus Paget.

After the Queen had described those photographs as 'outrageously beautiful', and after reports about the character and health of the seventeen-year-old Princess had proved to be equally satisfactory, the Prince Consort[6] took his son (15 April 1861) into his confidence. He informed him that, if he were interested, all family and diplomatic objections would be overlooked or overcome, and he warned[7] him (10 June) that 'it would be a thousand pities if you were to lose her'. He had written[8] (12 April) to his daughter in Germany:

If he does not marry until he is twenty-three, the Princess will be already twenty, and we could hardly expect her to be kept free so long. . . . We dare not let her slip away; on the other hand we have no right to bind Bertie . . . If the match were more or less your work . . . it would open the way to friendly relations between you and the Danes, which might later be a blessing and of use to Germany.

Defying German nationalist sentiment, the Crown Princess, as well as her husband whom she dominated, did everything possible to help. They arranged to meet Princess Alix and her parents privately at Strelitz from 29–31 May at the Palace of the Grand Duchess Augusta of Mecklenburg-Strelitz (a British princess who lived until 1916); and their glowing accounts were forward by the Prince Consort to the Prince of Wales, who asked that an early meeting should be arranged.

While the Crown Princess was perfecting arrangements for a secret meeting during September between her brother and Princess Alix, the Prince Consort's brother, the Duke of Coburg, tried to interfere. As an ardent German nationalist, the Duke, supported by old Stockmar in his dotage, was opposed strongly to any suggestion of a Danish marriage for the Prince of Wales; and the Prince Consort rebuked[9] him (22 July):

What has that got to do with you . . . Vicky has racked her brains to help us to find someone, but in vain. . . . We have no choice. . . . Bertie wishes to get married soon, and it is also in his interest, morally, socially and politically to do so. . . . It is of the utmost importance that this marriage should not appear to be a Danish trump against us and Prussia, but that it was started by our Prussian children, quite without the knowledge of Denmark or any action by our Ministers. Only in this way can the political aspect be kept out of the affair as far as is possible.

Preoccupied by that exciting and disturbing prospect of marriage, as well as by the need to choose a country property which his father proposed to buy for him out of the accumulated revenues of the Duchy of Cornwall, the Prince of Wales reached the Curragh Camp in Ireland on 29 June 1861. He was cheered by large crowds while driving through the streets of Dublin with the Viceroy, Lord Carlisle; but he made slow progress with his drill, and Bruce had to report [10] (15 August) the abandonment of all hope that he might be fit to command a battalion by the end of the month.

The fault lay not in the Prince but in the plan which had been devised for his much too rapid promotion. He felt sore, nevertheless, when ordered (23 August) to perform, in colonel's uniform, the duties of a subaltern on the occasion of the visit to the Curragh of the Queen, who was accompanied by the Prince Consort, the Duke of Cambridge and Lord Carlisle. The Prince of Wales pleaded vainly to be allowed to command a company, but his C.O., Colonel Percy, replied: 'You are too imperfect in your drill, Sir. Your word of command is indistinct. I will *not* try to make the Duke of Cambridge think you more advanced than you are.' Queen Victoria recorded [11] (24 August) in her diary that she had sent for Percy 'and thanked him for treating Bertie as he did, just as any other officer. Bertie likes him very much.'

Before he left the Curragh, a few of his brother Guards officers smuggled Nellie Clifden, a young actress whom they all knew well, into the Prince of Wales's quarters. News of that incident did not reach Bruce's ears, or those of the Queen and of the Prince Consort, until it was bruited widely in London some weeks later after the woman had bragged [12]; and in the meantime the young Prince continued to insist that he would not marry until he was quite sure that it would be a happy and successful marriage. 'In these days,' he explained [13] (1 August) to his mother, 'if a person rashly proposes and then repents, the relations – if not the lady herself – do not let him off so easily.'

On 11 September the Prince informed [14] his mother proudly that he had been allowed that day to manœuvre a brigade 'with expert assistance', and that he had come well through that ordeal. He left Ireland immediately for Germany to meet Princess Alexandra under cover of a plan for continuing his military studies by attending the autumn manœuvres of the Prussian Army near Coblenz, accompanied by his brother-in-law, the Crown Prince. Princess Alix left Copenhagen with her parents at the same moment to stay at Rumpenheim, which was situated conveniently, under cover of paying a health visit to Ostend.

Complete secrecy could not be preserved owing to intelligent guesswork by German journalists; but the Prince Consort wrote [15] (4 September) to his son:

Vicky has reported a long conversation which she had with your Uncle Ernest on the question of the Princess you are going to see. She said he was very violent, and that he would do what he could to dissuade you from such a marriage. ... He is going to the Rhine and will try his hand at this work.

Your best defence will be ... not to enter upon the subject, should he broach it. Saying nothing is not difficult. ...

He also said that the great point would be to prevent your meeting the Princess. ... In this respect, silence and the answer on which we agreed ... would be the best and wisest course – viz.: that you have only a few days and mean to spend them with your sister. ...

Should you be told that it is known that you will meet Princess A., your answer should be that you will be very glad to have an opportunity of seeing a young lady of whom you have heard so much good.

The Prince of Wales promised [16] his mother (11 September) to carry his father's letter in his pocket and to consult only the Crown Prince of Prussia, or Bruce, in case of trouble: 'I am afraid that I shall have many difficulties, but I feel sure that the best plan is not to be too precipitate. The newspapers, I see, have taken it up, and say that, if I marry a Danish Princess, there will be immediate rupture between the British and Prussian Courts.'

Defying the prejudices of her adopted country, the Crown Princess of Prussia presented her brother to Princess Alexandra of Schleswig-Holstein-Sonderburg-Glucksburg before the altar of St Bernard in the cathedral of Speyer on the morning of 24 September 1861; and the Prince of Wales wrote [17] (25 September) to his parents from Heidelberg:

Though we travelled incog., we were known immediately, and the Bishop insisted upon showing us about. There we met Prince and Princess Christian, and the young lady of whom I had heard so much; and I can now candidly say that I thought her charming and very pretty. I must ask you to wait till I see you, and then I will give you my impressions about her.

Princess Christian seems a very nice person, but is, unfortunately, very deaf. The Prince is a most gentlemanlike and agreeable person. After having thoroughly seen over the Cathedral we lunched at the hotel and then proceeded here. ... The Prince and Princess accompanied us and are living at the same hotel.

The Crown Princess wrote[18] also (25 September) from Heidelberg to her parents. She described how she had walked away with the Bishop, ostensibly to look at frescoes, 'but in reality to watch the course of their conversation'; and how, after some initial constraint, 'the reverse of indifference on both sides soon became quite unmistakable'. She wrote[19] again next day: 'I felt very nervous the whole time but ... I see that Alix has made an impression on Bertie, though in his own funny and undemonstrative way. He said to me that he had never seen a young lady who pleased him so much. At first, I think, he was disappointed about her beauty and did not think her as pretty as he expected, but as ... her beauty consists more in the sweetness of expression, grace of manner and extreme refinement of appearance, she grows upon one the more one sees her; and in a quarter of an hour he thought her lovely, but said her nose was too long and her forehead too low. She talked to him first, in her simple and unaffected way. She was not shy. I never saw a girl of sixteen so forward for her age; her manners are more like twenty-four ...'

When the Prince of Wales reached Balmoral on 30 September, Queen Victoria recorded[20] that he was decidedly pleased with Pcss. Alix, and described to me her manners, her pretty face and figure, but seemed nervous about deciding anything yet'. She wrote[21] more impatiently to her daughter next day: 'Bertie is extremely pleased with her, but as for being in love, I don't think he can be, or that he is capable of enthusiasm about anything in the world.'

That was the considered view of the Prince Consort, who drafted a characteristic memorandum[22] which he handed (7 October) to his son 'in order to make quite clear what appeared to me, in conversation yesterday, to be a little confused in your mind; and because the subject is of such vital importance to you that there should be left no chance of misapprehension'. The enclosure began:

Having expressed your desire to contract an early marriage after your coming-of-age, based on the consideration that it would be impossible for you to lead, with any chance or comfort to yourself, a protracted bachelor life ... you were most anxious to see Princess Alix of Holstein, of whose great charms and attractions you had heard so much, and who would, in all probability, be the object of desire of other young princes.

The political objections and difficulties ... were duly explained to you, but we admitted that they might give way to the primary object – your domestic happiness. Your sister and brother-in-law, at great political and personal disadvantages to themselves, succeeded in obtaining an interview with the Princess and her mother at Strelitz....

Despite extremely favourable reports, the Prince of Wales had insisted upon meeting before proposing to the Princess:

We considered this a very reasonable and proper wish, but felt a great difficulty in procuring such an interview without causing political alarm in Germany, and more or less compromising the parties concerned. A variety of plans were prepared ... and at last your sister succeeded, not without much trouble and inconvenience, both personal and political, to arrange the meeting ...

You have come back and given a most favourable report of the Princess, whose beauty appears to be almost perfect, whose manners and deportment you report as very distinguished, and whose education appears to have been remarkably good ...

The Prince of Wales, nevertheless, had still refused to commit himself, and had asked that the Princess and her parents should be invited to England before he finally made up his mind:

That is quite reasonable and proper, and it would, unless you had actually fallen in love (which after this apparent hesitation can hardly be supposed to be the case) have been imprudent on your part to go further in the matter without due reflection.'

Unfortunately, both parties had been compromised to some extent, and if Princess Alix and her parents were invited to Windsor:

We must be *quite sure*, and *you must thoroughly understand* that the interview is obtained in order that you may propose to the young lady, if she pleases you on further acquaintance as much as she did at the first.

Should the Princess fail to please, the Prince of Wales would have a duty to say at once that the affair was at an end, 'to avert further mischief, although a good deal will have been done already'. Any delay 'would be most ungentlemanlike and insulting to the lady and her parents and would bring public disgrace upon you and us'. The Prince Consort concluded by advising his son not to risk losing 'a positive and present advantage for the hope of future chances which ... probably may never occur'.

After the Prince of Wales had assured his father that he understood and agreed, Queen Victoria asked the Crown Princess to inform Princess Christian that the Prince of Wales wanted to know what impression he had made upon her daughter whom he was eager to see soon again. Princess Christian's reply was sent (30 October) to the Prince of Wales, at Cambridge, by his father, who described[23] it as 'very satisfactory, although the mother seems not to have put the important question to her daughter, and judges only from appearances'.

ii

A week later (9 November) Queen Victoria wrote[24] in her diary: 'Our dear Bertie's 20th birthday. May God bless and protect him and may he turn out well.' After one more week had passed, the Prince Consort sat down to write[25] (16 November) to his son 'with a heavy heart upon a subject which has caused me the greatest pain I have yet felt in this life.' Lord Torrington, 'one of the great gossips of London', had come into waiting recently, bringing 'a story current in the Clubs', which had been received with incredulity at Wind-

sor, that a liaison existed between the Prince of Wales and
an actress.

'A searching inquiry' had revealed that that story was
true, and that the liaison had been begun at the Curragh;
and the Prince Consort asked whether it provided the clue to
'the unsolved riddle' of his son's reluctance to marry, and of
the strange fear, which he had expressed sometimes, that
marriage might separate him from his friends. Prince Albert added that, although too heart-broken to see his son, he
was most anxious to protect him, as far as was possible, from
the full consequences of what had happened. He asked him,
therefore, to tell all, 'even the most trifling circumstance',
to General Bruce, who would try to forgive the deception
practised upon him and who had been instructed to serve
as the channel of further communication.

The Prince of Wales explained [26] that he had yielded to
temptation, after resisting for a time, and that the affair was
at an end. His contrition was expressed with heartfelt and
pellucid sincerity, and the Prince Consort commended his
son's firm refusal to name the officers who had led him into
error. 'It would have been cowardly', his father wrote [27]
(20 November), 'to sacrifice those who have risked themselves for you, even in an evil deed. We do not intend to
prosecute the inquiry to their detection. ... The past is past.
You have to deal now with the future.'

In forgiving his son for 'the terrible pain' which he had
inflicted upon both his parents, the Prince Consort urged
him to 'fight a valiant fight', while stressing the absolute
necessity for 'an early marriage. You *must* not, you *dare* not
be lost. The consequences for this country, and for the world,
would be too dreadful!' He travelled by special train on 25
November to Cambridge, where he stayed overnight at
Madingley Hall, and came away feeling much happier, after
a long and very satisfactory conversation with his son
whom he forgave completely. Unfortunately, he came away
also feeling physically exhausted, in consequence, the Queen
noted, [28] 'of Bertie's mistaking the road during their walk'.

The illness of his youngest son, Prince Leopold, and news
received on 12 November of the death from typhoid of his

cousin, the 25-year-old King Pedro V of Portugal, whom he had 'loved like a son'[29] had greatly depressed the Prince Consort. Confirmatory news of the Prince of Wales's scrape, which the Queen recorded[30] as 'the *one* great sorrow which cast him so utterly down', was received on 13 November; and the Prince Consort wrote[31] (29 November) to the Crown Princess: 'I am at a very low ebb. Much worry and great sorrow (about which I beg you not to ask questions) have robbed me of sleep during the past fortnight. In this shattered state I had a very heavy catarrh and for the past four days am suffering from headache and pains in my limbs which may develop into rheumatism.'

They were symptoms of typhoid, and after collapsing on 2 December, the Prince Consort died at 11 p.m. on 14 December 1861. The Prince of Wales, who had been taking examinations at Cambridge, had reached Windsor at three o'clock on the morning of that day, in response to a telegram despatched by his sister, Princess Alice, without the knowledge of the Queen who had refused to send for him earlier. She had formed the emotional and erroneous view that her eldest son had caused his father's illness.

For some months Queen Victoria was too much shocked and distressed to attend to pleas that she should view the matter, as men of the world would have done, in a more just and balanced perspective. She had heard her husband call frequently for Bruce in his delirium; she recalled doctors' statements that worry had undermined his strength; and, in response to an appeal from the Crown Prince of Prussia on behalf of the Prince of Wales, she wrote[32] (27 December) to her daughter:

Tell him that Bertie (oh, that Boy – much as I pity, I never can or shall look at him without a shudder, as you may imagine) does not know that I know all – Beloved Papa told him that I could not be told all the disgusting details – that I try to employ and use him, but I am not hopeful. I believe firmly in all Papa foresaw.

I am very fond of Lord Granville and Lord Clarendon, but I should not like them to be his Moral Guides; for dearest Papa said to me that neither of them would understand what we felt about Bertie's 'fall'. Lord Russell, Sir G. Lewis, Mr Gladstone, the Duke of Argyll and Sir G. Grey might. Hardly any of the others.

The Crown Princess continued to remonstrate with her mother, who wrote [33] again (18 January 1862):

All you say about poor Bertie is right and affectionate in you; but if you had seen what I saw, if you had seen Fritz struck down, day by day get worse and finally die, I doubt if you could bear the sight of the one who was the cause; or if you would not feel, as I do, a shudder. Still more, if you saw what little deep feeling about anything there is.... I feel daily, hourly, something which is too dreadful to describe. Pity him, I do.... But more you cannot ask. This dreadful, dreadful cross kills me!

The mental anguish suffered by the Queen, who had arrived, in any case, at the most trying period in a woman's life, stirred all men's chivalry to its depths. She refused to be convinced, however, when her husband's old friend, Colonel Francis Seymour, tried most gently but firmly to persuade [34] her (22 February) that Prince Albert's 'extraordinary pureness of mind' had caused him to take more deeply to heart than a normal father would have done 'a youthful error that very few young men escape', and that it was almost impossible 'to hope that the Prince of Wales should avoid'. The young Prince, who would have given anything to be able to help his mother, informed [35] Charles Carrington (19 December) and George Cadogan (25 December) that he had lost a father 'who was always kindness itself to me, though I fear I have often given him pain by my conduct', 'just at a time when I was most in need of his advice and counsel'.

It was evident that time would have to be allowed to perform a work of healing, and that the Prince of Wales's continued presence in England irked his mother. It was decided, therefore, that he should be despatched as quickly as possible upon a journey to Palestine and the Near East, scheduled to last for several months, which his father had planned as the crowning feature of his son's formal education. 'Bertie's journey is all settled', the Queen wrote [36] (11

January 1862) to the Crown Princess. 'Many wished to shake my resolution and to keep him here, to force a constant contact which is more than ever unbearable to me. ... The marriage is the thing, and beloved Papa was most anxious for it.'

On 29 January Queen Victoria saw the Prime Minister, 'for the first time since my great misfortune'. Lord Palmerston had come to discuss the Prince of Wales, and he said, the Queen recorded,[37] 'that the country was fearful we were not on good terms, as he was so much away from home. I pointed out that this was unavoidable, as Bertie's living in the house, doing nothing, was not a good thing. I said that he was a very good and dutiful son.'

The Prime Minister agreed fully with the Queen that the Prince of Wales must travel, and marry, and he said that the political objections to his marrying Princess Alexandra '*must* not be minded as they did not affect THIS country'. The Prince left England, accordingly, 'in the very strictest incognito', on 6 February 1862; and Queen Victoria recorded[38] that he returned for a moment, after he had said good-bye, 'and was low and upset, poor Boy. So was I.'

The Prince was accompanied by three equerries and a doctor, as well as by General Bruce, whose instructions required him to foster, above all else, the Danish project of marriage which had been formed by the Prince Consort on his son's behalf. Canon Arthur Stanley, Regius Professor of Ecclesiastical History at Oxford, who knew the Holy Land well, obeyed with great reluctance the Queen's urgent request that he should leave Oxford and travel independently to Egypt in order to assume the offices of chaplain and guide to the Prince of Wales.

Stanley's unselfish decision proved fortunate, for he found, to his surprise, that he relished the Prince's company very much. Furthermore, he was made Dean of Westminster soon after his return and he married Bruce's sister, Lady Augusta, who was the Queen's intimate friend.

The Prince of Wales was entertained in Vienna by the Emperor Francis Joseph; in Venice by the Empress Elizabeth of Austria; and in Trieste, where the royal yacht

Osborne had been sent to meet him, by the Emperor's brother, the Archduke Maximilian (who became Emperor of Mexico in 1864 but who was executed by his revolting subjects). The Prince paused, on his voyage down the Dalmatian coast, to visit Corfu, and to shoot wild boar in Albania; and letters to friends prove that he had become really happy again. In advising [39] Carrington, for example, who was still at Cambridge, to drop Nellie Clifden and '*occasionally* look at a book', he added (10 March) that his present way of life would be 'especially well adapted to a gay fellow like you'.

Joined by Professor Stanley at Alexandria on 1 March, the Prince stayed at Cairo in a palace, furnished and staffed on the most lavish scale, which the spendthrift Viceroy, Said Pasha, placed at his disposal. He enjoyed four days' strenuous sightseeing before starting up the Nile in two luxuriously equipped steamers which the Viceroy also provided; and Stanley, aged 47, was dismayed [40] at the outset by the Prince's 'levity and frivolity' in insisting that it would be much better to stop and shoot crocodiles than it would be to inspect 'tumble-down' old temples. At the First Cataract, nevertheless, he felt that he had succeeded in penetrating the mask of well-bred courtesy and indifference with which the Prince appeared to treat statues, viceroys and the members of his suite, and at Karnak, where he preached (16 March) in a corner of the great hall, the canon concluded that there was 'more in him than I thought'.

The tact and good feeling displayed by the Prince when he learnt, on returning to Cairo, that the canon's mother had died suddenly in England engaged Stanley's warm affection; and spirits were high when the entire party disembarked from *Osborne* at Jaffa on 29 October. Two days later, attended by fifty hand-picked servants, and escorted by a body of Turkish cavalry which was never less than a hundred strong, the Prince of Wales set out on horseback for Jerusalem.

That expedition camped, like a miniature army, every night, and the Prince grew a splendid beard. Breakfast was at seven; carpets were spread at noon for luncheon which lasted, with a siesta, for two hours; and local notables were often invited to dinner. Jerusalem, Bethlehem, Jericho were thoroughly explored, and trouble arose only at Hebron where the local Governor, fearing an outbreak of Moslem fanaticism, asked the Prince not to enter the Mosque where Abraham, Isaac and Jacob were reputed to lie buried with their wives.

Having failed to procure admission on a previous expedition, Stanley was resolved not to be baulked a second time, and Bruce conveyed, accordingly, an expression of the Prince of Wales's 'extreme displeasure' to the Governor-General of Palestine, Suraya Pasha. Arriving (7 April) with a regiment of cavalry, Suraya escorted his Christian guests personally into the Mosque; and Stanley told the Prince that his name had been the talisman which had unsealed the tombs of the Patriarchs. 'Well, you see,' the Prince remarked slyly, 'exalted rank has some advantages, after all!' 'Yes, sir,' Stanley retorted, rather ponderously, 'and I hope that you will always make a good use of them.' [41]

Good Friday was spent at Nazareth; Easter at Tiberius; and on 28 April the Prince rode into Damascus, where he was amused by Lady Ellenborough, who had married, as her third husband, a sheikh from Palmyra. Stanley preached (4 May) in the temple at Baalbek; and throughout that tour the Prince shot a great quantity of partridges, quails, owls, larks, vultures, gazelles, hares, and even lizards when nothing more interesting crossed his path. He had many specimens stuffed and was never parted from his guns; and he collected, at the same time, flowers and leaves which he had dried for the Crown Princess of Prussia.

Embarking again in *Osborne* (6 May) at Beyrout, the Prince visited Tyre, Sidon, Tripoli (whence he explored the cedars of Lebanon), Rhodes, Anti-Paros, Patmos and Smyrna. He anchored for some hours off the Dardanelles to allow the British Ambassador to Turkey, Sir Henry Bulwer, and some high-ranking Turks to come aboard, and he arrived at Constantinople on 20 May. He was received at once in an audience, which he described [42] as 'longish' and 'rather stiff', by the Sultan, Abdul Aziz, and he thoroughly enjoyed a week's stay at the British Embassy in the capital of the great Turkish Empire.

A most affectionate letter from Queen Victoria was delivered in Constantinople to the Prince; and Bruce wrote [43] (29 May) to his sister, Lady Augusta: 'I wish you could have seen the face of the Prince of Wales when he read the Queen's letter to him. It was actually beaming with pleasure. He felt that he had really deserved the genuine outpouring of a mother's tenderness and affection. It is a hopeful feature in his character that he has a strong love of approbation.'

Although much vexed by news, conveyed to him by Bulwer, that the Cabinet had vetoed, as unnecessarily provocative to Russia, a proposed extension of his journey to include the battlefields of the Crimean War, the Prince quickly recovered his poise and the Ambassador's verdict was very favourable. Bulwer informed [44] the Foreign Secretary, Lord Russell (June 1862), that the Prince possessed diplomatic gifts of a high order, and that the best method of handling him 'is never to maintain any argument at the time about this thing, or that thing, but simply to state an opinion; and, if that opinion is the right one, I have seen him always, and after a little time, coming round to it'.

The Prince reached Athens on 29 May and stayed at an hotel. His father had hoped that he would spend some weeks visiting classical sites in Greece, but that was impossible. King Otho, a Bavarian, who was deposed, deservedly, a few months later, had disgusted his subjects and provoked unrest, and the Prince of Wales departed on his homeward voyage after two days' sightseeing, wearing the Order of the Redeemer of Greece. He called at several islands, including Ithaca, before disembarking (10 June) at Marseilles, whence he travelled overnight to Paris and stayed with Lord Cowley at the British Embassy.

General Bruce, who had become gravely ill of a fever contracted in Palestine, was conveyed to an hotel in a state of collapse, and was replaced by Sir Charles Phipps, the Keeper of Queen Victoria's Privy Purse. The Prince of Wales, who bought jewellery and other pretty gifts in Paris for Princess

Alexandra, found time to visit the French Emperor at Fontainebleau, before returning on 14 June to Windsor, where
he was welcomed by his mother as a returned prodigal.

'Bertie arrived', the Queen recorded[45] (14 June) 'at ½
past 5, looking extremely well. I was much upset at seeing
him and feeling his beloved father was not there to welcome
him back. He would have been so pleased to see him so improved, and looking so bright and healthy. Dear Bertie was
most affectionate and the tears came into his eyes when he
saw me.' A week later (21 June), she recorded[46] again: 'His
time away has done him so much good; he is so improved in
every respect, so kind and nice to the younger children, more
serious in his ways and views, and most anxious for his marriage. He is naturally very distressed about General Bruce.'

The Prince assured his mother repeatedly that he wanted
to do everything she wished and, in particular, to meet and
propose marriage to Princess Alexandra at the earliest possible moment. He was 'furious'[47] with his Uncle Ernest,
Duke of Coburg, whose detestation of that Danish marriage
project had reached such a pitch that he was believed to
have written to Princess Christian about the affair at the
Curragh, and to have suggested that the Prince of Wales
would be an unsatisfactory husband. With her son's consent, accordingly, Queen Victoria suggested[48] (18 June) to
the Crown Princess that 'It would be well if Wally Paget
could let Princess Christian know the truth'.

In commissioning Mrs Paget to discharge that delicate
task in Copenhagen, the Crown Princess wrote[49] (28 June)
that the Queen was '*very* confident' that the Prince of Wales
'*would* make a steady Husband'; that she 'looked to his wife
as being his Salvation, for that he was very domestic and
longed to be at home'; and that the Queen 'was exceedingly
satisfied and pleased with him since his return to England,
and thought him immensely improved'.

The death on 27 June of General Bruce, who had been entitled 'Governor' and who was aged fifty-nine, was regretted
sincerely by the Prince of Wales who accepted the sixty-
year-old General (Sir) William Knollys as 'Comptroller and
Treasurer'. The Queen informed[50] her son (9 July) that he

was 'now too near 21 to have a Governor freshly appointed', but that Knollys, who was 'very fond of *young people*', would be 'the person to whom you would go for advice and assistance on all occasions', and who would also be 'responsible to me to a great extent for what took place'.

'I thank you very much', the Prince wrote [51] (9 July) to his mother, 'and perfectly agree that General Knollys would do very well. . . . I do not know him very well, but what I have seen of him I like very much. . . . As you feel sure that dear Papa would have approved of the appointment, that will make it doubly my duty to like and get on well with him.' On that letter, Sir Charles Phipps minuted [52]: 'Anything *more* cordial could hardly have been so sincere'; and the Prince continued invariably to be as conciliatory and amiable as was humanly possible. He lost his temper once, but only for a moment, on 14 July, when the Queen told him of her resolve to speak to Knollys about the affair at the Curragh Camp; but he wrote [53] next day to apologize: 'I have reflected and now think that it is certainly better that General Knollys should know. . . . Hoping that this may be the last conversation that I shall have with you on this painful subject. . . .'

Travelling as Countess of Balmoral, Queen Victoria stayed with her Uncle Leopold, King of the Belgians, at his Palace of Laeken, outside Brussels, from 2 – 4 September, on her way to visit the scenes of her dead husband's childhood at Coburg. Prince and Princess Christian, with their daughters Alix and Dagmar,* had already reached Laeken from Ostend where they had been staying; and Queen Victoria recorded [54] (3 September) that 'Alexandra is lovely, such a beautiful refined profile, and quiet ladylike manner, which made a most favourable impression'.

In a private talk with Prince and Princess Christian, the Queen expressed [55] her hope that 'their dear daughter would feel, should she accept our † son, that she was doing so with

---

* Marie Sophia Frederika Dagmar (1847–1928) subsequently Empress Marie Feodorovna, wife of Emperor Alexander III of Russia.

† Queen Victoria's use of that 'our', and of the royal 'we', was inspired by a wish to convince the world that her dead husband remained associated with her daily life.

her whole heart and will. They assured me that Bertie *might hope* she would do so, and that they trusted *he* also felt a like inclination. ...' Next day (4 September) Queen Victoria resumed her journey to Coburg, while the Danish family returned to Ostend.

The Prince of Wales spent 5 September with Princess Alexandra at Ostend, on his way to Brussels where he stayed at an hotel and drove over to Laeken every day. The Danish family returned on 8 September to Brussels where they stayed at the same hotel as the Prince of Wales; and the next day the Prince of Wales wrote [56] his mother what she described [57] as 'a touching and very happy letter' which 'would have pleased his beloved Father'. It began:

> The all-important event has taken place to-day. I proposed to the Princess at Laeken and she accepted me; and I cannot tell you *how* grateful I am for it. Though I still feel as if I was in a dream, I will give you an account of everything from the beginning.

The Prince of Wales explained that after lunching with Prince and Princess Christian and their family at their hotel in Brussels on 8 September:

> I begged Prince Christian to come to my room, and then I told him how I loved his daughter and how anxious I was that she should be my wife. I told him that I had quite made up my mind, and that I knew you had told him the same. I don't think I ever saw anybody so much pleased as he was. We then went out driving.... On our return, I saw the Princess Christian and told her the same as I had told her husband. She said she was sure I should be kind to her ... we then arranged that I should propose to her to-day out walking.
>
> Last night, at dinner (at Laeken) I sat between Princess Christian and her daughter. Though rather shy, we conversed a good deal together, and I fell in increasing love towards her every moment.

Next morning, the entire party drove to Laeken, where the King 'spoke most kindly to us all. He then proposed that we should go into the garden, which we did', and the Prince of Wales 'walked with Alexandra, some distance behind'. The account continued:

After a few commonplace remarks, Alexandra said that you had given her the white heather. I said I hoped it would bring her good luck. I asked how she liked our country, and if she would some day come to England, and how long would she remain. She said she hoped some time. I said that I hoped she would remain always there, and then offered her my hand and my heart. She immediately said *Yes*. I then kissed her hand and she kissed me.

We then talked for some time, and I told her that I was sure you would love her as your own daughter and make her happy in the new home, though she would find it very sad after the terrible loss we had sustained. I told her how *very* sorry I was that she could never know dear Papa. She said she regretted it deeply and hoped he would have approved of my choice. I told her that it had always been his greatest wish; I only feared that I was not worthy of her.

I then spoke to Princess Christian, and on returning to Laeken saw the Prince and Princess and their daughter alone in a room, and asked their permission that she should be my bride. They consented at once, and then I kissed Alexandra, and she me. We then went to luncheon....

I cannot tell you with what feelings my head is filled, and how happy I feel. I only hope it may be for her happiness and that I may do my duty towards her. Love her and cherish her you may be sure I will to the end of my life.

May God grant that *our* happiness may throw a ray of light on your once so happy and now so desolate home. You may be sure that we shall both strive to be a comfort to you.

You must excuse this hurried account, as I have been so often disturbed that I really don't know whether I am on my head or my heels....

4

Social Sovereignty

1862–68

i

'I FRANKLY AVOW to you', the Prince of Wales wrote[1] (11 September 1862) to his mother, 'that I did not think it possible to love a person as I do her. She is so kind and good, and I feel sure will make my life a happy one. I only trust that God will give me strength to do the same for her.' The engagement was made public on 16 September, after the Prince had joined the Queen in Coburg, and the news, received in England with rejoicing, aroused German discontent.

In the tedious dispute between Germany and Denmark about Schleswig-Holstein, the sympathies of Queen Victoria were warmly pro-German; and the Queen was grieved, although not surprised, to learn from her acting secretary, General Grey, that old Stockmar's 'rage and fury' at her son's Danish engagement 'knew no bounds.'[2] Although the British Government attached no political significance to that engagement, Danish public opinion was tempted to base some hopes upon it, and Queen Victoria was afraid less chivalrous motives might transform her son into a partisan.

That fear provided the Queen with a pretext for asking Prince Christian to bring his daughter to England at the beginning of November, and to depart immediately, leaving her at Osborne and Windsor for some four to five weeks. Princess Alexandra knew that the Queen wished to advise her about her future conduct, and to ensure that she would never use her influence to make the Prince of Wales a political partisan; but she protested[3] that she would be made to feel 'on approval'; and the Prince of Wales, assisted by the

King of the Belgians, tried very discreetly, but without success, to change his mother's purpose.

In asking the Prince of Wales to remain abroad while Princess Alexandra was in England, Queen Victoria placed a royal yacht at his disposal for a Mediterranean cruise. The Prince felt constrained to agree, although that arrangement, which evoked critical comment, involved separation from his betrothed, as well as the prospect of spending his twenty-first birthday (9 November) abroad.

At Queen Victoria's suggestion, the Crown Prince and Crown Princess of Prussia accompanied the Prince of Wales. A grave constitutional crisis had arisen in Prussia, where Otto von Bismarck was inaugurating a policy of 'blood and iron'; and the Crown Princess had incurred odium in her adopted country by her tactless manner of advertising her liberal English outlook, as well as by the active part which she had played in facilitating her brother's Danish engagement. The atmosphere was tense; the Crown Prince was becoming increasingly estranged from his father; and it appeared convenient that he and his English wife should go abroad for a time.

The Crown Prince and Crown Princess of Prussia with the Prince of Wales and General Knollys left Coburg, accordingly (6 October), on a fortnight's tour of Switzerland before embarking (22 October) at Marseilles for a Mediterranean cruise aboard *Osborne*. They called on the Bey of Tunis who showed them the ruins of Carthage, and visited Sicily, Malta, and Naples where the Prince of Wales celebrated his coming-of-age. He was promoted, on that occasion, to the rank of general; and he spent ten days subsequently with his sister and brother-in-law in Rome.

Although he secured the Queen's permission to meet Princess Alexandra and Prince Christian at Calais, on their return journey to Copenhagen, and to spend two days (28–29 November) in their company, the Prince of Wales was required to promise not to set foot upon Danish soil. The reason was explained[4] with devastating frankness by General Grey to Augustus Paget, the British minister at Copenhagen in a letter dated 13 December:

It was not so much the political question, and the storm that would be raised among her German connections, were any extra civility to be shown towards Denmark (though this consideration also has much weight with H.M.), but it is the fear – I might almost say the horror – the Queen has of the Princess's mother's family. The Prince [Consort], in promoting the marriage, had *much* to get over, and it is no small compliment to Princess Alexandra to say that her personal qualities are thought sufficient to outweigh the dislike that is felt to many of her connections.

The Queen's own expression is, 'The Prince of Wales is so weak that he would be sure to get entangled with Princess Louise's * relations, and it would be *too* horrid if he should become one of *that* family.'

These are reasons which cannot be stated; but I cannot tell you how firmly rooted they are in the Queen's mind, and how utterly hopeless it is to expect that, entertaining them, she would ever consent to the visit to Copenhagen.

During her visit to Osborne and Windsor, Princess Alexandra had entirely captivated Queen Victoria, who wrote[5] (12 November) to the Crown Princess: 'I can't say how I and we all love her! She is so good, so simple, unaffected, frank, bright and cheerful, yet so quiet and gentle that her *umgang* [companionship] soothes me. Then *how* lovely! ... This jewel! *She is one* of those sweet creatures who seem to come from the skies to help and bless poor mortals and lighten for a time their path!'

'How beloved Albert would have loved her!', the Queen recorded[6] in her diary that day; and the Princess, who spoke English fluently with a strong accent, promised everything which the Queen asked. She made herself at home and was delightfully spontaneous, as well as most anxious to be of use to her future husband, and she understood perfectly when the Prince of Wales felt obliged to support his mother in a dispute with Princess Christian about the duration of Princess Alexandra's stay in England. Writing[7] (20 October) from Lyons to inform Mrs Paget in Copenhagen that he had received a letter from Princess Christian

* i.e. Princess Christian.

announcing that she insisted upon having 'her daughter back for her birthday on December 1st,' the Prince added:

I have not the remotest doubt that P[rince] F[rederick] of Hesse, or some other relation, has put Princess Christian (to use a slang expression) up to this dodge, either to frustrate the Queen's arrangements, or to force me to come to Copenhagen. This is decidedly very unfair. . . .

I have answered Princess Christian's letter. . . . and what I now beg of you is to explain to her, in the most forcible way you can, that she is bound to keep her promises to the Queen regarding the stay of her daughter in England; and both my sister and brother-in-law think, and I quite agree, that the Queen's wishes ought to be obeyed strictly in this matter, as, when I was accepted as the future husband of their daughter, they ought to have been prepared to put up with some little inconveniences.

While negotiating the Marriage Treaty in Copenhagen, Augustus Paget was instructed [8] to reject the King of Denmark's request that Queen Victoria should ask for his consent to the marriage; but the obstinacy, or firmness, of Princess Christian compelled Queen Victoria to allow Princess Alix to leave England in time for her birthday. The Princess of Wales used to refer with merriment, in later life, to the three weeks' ordeal which she had undergone while 'on approval'; and although she learnt, during that time, to love and to understand Queen Victoria, she could not help remembering that her mother, from whom she had never been parted previously, had not been invited to England, and that her father, when he brought her over and when he returned to fetch her home, had been compelled to stay overnight at an hotel in London because the Queen had not asked him to be her guest.

Delighted almost beyond measure by her prospective daughter-in-law, Queen Victoria was well satisfied also with the Prince of Wales, who escorted Princess Alix and her father as far as Hanover, on their way back to Copenhagen. 'Bertie arrived', Queen Victoria wrote [9] (3 December 1862) to the Crown Princess, 'looking extremely well, and really

very much improved. It is such a blessing to hear him talk so
openly, and sensibly, and nicely, with such a horror of what
is bad, that I feel God has been listening to our prayers ... I
hope you have "germanized" Bertie as much as possible, for
it is most necessary.'

The wedding was fixed for 10 March 1863; and the Prince
of Wales discovered that he had inherited an annual personal income of about £50,000 from the Duchy of Cornwall, which had been nursed most efficiently by his father,
as well as a capital sum of about £600,000. Out of that capital, which had accumulated during his minority, £22,000
had been used a few months earlier to buy a 7,000 acre property at Sandringham from the Hon. C. S. Cowper, who had
chosen to live abroad after marrying his former mistress,
Lady Harriet d'Orsay.

Before his marriage, the Prince of Wales contributed
£10,000 towards the building of the Mausoleum at Frogmore, and spent another £100,000 on furniture, carriages
and jewellery, while the Government spent £60,000 on the
drastic modernization of Marlborough House which became his London home. He was left with an invested capital
of about £270,000 which served, with the Sandringham rent
roll of between £5,000 and £7,000, to raise his annual income
to a little less than £65,000.

Radicals argued that that sum ought to suffice; but extensive improvements were known to be necessary at Sandringham, and the Chancellor of the Exchequer, W. E. Gladstone,
insisted that the Prince's total income ought not to amount
to less than £100,000. Sir Charles Phipps warned [10] Gladstone (29 January 1863) that 'even with that he will be unable to do much that will be expected from him'; Lord Palmerston considered that the Prince was being treated shabbily; but Parliament was asked to vote only an additional
£50,000, of which £10,000 was apportioned as 'pin money'
to the Princess, who had nothing of her own. Paget reported [11] (24 December) from Copenhagen to Lord Russell
that Prince Christian, when informed about the 'pin money'
which his daughter would probably receive, had remarked,
ruefully and confidentially, that it was £8,000 more than his

total income of £2,000, which had been increased, some years earlier, from a beggarly £800.

The Prince of Wales was warned by *The Times* (20 February 1863) that he would be expected, on an annual income of £100,000, to outshine every subject; but Queen Victoria remained permanently, and not merely temporarily, withdrawn in eccentric and unpopular seclusion. The Prince was required, therefore, to provide the capital city of the richest and most powerful Empire on earth with a substitute Court on an income which, even when viewed against a background of Victorian money values and in the livid glare of a twentieth-century social conscience, must appear inadequate.

Precise details about the annual personal expenditure of individual Victorian territorial magnates are not available*; but the Prince of Wales's income was small in comparison with the incomes of many of his friends and acquaintances. Five great London landlords, the Duke of Bedford, Lord Cadogan, the Duke of Norfolk, the Duke of Portland and the Duke of Westminster (the richest man in Great Britain) — who all possessed ample resources elsewhere – derived larger personal incomes, from metropolitan rents alone, than the income enjoyed by the Prince of Wales, and forty-four individual landowners owned more than 100,000 acres.

Princely personal incomes were derived by many territorial magnates from annual rent-rolls very much larger than the rent-roll of the Prince of Wales. The Duke of Buccleuch, for example, derived £217,000 from 460,000 acres; Lord Bute £150,000 from 100,000 acres; Lord Derby £163,000 from 69,000 acres; the Duke of Devonshire £181,000 from 200,000 acres; the Duke of Northumberland £176,000

---

* Much very interesting, but incomplete and sometimes misleading information is contained in *Parliamentary Papers*, 1874, LXXII, *Return of Owners of Land* 1872–3. That famous report in many bulky volumes, dubbed popularly 'The New Doomsday Book', provided the first official survey of British land ownership since 1086. It was creamed by John Bateman in one small book entitled *The Great Landowners of Great Britain and Ireland* (fourth and last edition, 1883).

from 186,000 acres; and the Duke of Sutherland (the largest landowner in Great Britain) £141,000 from 1,358,000 acres. All those fortunes were supplemented very substantially by personal income derived from dividends on stocks and shares, royalties on docks and minerals, wives' fortunes and so forth.

Taxation was no hardship until the turn of the century; and the steep fall in agricultural rents, which ruined many squires owning properties of between three thousand and thirty thousand acres during the last two decades of the nineteenth century, was felt much less severely by great landowners. Most magnates were able not merely to compensate their loss but to increase substantially their annual revenues as a result of steady rises in the values of urban property, docks, minerals and industrial shares, and several enjoyed incomes of over £300,000.

A few magnates, like the Duke of Buckingham and the Marquess of Hastings, went under through gambling and other follies, and more would probably have extinguished themselves if the Prince of Wales had not provided many rich men, who lacked balance and occupation, with the solace of orbiting in a beguiling but disciplined and regular, if expensive, social round. Some, like the Duke of Marlborough (£37,000 from 24,000 acres) and Lord Rosebery (£24,000 from 23,000 acres), reinforced their foundations by marrying heiresses – a Vanderbilt and a Rothschild – who brought millions to garnish historic houses and to endow illustrious names.

In those circumstances it is remarkable that the Prince of Wales's annual expenditure did not, from the outset, exceed his income of £110,000–£115,000 by more than £20,000 a year.[12] That annual deficit was met out of his capital until that was exhausted, and the Prince was then wise enough to consult and to profit from the expert advice of such famous and successful financiers as the Rothschilds, Maurice Hirsch and Ernest Cassel, who relished the society of territorial magnates, although deriving an insignificant fraction of their immense incomes from land.

It was more difficult to devise an occupation than it was

to provide an income for the Prince of Wales, whose attention was absorbed by the preparations for his marriage. He took his seat in the House of Lords (5 February), and held (25 February) his first levee, and he paid many visits to his celebrated tailor, Poole in Savile Row, who served as a kind of post office in helping him to keep in touch with friends.

At 11.20 a.m. on 7 March 1863, accompanied by her parents, her two brothers and three sisters, as well as by her uncles, the Duke of Glucksburg and Prince Frederick of Hesse, Princess Alexandra disembarked at last at Gravesend. The Prince of Wales, who had very nearly arrived late at the quayside, almost ran aboard *Victoria and Albert*, which had been despatched to bring the bridal party from Antwerp, and he aroused a storm of cheering by kissing the eighteen-year-old Princess in full sight of the assembled crowds.

After presenting the members of his Household, which consisted of the Comptroller (General Knollys); the Groom of the Stole (Lord Spencer); the private secretary (H. W. Fisher); two Lords and two Grooms of the Bedchamber (Lords Mount Edgcumbe and Alfred Hervey; C. Wood and R. H. Meade); the librarian, Maurice Holzmann; and Francis Knollys (once a clerk in the Audit Office, who had been appointed private secretary to his father, the Comptroller), the royal party entrained for the Bricklayers' Arms at Southwark, where a carriage procession was formed.

Entering a carriage with the Princess and her parents, the Prince of Wales drove over London Bridge and by way of Temple Bar, Pall Mall, St James's Street, Piccadilly and Hyde Park to Paddington Station, and on that long and memorable drive Princess Alexandra, arrayed in a grey silk dress and violet jacket trimmed with sable and wearing a white bonnet with red rosebuds, took the hearts of the British people by storm. She appeared quite unmoved when the crowds got out of hand in the City, owing to the incompetence of the police, so that many people were crushed and a way had to be cleared, at one point, by a charge of the Life Guards with sabres drawn.

Although the King of Denmark, whose private life was a public scandal, was not invited to the wedding, popular enthusiasm was uninhibited, and some ringing verses by the Poet Laureate, Alfred Tennyson, expressed the mood of the hour. They stressed, inevitably, the Danish element in the marriage:

> 'Sea Kings' daughter from over the sea,
> Alexandra!
> Saxon and Norman and Dane are we,
> But all of us Danes in our welcome of thee,
> Alexandra!'

At Slough Station another carriage procession was formed, which passed through Eton where the schoolboys cheered themselves hoarse. The Queen greeted her guests on arrival but felt too 'desolate' to appear at dinner, which she took in a separate room with a lady-in-waiting. She noted,[13] however, that immediately before dinner, 'Alix knocked at the door, peeped in and came and knelt before me with that sweet, loving expression which spoke volumes. I was much moved and kissed her again and again.'

Queen Victoria never forgot that characteristic gesture. She took the Princess with the Prince of Wales and the Crown Prince and Crown Princess of Prussia on 9 March into the Mausoleum at Frogmore where the Prince Consort had been buried, and her diary recorded: 'I opened the shrine and took them in. Alix was much moved and so was I. I said, "*He* gives you his blessing!", and joined Alix's and Bertie's hands, taking them both in my arms. It was a very touching moment and we all felt it.'

At the wedding service in St George's Chapel, Windsor, on 10 March, 1863, the bride looked very lovely indeed in a white satin gown trimmed with garlands of orange blossom and puffings of white tulle with Honiton lace. She had cried during the morning, at parting from her mother, but she exclaimed with spirit to the Crown Princess of Prussia: 'You may think that I like marrying Bertie for his position; but if he were a cowboy I would love him just the same and would marry no-one else.'

The Prince of Wales, plump and nervous, but radiant in Garter robes and gold collar over a general's uniform, 'looked', Lord Clarendon recorded,[14] 'very like a gentleman and more *considerable* than he is wont to do'. He was supported at the altar by the Crown Prince of Prussia, and by his uncle Ernest, Duke of Coburg, who had swallowed his pride and his objections to the marriage in order to be present in such a role.

All the men present wore uniform, while the women blazed with diamonds in full Court dress, but without trains; and the beauty of the scene was enhanced by the mediaeval costumes of attendant beefeaters and heralds, and by the coats of cloth of gold worn by the State trumpeters who announced the arrivals of the separate processions of the clergy, Knights of the Garter, royalties, the bridegroom and ten minutes late – the bride. The Prince, while he waited, glanced constantly at his mother, who had taken no part in the procession of royalties, but who had walked from the Deanery, by a specially prepared covered way along the leads, to a gallery overlooking the Chapel. She sat there, surrounded by her ladies, and the mourning clothes and tightly-fitting black widow's cap which she wore were relieved only by the ribbon, badge, and star of the Garter, and by a diamond brooch enclosing a miniature of the Prince Consort.

The fantastically long silver train of Princess Alexandra, who was given away by her father, was borne by eight British bridesmaids, among whom Lady Diana Beauclerk was the prettiest. Four Bishops as well as the Dean of Windsor assisted the Archbishop of Canterbury, C. T. Longley, in conducting the service, and as the organ pealed a chorale composed by the Prince Consort, which the choir sang with Jenny Lind's glorious notes ringing over all, Princess Alexandra cast her eyes shyly down like a rosebud princess in a fairy tale, while Queen Victoria raised her eyes towards heaven with an expression which moved all who beheld it. The scene was commemorated in a painting by W. P. Frith, who had been installed in a corner with his sketch-book.

After lunching with thirty-six other royalties (but not

with the Queen), the Prince and Princess of Wales left Windsor at four o'clock for a week's honeymoon at Osborne, which was described caustically and unkindly by the Crown Prince of Prussia as one great gloomy vault, filled with relics of the Prince Consort. They returned to Windsor, in order to be near at hand while workmen put finishing touches to reception rooms at Marlborough House, which was large enough for the whole of what was known in 1863 as London society to be entertained at a single ball. 'Alix looked so sweet and lovely at luncheon', the Queen recorded[15] on 17 March, 'and Bertie so brightened up.' They went to Sandringham on 28 March and moved into Marlborough House on 7 April.

Then began such a season as London had never previously known, and Disraeli described it as a royal honeymoon extended over months. As ball succeeded ball amid a whirl of fêtes and receptions, processions and ceremonies, the Prince of Wales, in the flower of his lusty youth and with the most beautiful Princess in Europe at his side, inaugurated, with startling suddenness and inimitable gusto, a social sovereignty which endured until he died.

ii

The society which acclaimed the Prince and Princess of Wales in 1863 was supported by twenty-five million inhabitants of the British Isles who were being transformed with increasing rapidity into an urban proletariat. Housing conditions were appalling, but an expanding economy was raising the living standards of all except the weakest and poorest, who existed almost like animals.

The top section of the artisan class, organized in trade unions on lines recommended by Samuel Smiles in his famous book (*Self Help*, 1859), was enfranchised in 1867, when it became an important political factor; and the vast mass of the common people – as they were usually termed – displayed great deference towards the upper class. It had dreamed, a generation earlier, about manning barricades; but it had renounced all thoughts of violence, and the quality – as it was often termed – slept more securely in its beds in consequence.

The quality appeared to dream, in the home counties at any rate, about laying out the whole of England in a series of great privately owned parks, and the only barricades of which anyone was conscious were a consequence of the extreme tightness of the market in land. Pressure of population at the start of the nineteenth century had caused an increase in agricultural profits and rents, and the difficulty of acquiring land made the gentry class an increasingly exclusive one until the onset of the great agricultural depression at the end of the 1870s. At that time, less than seven thousand people owned four-fifths of all land in the United Kingdom; but thereafter it became much easier for merchants and manufacturers to buy land almost wherever they wished from the decaying gentry class. As tenanted land passed also, at an accelerating pace, into the outright possession of its farmers, the ancient yeomen class, which was thought once to have disappeared, returned in a different form into its own.

Throughout the lifetime of the Prince of Wales, the outlook and interests of the grandees differed widely from those of the gentry. As a class, the great territorial magnates had qualified themselves to lead the new industrial society, and had made themselves almost independent of agriculture, by using their capital to exploit iron and coal, for example, during the eighteenth century, by cutting canals and by building their own docks and communications. They had made industry fashionable, and, as industrial rentiers during the nineteenth century, they were content to sacrifice the agricultural interests of the doomed class of gentry. They maintained their political power after the repeal of the Corn Laws by placing the Tory and Liberal Parties upon a new commercial and industrial foundation, and they fitted themselves in that way for long-term economic and social survival.

A conspicuous and swollen class of plutocrats, envied and despised by the gentry, was welcomed and patronized by most great territorial magnates for realistic political reasons;

and, in ignoring class barriers, the Prince of Wales followed wise and traditional English practice. The class structure has always been comparatively fluid in Great Britain, where the political and military exigencies which hardened continental European aristocracies into closed castes were virtually unknown.

The European upper class formed part of a linked, French-speaking aristocracy which was conscious of certain common interests before 1914, and which acknowledged, as he grew older, the social leadership of the Prince of Wales. But the Prince's efforts to induce that class to assimilate new elements met with no success outside the British Isles. Members of the continental European patrician caste who maintained, by means of large-scale land-ownership, Austrian, German, Hungarian and Russian ascendancy over territories inhabited by allegedly inferior Czech, Croat, Polish, Serb, and Slovak peasantries were employed also to officer the great conscript European standing armies. Within the British Isles, however, similar conditions of land ownership existed only in Ireland; and the army was insignificant.

Even in the United States a profound sense of insecurity after the Civil War had caused a mushroom growth of artificial social criteria which appeared to be more absurd, as well as less elastic, than any which existed in England. They always amused the Prince of Wales, who loved to tease American acquaintances at Austrian spas, or on the French Riviera, by asking with mock seriousness why, for example, Arthur Leary, whose father was a hatter, should be 'in', while his three brothers were 'out'; or why the entire Vanderbilt family should have been 'out' until one of its members married the Duke of Marlborough. In England it had been possible always for outsiders to enter society, if they made themselves sufficiently agreeable.

A man's status in English society has always depended primarily upon his self-consciousness; for the English ... perceive and accept facts without anxiously inquiring into their reasons or meaning. Whatever is apt to raise a man's self-consciousness – be it birth, rank, wealth, intellect, daring or achievements – will add to his stature; but it has to be translated into the truest expression of a man's subconscious self-valuation, uncontending ease, the unbought grace of life.

Classes are more sharply marked in England because there is no single test for them, except the final incontestable result; and there is more snobbery than in any other country, because the gate can be entered by anyone, and yet remains, for those bent on entering it, a mysterious, awe-inspiring gate.[16]

The British upper class was associated traditionally with public service, and society resembled a club and not a caste. Membership had always been open to plutocrats; but manners and standards were menaced to an unprecedented extent by a flood of new wealth during the nineteenth century, and that process of deterioration was depicted inimitably by Anthony Trollope's novel, *The Way We Live Now* (1874).

In a letter to General Knollys, which he was asked to show to the Prince of Wales, Queen Victoria wrote[17] (10 June 1866) that society had become 'so lax and so bad' that the Prince and Princess of Wales had a duty 'to deny themselves amusement in order to keep up that tone in Society which *used* to be the pride of England'. The Queen explained that she and her husband had always been 'civil to, but kept at a distance from, the fast racing set', although, during her youth, 'its manners at least were good and none knew its faults'. Latterly, she added, the manners of its members had worsened to such an extent, and their faults had become so widely known, that the Prince of Wales was bound to mark his disapproval by 'not asking them to dinner, nor down to Sandringham – and, above all, not going to their houses'.

A small section of the upper class agreed with Queen Victoria in holding that the right, for whatever it might be worth, to the descriptive term 'well-bred' was passing from the society which orbited around Marlborough House, to the cultivated and dominant upper middle class, with which the Prince Consort had felt an affinity. In a reminiscent chapter entitled 'The Old Order', Lord Percy of Newcastle (a son of the 7th Duke of Northumberland) noted[18] that his parents had always impressed upon him 'the superiority of

English middle-class manners' over those displayed generally in Society. Too many patricians, furthermore, contrived to combine a bewitching and genuinely modest demeanour, which won the love of everyone whose acquaintance they were willing, for any reason, to accept, with an arrogant public mask.

The masks worn by the great Lord Castlereagh, or by the otherwise admirable hero of Jane Austen's novel, *Pride and Prejudice*, Mr Darcy, are obvious examples, and that arrogance left its imprint upon history. It affronted strangers, and caused much harm, for example, to Anglo-American and Anglo-Irish relations during the nineteenth century, besides injecting poison into Tory–Radical politics between 1905 and 1914.

Detesting arrogance and despising snobbery, the Prince of Wales helped to adapt Society, which he regarded as an organic growth, to the changing spirit of his age. He never doubted that the tastes and interests of all classes were fundamentally the same, except when cramped or distorted by economic difficulties, and he shared with the mass of his fellow-countrymen a temperament and character which had contributed much to making England rich, merry and great.

Using the social leadership thrust upon him to satisfy an autocratic instinct which might otherwise have been expended upon his children with whom his relations were supremely happy, the Prince's unquenchable vitality, curiosity and zest, in combination with a formidable dignity, secured the foundations of the monarchy deep in public opinion. Exaggerated rumours about gambling did his reputation harm at times, against a background of widespread poverty; but similar rumours about amorous adventures were less damaging. Such stories had not hurt the reputations of Wellington, Melbourne, or Palmerston; and Jupiter himself had given vicarious satisfaction to millions of loyal worshippers by descending occasionally from Olympus in a shower of gold.

The nineteenth-century social code made allowance for frailty in high places by licensing fusion between husband,

wife and lover, on condition that no confusion was permitted to occur. Everyone intimately concerned had to be
consenting parties, and all who possessed the freedom of
Vanity Fair were required to behave with the utmost decorum in order to prevent the innumerable irregular liaisons,
which beguiled the tedium of excessive leisure and about
which they loved to gossip privately, from becoming publicly known. Any indiscretion which impaired Society's
prestige invited a sentence of social death which was ruth-
lessly executed.

The Prince of Wales inaugurated, in 1863, the indispensable task of democratizing the monarchy by broadening,
in innumerable personal contacts, the basis of its appeal; but
his outlook was always conservative. The human and practical experience of democracy, which Americans absorbed in
their effort to tame a continent, reached England for the
first time by way of the trenches in the First World War.

That community of death and suffering dealt a mortal
blow to the arrogance which clung to some, and to the snobbery which clung to most sections of the swollen, amorphous
and cliquish society which surrounded the Prince of Wales
after as well as before he ascended the throne. Existing for
amusement, and often morbidly conscious of its identity, it
comprised a few thousand people and spread its branches
throughout the kingdom into some hundreds of country
houses which, except in the matter of bathrooms, became
ever more luxurious. In those homes, unmenaced by surtax
or death duties, set in extraordinarily variegated environ-
ments of great beauty and dependent upon an inexhaustible
supply of hordes of indoor and outdoor servants who never
dreamed that their descendants might become ladies and
gentlemen some day, life, whether dedicated to service or
frivolity, was synonymous with dignity, influence and ease.

Queen Victoria's intense dislike of the social leadership
assumed by the Prince of Wales, as well as her reasons for
entertaining that dislike, were expressed very clearly in
many letters which she wrote to him and to others during
the 1860s and even later. As early as 25 April 1863, after
a trifling disagreement with her son, who had only been

installed in Marlborough House for a fortnight, the Queen wrote [19] to the Crown Princess: 'Bertie is not improved since I last saw him, and his ways and manners are very unpleasant. Poor dear Alix! I feel so for her.'

On 8 June 1863, the Queen wrote [20] again to her daughter:

Bertie and Alix left Frogmore to-day, both looking as ill as possible. We are all seriously alarmed about her. For although Bertie says he is so anxious to take care of her, he goes on going out every night till she will become a Skeleton, and hopes there cannot be.

Oh, how different poor foolish Bertie is to adored Papa, whose gentle, loving, wise motherly care of me, when he was not 21, exceeded everything!

On 24 June, the Queen described [21] her son and daughter-in-law as in process of becoming 'nothing but puppets, running about for show all day and all night'; and three days later she wrote [22]: 'Oh, what will become of the poor country when I die! I foresee, if Bertie succeeds, nothing but misery, and he would do anything he was asked and spend his life in one whirl of amusements, as he does now. It makes me very sad and anxious.'

The root of Queen Victoria's objection to the 'frivolous' life which the Prince of Wales continued to lead can best be illustrated by an exchange of letters between mother and son in January, 1868. The Prince had written (14 December 1867), during a series of Irish bomb outrages in London and the provinces, to warn [23] his mother that the Government:

... should use the high hand, be firm, and deal with these rebels (for they are nothing else) most summarily. If they do not, the lower classes who already have a much greater power than they, I think, have any idea of, will be very difficult to manage; and then it will cause bloodshed and that, indeed, ought to be avoided.... At the present moment the new laws about cabs and traffic in London cannot be enforced, and everything that the Government gives in to is a feather in the cap of the lower orders.

To that letter, the Queen replied [24] (7 January 1868) that the bomb outrages, of which her son had complained, were the work of a mere handful of ruffians, and that 'the country never was so *loyal* or *so devoted to their Sovereign as now*'. She continued:

But there is one *great danger*, and one which it is the *duty* of *all* to *try* to *avert*, or the result may be *very* disastrous. This danger lies *not* in the *power given to the Lower Orders,* who are daily becoming more well-informed and more intelligent, and who will *deservedly* work themselves up to the top by their own merits, labour and good conduct, but in the conduct of the *Higher Classes* and of the *Aristocracy*.

Many, many, with whom I have conversed, tell me that at no time for the last 60 or 70 years was frivolity, the love of pleasure, self-indulgence, luxury, and idleness (producing ignorance) carried to such an excess as now in the Higher Classes, and that it resembles the time before the first French Revolution; and I must – alas! – admit that this is *true*. Believe me! It is *most alarming*, although you do not observe it, nor will you *hear* it; but those who do not live *in* the gay circle of fashion, and who view it calmly, are greatly, seriously alarmed. And in THIS lies the REAL *danger* of the *present* time!

The Aristocracy and the Higher Classes must take *great care*, or their position may become *very* dangerous. I shall do what I can in this direction, but as you mix much with the gay and the fashionable, you can do more, and so can dear Alix, to whom I wish you to show this letter, as I have often talked to her on these subjects.

That very kind and wise letter was in part the fruit of Queen Victoria's vivid recollection of the quasi-revolutionary agitation of the 1820s, '30s and '40s which had coloured her childhood and youth. It had been burned so deeply into her mind that she noted [25] occasionally with disapproval that even Princess Alix was becoming 'a little grand'; and she wrote [26] (30 August 1868) to warn the Crown Princess, who had complained about the pride shown by her eldest son (the future Emperor William II), that 'in the twinkling of an eye, the highest may find themselves at the feet of the poorest and lowest'.

Besides that fear of seeing a revolution provoked by the ostentatious frivolity and extravagance of the higher classes,

Queen Victoria was moved also by a sense of social injustice. She observed,[27] for example (26 July 1872) to the Crown Princess, that 'every sort of vice' was tolerated in the aristocracy, 'whereas the poorer and working classes, who have far less education, and are much more exposed, are abused for the 10th part less evil than their betters commit without the slightest blame. The so-called immorality of the Lower Orders is not to be named on the same day with that of the High and Highest. This is a thing which makes my blood boil.'

Queen Victoria was fond of saying that a prince, in the modern world, could only maintain his position by his character; and her husband, who had regarded princes as the future regenerators of society, had descried significant analogies between the obligations imposed by the priestly and the princely offices. As early as 10 February 1863, the Queen told [28] Lord Granville that the Prince and Princess of Wales 'should not go out to dinners and parties' during the London season, and that their social lives ought to be restricted to occasional visits to the houses of two or three high-ranking Cabinet ministers – 'Lord Granville, Lord Palmerston, and possibly Lord Derby' – and to the very few privileged great houses – Apsley, Grosvenor and Spencer Houses – but 'not to *all* these the *same* year'.

The restraints to which he had been subjected as a boy caused the Prince of Wales to dive headlong into all the varied delights which a rich and sophisticated society had to offer, and he paid no attention to his mother's reiterated objections to the conduct or characters of some of his most intimate friends, including the Duke of Sutherland and the Duchess of Manchester. It was natural and inevitable that the view taken by the Prince of the society which orbited around him should be opposed directly to that of the Queen; but both views reflected facets of a single ineluctable truth.

Material values and a selfish love of pleasure are no natural monopoly of an upper class. They are endemic in human nature, and, as British prosperity became more widely diffused, the same high proportion of members of all classes began to display the same material and frivolous outlook. For that reason, the late G. M. Young concluded his analysis of Victorian England by stating,[29] with rare acidity, that 'fundamentally, what failed in the late Victorian age, and its flash Edwardian epilogue, was the Victorian public. . . . Compared with their fathers, the men of that time were ceasing to be a ruling or reasoning stock.'

The economic advantages which Great Britain enjoyed, in comparison with other nations, precluded all risk of violent upheaval after Chartism fizzled out in 1848; and the concentration upon frivolity of a high proportion of the British upper class afforded useful adventitious opportunities to members of other classes for a time. After their minimum ambitions had been satisfied the British middle and lower classes soon ceased to appear more virtuous and high-minded than the upper class did; and there existed always a minority of patricians who were proud to devote their entire lives to public service.

The Prince of Wales's view of the society over which he ruled after 1863 is well illustrated in the robust reply which he wrote [30] (10 January 1868) to the heartfelt letter about the danger of social revolution which Queen Victoria had sent him three days earlier (7 January):

I do not think you quite understand what I meant in my former letter.

I did not mean that the really hardworking labouring classes were getting too much power, because they indeed deserve to be noticed when they attain a higher sphere of existence by their own merits and industry. But I alluded to ... what are known as 'roughs', and they, to a much greater extent than people are aware of, are getting a greater power. They are the people ... who broke into Hyde Park and attended the meetings at Trafalgar Square last year. At present their power is not really very great, but it may increase if law and order are not kept up....

With regard to what *you say* concerning the Aristocracy, or Upper Ten Thousand, I quite agree that, in many instances, amusement, self-indulgence, etc., predominate; but it is hard to say that all are so. I know of so many instances where those of the highest rank are excellent Country Gentlemen, are Chairmen of Quarter Sessions, Magistrates, etc., and the ladies attend to their duties also.

In every Country a great proportion of the Aristocracy will be idle and fond of amusement, and have always been so; but I think that in no Country more than ours do the Higher Classes occupy themselves, which is certainly not the case in other Countries.

We have always been an Aristocratic Country, and I hope we shall always remain so, as they are the mainstay of this Country, unless we become so Americanized that they are swept away. And then the state of things will be quite according to Mr Bright's views, who wishes only for the Sovereign and the people, and no class between!

But I quite agree that in these days much depends on the Aristocracy maintaining their proper position and leading a useful life, though some pleasure cannot be denied them, and so-called 'Society' cannot quite cease to exist.

Much depended, as the Prince observed, upon the way in which members of the aristocracy maintained their positions by leading useful lives which inspired respect; and the question of his own occupation posed a difficult problem. The Constitution, which provides the sovereign with whole-time occupation, makes no such provision for the heir to the throne; and previous Princes of Wales had focused the hopes and activity of the Parliamentary Opposition. As such conduct had become unthinkable, and as social sovereignty was regarded as inadequate, it appeared likely that the Prince of Wales would be constrained to seek new paths.

5

An Unemployed Youth

1863-9

i

Two of Queen Victoria's younger sons, Alfred, Duke of Edinburgh, and Arthur, Duke of Connaught, enjoyed useful careers in the Navy and Army; but the problem of devising a suitable occupation for the Prince of Wales was discussed intermittently for years, before being raised artificially to the level of a crisis by Gladstone in 1871-2. The Queen's original intention* that her eldest son, who had been taught to regard himself as belonging to the nation as a whole, should 'early be initiated into the affairs of State', was abandoned for ten years after his father's death; and Queen Victoria's diary recorded[1] with habitual candour on 8 July 1871: 'After '61 I could hardly bear the thought of anyone helping me, or standing where my dearest had always stood; but, as years go on, I strongly feel that to lift up my son and heir and keep him in his place, near me, is really what is right.'

In the meantime, Queen Victoria had warned[2] Lord Granville (10 February 1863) that the Prince of Wales should *upon no account* be put at the head of any of those Societies or Commissions, or preside at any of those scientific proceedings in which his beloved great Father took so prominent a part'; and she had rejected consistently her ministers' advice that the Prince should be permitted to represent her in public, as his father had done. She wrote,[3] for example (9 July 1864), through Sir Charles Phipps to the Home Secretary, Sir George Grey:

Her Majesty is very much opposed to the system of putting the Prince of Wales forward as the representative of the

* See p. 22 above.

Sovereign. She thinks it is not fair to the Prince of Wales, as placing Him in a position to which He is not entitled, and accustoming people to regard Him in a full light.

Properly speaking, no one can represent the Sovereign but Her, or Her Consort. There are certain duties and forms which ... as the Queen is unable to perform them, She can and does depute someone else to perform ..., but Her Majesty thinks it would be most undesirable to constitute the Heir to the Crown a general representative of Herself, and particularly to bring Him forward too frequently before the people.

This would necessarily place the Prince of Wales in a position of competing, as it were, for popularity with the Queen. Nothing ... should be more carefully avoided.

By the end of the 1860s Queen Victoria had become habituated to a life of secluded invisibility and strenuous desk work at Osborne and Balmoral. She did not visit London for years on end, whereas the Prince of Wales had established an equally set annual routine of a very different kind. It dovetailed geographically with that of his mother only at the beginning of August, when he yachted at Cowes, near Osborne, and during October, when he shot at Abergeldie, near Balmoral; and Queen Victoria started to enlist, in a semi-secretarial capacity, the services of her younger children, and especially those of Prince Leopold (Duke of Albany), whose health was always indifferent.

Throughout January and February, the Prince of Wales was based upon Sandringham, which he regarded as home, and where shooting had become a way of life. Guests noticed that he enjoyed practical jokes, that he made a point of arranging personally such details as bedroom allocations and seatings at meals, and that the Sunday ritual never varied.

Too impatient to sit through an hour's morning service, the Prince of Wales entered the church in his park, with his male house guests and to the accompaniment of a fresh peal of bells, immediately before the sermon which was limited strictly to ten minutes, and at the moment when the service was half way through. After luncheon, all guests were conducted by the Prince and Princess on a lengthy tour of the stables, kennels, gardens, model farm, stud farm and, lastly, a school established by the Princess for training local boys in arts and crafts.

At the beginning of March the Prince liked to visit the French Riviera, *en garçon* for five weeks, which included a few days in Paris at either end. He sent ahead his yacht, which he often made his headquarters, and he attended fêtes, dinners, balls and suppers almost every night before returning refreshed to Marlborough House to face the rigours of the London season.

Most of the Prince's public engagements were undertaken during the summer months, and especially during July; and he made a point of visiting many artists' studios, in Paris as well as in London, and in other capital cities when he had the opportunity. To the Court which he had established at Marlborough House, achievement, beauty, riches, sophistication and wit provided equally valid criteria of admission; and he attended race meetings, and the theatre, as often as possible.

At Newmarket the Prince stayed sometimes in private quarters which he retained at the Jockey Club, and sometimes at friends' houses in and near the town, and his extraordinary vitality made the atmosphere electric wherever he went. He needed perpetual diversion, and expected members of his intimate circle to come to Marlborough House at short notice, or to arrange small supper parties for him at equally short notice elsewhere.

At the end of July the Prince yachted at Cowes for two or three weeks before leaving, sometimes with the Princess and sometimes *en garçon*, for a holiday at some German or Austrian spa, where he tried to reduce his weight. He drank comparatively little, but smoked innumerable cigars and cigarettes, and indulged a tremendous appetite for rich food. Returning home early in October, the Prince enjoyed a month's grouse shooting and deerstalking at Abergeldie, before going to Sandringham, where he invariably spent his own and the Princess's birthdays (9 November and 1 December) as well as Christmas.

Within the framework of that routine, the Prince accumulated a number of honorary presidencies, chairmanships, governorships and colonelcies. He became, for example, President (1863) of the Society of Arts, Chairman (1864) of the Governors of Wellington College, a Governor (1865) of the Charterhouse and of Christ's Hospital, Regimental Colonel (1863) of the 10th Hussars, Captain-General and Colonel (1863) of the Honourable Artillery Company and Colonel-in-Chief (1868) of the Rifle Brigade.

On an average of twenty-seven days a year during the late 1860s, the Prince of Wales attended public dinners, laid foundation stones, opened buildings or inspected institutions; and the light in which he regarded those duties was shown in a letter which he wrote to a former tutor. F. W. Gibbs had expressed a hope that the Prince would not decline to open the new buildings of Glasgow University, and the Prince replied [4] (15 September 1868):

I quite agree with you that the duty (which, after all, will be a very easy one) which I shall have to perform, has, for its object, a National one; and I shall never shrink from coming forward (however inconvenient to myself) when asked for such an occasion.

But I am asked, if once, at least thirty times in the course of the year to do things which only make me an advertisement, and a puff to the object in view; and I think you will agree with me that I ought to think twice before (using a slang expression) being 'let in' to such things.

The public sector of the nation's economy was extremely narrow at that time; but the Prince duly opened the new buildings at Glasgow on 7 October 1868. He had become an accomplished and fluent public speaker, and he never used notes on such occasions after passing a difficult test on 18 June 1865. He was called upon unexpectedly to propose or respond to five toasts that evening at a dinner in aid of the Duke of Cambridge's Homes for Soldiers' Wives, and his diary recorded [5]: 'all went off very well, but it was a great ordeal for me to go through'.

The Prince loved the company of the Commander-in-Chief, the Duke of Cambridge, who was his mother's first cousin and whom he called 'Uncle George'; but he saw no active service, and some murmuring was aroused on that account in the Army when the Prince was made a field-marshal in 1875. The Queen complained[6] in a memorandum (21 February 1866) that he took no interest in the troops; others held that he paid a disproportionate amount of attention to buttons and uniforms; and the Prince was hurt when the Government rejected his offer to serve in the field with the Egyptian expedition of 1882. Much as he hated the policies which drove Prussia into war successively with Denmark, Austria and France, he envied his brother-in-law, the Crown Prince of Prussia, who saw active service in high command in all three victorious campaigns.

'Mind you vote against the Reform Bill', the Prince of Wales wrote[7] (15 April 1866) to Charles Carrington, who laughed and voted for it in the Commons, while retaining the Prince's goodwill. In public the Prince maintained invariably an attitude of strict neutrality; but he relished contacts which he made by attending committees of the House of Lords. Selecting subjects – cattle plague, supply of horses, public schools – which excited no controversy on Party lines, the Prince attended committees or debates on an average of twenty-five days a year during the late 1860s, and he supported consistently, by voice and vote, a Bill, which was thrown out time after time, to legalize marriage with a deceased wife's sister.

Besides telling dissident bishops, with perfect good humour, that he had as much right as they or anyone else had to express a view upon that issue, the Prince had a private motive for persisting after the death of his sister, Princess Alice, in 1878. The Princess had married the Grand Duke of Hesse; and her brother hoped, for a time, that his youngest sister, Princess Beatrice, might become the Grand Duke's second wife.

The invasion of Denmark by Prussian and Austrian armies in January 1864, moved the Prince of Wales to ask his mother to accord him the privilege of direct access to Foreign Office despatches. Through General Grey, however, Queen Victoria informed[8] the Foreign Secretary, Lord Russell, that she did not wish the Prince of Wales to enter into 'separate and independent communication with the Government', and that she proposed, therefore, to have 'a précis made of such despatches, sent to Her, as She thinks the Prince of Wales should see'. Grey added that the Queen 'would thus be enabled to exercise some control over what is communicated to Him – a control which is very necessary, as She must tell you confidentially, that His Royal Highness is not at all times as discreet as He should be'.

To a letter of protest which the Prince wrote when informed of that decision, the Queen replied[9] (3 June) that it was final, and that '*you* could not well have a Government key which only Ministers, and those immediately connected with them, or with me, have'. The Prince had not asked specifically before for a key to the red despatch boxes in which Cabinet papers were circulated, but he considered that he was as much entitled as his father had been to regard himself as 'immediately connected' with the Sovereign; and he initiated a struggle, to secure possession of such a key, which lasted for a quarter of a century and which caused him great annoyance and frustration.

The father of the Princess of Wales, after succeeding, on 15 November 1863, to the throne of Denmark as King Christian IX, was constrained by his subjects to ratify immediately the full incorporation of Schleswig into his kingdom. German troops crossed the border two months later, and the British family was divided most painfully; but Danish resistance was crushed after a campaign which lasted five and a half months.

The British Government, press and public opinion were very strongly pro-Danish, to the immense and unconcealable satisfaction of the Prince and Princess of Wales. Queen Victoria, on the other hand, and her daughter, the Crown Princess of Prussia, were vehement advocates of the hereditary claim of Duke Frederick (Fritz) of Augustenburg to rule, as a German princeling, the Duchies of Schleswig and Holstein in place of King Christian of Denmark.

The father of Fritz Augustenburg had renounced, in 1852, in return for a payment of £350,000 his claim to succeed to the disputed duchies; but the Crown Princess of Prussia warned[10] the Prince of Wales (20 November 1863) that that renunciation had been 'contrary to natural justice'. She explained, at great length, that there would be 'an end to all legal rights in Europe' if a Congress of Great Powers were permitted to dispossess a reigning German House 'without even so much as assigning a reason'; and that, as the German Confederation had 'the duty of protecting Princes, who are its members, in their rights ... a voluntary cession could only be in favour of a member of the Confederation, and consequently not to the King of Denmark, as King of Denmark'.

To that letter the Prince of Wales was content to retort [11] (21 November) that his sister appeared to have succeeded at last in becoming a thorough Prussian, and that 'a grand outcry' would occur in England 'if we don't do something in the matter'. Palmerston had used language in the Commons in July 1863, which gave the Danes cause to think that British aid would be forthcoming; but, after war had broken out, Queen Victoria informed [12] the Prince of Wales (8 February 1864) that the Prince Consort had foreseen all that had happened, and that the Crown Princess's view on the merits of the quarrel coincided with that of both her parents.

Disregarding the very strongly expressed expostulations of Queen Victoria, who remained warmly pro-German, Palmerston and Russell pursued a policy which Lord Derby characterized aptly as one of 'meddle and muddle'. They interlaced fierce threats with offers of mediation and with specific proposals for a peace of compromise, and war with Germany was averted only as a result of the British Government's failure to discover any continental ally.

The Prince of Wales was often violent in abusing Prussia, but Clarendon, who was sent by the Queen to enjoin greater caution, reported [13] reassuringly on 20 May. Although warmly pro-Danish, and naturally very sympathetic 'with the Princess, who passed sleepless nights and was miserable about the trials that her parents were undergoing', the Prince of Wales had (19 May) written to warn his father-in-law to abandon even 'the slightest hope' that England would intervene actively on Denmark's behalf. The Prince had suggested to Clarendon that occasions might arise when he could be 'of more use than Sir A. Paget' in serving as the channel of communication between the British Government and the King and Queen of Denmark, and had added 'that it would be a great satisfaction to him to be so employed'.

Queen Victoria considered that her son's offer could only be accepted, if at all, '*with extreme caution*'; and Russell, under restraint by the Queen, displayed the utmost reserve. Exasperated in consequence, the Prince started, in concert with the Duke of Cambridge, to consult leading members of the Conservative Opposition.

In begging Clarendon, 'as a personal friend of the Prince Consort', to burn her letter and to speak very seriously to the Prince of Wales about a matter 'which causes the greatest anxiety', Queen Victoria wrote [14] (26 June): 'Our poor Boy stands so alone, alas! – has the best intentions, but is *not* discreet. ... She therefore earnestly appeals to Lord Clarendon to help him and her. The Queen has not felt it safe to tell him the decision of the Cabinet'.

The Cabinet had decided, on the previous day, that Prussia and Austria would have to be left in possession of the Duchies of Schleswig and Holstein, and that no action by the British Government was possible to save Denmark from the consequences of defeat in war. That was the only occasion during his life on which the Prince displayed any disposition to imitate former Princes of Wales by becoming entangled with the Parliamentary Opposition, and it frightened Queen Victoria. In reassuring her, after two conversations with the Prince at Chesterfield House and at Devonshire House, Claredon asked [15] that full allowance should be made for the Prince's youth and inexperience, as well as for his 'extreme anxiety for the family of the Princess and the political existence of Denmark'.

Queen Victoria's doubts about her son's discretion had been reinforced by his action in flouting her known wishes when he called (22 April 1864) upon the Italian revolutionary leader, Guiseppe Garibaldi, who had been acclaimed rapturously in England, and who was staying in London with the Duke of Sutherland at Stafford House. Palmerston and

Russell (but not Disraeli) had entertained the hero already, and another member of the Cabinet, Lord Granville, explained[16] (21 April) to the Queen that 'the joining of the aristocracy, including some Conservative leaders', with 'the middle and lower classes' in honouring Garibaldi had 'taken the democratic sting (as to this country) out of the affair'. Although 'a goose', in a 'mountebank dress which betrays a desire for effect', Garibaldi was 'physically and morally brave'; there had been 'tomfoolery and much vulgarity, but there has also been much that is honourable to the English character'.

Reflecting that character admirably, the Prince of Wales wrote[17] (23 April) from Sandringham to his mother:

> ... I had to go to London yesterday for a Duchy of Cornwall Council ..., and the Duke of Sutherland having written several times to General Knollys about Garibaldi, offering to bring him here, which was, of course, declined, I agreed with General Knollys that the best plan would be to call at Stafford House *quite privately* ..., as you will naturally understand that I was anxious to do nothing which might possibly, politically or otherwise, embarrass you or the Government....
>
> I was much pleased with him. He is not tall, but such a dignified and noble appearance, and such a quiet and gentle way of speaking – especially never of himself – that nobody could fail to be attracted to him.... He asked a great deal about you, and ... referred to Denmark and said how much he felt for all the brave soldiers who had perished in the war.
>
> Though, of course, it would have been very different for you to see him, still I think you would have been pleased with him, as he is *uncharlatanlike*, if I may use such an expression .. and though his undertakings have been certainly revolutionary, still, he is a patriot, and did not seek for his own aggrandisement.

The Queen informed[18] General Knollys (25 April) that she held him responsible; that she was '*very* much shocked'; and that 'for the future she must *insist* that no step of the *slightest political importance* shall be taken without due consultation with the Queen'. Knollys replied[19] (27 April) that he had done 'what he could to make that which he could not prevent as little annoying as possible to Your Majesty;' but the Prince, who had been rebuked also by his mother, replied in a different strain. He had selected his ground carefully, and he wrote [20] (27 April) that he could not admit that he had been wrong, or imprudent; that his visit to Garibaldi had been 'hailed with joy throughout the country'; and that he had always believed firmly 'in the Unity of Italy, which is the avowed policy of the present Government'. Adding that Knollys had been rebuked unjustly, the Prince concluded:

I feel he feels it very much, as he is not, and cannot be, responsible for my actions. I have now been of age for some time and am *alone* responsible, and am only too happy to bear *any* blame on my shoulders. . . .

You will, I am sure, excuse my perhaps having written rather bluntly; but, as I know you like my confiding in you and letting you openly into my thoughts, I have done so now.

That was the first of a number of occasions on which the Prince found it necessary to assert his personal independence; and he did so always with tact and unruffled courtesy. He had become a father three months earlier, two months before the expected date, and he had to fight during the summer for permission to escort the Princess at the earliest opportunity on a visit to her parents at Copenhagen.

On 8 January 1864, while staying at Frogmore, near Windsor, the Princess of Wales drove to Virginia Water to watch her husband play ice hockey. After being whirled over the ice in a sledge, the Princess felt unwell, and she drove home with her lady-in-waiting, Lady Macclesfield, before giving birth to a prince at ten minutes to nine.

No preparations had been made; the Home Secretary could not be summoned, and a local practitioner, Dr Brown, who was knighted for his exertions, arrived at a gallop only a short time before the baby was born. Queen Victoria, who arrived next day and took command, recorded [21] in her diary that Lady Macclesfield, who had borne twelve children of her own, had acted as nurse 'in every sense of the word', and that there had been 'no clothes for the poor little boy, who was just wrapped in cotton wool'.

In insisting that the baby should be christened Albert Victor, the Queen explained [22] (14 January) her wish that the Prince of Wales should be known as Albert Edward when he became King, and that all his descendants should bear the names of Albert or Victoria until the end of time. The Prince avoided carefully making any promise, while observing [23] (15 January) that no English sovereign had as yet borne a double name, 'although no doubt there is no absolute reason why it should not be so'.

As soon as she was well, the Princess started to agitate for permission to visit her parents in Copenhagen, and the Prince, who had never visited Denmark, supported most warmly that request. Queen Victoria acquiesced with great reluctance, on condition that the strictest incognito should be preserved; that Germany should be included in the itinerary, and that the baby should be sent home after an absence of three weeks.

On 1 September 1864, the Queen drove to Abergeldie, 'where' she noted [24] in her diary, 'I saw Alix washing the dear Baby, which certainly looks a frail little thing'. Two days later, accompanied by the baby, as well as by Lord and Lady Spencer, Sir William Knollys, and two doctors, the Prince and Princess of Wales embarked at Dundee aboard *Osborne* for Copenhagen.

ii

The Princess's interests were centred always in her children and family, with a passionate and possessive intensity, and she was overjoyed at being re-united with her parents. Missing her favourite, slim and very handsome nineteen-year-old brother, William, who had been elected to the throne of Greece as King George I, she looked forward eagerly to meeting the Grand Duke Nicholas (eldest son of the Emperor Alexander II of Russia), who was due in Copenhagen before the end of the month, and who became engaged (28 September) to Princess Dagmar.

Afflicted by fearful loss, the Danish people accorded their English visitors such a rapturous and generous welcome that Queen Victoria was alarmed. She had directed the Prince and Princess to go to Stockholm and to stay at an hotel, or at the British Legation, while the Grand Duke Nicholas was wooing Princess Dagmar in Copenhagen; but they stayed instead for ten days at the Palace with King Charles XV of Sweden, who took the Prince of Wales on a much publicized elk hunt.

Besides reproaching her son for having broken his incognito, Queen Victoria wrote several times to ask that the baby should be despatched home immediately with the Spencers in the royal yacht, as had been promised; and, in yielding reluctantly, the Prince wrote [25] bluntly (7 October) to his mother. He explained that the Princess hated being compelled for the first time to part with 'her little treasure', against the doctors' advice, and he refused to apologize for having stayed at the Palace in Stockholm. The hotels in the Swedish capital were squalid; the Legation was cramped in lodgings, 'and I have not the intention of letting Alix be uncomfortably lodged if I can help it. Besides, as I said before, the King was immensely gratified by our visit, and what would have been the good of annoying him by not going to the Palace? ... You may be sure that I shall try to meet your wishes as much as possible, but .... if I am not allowed to use my own discretion we had better give up travelling altogether.'

Infuriated by that letter, which she received on 9 October, Queen Victoria retaliated immediately by telegraphing a curt order to the Prince and Princess of Wales. She had warned [26] them already (3 October) that on their homeward journey, they must observe 'a real incognito' in Paris, 'stop at an hotel', and 'not lodge with the Emperor and Empress' at Compiègne or Fontainebleau, 'the style of going on there being quite unfit for a young and reputable Prince and Princess like yourselves'; and she now ordered that their journey through France should be cancelled, and that they should return through Belgium instead.

In notifying [27] Lord Russell (9 October) that she had 'not hesitated a moment' to exercise her authority 'after the extraordinary publicity of the visit to Stockholm, *contrary to the express agreement beforehand*', Queen Victoria explained that her beloved husband would have applauded her action, and that every member of the Cabinet 'except Lord

Palmerston', would appreciate her motive. She added that her son would be required to pay several visits to relatives in Germany on his way home, 'to show that he is not only the Son-in-Law of the King of Denmark, but the Child of his Parents'.

Startled by the Foreign Secretary's intimation that his duty impelled him to suggest, with profound respect, that her action had been hasty and imprudent, Queen Victoria consulted her Household about the best method of handling the Prince of Wales in future. Sir Charles Phipps minuted [28] (17 October) that it was 'of the highest importance' that the extent of the Queen's authority 'should be distinctly defined and constantly supported and maintained by the Government ... but the Government should lay it down, so that control should not constantly be associated in the Prince of Wales's mind with Your Majesty's authority, for which He should feel nothing but confiding affection'.

After visiting Hanover and Darmstadt, the Prince and Princess of Wales met the Crown Prince and Crown Princess of Prussia at Cologne; but war memories were still bitter, and that encounter, which was not a success, had been difficult to arrange. When the Crown Princess complained to her mother that her brother did not reply to letters, Queen Victoria replied [29] (11 October) that she was 'shocked', but that 'Bertie ... is becoming quite unmanageable'.[30] She added that he was entirely in the hands 'of that most mischievious Queen of Denmark', and that 'Alix, good as she is, is not worth the price we have had to pay for her in having such a family connexion. I shall not let them readily go there again.'

The Prince of Wales complained [31] (7 November) to Lord Spencer about the tactlessness of his brother-in-law at Cologne: 'It was not pleasant to see him and his A.D.C. always in Prussian uniform, flaunting before our eyes a most objectionable medal ribbon which he received for his *deeds of valour* ??? against the unhappy Danes.' A little time was needed before harmony in that quarter could be restored; but all misunderstanding with Queen Victoria was dispersed at once.

The Prince and Princess of Wales stayed at Osborne immediately after returning home, and the Queen described that visit as 'most satisfactory'. She promised to make the King of Denmark a Knight of the Garter, and wrote [32] (19 November 1864) to the Crown Princess: 'Alix is really a dear, excellent, right minded soul, whom one must dearly love and respect. I often think her lot is no easy one, but she is very fond of Bertie, though not blind. . . .'

Frequently as Queen Victoria and the Prince of Wales differed thereafter, and widely as their ways of life inevitably diverged, it is pleasant to record that nothing occurred at any time which threatened to damage the deep bonds of affection, respect and understanding which united them. On the rare occasions when the Prince was in trouble, his mother sprang like a tigress to his aid, and her letters to the Crown Princess of Prussia were filled constantly with tributes to him. 'Bertie', she wrote,[33] for example (15 December 1865), 'has a loving affectionate heart, and never could bear to be long in disagreement with his family.' 'Really,' she wrote [34] (9 November 1867), 'Bertie is so full of good and amiable qualities that it makes one forget and overlook much that one would wish different'; and again [35] (3 July 1869): 'He was affectionate and simple and unassuming as ever. I am sure no Heir Apparent was ever so nice and unpretending as dear Bertie is.'

The quality which most impressed contemporaries was the extraordinary energy displayed by the Prince as he rushed day after day from one social engagement to another. He could make do with little sleep; he liked his diary to show a crowded schedule, and he hated to be kept waiting even a moment. Gregarious and not domestic by nature, he was worried by the Princess's perpetual unpunctuality. 'I don't think she makes his home comfortable', Queen Victoria informed [36] the Crown Princess (11 August 1866). 'She is never ready for breakfast, not being out of her room till 11; and often Bertie breakfasts alone, and then she alone.'

Sometimes the Prince would summon a few friends to Marlborough House late at night for what he termed, during the 1860s, 'a baccy' which would be prolonged into the small hours with supper and whist. At other times he would sally forth with a party, which might include the Duchess of Manchester or Lady Filmer, and explore the night life of the capital. He used hansom cabs on such occasions, and ended up normally at the Cremorne Gardens in Vauxhall, or even at Evans's Music Hall in Covent Garden, where he would sit in a reserved box, protected by a screen from the public gaze.

Whenever a big fire occurred in the capital the Prince liked to be alerted by Captain Eyre Shaw, who had organized the Metropolitan Fire Brigade and who was one of the most popular men in London. Accompanied, if possible, by the Duke of Sutherland and other friends, the Prince would race to the scene and offer assistance, protected from publicity because a popular press scarcely existed, and because newspapers were still incapable of reproducing photographs.

The Duke of Sutherland indulged a passion for driving railroad as well as fire engines, and Queen Victoria implored [37] her son (30 December 1865) not to stay with the Duke at Dunrobin, explaining that 'he does not live as *a Duke ought*'. 'If you knew him as well as I do,' the Prince retorted [38] (2 January 1866), 'I am sure you would like him, as he is a clever and most straightforward man in spite of certain eccentricities and, formerly, faults.' He reminded the Queen that the Duke's mother had been one of her 'oldest and most devoted friends', and warned her that, if the visit were cancelled, 'we should, of course, be obliged to use your name, which would not be pleasant'.

Queen Victoria, who always knew when she had gone far enough, was much distressed to hear [39] from Lord Palmerston, at the beginning of April, that the Prince was drawing extensively upon his capital in order to pay gambling losses. The Prime Minister offered to remonstrate privately with the Prince; but Sir William Knollys informed [40] the Queen (11 April), through Sir Charles Phipps, that he had remonstrated already, 'in writing, having ascertained on more than one occasion that that was the best, if not the only mode of making a lasting impression ... and His Royal Highness testified no displeasure at my having done so'.

Sir William Knollys recorded [41] categorically (13 August 1867) that 'were it not for the outlay at Sandringham, I should have had no difficulty up to the present time in keeping the P.'s expenditure within his Income'; and he estimated the cost of alterations and improvements in hand at that time at £80,000. Palmerston always regretted that the Chancellor of the Exchequer declined absolutely to consider asking Parliament to vote a larger income for the Prince of Wales, but Gladstone adhered inflexibly to his opinion that Queen Victoria had a duty to assist her heir. For that reason he refused, after a troublesome correspondence, to contribute one penny from public funds towards expenses when the Prince went on 7 May 1865, to open an International Exhibition at Dublin.

When the Conservatives returned to office, Benjamin Disraeli was more generous in conceding expenses, but equally reluctant to approach Parliament about voting the Prince a larger income. 'I gave him [Disraeli]', Knollys recorded [42] (29 May 1867) 'an abstract of my account of the Prince's expenditure for the last 4 years, shewing that we exceeded our income by £20,000 in each year.... He alluded to the difficulty and delicacy of bringing it before the House of Commons without prejudice to the Queen. "But", he said, "I will take a favourable opportunity for doing it, after speaking to Lord Derby. I must take my own time. I see you have no debts?" "No", I replied, "because I am obliged to sell out from the capital." "Then you must continue to do so", he replied, "in the interim".'

Despite that promise, an approach to Parliament was held to be inopportune, and unjust rumours continued to circulate that the Prince was pressing men and boys to play whist for higher stakes than they could afford. Many with whom he played could afford higher stakes than he; and his diary [43] proves that in March 1865, when Palmerston saw fit to worry Queen Victoria, the largest sums which changed hands in any single evening were on 16 March, when the Prince lost £138 in eight rubbers to the Duke of St Albans, Sir Robert Peel and Lord Sefton; and on 21 March, when he lost £101 to Lord Bath, Percy Fielding and Lord Methuen.

Among rich men such sums were innocuous, but, after failing in a determined effort to dissuade the Prince from joining the Jockey Club and White's, Knollys recorded [44] losses of £400 and £300 – 'no large sums but the beginning of larger, – at White's on the nights of 12 and 13 August 1867. Gambling on a greater scale than that would have been dangerous, but the Prince, who was quite a good whist player, was content not to exceed it; and the bets which he placed on horses were kept also within reasonable bounds. He wrote,[45] for example, (27 April 1866) to Charles Carrington, in Paris:

As you probably will not be back in time to settle my account at Tattersall's, do you mind writing or telegraphing to some friends to do so in *your* name?

Our account is – I win £300 on *Vauban* – lose £100 on *Plaudit* – and win £75 on *Plaudit* – making a total of £275, I win. This is, I hope, correct. At any rate I have put it in my book. . . . Remember me to those wicked boys, Blandford * and Oliver.†

Yachting at that time strained the resources of the Prince of Wales, who could not afford to consider even the bare possibility of owning racehorses; but members of the older generation contemplated with extraordinary satisfaction the way of life which he had adopted in Norfolk as a county magnate. Because they looked backwards to the previous century, they had feared that a political faction might be formed around the Prince, who was amazed at the thankfulness which they expressed sometimes at seeeing that risk averted.

A most eager sportsman, attracted especially by shooting, the Prince increased gradually the total head of game killed annually at Sandringham from 7,000 to 30,000, while remaining dissatisfied with the limited facilities which Sandringham offered. He rented neighbouring shoots accordingly, went North for grouse and deer, and abroad for fresh experience.

The Prince had no ambition to become a first-class shot, but he liked being out-of-doors as much as possible, and he therefore imitated his neighbour, Lord Leicester, by order-

* Marquess of Blandford.   † Hon. Oliver Montagu.

ing that all clocks at Sandringham should be put forward permanently by half an hour in order to economize daylight. He liked a high partridge and a rocketing pheasant, but derived his principal enjoyment from the fresh air and exercise, and from seeing everybody around him as happy and carefree as himself.

At Sandringham, as elsewhere at that period, shooting was organized much more luxuriously than it had been a generation earlier, when game was walked up with dogs and shot with muzzle-loaders. The introduction of breech-loaders, and the new practice of employing a small army of beaters, had transformed the sport into a quasi-military operation; and keepers, who were rewarded for rearing the maximum possible quantity of game, were ordered to report about anything which might impair its preservation.

Tenant farmers were expected to subordinate their interests to those of game preservation, and to see their crops suffer in consequence. If they consented cheerfully, they enjoyed happy personal relations with their landlord, and could count upon generous help in sickness or old age; but two farmers on the Sandringham property fought the Prince of Wales hard but unsuccessfully on that issue of game preservation which almost all young men carried to excess.

Sir William Knollys recorded [46] moodily (12 August 1867) that 'the cost to H.R.H.... of these competitions for the largest game bag' would 'consist chiefly in the loss of his good name'; and one of the rebel farmers, Mrs George Cresswell of Appleton, published anonymously in London an astringent account of her quarrel with the Prince of Wales, before migrating in despair to Texas. Most copies of that tiresome but amusing book were bought up and destroyed by the agent at Sandringham; but the worst personal charge which the author could find to bring [47] against the Prince was a 'fatal habit of listening to tales from any quarter without taking the trouble to inquire into the truth of them'. Mrs Cresswell attributed that fault to the Prince's 'not having passed through the wholesome discipline of a public school, where boys contract a horror of sneaks or sneaking';

and all who knew him agreed that the Prince was very impressionable. Amiable but hasty, shrewd but careless, he adopted readily friends' opinions which were often less reliable than those which he would have formed himself if he had been willing to reflect.

The Prince and Princess earned immense personal popularity in Norfolk, and the county's radical tradition appeared to dissolve in the sunshine of their affability. They gave county, farmers' and servants' balls at regular intervals, and delighted labourers who earned extra money by serving as beaters on shooting days. Queen Victoria begged [48] her son (31 January 1870) to use his influence to try to stop excessive game preservation and, in particular, 'to do a little away with the *exclusive* character of shooting.... With hunting (much as I dislike it, on account of the danger of it) this is the case, and that is what makes it so popular.'

Although he hunted often with enjoyment, the Prince was never much addicted to that sport. After saving £2,000 a year by selling the Windsor Harriers in 1869, he informed [49] Queen Victoria (5 September) that he preferred 'staghounds to foxhounds' – a point of view which few hunting enthusiasts would share; but he lived in a shooting and not a hunting county.

The Prince was sensitive also about his increasing girth, which caused some people to call him 'Tum Tum' behind his back. His personality was so formidable that he seldom had occasion to put down familiarity, but the story of a scrape in which Sir Frederick Johnstone involved himself at Sandringham was widely repeated. The baronet was behaving rather wildly late at night in the billiard room, when the Prince put his hand on his shoulder and remarked with a kindly smile: "Freddy, Freddy, you're very drunk." Sir Frederick pointed immediately to his host's middle before exclaiming in imitation of his host's habit of rolling his 'r's, "Tum Tum, you're ve*rrr*y fat!" The Prince turned on his heel, beckoned an equerry, and told him to make sure that Johnstone left the house before breakfast the following morning.

The Prince accepted Johnstone's apology after a proper

interval, as he forgave, later, other friends for very much worse offences on the rare occasions when they hurt or injured him. He was sensitive and quick-tempered but generous and placable, and he would go to extraordinary lengths to help any friend in trouble.

Fishing bored the Prince, who could never bear to be alone even for a moment, but his passionate enthusiasm for horse-racing earned immense popularity. Queen Victoria urged him constantly to cut down the number of race meetings which he attended; but in chiding her gently for the annual 'jobation' which she gave him on that subject, he insisted upon his right to exercise his personal discretion. 'When I have seen young men I know betting', he informed [50] her (16 June 1869), 'over and over again I have warned them of the consequences'; and he argued [51] (5 June 1870) that it was better 'to elevate' a national sport by royal patronage, than 'to win the approval of Lord Shaftesbury and the Low Church party' by abstaining from it.

After the birth (3 June 1865) of her second son, the future King George V, the Princess of Wales recovered in time to race at Cowes at the end of July in her husband's new cutter, *Dagmar*, before accompanying him to Germany. They stayed at Rumpenheim, where the atmosphere, as always, was bitterly anti-Prussian, and travelled to Coburg to see Queen Victoria unveil a statue of the Prince Consort on 26 August in the presence of her nine children. The Queen herself was disgusted with Prussia at that time, on account of an agreement, concluded on 10 August, whereby Schleswig was assigned to Prussia and Holstein to Austria, while the claims of the Duke of Augustenburg were set aside. She tried without success to avoid meeting the King of Prussia, and consented to an engagement between her daughter, Princess Helena, and the Duke of Augustenburg's younger brother.

The Princess of Wales refused absolutely to meet any member of the Prussian royal family, and the Prince was troubled by a scene which she made on the way home. The Queen of Prussia had travelled to Coblenz to greet them, but the Princess would not leave the train. She insisted upon continuing her journey, and left the Prince behind to explain her pointed action as best he could.[52]

The coldly calculated aggressive war which Prussia launched against Austria in June 1866 raised to fever-pitch the anti-Prussian sentiment of the Prince and Princess of Wales. Austria was crushed in a seven weeks' campaign; Prussian hegemony was established throughout Germany; and Schleswig Holstein was annexed by Prussia.

Many relatives and friends whom the Prince and Princess enjoyed meeting at Rumpenheim suffered fearful loss through having fought upon the losing side. All the territories of the Landgrave of Hesse-Cassel (who was the Princess's uncle) as well as those of the King of Hanover and the Duke of Nassau were annexed by Prussia; and part of the territory of the Grand Duke of Hesse was similarly annexed. The personal fortune of the King of Hanover was sequestrated; and a heavy indemnity was levied upon the unfortunate subjects of the Grand Duke.

The Prince of Wales's abuse of Prussia was robust and indiscreet, while the hatred for everything Prussian felt thereafter by the Princess of Wales became obsessive, personal and, for that reason, embarrassing. Because she was expecting another baby she could not travel to St Petersburg to be present at her sister's marriage to the heir to the Russian throne; but the Prince, who told[53] Lord Derby (13 October 1866) that he would be 'only too happy to be the means in any way of promoting the *entente cordiale* between Russia and our own country' was determined to go. He informed[54] the Queen (14 October) that Derby approved, and that 'besides the pleasure of being at Dagmar's marriage, it would interest me beyond anything to see Russia'.

Queen Victoria let him go, on condition that he broke his journey in Berlin and stayed with the Crown Princess, who reported that he had been most conciliatory and amiable; and he was greeted at the railway station in St Petersburg by the Emperor Alexander II, the Crown Prince of Prussia, and the Grand Duke Alexander. After the death from tuberculosis of the Grand Duke Nicholas, to whom she had first been engaged, Princess Dagmar's affections had been transferred to the younger brother, the Grand Duke Alexander whom she married at a splendid ceremony in the Winter Palace at St Petersburg on 9 November.

The Prince went on to Moscow, where he was again magnificently entertained; and Disraeli contributed one thousand pounds towards his expenses from government funds.[55] On his return, the Prince found that the Princess's health was unsatisfactory, and she became seriously ill with rheumatic fever on 15 February 1867, five days before giving birth to a daughter, Princess Louise. Great anxiety was felt; the Queen of Denmark stayed for two months at Marlborough House, and the Princess was unable even to be wheeled into the garden until 3 July. One of her knees remained stiff for the remainder of her life, and some society ladies adopted, in consequence, what they termed the 'Alexandra limp'.

The Princess was still crippled when, accompanied by a lady-in-waiting, two doctors and twenty-five servants, she left on 18 August 1867, with the Prince of Wales to try the baths at Wiesbaden; and the Prince was exceedingly restless throughout their two months' stay. 'I have been greatly concerned', Sir William Knollys recorded[56] (24 August) in his most solemn manner, 'by a conversation with Mr Paget [one of the doctors], in which he spoke out very forcibly and, as I fear, truly, on the tone people in his own class of society now used with respect to the Prince, and on his neglect of the Princess, and how one exaggeration led to another....'

At Darmstadt, on 14 October, Princess Louis of Hesse told[57] Sir William that scandalous gossip about attentions paid to pretty ladies by her brother, the Prince of Wales, in St Petersburg and Moscow during November, as well as in Paris which he had visited during May in order to open the British section of an international exhibition while the Princess was unwell, had shocked King William and Queen Augusta of Prussia. The stories were probably exaggerated, but the Prince was young, impressionable and gay; and Princess Louis added that he had taken her lecture 'most good-humouredly'.

Alerted by the Queen of Prussia, Queen Victoria made

every effort, unavailingly, to dissuade the Prince of Wales from attending the races at Baden from 4–10 September. Queen Victoria and Queen Augusta were agreed that Baden society was so disreputable that 'no one can mix in it without loss of character'; and the Prince found it necessary to write [58] (27 August) to his mother: 'I know that Vicky has written to you on the subject, but one would imagine that she thought me 10 or 12 years old, and not nearly 26.'

After the Prince had left for Baden with his equerry, Christopher Teesdale, and Charles Carrington, Knollys wrote [59] (4 September) to Queen Victoria that although he deplored the failure of his efforts, 'he thinks he owes it to himself to beg Your Majesty's pardon for his freedom in saying that in no points will His Royal Highness brook Sir William's interference less than in any matter, connected with his plans and intentions, which has already formed the subject of correspondence and conversation with Your Majesty ...'.

The Grand Duke Alexander (the Czarevitch) and the Grand Duchess (formerly Princess Dagmar) as well as the Queen of Denmark came to stay with the Princess of Wales, and the Prince complained [60] about his Russian brother-in-law's bashfulness and lack of initiative. He obtained invitations for him to shoot with a variety of amusing hosts, including a rich wine merchant; laughed [61] at suggestions that some of the people whom he would meet would be unsuitable, and took him to Rumpenheim, where Knollys recorded [62] (23 September): 'I found, as I had heard that I should, a most rabid anti-Prussian feeling at Rumpenheim. They all seemed to have been bit by some Prussian mad dog, and the slightest allusion set the whole party – and we were 36 at dinner – into agitation.'

Encouraged by the Princess of Wales, the Grand Duchess Alexander had refused to meet the King and Queen of Prussia; and a most awkward situation arose when the King telegraphed (19 September) an offer to visit the Princess of Wales at Wiesbaden at a time convenient to her. After trying vainly to persuade the Princess to appoint a day and time, the Prince of Wales was obliged to reply that she was still feeling too unwell; but, as it was known that she was better, great offence was taken.

Queen Augusta complained to Queen Victoria that the King had been insulted and that the mind of the Czarevitch was being poisoned against Prussia; and the Prince of Wales paid separate conciliatory visits to the Prussian King and Queen. The Princess refused to accompany him on either occasion and he wrote [63] (4 October) to his mother:

I myself should have been glad if she had seen the King, but a lady may have feelings which she *cannot* repress, while a man *must* overcome them. If Coburg had been taken away as Hanover, Hesse (Cassel) and Nassau have been, I don't think you would much care to see the King either.

You will not, I hope, be angry, dear Mama, at my last sentence; but it is the only way that I can express what dear Alix really feels.

In obedience to their mother, the Crown Princess of Prussia and Princess Louis of Hesse applied strong pressure to the Prince of Wales. They suggested that it was his duty to heal family feuds by ordering the Princess to issue an invitation to the King of Prussia; and the Prince summoned Queen Louise of Denmark to his aid. He told [64] Knollys that 'she was so sensible, and would make her daughter do what was proper'; but the mother had no better success than the husband had had.

A crisis arose on 9 October when the Crown Prince of Prussia telegraphed another request that the Princess of Wales should name a date and time when it would be convenient for the King to call, and a painful conference was held in the library of the house which the Prince had rented at Wiesbaden. The Prince of Wales and Sir William Knollys appealed to the Queen of Denmark, who replied weakly, that 'she was ready to sacrifice herself and see the King if he came to-morrow', but that she had not the heart to distress or try to persuade her daughter any more:

She left me [Knollys recorded] [65] to fight the battle in support of the Prince, who used every argument, but in vain, to persuade the Princess. It was a question of feeling with the Princess, and she would not listen to reason of any kind.

After a long discussion the Princess ended it by getting up and walking out of the room by the aid of her stick. ... The Prince was in despair what to do next.

After exchanging glances with Knollys, the Prince scribbled a telegram inviting the King of Prussia to breakfast the following morning, while the Queen went to her daughter's room to comfort and prepare her. The Prince followed and waved the telegram in the Princess's face, before returning and asking Knollys 'to send it off instantly, which I lost no time in doing'. After more telegrams had been exchanged, it was settled that the King of Prussia should come to breakfast on 11 October; but the Queen of Denmark retired to Rumpenheim and sent her son, the King of Greece, to take her place.

Immediately before the King of Prussia arrived, Knollys displayed some tactlessness. 'I saw the Princess', he recorded,[66] 'and remarked, as she entered the drawing-room, that she was looking pale, and expressed my fear that she had caught cold, and my regret that she was looking pale in consequence. "Yes," she said, "I may be pale, but it is from anger at being obliged to see the King of Prussia, and not from cold."'

While the Princess was telling Knollys exactly what she thought at that moment about the action of the Prince of Wales's sisters – 'I am afraid she said "those two interfering old women", tho' not much older than herself – the door was thrown open and King William I of Prussia marched in triumph into the room, followed by the Prince of Wales and the King of Greece, who had met him at the station. The unwelcome guest, who exuded cordiality, insisted upon staying to luncheon as well as to breakfast, but the Princess of Wales was 'very *civil*', under effort, and Princess Louis of Hesse informed[67] Knollys subsequently 'that the King was quite satisfied with his reception'.

6

A Proposed Employment

1868–72

AFTER sending Carrington (10 October 1867) a jewelled
tie pin in token of 'two or three lucky coups'[1] at the gaming
tables, the Prince returned with the Princess (18 October) to
Marlborough House and went to Windsor on a visit to
Queen Victoria. She forgave, without effort, anything which
she felt that she ought to regret, and praised warmly her
son's manliness, gentleness and sincerity; but she told[2] Sir
William Knollys (13 November) that she trusted that the
doctors would not recommend another visit to Wiesbaden.

The Princess's recovery was not complete for some
months, and the year 1868 was devoted almost entirely to
convalescence and pleasure. The Prince amused Londoners,
but provoked some tart newspaper criticism, by a great day's
run with the Royal Buckhounds on 2 March 1868, when a
carted deer was chased from Harrow through Wormwood
Scrubs to the Goods Yard at Paddington Station. It was
killed there before the astonished eyes of railway guards
and porters; and the Prince and his friends rode merrily
through Hyde Park and down Constitution Hill to Marlborough House.

From 15–24 April, the Prince and Princess visited Dublin
at the suggestion of the Prime Minister, Disraeli, who
wanted to allay Irish discontent; and the Queen acquiesced
on condition that the Government should pay all her son's
expenses. She insisted[3] also that Disraeli should forget his
request that the Prince of Wales might rent a residence and
hunt in Kildare or Meath, in order to associate the royal
family more closely with Ireland, while combining 'duty
with pastime' in a manner befitting 'a princely life'.

The Prince's visit to Dublin was most successful, and the Viceroy, Lord Abercorn, was delighted. Two impressive moments in a crowded programme of balls, reviews and race meetings were the Prince's installation as a Knight of St Patrick in the Protestant cathedral, and his unveiling, outside Trinity College, of a statue of Edmund Burke.

While Gladstone pursed his lips and Disraeli jested about 'Prince Hal', a whispering campaign about aspects of the Prince's private life ran through some sections of the community and found expression in *The Times* and other newspapers. His name was coupled vulgarly with that of the actress, Hortense Schneider; and amid much absurd exaggeration, Sir William Knollys recorded [4] his view that reputation could be 'equally affected by the true and the false'. Queen Victoria begged her son to forgo the London season and to spend a few weeks in the country for the sake of the Princess, who was expecting another baby; but the Prince retorted [5] (1 May) that 'we have certain duties to fulfil here, and your absence from London makes it more necessary that we should do all we can for society, trade, and public matters'.

Queen Victoria's reply [6] (4 May) was humble, moving and irresistible. She asked the Prince to forgo the Derby for once, and to 'run up' to Balmoral for a night or two instead, 'to spend my sad birthday with me' and 'shed a little sunshine' over the house. The Queen said that she hoped that 'dearest Alix would not mind if he came alone; and the Prince agreed at Balmoral that a holiday which he and the Princess had been planning to take that winter should be extended to last for several months.

After giving birth to her fourth child (Princess Victoria) on 6 July, 1868, the Princess of Wales set her heart on taking her three elder children as far as Copenhagen on the first stage of a six months' tour of Europe and the Near East. Queen Victoria held that that wish was selfish, and that the children, as 'the Children of the Country', should be left in her care; but the Prince, who would not allow the Princess to be called selfish, wrote [7] (5 November) to his mother: 'None of us are perfect, and she may have her faults; but she certainly is not selfish and her whole life is wrapped up in her children. It seems hard that because she wishes (with a natural mother's pride) to take her 3 eldest children to her Parents' home, every difficulty should be placed in her way....'

Queen Victoria yielded, on receipt of that letter; and the Prince and Princess of Wales left England on 18 November for Paris to spend a few days with the Emperor Napoleon III. They travelled with a doctor and thirty-three servants, and with a suite which consisted of Lord Carrington, Arthur Ellis, the Hon. Mrs William Grey, the Hon. Oliver Montagu and Christopher Teesdale, V.C.

The Princess of Wales's success at a ball which the French Emperor gave for her at Compiègne was remembered for many years; and on 26 November the Prince and Princess left Paris to spend six weeks with the King and Queen of Denmark. They broke their stay before Christmas to spend a week with the King of Sweden, who shocked Queen Victoria by making her son a freemason. 'I quite agree', the Prince wrote [8] to his mother (25 December), 'that secret societies as a rule are to be deprecated; but I can assure you that this has unpolitical signification. More than that I may not say, and I feel convinced that I shall have many opportunities of doing great work in my new capacity.' He relished the wide range of fresh contacts which he gained through freemasonry, and he was installed as Grand Master of the Order in England in April 1875, after Lord Ripon had resigned on turning Roman Catholic.

In other letters to his mother, the Prince expressed great regret at the change of Government in England which had brought Gladstone and the Liberals into power. It was useless, he wrote [9] (26 February and 4 April, 1869), to make concessions to the Irish, because 'they will afterwards want more concessions, and where are you to stop?' He suggested that 'the safety of the Crown itself' was endangered by Gladstone's attack upon the Anglican Church establishment in Ireland, and added: 'I suppose the law of Primogeniture will be attacked next ... we are living in strange times.'

The Queen noted [10] in her diary (4 March 1869) that she

had seen Gladstone and discussed with him 'Bertie's affairs –
his expenses, etc.'. She informed the Prime Minister that she
knew that her son 'hoped' and 'expected' that the House of
Commons would vote him a larger income, but Gladstone
replied that there was 'no intention, or disposition, to give
him any addition'.

Leaving Copenhagen on 15 January, the Prince and Princess saw their children off to England from Hamburg in a
royal yacht, and Queen Victoria wrote to express concern
that no governess had been appointed to discipline them.
'If,' the Prince replied [11] (26 February), 'children of that age
are too strictly, or perhaps too severely treated, they get shy,
and only fear those whom they ought to love; and we should
naturally wish them to be very fond of you, as they were in
Denmark of dear Alix's Parents. I quite agree with you that
the question of a governess being appointed must be considered on our return.'

From Hamburg the Prince and Princess of Wales went to
stay for three days in Berlin with the Crown Prince and
Crown Princess of Prussia; and the King, after his triumph
at Wiesbaden, exerted himself to be agreeable. He invested
the Prince with the Order of the Black Eagle, but the Queen
of Prussia took offence when the Princess of Wales, whom
she had treated with marked coldness, addressed her in consequence at a ball as Your Majesty instead of Aunt Augusta,
as she had been instructed to do. After informing the Princess that she had been rude, the Queen turned her back, but
repented later and sent a green and gold porcelain dinner
service as a peace offering.[12]

The atmosphere at Vienna was much more congenial, and
the Prince and Princess were entertained for a week at a
series of balls, concerts and race meetings. The Ambassador's wife, Lady Bloomfield, informed [13] Queen Victoria
confidentially (26 January) that all attempts to maintain the
private character of the visit had been broken on the rock of
Austrian aristocratic formality; that one entire day had had
to be devoted to paying calls on members of the Hapsburg
family, and that 'as there are 27 Archdukes now at Vienna,
it was hard work'.

On 18 January Queen Victoria wrote [14] to inform her son that she had been distressed to hear that Sir Samuel Baker, whom she described as 'unprincipled', as well as the Duke of Sutherland, were waiting in Egypt to join the Prince's party: 'If you ever become King, you will find all these friends *most* inconvenient, and you will have to break with them *all*.' Besides defending the Duke, the Prince replied [15] (26 January) that Baker, who had discovered the source of the Nile, knew the country well and was 'a good sportsman; and, whatever his principles may be, he is not likely to contaminate us in any way. Besides, he will not be on the same boat with Alix and me.' He counter-attacked gently by suggesting that his mother would do well 'to go oftener and remain longer in London ... as the people – not only Londoners – cannot bear seeing Buckingham Palace always unoccupied'; and he added that he had been sorry to observe, in Vienna, the way in which Crown Prince Rudolf – 'a very nice young man, but not at all good-looking' – was 'treated almost like a boy by his Parents'.

When Queen Victoria expressed astonishment that her son should be unaware that the noise of London was bad for her nerves, the Prince attacked [16] gently again (26 February) from Korosko, on the Nile:

If you sometimes even came to London from Windsor – say for luncheon – and then drove for an hour in the Park (where there is no noise) and then returned to Windsor, the people would be overjoyed – beyond measure. It is all very well for Alix and me to drive in the Park – it does not have the same effect as when you do it; and I say thank God that is the case. We live in radical times, and the more the *People see the Sovereign* the better it is for the *People* and the *Country*.

After embarking at Trieste (27 January) for Alexandria in the frigate *Ariadne*, which had been refitted as a yacht to accommodate them, the Prince and Princess of Wales were welcomed by the Khedive Ismael of Egypt in Cairo on 3 February. The Esbekiah Palace had been refurnished in their honour in what the Prince described as a style of useless extravagance; and their bedroom, which was nearly fifty yards long, contained massive twin beds in solid silver, and chairs covered in beaten gold which were far too heavy to move. The gardens, ablaze with flowers and dotted with sculptured fountains illuminated at night and playing continuously, accommodated troupes of dancers and acrobats in tents, as well as a private menagerie.

Besides Sir Samuel Baker and the Duke of Sutherland, the Prince added a number of people to his party when he reached Cairo. They included W. H. Russell, the well-known journalist whom he dubbed his historian; Professor Richard Owen, head of the Natural History Department of the British Museum; Prince Louis of Battenberg, a midshipman in *Ariadne* and 'really a remarkably nice boy'; John Fowler, an engineer who knew 'all about the Suez Canal'; Colonel Edward Stanton, British Consul-General in Cairo; two westernized members of the Khedive of Egypt's Cabinet; and some relatives of the Duke of Sutherland. 'You will doubtless think', the Prince wrote [17] (9 February 1869) to Queen Victoria, 'that we have too many ships and too large an entourage, but ... in the East so much is thought of show, that it becomes almost a necessity.'

On 6 February the Prince's party started up the Nile in six blue and gold steamers, each towing a barge filled with luxuries and necessities including four riding horses, and a milk-white donkey for the Princess; 3,000 bottles of champagne and 4,000 of claret; four French chefs and a laundry. No expense had been spared by the generous Khedive, and although the panelled décor of the steamers, on the theme of Anthony and Cleopatra, was garish, the double pile carpets and solid English furniture had been chosen personally on the Khedive's behalf by Sir Samuel Baker, who 'has really', the Prince informed [18] his mother, 'taken a great deal of trouble to make all the necessary arrangements for our comfort, in which he has most thoroughly succeeded.... I cannot say how glad I am to have asked him to accompany us.'

Throughout that thousand-mile voyage to Wadi Halfa and back, the Prince took the services and read the lessons on Sundays, and the captain and sailors turned towards Mecca at six o'clock every evening and touched the decks with their foreheads. Famous monuments and ruins were explored, and the Prince, who killed his first crocodile – a female, nine feet long, containing eighty eggs – with an expanding bullet on 28 February, failed to shoot a hyena, but killed quantities of cormorants, cranes, doves, flamingoes, hawk-owls, herons, hoopoes, mallards, merlins and spoonbills.

The Prince and Princess returned to Cairo on 16 March with thirty-two mummy cases, an immense sarcophagus, and a ten-year old chocolate-coloured orphan boy, Ali Achmet, who was loathed by the English servants and who was despatched, in consequence, with a mass of other trophies to Sandringham, where he served coffee in native dress. The Khedive's hospitality in Cairo was so overwhelming that the Prince climbed the Great Pyramid for exercise – and vowed that he would never do so again – while the Princess visited harems and teased her husband about the pretty unveiled faces.

After inspecting the Suez Canal in the company of its designer, Ferdinand de Lesseps, the Prince and Princess of Wales were welcomed (1 April) in Constantinople by the Sultan of Turkey, Abdul Aziz, who conducted them over the palace of Saleh Bezar, which enjoyed charming views over the Bosphorus, and asked them to consider it as their own for as long as they cared to stay. The Prince knew, from experience, that European notions about the privilege attached to gentility were not understood in Turkey, but he thought it right to present every member of his suite. As he did so, he was amused by the unconcealed smirk of supercilious disdain and boredom which his host displayed.

The Turkish officers who were attached to the Prince's suite, and who had to be given costly presents, were civilized and agreeable, and the perfectly trained servants were French-speaking. An orchestra of eighty-four musicians was eager to play even at breakfast, and it was impossible to leave or enter the house without causing unseen batteries to thunder in salute, bands to start playing *God Save the Queen* and guards to turn out, looking as if they wanted to be inspected. In those circumstances the Ambassador, H. G.

Elliot, contrived an escape through a side entrance for the Prince and Princess, who mingled occasionally on foot as 'Mr and Mrs Williams' with tourists in the streets and bazaars.

The Prince, who had entertained the Sultan in London during the summer of 1867, was amused by a dinner (3 April) which the Sultan gave at his Palace. Abdul Aziz had never sat down to dine before with ladies in his own dominions; and no Turk, except the Grand Vizier, had ever sat in his master's presence. As half the twenty-four guests were Turks who could not conceal their fright, the Prince told[19] his mother that the event 'may even be called a historical one'.

After 'a wonderfully happy visit', the Prince and Princess embarked (10 April) in *Ariadne*, with a British naval escort, for Sevastopol. The British Ambassador to Russia had been summoned from St Petersburg and attached to the Prince's suite, and the Prince joked with him during the voyage about the immense number of gold boxes, many jewelled, which he had had to distribute in Constantinople. He said that he would be ruined unless the Government agreed to pay, and complained that although no one took snuff, everyone appeared to expect to be given a jewelled snuff-box.

At Sevastopol on 12 April the Prince and Princess were greeted by the Governor, General Kotzebue, who showed them the ruins of the fortress which he had helped to defend, and who took them on a tour of the Crimean battle-fields: 'We got back to the ship at 6.00 p.m.', the Prince wrote[20] (13 April) to Queen Victoria, 'after one of the most interesting days that I can remember. But one cannot but feel sad to think that over 80,000 men perished – for what? For a political object! I could write you many pages more on the subject. ...'

Those further reflections were not committed to paper; and after an excursion to Yalta the royal party embarked for Athens where they stayed with King George (the Princess's favourite brother, 'Willy') and Queen Olga (born a Russian Grand Duchess). The King and Queen of the Hellenes accompanied their guests to Corfu, which had recently been ceded to Greece by Great Britain, and after a boar-hunt arranged by the Turkish authorities on the Albanian coast, *Ariadne* took the Prince and Princess to Brindisi, whence they travelled by special train to Paris, and stayed (6-11 May) at an hotel.

The Emperor Napoleon gave the Princess another ball and took the Prince to a military review; and Queen Victoria wrote [21] (4 May) to her son:

> You will, I fear, have incurred immense expenses, and I don't think you will find any disposition (except, perhaps, as regards those which were *forced* upon you at Constantinople) to give you any more money.
>
> I hope dear Alix will not spend much on dress at Paris. There is, besides, a *very* strong feeling against the luxuriousness, extravagance and frivolity of Society; and everyone points to *my* simplicity. I am most anxious that *every possible* discouragement should be given to what, in these radical days, added to the many scandalous stories current in Society ... reminds me of the Aristocracy before the French Revolution. ...

The rise of a republican movement in the great cities was causing British ministers some anxiety at that time; and the Prince replied [22] (7 May 1869) from Paris to his mother:

> Our journey has been rather expensive, but it won't ruin us; and I am much too proud to ask for more money as the Government don't propose it. But I think it would be fair if the Foreign Office were to pay some of the expenses at Constantinople. ...
>
> You need not be afraid, dear Mama, that Alix will commit any extravagances with regard to dresses, etc. I have given her two simple ones, as they make them here better than in London; but if there is anything I dislike, it is extravagant or outreé dresses – at any rate in my wife.
>
> Sad stories have indeed reached our ears from London of 'scandals in high life', which is indeed much to be deplored; and still more so the way in which (to use a common proverb) they 'wash their dirty linen in public'.

The Prince's habit of inserting homely proverbial sayings, enclosed within quotations marks, into his letters remained always much the most characteristic feature of his correspondence. He appeared to derive confidence from them, and his secretaries noticed, and complained occasionally, of another habit. He never failed, Sir William Knollys recorded [23] (25 August 1867) 'to alter *something* in any copy made for him either of a speech or of a letter', even although the alteration might appear to lack any significance.

That second trait was symptomatic of a sense of boredom and frustration which caused the Prince, immediately after his return to London (12 May 1869), to quarrel with the committee of White's Club. The older members contrived to secure the rejection of his motion that smoking should be allowed in the morning room, and he resigned forthwith. He had no difficulty in coaxing one or two rich acquaintances into providing the money to found a new club at 52, Pall Mall, almost opposite Marlborough House; and of that club, which was named the Marlborough, the Prince of Wales became the very active ruler.

Thereafter, the Prince insisted that his friends should join the Marlborough, which he used constantly, and to which no one could be elected without his approval. He made few mistakes and, although horrified once by the discovery that he had admitted a plausible American card-sharper whom the police of both countries were attempting to trace, most members of the Marlborough would have been equally acceptable elsewhere. Many did belong also to Boodle's, Brooks's or White's; to the Guards', the Travellers or the Turf; and the Marlborough flourished as a charming club until 1914. Thereafter it ran into increasing difficulties which culminated in its dissolution in 1952.

While the Princess went usually to Denmark during the early autumn in order to be reunited with her clannish family, the Prince tried out many new acquaintances at German spas. He was happy to be of use to, and to be made use of, by men whom he found congenial; but friendship with the Prince of Wales involved expense. Lord Hardwicke, for example, who perfected the top hat; Lord Dupplin, who invented the dinner jacket; Charles Buller, the handsome son of an Indian judge who stole all hearts but had less than a thousand pounds a year to live on; and Christopher Sykes, a singularly lovable and sweet-natured snob, whose story has been immortalized by his nephew,[24] all beggared themselves.

Most of the Prince's friends, on the other hand, were rich men who loved pleasure; and among them the Prince discovered a special affinity with Jews. He started with members of the Rothschild family, whose ornate palaces, replete with superb paintings and furniture, arose to dominate the Buckinghamshire landscape. Old Sir Anthony de Rothschild, as the Prince's earliest independent financial confidant, was a frequent and privileged guest at Sandringham before his death in 1876; and the Prince was on terms of close friendship with Sir Anthony's nephews. Alfred was his favourite, but he stayed equally often with Leopold, and with Nathaniel who became the first Jewish peer in 1885.

The surprise appointment of Lord Rothschild, in preference to Lord Cottesloe, as Lord Lieutenant of Buckinghamshire in 1889 was attributed to the influence of the Prince of Wales, who was attracted also to members of the French and Austrian branches of the Rothschild family. As social phenomena, the Rothschilds' quizzical detachment from the familiar European class pattern fascinated the Prince, who relished their sensible cosmopolitan outlook, public spirit, geniality and panache, as well as their generosity and the invaluable advice and help which they gave. All were welcome and frequent guests at Sandringham.

The Prince's social outlook was as liberal as that of his sister, the Crown Princess of Prussia, but his political views were more strictly conservative; and he wrote,[25] for example (24 October 1869), to Queen Victoria: 'I heard that there was a tremendous crowd in the Park, and I have no doubt much treason was talked. The Government really ought to have prevented it. ... The more the Government allow the lower classes to get the upper hand, the more the democratic feeling of the present day will increase. ... I hear some speakers openly spoke of a Republic!'

After taking the Princess to Wildbad that autumn, for further treatment of her knee, the Prince flitted between Homburg, Rumpenheim and Baden before going up to the

Scottish Highlands to shoot grouse and stalk deer. On 26 November, the Princess gave birth in London to her fifth child, Princess Maud; and, while Sandringham was being rebuilt on a larger scale, the Prince rented Gunton Hall, near Cromer, from Lord Suffield.

At a ball which the Prince gave at Gunton on 10 January 1870, it is on record [26] that his friend, Christopher Sykes, became so drunk that he collapsed and had to be put to bed, and that his host retaliated by ordering that a dead sea-gull should be laid beside him. The joke answered so well that a live trussed rabbit was substituted on the following night.

Three weeks later the Prince experienced an extremely unpleasant shock when his acquaintance, Sir Charles Mordaunt, filed a petition for divorce from his twenty-one-year-old wife, citing two of the Prince's friends, Lord Cole and Sir Frederick Johnstone, as co-respondents. A counter-petition was filed, alleging that Lady Mordaunt was insane; and the Prince of Wales, who had written her a number of letters and who had paid her some visits, was served by Lady Mordaunt's counsel with a subpœna to appear as a witness at the trial.

The Prince took the Princess into his confidence immediately, and consulted Lord Hatherley, the Lord Chancellor. He was innocent; and, after reading the trifling letters which he had written to Lady Mordaunt, Hatherley wrote [27] (9 February 1870): 'I find it difficult to believe that any useful object can have been had in view in taking the extraordinary step of sending a subpœna to Your Royal Highness's solicitors requiring your attendance.' He advised him, nevertheless not to raise any question of privilege, and to be the first to inform Queen Victoria.

The Prince wrote [28] accordingly (10 February) to his mother, enclosing the Lord Chancellor's letter:

It is my painful duty (I call it painful because it must be so to you to know that your eldest son is obliged to appear as a witness in a Court of Justice) to inform you that I have been 'sub-pœnaed' by Sir C. Mordaunt's Counsel to appear as a witness on Saturday next at Lord Penzance's Court. ...

Alix has been informed by me of everything concerning this unfortunate case. . . .

The Queen telegraphed immediately her complete confidence in her son, to whom she wrote also a moving and tenderly affectionate letter, asking only that he should try to be more circumspect. 'I cannot sufficiently thank you', the Prince replied [29] (12 February), 'for the dear and kind words which you have written to me. . . . I shall remember all the kind advice you have given me, and hope to profit by it.'

Sir William Knollys assured the Queen that he had reason to know that Lord Penzance would protect the Prince, 'should any improper questions be put by the Mordaunt counsel'; but the Prince was on tenterhooks, and he wrote [30] (17 February) to his mother:

I shall be subject to a most rigid cross-examination by Sergeant Ballantine, who will naturally try to turn and twist everything that I say in order to compromise me.

On the other hand, if I do not appear, the public may suppose that I shrink from answering these imputations which have been cast upon me.

Under either circumstance I am in a very awkward position, and you can easily imagine how I am worried, dearest Mama. . . .

The Lord Chancellor reassured the Queen, who ended her letter [31] of thanks (21 February):

Still, the fact of the Prince of Wales's intimate acquaintance with a young married woman being publicly proclaimed, will show an amount of imprudence which cannot but damage him in the eyes of the middle and lower classes, which is most deeply to be lamented in these days when the higher classes, in their frivolous, selfish and pleasure-seeking lives, do more to increase the spirit of democracy than anything else.

The Prince's demeanour during a seven minutes' examination by Lady Mordaunt's counsel in the witness box on 23 February 1870, was perfect. He denied that he had committed adultery; no cross-examination followed; and Sir Charles's petition failed at that time on the ground that his wife was disabled by insanity from being a party to the suit.

At the Queen's request the Lord Chancellor wrote[32] (25 February) to remind the Prince that his life was like 'a city set upon a hill'; and Gladstone wrote[33] (23 February):

> The conviction of my mind, based on no short experience, is that, so long as the nation has confidence in the personal character of its Sovereign, the Throne of this Empire may be regarded as secure; but that the revival of circumstances only half a century old tend rapidly to impair its strength and might bring about its overthrow.
>
> Even suspicion ... would produce much of the evil attaching to proof, and such nearness to the Throne as that of Your Royal Highness for this purpose is almost identical with its possession.

Most of the nation's traditional institutions had been adapted by law, after Parliamentary inquiry, to meet nineteenth-century needs; but the Monarchy had been left to adapt itself and was passing through a phase of temporary unpopularity. Queen Victoria was criticized for neglecting her ceremonial duties and for living in quasi-oriental seclusion; while the Prince of Wales was criticized because pleasure and frivolity appeared to be his sole aim and occupation.

In those circumstances, an anonymous pamphlet (by George Otto Trevelyan), entitled *What Does She Do With It?*, enjoyed a wide circulation. It alleged that Queen Victoria was hoarding treasure in a miserly and eccentric way; and it was matched by scurrilous publications about the Prince of Wales. *The Coming K——*, for example (a dull but clever parody of Tennyson's *Idylls of the King*), purported in 1870 to strip the veil from the Prince's private life by drawing upon apocryphal stories current in Paris and in the London underworld.

For some weeks after the Mordaunt trial, the Prince and Princess of Wales were hissed from time to time as they drove about the streets of the capital; and an unpleasant incident occurred when they visited the Olympic Theatre on 1 March. Forewarned of trouble, the owner had planted a few cheer-leaders in the gallery, but their well-meant efforts provoked a storm of booing and cat-calls as soon as the Prince and Princess, accompanied by the Duchess of Manchester and Oliver Montagu, entered their box. A startled attempt at a counter-demonstration from the stalls produced an ugly situation for a few moments; and as late as 13 June, at Ascot, the Prince had a bad reception as he drove up the course. When, however, a horse in which he was supposed, rightly or wrongly, to have a private interest as part-owner, won the last event, a crowd cheered him in the royal stand: 'You seem to be in a better temper now than you were this morning, damn you!', the Prince told them smiling genially, as he raised his hat and lit a cigar; and that bonhomie elicited fresh cheers.[34]

While Queen Victoria's children tried hard to persuade their mother to overcome her nervous shrinking and to appear in London and in public, she redoubled her efforts to persuade the Prince of Wales to renounce frivolous society. She begged[35] the Princess, for example (13 March 1870), to drop the Duchess of Manchester on the ground that, although 'she may not, and, I believe, *does not* do anything positively wrong', she had 'done more harm to Society from her *tone*, her love of admiration and "fast" style, than almost anyone'; but the Prince and Princess would brook no interference in their private affairs from any quarter. When the Prince's secretary, Herbert Fisher, resigned in June 1870, the Prince rejected his mother's emphatic advice that he should not appoint Francis Knollys, Sir William's son, in his place: 'He has had so much to do for me lately', the Prince wrote[36] (2 July) to Queen Victoria, 'that I am convinced he will suit me in every way; and I have already told him of my intention.'

When France put herself in the wrong by declaring war with startling suddenness upon Prussia on 15 July 1870, the Princess of Wales, who had been deeply hurt by the Mordaunt trial, was in Copenhagen on a visit to her parents which was expected to last for a considerable time. The Prince left England on 22 July to bring home the Princess, who hoped from the bottom of her heart that Prussia would be annihilated.

The surrender of the French Emperor and the proclamation of a Republic in Paris after the Battle of Sedan (2

September), and the proclamation of the German Empire (18 January 1871) in the Hall of Mirrors at Versailles astonished the Prince of Wales, who had expressed to the Austrian Ambassador, Count Apponyi, while dining at the French Embassy, his belief that Prussia would be taught a lesson at last. Count von Bernstorff, the Prussian Ambassador in London, complained immediately that that belief had been expressed in the form of an unneutral wish; and the Prince, before leaving for Denmark, informed [37] Queen Victoria (19 and 20 July) that Bernstorff was 'an ill-conditioned man, and I only long for the day when he will be removed from here. Of course I consider the French quite in the wrong, and, as all our relations are in Germany, it is not likely that I should go against them. . . . I am afraid that Alix's feelings are strongly against Prussia. They have always been so since that unfortunate Danish war.'

'I rejoice', the Prince wrote [38] (28 August) to Lord Harting-ton, who sat in the Cabinet as Postmaster General, 'that the Cr. Prince has done so well, and with such a splendid Army'; but his discretion continued to be suspect, and ingenuous offers (August 1870) to travel anywhere if he could be given letters of friendly advice from the British Government for delivery to the Emperor Napoleon and to King William of Prussia were disregarded. At a time when they were overwhelmed with work, Gladstone and Granville were tempted to dismiss [39] as 'royal twaddle' the Prince's views about methods of effecting a settlement; and on 18 November Granville reported [40] to Gladstone that the Prince had been 'more than usually unwise in his talk'.

The Prince had been stressing the need for insisting that France should retain a monarchical government; and Gladstone described [41] that report (19 November) as 'wonderful'. But the fall of the French monarchy encouraged the formation and activities of at least fifty republican clubs in British cities and towns, including Aberdeen, Birmingham, Cambridge, Cardiff, London, Norwich and Plymouth; and Gladstone was worried increasingly about what he termed the 'royalty question'. Taking advantage, accordingly, of 'a partial and momentary lull', the Prime Minister opened [42] his mind secretly to the Foreign Secretary on that subject (3 December 1870):

For our time as a Government, and my time as a politician, Royalty will do well enough in this country, because it has a large fund to draw upon, which was greatly augmented by good husbandry in the early and middle part of this reign, and which is not yet exhausted.

But the fund of credit is diminishing, and I do not see from whence it is to be replenished as matters now go. To speak in rude and general terms, the Queen is invisible and the Prince of Wales is not respected. ...

Because, after trying hard, he saw no prospect of being able to induce Queen Victoria to alter her way of life and to attend to her ceremonial duties, Gladstone concentrated upon a plan for bringing forward the Prince of Wales. It postulated, when fully formulated, that the Prince should spend all his winters in Ireland, learning the art of constitutional sovereignty, and that he should deputize for the Queen at Buckingham Palace during the summer months.

In outlining the Irish part of that plan to Lord Granville on 3 December, Gladstone noted that the office of Viceroy, or Lord Lieutenant of Ireland, would 'disappear', leaving the Irish Secretary (who had a seat in the British Cabinet and an office in Whitehall) as 'the only responsible agent, instead of having a joint responsibility with the Lord Lieutenant'. The Prince would perform in Dublin the ceremonial and external duties of the former Viceroy; he would receive the Viceroy's official salary and allowances; and 'the sacrifice of personal freedom and pleasure' which he made, 'would be more than repaid, if repayment is wanted, in the general estimation which accompanies the discharge of public duty'.

Gladstone saw 'no reason why the Prince should not have a relation to the Irish Minister resembling in some points that of the Sovereign to the Cabinet; though without the final authority which is not, in fact, represented in the Irish, but in the British, Government'. He considered that the Prince, who possessed 'that average stock of energy, which enables men to do that which they cannot well avoid doing, or that which is made ready to their hands', would, in that way, 'obtain a very valuable political education'.

The campaign which he waged secretly on the Prince of Wales's behalf during the two years which followed, to procure the implementation of that plan, was regarded by Gladstone as an event of outstanding importance in his life. It involved him, however, in head on collision with Queen Victoria, and he was most anxious for that reason that the utmost reticence should be observed during his lifetime as well as during the lifetimes of the Queen and of the Prince of Wales.

Despite many bitter things which he had to say in later life about the West End of London, the Upper Ten Thousand and the House of Lords, Gladstone was imbued always with a most profound veneration for the Monarchy, and with a chivalrous devotion and loyalty to Queen Victoria, who mortified him and who vetoed his plan. 'She must say', she wrote [43] (18 November 1874) to her private secretary, General Ponsonby '... that *she* has felt that Mr Gladstone would have liked to *govern* HER as Bismark governs the [German] Emperor'; and she never forgave that desperate and extremely hard-fought attempt at interference with what she regarded as her private and family affairs.

While Gladstone was still engaged in preliminary skirmishes with Queen Victoria, the Princess of Wales gave birth to a sixth child, a boy (6 April 1871), who lived only twenty-four hours. Friends wondered whether the Princess had been sufficiently careful or whether, aware of the temptations which beset her husband, she had been too eager to remain until the last moment at his side. The Prince was accused in consequence of having, through carelessness, encouraged his wife to neglect her health, and the Dean of Windsor spoke to him on that subject at Queen Victoria's request. The Dean reported [44] (18 April) to the Queen that he had had a serious talk with the Prince who was 'evidently deeply attached to the Princess, despite all the flattering distractions that beset him in Society; and the Dean hopes and believes that he will be more careful about her in future. We shall see.'

The Prince wrote [45] himself (10 April) to Queen Victoria:

Want of feeling I never could show, but I think it is one's duty not to nurse one's sorrow. ... I shall also be glad when Alix resumes her social duties (with, of course, due care for her health). ...

Besides our social duties, which are indeed very numerous in the Season, we have also many to do as your representatives. You have no conception of the quantity of applications we get, in the course of the year, to open this place, lay a stone, attend public dinners, luncheons, fêtes without end; and sometimes people will not take NO for an answer. I certainly think we must be made of wood or iron if we could go through all they ask and all these things have increased tenfold since the last ten years.

After exploring the battlefields of Sedan and Metz (August 1871) in the strictest incognito, the Prince joined the Princess at Oberammergau, where they saw the Passion Play together and went on to stay with the Hesse Darmstadt family at Jugenheim. The large party assembled there included the Emperor and Empress of Russia, with all their children, as well as the Prince's brother, the Duke of Edinburgh; and while the Duke paid court to the Emperor's daughter, the Grand Duchess Marie, the Prince of Wales flitted to Homburg, where his activities evoked critical comment. *Reynold's Newspaper*, for example, which enjoyed at that time the largest guaranteed circulation (over 300,000) of any newspaper in the world, reported (24 September) that while 'the Heir Apparent to the British Throne' was 'staking his gold upon the chances of a card or the roll of a ball – gold, be it remembered, that he obtained from the toil and sweat of the British working-man, without himself producing the value of a halfpenny ... foreigners, and his own countrymen, stood six deep' around his table.

'Send for and read *Reynolds Newspaper* of last Sunday on the gambling at Homburg', Gladstone wrote [46] to Granville. 'These things go from bad to worse. I saw *What Does She Do With It?* advertised on the walls of the Station at Birkenhead.' That was very shocking, but chance intervened suddenly to produce the most dramatic explosion of popular loyalty to the throne since the happy restoration of Charles II.

At the end of October 1871, the Prince of Wales was infected with typhoid fever by foul drains while staying with Lady Londesborough at Londesborough Lodge, near Scarborough. A fellow guest, Lord Chesterfield, died on 1 December of that disease, and the condition of the Prince was regarded as desperate by the end of that week.

The Queen and the royal family assembled at Sandringham, where the Princess rarely left her husband's bedside except to pray in the little church; and the gloomy note struck in the bulletins, which were issued several times a day for an entire fortnight by the Court physicians, Sir William Jenner, Dr Gull and others, caused the nation and empire almost to abandon hope. Death was popularly depicted in the guise of a panther toying with its royal victim; and a future Poet Laureate, Alfred Austin, caught the mood of the hour in one couplet which plumbed the depths of pathos and which, although subsequently suppressed, forecast also the poor quality of his later work:

> Flash'd from his bed, the electric tidings came,
> He is not better; he is much the same.

The approach of the fatal anniversary (14 December) of the Prince Consort's death from typhoid, ten years earlier, heightened the sense of impending catastrophe; and, while snatching a few hours sleep on a mattress in the bedroom of the Princess of Wales, Queen Victoria was informed at 7 p.m. on 11 December that the end must be expected during the night. Nevertheless, next morning, some slight improvement was reported in the condition of the Prince, who raved incessantly thereafter for thirty-six hours, talking, singing, whistling, with rare intermissions marked by laborious groans for breath.

'In those heart-rending moments', Queen Victoria recorded,[47] 'I scarcely knew how to pray aright, only asking God, if possible, to spare my beloved Child.' 14 December was a day of crisis, but that evening the fever departed, leaving the Prince utterly exhausted and sleeping peacefully like a child. He advanced slowly, but by easy stages, through convalescence to recovery; and an elemental upsurge of loyal emotion destroyed republicanism overnight as a significant factor in British radical politics.

Gladstone was resolved to seize that chance to bring the royalty question to a happy and profitable issue: 'We have arrived', he wrote [48] (22 December) to Granville, 'at a great crisis of Royalty: only it is a crisis which may be overlooked, because the issue is in a remote future. Not the less it is true that *this*, in all likelihood, is the last opportunity to be given us of effecting what is requisite.' He told his wife and family that the royalty question, upon which he had been engaged in painful controversy for months with Queen Victoria, was the only consideration which prevented him from quitting public life.

Gladstone had begun by taking up a suggestion, which Disraeli had dropped when the Queen objected to it, for acquiring a royal residence in Ireland. That residence, which would have been maintained out of public funds, would have been used by any member of the royal family who cared to hunt or shoot there, and to show the Irish that they were not forgotten; but that simple proposal was superseded quickly by what Gladstone termed his 'greater plan'. It envisaged the abolition of the Viceroyalty, and the despatch of the Prince of Wales to Dublin as the Queen's permanent non-political representative during the winter months.

Gladstone had warned [49] Queen Victoria as early as 25 June 1871, that that plan was 'to be regarded by no means as an exclusively Irish question, but as one likely to be of great utility in strengthening the Throne under circumstances that require all that can be done in that sense, if indeed we can make it the means of putting forward the Royal Family in the visible discharge of public duty'. The Prince's recovery prompted Gladstone to enlarge still further the 'greater plan' by insisting that Queen Victoria should either emerge from retirement, or permit the Prince and Princess of Wales to deputize for her in London, at Buckingham Palace during the summer months.

The Queen had been exasperated already that summer by Gladstone's strongly-pressed advice that she should prorogue in person the Parliamentary Session which had been prolonged into mid-August by pressure of business. She suggested that the Prime Minister was seeking to make use of her for a Party political object, and Gladstone was very angry. 'Upon the whole,' he wrote [50] (16 August 1871) to Ponsonby, 'I think it has been the most sickening piece of experience which I have had during near forty years of public life. *Worse* things may easily be imagined; but smaller and meaner causes for the decay of Thrones cannot be conceived. It is like the worm which bores the bark of a noble tree and so breaks the channel of its life.'

Staying that autumn at Balmoral, Gladstone found himself 'upon a new and different footing' with Queen Victoria, who became ill through depression and worry. He told [51] his wife (1 October) that 'the repellant power, which she knows so well how to use, has been put in action against me for the first time since the formation of the Government'. He was encouraged warmly, nevertheless, to press his plan of providing the Prince of Wales with suitable employment, by all members of the Prince's Household, including the new private secretary, Francis Knollys, as well as by the Duke of Cambridge, Princess Louise, Lord Granville, Henry Ponsonby and the Dean of Windsor, Gerald Wellesley, who begged only that he would show more tact.

As soon as it became clear that the Prince of Wales would not die from typhoid, Ponsonby sent [52] Knollys (17 December) a memorandum which began: 'It is assumed that the Prince of Wales, on his recovery, will gladly accept the advice of those who think that employment is desirable for him; and that the present may be a turning point in his life, if properly managed.' The possibilities were listed under the five headings of philanthropy; arts and sciences; the army; foreign affairs; and Ireland.

In reply [53] (19 December) Knollys started from the proposition that, unless the Prince were really interested, 'I should fear that, with his disposition, he might become irretrievably disgusted with business of every description.' Knollys added that an 'intimate knowledge of his character and tastes' had caused him to strike philanthropy, as well as arts and sciences, without hesitation from the list of possibilities.

Knollys explained that 'the Philanthropist, to succeed, should possess certain qualities which I do not think exist in the Prince of Wales. ... The same objection applies to Science and Art. He has been connected, more or less, for several years with the South Kensington Museum, and with several Exhibitions; but I cannot say that he has ever shown any special aptitude in that line.'

After dismissing the army also, as unsuitable, Knollys described the Irish plan as 'undoubtedly the best means' of providing employment for the Prince of Wales. But after discussing the Queen's objections, and the danger of allowing the best cause to become the enemy of the good, Knollys recommended foreign affairs, 'which have afforded occupation to even the most indolent of Princes'. He asked, accordingly, that the Prince of Wales should be invited to imitate the Prince Consort by writing comments for the Queen on despatches submitted by the Foreign Secretary.

The Foreign Secretary and the Prime Minister objected strongly, for different reasons, to that proposed solution. Granville informed [54] Ponsonby (26 December) that intolerable delays would occur if everything had to be submitted to the Prince who would quickly become discouraged at finding his suggestions 'snubbed by the Queen, or necessarily argued against by me. And as to really confidential matters, will they remain secret. He asked me to keep him informed during the War. One evening I got 4 messages from different friends, telling me to be careful. One of my first notes to him had been handed round a dinner party....'

Gladstone was wedded exclusively to his greater Irish plan; but Ponsonby had to inform [55] him (8 March 1872) that the Prince was 'even more opposed than the Queen to going in any official capacity to Ireland; and nothing but the most urgently expressed wish from the Queen would induce him to go'. The Prince had asked to be 'successively attached' to each of the great Government offices in Whitehall, 'where he would learn the habits of business in general, and the work of the Department in particular'.

While Gladstone battled with Queen Victoria on behalf of the plan which he had prepared, the Prince of Wales was recuperating at Osborne; and the Queen wrote [56] (14 February) to the Crown Princess of Prussia about his progress. She described him as very weak and drawn, but 'quite himself, only gentler and kinder than ever; and there is something different, which I can't exactly express. It is like a new life – all the trees and flowers give him pleasure, as they never used to do, and he was quite pathetic over his small wheelbarrow and little tools at the Swiss cottage. He is constantly with Alix, and they seem hardly ever apart ! ! !'

On 27 February 1872, a Thanksgiving Service in St Paul's Cathedral was attended by 13,000 people; and the Queen, with the Prince and Princess of Wales, were received with a ceaseless thunder of applause as they drove in procession through the streets of the capital. A fortnight later (9 March), Gladstone drew up a secret memorandum for a committee of the Cabinet consisting of himself, Granville, and Lord Halifax (Lord Privy Seal). The preamble stated [57] that Gladstone's Irish plan was necessary and urgent, and that its object was to improve 'the relations between the Monarchy and the Nation by framing a worthy and manly mode of life quo-ad public duties for the Prince of Wales', who left England with the Princess on that day for a three months' sunshine holiday in the Mediterranean.

7
India

STOPPING in Paris on the way to Cannes, the Prince of Wales called on President Thiers and met a number of representatives of the new republican regime which had been recognized by the British Government. He visited the Jockey Club, of which he was a popular member, and entertained at his hotel the Comte de Paris and other members of the Bourbon-Orleans family whose banishment, enforced by the Second Empire, had been cancelled as a gesture of confidence by the Third Republic.

From Cannes the Prince and Princess went in the royal yacht to Rome, where they were joined by the King and Queen of Denmark and entertained by King Victor Emanuel. The Prince exchanged civilities with the Pope who had immured himself in the Vatican, and, after staying in Florence, Venice and on Lake Como, he returned to Marlborough House on 1 June in good health and stouter than before his illness.

Francis Knollys, who had stayed in England, had been in communication with the Prince, as well as with Gladstone, about the Prince's employment problem. On 27 April, Knollys informed[1] Ponsonby, who told Gladstone, that the Prince did not wish to be faced with a 'cut and dried' plan when he returned to England, and that he was 'a little afraid' Gladstone might say: 'There – this is the plan we have prepared for you. It is quite ready and everything is settled. Take this, or nothing, *and* the consequences.' The Prince, who asked for an opportunity to talk privately with Gladstone and Granville, 'as soon as he had had time to turn himself round', announced that he was quite prepared 'to discuss the

Irish plan on its merits, and that, upon the whole, he looked on it in a more favourable light than was formerly the case'.

In those circumstances Gladstone very much regretted and resented the Queen's insistence that he should communicate exclusively with her and leave her to explain his views to the Prince of Wales; but the Prince acquiesced and the Prime Minister was compelled to concede the point. He sent the Queen, accordingly (5 July 1872), a very long letter [2] outlining his proposals.

Gladstone argued that 'no person would dream of proposing, for the Heir Apparent, public occupation beyond the limits of the United Kingdom'; that a succession of fragmentary attachments to different government offices could never inculcate business habits or a sense of responsibility; that all suggested alternatives were equally illusory; and that the only hope lay in Ireland. He said that there would be no difficulty about abolishing the Irish Viceroyalty, or about arranging for the Prince of Wales to stand in the same kind of constitutional relationship to a new Minister for Ireland (who would have a seat in the Cabinet) as that in which the Queen stood to her Prime Minister:

The nature of his duties would afford an admirable opportunity for giving the Prince the advantage of a political training which, from no fault of his own, he can hardly be said hitherto to have enjoyed. Administrative business might without difficulty be brought under his view in its daily course. He would have the opportunity, in all but extraordinary cases, of forming his judgement and offering his remarks while it was still under consideration, and with a view to practical results. He would at the same time be completely shielded from political responsibility in its technical sense. . . .

After pleading, in excuse for the liberty which he was taking, the unique opportunity afforded by the Prince's providential recovery, as well as his great anxiety for the stability of the Throne, Gladstone approached, 'with the utmost deference and reserve', the most delicate portion of his subject. He observed that the vitally important task of elevating the entire moral tone of Society, which the Queen had discharged to perfection 'by over twenty years of indefatigable activity', had been neglected completely since her widow-hood.

If the Queen were to decide that she had become incap-able of performing 'the social and visible functions of the Monarchy', Gladstone asked that she should invite the Prince and Princess of Wales to reside at Buckingham Pal-ace in her absence, and to perform them on her behalf. He explained that 'the accession of personal consideration and respect which would accrue' to the Prince of Wales as a result of 'the discharge, during a portion of the year, of duties in Ireland, such as those to which allusion has been made', would enhance the power of the Prince and Princess 'to serve Your Majesty with effect, and to confer benefit upon all society, but especially upon the higher society of Lon-don'. He added that, in that event, his proposals would em-brace 'the entire circle' of the Prince's year: 'Four to five months in Ireland, two or three in London, the autumn manoeuvres, Norfolk and Scotland, with occasional frac-tions of time for other purposes, would sufficiently account for the twelvemonth.'

In an interesting memorandum for Sir Henry Ponsonby, Queen Victoria noted[3] (9 July) that she had read Glad-stone's 'long paper with a good deal of irritation', and that 'an extraordinary want of knowledge of the world' had caused the Prime Minister to exaggerate her potential social influence in London, and even the badness of contemporary society. It was obvious that 'the Queen never could go out into society enough ... to have the slightest effect upon that independent, haughty, fault-finding fashionable set, which always was most inimical to the Prince [Consort] and her-self'. Explaining that she had never been supported when she had attempted, occasionally, to exclude certain people from 'great State entertainments' at Buckingham Palace, Queen Victoria suggested that it ought to have been much easier for the Prince and Princess of Wales to exclude *all doubtful* characters' from their smaller house and more in-timate society.

While admitting that the contemporary 'tone and style' of society were '*repulsive*, vulgar, bad and frivolous *in every* way,' Queen Victoria argued that society, nevertheless, was *'not near so bad* as it was 70 *or* 80 *years ago* when, as Lord Melbourne used to tell the Queen, there was hardly *one lady* of high rank whose character was not well known to be most reprehensible!! And as for the gentlemen, beginning with her *own uncles*, it was as bad as possible.' The Queen's memorandum continued:

To come to Ireland, and the training business, etc.; as regards the latter, any preparation of this kind is *quite useless;* and the P. of Wales WILL NOT do it, and unless you are absolutely forced *to do* it, you never will try. The Queen herself, though it was tried in all ways, *never* could *before* her accession take the slightest interest in public affairs; but, the moment she felt the responsibility, she bent her neck to the yoke and worked hard, though she *hates* it *all* as much now as she did as a girl.

The present King of the Belgians was considered as *unfit, idle* and *unpromising* an Heir Apparent as *ever was known*; and yet what an admirable King he has made!! Necessity and responsibility have forced this upon him and brought it about. No forced artificial position, like it would be in Ireland, will ever do this. To make the P. of Wales give up four to five months in Ireland is quite impossible.

After pointing out that Ireland was the least loyal portion of her dominions; that it would spell exile to the Prince of Wales, and that it would be bad also for his health, Queen Victoria concluded: 'Whoever knows the P. of Wales's character knows that he will always lean to a Party; and in Ireland he would be unable to withstand this, and would be beset by people who would force him into one extreme or the other.' In those circumstances, her reply to Gladstone took the form of an icy scrawl [4] (12 July) in three lines, enclosing a memorandum by Ponsonby, who suggested that as Ireland was in a state of fermentation, violent change seemed undesirable, and that the Prince would be more likely to display an indiscreet partiality for the Conservatives than to contract business habits. After expressing the Queen's view that the personal portion of Gladstone's letter 'more properly concerns herself to settle with members of her family as occasion may arise' Ponsonby added that the Queen would discuss it with the Prince of Wales.

Few men would have cared to continue that correspondence, but Gladstone recorded[5] his view that the Prime Minister had a special responsibility towards the Sovereign in matters of conduct which concerned the public interest. He told[6] Granville (16 July), who had implored him to desist, that he had to consider how much the Queen, and the country through her, had suffered in the past 'from want of plain speaking'; and he wrote[7] again (17 July) to the Queen: 'Were a Nation a being formed to act by pure and dry reason, without doubt it might be shown' that the Queen's neglect of her public and ceremonial duties since the Prince Consort's death had been due 'in no degree to an alteration of will on Your Majesty's part. But a Nation seems to be affected more powerfully and practically by other forms of motive than by mere reasoning ... it ceases fully to believe in what it does not see.' It had become the Queen's duty either to reappear in public, or to allow the Prince and Princess of Wales to adopt a scheme of life which would enable them 'to contribute in the highest degree of which the case admits to the maintenance of the strength and influence of the Monarchy'.

Enclosing a six-point memorandum which purported to meet all the Queen's objections, so far as he understood them, to his plan for remodelling the life of the Prince of Wales, Gladstone said that the plan had been formed to meet a public want and without reference 'to any interest personal to himself or peculiar to the present Government'. But the Queen, after waiting three weeks pointed out[8] (5 August) that 'as success could only ensue from the cordial desire of the Prince of Wales to undertake the duties suggested, and from the hearty approval of the Queen, it is evident that the experiment must fail'. She argued that Ireland was 'in no fit state to be experimented upon' and trusted, therefore, 'that this plan may now be considered as *definitely* abandoned'.

The Queen added that, although the Prince of Wales wanted to be 'left free to move as he pleased', he was 'anxious to be informed on all public matters which are of special interest, and to be assisted in forming an opinion on such subjects by communications from the members of the Government. He is also extremely desirous of being attached in some mode or other to the different departments of the State so as to learn the principles on which they are conducted; and he thinks that if he were appointed a member of the Indian Council he would be able to gain some knowledge of Indian affairs and find an interest in the discussions of that Body.'

After minuting his disgust at the rejection of his Irish plan, and at 'the illusory nature of the substitute recommended', as well as his belief that the Queen had prejudiced the Prince of Wales, Gladstone recorded [9]: 'Only one thing I cannot do. I cannot regard the reply as bringing the matter to a state in which it is to be put by, for I think it is of the weightiest character.' He explained,[10] therefore, in another long letter (28 August), to which a five-point memorandum was attached, that his object was to experiment not upon Ireland but upon the Prince of Wales; and that he wished to be allowed personally to explain to the Prince any points 'on which Mr Gladstone may not have enabled Your Majesty to place His Royal Highness in full possession of his meaning'.

It was to no purpose, and on 2 September the Queen wrote [11] that it was 'useless to prolong the discussion'. She advised the Prime Minister to consult 'such of his colleagues who best know the Prince of Wales', and to concentrate 'upon some other plan of employment'; and only then did Gladstone start to admit defeat in letters to a few of his colleagues. Complaining that his road had been blocked completely by the Queen, he informed [12] Granville (6 September) that 'it would be idle to attempt to force her, and I do not think it would be right for me to resign upon the matter, as it would do more harm than good'.

Writing (28 September) to Lord Hartington (Chief Secretary for Ireland) Gladstone observed [13] that although 'the Queen has now put an extinguisher upon my proposals with regard to the Prince of Wales, the Viceroyalty of Ireland, and the provision for a fuller discharge of the visible duties of Royalty ... it will, of course, be open to the Government to renew or press the proposals ...'. The Cabinet decided against that course, however; and Gladstone recorded [14] his view that the facts, when disclosed after his death, would have their 'proper place in any account of our relations with Ireland'.

The Prince of Wales (who had caused chatter in the meantime by going with the Duke of St Albans on a lark to Trouville, where he met and talked politics with the French President) asked his mother to continue to serve as his channel of communication with the Prime Minister. 'I need hardly assure you', Knollys wrote [15] (16 September) to Ponsonby, 'that the Prince of Wales's objections to the Irish Plan remain as strong as ever; and he feels them to be so good that he would on the whole rather prefer not to see Mr Gladstone on the subject.' At his mother's request he wrote [16] her a letter (27 October) which he asked her to show to Gladstone, and in which, while declining absolutely to go to Ireland, he stated that he 'would be very glad to have an opportunity of discussing with Mr Gladstone the subject of some useful employment which I could undertake as your eldest son, and which I am as anxious as ever to obtain'.

With mixed feelings, Gladstone accepted an invitation to stay at Sandringham for that purpose at the end of November, and he begged [17] the Queen (4 November) to play her part by trying to induce the Prince 'to adopt the habit of reading. The regular application of but a small portion of time would enable him to master many of the able and valuable works which bear upon Royal and Public duty'. Too casually for Gladstone's taste, the Queen replied [18] a fortnight later (18 November): '... She has only to say that the P. of W. has *never* been fond of reading, and that from his earliest years it was *impossible* to get him to do so. Newspapers and, *very rarely*, a novel, are all he ever reads.'

Although cosseted at Sandringham by the Princess, to whose beauty he was very susceptible, the Prime Minister felt too much discouraged to raise the subject of his host's employment problem. The Prince had been fully prepared and was willing to listen; and no one was more bitterly disappointed than Francis Knollys, who wrote [19] (8 December) to Ponsonby: 'I should have written to you directly after Mr Gladstone left here had anything as regards the question of employment resulted from his visit. But he did not even mention the subject to the Prince, and the latter said nothing to him. G. will never again have so good an opportunity and the whole thing is too disheartening.'

The minor question of providing a royal residence in Ireland was pursued intermittently but abortively for years; and, on Gladstone's behalf, the Viceroy, Lord Spencer, revived equally abortively in 1885 the suggestion that the Prince of Wales might go to Dublin as the Sovereign's permanent representative. As late as 1901, immediately after his accession to the throne, the Prince toyed with the idea of sending his son to Dublin in that capacity, but no employment was found in Ireland for the heir to the throne. Gladstone's hopes were wrecked completely, and Ponsonby described [20] (7 October 1876) in a letter to Lord Derby's secretary, Thomas Sanderson, how 'at last the most useless and the most objectionable of all the proposals, which the Foreign Secretary and the Foreign Office particularly disliked', had been adopted for the employment of the Prince of Wales. It had been decided that selected Foreign Office despatches should be sent to the Prince for information; but in October 1876, none had been sent for three months; and Disraeli ordered that nothing secret or important should ever be sent, because the Queen and he entertained doubts about the Prince's discretion.

The development of the overseas empire had not reached a point at which it would have appeared appropriate that the Prince of Wales should be employed as a peripatetic ambassador of goodwill; and the Prince's temperament rendered virtually insoluble the task of discovering an acceptable species of employment for the heir to the throne in that age. On the other hand, the growing volume of popular affection and sympathy which the Prince of Wales inspired was never inhibited by his evident incapacity to repeat the very useful role which his father had played in public affairs; and the Queen's intuition, founded on her own experience, that her son would bend his neck to the yoke only when compelled by necessity, was vindicated fully after he had succeeded to the throne.

It is impossible, nevertheless, not to deplore that missed opportunity in Dublin. It is unlikely that the Prince's presence would have influenced significantly the unhappy future course of Anglo–Irish relations, and the experiment might have failed; but those are not the primary points at issue. Whereas ordinary men and women take many successive personal decisions which determine the shapes of their careers, the Prince's life-pattern was moulded rigidly by extraneous factors, and the crisis which confronted him during the summer of 1872 was unique. The chance, boldly seized, and the experience, manfully endured, could have helped to relieve the Prince of a significant part of a great burden of frustration which tormented his mind until the end, and he might in consequence have become a happier man, and a less tense and moody king, if he had tried to follow the course charted by the Prime Minister.

As Walter Bagehot wrote in *The English Constitution* (1867), 'All the world and the glory of it, whatever is most attractive, whatever is most seductive, has always been offered to the Prince of Wales of the day, and always will be. It is not rational to expect the best virtue where temptation is applied in the most trying form at the frailest time of human life.' No evidence exists that the Prince ever read that book, which his son studied [21] for a time; and some of its most sparkling paragraphs read almost like an impertinent lecture addressed to the Prince of Wales, whom the author dubbed 'an unemployed youth'. 'He may form good intentions; he may say, "Next year I will read these papers; I will ask more questions; I will not let these women talk to me so." But they will talk to him. The most hopeless idleness is that smoothed with excellent plans.'

'So it is', Bagehot concluded, 'if the Prince comes young to the throne; but the case is worse when he comes to it old or middle-aged.' He might be nothing but 'a pleasure-loving lounger, or an active, meddling fool. ... It is easy to imagine that such a king would be the tool of others; that favourites should guide him; that mistresses should corrupt him; that the atmosphere of a bad Court should be used to degrade free government.'

ii

The Prince's life, accordingly, continued in its former rut, and it is on record,[22] for example, that Francis Knollys, who shared some of his master's tastes, invited the twenty-six-year-old Lord Rosebery in 1873 to lend his London house as a convenient rendezvous at which the Prince of Wales and the Duke of Edinburgh could meet 'their euphemistically named "actress friends"'. Rosebery excused himself, but other friends were more accommodating; and cockfighting figured sometimes among the amusements provided.

Social matters engrossed much of the attention of the Prince of Wales, who trumpeted his annoyance to the world when Gladstone and Granville asked him to stay away from the funeral of the ex-Emperor Napoleon III, which he had obtained the Queen's permission to attend. After the ex-Emperor died in exile at Chislehurst on 9 January 1873, hordes of Bonapartists flocked across the Channel, bent upon turning the occasion into a public demonstration against the Third Republic as well as against Germany; and the Prince consoled himself by inviting some of the most prominent to stay at Sandringham. In a letter (15 January) to Granville, Gladstone unkindly contrasted[23] the Prince's 'real good nature and sympathy' with his 'total want of political judgement, either inherited or acquired'.

The relationship in which the Prince stood to ministers at that time was illustrated in a letter which he wrote[24] (12 March 1873) to his friend, Lord Hartington, after the Government had been defeated on its Irish University Bill: 'Would you consider me very indiscreet if I asked you to let me know what steps the Govt. are going to take since the meeting of the Cabinet? You can perfectly rely on my keeping secret any communication you may think right (with Mr Gladstone's sanction) to make to me. Should you, however, think that my wish is an indiscreet one, please burn this and think no more about it.'

After attending the opening of an international exhibition in Vienna on 1 May 1873, the Prince and Princess of Wales spent a night or two in Berlin with the Crown Prince and Crown Princess of Prussia. All four abused Bismarck; family harmony was cemented; and Queen Victoria wrote [25] (25 May) to her daughter: 'It gives me such pleasure to hear you speak so lovingly of dear Bertie, for he deserves it. He is such a good kind brother – a very loving son and true friend – and so kind to all below him, for which he is universally loved – which poor Affie is not at all, either by high or low.'

Prince Alfred (Affie), Duke of Edinburgh, had become engaged to the Emperor of Russia's daughter, the Grand Duchess Marie; and disagreement arose about the precedence which should be accorded to her in England. The Russian Court claimed that the Emperor's daughter should take precedence over the Princess of Wales; but Queen Victoria would not consent, and the Grand Duchess, who was accorded precedence after the Princess of Wales but before all Queen Victoria's daughters except the Crown Princess of Prussia, was extremely dissatisfied.

The Prince of Wales played a helpful family part by inviting the Czarevitch and his wife to stay for two months (16 June – 13 August) at Marlborough House. They brought their children; and the eldest (the future Emperor Nicholas II) who never forgot that visit to England, became devoted to his Uncle Bertie, who spoilt him.

Popular interest was focused at that time not upon the Czarevitch but upon the unprepossessing Shah of Persia, who reached London on 18 June 1873. Because the Queen would not come to Buckingham Palace, the burden of entertainment was borne by the Prince of Wales, who piloted his guests everywhere. Many stories were told of the Shah's disgusting habits, and the Prince was never tired of repeating a comment made at Trentham, where both had spent the night as guests of the Duke of Sutherland. 'Too grand for a subject', the Shah had gravely observed. 'You'll have to have his head off when you come to the throne.'

Early in January 1874, the bookstalls started to sell a new and more malignant attack upon the Prince of Wales, by the authors of *The Coming K—*. Entitled *The Siliad*, it was filled with scurrilous social and political satire, but Gladstone explained [26] (5 January) to Granville that it would be wrong to give it adventitious importance by taking action to suppress it. Granville informed [27] Gladstone that the Prince of Wales and the Duke of Cambridge, whom he dubbed 'those two men of iron', were exhorting him to be '*firm*' against Russia in central Asia, and that the Prince's comments had been mingled with violent complaints about a new army uniform.

Because he loved uniforms the Prince was incensed by the Queen's refusal to allow him to accept the honorary colonelcy of a Russian regiment which Alexander II had offered him. The Duke of Edinburgh, as the Emperor's prospective son-in-law, was permitted to accept one, but Gladstone and Granville held that it would be contrary to precedent in the case of the Prince of Wales, who left England in consequence on 10 January, in order to attend his brother's wedding in St Petersburg, in a dissatisfied frame of mind.

That mood was dispelled by the lavishness of Russian hospitality, which placed palaces at the disposal of the Prince and Princess of Wales in Moscow as well as in St Petersburg. The Prince, who was delighted by a magnificent boar-hunt during which eighty beasts were slaughtered, was pleased also, while in Russia, by Disraeli's courtesy in writing (17 February) to notify him that he had again become Prime Minister after defeating Gladstone at the General Election.

Soon after the Prince's return, the Russian Emperor paid a State visit to England, and Gladstone as well as Disraeli was invited to meet him (15 May) at a great state banquet at Marlborough House. A very strenuous season followed which ended on 22 July when the Prince of Wales gave the most remarkable and elaborate ball of his career.

Fourteen hundred invitations were issued, and Sir Frederick Leighton superintended the decoration of Marlborough House. The Princess, wearing jewels of marvellous splendour, was superb in Venetian dress with her two young sons as pages, and the Prince appeared as Charles I. Wearing a long sword and his Garter badge, with the star on the left shoulder of the short black velvet cloak which partially covered a maroon satin and velvet suit embroidered with gold, the Prince danced until dawn, waving a mass of fair cavalier curls which flowed down his shoulders from under a black felt hat trimmed with one large white feather and looped up with an aigrette of cascading diamonds. Supper was served in two scarlet marquees, hung with rich tapestries; and *The Times* praised warmly that display of 'well-ordered magnificence' in the life of a Prince who 'proved himself last night well descended from Kings whose Courts have never been wanting in splendour'. The Prime Minister, who described the scene as 'gorgeous, brilliant, fantastic', was permitted to appear in uniform instead of fancy dress after dining and speaking at the Mansion House.

On 27 August the Prince and the Princess of Wales left England for Potsdam, where they stayed in the New Palace with the Crown Prince and the Crown Princess, and attended the Confirmation of their nephew, the future Emperor William II. All took Communion together after the Prince had summoned his nephew to his sitting-room and had read to him there a letter which Queen Victoria had written for the occasion, as well as a passage (selected by the Prince of Wales) from a Bible which was the gift of The Queen.

From Potsdam the Princess went to stay with her parents in Copenhagen, while the Prince went to Baden to drink the waters and gamble. Reports, which appeared in the British press about that visit to Baden, were associated with rumours that the Prince owed about £600,000; that Disraeli had been invited to ask Parliament to pay his debts; and that Queen Victoria and Rothschild were discharging the most urgent claims in the meantime.

The Prince had no debts at that time which were over a year old, and it was thought well to issue (18 September) a denial of reports that he was in financial difficulties. The Prince and Sir William Knollys reassured [28] the Queen about Rothschild; but Sir William Knollys expressed [29] (14 September) great anxiety on the score of gambling and betting: 'It is impossible to say what they may lead to, and, as Your Majesty was once pleased to observe to him, the Country could never bear to have George IV as Prince of Wales over again.'

Sir William explained that he had objected to the current visit to Baden, 'and should equally do so if another visit to Paris in returning be in contemplation. It is the most dangerous place in Europe, and it would be well if it were never revisited. In fact, remaining on the Continent, whenever it involves a separation of the Prince and Princess of Wales – whether Her Royal Highness is in Denmark or elsewhere – cannot be otherwise than most undesirable, and in the interests of both would be better limited to the shortest period. ...'

From Baden the Prince went to Denmark in order to spend a short time with the Princess and his parents-in-law, before embarking, *en garçon*, upon a tour of the castles of French friends in the Loire Valley. He had arranged to stay first at Esclimont, near Rambouillet, with the Duc de la Rochefoucauld-Bisaccia, who had just been dismissed from his post as French Ambassador in London for having advocated the claim of the Comte de Paris to the throne of France.

That French tour alarmed Queen Victoria, who begged Disraeli to stop it; and the Prime Minister warned[30] the Prince (3 October) to exercise great discretion. He explained,[31] however (4 October), to Queen Victoria that he knew the Prince's character well enough to be certain that he would have destroyed 'any little influence' which he might possess, if he had attempted rashly to interfere with his private life and plans.

After calling upon the French President, Marshal Mac-Mahon, who invited him to hunt at Marly, the Prince went by special train (15 October) to Rambouillet and was driven to Esclimont. He apologized for the unavoidable absence of the Princess, and was entertained sumptuously in one of the few great French houses which had retained a mass of pre-Revolution gold and silver plate. The Duchesse de la Rochefoucauld-Bisaccia had been born a Princess de Ligne, and the Prince's fellow-guests included the Comte de Breteuil, the Duc de Chartres, the Duc de Croy, the Duc de Doudeauville, the Marquis de Galliffet, the Marquis de Lau, the Duc de Mouchy, Barons Alphonse and Nathaniel de Rothschild, M. Standish and their wives, as well as the Duchesse de Luynes, whose husband had been killed during the war.

The Prince of Wales had been very much at home for some years in that society, which had its headquarters in the Faubourg St Germain. He understood perfectly the undertones governing the relationship between the pre-revolutionary aristocracy of land and birth, and representatives of the fallen imperial regime who were often associated with banking and commerce. In an increasing number of cases the freemasonry of wealth, and the exercise of tact, enabled those two social worlds to mingle harmoniously, and the Duc de Mouchy, for example, married a great-niece of Napoleon I, while the Duc de Grammont married a Rothschild. On the other hand, almost all representatives of the Third Republic were beyond the pale; and the social ascendancy enjoyed by the Prince in France was dependent upon his absolute refusal to make at any time the smallest attempt to bridge or to ignore that gulf.

Among a host of French friends and acquaintances, none were quite so close to the Prince of Wales as the Duc and Duchesse de Mouchy, the Princesse de Sagan, and M. and Mme Standish. All were frequent guests at Marlborough House and Sandringham; the Prince used their houses in Paris almost as his own, and they played the foremost part in enabling him to lead a different and less restricted life whenever he crossed the English Channel.

Beautiful and vivacious, Anna de Mouchy was a daughter of Prince Lucien Murat and a granddaughter of the famous Marshal Joachim Murat – the innkeeper's son – who was made King of Naples by his brother-in-law, Napoleon I, and who was executed by his former subjects, at last, as a public nuisance. Brought up as a Protestant by an American mother (Georgina Frazer of Baltimore), Anna Murat had turned Roman Catholic when she came of age, and had been recognized as a Princess of the Blood by Napoleon III.

He gave her an annual income of forty thousand pounds and much valuable jewellery when she married Antoine de Noailles, Duc de Mouchy, who bore one of the most illustrious names in France. Thereafter, the dislike which a parvenu imperial rank aroused among a legitimist patrician caste was dissolved very easily; and the Duchesse de Mouchy, an intimate friend of the Empress Eugénie, consolidated an undisputed social leadership.

Less vivacious but, if possible, even more beautiful than the Duchesse de Mouchy, the gorgeous and extravagant Princesse de Sagan bore likewise a historic name, but was of middle-class origin. A daughter of the rich banker, Baron Seillère, Jeanne de Sagan's gallantries were reputed to be as numerous as those of her husband from whom, except occasionally, she lived apart, and her name had been linked with that of the Prince of Wales as early as 1867. With the Princesse de Metternich and Baroness Poilly, the Princesse de Sagan was regarded as the arbiter of elegance; and after her husband's castle of Mello had been transferred to her banker brother (who married a daughter of the Prince of Wales's witty and light-hearted friend, the Marquis de Galliffet) she divided her time between her great mansion in the Rue St Dominique and her charming properties at Cannes and Deauville.

Frank and Hélène Standish were loved equally by the Prince and Princess of Wales, and their marriage, although childless, was famous for its happiness. Standish, whose mother had been a daughter of the Duc de Mouchy, was the grandson of an English squire who had settled in France after inheriting a large fortune. The Standish home in the Avenue d'Iéna was furnished and arranged in contemporary English taste, and Mme Standish, a firm ally of the Duchesse de Mouchy and a wise counsellor of the Princesse de Sagan, was born a Decazes and sprung from the purest patrician stock.

Hélène Standish invited ridicule by modelling her appearance and manner too openly upon that of the Princess of Wales, to whom she bore a remarkable physical resemblance, and who was always her intimate friend.

A great sportswoman who lived for pleasure, her fame has
perished; but she dispensed a generous hospitality for two
generations, and wore round her pretty throat a rope of
pearls which was celebrated throughout Europe.

From Esclimont the Prince went to Serrant (Duc de la
Tremouille); Dompierre (Duchesse de Luynes); Mello (Princesse de Sagan); Mouchy-le-Chatel (Duc de Mouchy); and
finally to Chantilly (Duc d'Aumâle). Newspaper readers in
France and England derived vicarious pleasure from long,
printed accounts of festivities staged, game slaughtered and
succulent luncheon and dinner menus; and after a final stag-
hunt with the President at Marly, and a dinner which he
gave jointly with the Comte de Paris at the Jockey Club,
the Prince of Wales returned well satisfied on 29 October to
Marlborough House.

The Prince of Wales had offended no one while contribut-
ing that modest fillip to the French legitimist cause, and he
took the Princess immediately to stay at Packington with
Lord Aylesford. Thence, on 3 November, he toured three
factories in Birmingham, and was entertained in the Civic
Hall at a luncheon which aroused widespread curiosity. The
Mayor of Birmingham, Joseph Chamberlain, was a Radical
demagogue who had advocated a republic; but the four
speeches which he made that day combined loyalty with
manliness and courtesy to perfection. All struck precisely
the right note, and although three years passed before he
dined for the first time at Marlborough House, the process
whereby he was transformed into a Tory statesman, while
his eyes were raised from municipal drains to the imperial
horizon, was assisted materially by the Prince of Wales.

After leaving Packington on 7 November, the Prince and
Princess visited Coventry, where the Prince of Wales perpetrated one of his most famous practical jokes. He was
accompanied by Lord Hartington and by the Duchess of
Manchester, whose liaison was known to, and accepted by,
the whole of Society.

That liaison had been interrupted for a short time by an
attachment which Hartington had formed with the celebrated *demi-mondaine*, Catherine Walters, known widely

and affectionately as 'Skittles'. The Prince asked an equerry
to arrange that a bowling alley should be included in their
tour of the town, and that the Mayor of Coventry should be
instructed to make a point of informing Lord Hartington
that the Prince had particularly requested its inclusion, in
tribute to his friend's democratic enjoyment of the game of
skittles.

All went as planned, and when Hartington, in his gruff way,
showed no interest in a bowling alley, the Mayor exclaimed
in all innocence: 'His Royal Highness asked especially for
its inclusion, in tribute to your lordship's love of skittles.'

iii

During the winter of 1874–5 the Prince of Wales concentrated upon the task of extracting from Queen Victoria, and
from ministers, permission to tour India at the Government's
expense. He told [32] his librarian at Sandringham to start
collecting books about India, and he corresponded with
Disraeli, who began his letters always with 'Sir, and dear
Prince'. The position reached at the end of March 1875, was
described [33] by the Prime Minister, after a visit to Windsor,
in a letter (30 March) to the Secretary for India, Lord Salisbury:

The Indian Expedition!
It seems that our young Hal [the Prince of Wales] kept it a
secret from his wife and induced his Mother to give her assent
on the representation that it was entirely approved by her
Ministers.
The Wife insists upon going! When reminded of her children, she says, 'the husband has first claim'.
The Mother says that nothing will induce her to consent to
the Princess going, and blames herself bitterly for having sanc-
tioned the scheme without obtaining on the subject my opinion,
and that of my colleagues.

Disraeli explained that he had undertaken the entire
management of the affair; that finance was a great problem;
and that the Prince could not, while the Queen would not,
make any contribution: 'Where is the money to come from?
He has not a shilling; she will not give him one. A Prince

of Wales must not move in India in a *mesquin* manner.
Everything must be done on an imperial scale, etc., etc. This
is what she said. ...'

Despite Radical opposition to expenditure of public funds
on another pleasure trip for the Prince of Wales, Disraeli
obtained a supplementary vote of £112,000 from the Commons. He said that the Prince would be the Viceroy's guest
in India, and that the Indian Government would contribute an additional £30,000 towards the Prince's personal
expenses; but although that contribution was raised subsequently to more than £100,000, the Prince felt keenly the
position in which he was placed of having to give presents of
far less value to the Indian princes than those which they
lavished upon him.

Responsible opinion (e.g. *The Times*, 10 July 1875) held
that the Prince had been treated shabbily by Parliament:
and Disraeli, who had done his best, was invited to Sandringham to hear the Prince's complaint that he had not been
given enough money. The Prime Minister suggested that his
parsimony had been prudent, because it had changed public
opinion: 'The general sentiment now – and it will remain
for a long time – is that the Prince of Wales is not spending
enough. If Your Royal Highness is wise, and I am sure you
will be, this feeling may be turned to good account.' Disraeli reported [34] (16 October) to Lady Bradford that the
Prince had appeared 'amused and satisfied'; but that he was
still liable to talk 'big' when among his 'creatures' about
'spending, if requisite, a million, and all that...'

In the prevailing confusion, for which Disraeli apologized [35] (10 August) to the Prince, saying that there had
been 'too many cross purposes', the Queen offended her son
by ordering that all detailed proposals should be submitted
directly to her by Disraeli or Salisbury, instead of being
settled by them in consultation with the Prince. Francis
Knollys informed [36] Ponsonby (4 June) that the Prince
particularly regretted the Queen's want of confidence in this
instance, after trying all his life to set an example of obedience to her wishes, and that, as 'the idea of this visit emanated *entirely* from the Prince of Wales', it was natural that

'as far as practicable, he should wish to keep the arrangements connected with it in his hands'.

After a stormy interview with Disraeli in Downing Street, during which the Prince 'manifested extraordinary excitement' and refused to consent to any change in the suite which he had personally chosen, the Prime Minister advised[37] the Queen to give way. She agreed, reluctantly, saying that she wanted 'some more eminent men'; and the final list contained eighteen names: Lord Aylesford (personal guest); Lieut. Prince Louis of Battenberg, R.N. (A.D.C.); Lieut. Lord Charles Beresford, R.N., M.P. (A.D.C.); Lord Carrington (personal guest); Canon R. Duckworth (chaplain); Lieut.-Col. Arthur Ellis (equerry); Dr Joseph Fayrer (physician); Augustus FitzGeorge (A.D.C. – son of the Duke of Cambridge); Sir Bartle Frere (leader); Albert Grey (secretary to Sir Bartle Frere); Sydney Hall (artist); Francis Knollys (secretary to the Prince of Wales); Lord Alfred Paget (representing the Queen); Major-General Dighton Probyn, V.C. (equerry); W. H. Russell (honorary private secretary to the Prince, and historian); Lord Suffield (Lord-in-Waiting); the Duke of Sutherland (personal guest); Lieut.-Col. Owen Williams (commanding the Blues – equerry).

Non-members of the suite were a zoologist (Bartlett); a botanist (Mudd); and 'a clerk of great merit' from the India Office (Isaacson) whose assistant ranked as an 'upper' servant with the Prince's valet, stud-groom, page, three chefs, and the Duke of Sutherland's piper. The Prince, who was forced to abandon his plan of taking a detachment of Life Guards, travelled with twenty-two ordinary 'lower' servants.

Queen Victoria objected only to the inclusion of Lord Charles Beresford and Lord Carrington; and, although the expedition was exclusively masculine, the Princess of Wales was never reconciled to her exclusion. She begged Disraeli vainly to intercede for her, and wrote[38] many years later (12 November 1913) to Lady Hardinge of Penshurst: 'How I wish I could have paid you a visit in beautiful India – the one wish of my life to see that *wonderful*, beautiful country! But, alas, it was never to be, and when I might have gone –

that time with my dear husband – he would not let me, and to this day I do not know why, excepting that he said at that time it was difficult for ladies to move about there – as if that would have mattered to me!'

Leaving England on 11 October 1875, the Prince of Wales lunched in Paris with President MacMahon before dining and going to a theatre with the Comte de Paris and other friends. The Prince reached Brindisi by special train, and embarked (16 October) for Bombay in the specially converted troopship *Serapis* (Capt. the Hon. H. Carr Glyn, R.N.), which was escorted by the frigates *Hercules* and *Pallas*, with the royal yacht *Osborne* in attendance. Disraeli had noted at Sandringham at the beginning of October that the Princess of Wales had looked as though she were preparing to commit suttee; and the Prince, after saying good-bye to her at Calais remained depressed for three weeks: 'We are more like a lot of monks than anything else', Carrington wrote [39] to his mother (20 October). 'No jokes or any approach to them. ... He [the Prince] was tremendously low in Paris, and even yet isn't up to his usual form'; and he added (5 November): 'The Prince of Wales ... looks wonderfully well ... the quiet and early hours and the regularity of the living here have done him no end of good ... No news – all well – no whist and no sprees, or bear-fights, or anything!'

Every member of the Prince's suite took pride in observing strict formality upon all public occasions. They felt that their country's honour was entrusted to their hands; and officers and civilians all wore for dinner a costume approved by the Prince of Wales, which signified the birth of the dinner jacket. Mess dress and swallow-tail coats were discarded in favour of a short dark blue cloth jacket which was worn with black trousers and a black bow tie.

After brief but ceremonial visits to Athens, Cairo and Aden, the Prince of Wales was welcomed on 8 November 1875, at Bombay by the Governor, Sir Philip Wodehouse, and by the Viceroy of India, Lord Northbrook, amid a thunder of naval and military salutes. The Viceroy, who ceded precedence to the Prince, attended a banquet that evening at Government House but left early next morning for Calcutta.

Among additions made in India to the Prince of Wales's suite were Major-General Sam Browne, V.C., who had lost an arm in the Mutiny, and Major Edward Bradford, who had lost one to a tiger. Sam Browne took charge of transportation, and Edward Bradford, 'the head of the secret police in India', who never left the Prince's side, was made responsible for security.

The suite had orders to surround the Prince at all times and its members took turns in sitting up all night outside any room or tent in which he slept. Those precautions fidgeted the Prince much less than did the innumerable telegrams about his health which Queen Victoria despatched constantly, often *en clair*, and sometimes so worded as to provoke ridicule.

The main task of the Prince of Wales in India – unforeseen at the outset – was to show himself to princes, soldiers, peasants and workers as the incarnation of the British Raj, which had previously been no more than a remote and abstract symbol, represented by officers and officials who extorted varying degrees of love, respect, fear and, occasionally, hatred. The Prince, with his Royal Standard, made an indelible impression wherever he went, and his passion for big game, which exhausted some members of his suite including the Duke of Sutherland who invented an early excuse to go home, enhanced his standing in the eyes of princes and chiefs who were much the most politically conscious and articulate members of the community at that time. In that way a mood was aroused quickly which helped to prepare public opinion for Disraeli's Bill to proclaim Queen Victoria as Empress of India, which was introduced into Parliament before the Prince of Wales returned home.

The Princes's manner while in contact with all classes of his future Indian subjects could not have been bettered, and it was rightly and universally praised. It combined dignity with ease; and he protested hotly to Lord Salisbury about the 'disgraceful' way in which some British officers constantly referred to the natives as 'niggers'. 'Because a man has a black face and a different religion from our own,' he wrote [40] (30 November) to Lord Granville, 'there is no reason why he should be treated as a brute.'

Manifestations of racial or religious prejudice were anathema to the Prince of Wales; but the attempt of his friend, Lord Lytton, who succeeded Northbrook as Viceroy of India in January 1876, to alter the intransigent social outlook of Englishmen serving in India was resented in some circles and attributed to 'the malign influence' of the Prince of Wales. The Prince wrote [41] as early as 14 November 1875, from Poona to complain to Queen Victoria about 'the rude and rough manner with which the English political officers (as they are called), ... treat the princes and chiefs upon whom they were appointed to attend'; and the Queen, greatly concerned, spoke strongly to Disraeli and Salisbury on the subject, as well as to the Viceroy designate before he left for India. Lytton was warned when he reached Calcutta that Indian princes relished opportunities to short-circuit official channels, and was met by hints that the Prince of Wales regarded all hereditary potentates as members of one great trades union.

While driving through the streets of Bombay the Prince noticed a number of illuminated signs which read 'Welcome to our Future Emperor', and he sat at Government House in something very like imperial state on the mornings of 9 and 10 November while receiving a number of major and minor native potentates. The most impressive was the twelve-year-old Gaekwar of Baroda, whose trim little figure and face of extraordinary beauty and dignity appeared like a crystal rainbow out of a cascade of diamonds said to be worth six hundred thousand pounds. With shining eyes the boy parried the Prince's questions about his lessons, and said that he loved only hunting and cricket. He brought six heavy gold cannon, worth forty thousand pounds apiece, as presents; but they were returned discreetly to his treasury.

After a brief excursion to Poona, the Prince visited Baroda, where Wodehouse and Frere hoped that he would lend prestige to the young Gaekwar's government. The former Gaekwar had been deposed for tyranny and corruption, and his predecessor's widow, on being asked to find a successor, had chosen the handsome boy who had amused the Prince in Bombay, and who had played formerly, half naked, in the streets of Baroda. The Maharanee, a civilized and charming woman, who had discarded the veil, talked easily to her guests and pleased the Prince.

During that happy visit the Prince hunted cheetah and black buck and enjoyed some pig-sticking; and he wrote [42] (21 November) to his little son, Prince George, to describe some 'very curious' wild beast fights which had been staged for his amusement. Elephants, rhinoceros, buffaloes and rams had been pitted against each other, 'but none was hurt excepting one buffalo who had his horn broken, which I fear must have hurt him a good deal'.

An outbreak of cholera caused the abandonment of a plan for a visit to Mysore, after the population had been alerted for a hundred miles around, and many thousands of pounds had been spent upon preparations. Instead, the Prince left Bombay (25 November) in *Serapis* in order to shoot elephants in Ceylon; and a vessel filled entirely with British, Indian and foreign newspaper correspondents was added to his escort.

After a brief visit (27 November) to Goa, and a gay dinner given (30 November) at sea to celebrate Lord Charles Beresford's promotion to the rank of commander, the Prince of Wales landed (1 December) at Colombo, where he knighted, on the Queen's behalf, William Gregory, the Governor of Ceylon. The Prince went up to Kandy, where elaborate preparations had been made, and on 6 December, he killed his first elephant, after knocking over another which lay quiet and looked as though it were dead. The Prince often told the story of the first elephant which he thought that he had killed. He hacked its tail off, while Charles Beresford climbed on to its rump and started to dance a hornpipe; but the beast rose unexpectedly to its feet and tottered off into the jungle before anyone could grab a rifle and fire. The Prince wrote fully to his sons, promising to bring a baby elephant to Sandringham for them to ride, and he complained of the jungle leeches 'which are very bad, and climb up your legs and bight [sic] you'.

Disembarking at Tuticorin on 10 December, the Prince was welcomed at Madras three days later by its Governor, the Duke of Buckingham, who had invited many pretty and vivacious English ladies to entertain his guest. The Duke's combination, at Government House, of every English domestic amenity with the style of life of an oriental satrap was highly congenial to the Prince of Wales, who was taken to the races as well as to hunt jackal.

The Indian capital, Calcutta, was reached on 23 December, and the guns of all ships, forts and batteries thundered in unison as the Prince of Wales disembarked in the full dress uniform of a field-marshal, wearing his Garter badge and the Star of India, and with the Viceroy, Lord Northbrook at his side. A reception hall had been specially built near the landing stage, and the Prince received a large number of European and Asiatic notables.

After a State banquet at Government House, where he stayed, the Prince held a Durbar in the throne room, next morning, by special commission (which the Viceroy proclaimed) from the Queen. Gigantic troopers of the Viceroy's bodyguard, in tunics and cummerbunds of scarlet and gold, wearing zebra-striped turbans, buckskin breeches and jackboots, were arranged like statues between each pair of marble columns, and the place swarmed with officers and civilians in gorgeous uniforms. Eight important bejewelled potentates bearing rich presents were presented personally and successively to the Prince of Wales. They were the Maharajahs of Gwalior, Jaipur, Jodhpur, Kashmir, Patiala and Rewa; the Maharajah Holkar of Indore, who was as fat as Henry VIII; and the Begum of Bhopal, who would not raise her veil, but who was agreeably talkative.

A week of strenuous sightseeing, visits and races and receptions followed, at the end of which, on New Year's Day, 1876, the Prince held an investiture of the Order of the Star of India in camp on the Maidan. After joining the Viceroy and the Commander-in-Chief (Lord Napier of Magdala) in a stately procession of Knights Grand Commander, the Prince proceeded to invest new members individually with the different grades of the Order to which they had been appointed; and he rounded off the day by unveiling an equestrian statue of the Viceroy, Lord Mayo, who had been assassinated in 1872; by watching a polo match on the Maidan and a display of fireworks on the racecourse; and by attending at 10.15 p.m., after a banquet at Government House, a performance of one of his favourite farces, *My Awful Dad*.

On 5 January the Prince began a tour of North India, starting at Benares, where he was welcomed by the Governor of Bengal, Sir Richard Strachey. He received, very quietly, on the morning of his arrival, six male descendants of the former Mogul Emperor of Delhi who were living upon a bare pittance from their British conquerors, but who bore themselves with dignity which extorted admiration; and that evening he dined with the universally respected Maharajah of Benares – a famous warrior and scholar – who sent a golden litter to convey the Prince into his palace, and silver litters and chairs for his companions.

At Lucknow, where he sensed a latent hostility for the first time, the Prince of Wales laid the foundation stone of a memorial to the native heroes who had died nineteen years before while helping to defend the Residency against the fanatical assaults of 60,000 mutinous and malignant Sepoys; and at Cawnpore he visited the memorial and monument standing over the well into which Nana Sahib had pitched the bodies of his Christian victims. There, as at Agra, and at every other place which he visited, the Prince was indefatigable in holding levées and receptions, and in paying visits of inspection and ceremony; and at Delhi, where he was welcomed by Lord Napier of Magdala, he spent an entire week in camp with the army.

After reviewing 18,000 troops and attending some large-scale manœuvres, during which he led his own regiment, the 10th Hussars, in a cavalry charge, and dined, on successive nights, with it and with officers of the Rifle Brigade, of which he was also Colonel-in-Chief, the Prince travelled to Lahore. He entered the gaol there and enjoyed a long conversation with an aged and notorious thug, whose life had been spared when he turned Queen's evidence, and who discussed coolly and factually some of the 250 murders which he claimed to have committed before he was laid by the heels.

Thereafter the Prince's attention was concentrated exclusively upon big game; and he placed himself in the hands of a famous hunter, Henry Ramsay, whom he knighted, and who ruled, as High Commissioner, the frontier districts along the Nepalese border. Carrington and Prince Louis of Battenberg broke their collar-bones while pig-sticking, but the Prince, who was as fearless as anyone, suffered no mischance and was superlatively happy. He stayed successively with the Maharajahs of Kashmir, Patiala, Gwalior (who took a special pride in his army, which the Prince reviewed) and Jaipur (in whose company on 5 February the Prince killed his first tiger – a female, 8½ feet long, with three cubs in her womb). All four potentates competed for the honour of showing the best sport, and of staging the most gorgeous display of fireworks in which the Prince always revelled, and of which he became a connoisseur.

On 20 February 1876, at a camp formed in jungle country at Bonbussa, on the Sardah river which formed the boundary between India and Nepal, Sir Jung Bahdur, the sixty-year-old Prime Minister and virtual ruler of Nepal, whose king had been turned into a puppet, accepted from Sir Henry Ramsay the honour of showing sport to the Prince of Wales. Blazing with diamonds and wearing in his helmet, in addition to bird of paradise plumes, an immense ruby which was the gift of the Emperor of China, Sir Jung's manner was too obsequious to win the goodwill of the Prince of Wales. Sir Jung, who had visited England in 1850, had rendered valuable aid during the Great Mutiny, but he was reputed to be of low extraction, and the best that any member of the Prince's party could find to say about him was put brutally by Arthur Ellis into a letter [43] (20 March) to Queen Victoria: 'He is the most energetic specimen of a native we have met. This quality, being so rare, it is greatly admired. He is a remarkable savage.'

Sir Henry Ramsay had collected 200 riding elephants and 2,000 coolies; but Sir Jung had collected, on the Nepalese side of the river, 1,000 riding elephants and at least 10,000 soldiers

to act as servants and beaters and to attend on the needs of
less than twenty sportsmen in a camp known as Jumoa,
which covered many square miles of forest. On his first full
day in Nepal (21 February) the Prince of Wales, seated in a
howdah on the back of an elephant, killed six fully grown
tigers; and every night in the various camps which were
used, he enjoyed a hot bath, changed into evening dress,
and gave a dinner party in a large and richly furnished tent.

'Since I last wrote to you,' the Prince informed[44] (23
February) his sons, Prince Eddy and Prince George, 'I have
had great tiger shooting. The day before yesterday I killed
six, and some were very savage. Two were man-eaters. To-
day I killed a tigress and she had a little cub with her.' He
said that he hoped to bring some cubs home to England, and
added that 'two little bears and an armadillo got loose in
Mr Bartlett's tent last night and frightened him so that he
did not know what to do ...!'

Lord Charles Beresford may have been responsible for
playing that prank upon the expedition's official zoologist;
but on 20 February the Prince had been dearly troubled to
hear news of a far more serious prank which was being
played at that time in England upon his personal guest and
intimate friend, Lord Aylesford, 'Sporting Joe'. 'Letters!!!',
the Prince recorded[45] laconically in the jejune diary which
he kept; and on that day Aylesford received a note from his
wife announcing that she intended to elope with another of
the Prince's friends, Lord Blandford, who had decided, for
her sake, to desert Lady Blandford.

The Aylesfords and Blandfords belonged to the inner
circle of the Marlborough House set, and it was certain that
the scandal would convulse society. With the Prince's consent, Colonel Owen Williams, who was Lady Aylesford's
brother, had left for home on 16 February in response to an
urgent appeal from his family; and the Prince now agreed
that Aylesford should follow at the first opportunity.

Aylesford left accordingly (28 February) on an elephant's
back on the first stage of his journey to the railhead at
Bareilly. Carrington wrote[46] (1 March) to his mother (Lady
Carrington): 'He has gone home broken-hearted at the

disgrace ... and the misery it all entails is terrific. ... Our party is much reduced now, as we have lost the Duke of Sutherland, Grey, Owen Williams and Joe Aylesford. Old Alfred Paget, too, is dying to get home. ...' Lord Alfred Paget was a great favourite with Queen Victoria and, in a letter[47] (23 February 1876) to the Queen, Francis Knollys said that he would never dare to repeat to her the barrack-room expressions with which the game but explosive old man relieved his feelings as he retired exhausted to his tent at the end of each day's sport.

After denouncing Blandford as 'the greatest blackguard alive', and after expressing warm sympathy with Aylesford, the Prince of Wales enjoyed an elephant hunt on 25 February which Carrington described as 'probably the finest day's sport ever seen'. Other good days followed, and on 24 March Sir Bartle Frere summed up, for Queen Victoria, the effects of the expedition as a whole. He declared[48] that the last part, in Nepal, had been as great a success 'as any of the earlier phases', 'not only on account of the wonderful sport' which Sir Jung Bahadur had shown the Prince of Wales, and which newspaper correspondents had fully reported, but much more on account of 'the impression it made on people at a distance – an impression of manly vigour and power of endurance which pleased everyone, Europeans and natives alike ... It was like winning a battle and proved he possessed Royal qualities of courage, energy and physical power.'

For the rest, Frere suggested that the Prince of Wales had succeeded in winning the affection of the common people of India, as well as the respect and admiration of India's princes and nobles. His manner had invariably been perfect; and, just as the Queen would in future be Empress of India and not merely the Sovereign of India's British conquerors, so the Prince of Wales had infused a new hope into an entire sub-continent. Frere added that the Prince had made all India's inhabitants feel that he stood to them in exactly the same relationship as that in which he stood to the British, and that he had conferred a new dignity upon them by coming for a time to share their mundane lives, and to dwell and travel in their midst.

8

A Personal Quarrel

1876–80

i

AFTER distributing many presents, the Prince of Wales left Nepal on 5 March. He warned Sir Jung Bahadur that he would not be well received on his next visit to England unless he contrived to prevent his favourite daughter from committing suttee when her husband, who was dying, was cremated. Sir Jung defied his priests, accordingly, and refused to allow his daughter to be burned to death on his son-in-law's funeral pyre; but when he was murdered shortly afterwards in Katmandu, his three widows vexed the Government of India by committing suttee in the traditional manner. The senior widow wrote very courteously to announce her intention to the Prince, leaving insufficient time for a reply.

After knighting Sam Browne, Dighton Probyn and Dr Fayrer at Allahabad, and after paying a visit to the Maharajah Holkar of Indore (who gave him a waist-belt of pearls for the Queen, a diamond necklace for the Princess and a diamond ring for himself which he sometimes wore), the Prince sailed (13 March) in the *Serapis* on the homeward voyage from Bombay. Attended by the royal yacht *Osborne* and escorted by the frigate *Raleigh*, he took with him a valuable collection of jewellery and trophies (most of which were loaned to museums and all of which he obtained permission to import free of duty), as well as two native A.D.C.s, a Madras curry cook, and a quantity of flora and fauna including orchids, bears, birds, deer, elephants, horses, leopards and tigers.

Before the Prince reached Cairo (25 March) London society buzzed with the news that Lord Aylesford intended to divorce his wife, citing Lord Blandford as co-respondent, and that the Prince of Wales had denounced Blandford's conduct in scorching terms. Aylesford, in his great trouble, had trumpeted the Prince's views, and it seemed likely that the lives of Lady Aylesford and Lord Blandford would be blasted by public scandal which would impair the prestige of society and which might even involve the Prince of Wales.

In those circumstances, the member of Parliament for Woodstock, Lord Randolph Churchill, rushed in a chivalrous but reckless way to the aid of Blandford, his elder brother. He began by imploring the lovers not to elope, and by telegraphing to ask the Prince of Wales to use his influence with Aylesford in order to stop divorce proceedings from being started. No elopement took place; the Prince declined to interfere; but Colonel Williams urged Aylesford to call out Blandford. Lord Hartington and Lord Hardwicke had difficulty in persuading Lord Aylesford that duelling was out of date, and they failed to persuade him to alter his decision to divorce his wife.

While the Prince of Wales held that no one was entitled to interfere in Aylesford's private affairs, Lord Randolph Churchill convinced himself that the Prince had conspired with Aylesford to throw Lady Aylesford into Blandford's arms. He told everyone that the Prince, while fully cognizant of Blandford's liaison with Lady Aylesford, had insisted upon taking Aylesford with him to India, although Lady Aylesford, fearful of her own frailty, had urged her husband to remain behind. The Prince's papers prove[1] that Lady Aylesford had in fact urged her husband to accept the Prince's invitation; but Churchill argued, nevertheless, that the Prince's condemnation of Blandford's conduct was hypocritical.

The Prince would have continued to treat the liaison with amused tolerance if the lovers had been discreet. Aylesford would have had to have been a deceived or a consenting party, but the Prince would never tolerate public scandal, and he denounced Blandford on principle when public scandal appeared likely to result. Blandford's infatuation made him utterly reckless, but Lady Aylesford's sisters made her appreciate at the eleventh hour the treacherous nature of the ground upon which she stood. Divorce entailed social ostracism which she had no wish to incur, and she therefore gave Blandford a packet of letters which the Prince of Wales had written to her some years before. Blandford handed them to his younger brother, Lord Randolph, who undertook to use them as a means of compelling the Prince to bring pressure to bear upon Aylesford to drop the idea of a divorce.

Fortified by the opinion of his solicitor (W. D. Freshfield) that the letters, if made public, would damage and greatly embarrass the Prince of Wales, Randolph Churchill informed[2] his friends with a strange absence of discretion that he held the Crown of England in his pocket. Dragging with him an older friend, Lord Alington, who ought to have known better, but whose judgement was upset by frantic appeals made to him by Lady Aylesford's sisters, Churchill called upon the Princess of Wales at Marlborough House, and told[3] her that 'being aware of peculiar and most grave matters affecting the case, he was anxious that His Royal Highness should give such advice to Lord Aylesford as to induce him not to proceed against his wife'.

After explaining[4] to the distressed Princess that 'he was determined by every means in his power to prevent the case coming before the Public, and that he had those means at his disposal', Churchill referred to the letters which he had acquired and said that they were of 'the most compromising character'. He warned the Princess that, in the opinion of lawyers whom he had consulted, the Prince would be subpoenaed to give evidence if Aylesford sued for divorce; and that, if published, the Prince's letters to Lady Aylesford would ensure that His Royal Highness 'would never sit upon the Throne of England'.

Churchill added, as he departed, that he would inform the Prince as well as Aylesford about the turn which events had taken; and the reflections of the Princess, whose memory of the Mordaunt case was vivid and painful, may be imagined. The Prince of Wales received that news in Cairo, at the Gezireh Palace, which the bankrupt Khedive had lent him, and where, in the intervals of shooting quail and listening to the music of Offenbach at a gorgeous new opera house, he was being entertained at a series of luncheon and dinner parties. He wrote at once to ask Lord Hardwicke to represent his interests in England and to confer urgently and secretly with the Prime Minister.

The existence, in hostile and unscrupulous hands, of a packet of imprudent letters was unfortunate and dangerous but less ostensibly compromising than Churchill supposed. 'I quite understand and feel', the Lord Chancellor (Lord Cairns) wrote [5] (26 July 1876) to Lord Hartington after the Prince had returned home, 'that there is a degree of difficulty in speaking as to the character of the letters. ... Any letter from a person in high position, written in a strain of undue familiarity and containing many foolish and somewhat stupid expressions, must, when displayed to the public, be injurious and lowering to the writer'. The Prince had enjoyed an innocent flirtation with Lady Aylesford, but similar innocence, in the case of Lady Mordaunt, had not sufficed to avert great trouble and embarrassment.

In a mood of frustration and of ungovernable rage at the insult, injury and pain to which the Princess of Wales had been subjected at the hands of a man whom he had regarded as an intimate friend, the Prince of Wales despatched Lord Charles Beresford aboard *Osborne* from Alexandria to Brindisi. Beresford was instructed to reach London by the quickest available means; to request Churchill to name his seconds; and to arrange a convenient time and place on the north coast of France for a meeting with pistols between Lord Randolph Churchill and the Prince of Wales before the Prince arrived home.

That unwise step gave Churchill the opportunity to write what Carrington termed [6] 'a dreadful letter to the Prince of Wales'. It stated that the idea of a duel between the Prince and the writer was impossible and absurd, and that no one understood that better than the Prince. Beresford delivered that curt and insolent reply to the Prince of Wales at Malta on 9 April 1876.

After seeing Hardwicke, Disraeli sent (14 March) for Lords Alington and Randolph Churchill, but the latter remained obdurate, Alington, on the other hand, wrote [7] an abject apology to the Prime Minister immediately after the interview, and before explaining [8] to Hardwicke that, 'as an available man worked on by the sisters of Lady Aylesford', he had acted 'on the spur of the moment' in the desperate hope of saving her 'from a terrible future'.

The Prince of Wales defied Lord Randolph Churchill to do his worst. He appealed to the Queen to stand by him; assured her of his innocence, and offered to delay his home-coming, if that course were deemed expedient. Queen Victoria telegraphed immediately her confidence in him, and Ponsonby wrote [9] (19 April) to Knollys:

The Queen has such perfect confidence in the Prince of Wales, that His Royal Highness's disclaimer of any evil intentions is sufficient to convince Her Majesty that the letters are per-fectly innocent. But the publication of any letter of this nature would be very undesirable, as a colouring might be easily given and injurious inferences deduced from hasty expressions. The Queen, therefore, regrets that such a correspondence, harmless as it is, should be in existence; but Her Majesty thinks it quite right that His Royal Highness should not interfere in Lord Aylesford's affair in consequence of this threat. . . .

The Queen feels very deeply the pain this matter has caused the Prince of Wales, and had there been any probability of a public scandal into which his name could be dragged by these villains, she would have agreed in thinking it advisable that he should not return until a frank explanation had been publicly made. But, as it is to be hoped that there is no prospect of any such misfortune, Her Majesty hopes that, conscious of his in-nocence, he will discard all thoughts on the subject and enjoy the welcome he will find on his return, when she hopes he will take as much rest and quiet as he can.

Prodded by Disraeli, Hardwicke did his utmost to dissuade Aylesford from suing for a divorce, while the Prince of Wales fretted because that issue hung fire. He was most deeply touched by his mother's understanding attitude, but irked by having to rely upon Disraeli to handle the recalci-trant back-bencher, Randolph Churchill. Lord Randolph's parents, the Duke and Duchess of Marlborough, who were close friends of the Queen, were plunged into gloom, and the situation appealed to the Prime Minister's sense of irony which always set the Prince of Wales on edge. For that reason the Prince felt more relaxed usually with Gladstone than he did with Disraeli, and he injected a touch of asperity into a letter which he caused Knolly to write [10] (5 April) to the Prime Minister's secretary. The Prince was angry that he had been left to learn from the newspapers about the Government's intention to proclaim the Queen as Empress of India: 'He is certain that in no other country in the world would the next Heir to the Throne have been treated under similar circumstances in such a manner. ... The English Monarchy is not an elective one ... and the present Prince of Wales possesses the same rights and vested interest, as regards the future of the Crown, as any of his predecessors.'

Disraeli smoothed the Prince's ruffled feelings, and informed him privately that, on the Queen's birthday, Knollys would be made a C.B., Suffield a K.C.B., and Bartle Frere a G.C.B. and a Baronet in official recognition of the great success of the Indian expedition. The Prince, who was delighted by that news, visited Madrid on 25 April and Lisbon on 1 May, before disembarking at Portsmouth on 11 May.

In what the Princess of Wales described [11] (14 April) to the Queen as 'a very dear letter from my Bertie', the Prince informed the Princess that he was particularly anxious to see her '*first and alone*' and that she should board *Serapis* off the Needles. Everyone else, including their children and the Dukes of Edinburgh and Cambridge, waited at Portsmouth; and after being drawn to London by special train and taking part in a carriage procession through the streets of the capital, the Prince and Princess of Wales attended a gala performance of Verdi's *Ballo in Maschera* at Covent Garden, within an hour of the traveller's return to Marlborough House.

The Prince wrote [12] (2 May) to the Queen that he would 'infinitely' have preferred to dine alone with the Princess at Marlborough House, or to take her to dine very quietly at Buckingham Palace, but that, in view of the scandal with which his name had been linked, he had thought it right to

appear in public in order to give society an immediate opportunity to express its feelings. The standing ovation, prolonged for several minutes and revived before the start of
every act as well as at the close of the performance, was
immensely gratifying to the Prince and Princess of Wales.
It conveyed a private and particular message to them; but,
as Frere informed [13] Carrington, the idolatry lavished upon
the Prince of Wales by the great mass of the British people
did not depend in the least upon society, and was not diminished by the few human faults which he was much too
straightforward to attempt to conceal. The Prince Consort,
despite his outstanding qualities and virtues, had never inspired a tithe of the loyalty and affection which his son
commanded without effort because he was regarded as the
typical Englishman, living the kind of princely life which
the majority of his fellow-countrymen wished to see him
live in that age, and which, in his position, they would have
lived and enjoyed themselves.

On 12 May 1876, within twenty-four hours of the Prince's
return home, Lord Aylesford told Lord Hardwicke that, in
order to avoid great public scandal and mischief, he had
renounced his intention of divorcing his wife. Hardwicke
drove immediately to Marlborough House, where he saw
and informed the Prince of Wales; and he wrote that evening to inform [14] Queen Victoria (through Ponsonby) that
everything was 'settled', and that Aylesford 'will arrange
matters privately and will separate from his wife, making
proper provision for her, etc.'. The Queen and the Prince
were exceedingly warm in praise of Hardwicke, who warned
Aylesford to show tact and to keep out of the Prince of
Wales's way for a time; and although Aylesford did attempt
to divorce his wife some years later, the suit was dismissed,
after the intervention of the Queen's Proctor, and as a result
of evidence about the nature of his own private life. Lady
Blandford obtained a deed of separation from her husband
(whom she divorced in 1883); and a cataract of execration
descended in May, 1876, upon the head of Lord Randolph
Churchill.

Lord Randolph departed, in consequence, with his very

attractive American wife, Jennie Jerome, on a tour of the United States after despatching (12 July) a letter of apology to the Prince of Wales which was not acknowledged. Queen Victoria asked Disraeli to try to effect some kind of settlement, for the sake of her old friends, the Duke and Duchess of Marlborough, who were looking dreadfully ill and wretched; and under pressure from the Queen, as well as from Disraeli and Lord Hartington, the Prince agreed in principle to accept an apology from Lord Randolph on condition that it was couched in language dictated by the Lord Chancellor and approved by Disraeli and Lord Hartington.

A form of abject apology, very wounding to Marlborough's family and parental pride, was drawn up immediately by Lord Cairns and shown to the Duke after being approved by Queen Victoria, the Prince of Wales, Disraeli and Lord Hartington. It was sent by Hartington to Churchill, who signed it with intentional irony on 26 August at Saratoga, where General Burgoyne, a century earlier, had insisted that he was signing a convention and not a capitulation when he surrendered his army to the Americans. Churchill added,[15] in a postscript that 'as a gentleman' he felt bound to accept the word of the Lord Chancellor for the phrasing of the document which he had signed; and Marlborough, who forwarded it (13 September) to Knollys, explained [16] (17 December) to Disraeli that its wording had reflected the disparity between his son's rank and that of the Prince.

The Prince sent the Duke a formal acknowledgment, but declined to do more on the ground that the postscript was unacceptable. The Lord Chancellor characterized it as ungracious; and the Prince held strongly at that time, and his friends agreed, that Churchill had forfeited for ever the right to describe himself, or to be described as, a gentleman. Disraeli told Lady Bradford and others that the Prince of Wales's private affairs were 'almost as troublesome' as the great crisis which had arisen in the Balkans; but, under pressure, the Prince indicated through Knollys in December that his formal acknowledgment could be construed to imply acceptance of Randolph Churchill's apology, and at that point, despite further correspondence, the affair came to rest.

As early as 12 May the Queen, after consulting Disraeli, had risked her son's displeasure by inviting Lord and Lady Alington to a drawing-room at Buckingham Palace; and on Christmas Day, 1876, she wrote[17] to inform the Prince that she could not entirely exclude Lord Randolph Churchill from Court festivities now that his apology was accepted. The Prince replied that on such occasions he would bow without speaking to Lord Randolph, but he caused it to be known that he and the Princess would boycott any house or family which should at any time offer hospitality to, or accept hospitality from, the Randolph Churchills. Lord Randolph and his wife incurred in consequence the dire penalty of a social ostracism which was enforced rigorously for some years, and Churchill's subsequent career reflected the bitterness which ate into his mind.

At the cost of severe financial embarrassment which led to a sale of art treasures from Blenheim, the Duke of Marlborough, who was not rich in comparison with other dukes, accepted Disraeli's offer of the Viceroyalty of Ireland and took his sons with him to Dublin in December. The Prime Minister explained[18] (22 July) to the Prince of Wales that no office was more difficult to fill because to carry out 'the duties in a becoming manner requires £40,000 a year.... The salary is only half that sum'. Marlborough had declined that office on the formation of the Government, but he accepted it now on the ground, stated by Disraeli in a letter to the Prince, that 'the dignified withdrawal of the family from metropolitan and English life at the moment and for a time' had become desirable.

The Prince told[19] the Prime Minister in jest (27 October) that he would have done better to find some desert island to which Blandford and Randolph Churchill could be banished; and eight years passed before he spoke to Lord Randolph again. He ended the social boycott by consenting to meet him on 8 March 1884, at dinner with the Attorney-General, Sir Henry James, in Wilton Crescent, when the Gladstones were also present.

The Prince informed the Queen (9 March 1884) that all had gone well; and he dined again with Lord and Lady Randolph Churchill, Sir Henry James, J. Gordon Bennett and others at the Café Anglais in Paris on 2 June. But he did not consider that he had forgiven Lord Randolph until he dined, on 16 May 1886, with the Churchills at their house in Connaught Place, after his host had become Secretary for India and after Blandford, who was a fellow-guest, had succeeded his father as Duke of Marlborough.

Even then the Prince felt that he owed an explanation to his younger son, Prince George, to whom he wrote [20] (18 May) that 'after $10\frac{1}{2}$ years' he had 'thought it best to be on speaking terms' with Lord Randolph, 'though we can never be the same friends again that we were formerly'. They could be, however, and they were, because they had interests in common, and the tact and very great American charm of Lady Randolph Churchill cast a new spell over an old friendship when it was at long last fully restored.

ii

Even before the Prince of Wales returned from India, a peasants' revolt in the Balkans had again divided the political sympathies of the British royal family. Russian expansionist ambitions, expressed in the guise of aggressive sympathy for oppressed Christian Slavs in South-East Europe, clashed with the British Government's resolve to buttress Turkey as a barrier against Russia, and with Disraeli's desire to raise British prestige.

Queen Victoria, the Prince of Wales and the German Crown Princess were strongly anti-Russian, while the Princess of Wales, who relied always upon the Czar to maintain her brother upon the throne of Greece, and whose sister had married the Czar's heir, was equally strongly pro-Russian. She was supported by the Czar's son-in-law, the Duke of Edinburgh, as well as by the entire Hesse-Darmstadt family into which Princess Alice had married; but all behaved with great discretion and restraint.

While the revolt in the Balkans spread like a forest fire,

British opinion was inflamed by reports of massacres perpetrated by Turkish troops. Gladstone called upon the Russians
to intervene in the names of religion and humanity, and to
drive the Turks 'bag and baggage' out of Europe; but Disraeli had anticipated him by sending a British fleet to Besika
Bay to protect Constantinople.

The Prince of Wales wrote [21] (14 September 1876) to Disraeli: 'I deeply deplore the present agitation with the so-
called Bulgarian atrocities, which is now so prevalent
throughout the country. It must, I fear, weaken the hands of
the Government, who are so anxious to do all in their power
to maintain peace.' Disraeli replied that an honourable
peace was still obtainable, and that, had it not been for
Gladstone's factious and short-sighted agitation about 'the
Bulgarian horrors', England's position would have been
much stronger.

After the failure of a conference (December 1876–January
1877) at Constantinople, the British representative, Lord
Salisbury, complained [22] to his wife about the anti-Russian
proclivities of the Marlborough House 'clique', including
especially those of the Prince of Wales and the Duke of
Sutherland. The Prince had formed the view that war with
Russia was probably inevitable, and had started, accordingly, to institute private inquiries about the possibility of obtaining a military command.

The Prince was assiduous, as always, in collecting excellent
first-hand information from a great variety of friends, to
whom he remained loyal in all circumstances. Valentine
Baker, for example, had commanded the Prince's regiment,
the 10th Hussars, until 1875 when, on evidence which the
fashionable world thought inadequate, he was cashiered
from the Army and imprisoned for twelve months for an
assault upon a governess in a railway carriage. After the
sentence had been served, the Prince helped his friend to
obtain employment as a general in the Turkish Army; and
when Baker passed briefly through London in December
1876, the Prince begged [23] Disraeli vainly (10 December) to
confer with him about Turkish military dispositions in the
Dardanelles.

The Prince also tried vainly to procure for Baker a sympathetic message from Queen Victoria, who was better pleased by her son's attitude towards the Russian question: 'I fear', the Prince wrote [24] (1 August 1877), to his mother, 'we shall cut a very ridiculous figure in the eyes of the world, as we can bark but dare not bite, and we shall soon find ourselves left out of the councils of Europe and shall only have ourselves to blame for it.' He informed [25] his mother (2 October) that Gladstone and the Czar had made his 'blood boil with indignation', and Queen Victoria wrote [26] (26 October 1877) to the German Crown Princess: 'I am glad to say Bertie is as right about the whole thing as can be. He is *furious* with the Russians, and with the folly of the people here; and all for checking Russia in every possible way.'

While the issue of peace or war hung balanced on a razor's edge, Disraeli's Cabinet was torn by dissensions, and the ban imposed upon the despatch of secret papers to the Prince of Wales was rigorously enforced. That slur upon his discretion was made harder to bear when Queen Victoria obtained, in April 1877, a key to the Cabinet boxes for her youngest son, Prince Leopold (Duke of Albany), whose services she was employing in a secretarial capacity; but the Prince of Wales repressed his feelings and accepted that situation with his customary dignity.

Seeking diversion, the Prince flirted mildly with an American ingénue, Miss Chamberlayne, from Cleveland, Ohio, who was nicknamed 'Chamberpots' by the Princess of Wales; and he invited to Sandringham – 'without even saying a word to me', Queen Victoria complained [27] (7 November 1877) to the Crown Princess – the Prince of Orange whose private life was a European scandal and whom he had nicknamed 'Citron'. Not long afterwards he made one of his rare mistakes in judging men. He met on the Riviera and brought to England a young, mysterious but good-looking and evidently well-bred Count Miecislas Jaraczewski, who became known at Sandringham, where he stayed constantly as well as at the Marlborough and Turf Clubs where he was well liked, as 'Sherry and Whiskers'. The Count lived on his wits until March, 1881, when he ended his life, as a nobleman should, to avoid arrest and exposure.

After calling upon the Prince at Marlborough House, the Count attended a ball (12 March), gave a gay supper at the Turf Club in the small hours, and returned to his lodgings in Bennett Street, where he swallowed prussic acid. An inquest was dispensed with; Sir Dighton Probyn took possession of the dead man's papers; and the Prince of Wales, who attended the funeral, laid a wreath on his own behalf and another on that of the Princess.

The Prince of Wales was fascinated at that time by the actress, Sarah Bernhardt, of the Comédie Française, whom Lady Frederick Cavendish described [28] unkindly (30 June 1879 as 'a woman of notorious, shameless character.... Not content with being run after on the stage, this woman is asked to respectable people's houses to act, and even to luncheon and dinner; and all the world goes. It is an outrageous scandal!' Many people thought differently, because London society was larger and more diverse than it had been twenty years earlier, and its more strait-laced sections were much too dull to attract or satisfy the Prince of Wales. Hostesses had to compete to secure his presence at balls and dinners, and the intensity of that competition at the end of the 1870s was mainly responsible for the cult of the so-called 'professional beauties'.

Its priestesses were certain fashionable ladies, whose beauty was transformed by the camera – that early engine of democracy – from a social into a popular cult. Photographs of Mrs Cornwallis-West, Mrs Edward Langtry, Mrs Luke Wheeler, were displayed in shop windows and became best sellers; and the fame of Mrs Langtry, in particular, spread like fire.

On 24 May 1877, while the Princess of Wales was staying in Athens with her brother, King George of Greece, the Prince, after attending the opera, took supper with the Arctic explorer, Sir Allen Young. In Sir Allen's house that evening he met, by pre-arrangement and for the first time, a colourless sportsman, Edward Langtry, and his twenty-three year-old wife, Lillie, daughter of W. C. Le Breton, Dean of Jersey.

Discovered only a month earlier by Lord Ranelagh, the face and figure of 'the Jersey Lily' had taken society overnight by storm. Dragging a most reluctant husband in her wake, Mrs Langtry had attended all the gay parties; her photographs had appeared everywhere; and, within a month of her first meeting with the Prince of Wales, crowds started to collect whenever, alone or in his company, she drove, rode or walked abroad.

No public scandal was caused when the Prince of Wales became Mrs Langtry's lover, because the situation was accepted by the Princess, as well as by Langtry who faded into the background and disappeared. It was accepted also for that reason by society, which was convulsed and far more concerned at that time by the imminent prospect of another major European war, as Russian armies surged almost up to the walls of Constantinople and caused a panic on the London Stock Exchange.

On 23 December 1877, the Prince of Wales warned[29] Queen Victoria that unless war were declared immediately upon Russia 'we shall never be able to hold our head up again in the eyes of the world. This is our last chance, now. Forgive me for writing thus plainly.' As Disraeli made a series of warlike moves, the excitement in England was greater than at any time since the escape of the great Napoleon from Elba; but Lord Derby, the Foreign Secretary, resigned in protest.

After a prolonged crisis, Lord Salisbury, who succeeded Derby, attended with Disraeli a conference which opened in Berlin on 13 June 1878, in an effort to resolve the Anglo-Russian deadlock. Under Bismarck's chairmanship a satisfactory compromise was arranged, and Disraeli informed[30] the Prince (22 June) that, at five o'clock on the previous afternoon, the Russians had 'surrendered unconditionally' to a threat that he would break up the conference: 'Dearest Prince,' the Prime Minister added excitedly, 'I am almost ashamed to send you this not only illegible but illiterate scrawl'; but 'Turkey is in my pocket', and Russia is 'now, more hopelessly than ever, excluded from the Mediterranean'.

A fortnight later (6 July 1878) Disraeli explained [31] equally characteristically to the Prince how he had acquired Cyprus, and secured a minor rectification of the Greek frontier to please the Princess of Wales:

England enters into a defensive alliance with Turkey as respects all her Asiatic dominions; and, with the consent of the Sultan, we occupy the island of Cyprus. It is the key of Asia and is near to Egypt. Malta is too far as a military base for these purposes.

I did yesterday something for Greece. It was very difficult, but is by no means to be despised. It was all done for Her Royal Highness's sake. I thought of Marlborough House all the time, and it was not decided, after many efforts, until the last moment.

In great haste, ever Sir and dear Prince. . . .

French opinion was enraged by the British acquisition of Cyprus. It foresaw that that island might serve as a springboard for a British invasion of Egypt, which was regarded as a French preserve; and the Prince found scope for his diplomatic gifts in attempts to allay French discontent. He was constantly in Paris in 1878, as President of the British section of an International Exhibition which opened on 1 May; and at a banquet in Paris on 3 May he expressed his conviction that 'the *entente cordiale*, which exists between this country and our own, is one not likely to change'.

Warned by Lord Salisbury, after the Cyprus convention, that he would risk being insulted if he returned to Paris, the Prince of Wales did not hesitate. He had formed a warm acquaintanceship with a rabid republican, Léon Gambetta, an ugly, one-eyed war hero who held no office but who dominated the Chamber of Deputies and was extremely influential. The Prince was so successful in charming Gambetta, and in allaying French suspicions through him, that Salisbury wrote [32] most appreciatively (24 July): 'The crisis has been one of no little delicacy; and, if the leaders of French opinion had definitely turned against us, a disagreeable and even hazardous condition of estrangement between the two countries might have grown up.... Your Royal

Highness's influence over M. Gambetta, and the skill with which that influence has been exercised, have averted a danger that was not inconsiderable.'

The Prince replied,[33] the same day, that he was 'beyond measure pleased to hear' that he was thought by the Government to have helped 'to allay the irritation which was manifest in France at our taking Cyprus ... as nobody would have deplored more deeply than I should that any estrangement between the two countries should occur'. He continued to visit Paris constantly and to cultivate, with French ministers, contacts which had to be kept rigorously separate from friendships in the social world.

With habitual generosity the Prince of Wales despatched to Paris a former friend, Charles Buller, who had resigned his commission in the Blues after running into serious financial trouble, and who accepted a fee for looking after the Prince's Indian collections. They formed part of the British section of the Paris Exhibition and, after warning Buller to be 'on parade', the Prince, late one evening, brought some of his dinner guests, including the Duke of Beaufort, the Duc de Chartres, Lord Lyons (the British Ambassador), Prince de Sagan and Prince Trauttsmansdorff, to inspect them. Instead of being received by Buller, however, the party was insulted by a drunken workman who had been asleep behind one of the showcases.

The Prince scribbled a stern rebuke next day to Buller, who had been so spoilt and petted that he sent a casual and insolent reply which ended his friendship with the Prince of Wales. The Prince was too amiable, nevertheless, to harden his heart completely, and he continued to try to help, even after Buller had been sent to gaol for issuing a worthless cheque.

Back in England, the Prince took a very warm personal interest in the troubles of Sir Bartle Frere, who had conducted his Indian tour, and who was an extremely able man and greatly liked. He had been sent to South Africa, as High Commissioner and Governor of the Cape; but, in a tradition which he had imbibed while serving as a young man in India, he provoked a war against the Zulu nation without obtaining specific authority from the Colonial Office.

Frere's policy of conciliating the Boers in the recently annexed Transvaal, while crushing their enemies, the Zulus, as a prelude to the federation of the sub-continent, was statesmanlike and far-sighted. Disraeli would have acclaimed it and British opinion would have acquiesced, if his war had gone according to plan. But Lord Chelmsford's invading army was defeated at Isandhlwana on 22 January 1879, when 800 British soldiers and 600 of their black auxilaries were killed. Strong Liberal and Radical protests were voiced in Parliament and the Press; Disraeli was greatly shaken, and the electoral prospects of the Conservative Party suffered damage.

Chelmsford retrieved his reputation by destroying the Zulu power at Ulundi on 4 July; and the Zulu King, Cetewayo, was conveyed to England, lectured by the Colonial Secretary on statecraft, and presented to Queen Victoria at Balmoral. But a pathetic incident before that victory dismayed the British public and caused acute distress to the Prince of Wales.

The Prince had made a favourite of the daring and very popular Prince Imperial of France (only child of the widowed ex-Empress Eugénie) and had helped to secure permission for his protégé to take part in the campaign. On 1 June, however, the Prince was killed during a reconnaissance, after a Captain Carey, detailed by Lord Chelmsford to restrain his boyish ardour and protect him, had purchased life, with infamy, by flight.

Frere's great reputation was blasted irrationally by those untoward events; and Disraeli, who was contemplating a General Election, despatched General Sir Garnet Wolseley to control Frere and to reverse his policy. Wolseley was ordered to display toughness towards the Boers, who rebelled soon afterwards, and to withdraw British authority from Zululand, which had been plunged into anarchy by being deprived of its king; but the British Government did not choose to incur the odium of recalling Frere.

Frere's policy continued to command the unanimous support of white opinion in South Africa, and to commend itself also to the Prince of Wales and to large sections of British Conservative opinion. But the Prince warned [34] Frere (16 September 1879) that he ought to follow Chelmsford's example, and to resign, instead of remaining as an impotent and disarmed sentry at his post. Frere insisted, [35] nevertheless, (30 October) that it was his duty to compel the Government to incur the odium of dismissing him, and that history, after exposing the hypocrisy of Disraeli, would vindicate the wisdom of his war. He stayed in South Africa, therefore, at the cost of his dignity, while Disraeli, who mocked his self-righteousness, left Gladstone to order his recall after the Liberals had won the General Election.

At Abergeldie, where he stayed from 9–13 October 1880, Frere admitted that he ought to have resigned and that he had made mistakes; but the rancorous grudge, which he nursed against Disraeli, poisoned his mind. The Prince considered that Frere had been sacrificed on the altar of political expediency, and after his friend's death in May 1884, he sponsored an appeal for funds to erect a statue which he unveiled (5 June 1888) on the Thames Embankment.

While corresponding with Sir Bartle Frere in South Africa, the Prince of Wales toyed with the idea of touring that sub-continent and of extending his journey to Australia. He was in advance, however, of public opinion, which would have regarded that voyage critically as another pleasure trip. The cost of sending both the Prince's sons on three educational voyages round the world was being defrayed out of public funds at that time; and the Prince of Wales was warned that he could not expect the new Liberal Government to contribute one shilling, in those circumstances, towards the enormous expense which he would be certain to incur if he, too, were to embark upon a world cruise.

The Prince of Wales had intended to send his elder son, Prince Albert Victor (Eddy), born in 1864, to Wellington College, of which he was a governor, and which had been founded to prepare sons of middle-class parents for a military career. The Prince was anxious that both his sons should enjoy the advantage of mixing on equal terms with a wide variety of boys, and he intended that his younger son, Prince George, born in 1865, should enter the Royal Navy.

An admirable tutor, the Rev John Neale Dalton,* who had obtained first-class honours in theology at Cambridge, was appointed in 1871 to prepare both boys; and no trouble was experienced with the younger, who was bright, handsome and satisfactory in every way. Prince George alone, however, appeared to be capable of arousing an occasional spark of interest and activity in his lethargic elder brother, who was destined to succeed to the throne; and for that reason the Prince of Wales accepted Dalton's advice that it would be unwise to separate the brothers at that time.

Prince Eddy and Prince George were entered together, accordingly, as cadets in the naval training ship *Britannia*; and their father continued to hope that the elder might improve sufficiently to be sent later to Wellington. The brothers remained great friends, but Dalton had to report [36] (9 April 1879) that while Prince George had done well and earned golden opinions, Prince Eddy 'fails, not in one or two subjects, but in all' and that 'the abnormally dormant condition' of his mind, which deprived him of power 'to fix his attention to any given subject for more than a few minutes consecutively' ruled out any lingering hope that it might be possible to send him to a public school.

Arguing that a public school would, in any case, have exposed a weakness which had been more or less 'masked' in *Britannia*, Dalton advised that a private tutor would be a fatal mistake owing to lack of stimulating competition. He urged, therefore, that both Princes should cruise round the world for two years, and that, in order to spread the risk and to allow Prince Eddy's special needs to be met by the appointment of a suitable staff of tutors skilled in handling backward boys, the Admiralty should be invited to provide a separate warship for each Prince.

Because he and the Princess valued the warm friendship existing between his sons, the Prince of Wales decided that both should travel in one ship; and the matter was brought

* The Rev. J. N. Dalton, K.C.V.O., C.M.G. (1839–1931); Canon and Steward of St George's Chapel, Windsor.

before the Cabinet on 19 May 1879, by the First Lord of the Admiralty, W. H. Smith, who recommended that the Princes should be separated and that two warships should be provided. The Prince of Wales, who was really enraged by that interference with his parental authority, did not hesitate to send at once for the Prime Minister, who surrendered and apologized, after the Prince had used very strong language.[37]

Disraeli accepted responsibility, but Dalton had been to blame and he tendered his resignation when the Prince of Wales forbade further discussion about the possibility of two ships. He withdrew that resignation (11 September) less than a week before he sailed (17 September) with both Princes and a hand-picked complement of officers and tutors aboard *Bacchante* (4,000 tons), which was commanded by Lord Charles Scott, after the Admiralty had carried out a series of rigorous tests of the vessel's seaworthiness. Three cruises, undertaken during the three years which followed, were commemorated by Dalton in two ponderous tomes [38] dedicated to the Prince of Wales.

The Prince of Wales's daughters posed no educational problem, and the Princesses Louise, Victoria and Maud were instructed by governesses on restricted but conventional contemporary lines. They were always with their mother, who was much the strongest personal influence in the lives of all her children, and who was known to them all, always, as 'Darling Motherdear'. Gay and spontaneous, dignified and dutiful, the perspective of the Princess of Wales became as domestic as that of her husband was gregarious. She lavished affection upon her children, upon her brothers and sisters, and upon her parents, as she lavished money upon charity with an equal degree of reckless generosity and extravagance; and the adoration which she received in return compensated for the troubles of her married life.

Those troubles never impaired, at their roots, the ties of affection, sympathy and respect which knit husband and wife together; but increasing deafness destroyed a large part of the Princess's ability to continue to share without exhaustion her husband's intense enjoyment of the society over which he reigned for half a century. Her unpunctuality tormented the Prince of Wales, who was invariably on time and who insisted that punctuality was the courtesy of princes; she had no aesthetic outlets, except music; but she was sustained by a pure religious faith which she had been taught as a child and which she was never tempted to question.

The Members of her Household were devoted to the Princess of Wales, but no one approached remotely at any time the place held in her affections by her husband's unmarried equerry and friend, Colonel the Hon. Oliver Montagu, who commanded the Blues (Royal Horse Guards). He loved the Princess with that exalted, chivalrous and selfless passion which inspired knights in mediaeval romances to dedicate their lives to the service of beautiful princesses and queens. Oliver Montagu would have perished gladly to spare the Princess of Wales the least shadow of reproach or annoyance, and his untimely death in 1893 left in her heart an aching void which was never filled.

9
Egypt

1880–84

THE departure of his sons in *Bacchante*, and his pre-occupation with Mrs Langtry, caused the Prince of Wales to be even more indulgent than usual to the wishes of the Princess. He was too restless to enjoy staying for any length of time at the Danish Court, but in the autumn of 1879 he renounced his custom of going *en garçon* to Homburg and took the Princess to Denmark instead. They stayed for a month with the King and Queen at Bernstorff, where the Czarevitch and his wife were fellow-guests.

Queen Victoria doubted the prudence of that meeting between the heirs to the British and Russian thrones so soon after the crisis which had brought the two Governments to the brink of war; and the Princess became impatient. The Czarevitch warned [1] the Prince that Disraeli would have to disappear before the happy personal relationship between the Russian and British royal families could be extended to the political field; and the Prince explained [2] (17 September 1879) to Queen Victoria: 'I shall, of course, avoid politics as much as possible, but as he married dear Alix's sister, who I am very fond of, I am most anxious that our relations should not be strained.'

The Prince and the Czarevitch vied with each other in giving grand parties on their yachts, *Osborne* and *Dirjava*, which were kept standing by throughout their stay. 'Last Saturday', the Prince wrote [3] (15 October) to his sons, 'we had a very pleasant cruise in the *Osborne* to Helsingborg. All the Relations and Cousins came, also the Crown Prince of Sweden. ... We had an enormous luncheon on board and the Russian band to play. ... Uncle Sasha [the Czarevitch] gave a luncheon last week to officers of the Danish Guards on board the large Imperial yacht *Dirjava*, and I gave one on Monday last on *Osborne* to the officers of the Danish Hussars.'

On the journey home the Czarevitch and his wife accompanied the Prince and Princess of Wales to Paris, where all four spent a happy and crowded week in a whirl of luncheon, dinner, theatre and supper parties. The Prince and the Czarevitch called hand in hand upon President Grévy in order to demonstrate to the world that, as far as they personally were concerned, the Anglo-Russian Breach was healed; and the Czarevitch, after escaping from his large suite, strolled unrecognized along the boulevards with his brother-in-law acting as guide.

Disraeli grumbled[4] (9 and 11 November) to Lady Bradford that the Prince of Wales appeared to have 'ratted', and that he had come home very pro-Russian; but everyone who knew the Prince well had cause to make analogous complaints at times. He had to be guarded for many years against excessive impressionability, but he tried hard to learn to guard himself and became, in consequence, at the end of his life, a little too inflexible.

Contemporary critics enjoyed compiling summaries of the way in which the Prince apportioned his time; and his diary proves[5] that in 1879, which was a typical year, he performed the following twenty major public engagements:

14 April	Open Convalescent Home at Hunstanton, Norfolk.
26 April	Dine with Royal Institute of British Architects.
12 May	Attend Grand Military Assault at Arms and Gymnastic Display at Albert Hall in aid of Widows and Orphans of Zulu War.
24 May	Drive in procession over Lambeth, Vauxhall, Chelsea, the Albert and Battersea bridges, pausing to declare each one free of tolls in perpetuity.
17 June	Lay foundation stone of Norfolk and Norwich Hospital.
21 June	Visit Plymouth and lay foundation stone of new Eddystone lighthouse [but a gale caused the ceremony to be cancelled at the last moment].

24 June	Open new school and other buildings of Alexandra Orphanage at Hornsey Rise.
26 June	Preside at annual dinner of West London Hospital.
27 June	Attend conversazione at Royal Colonial Institute.
30 June	Inaugurate International Agricultural Exhibition at Kilburn. [The Prince wrote[6] (3 July) to Prince George that 'amongst other animals ... an enormous French donkey with a gigantic beard was shown. He was called "Christopher" – why, I cannot conceive!' But he had called it so himself, because it reminded him of his favourite butt, Christopher Sykes].
5 July	Conduct Queen round International Agricultural Exhibition.
7 July	Attend Fancy Fair at Albert Hall in aid of French charities in London.
8 July	Lay foundation stone of new wing of Royal Hospital for Incurables at West Hill, Putney Heath.
9 July	Visit Royal Normal College and Academy of Music for the Blind, when Princess presents prizes.
15 July	Visit National Orphan Home, Ham Common, when Princess presents prizes.
17 July	Lay foundation stone of new wing at Hospital for Consumption and Diseases of the Chest at Brompton.
18 July	Visit North London Collegiate School for Girls, where Princess presents prizes.
22 July	Stay with Lord Yarborough at Brocklesby House [where a house-party of twenty-two guests included the Duke and Duchess of St Albans, Lord and Lady Castlereagh, Lord Macduff, Lord Suffield, Count Jaraczewski, Lord Marcus Beresford, Oliver Montagu and Christopher Sykes] and unveil new statue of Prince Consort at Grimsby.
26 July	Visit Royal Hospital School at Greenwich and present prizes.
3 November	Visit St Bartholomew's Hospital; open new museum classroom and library; and lunch in Great Hall.

The Prince visited many artists' studios, and attended

twelve formal Committee meetings during 1879. He held four levees, besides attending two drawing-rooms and two state concerts at Buckingham Palace; and on seven of the eighty occasions on which he went to the theatre, opera or ordinary concerts, the proceeds of the performances were devoted to charities.

The Prince attended the House of Lords nineteen times during 1879; and on 3 May he spoke for three minutes in presenting a petition, bearing 3,258 signatures, in favour of Lord Houghton's Bill to legalize marriage with a deceased wife's sister. He had organized an agitation in Norfolk and had persuaded farmers and others to sign; but the Bill was defeated by 101 votes to 81 on its second reading on 6 May, when the Prince voted with the minority.

The Government was much worried throughout 1879 by a very serious and deepening agricultural and trade depression, which caused Disraeli to contemplate the appointment of a Parliamentary Committee of Inquiry, and the launching, in the Queen's name, of a national appeal to relieve distress. He wanted the Prince of Wales as well as 'moderate members of the Opposition' to serve on that Committee and to be associated with the appeal, and he outlined[7] his proposals (22 December 1878) to the Prince, who replied[8] on Christmas Day: 'I am entirely at your disposal, and ready to do anything you may think proper.'

Because the Opposition suspected Disraeli of a wish to steal a Party advantage, an ordinary Royal Commission on the Agricultural Depression was appointed instead. The Prince was not invited, and showed no inclination, to serve upon it; but, on 29 May 1880, his appointment as Colonel-in-Chief of the Household Cavalry (1st and 2nd Life Guards and Royal Horse Guards) realized a long-standing and deeply cherished ambition.

The Duke of Cambridge pressed that appointment warmly upon Queen Victoria, who had opposed it for many years; and Sir Henry Ponsonby minuted[9] (17 February) that 'there might be just enough occupation ... to interest His Royal Highness'. The Duke wanted to enlist the Prince of Wales's support against Sir Garnet Wolseley, who was his principal military critic, and who returned from South Africa in May 1880 to become Quartermaster-General at the War Office.

A passion for army reform threw Wolseley into violent opposition to the Duke of Cambridge, who obstructed all reform for half a century; and Gladstone wanted a peerage to be conferred upon Wolseley in order to give the reformers an expert spokesman in the House of Lords. Angered by that proposal, the Duke threatened to resign; the Prince of Wales supported the Duke; and Wolseley had to wait for his peerage until he had conquered Egypt in September 1882.

Although prejudiced against Wolseley on account of Sir Bartle Frere, the Prince of Wales was convinced by Lord Hartington, who was Secretary of State for War from 1883–1885, that the problem of army reform was urgent. The reformers were able to count thereafter upon the benevolent neutrality if not always upon the active support of the Prince of Wales, whose principal complaint was that all promotions went automatically to Wolseleyites: 'The whole matter resolves itself into this', he wrote [10] (17 September 1884) to Lord Hartington, 'however competent or able an officer may be – unless he belongs to the "mutual admiration society" he had no chance of getting the "good things" in his profession.'

That was true; and until he came to the throne the Prince of Wales admired without much liking Lord Wolseley, whilst he relished the company of the Duke of Cambridge, whose faults he appreciated. He had started during the late 1860s to laugh at the Duke's fumbling and perfunctory attempts to convey remonstrances from Queen Victoria about his personal conduct; and he knew that the Duke, with whom he shared many tastes, detested those missions which were entrusted [11] to him, nevertheless, from time to time. On the other hand, the Prince was very proud that a member of the royal family should hold the office of commander-in-chief; and he hated to see Lord Wolseley succeed to that office instead of the Duke of Connaught, when the Duke of Cambridge resigned at long last in 1895.

Before appointing the Prince of Wales to be Colonel-in-Chief of the Household Cavalry in 1880, Queen Victoria insisted that he should surrender the Colonelcy-in-Chief of the Rifle Brigade to the Duke of Connaught. She asked the Prince of Wales to say nothing, because she wished his younger brother's appointment to be a surprise; but the Prince made a bargain with the Dukes of Cambridge and Connaught that he should be allowed to continue to wear the black buttons of the Rifle Brigade whenever he chose.

That arrangement, concluded behind her back, vexed Queen Victoria, who accused the Prince of Wales of a breach of confidence: 'I do not think', he replied [12] (7 June 1880) 'that I am prone "to let the cat out of the bag" as a rule, or to betray confidences; but I own it is often with great regret that I either learn first from others, or see in the newspapers, hints or facts stated with regard to members of our Family.'

Queen Victoria was equally vexed by the Prince's attempts to be of use when the Conservatives were thrown out of office at the General Election of March 1880. She was so unhappy at losing Disraeli as Prime Minister that she became temporarily overwrought, and informed [13] Ponsonby (4 April) that she would 'sooner *abdicate*' than send for Gladstone, '*that half-mad firebrand* who would soon ruin everything and be a *Dictator*'.

Despite the decisive personal part which he had played in winning the General Election, Gladstone had renounced the Liberal leadership in January 1875. He had retired into private life in order to devote himself to the defence of Christian dogma against scientific assaults; and Queen Victoria proposed, accordingly, to invite Lord Hartington to become Prime Minister. Lord Hartington and Lord Granville, who were the official leaders of the Liberal Party, were most anxious that the Queen should send for Gladstone, for whom the country was calling insistently; and with their approval the Prince of Wales wrote [14] (21 April 1880) to Sir Henry Ponsonby:

I think it right to let you know that I had a long conversation again with Hartington yesterday evening, and he is *more* anxious than ever that the Queen should send for Mr Gladstone to form a Government instead of sending either for Lord Granville or himself. ... It would get over many difficulties, make the Queen most popular, and a more moderate Government would be formed than one Hartington would have to constitute. He saw Mr G. yesterday and he told me that nothing could be nicer than the way the latter spoke of the Queen – how much he felt for her. ... From what he told me, Mr G. will, I am sure, do all he can to meet the Queen's wishes and be conciliatory in every possible way. ... Far better that she should take the initiative than that it should be forced on her.

With the Prince's consent, Ponsonby laid that letter before the Queen, who minuted [15] it (22 April), immediately before she saw Lord Hartington: 'The Prince of Wales may be told, but *very shortly* what the consitutional course is, which is *quite* clear. He has *no* right to meddle and *never* has done so *before*. Lord Hartington must be told, when he leaves, that the Queen cannot allow any private and intimate communications to go on between *them*, or all confidence will be *impossible*.'

After that severe snub, the Prince of Wales confided to Lord Hartington at the Turf Club, and to Lord Granville, his regret at the influence which his brother, Prince Leopold, was exercising over the Queen. Prince Leopold was still helping his mother in a secretarial capacity, and the Prince of Wales considered that he was doing his utmost also to induce her to regard Gladstone as a disloyal enemy of the royal family. After persuading Queen Victoria to acknowledge (22 April) Gladstone's profound personal loyalty to the throne, Hartington promised to ask Gladstone formally whether or not he would be willing to serve in a subordinate capacity in a new Liberal government.

Gladstone replied that he would not, but that he would give loyal support to any government which Hartington or Granville might form; and Lord Hartington and Lord Granville went together to Windsor with that reply on the morning of 23 April. They told the Queen that the nation was clamouring for Gladstone's return to office as Prime Minister; and with a heavy heart on the evening of that day she sent for Gladstone at last and asked him to form a government.

Although out of sympathy with the new Prime Minister's policy, the Prince of Wales had no difficulty in maintaining a happy personal relationship. He paid him little attentions, and Gladstone's very complex nature responded in a characteristic way. The failure of all his efforts to secure employment for the Prince had involved Gladstone in what he regarded as the most mortifying experience of his entire career; but an intense love of being mortified is the master-key to an understanding of his character. He warmed, accordingly, towards the Prince, and greatly enjoyed dining or staying with him; and on such occasions he would even lay aside his hatred of smoking, and exhale tobacco smoke slowly and reflectively through his nostrils, as the Prince did.

The Prime Minister went even further in his efforts to please the Prince of Wales. He knew that the Prince wanted his friend, Mrs Langtry, to be received and not cold-shouldered in society, and in his innocent and ingenuous way, he decided to call upon her himself. He found her charming, gave her copies of his favourite 'goody' books to read, and allowed her to make social capital out of the acquaintance. With his habitual unworldliness, he also gave her the code sign which enabled a very few privileged people to send him, when they wished, letters enclosed in double envelopes which escaped being opened by his private secretaries.[16]

Despite more than one strongly-worded protest from the Prince of Wales, the Queen continued the ban upon his seeing secret official papers, and a coolness developed in consequence between the Prince and the new Foreign Secretary, Lord Granville. The Prince felt that Granville, as an old friend, might reasonably have exercised some degree of personal and informal discretion; but he cultivated an agreeable and profitable friendship with Granville's Radical Under-Secretary of State for Foreign Affairs, Sir Charles Dilke, who was hated by the Queen on account of the republican views to which, in the past, he had given uninhibited expression.

The Prince laid himself out to charm Dilke when they met for the first time at dinner with Lord Fife on 12 March 1880. They discussed French politics and the Greek question; their friendship developed rapidly; and Dilke, who was a very clever man and who enjoyed his popularity at Marlborough House, contrived thereafter to feed the Prince of Wales with information for which he was hungry, in the spiced conversational form which he relished.

The sketch which Dilke drew and the judgement which he formed of the Prince of Wales at that period were quite kindly. He was amused by a great dinner which the Prince gave on 6 June 1880 at Marlborough House for the King of Greece, when the Gladstones and Lord Granville were present. After the ladies had retired, a Greek colonel, who was one of the King's equerries, showed plainly that he had drunk too much champagne: 'He's a good little King, but not what I call a fashionable King', he exclaimed,[17] waving an arm in his Sovereign's direction; and then, pointing at the Prince of Wales, he added: 'Now that's what I call a fashionable Prince – *un Prince vraiment chic* – He goes to bed late, it is true, but he gets up – well never! That's what I call a really fashionable Prince. My King gets up at six!'

The Prince seldom rose late, in fact, because he could do with little sleep for long periods; but he betrayed himself sometimes. Dilke watched[18] him closely on 14 March 1881 at the Russian Chapel in Welbeck Street, where a requiem mass was being sung for the Emperor Alexander II of Russia, who had been assassinated on the previous day: 'On this occasion I saw the Prince of Wales go to sleep standing, his taper gradually turn round and gutter on the floor.'

On 1 July 1881, Dilke attended a midnight supper party given at the Prince of Wales's request by Ferdinand de Rothschild, at his house in Piccadilly, in order to allow the Duc d'Aumâle to meet Sarah Bernhardt: 'All the other ladies present were English ladies who had been invited at the distinct request of the Prince of Wales. It was one thing to get them to go, and another to get them to talk when they were there; and the result was that, as they would not talk to Sarah Bernhardt, and the Duc d'Aumâle was deaf and disinclined to make conversation on his own account, nobody talked at all, and an absolute reign of the most dismal silence ensued.'[19]

Before his career was blasted by public scandal in 1886, Dilke attended many gayer and more successful supper parties in the company of the Prince of Wales, who did his utmost to assist his friend's promotion to Cabinet rank. He forgave Dilke for refusing, on principle, to support a grant of £2,000 which was voted by Parliament towards the expenses (amounting to £3,500) which he incurred while attending Alexander II's funeral in St Petersburg; and he relished the part which he played behind the scenes in securing for Dilke the Presidency of the Local Government Board when Gladstone reconstructed his Government in December 1882. Queen Victoria approved of that appointment because it reduced to a minimum any possible occasions of contact between Dilke and herself; and Dilke noted[20]:

During the whole of the month while my position in the Cabinet was under hot discussion, I saw a great deal of the Prince of Wales, who wished to know from day to day how matters stood, and I was able to form a more accurate opinion of himself and of the Princess, and of all about them, than I had formed before. The Prince is, of course, in fact a strong Conservative, and a still stronger Jingo, readily agreeing in the Queen's politics, and wanting to take everything everywhere in the world, and to keep everything if possible; but a good deal under the influence of the last person who talks to him, so that he would sometimes reflect the Queen and sometimes reflect me, or Chamberlain, or some other Liberal who had been shaking his head at him. He has more sense and more usage of the modern world than the Queen, but less real brain power. He is very sharp in a way – the Queen not sharp at all, but she carries heavier metal, for her obstinacy constitutes power of a kind.

The strongest man in Marlborough House is [Sir Maurice] Holzmann, the Princess's secretary and the Prince's librarian. He is a man of character and solidity, but then he is a Continental Liberal. ... The Princess never talks politics. ... It is worth talking seriously to the Prince. One seems to make no impression at the time ... but he does listen all the same, and afterwards, when he is talking to somebody else, brings out everything that you have said.

On another occasion Dilke noted [21] that 'the only two subjects on which the Prince agrees with any Liberals' were those of the government of London, which he wanted to see reformed, and Lord Randolph Churchill, whom he continued to boycott despite the involuntary admiration which he accorded to the brilliantly audacious attacks upon Gladstone with which Lord Randolph was earning a meteoric reputation. Success appealed strongly always to the Prince of Wales, who was depressed and baffled by a series of reports from Dalton about the total failure of all efforts to help and educate Prince Eddy.

On 1 May 1880, for example, Dalton wrote [22] in glowing terms about the younger boy, Prince George, while describing the problem presented by the elder as insoluble. Prince Eddy, despite every possible encouragement from a select and experienced body of tutors and naval officers, 'sits listless and vacant, and ... wastes as much time in doing nothing, as he ever wasted. ... This weakness of brain, this feebleness and lack of power to grasp almost anything put before him, is manifested ... also in his hours of recreation and social intercourse. It is a fault of nature. ...'

The Prince of Wales, who had just acquired a new racing yacht, *Aline* (216 tons), which he named after a daughter of Baron Gustave de Rothschild of Paris, and who was building a new ballroom at Sandringham, sought comfort and displayed optimism in a characteristic way. He loved both boys equally, and tried hard to regard them for as long as possible as a single entity, in the hope that the younger, who had 'passed all his examinations for midshipman rating exactly as any other boy would do', would cure the defects of the elder: 'The older they get,' he suggested [23] (22 May) to the Queen, 'the more difficult we see is the problem of their education, and it gives us many an anxious thought and care'.

Queen Victoria emphasized constantly the need for protecting both Princes from contamination by the society in which their parents delighted; and the Prince of Wales wrote [24] (22 May 1880) that 'our greatest wish is to keep them simple, pure and childlike for as long as possible'. He assured [25] her (11 July 1880), 'as I have had reason to say before', that they were in no danger at all: 'We both hope and think that they are so simple and innocent, and that those they have come in contact with have such tact with them, that they are not likely to do them any harm.'

On 14 January 1881, the Prince of Wales delighted the Jewish community of London by attending a synagogue and signing the register at the wedding of Leopold de Rothschild with Marie Perugia of Trieste, a sister of Mrs Arthur Sassoon whose beauty the Prince admired; and he left England a month later in order to attend (27 February) the wedding of his German nephew, Prince William. The Princess of Wales, who was never reconciled with the Prussians, did not accompany her husband; but the marriage was welcomed warmly by Queen Victoria because the bride, Princess Augusta Victoria, was a daughter of Duke Frederick of Schleswig-Holstein-Sonderburg-Augustenburg whose claims to the Duchy of Holstein had been contemptuously brushed aside sixteen years earlier by Bismarck.

Duke Frederick's younger brother, Prince Christian, had married Queen Victoria's daughter, Princess Helena; and Prince William's wedding was regarded by most members of the British royal family as a lucky act of happy reconciliation. The Prince of Wales, who was welcomed rapturously in Berlin, noted [26] that no less than fifty-four relations had sat down on 1 March at a family dinner given by his sister, the Crown Princess.

On 2 March the Prince had a long interview with Prince Bismarck, who gave his visitor little opportunity to express his views on world affairs; and shortly after returning home, he left England again (23 March), with the Princess, to attend the funeral in St Petersburg of the murdered Russian Emperor, Alexander II. The new Emperor, Alexander III, came to join his English guests in the Anitchkoff Palace, where they were lodged, because his Empress, Marie Feodorovna (formerly Dagmar), wished to be under one roof with her sister, the Princess of Wales; but the atmosphere was gloomy, and the extraordinary strictness of the security precautions gave the Prince a feeling of claustrophobia which he could scarcely endure.

After investing Alexander III with the Garter on 28 March, the Prince returned home, leaving the Princess behind with her sister for one week. Queen Victoria deplored that arrangement, but the Princess wrote [27] (6 April) from St Petersburg to the Queen: 'It really was very kind in my Bertie to let me stop ... and, after all, it would have mattered much less if anything had happened to me than to him! Besides, I think one is bound to try and help those who are near and dear to us.'

After attending Disraeli's funeral on 28 April, the Prince again left England, but without the Princess, on 4 May 1881, to attend the wedding in Vienna (10 May) of the Crown Prince Rudolf and Princess Stephanie of Belgium. He stayed, tactfully, at an hotel, because he wanted to be free to receive and to accept hospitality from members of the Austrian branch of the Rothschild family without embarrassing the Emperor. Some, but not all, of the archdukes cold-shouldered the Rothschilds, who were liked and encouraged by the Crown Prince; and the Prince of Wales spent a day or two in Budapest and a full and lively week in Paris before returning on 23 May to Marlborough House.

During the London season which followed, the Prince amused society by paying extraordinary attentions to the reactionary King Kalakaua of Hawaii, or, as the Prince preferred to call it, the Sandwich Islands. He was anxious that Kalakaua, who reigned from 1874–1891, should cease to woo the United States, and that he should consent to the annexation of the islands by Great Britain. At a party given by Lady Spencer on 13 July, the Prince insisted that the King of Hawaii should be accorded precedence over the German Crown Prince, who protested without avail. The Crown Prince was silenced by his brother-in-law's robust retort: 'Either the brute is a King, or he's a common or garden nigger; and, if the latter, what's he doing here?'

The Prince of Wales took Kalakaua on 16 July to a Lord Mayor's banquet at the Mansion House, and to a Trinity House banquet four days later. He found him amiable and very interesting, and gave him a luncheon at Marlborough House. He made Christopher Sykes, Lord Charles Beresford and other friends give parties in Kalakaua's honour, and at the Marlborough House ball on 22 July, which ended the London season, he again relegated his German brother-in-law to second place by asking King Kalakaua to open the royal quadrille with the Princess of Wales.

Queen Victoria was hurt by the Prince of Wales's refusal to postpone that ball in consequence of the death (18 July) of Arthur Stanley, Dean of Westminster, who was her greatest friend, and who had conducted the Prince's tour of Palestine in 1863. In a letter (27 July) to her son the Queen wrote [28] that Stanley was 'more than any Bishop or Archbishop'; that he had 'stood alone, earning an immortal name for himself'; and that she deplored her son's heartless frivolity in arranging that the funeral should be held a day earlier than had been intended in order to avoid a clash with Goodwood Races.

On 21 December 1881, the Prince of Wales wrote [29] to his younger son, Prince George:

Yesterday we went to a morning performance at Haymarket Theatre and saw Goldsmith's comedy, *She Stoops to Conquer*, in which Mrs Langtry acted with a professional company. It was her début, and a great success. As she is so very fond of acting, she has decided to go on the stage and will, after Christmas, join Mr and Mrs Bancroft's company at the Haymarket.

That performance was held in aid of the Royal General Theatrical Fund, and *The Times* reported that Mrs Langtry had attracted the most distinguished audience ever seen in a theatre. Her social and financial position had become precarious after the birth of a daughter, the bankruptcy of her husband, and the circulation of rumours (which landed a magazine publisher in gaol) about a scandalous impending divorce, and many doors were shut heartlessly in her face. Her life needed to be rearranged; and the Prince of Wales, staunch always in friendship, procured an opening for her with the actor-manager [Sir] Squire Bancroft who controlled the Haymarket and the Prince of Wales's theatres.

Early in 1882, accordingly, Mrs Langtry appeared at the Haymarket as the heroine in *Ours*, a comedy about the Crimean War by Tom Robertson. The Prince, who came up from Sandringham on 28 January to see it, went again on 13 February and on 15 March; and he did everything in his power to help and encourage the inexperienced actress. On 26 February, when it had become clear that the play was a triumphant success, he attended with the Duke of Cambridge a midnight supper party which Mrs Langtry gave; and the glamour of his name and interest ensured a semi-royal reception for his friend when she first toured the United States during the winter of 1882-3. Mrs Langtry continued, thereafter, to make a conspicuous success, in America as well as in England, of a light-hearted and unconventional career. In addition to beauty, business acumen, and a tough constitution, she possessed courage, grit and talent; and no one could have been more delighted than the Prince of Wales was to see her become, within the brief space of two years, a rich woman and a patron of the turf.

The gratitude and goodwill felt by the Prince of Wales towards the theatrical profession which had welcomed his friend so generously and without fuss or jealousy at a critical moment in her life, found expression in a much publicized dinner which he gave on 19 February 1882 at Marlborough House. The thirty-seven guests included Squire Bancroft, Francis Burnand, George Grossmith, John Hare, Henry Irving, William Kendal, G. A. Sala and Charles Wyndham; Lord Aylesford, the Duke of Beaufort, Lord Carrington, Lord Fife, Prince Leiningen, Lord Londesborough, Lord Lytton and Lord Torrington; as well as George Lewis, the solicitor whose practice was unique, because the bulk of it lay in cases involving the follies and indiscretions of the rich which might have caused acute embarrassment or disaster, but which his adroit handling preserved for ever from the light of day.

The menu, which consisted of nine courses only, was acclaimed by the Press as an impressive rebuke to ostentation;

and Lord Carrington informed [30] his wife 20 February) that 'Tum Tum' had excelled himself; that the affair had been well received; and that it would certainly raise actors' social standing. 'They were sandwiched between ordinary mortals with more or less success. I sat next to Kendal, a good-looking bounder, who distinguished himself later in the evening by singing a very vulgar song which was not favourably received in high quarters. . . . Irving and Bancroft were the great guns . . . but it was a dullish evening.'

In July 1882, in response to a strange sequence of events, Gladstone felt constrained to order the bombardment of Alexandria and the despatch of a British army to invade and occupy Egypt. That country's importance had been greatly increased since the opening of the Suez Canal, but Gladstone, who had disliked very much the *coup* whereby Disraeli had acquired the Khedive's shares, had described the subsequent process, whereby France and England had established a joint control over the bankrupt Egyptian treasury in the interests of European bondholders, as one of Disraeli's 'mischievous and ruinous misdeeds'.

Gladstone had incurred odium already by a clumsy handling of the problem of the Transvaal, which Disraeli had annexed. Liberals had castigated that action so severely that the Boers expected an immediate grant of self-government when the Conservatives were thrust out of power, and they rose in revolt when informed that they must first set their house in order. At Majuba Hill a British army suffered another humiliating reverse; and Gladstone proceeded at once to concede, from weakness, an independence which he would have done much better to concede, at the outset, from strength.

After outraging Jingo sentiment by the unfortunate timing of that imprudent concession, Gladstone was placed in a worse dilemma when a nationalist revolt exploded in Egypt in 1882. Directed against Europeans, it was headed by a Colonel Arabi who exploited the discontent felt by native army officers at seeing their salaries reduced, and their prospect of promotion impaired, by their government's need to pay interest on foreign loans. Arabi's remedy was to discontinue such payments, and Gladstone was appalled equally by the threat which the Colonel represented to political morality by establishing a military dictatorship, and to financial morality by that brazen act of repudiation.

The Prince of Wales, who did his utmost to persuade the Government to employ force against Egypt, showed Lord Granville a number of letters which he had received from Lord Charles Beresford. Beresford, who had lost his seat in Parliament, and who commanded the gunboat *Condor* at Alexandria, had described with uninhibited frankness the steps which he was taking to inspire a Press campaign at home against the Government's supine inactivity; and Granville infuriated the Prince by reporting that conduct to the First Lord of the Admiralty, who proposed to order the immediate arrest of Lord Charles and his trial by naval court martial.

A quarrel between the Prince of Wales and Lord Granville was averted by a promise that no action would be taken against Beresford for supplying confidential information to the Press; and the Government tried vainly to persuade the Great Powers to intervene jointly in Egypt on behalf of defrauded European bondholders. All declined, and even France drew back at the last moment in consequence of a political convulsion. The French were afraid that a sinister motive might lie behind Bismarck's unconcealed wish to see French troops locked up in Egypt, in addition to those which were already committed in Tunis and Algeria; and the French fleet was ordered, accordingly, to quit Alexandria, and to leave the British on their own.

After a riot in Alexandria in which fifty Europeans were killed, Arabi started to mount guns which were a threat to all British ships in the harbour. No reply was received to an ultimatum requiring that work to stop at once, and after the British fleet had opened fire on 11 July 1882, the Prince's friend, Charles Beresford, played such a spirited part ashore that he became overnight a popular hero in England. By the evening of 11 July the city of Alexandria had been reduced, mainly by rioters, to a smoking ruin; anarchy ensued in Egypt; and a British army, commanded by Sir Garnet

Wolseley, was landed on 19 August at Port Said with orders to take Cairo, smash the Egyptian army, and restore good government.

In that army the Duke of Connaught was given command of the Guards Brigade; and the Prince of Wales, supported by the Duke of Cambridge, pleaded with Queen Victoria, and with the Government, for permission to serve with the expedition in any capacity. He had been stung by French and German caricatures depicting him as a field-marshal whose experience of war was limited to the annual battle of flowers on the French Riviera, and by an uncouth and untrue taunt – attributed to Bismarck – that his love of uniforms was matched only by his fear of powder; but his fervent offer of service was rejected by the Cabinet.

Granville wrote [31] (31 July) to congratulate the Prince of Wales on the 'spirit and pluck' which he had displayed; and Ponsonby wrote,[32] in courtly language and at length, to explain how greatly the Prince's 'gallant offer of joining the expedition to Egypt' had troubled the Queen:

... Her Majesty, I may almost say, fully agreed with Your Royal Highness's desires to be of use, warmly appreciated the gallant wish to see service, and was proud that the Prince of Wales should not shrink from sharing the dangers and privations of her troops.

But, on the other hand, the imperative demands of public duty compelled Her Majesty to point out the grave difficulties, and inconvenience, of such a proceeding; and, having been advised by the Government, as well as by several leaders of the Opposition, that it would be inexpedient and most unwise, considering Your Royal Highness's rank and position, to join the expedition as a spectator, and impossible for Your Royal Highness to be attached to it on duty, the Queen finally and conclusively decided that it was necessary to ask Your Royal Highness to abandon the idea.

One difficulty was that whereas the Duke of Connaught was by any standard, a competent and well trained brigadier, the Prince of Wales had had no experience in command of troops. No suitable post existed and, although bitterly disappointed and depressed, the Prince accepted that decision and gave a dinner (31 July) at the Marlborough Club to twenty-three officers of the Household Cavalry, including Oliver Montagu, on the eve of their jubilant departure. He was in constant correspondence with many of them before and after they had helped to fulfil the highest British hopes by annihilating the Egyptian army on 13 September at Tel-el-Kebir; and he was informed [33] by Oliver Montagu, two days before that battle, that the army's hospital arrangements were 'a disgrace to England'.

While the Prince did what he could to stir the War Office to provide a more adequate medical service, Cairo surrendered to a spirited dash by British cavalry, and Egypt lay, broken and bankrupt, at the conquerors' feet. Within a few months the Prince of Wales was called upon to preside at a series of dinners in honour of the victorious naval and military commanders, Lord Alcester and Lord Wolseley, who were awarded peerages, money grants and the thanks of Parliament; as well as to open an exhibition of war photographs in Bond Street, and a great panorama of the battlefield of Tel-el-Kebir.

Because force is the bedrock of government, the first need was to form a new Egyptian army, officered by Britons and trained on British lines; and the Prince of Wales flung himself chivalrously into the task of securing the command of that army for his unfortunate friend, Valentine Baker. Lord Wolseley approved; the Khedive of Egypt, whose authority Wolseley had been instrumental in restoring, made the appointment; and Baker resigned his commission as a major-general in the Turkish army. He had already left Constantinople for Cairo, when a puritan outcry arose in England, and the Cabinet decided, in consequence, that Baker was unacceptable as Commander-in-Chief.

The Prince implored [34] Gladstone vainly (3 December) to relent: 'It is not for me to comment on the decision of the Cabinet, but I must confess that I think Baker Pasha has been very hardly and unfairly treated. ... To deprive him now of the important command, which the Khedive has conferred upon him, is simply to ruin him.'

The Duke of Cambridge agreed with the Prince of Wales in holding that Baker's former disgrace and imprisonment in England had fully expiated the attempted rape of which he had been convicted; and the Prince begged [35] Lord Wolseley (3 December) to intercede with the Government and not to allow his friend 'to fall between two stools'. It was to no purpose, however, and Sir Evelyn Wood was made Commander-in-Chief of the Egyptian army, while Baker had to be content with the command – for which he was wholly unfitted – of the Egyptian police.

While the Egyptian campaign was in progress, the Prince of Wales started for the first time to play lawn tennis, which had been invented a few years earlier. He added that game to fencing as a means of reducing his weight, and as soon as his interest was known courts appeared at Homburg, in time for his visit in August and September, 1882, and again at Cannes, in January and February, 1883. He played with sporadic enthusiasm for several years, and the game acquired immediate prestige.

After returning (15 February 1883) from Cannes, the Prince again left England *en garçon* on 24 February in order to attend the silver wedding celebrations of his sister, the Crown Princess, in Berlin. He was immensely pleased at being made Colonel of the 5th Pomeranian Hussars, but the Princess of Wales, who disapproved strongly of his wearing a Prussian uniform, informed [36] Queen Victoria (1 October) that she and her husband had agreed not to discuss that subject. The Prince reported gleefully to Gladstone, whom he saw frequently, and who trusted him with a growing amount of secret information, that Bismarck had expressed cordial approval of the British action in Egypt.

Because that action had exasperated French opinion, the Prince cancelled his visit to Paris in the spring of 1883; but he spent more than two months on the Continent that autumn. He went first (14 August) to Homburg, and thence to stay at Baden with the Dowager Duchess of Hamilton, who had been born a Princess of Baden. Her son, the Duke of Hamilton, and her daughter and son-in-law, Count and Countess Festetics, as well as Lord and Lady Charles Beres-

1. Queen Victoria and the Prince Consort, 1 March 1861

2. Queen Victoria (and bust of the Prince Consort) with the Prince
and Princess of Wales on their wedding day, 1863

3. The Princess of Wales, 1866

4. The Prince of Wales, 1870

5. Lillie Langtry (Emilie Le Breton, wife of Edward Langtry), 1886

6. Lady Brooke (formerly Frances Evelyn Maynard, later Countess of Warwick), 1890

7. Prince Frederick William of Prussia (later the German Emperor Frederick III), 1857, by Franz Krüger

8. Victoria, the Princess Royal (later the Empress Frederick), wife of the Crown Prince Frederick, 1876, by Heinrich von Angeli

9. At Marlborough House, 1889. (*Standing, left to right*) Duke of Clarence, Princess Maud (later Queen of Norway), the Princess of Wales, Princess Louise (later Duchess of Fife), the Prince of Wales. (*Sitting*) Prince George, Princess Victoria

10. The Prince of Wales and his brothers, the Duke of Connaught and the Duke of Edinburgh, at the wedding of the Duke of York (later George V), 6 July 1893

ford, Christopher Sykes, Henry Chaplin and the Duchess of
Manchester were fellow-guests; and the principal amuse-
ments were baccarat and horse-racing. On 30 August the
Prince ran, unsuccessfully, a horse called *The Scot* for the
International Steeplechase.

After returning to Homburg the Prince of Wales, in
Prussian uniform, attended the autumn manoeuvres of the
German army at the Emperor's invitation. He was impressed most of all by the endurance of the infantry, which
was matched by that of the old Kaiser, aged eighty-six,
who rode for hours at the head of his troops; and the Prince
noted [37] (20 September) in his diary: 'Dine with Emperor
& Empress, Kings of Spain, Saxony & Servia, Cr. P. & Cr.
Pss. of Germany, Cr. Pr. of Portugal, Etc. Etc. at Schloss
(Family Dinner) 7.30. Great "Tattoo" [sic] in Courtyard 9.00
(upwards of 1,000 musicians).'

On 29 September the Prince of Wales joined the Princess
at Fredensborg in Denmark where fellow guests included the
King and Queen of Greece, as well as the Emperor and Empress of Russia who enjoyed escaping as often as possible to
the comparative freedom of Denmark. Returning on 17
October to Marlborough House the Prince took his eldest
son, Prince Eddy, to Cambridge on the following day, and
left him at Trinity College as an undergraduate.

While Prince George was settling down extremely happily
to a naval career, Prince Eddy had been crammed for Cambridge throughout the summer of 1883. A staff of tutors from
Eton and Trinity had done their best at Sandringham,
under the direction of J. K. Stephen, whose reports were
discouraging: 'I do not think', he wrote [38] (31 August) to
Dalton, 'he can possibly derive much benefit from attending
lectures at Cambridge. ... He hardly knows the meaning of
the words *to read*.'

After dividing the remainder of the year between Newmarket and Sandringham, the Prince wrote [39] (1 January
1884) to thank the Queen for an advance copy of her new
book, *More Leaves from a Journal of Our Life in the Highlands*. He annoyed her by expressing 'grave doubts whether
your private life ... should be, as it were, exposed to the

world'; begged her to restrict the book to private circulation, and explained: 'You will, dearest Mama, I am afraid not agree in this, but I hold very strong views on the subject.'

The Queen retorted [40] (3 January) that if she did what the Prince suggested, her book would only reach members of society, who were the people least qualified to appreciate 'simple records'. She added: 'I know that the publication of my first book did me more good than anything else, and dear Papa's *Life* also'; and that was true. Two large editions of the new book were sold out almost as soon as it was published; and some of the Prince's friends expressed surprise that his name was not mentioned. He asked [41] the Queen accordingly (26 February) to insert in the third edition some account of a visit which he had paid to Balmoral in 1875: 'Though I am well aware that the inner object of your book is to describe your life in the Highlands, still, as it is now a work which is finding its way all over the world, it might create surprise that the name of your eldest child never occurred in it.'

That unfortunate letter gave the Queen an opportunity of which she could not resist taking advantage. She agreed to make the suggested insertion, but asked [42] (27 February) whether the Prince had actually read the book, or whether he had commissioned 'so-called friends', who were bent upon making mischief, to read it on his behalf. If he had been kind enough to read the book carefully, he must have seen that his name was in fact mentioned on pages 1, 5, 8, 331, and 378. Queen Victoria added that it would have been mentioned many times more often if he had come more often to see her at Balmoral.

The Prince, who apologized [43] (28 February) for having been hasty and inaccurate, had accepted nomination (22 February) as a member of a Royal Commission on the Housing of the Working Classes. Other members included Lord Brownlow, Lord Carrington, Jesse Collings, Sir Richard Cross, Sir Charles Dilke (Chairman), G. J. Goschen, Cardinal Manning and Lord Salisbury; and, despite support from Dilke, the Prince failed in an attempt to have Miss Octavia

Hill added to the Commission. Gladstone considered that the appointment of a woman would constitute too great a departure from precedent; but the Prince established another precedent by insisting that Manning, as a Prince of the Church, should rank immediately after himself, and before Lord Salisbury, on the Commission.

The Prince accepted with alacrity Lord Carrington's suggestion that they should explore together, in disguise, some of what the Prince, in addressing the House of Lords, termed 'the worst and poorest' slums in Clerkenwell and St Pancras; and, early on 18 February, he, Carrington and Dr Buchanan, who was Chief Medical Officer of Health in the Local Government Board, changed into workmen's clothes in Lord Carrington's mansion in Whitehall, before driving in a four-wheeler to the slums with a police cab as escort. Horrified by what he saw, the Prince wandered from alley to alley, after dismissing impatiently his police escort which tried to restrain him. In one unfurnished room he was deeply moved by the sight of a gaunt, shivering woman, lying on a heap of rags with three almost naked children who were too cold, and too much starved, to make any response whatsoever. He pulled a fistful of gold from his pocket, but put it back when Carrington and Buchanan warned him that the news would spread like wildfire, and that they might all be torn to pieces by the other denizens of the alley who would be driven crazy by the sight of so much wealth.

When they emerged, Carrington had difficulty in hailing a cab which took them to a rendezvous with a junior medical officer of health who had not been let into the secret of the Prince's identity. The Prince accepted Carrington's suggestion that he should sit with his back to the horses, while the ill-bred bureaucrat, misinterpreting the Prince's natural hauteur, displayed resentment by treating him with familiarity. He started to slap him on the back, exclaiming, 'What do you think of that Old Buck!'; but Carrington noted [44] that the Prince 'kept his temper and behaved very well. It was a droll sight! We visited some very bad places in Holborn and Clerkenwell, but we got him back safe and sound to Marlborough House in time for luncheon.'

Four days later (22 February 1884), the Prince of Wales delivered the only speech of substance which he ever made as a member of the House of Lords. After describing, in scorching language, some scenes which he had witnessed in Holborn and St Pancras, he referred very modestly to the provision which he had made for his own labourers at Sandringham, and demanded that the Government should take drastic and urgent action to improve housing conditions: 'Our Commission', he informed [45] Prince George (15 March), '... sits now regularly twice a week for 3 hours, and I have attended all the meetings as yet.'

Two meetings only had been held at that time, and the attention of the Prince of Wales was distracted almost at once by the sudden death at Cannes on 28 March 1884 of Prince Leopold (Duke of Albany). After bringing home his brother's body, he left England again a month later to attend the wedding at Darmstadt (30 April) of his niece, Princess Victoria of Hesse, and his friend, Prince Louis of Battenberg, and he remained abroad on that occasion for seven weeks. Strict mourning for the Duke of Albany, which barred all social activity, had made England appear quite intolerable; and the Prince wrote [46] (3 May) to his fellow-commissioner, Lord Carrington: 'I deeply regret being away from the Commission, and am completely losing the thread of the inquiry; but I fear it cannot be helped.'

That autumn, nevertheless, the Prince did not go to Homburg, but remained in England in order to attend to the business of the Commission; and when it stood adjourned on 5 December he had attended nineteen out of fifty-one meetings. Immediately after that adjournment, he invited his Radical working-class colleague, Henry Broadhurst, M.P., to spend the week-end of 12–15 December at Sandringham; and that experiment was a success.

Broadhurst recorded [47] that, 'in order to meet the difficulties in the matter of dress, dinner was served to me in my own rooms each night'; and the social climate made that arrangement appear natural. Broadhurst, who was much gratified, would otherwise have been embarrassed, but he enjoyed many frank discussions with his host and hostess, as well as with Prince Eddy and Prince George; and he noted happily that he 'left Sandringham with a feeling of one who had spent a week-end with an old chum of his own rank in society ...'

10
Germany

BOREDOM and frustration afflicted the society which revolved round the Prince of Wales. Admirably organized as
it was for assimilating new elements, and endowed, as most
of its members were, with tradition and an elevated
patriotism, comparatively few did themselves justice. Their
true quality was obscured in a hothouse world of game preservation, gold plate, jewels and other luxuries, and their
sense of complete security was buttressed by the gaping
servility of a host of inferiors. Some, in those circumstances,
had recourse to gambling and other absorbing hazards, and
most convinced themselves that they personally embodied
English history; that the Empire belonged peculiarly to
them; and that the future of both, as well as their own
survival, depended upon the maintenance of privileges
which they accepted as rights.

Many fought with every weapon in their armoury, including financial, political and social power, to preserve those
privileges until 1914; and the strenuous atmosphere
engendered by that contest afforded some relief from boredom and frustration. After much of the gilded fabric of the
1880s and the 1890s had dissolved like a dream, patricians
displayed a disproportionate ability to compete, prosper and
prevail; but, until put to that test, most remained idle out of
habit.

A combination of unlimited leisure with unprecedented
wealth fostered a restless pursuit of pleasure which failed to
procure contentment. The Prince of Wales displayed many
symptoms of that *malaise* which afflicted most members of
the society over which he reigned, and the task of keeping

him amused was regarded as a major social problem throughout the last decades of the nineteenth century. A variety of frivolous stratagems were devised in an effort to charm away the tedium of assembling again and again in the same great country houses; and some hostesses were prepared always to divert their guests, including the Prince, by a discreet allocation of bedrooms in accordance with their known but unexpressed wishes.

Politically, the Prince's mind remained open to argument in some fields until the formation of the great Liberal Government of 1905. He welcomed, for example, the Third Reform Bill which increased the electorate from three to five millions in 1884 by extending to country dwellers the principle of household suffrage which had been conceded to townsmen in 1867. Convinced by Lord Rosebery that the Bill was just and necessary, the Prince of Wales congratulated[1] his friend (8 July 1884) upon a speech which he had made during a debate on its second reading in the House of Lords: '... It was simply splendid, and so much to the point in every sense of the word. You spoke for upwards of an hour – and it seemed to me like ten minutes. Tell me candidly your opinion, whether you think that there would be any Constitutional objection if, in my position, I voted with the Government.'

It was impossible, of course, for the Prince to vote on that issue, and he was unhappy when the Lords rejected the measure by 205 votes to 146. Before the resultant crisis was resolved during November by a conference at Downing Street between the leaders of both Parties, the Prince invited himself, with the Princess and their daughters, to luncheon at Lord Carrington's house in Whitehall to witness a reform procession which took three and a half hours to pass on 21 July.

Carrington, an ardent Liberal, sent[2] immediately for the organizers of the demonstration and arranged that every marcher should demonstrate his loyalty, while passing Carrington House, by turning his eyes right, doffing his cap and cheering the Prince of Wales. He arranged, furthermore, that, whenever a band passed, the entire procession should halt while the marchers sang 'God Bless the Prince of Wales'.

The atmosphere at luncheon was a shade too militant to please the Prince of Wales, who warned[3] Lord Rosebery that attacks upon the House of Lords could harm the Crown by involving the hereditary principle. Rosebery retorted that Liberals valued the use, while deploring the abuse, of the hereditary principle; and that the Crown was above controversy because it never attempted to resist the people's will or to dictate, as the Lords did, to the Commons.

At that moment, flanked by mounted police, and carrying red banners denouncing hereditary legislators, the heads of the procession appeared behind massed bands playing the *Marseillaise*; and the Prince remarked drily to his host:

'Hey, Charlie! This don't look much like being a pleasant afternoon.'

'Wait a bit, sir. I think and hope you're about to get *the* reception of your life.'

The Prince's brow darkened, but all went as planned; and the roars of applause, which the Prince and Princess acknowledged continuously from the balcony, might almost have been heard at Windsor. The Princess complained presently of a headache and said that she would lie indoors upon a sofa, but, at her disappearance, the cheers became punctuated by rude catcalls and groans, and she had to be asked to return at once and to endure as best she could the intense heat and the renewed noise of cheering.

Conservatives complained loudly that Carrington had entrapped the Prince of Wales into taking part in a reform demonstration. The Carlton Club was furious, but the Prince was unmoved. He told Carrington that he had enjoyed an experience which had been instructive as well as interesting.

In private that summer the Prince was strongly critical of the Government's mishandling of a dangerous situation in the Sudan. A nationalist revolt under the Mahdi had placed a number of scattered Egyptian garrisons in deadly peril; British opinion insisted that they should be rescued; and a major-general of Engineers, Charles Gordon, C.B., had been despatched to Khartoum to advise about ways and means.

Sword in hand and Bible in pocket, Gordon had enjoyed a romantic career of warfare in three continents. He had cast an extrordinary spell over his countrymen whose thoughts were focused upon the lonely, lion-hearted but perverse hero who had turned his orders inside out. He refused to retreat while he could; he bombarded the British and Egyptian Governments with plans for crushing the Mahdi and for conquering the Sudan; and the mischievous comments which he confided to his journal about the dilemma into which he had plunged Gladstone's Government read like ghostly schoolboy chuckles echoing faintly through the mist of years.

Public opinion compelled Gladstone to authorize in August 1884, the despatch of an army to Khartoum; and before it started (5 October) after inexcusable delays on its mission to rescue Gordon, the Prince of Wales pleaded vainly once more for permission to accompany it and to serve under Lord Wolseley's command. 'Indeed I wish it were possible that you, sir, would take part', Wolseley wrote [4] (28 August) to the Prince, who trumpeted his disappointment to the world; and in order to please the Prince, Wolseley agreed to take Charles Beresford as his naval A.D.C. and Valentine Baker, who had not made a success of his command of the Egyptian police, as his principal intelligence officer.

The Prince was disgusted when the War Office again vetoed Baker's appointment, and he was mortified by a fresh spate of unkind continental caricatures. They mocked his alleged unwillingness to risk his life and sacrifice his ease; but he was more deeply wounded by an undercurrent of unfair criticism in a few bone-headed sections of the British Army.

That criticism, which was never voiced publicly, found a vent in an incident three years later when the Prince of Wales's horse, *Hohenlinden*, won the Grand Military Hunt Cup at Sandown amid the cheers of the crowd. The owner of the horse which came in second was induced to lodge an objection, on the ground that the race was open only to owners who had seen active service.

That dubious and malicious objection was allowed stupidly by the stewards, and the prize was awarded to the owner of the second horse. The Prince, who was always extremely sensitive, preserved a dignified silence; and to spare his feelings the disqualification of *Hohenlinden* was attributed to a technical hitch. The horse was alleged to have been entered in error as a six-year-old, when it was really older, and no further information was vouchsafed.

So many officers bearing famous names accompanied Lord Wolseley that Gladstone's disgruntled Radical followers denounced the relief expedition as a social stunt. It was badly managed, and Wolseley admitted[5] (28 December 1884) in a private letter to the Prince of Wales that 'this venture ... is not one after my own heart as the General responsible for the Campaign, although I should have gloried in it if I held a subordinate command'. He explained that he could see sometimes, in his 'mind's eye, the little boys running along Pall Mall with great printed placards announcing the DEATH AND DEFEAT OF LORD WOLSELEY'.

The Prince of Wales was at Cannes taking part in the battle of flowers with the Princesse de Sagan, the Duchesse de Luynes and other friends, when news reached London (5 February 1885) that Khartoum had fallen; that Gordon was killed; and that the relief expedition had arrived two days too late. Returning home on 19 February, the Prince associated his name as publicly as possible with the movement to found a national memorial to the dead hero; and he endorsed the view, which Gladstone rejected after some hesitation, that the disaster ought to be avenged immediately by the annihilation of the Mahdi and by the conquest, or liberation, of the Sudan.

On 18 March the Prince of Wales, accompanied by Prince Eddy, left England again to attend in Berlin the 88th birthday celebrations of the German Emperor and King of Prussia, William I. While Anglo-French relations were clouded by ill-feeling engendered by the Egyptian entanglement and other problems, the Prince did his best, between 1884 and 1888, to woo German opinion. Because he had too little to do, however, he interfered (in a role described[6] by Frederick von Holstein, of the German Foreign Office, as that of 'Matchmaker-in-chief') in a love affair which had political as well as personal repercussions; and in that way he incurred the bitter enmity of his twenty-six-year-old nephew, Prince William (eldest son of the Crown Prince), as well as the distrust of the Imperial Chancellor, Prince Bismarck.

Princess Victoria, aged nineteen, who was the Prince of Wales's niece and a daughter of the German Crown Prince and Crown Princess, had fallen blindly in love with the thirty-year-old Prince of Bulgaria. When a Russian army had liberated Bulgaria from Turkish oppression in 1879, Prince Alexander of Battenberg had been chosen to rule it as a Russian nominee and puppet but, although dependent entirely upon Russian gold and goodwill, he made himself a dictator and sought to gratify his subjects by playing an independent and ambitious role.

Known to his Russian, German and British relatives as Sandro, Prince Alexander was the very handsome and attractive child of a morganatic marriage between a prince of the Hesse-Cassel family and a Polish lady of bourgeois extraction. Because one of his aunts had married the Russian Emperor Alexander II, he was a first cousin of Sasha (the Emperor Alexander III), and he was very closely connected also with the British royal family.

Sandro's brother, Prince Louis of Battenberg, married in 1884 a daughter of the Prince of Wales's sister, Alice, the Grand Duchess of Hesse; and another brother, Prince Henry of Battenberg (Liko), married in 1886 the Prince of Wales's sister, Princess Beatrice. The Hohenzollern family, nevertheless, thought it unsuitable that the morganatic Battenbergs should seek to ally themselves with the great dynastic houses of Europe.

With her liberal English outlook, the German Crown Princess despised and laughed at that prejudice; and her view was endorsed warmly by Queen Victoria and the Prince of Wales. The political objections, nevertheless, to a marriage between the Crown Princess's daughter and the Prince of Bulgaria outweighed considerations of protocol. The Russian Emperor, Alexander III, had begun to hate his father's former protégé, and the Russian Government was toying already with plans for effecting Sandro's deposition or assassination. At the same time, a good understanding with Russia was the keystone of Bismarck's foreign policy.

The defeat of France in the war of 1870-71 had altered, to the disadvantage of Russia, the former balance of power in Europe. For that reason Bismarck was resolved at any cost to avoid the infliction of pinpricks which might provoke what he most dreaded – a hostile Franco-Russian alliance; and it appeared most undesirable to allow the Prince of Bulgaria to improve his position by marrying a German imperial princess. The affair was regarded in Berlin as an English intrigue, and the interference of the Prince of Wales on behalf of the lovers was resented as a mischievous presumption.

At the wedding of Prince Louis of Battenberg in Darmstadt, in April 1884, the Prince of Bulgaria had bewitched Queen Victoria, who wrote[7] (15 December 1886) to the Crown Princess: 'I think he may stand next to beloved Papa, and he is a person in whose judgement I would have great confidence. I think him very fascinating, and (as in beloved Papa's case) so wonderfully handsome.'

That was, indeed, high praise; and, after Prince Louis's wedding in Darmstadt, the Prince of Wales neglected meetings of the Royal Commission on the Housing of the Working Classes in order to escort the Prince of Bulgaria to Berlin. He helped his sister to talk the Crown Prince round to their view of the projected marriage; and Holstein noted[8] (12 May 1884): 'At the banquet at the New Palace two days ago, the Crown Prince, who was sitting between the Prince of Wales and the Prince of Bulgaria, treated the latter with quite unusual cordiality. A few days earlier he had spoken with the loftiest disdain of all Battenbergs. So the Crown Princess has got him round once again.'

Bismarck had already persuaded the Emperor to send Prince William, instead of the Crown Prince, to represent Germany at the 16th birthday celebrations of the Czarevitch Nicholas, elder son of Alexander III, and to reassure the Russian Emperor about the Bulgarian project of marriage. A stinging rebuke was administered in that way to the

Crown Prince and to his English wife; and Prince William, who was in violent revolt against his parents' liberal ideas and English ways, embarked upon a correspondence with the Czar and the Czarevitch which contained many gibes in poor taste about the Prince of Wales.

Bismarck warned [9] the Prince of Wales that the affections of princesses counted for nothing when weighed in the balance against German political interests; and the Prince, taken aback, retorted only that that seemed 'rather hard'. He thought it hard also that the old Kaiser should have rebuked the Crown Prince for having allowed the Prince of Wales to bring the Prince of Bulgaria to make trouble in Berlin, like some hero in a comic opera.

When the Kaiser forbade any further meetings between the lovers, the Prince of Wales arranged [10] a secret one, with his sister's connivance, at Potsdam, where politics were consigned to perdition and vows of eternal fidelity were exchanged. Prince Bismarck professed to believe that England wanted to drive a wedge between Germany and Russia; but the only wedge driven home was that between Prince William (who saw eye to eye with his grandfather and with Bismarck) on the one hand, and his parents and the Prince of Wales on the other.

When the Prince of Wales returned to Berlin in March 1885 the Crown Princess was aware that the Kaiser had ordered [11] the Prince of Bulgaria (18 March) to renounce formally all claim to the hand of Princess Victoria, and that Sandro, after being subjected to heavy pressure for months, was about to obey. Sandro begged the Kaiser (8 April), in return, to intercede on his behalf with the Czar; and the Prince of Wales reported [12] (21 March) to Queen Victoria that his sister was looking ill, 'low-spirited and preoccupied, as you may easily imagine'.

Bismarck provoked some indignant comment in British newspapers by failing to return personally the Prince of Wales's call. He sent his son, Herbert, to return it instead; and the Prince, who dined with the Kaiser at what he termed [13] the 'dreadful hour!' of four o'clock, appreciated that nothing could be achieved while the old Kaiser lived.

On the other hand, William I was aged eighty-eight; the Crown Prince could expect to succeed before long; and it seemed likely that the Crown Princess would then rule Germany through her husband.

So the Crown Princess's daughter continued to dream about her beautiful Bulgarian lover, after her sympathetic uncle had returned home in order to pay a state visit to Ireland. The Viceroy, Lord Spencer, had suggested it; Gladstone had endorsed it; but the Prince of Wales was vexed by the way in which it had been handled by the Prime Minister.

As early as 7 December 1884, Queen Victoria had minuted [14]: 'If the Government wish for it, *they* must pay for the visit.' But Gladstone argued that the Prince ought not to be cajoled and bribed by the Cabinet into doing what was right in the national interest; and that he had a clear duty to visit Ireland at his personal expense, or at that of the Queen.

On the Prince's instructions, Francis Knollys explained [15] (26 January 1885) to Ponsonby, for the Queen's eye:

I have written to Lord Spencer, with the Prince's approval, that the Government (with one or two exceptions) are invariably indifferent to what H.R.H. does, or does not, do; and that this is annoying to him sometimes; that unless the Cabinet really think it desirable that he should undertake the proposed visit, he is reluctant to embark in it; that he feels that Mr Gladstone, on behalf of the Cabinet, should communicate with him on the subject ... and that ..., if the visit does take place, he should go to Ireland at the *express wish* of the Government; ... that he imagines that neither the Queen nor the Cabinet can suppose that he expects to derive any *personal pleasure* from the visit ...'

Queen Victoria begged Gladstone not to create difficulties, and to send a suitable letter to the Prince of Wales; but the Prime Minister had been overworking and his mood was perverse. He wrote, [16] accordingly (3 February), to express the 'very lively satisfaction' with which he had noted the Prince's public-spirited decision to visit Ireland on his personal initiative and in the national interest; and he said nothing about expenses.

Writing [17] (6 February) from Cannes to the Queen, the Prime Minister and the Viceroy, the Prince of Wales declined absolutely to set foot in Ireland unless the strong wish of the cabinet that he should do so at their expense and request, and on their advice and responsibility, was conveyed to him first, unequivocally and in writing, by the Prime Minister. He begged Lord Spencer to make Gladstone understand the kind of letter which he required and, after some delay, he received it.

The Chief Secretary for Ireland, Henry Campbell-Bannerman, considered that Gladstone was wasting a trump card. He argued that a clear statement of the Government's policy, if it had one, would have been more useful than a royal visit at that time; but Gladstone and Spencer held that the visit would provide a useful means of testing the temper of the Irish nation.

Accompanied by Prince Eddy, the Prince and Princess of Wales toured Ireland from 8–27 April 1885. Their reception in Dublin was loyal and enthusiastic, and they left on 13 April for the south where they stayed near Cork at Convamore with Lord and Lady Listowel.

On 14 April, Lord Waterford (Charles Beresford's eldest brother) invited sixty guests to meet the Prince and Princess at luncheon at Curraghmore – a splendid house and property of 100,000 acres, including 7,000 acres of park; but a visit paid to Cork on the following day was much less enjoyable. 'The loyalists', the Prince of Wales wrote [18] (17 April) to Prince George, 'received us with the greatest enthusiasm, but the nationalists, who are virtually separatists, as badly as possible.'

The Prince's equerry, Arthur Ellis, wrote [19] (15 April) to Queen Victoria: 'The truth (and Your Majesty will wish to know the truth beyond every other thing) is that the lower class, the *lazzaroni* of Cork, which exists in overpowering numbers, were rabid rebels. No other word can convey their hostility and behaviour…. and no one who went though this day will ever forget it…. It was like a bad dream. The Prince of Wales showed the greatest calmness and courage.'

A well-dressed middle-class crowd cheered the Prince and

Princess outside the Protestant cathedral, but elsewhere the royal visitors were booed continuously and even pelted with onions. The Prince rejected all suggestions that the programme should be altered or curtailed, and he drove with the Princess, accordingly, through what Arthur Ellis described to Queen Victoria as 'streets filled with sullen faces – hideous, dirty, cruel countenances, hissing and grimacing into one's very face, waving *black* flags and *black* kerchiefs – a nightmare!'

Deeply hurt by that reception, which he refused to discuss, the Prince was more concerned about an incident in Afghanistan which brought the British and Russian Empires again to the verge of war. Appreciating that British attention was concentrated upon the Nile valley, the Russians contemplated an advance in the valley of the Oxus, and they staged a sanguinary affray at Pendjeh, a few miles inside Afghanistan, on 30 March 1885, in order to test the temper of the British nation.

Having suffered much worse things at Disraeli's hands, the Afghans remained calm; but the Government of India was alarmed, and a wave of anti-Russian sentiment convulsed Great Britain and caused a panic on the Stock Exchange. After announcing that all British naval and military forces would be concentrated against Russia (and that the Sudan would be abandoned, in consequence, to the Mahdi), Gladstone obtained a vote of credit of eleven million pounds from the Commons; and, in face of that unexpectedly resolute action, the Russians agreed to submit the incident at Pendjeh to arbitration.

'I hardly see how we can avoid going to war with Russia now', the Prince of Wales wrote [20] (10 April) to Prince George; and he was vexed at being left in the dark. 'It is needless to say', he informed [21] Queen Victoria (19 April), 'that I am kept in perfect ignorance as to what is going on. I very much fear that the Government will give way and believe Russian promises and assurances which are of no value whatever. The result will be that ... our position in India will be imperilled.'

ii

Continuing his Irish tour, the Prince of Wales visited Killarney and Limerick before leaving for loyal Belfast and Londonderry. Everywhere in the North the royal visitors were received with full-throated cheers; and, while staying at Baronscourt with the Duchess of Abercorn, the Prince wrote [22] (26 April) to assure Queen Victoria that more royal visits were necessary to destroy 'the influence, which undoubtedly exists, of those abominable agitators who wish to separate this country from Great Britain'.

After congratulating the Prince of Wales, Gladstone tried again to persuade Queen Victoria to lift the ban upon the Prince's access to Cabinet and Foreign Office papers. He asked only to be allowed to supply, regularly and openly, information which Disraeli had communicated irregularly and surreptitiously; but the Queen replied that the Prime Minister must have been misinformed about Disraeli's habit and that she would tolerate no unauthorized communication between Gladstone and the Prince of Wales.

'I agree, respectfully and decidedly', Gladstone wrote [23] (30 May) to Ponsonby, 'in the opinion that communications to the Prince of Wales as to matters treated in the Cabinet should be by the immediate authority and under the immediate control of the Sovereign. On the other hand, the admission of the Prince of Wales, at his time of life, to an interior knowledge of affairs, appears to me very judicious. …' It was to no purpose, however; Queen Victoria would not agree, and Gladstone felt justified in exercising a personal discretion in communicating privately with the Prince from time to time.

On 22 August 1885 the Prince left Aberdeen aboard *Osborne* on the first stage of a nine weeks' continental holiday. After cruising with a party of friends in Norwegian waters, he went to Drottningholm to stay with the King of Sweden, and subsequently to Bortanga, to stay with Baron Oscar Dickson who staged an elk hunt on his 14,000-acre estate. Four hundred beaters served forty-six guns who were extended over a great distance, and on one day (10 September) an unprecedented total of fifty-two elk were killed.

Refreshed by that novel experience, the Prince of Wales joined the Princess, the Emperor and Empress of Russia, and the King of Greece in Denmark; and he wrote [24] (18 September) to Prince George: 'Our days here are very quiet and pleasant. 9.30, breakfast. Walk immediately afterwards. 1, luncheon. Then driving, riding or walking. Dinner at 6 or 6.30. Tea at 9.30. Then whist and to bed between 11 and 12. ... Unfortunately on the night of 22nd I must leave, as I have promised to pay Count Festetics a visit at Bergeneze in Hungary for the stalking before the season is over.'

At Bergeneze, on Lake Balaton, Tassilo Festetics had assembled a gay party of Hungarian magnates who accompanied the Prince every morning at four-thirty to stalk deer. Returning to breakfast at nine-thirty, the Prince went out again for three hours at 4 p.m.; but one entire day was devoted to partridges when eight guns killed 419 brace.

In Budapest, where he stayed from 3 to 11 October with Count Karolyi, the Prince of Wales was stated [25] by Holstein to have 'led such a fast life ... that even the Hungarians shook their heads'; but evidence exists* that that comment was malicious and that the Prince enjoyed only the routine pattern of the gay life of a Hungarian magnate. He saw much of the Crown Prince Rudolf, and he telegraphed a request that his nephew, Prince William, should come urgently from Berlin to Budapest, as he had something private and important to say to him.

After waiting for his nephew, who made no attempt to hurry, the Prince of Wales wrote [26] (14 October) to condole with Prince George, who had just missed obtaining a first class pilot's certificate in an examination which he had taken: 'You have, I hope, got over your disappointment

* Before he died, Count Geza Andrássy spoke to Sir Michael Adeane about this period, which he remembered, in the life of the Prince of Wales. The only shock ever administered by the Prince in Hungary to a society which was admittedly almost shock-proof was caused by his attempt a few years later (see page 277 below) to introduce Baron Hirsch into its midst.

about a First. It would, of course, have been *better* if you *had* obtained it; but being only within 20 marks is *very* satisfactory, and shows that there is no favouritism in your case.'

Prince William, who reached Budapest on 11 October, was informed [27] by his uncle that evening that his projected visit to Sandringham during November would have to be cancelled. The Prince explained that his nephew could not well come to Sandringham without calling at Windsor upon Queen Victoria; but that the attitude which he had adopted towards his sister's affair with the Prince of Bulgaria had annoyed Queen Victoria so greatly that she had no wish to see her grandson.

Prince William was well aware that his mother was only waiting for the old Kaiser's death to announce his sister's engagement to Sandro, who was regarded by Queen Victoria, as well as by the Crown Princess, as a matchless hero of romance. He appreciated that the Prince of Wales had clutched thankfully at a weak excuse to avoid entertaining him at Sandringham; and, on his return to Berlin, he informed [28] Herbert Bismarck that 'he was very glad he now had a weapon he could use against his mother if she should reproach him with not being sufficiently well disposed towards the Queen of England', whom he dubbed, rudely, 'the old hag'.

Three years later, after succeeding prematurely to the throne, Prince William was able to take revenge; but the Prince of Wales understood his sister's weakness. At the suggestion of Lord Rosebery he had written, [29] during the summer of 1885, to reproach her for having inflamed German opinion unnecessarily against England through her tactlessness in flaunting too openly her English nationality and outlook, regardless of German susceptibilities.

After settling his business with Prince William, the Prince of Wales travelled (12 October) to Vienna and to Paris, before returning to Marlborough House in time for breakfast on 27 October. He left before luncheon for the Jockey Club at Newmarket, and was concerned by the prospect of a tremendous political crisis on the issue of Irish Home Rule to which he was most strongly opposed.

The defeat of Gladstone's Government by a combination of Conservatives and Irish Nationalists during a Budget debate in June 1885 had not resulted in an immediate General Election because new electoral registers could not be completed until November. Lord Salisbury had formed a minority Conservative Government; and the General Election of November 1885 left the Irish members holding the balance of power. 335 Liberals faced 249 Conservatives, and 86 Irish Nationalists united under Charles Parnell; and Salisbury continued in office until his Government was defeated on 27 January 1886.

The real (although not the ostensible) cause of that defeat was the Government's announcement of its intention to introduce a new Irish Coercion Bill, and to apply it with rigour. Gladstone's secret conversion to Home Rule had become known in mid-December, as a result of his son's indiscretion; and his right wing was already in revolt when he received (30 January 1886) a summons from Queen Victoria to form his third administration.

Instructed by Queen Victoria, Ponsonby sent a detailed summary of the situation to the Prince of Wales, who replied [30] (31 January):

... I am very grateful to the Queen for having instructed you to give me some information regarding the present Ministerial crisis. I purposely have not written to her, knowing how much she has to do and think of, and deeply sympathize with her in the great difficulties she has to contend with. ...

You say that when you saw Mr Gladstone (at midnight) he did not enter very deeply into his policy, but that the chief features related to Ireland, and to some means, if the Irish members are reasonable, of meeting the wishes of the people of that country and of preserving the integrity of the United Kingdom, under the paramount rule of the Queen and Imperial Government! That sounds like an Irish bull!

Either Mr Gladstone's Government must go in for Home Rule, or for coercive measures. I see no alternative. If the former, which means 'meeting the wishes of the Irish people', the integrity of the United Kingdom cannot be maintained. If the latter, then only can it exist.

The Prince added that he knew for certain that Lord

Hartington, G. J. Goschen and Sir Henry James would never join a Home Rule government, and that he believed that others also would refuse: 'If Lord Spencer is "talked over", I lose for ever all the high opinion I have ever held of him as a politician and a man of honour.' He suggested Lord Rosebery for the Foreign Office, because Lord Granville's health was failing visibly, and added that the Duke of Cambridge would be happy if Henry Campbell-Bannerman became Secretary for War.

On 1 February, Ponsonby thanked [31] the Prince for his 'very valuable' suggestion about Campbell-Bannerman, which was adopted after Gladstone had attempted vainly to force H. C. E. Childers upon the Queen. The Queen was eager at first to persuade Gladstone to make her son-in-law, Lord Lorne, Under-Secretary for the Colonies, but the Prince dissuaded her, and Lorne came round to the Prince's view: 'I hardly think', the Prince wrote [32] (2 February) to Ponsonby, 'that the Queen's son-in-law should form part of the Government, no matter what Party is in power. And how could he form part of a "Home Rule" Government! I am very strong on that point. ...'

On a hint from the Queen, the Prince had postponed his annual visit to the South of France until the new Government was formed, although he told Ponsonby: '*Entre nous*, I cannot see how I can be of any use to the Queen and her Government, much as I should like to be.' He left on 21 February with Prince George, who joined his ship at Genoa on 4 March; and on 5 March the Prince wrote [33] to him from Monte Carlo:

On seeing you going off by the train yesterday, I felt very sad, and you could, I am sure, see that I had a lump in my throat when I wished you good-bye. We have been so much together, and especially lately, that I felt the parting doubly. ...

On returning to Cannes to-day I shall miss you more than ever, my dear Georgy, and at the ball at Baroness Hoffmann's – How I wish you could be at it!

Now God bless you, my dear boy, and may He guard you against all harm and evil, and bless and protect you. Don't forget your devoted Papa, A.E.

On returning to London, the Prince of Wales informed [34] Prince George (11 April) that nobody expected Gladstone's Home Rule Bill to pass, and that, from the Peer's gallery in the House of Commons, he had heard three eminent Liberals – Lord Hartington, Joseph Chamberlain and G. O. Trevelyan – deliver 'most damaging' speeches against it. Foreseeing a crash, he wrote [35] (14 May) to Lord Carrington, who had gone out to govern New South Wales: 'Another General Election, so soon again, will be a very serious matter; and a most untoward event in the middle of the London Season!'

93 Liberals voted with the Conservatives in the Commons when the division was taken on the second reading of the Irish Home Rule Bill during the early hours of 8 June 1886. The Bill was rejected; a General Election followed at once; and the Liberal Party was crushed and split. 316 Conservatives, supported by 78 Liberal Unionists, were returned with a combined majority of 118 over 191 Gladstonian Liberals and 85 Irish Nationalists.

On returning to power, Lord Salisbury authorized his Foreign Secretary, Lord Iddesleigh, to continue a practice, initiated earlier that year by Lord Rosebery on his personal responsibility, of sending copies of some secret Foreign Office despatches to the Prince of Wales to read. Salisbury was kind to the Prince, who was most careful to be discreet, and who asked the Prime Minister to find a good post for Lord Cadogan, and to make Lord Charles Beresford, who was bored in the House of Commons, 'head of the Irish Police Force'.

Salisbury made Cadogan Lord Privy Seal, and Beresford Fourth Sea Lord, after promising the Prince that he would try to find something more important for the latter in due course; but Beresford caused constant trouble. When he resigned, in January 1888 the Prince of Wales explained [36] (15 January) to Prince George that their friend had 'resigned his seat in the Admiralty for the 100th time and it has been accepted as I fancy his colleagues could not get on any more with him, as *entre nous*, he laid down the law too

much'. Private motives prompted* Beresford to apply for a
return to active service in December 1889; and he was given
command of the cruiser *Undaunted*.

Lord Randolph Churchill, who was appointed Chancellor
of the Exchequer and Leader of the House of Commons in
August 1886, when he was aged 36, became the Prince's
principal political confidant, in place of Sir Charles Dilke.
Dilke might have succeeded ultimately to the leadership of
the Liberal Party if his career had not been blasted by a disastrous divorce scandal; and the Prince informed [37] Lord
Carrington (14 March 1886) that their friend had 'played his
cards very badly, and been badly advised'.

Other friends who joined the Prince's inner circle during
the late 1880s were three members of the Sassoon family
(Albert, Arthur and Reuben) who belonged to the *Haute
Juiverie* and who had reached England from Bagdad, via
Bombay, and the Comte de Paris, Pretender to the French
throne, who made his home in England after being exiled
permanently from France in June 1886. Two new friends
were Lord Brooke (Lord Warwick's heir) and his wife
Frances (Daisy) who was aged twenty-six in 1886, and who
was the very beautiful heiress of her grandfather, the last
Lord Maynard.

The Prince of Wales did not accompany the Princess to
Denmark in September 1886, because very recent events had
made him unwilling to meet his brother-in-law, Sasha, the
Emperor of Russia. On the night of 21–22 August, agents of
the Czar had surrounded the Prince of Bulgaria's palace in
Sofia, abducted Sandro and compelled him to abdicate at
pistol point. Queen Victoria and the German Crown Princess
were almost prostrate with grief and rage; the Prince of
Wales was exceedingly angry; and the young Prince William rejoiced. Those personal attitudes, however, were of
little consequence except in so far as they reflected those of
the Great Powers.

In November 1885 the Prince of Bulgaria had fought a victorious campaign against King Milan of Serbia, who was a
client of the Emperor Francis Joseph, and relations between

* See p. 290 below.

Austria–Hungary and Russia were strained in consequence. Bulgaria was regarded by the Great Powers as a Russian sphere of influence, although Sandro, encouraged by England, his subjects and personal ambition, had made himself odious to the Russian Government; and a serious dispute between Austria–Hungary and Russia could have drawn all Europe into war.

Bismarck had formed with Austria-Hungary, behind Russia's back in 1879, a secret alliance which was transformed, by the adherence of Italy, into the Triple Alliance in 1882. Germany was pledged to aid Austria if any dispute in the Balkans should precipitate an Austro-Russian war, but Bismarck did his utmost, while he lived, to foster good relations between Russia and Austria.

That Austro–German alliance helped to precipitate the supreme catastrophe of 1914, but Bismarck held that Germany, after 1871, had nothing more to gain by war. For that reason he restrained Austria–Hungary in November 1885, and was delighted when Prince Alexander of Battenberg disappeared from the scene. Sandro had forfeited everyone's confidence, except that of his subjects, and of England; and a new and more amenable prince, Ferdinand of Coburg, who was accepted in Vienna and tolerated in St Petersburg, was chosen in July 1887 to rule Bulgaria after Prince Waldemar of Denmark, a younger brother of the Princess of Wales, had been unsuccessfully approached.

The ex-Prince of Bulgaria * was staying at Windsor Castle with Queen Victoria on 20 December 1886, when Lord Randolph Churchill arrived to dine and stay the night. The Chancellor of the Exchequer, who despatched on Windsor Castle notepaper a letter of resignation to Lord Salisbury, said nothing about it to the Queen who was justifiably angry at being left to learn the news when she opened *The Times* on 23 December. Lord Randolph had not expected that his

---

* After returning to his father's home in Darmstadt, Prince Alexander of Battenberg fell in love with an opera singer whom he married secretly in February 1889. He took the name of Count Hartenau, retired into private life and died at Graz, aged thirty-six, in 1893.

resignation would be accepted, and the Prince of Wales informed [38] Prince George (27 December) that, when lunching alone with Lady Randolph on 22 December, both had been in complete ignorance of what had occurred.

The shock was profound, and Lord Randolph, who wrote (23 December) to explain his reasons to the Prince of Wales, enclosed a sheaf of recent correspondence with his colleagues. He had been anxious to pare the Service Estimates in order to keep the Budget down to £94½ millions, while doubling Local Government grants and carrying out reforms in that field in accordance with the principles of the Tory democracy which he had preached for some years. He had trusted that his colleagues would accept those demands and implore him to stay in office; but, when his resignation was accepted, he found it impossible to make any satisfactory public statement because Budget details were secret.

The Prince forwarded Lord Randolph's letter, with its enclosures, to the Queen, who was incensed at what she termed a 'most objectionable ... and even dangerous correspondence'. She asked Ponsonby to see that it was broken off forthwith, and Ponsonby and Knollys were at a loss to find a means of relaying that demand in a form which was likely to be acceptable to the Prince of Wales, who wrote [39] (22 January 1887) to his mother at considerable length:

You are, if you will allow me to say so, rather hard on Lord R. Churchill. I do not enter into the question whether he was right or wrong in resigning on the point at issue between him and his colleagues, but he has at any rate the courage of his opinions. ...

Ld Randolph is a poor man and a very ambitious one, but he gave up £5,000 a year in ceasing to be Chancellor of the Exchequer. Now that he has left office I am not likely to see much of him as he goes but little in society. Though I certainly do not agree in all his public views (and I have often told him so) still, I cannot help admiring many of his great qualities. Should his life be spared (and he has not a good life) he is bound to play sooner or later a prominent part in the politics and the destinies of this country.

You remind me, my dearest Mama, that I am 45, a point I

have not forgotten, although I am glad to say that I feel younger. You are, I think, rather hard upon me when you talk of the round of gaieties I indulge in at Cannes, London, Homburg and Cowes. ...

I like Cannes excessively, especially for its climate and scenery, just the same as you do Aix, which you tell me you are going to this year. To be away from England in the South for 3 weeks is a very beneficial change to me. ... It is certainly my intention to stay a short time at Cannes, and I shall have the great happiness to see dear Georgy who is coming over from Malta. ...

With regard to London, I think, dear Mama, you know well that the time we spend there is not *all* amusement, very much the reverse. To Homburg I only go for my health and to Cowes to get the sea breezes and yachting which, after the fatigue of the London Season, are an immense relaxation. Nobody knows better than I do that I am not perfect – still I try to perform the many and ever-increasing duties which lie before me to the best of my ability, nor do I shirk many which I confess I would prefer not to have to fulfil. There is an old English saying that 'all work and no play makes Jack a dull boy' – and there is a great deal of truth in it. ...

The Prince went to Cannes in February 1887 and took part in the battle of flowers; and in March to Berlin where he helped to celebrate the ninetieth birthday of the old Kaiser. He went to Homburg in August after writing [40] (13 August) to Prince George:

When I wished you good-bye on Thursday in your cabin I had a lump in my throat which I am sure you saw. It is the greatest bane in one's life saying good-bye, especially to one's children, relations and friends. ...

I was sorry to learn from hints that you had dropped that you were not as keen about the Navy as formerly. This I should greatly deplore – as no finer profession for an Englishman exists in the world, and our great wish is that you should be fond of it. Every year as a profession it becomes more interesting, and some members of our family ought always to be actively employed in it. If you left the Navy, what would you do? Would you like to lead an idle life? I feel sure not.

Prince Eddy, who had left Cambridge, where he had been awarded the honorary degree of Doctor of Law, was serving with his father's regiment, the 10th Hussars, in which he was unhappy; but Prince George reassured his father about his own satisfaction with the Navy. The Prince of Wales told [41] him (20 August) that Homburg was full of visitors, 'most of whom I know, more or less'; and that he had enjoyed a series of picnic parties given by Reuben Sassoon, on one occasion for as many as seventy guests.

From Homburg the Prince went to Fredensborg in Denmark, where he joined the Princess and resumed his friendship with the Emperor and Empress of Russia, who were fellow guests: 'You can picture our life here', he wrote [42] (9 September 1887) to Prince George, 'and all the noise and racket; but "we are a very happy Family, *we are*!" You are the only one wanting to make it complete.'

The average annual number of public engagements undertaken by the Prince of Wales increased to forty-two during the 1880s. That average continued to increase, even discounting 1887 which was an exceptionally busy year because he bore most of the burden of entertaining Indian, colonial and foreign visitors who attended the Jubilee celebrations of the fiftieth anniversary of Queen Victoria's accession to the throne. Apart from Indian maharajahs, blazing with diamonds, the tall German Crown Prince, Frederick William, made the greatest impression upon the British public, although his health had begun visibly to fail. The Prince of Wales was constantly at his brother-in-law's side, but Prince William, who accompanied his father, complained [43] that his uncle had ignored him almost to the point of appearing to be unaware of his existence.

The Jubilee celebrations, which released a surge of emotion, tempted the Prince of Wales to establish a permanent memorial. He appealed for funds to found in South Kensington an Imperial Institute, which was intended to promote wider public knowledge of the life, scenery and industries of India, the Colonies and the United Kingdom; and also to give scientific and technical advice about the exploitation of natural resources.

The Prince loved shows and had been associated with exhibitions all his life. They stemmed from the Great Exhibition of 1851, and the most recent had been a Colonial and Indian Exhibition, opened by the Queen in South Kensington in 1886, and known colloquially as the 'Colinderies', which became the genesis of the Imperial Institute. A profit of £25,000, made by the Colinderies, was handed over to the Imperial Institute; and the Prince of Wales would have liked to perpetuate a scheme which he had initiated for the cheap admission of artisans.

In welcoming a deputation of trades union leaders, which included Henry Broadhurst, M.P., in his ballroom at Sandringham on 15 November 1886, the Prince observed that two and a half million 'artisans' certificates' had been distributed throughout the country 'at my request'; and that 1,232,010 working class people had in consequence 'derived, as I sincerely trust and believe, useful instruction together with rational relaxation and amusement' by visiting the Colinderies. He continued:

I trust that before you leave for your return to London, you will judge for yourself of the manner in which I have attempted to discharge some of my duties as a country gentleman; and that you may be convinced, by what you see, that I have not been unmindful of my obligations as a landlord and employer of labour.

After personally conducting the trades union leaders over his house, the Prince left for Newmarket. He deputed to his agent, Edmund Beck, the task of showing the deputation his gardens, farm buildings and a few cottages, and of entertaining them to a high tea in the Sandringham Working Men's Club.

Two or three maharajahs responded generously to the Prince's appeal for funds for the Imperial Institute, but the Indian and Colonial Governments disgusted the Prince of Wales by refusing to subscribe. The British public, and even his personal friends held back; and he wrote [44] (12 August 1887) to Lord Carrington: 'What a pity that the Imperial Institute does not find favour among those whom you are now governing; but we must have patience, and I trust that when New South Wales hears that the edifice is actually built, they will not hang back but give a handsome donation.'

Few handsome donations were received, and the public showed its boredom after Queen Victoria had opened the building at last in 1893. The Prince of Wales lost all interest* in consequence, and blamed the colonial governments for what he regarded as a dismal failure.

Leaving England on 10 February 1888, the Prince went to San Remo to see his brother-in-law, the Crown Prince Frederick, who had developed cancer of the throat and upon whom a tracheotomy had been performed in order to avert suffocation: 'Poor Aunt Vicky is worried to death', the Prince of Wales informed[45] Prince George (18 February). 'There are 7 doctors and some 50 reporters of different newspapers! The former do not alas!, agree among themselves. It is all very sad.' He added that he had relieved his feelings by taking part at Nice on 16 February in the battle of flowers, 'and it was capital fun, though there were not so many carriages as usual'.

The Queen and the Foreign Office had been disturbed, in the meantime, by the consequences of the Prince's action in handing to Lord Randolph Churchill a personal letter of introduction from the Princess of Wales to her sister, the Empress of Russia. The Churchills were lionized by Russian society during the winter of 1887–8; and Lord Randolph, who charmed the Emperor and Empress, contrived to convey an impression to the public that the Prince of Wales had sponsored his journey and that the British Government desired an Anglo-Russian understanding.

Lord Randolph's long reports to the Prince of Wales were extraordinarily bright and vivid, and although the Prince assured the Queen and Lord Salisbury that the visit was devoid of political significance, the Queen begged[46] her son (3 January) to cease all correspondence with someone so

* The Imperial Institute was transferred to London University in 1899; and in 1946 the Minister of Education became responsible for its administration and finance. The Institute (which changed its name to Commonwealth in 1958) continues to discharge its educational functions, but its scientific and technical activities are controlled by various departments. It receives annual grants-in-aid from Parliament, as well as from commonwealth and colonial governments.

unreliable and indiscreet. The Prince continued, nevertheless, to treat Churchill as an intimate friend and to cultivate
the friendship of Baron de Staal, the Russian Ambassador in
London, whom he found very congenial; and Lord Salisbury caused an official statement to be issued that Lord
Randolph represented no one except himself.

On 10 March 1888, the Prince and Princess of Wales celebrated their silver wedding anniversary at Marlborough
House. Queen Victoria, who came to dinner, brought an
immense loving-cup, and other presents included a diamond
and ruby cross from the Prince to the Princess; a diamond
and ruby necklace from the Emperor and Empress of Russia; some old Dresden vases from the German Emperor and
Empress; a personal letter and the honorary colonelcy of the
12th Hungarian Hussars from the Emperor Francis Joseph;
a diamond tiara from 365 society ladies; a diamond butter-
fly from the United Grand Lodge of Freemasons; a silver
model of the proposed Imperial Institute from the Lord
Mayor and Corporation of London; 'a pair of the largest
diamond and pearl solitaires ever seen' from Lord Rothschild, and a gold bouquet holder 'encrusted with precious
stones' from Lady Rothschild; an engagement book bound
in gold and 'encrusted with precious stones' from Leopold de
Rothschild; and two leading articles in *The Times*.

The first article suggested that while the occasions were
rare when the Prince's 'conduct is less free from reproach
than his well-wishers could desire', he could do well to conquer 'the unfortunate weakness which has led him to
patronize American cattle-drovers and prize-fighters'; and
the Princess was praised for weaning her 'good-natured and
tolerant' husband from the 'cruel practice' of shooting live
pigeons on rifle ranges. The second article, although even
more pompous, was wholly laudatory. The Prince was praised
for all his 'charitable, educational, industrial, artistic and
scientific' endeavours, as well as for his services 'to what may
be called the religion of the family throughout England.'

On 16 March 1888, the Prince of Wales represented the
Queen in Berlin at the funeral of the old Emperor, William
I, who had been born in 1797 and governed by Prince Bis-

marck for many years. His gentle successor, Frederick III, who had displayed military capacity in three wars, was regarded, nevertheless, as un-Prussian in outlook, and had been excluded from political influence.

Although too ill to attend his father's funeral in the biting wind of 16 March 1888, the Emperor Frederick rallied sufficiently to be present, with the Empress and the Prince of Wales, at the wedding of his younger son, Prince Henry, and Princess Irene of Hesse on 24 May. The Prince of Wales was distressed by the complaints which the Empress poured into his ears about the conduct of her eldest son, Prince William; and he was furious when Count Herbert Bismarck suggested that an Emperor who could not speak should not reign.

Frederick III died after a reign of 99 days on 15 June, aged fifty-seven; and the Prince of Wales, accompanied by the Princess and Prince Eddy, attended the funeral. Because she hated Prussia so bitterly, the Princess of Wales had not visited Berlin for eleven years, but she believed that the Emperor Frederick had intended to make some reparation to Denmark, and Queen Victoria noted [47] in her diary that she 'was greatly relieved to hear that dear Alix would go with Bertie to Berlin, as I begged her to'.

The Prince tried to console the widowed Empress Frederick by suggesting that her son, William II, whom he dubbed privately William the Great, would acquire wisdom and behave modestly; but his sister could not agree. Her hopes had been blasted by her husband's cruel death, and the Prince of Wales was almost equally dismayed. It would be unprofitable to speculate about the possible effects of the conflicting pressures to which the Emperor Frederick III would have been exposed, had he lived, but his mental agony might have exceeded the physical suffering caused by his illness.

Frederick III's private secretary, Lieut.-Colonel Summerfield, considered [48] (in 1885) that it was 'absolutely inconceivable' that his master 'should ever, no matter what the circumstances, assert his own will in opposition to his wife's. You have only to look at what she's made of him. But for her, he'd be the average man, very arrogant, good-tempered, of mediocre gifts and with a great deal of common sense. But *now*, he's not a man at all. ... He's a mere cipher. ...'

With that disposition the Emperor Frederick would have had to choose between Bismarck, advocating the maintenance of the *status quo* and a firm understanding with Russia; young Germany, represented by Prince William, advocating a forward policy upon all fronts; and the Empress and her brother advocating what the vast majority of Germans would have denounced as a policy of subordinating German interests to those of England. The policies which were pursued after Frederick III's untimely death, and which led Germany along the road to 1914, were shaped by elemental forces which only the greatest strength and wisdom could have controlled.

The Prince of Wales wrote [49] (16 June) to Prince George: 'Try, my dear Georgy, never to forget Uncle Fritz. He was one of the finest and noblest characters ever known. If he had a fault, he was *too* good for this world.' He wrote [50] two days later to Queen Victoria: 'I felt, on leaving the Church, that I had parted from the noblest and best man I had ever known, except my ever-to-be-lamented Father.'

11

William the Great

1888–90

IF FREDERICK III had lived, the Prince of Wales' ambition to serve his country by supplementing regular diplomatic channels would have been realized to the full. As the friend and brother-in-law of the Kaiser (Fritz) as well as of the Czar (Sasha), he had looked forward to many years of useful and thoroughly congenial para-diplomatic activity, but his nephew, William II, obstructed that plan. Refusing to take his uncle seriously, he snubbed and ignored him, and employed his imperial rank to challenge the European social primacy which the Prince of Wales, whom he dubbed 'the old Peacock', had hitherto enjoyed.

For that reason the death of Frederick III after a reign of less than one hundred days was a bitter political as well as personal loss to the Prince of Wales: 'He was one of those men', he informed[1] Lord Carrington (9 August 1888), 'you sometimes hear of, but rarely see ... but short as his reign was, his name will not be forgotten, though those wicked Bismarcks wish that it should be, because his politics were liberal and theirs are not.'

The Prince of Wales imagined, mistakenly, that his nephew's policy was likely to remain in tune with that of the Imperial Chancellor, Prince Bismarck, and with that of Bismarck's son, Count Herbert Bismarck, who was German Secretary of State for Foreign Affairs; but the supreme aim of the old Chancellor was to preserve the *status quo*. The dynamic young men who surrounded the young Kaiser were eager, on the other hand, for a forward policy in the Balkans, Asiatic Turkey and Africa; and William II made up his mind, accordingly, to dismiss Bismarck and to govern Germany himself.

There was nothing in the German constitution to restrain

the young ruler whose charm, when he chose to exert it, rivalled that of the Prince of Wales, and who became the spoilt darling of Europe. His intention was divined at once by the shrewd and hard-working Emperor, Alexander III. The Czar appreciated that Bismarck stood in the way of the adoption by Germany of an anti-Russian policy; and Bismarck's fall in March 1890 was the prelude to the formation of a Franco-Russian treaty of alliance which Bismarck had striven to avert.

Before his fall, Bismarck tried hard to improve German relations with Great Britain and France, as well as with Russia; and Count Herbert Bismarck came to London in March 1889 to promote an open Anglo-German alliance. That proposal which would have operated against France, and for which Parliamentary ratification was requested specifically by Bismarck, was rejected by Lord Salisbury who believed, nevertheless, in the possibility of an enduring Anglo-German understanding, and who did his utmost to woo that untried but very important political factor, Kaiser William II.

The Prince of Wales was on bad personal terms with Herbert Bismarck, to whom he had talked indiscreetly in Berlin three days after the funeral of Frederick III. In the presence of the Princess he had asked, disingenuously, whether, if Kaiser Frederick had lived, concessions would have been made by Germany on the questions of Alsace-Lorraine, North Schleswig and the sequestrated property of the Duke of Cumberland, who had married the youngest sister of the Princess of Wales.

The Duke of Cumberland was the son and heir of the last King of Hanover, who had fought on the losing side during the Austro-Prussian war of 1866. His kingdom and fortune had been swallowed by Prussia in consequence, and the Prince of Wales had offended many of his Prussian kinsfolk by parading frequently his sympathy with the misfortunes of the Hanoverian family.*

* Four years later, Kaiser William II caused the Duke of Cumberland's personal fortune to be restored; but it is unlikely that that overdue act of restitution was influenced by the Prince of Wales.

Young Bismarck complained that only the presence of the Princess of Wales had prevented him from couching in more vigorous language his replies to the Prince's tactless questions; and William II resented his uncle's interference. He was determined to teach him a lesson, and in a speech at Frankfurt-an-der-Oder on 16 August, he described as intolerable insults all reports that his revered father would ever have consented to yield voluntarily what the Prussian sword had won.

The Prince of Wales moved to Sandringham after the Emperor Frederick's funeral, because Court mourning made London appear intolerable. He had felt constrained even to forgo his daily ride in Rotten Row, and he was amazed to hear that his nephew, 'William the Great', was proposing to pay a State visit to Russia within a month of his father's death.

The Prince of Wales chose that moment to fling himself into a quarrel which he had helped personally to open between his friend, Sir Robert Morier, the British Ambassador in St Petersburg, and Count Herbert Bismarck. The Prince warned the Ambassador that young Bismarck was spreading a lying story which reflected upon his professional honour, and that the elder Bismarck regarded him as a personal enemy.

Herbert Bismarck alleged that Morier, while serving in the British Legation at Darmstadt during the Franco-Prussian War, had revealed to the French Marshal Bazaine the operational Plan of the Crown Prince Frederick's army. Herbert Bismarck, who had been serving with that army, had been wounded in the battle which followed, but his motive in spreading that story so belatedly was to discredit Morier's friend, the Empress Frederick, as well as to blast Morier's reputation and to compel him to resign.

Morier had convinced the Prince of Wales, while staying at Sandringham, that an Anglo-Russian understanding was not merely desirable but possible; and the Bismarcks considered that Morier's efforts to drive a wedge between Germany and Russia were meeting with success. Because he was extremely sensitive on that subject, Prince Bismarck told [2]

Sir Edward Malet, the British Ambassador in Berlin (who alerted the Prince of Wales), that he regarded Morier as a personal enemy.

After consulting together in Berlin, Morier and Malet called on 23 July 1888 at Marlborough House upon the Prince of Wales, who assured them that his sole motive was to clear the Honour of the Empress Frederick from the disgraceful imputation that she had betrayed her husband's military secrets to Morier. He urged them to press Lord Salisbury to demand an official explanation from the German Government; but Salisbury informed[3] the two angry ambassadors that he was not prepared to jeopardize his policy by quarrelling with the Bismarcks.

Morier obtained easily (8 August), from Marshal Bazaine, a categorical denial in writing of the lie which Herbert Bismarck had spread; but Salisbury argued that the matter was too vague to support serious analysis or discussion. He suggested[4] (16 October) that the Prince of Wales had been impulsive and indiscreet, but added that 'even a tempest in a teacup can at times be inconvenient'.

'It is inconceivable to me', the Prince wrote[5] (31 July) to Queen Victoria, 'that Lord Salisbury does not see the gravity of the matter.' He assured his mother that Herbert Bismarck lacked 'the instincts of a gentleman'; that 'if he were tackled he would give way at once'; and that 'Lord Palmerston or the late Lord Derby would never have permitted such insults heaped on one of your ambassadors to be passed unnoticed'. Queen Victoria was anxious to clear her daughter's reputation, and, on that account, Salisbury authorized Malet reluctantly to ask Herbert Bismarck for a personal explanation. No satisfaction could be obtained and, after a letter from Morier to Herbert Bismarck had elicited an insulting reply, Prince Bismarck proceeded to implement his maxim : 'courtesy in diplomacy – rudeness in the Press'. German newspapers launched attacks, accordingly, against the Prince of Wales, the Empress Frederick and Sir Robert Morier, and much ill-feeling was caused.

While the Princess of Wales and her daughters went to stay with the King of Denmark and later, with the Duke of

Cumberland, the Prince left Cowes (14 August) for Homburg where he played a great deal of lawn tennis. He was much distressed at the start of that ten weeks' holiday to receive news of the sudden death of his Canadian friend, Sir John Rose. After managing the Prince's Canadian tour, Rose had settled in England where he became the mainstay of the Duchy of Cornwall, of the Imperial Institute and of all the exhibition work with which the Prince's name was associated. He had made himself indispensable; the Imperial Institute suffered by his death, and the Prince described his loss as 'irreparable'.

On 15 August and again on 2 September the Prince of Wales wrote[6] to the Kaiser to ask the exact date on which his nephew proposed to pay his State visit to Vienna. The Prince said that he would interrupt a hunting trip, if necessary, in order to be present with the Emperor Francis Joseph and the Crown Prince Rudolph when the Emperor William arrived; but he had received no reply to either letter when he reached the Grand Hotel, Vienna, on 10 September 1888 in time for breakfast.

Immediately after breakfast, the Prince of Wales donned his red and gold uniform as Honorary Colonel of the 12th Hungarian Hussars, in order to receive the Austrian Emperor and Crown Prince who asked how he would like to be entertained. A programme was produced which involved the absence of the Prince of Wales from Vienna on 3 October; and, after the Prince had approved it in principle, the Emperor remarked casually that the Kaiser was due to arrive on 3 October.

The Prince of Wales said[7] immediately that he would return to Vienna on that day; that he would remain there throughout his nephew's visit; and that he would send to Berlin in good time for his uniform as Honorary Colonel of the Blücher Hussars. His visitors departed without offering any comment, and the Prince, after paying a number of calls, dined that evening with the Emperor at the Burg.

On the following day, after being photographed in his gay Hungarian uniform and after paying more calls, the Prince returned to his hotel to entertain the British Ambassador, Sir Augustus Paget, and Lady Paget to luncheon. Paget arrived early at the hotel and asked to see the Prince's senior equerry, Major-General Arthur Ellis, alone and at once.

Paget said that he had a most disagreeable communication to make. He had seen the Foreign Minister, Count Kalnoky, who had given him to understand that the presence of the Prince of Wales in Vienna during the Kaiser's visit would be unacceptable to the Emperor William and therefore embarrassing to the Emperor Francis Joseph.

Paget explained that he had seen Kalnoky immediately after the Foreign Minister had seen the German Ambassador, Prince Reuss, and that there could be no possibility of a misunderstanding. That news was broken to the Prince of Wales, who was astonished and indignant and who racked his brains to discover a reason. He told [8] Paget that he was on good terms with his nephew and that he had been afraid of exciting ill-natured gossip by absenting himself from the capital while the Kaiser was there; but within twenty-four hours all Vienna was buzzing with the report that the Kaiser had threatened to cancel his visit unless his uncle was asked to depart.

That afternoon the Prince went to the races before attending at five o'clock a gala dinner given by the Emperor in honour of the Czar's birthday. He entrained after dinner, with the Emperor and the Crown Prince, for Croatia, to attend the autumn manœuvres of his host's army; and ridiculous articles in the Austrian and German press suggested that, under cover of a pursuit of pleasure, the Prince of Wales wanted to interfere in the forthcoming conversations between the Austrian and German Emperors, to embroil both with Russia and to make mischief on behalf of France.

After informing the Austrian Emperor that he would visit Rumania during the German Emperor's stay in Austria-Hungary, the Prince of Wales made a dignified effort to reach an accord with his tiresome nephew. He dictated (12 September) a letter [9], for General Ellis's signature, to the British military attaché in Berlin, Colonel Charles Swaine, who was instructed privately to find means of ensuring that it was actually read by the Kaiser. The key passage read:

... Of course someone may have made mischief, but ... the Prince of Wales only regrets that, if the Emperor had any personal grievance against him, he did not write to him himself, rather than send messages through the Ambassador, which at once assumes an official aspect.

I am now authorized by the Prince of Wales to ask you to ascertain from H.M. *what is the meaning of all this?* – as you can imagine the very false position towards his Imperial host in which H.R.H. now finds himself....

Swaine had been treated in the past as a personal friend by the Kaiser as well as by the Prince of Wales; but at the German army's autumn manœuvres the Kaiser cut him. Swaine, in consequence, had to enclose Ellis's letter with a personal one of his own which the Kaiser, treading on air, professed to regard as a gross presumption. When it became clear that no reply would be vouchsafed, Sir Augustus Paget, after reporting the facts to Lord Salisbury, wrote [10] privately (25 September) to impress upon the Prince of Wales:

the *all importance* of Your Royal Highness being *more than guarded* in anything you say about the Emperor William.

I am perfectly certain, from what has been told me, that all the present trouble comes from stories having been repeated to His Imperial Majesty of what Your Royal Highness has said. Some of those stories have been repeated to me. I need not say that I do not believe them, but it is necessary to avoid saying anything *whatsoever* which may be made use of as a foundation for the gossip of the malevolent or idle....

One of the Prince's stock remarks about his nephew was that 'William the Great needs to learn that he is living at the end of the nineteenth century and not in the Middle Ages'; and he was too careless about the company in which he spoke. Count Tassilo Festetics, at whose castle on Lake Balaton the Prince went to stay, was notoriously indiscreet, as also was the Crown Prince Rudolf.

Before leaving Budapest by steamer (2 October) for Rumania, the Prince of Wales enjoyed a few gay days and nights in Vienna, Budapest and their environs with the Crown

Prince Rudolf, whose company he found very congenial, and on whose private life he turned an indulgent eye. He was charmed by the King and Queen of Rumania, who entertained him with charades and amateur theatricals at Sinaia, and he informed [11] his mother (5 October) that he felt 'thoroughly at home'. He added: 'I felt sure how pained, surprised and indignant you would be at William's conduct to me. The more I think the matter over the more unaccountable it seems to me. I propose, however, to take no further steps until I have heard from or seen Sir A. Paget.'

After three days at Sinaia, the Prince of Wales departed to shoot bear at Gorgeny in Transylvania with the Crown Prince Rudolf, but no bears were shot, or even sighted, because they had withdrawn into the high mountains from the dry heat of the foothills. 'It was *most* disappointing,' the Prince wrote [12] (12 October) to Prince George, 'and the Crown Prince was dreadfully put out. ... But we were a very cheery party – capital cook, Hungarian band, and splendid weather.'

Returning to Vienna after the Kaiser's departure, the Prince dined (14 October) with the Emperor before leaving by the night train with the Crown Prince for Neuburg in Styria. There, on the following day, seven rifles killed thirty chamois in three hours, and the Prince of Wales, who killed four and wounded two and who described [13] that as 'the prettiest sport I have ever seen for a long time', departed (16 October) for Paris.

From Paris the Prince wrote [14] (20 October) to Prince George: 'I have been twice to the theatre and, last night, to a circus where water was introduced into the arena, and there was a mimic sea-fight. Yesterday I visited M. Pasteur's laboratory and saw 20 patients inoculated. ...' He left Paris on the evening of 21 October after a day's shooting with Alphonse de Rothschild at Ferrières; and he discussed the Vienna incident next day with Lord Salisbury for half an hour at Marlborough House before leaving for three days' racing at Newmarket.

Lord Salisbury explained [15] that, according to Count Hatzfeldt, the German Ambassador in London, the Prince of Wales's presence in Vienna, during the German Emperor's visit, might have aroused Russian suspicions 'at a moment when matters were very delicate, without offering to Germany any substantial compensation in the shape of a genuine English alliance'. The Prime Minister added that the Prince appeared also to have offended the Kaiser by talking unguardedly about North Schleswig and Alsace-Lorraine, by pressing the Duke of Cumberland's claims upon the Bismarcks and by sending them a memorandum on the subject, as well as by treating the German Emperor 'as an uncle treats a nephew, instead of recognizing that he was an Emperor'.

Lord Salisbury warned [16] the Prince that the Kaiser, who appeared to be 'a little off his head' and 'not quite all there', had expressed a strong wish to pay a State visit to England. It was desirable that the personal issue between Prince and Kaiser should be settled first, but confidential discussions about that issue could not be allowed to 'affect the general policy of the two nations'. The Prince agreed to leave his personal interests in the hands of the Prime Minister, and in those of Queen Victoria who was boiling with indignation at her grandson's conduct.

Writing [17] (15 October) to Lord Salisbury, the Queen described as *'perfect madness!'* the Kaiser's wish 'to be treated in private as well as in public as "His Imperial Majesty".' The complaint that the Prince of Wales had treated him as a nephew, and not as a Emperor, was 'really too *vulgar* and too absurd, as well as untrue, almost *to be believed*' and '*if* he has *such* notions, he had better *never* come *here*. The Queen will not swallow this affront.' The Queen added that she had been informed by the Prince of Wales that the young Emperor had told the Crown Prince Rudolf:

> ... that if his uncle wrote him a very kind letter, *he might perhaps answer it!!* All this shows a very unhealthy and unnatural state of mind; and he *must* be made to feel that his grandmother and uncle will not stand such insolence. The Prince of Wales must *not* submit to such treatment.

As regards the political relations of the two Governments,

the Queen quite agrees that that should not be affected (if possible) by these miserable personal quarrels; but the Queen much *fears* that with such a hot-headed, conceited, and wrong-headed young man, devoid of all feeling, this may, at ANY moment, become *impossible*.

With Queen Victoria's approval, the Prince of Wales declined to receive Count Herbert Bismarck at Marlborough House in March 1889; but Lord Salisbury continued to regard the personal quarrel between Prince and Kaiser as an irritating side issue. He welcomed the Queen's action in sending her son-in-law, Prince Christian, to Berlin in April 1889 to effect, if possible, a family reconciliation; but he was positive that the Kaiser's State visit to England during the first week of August would have to take place, whether or not an apology had been rendered first to the Prince of Wales.

Prince Christian reported [18] (16 April) to the Prince of Wales from Berlin that the Emperor had denied verbally that he had expressed any wish not to meet his uncle in Vienna, but that he would write no letter because 'this is not a simple affair between uncle and nephew, but between Emperor and Prince of Wales'. Prince Christian reminded the Prince of Wales that 'the Emperor is still too young in his position to feel quite sure of himself. ... He is constantly apprehensive of doing something incompatible with his dignity.'

'Please let William clearly understand', the Prince of Wales wrote [19] (19 April) to Prince Christian, 'that unless I *do* receive a few lines from him, as I have asked for in my previous letters to you, I shall be unable to meet him when he comes to England this summer.' He added that he would 'take care that everyone knows the reason!', and explained: 'I have also my own dignity to uphold.'

Although Queen Victoria and the Empress Frederick encouraged him to continue to stand firm, the Prince of Wales appreciated shrewdly that no satisfaction was likely to be obtained. The cards were stacked in his nephew's hand, and on 15 May the German Ambassador in London, who appeared nervous and uncomfortable, informed [20] Lord Salisbury that he was instructed to state that 'great scandal and political damage' might follow if the Kaiser's verbal assurances were not accepted.

Salisbury advised [21] Queen Victoria accordingly (18 May) that her grandson's verbal disavowal of any intention to insult his uncle must be accepted as its face value. He argued that an insult ceased to be an insult when, as in the present case, it was impossible to prove that the denial was false; that the Kaiser might be trying to protect Prince Reuss, the Bismarcks, or even the Emperor Francis Joseph; and that irreparable harm might result if he were pressed too hard.

The Prince of Wales had warned the Empress Frederick not to involve herself in the quarrel, but he kept her informed constantly about its progress. 'If you only knew', he wrote [22] (15 May), 'how sick I am of the whole affair, and how annoyed that the mild efforts I have made to put matters straight have been of no avail. The best part of the joke (?) is that Hatzfeldt told Ponsonby that the Vienna incident never existed! ... After this you can see that I can do nothing more ... and I leave the matter entirely in dear Mama's hands, who must do what she thinks best.'

After much discussion with Lord Salisbury and others, the Queen sent the Kaiser a letter [23] (25 May) which the Prince of Wales described as 'rather too mild'. In it, after accepting her grandson's denial, the Queen wrote: 'I cannot understand how this mistake could have arisen, which might easily have led to very serious consequences, and I hope that you will inquire into the circumstances.'

The Kaiser's reply [24] (30 May) caused very deep offence to his English relatives, and the Queen, who described [25] it (1 June) to the Prince of Wales as 'incredible!!', expressed her fear that 'it will and *must* annoy you very much'. It stated that the so-called Vienna incident had been inquired into already, and that 'the whole affair is absolutely invented, there not being an atom of a cause to be found. The whole thing is a fixed idea which originated either in Uncle Bertie's imagination, or in somebody else's. Who put it into his head? I am very glad to hear that this affair has at last come to an end.'

On receipt of that disingenuous letter Sir Augustus Paget

was recalled immediately from Vienna for consultation; but, although the Queen wrote again, her grandson's reply was evasive. Sir Francis Knollys complained [26] bitterly (8 June) to Ponsonby that the Prince of Wales had been 'sacrificed by Lord Salisbury to political expediency'; and the Prince explained [27] (18 June) to the Empress Frederick that he could do no more, after having placed his interests unreservedly in their mother's hands: 'Lord Salisbury was consulted by her, and he gave her the worst possible advice, making us virtually to "eat humble pie"! What a triumph for the Bismarcks, as well as for Willy!'

The Prince of Wales was easily persuaded not to cause irresponsible chatter by absenting himself during the Kaiser's visit (2–8 August 1889), which proved to be a much greater success than his English relatives had dared to hope. From the moment when the Prince of Wales, wearing the uniform of an admiral of the fleet and accompanied by Prince Eddy and Prince George, boarded off Spithead the imperial yacht *Hohenzollern*, which had been escorted across the North Sea by twelve units of the infant German Navy, the Kaiser laid himself out to charm. He, too, was arrayed as a British admiral of the fleet, and was voluble in expressions of pride and delight in that honorary rank which had been conferred on him.

After a series of gala dinners and naval exercises and reviews, the Kaiser was entertained by a military review at Aldershot from which the Prince of Wales excused himself. A painful attack of phlebitis had made it difficult for him to mount a horse; but, after the Kaiser's departure, Francis Knollys reported [28] privately to Lord Salisbury (11 August) that 'the relations between the Emperor and the Prince of Wales are at present excellent, and the latter talks of going to Berlin in January for the Emperor's birthday'.

The Kaiser made no allusion to the Vienna incident, but the Prince of Wales resumed amiable personal relations with Herbert Bismarck. Causes of recent misunderstanding were discussed, but Knollys noted [29] that those relaxed talks had skimmed only the surface. The Prince, who proposed the Kaiser as well as Prince Henry of Prussia for membership of the Royal Yacht Squadron, continued to hope, with characteristic optimism, that his nephew's aggressive personality would change. He acknowledged cheerfully his nephew's superior cleverness, as well as his superior rank, and he was prepared to go to great lengths in an effort to remain publicly on good terms with him. He was repelled, however, by a boisterous flamboyance, which caused him to write [30] privately (20 May 1891) to his sister: 'Willy is a bully, and most bullies, when tackled, are cowards.'

The Prince of Wales continued to enjoy life with a schoolboy gusto, which was checked at increasingly frequent intervals by moods of boredom and frustration: 'The age of chivalry has, alas!, passed,' he wrote [31] (31 December 1888), to Sir Henry Acland, 'and one sees it daily both in political and social life. But one must go with the times and try and pick out the good and discard the bad!'

Disguised as the Devil, in scarlet and with horns on his head, the Prince of Wales enjoyed thoroughly the battle of flowers at Cannes in March 1889; but he was shocked by a series of matrimonial and other disasters among his friends. He had greatly liked the Austrian Crown Prince Rudolf, whose suicide in January 1889, after murdering his mistress at Mayerling, amazed him. He ascertained [32] that Rudolf had written to the Pope to ask for a divorce from his wife (whose voice was said to resemble a foghorn), and for permission to marry his mistress; that the Pope had sent the letter to the Emperor Francis Joseph, and that a scene had followed between father and son which led directly to the catastrophe.

The Prince was shocked and amazed again, in October 1889, when the superintendent of his stables, Lord Arthur Somerset, of the Blues, whom he had always called 'Podge' and treated as an intimate friend, was discovered in a homosexual brothel which the police raided in Cleveland Street, off the Tottenham Court Road. A rumbling scandal was caused when some of the facts became known a month later; but the Prince, who said at first, 'I won't believe it, any more than I should if they had accused the Archbishop of Canterbury', argued that any man addicted to such a filthy vice must be regarded as an 'unfortunate lunatic'. He expressed [33] (25 October) to Lord Salisbury his satisfaction that Lord Arthur had been allowed to flee the country, and asked that, if he should 'ever dare to show his face in England again', he should be allowed to visit his parents quietly in the country 'without fear of being apprehended on this awful charge'.

When in May 1889 Lord Rothschild was appointed to succeed the last Duke of Buckingham as Lord Lieutenant of Buckinghamshire, the Prince of Wales wrote [34] (10 May) to Lord Carrington, who disapproved: 'It would have been strange ten years ago, but times change. He is a good fellow and man of business, and he and his family own half the County!' The Prince was equally pleased when his eldest daughter, that summer, married outside the royal caste.

The wedding on 27 July 1889, of Princess Louise (aged twenty-two) and the Earl of Fife (aged forty), a rich Scottish landowner with a sound business head, gave satisfaction to the nation. As Lord Macduff, Fife had sat formerly as a Liberal in the House of Commons, but he was one of the Prince's friends of whom Queen Victoria approved warmly and she made him a duke on his marriage. She had no wish to do so, and she thought it unnecessary and even absurd, but she yielded to the plea of the Prince of Wales who turned that issue into a personal one.

When the Shah of Persia visited England for the second time in July 1889 the Prince of Wales groaned, but consented again to bear most of the burden and some of the expense of his entertainment. Several friends, including Lord Cadogan, Lord Rosebery, the Rothschilds and Sir Albert Sassoon, helped by staging princely festivities; but that London season had proved exhausting, and the Prince left thankfully for Homburg on 13 August on the first lap of a three months' holiday.

Annoyed by what he described [35] to Prince George (17 August) as the importunity of numbers of 'uninteresting and tiresome people', the Prince of Wales flitted back to Scotland to stay with his daughter and son-in-law at Mar Lodge, before joining the Princess of Wales (30 September) in Denmark. He moved to Venice after a fortnight's stay, and embarked (15 October) with the Princess and his unmarried children in *Osborne* for Athens.

What Queen Victoria used to describe as 'the royal mob' was assembling at Athens for the wedding (27 October) of the Prince of Wales's nephew, Constantine, Duke of Sparta, and the German Emperor's sister, Princess Sophie; and the Prince of Wales was escorted by the entire British Mediterranean fleet. The Kaiser, wearing the uniform of a British admiral of the fleet, warned his hosts at a luncheon which the Prince of Wales attended in the British flagship *Dreadnought*, that British naval strength in the Mediterranean was at a dangerously low ebb, and that the Fleet's dispositions ought to be reconsidered at once in the light of a plan which he had prepared and dictated.

Suppressing his mirth, the Prince of Wales assured[36] Queen Victoria (2 November) that no 'contretemps' had occurred at any time; that 'Willy' had 'seemed in high good humour'; and that Willy's wife, Dona, had also been 'most amiable and not at all on her high horse'. All went well, and other royalties in Athens included the Empress Frederick, the Czarevitch Nicholas and the King and Queen of Denmark.

While the Princess of Wales returned with her parents to Copenhagen, and while the Kaiser paid a State visit to Constantinople, the Prince, accompanied by Prince Eddy (who was *en route* for India) re-visited Egypt in the *Osborne*. He was met at Port Said by Sir Evelyn Baring, who ruled Egypt with the modest title of British Agent and Consul-General and whom he described[37] as 'a very able man but with no manners'; and he was lodged most opulently at the Ghizeh Palace in Cairo by the Khedive Tewfik, whom he described[38] as 'quite charming and full of conversation'.

Baring was tempted to treat the Prince of Wales as a schoolmaster might treat a pupil, and he urged him repeatedly to do everything in his power to enhance Tewfik's prestige. He was anxious that Tewfik, and not the Prince of Wales, should take the salute at a great military review on 2 November. The Prince responded by leading 1,700 men of the British occupation force and 4,000 Egyptians in a march past the Khedive, whom he saluted respectfully, while massed British regimental bands played the Khedival Hymn as well as 'God Save the Queen'.

Two days later the Prince attended a Mahommedan religious fête in honour of the Prophet's birthday, before embarking for home. He expressed a fervent wish to Baring and others that the British would stay in Egypt for ever; and he spent a few more days in Athens, and a few in Paris also, before returning (18 November) to Marlborough House.

A severe attack of bronchitis would have prevented the Prince of Wales from visiting Berlin privately, as he had intended to do, for the Kaiser's birthday at the end of January 1890. At the Kaiser's request, however, that visit was transformed into a State one six weeks later, and the Prince of Wales was treated as a Sovereign returning, on behalf of Queen Victoria, the State visit which the Kaiser had paid to England in August 1889. After opening the Forth railway bridge, the Prince of Wales accompanied by Prince George, started for Berlin on 19 March 1890, carrying a list of possible princesses, compiled by Queen Victoria, for his elder son to marry.

The first name on that list was the Kaiser's youngest sister, Princess Margaret (Mossy), who showed no enthusiasm for Prince Eddy; but the Prince of Wales was delighted by his visit and by many attentions paid to him. He wrote [39] (31 March) to Queen Victoria, before leaving Berlin for the South of France: 'When you next write to him [the Emperor William] please thank him, as he treated me quite like a Sovereign and considered my visit as in your name – in fact, as your representative; and I am very sorry to say that my expenses, in consequence, have been heavy.'

With the active cooperation and help of the Leader of the Opposition, W. E. Gladstone, the House of Commons had recently voted the Prince of Wales a capital sum of £60,000, and had increased his annual income by £36,000 to enable him to provide for his children. Radicals had protested strongly against that provision which fell short, by a long way, of the Prince's needs and hopes; and Gladstone argued [40] constantly, in private, that Queen Victoria ought personally to have allowed her heir an additional £50,000 a year 'in consideration of the extent to which she allows him to discharge her social duties for her'.

Because he was known to be embarrassed financially, the Prince was pestered constantly by moneylenders, and his hotels at Paris, Homburg and Cannes appeared to be ringed perpetually by touts. Writing very confidentially from Paris on 14 November 1889, the British Ambassador, Lord Lytton, informed [41] the Prime Minister, Lord Salisbury, that he had found it necessary to institute private inquiries through the head of the French police 'with a view to the protection of H.R.H.' from 'the abuse of his name and position' by financiers of doubtful repute.

Lytton's motive was to scotch persistent reports that the Prince of Wales owed large sums to unsuitable persons; and the Prefect of Police notified the British Ambassador that the Prince, after negotiating unsuccessfully for many months with various firms, had obtained funds which he needed urgently, from the French Rothschilds. Lytton leaned, nevertheless, to the view that the French police were mistaken, and that, as he informed [42] Lord Salisbury, 'if there be any truth in this information, it was probably Hirsch, and not Rothschild, who advanced the money'.

Baron Maurice de Hirsch had obtained an introduction to the Prince of Wales in December 1886 from the Crown Prince Rudolf of Austria, in consideration of a loan of 100,000 gulden which he had made to the Crown Prince. [43] The Prince of Wales arranged to confer with Hirsch in Paris on his way home from Berlin, where he dined (23 March) with Count Herbert Bismarck, after visiting at five o'clock the fallen Chancellor, Prince Bismarck, who had been dismissed five days earlier by the Kaiser.

Hirsch visited the Prince of Wales at the Hotel Bristol in Paris at tea-time on 1 April 1890; and the Prince lunched at Hirsch's house on the following day before embarking for Cannes. By origin a rich Bavarian Court Jew of the third generation, Hirsch, who was aged fifty-nine, became at once the Prince's unofficial financial adviser and confidant. He was an interesting man, civilized, and by no means devoid of charm; but, after amassing one of the largest private fortunes in history, out of banking, aggressive railroad promotion in Russia, Austria-Hungary and Turkey, as well as out of bold speculations which enabled him to corner repeatedly markets in sugar and copper, he had become embittered as a result of snubs provoked by his morbid social ambition.

After losing his only legitimate son in 1887, Hirsch announced that humanity would be his heir, and he gave between ten and eleven million pounds during his lifetime to a Jewish colonization association which relieved the needs and organized the emigration from Russia of large numbers of his oppressed co-religionists, who were re-settled, as agriculturists, in the Argentine, Canada and Anatolia. Hirsch contributed also on a princely scale to hospitals and other nonsectarian charities in France and England, where he raced successfully, joined the Marlborough and a few other clubs, and enjoyed the kind of social life on which his heart was set.

Social life in Germany had been closed to Hirsch by anti-semitism, and the position in Austria-Hungary, where he contributed huge sums to educational charities, was only a little easier. He was richer than the more cautious Rothschilds but, unlike them, he was never assimilated socially. He was excluded from the Jockey Club, cold-shouldered, or treated, at best, with a mortifying condescension by most archdukes and great magnates, and never received at Court. A problem of that kind fascinated the Prince of Wales, who promised that he would teach the Austrian nobles a lesson by coming to stay with Hirsch that autumn and by bringing with him a party of English friends.

The Prince returned to England on 19 April, after seeing Hirsch twice again in Paris on his way home from the Riviera; and, throughout the London season which followed, Hirsch was seen constantly with the Prince of Wales. He rented Bath House in Piccadilly, a country house near Sandringham and a shoot near Newmarket, and he was a frequent guest at the houses of all the Prince's friends. The

Prince of Wales was amused especially at what he described to Prince George as a delightfully mixed dinner party given by Lady Randolph Churchill in London on 21 July, when the guests included Henry Chaplin, the Gladstones, Hirsches, Roseberys, the Russian Ambassador and the Duke of Orleans.

Being very sensitive himself, the Prince of Wales resented hotly any affront offered to his new friend in any quarter, and he made a personal issue of Queen Victoria's refusal to invite Hirsch to a State concert at Buckingham Palace on 25 June. Knollys wrote [44] (26 June 1890) to Ponsonby: 'H.R.H. is *dreadfully* annoyed about it, and, as he looks on him as a personal friend of his (whether he is a good one or not is another question), looks upon the step which the Queen has taken as a personal slight.'

During that year 1890, the Prince performed some fifty public engagements, and that total rose steadily year by year as the century drew towards its close. He went nine times to the House of Lords in 1890 and sixty-seven times to the theatre; and he informed [45] Prince George (26 August 1890) that 'at the balls in London this year' he had danced only quadrilles and 'not a single valse ... because I am getting too old and fat'.

The affairs of Prince Eddy, who was created Duke of Clarence and Avondale in May 1890, caused his parents increasing anxiety. Because he was dissipated and unstable, an early marriage was obviously necessary; but he was rejected by Princess Alix of Hesse (who became the last Empress of Russia), and he refused to consider the even more eligible candidate, Princess Margaret (Mossy) of Prussia. Instead, despite a strongly expressed warning letter [46] (19 May) from Queen Victoria, the Duke fell head over heels in love with Princess Hélène d'Orléans, daughter of the Comte de Paris, who was Pretender to the French throne, and the young couple became engaged at the end of August 1890, while staying at Mar Lodge with the Duke of Fife.

Despite the very great religious and political objections, the Prince and Princess of Wales were delighted. They were profoundly grateful to Princess Hélène for her offer to defy her father by renouncing Roman Catholicism and by joining the Church of England, and they hoped that all other objections would be removed by that sacrificial act. The Prince of Wales could not bring himself to interrupt his cure at Homburg, but the Princess of Wales was staying at Mar Lodge. She liked Princess Hélène; she hated the idea of any German marriage; and with feminine subtlety she advised the lovers to take Queen Victoria by surprise and storm at Balmoral, and to turn her into an ally by making her their confidante.

The lovers acted on that advice successfully on 29 August; and the Queen, who was much touched and agitated, promised that she would do what she could to help them. She told A. J. Balfour, who was staying at Balmoral as minister in attendance, that it had been difficult not to say 'yes' at once; and Balfour wrote [47] characteristically (30 August) to his uncle, Lord Salibury:

We shall have a great deal of trouble over it all, but it is impossible not to see the humorous side of the business. Will it be believed that neither the Queen, nor the young Prince, nor Princess Hélène, see anything which is not romantic, interesting, touching and praiseworthy in the young lady giving up a religion, to which *she still professes devoted attachment*, in order to marry the man on whom she says she has set her heart! They are moved even to tears by the magnitude of the sacrifice, without it, apparently, occurring to them that at the best it is the sacrifice of religion for love, while at the worst it is the sacrifice of religion for a throne – a singular inversion of the ordinary views on martyrdom. ...

The Comtesse de Paris, a masculine woman who was sufficiently independent to smoke pipes while shooting and deer-stalking, and the Prince of Wales's best cigars after luncheon and dinner, was in favour of her daughter's immediate reception into the Church of England, followed by marriage; but her husband was opposed irrevocably to that plan. He refused to allow his daughter to become a Protestant, to the undisguised relief of the Prime Minister, Lord Salisbury, and of the Lord Chancellor, Lord Halsbury, who composed elaborate memoranda upon the political and legal aspects of the affair.

The Princess of Wales had divined that Princess Hélène was genuinely in love with her son, who possessed attraction for women although he was mentally immature; but she found Lord Salisbury difficult to convince. The Prime Minister was drily amused when she argued that apostacy ought to be accepted as conclusive proof of disinterested love; and the Prince of Wales asked casually whether it would be possible for Princess Hélène to remain a Roman Catholic, after giving an undertaking that all children would be brought up in the Church of England. He abandoned that idea immediately because Lord Salisbury warned him that the anger of the middle and lower classes might endanger the throne if it became known that he had advanced or ever contemplated it; and he wrote [48] (20 September) to Ponsonby: 'The Lord Chancellor is now being consulted, but till the Ct. de P. consents to the change of Religion one might just as well consult the Great Mogul.' He informed [49] Prince George (12 October): 'What the ultimate result may be, God only knows ... I am not very sanguine.'

On 23 November, the Prince of Wales reported [50] to Prince George that Prince Eddy's prospects were 'in a deplorable state, as Hélène went to see the Pope(!), who naturally pointed out the iniquity she would commit if she changed her religion. This brings everything to a deadlock; and it is a sad state of things and makes poor Eddy quite wretched.' The Prince of Wales kept his promise, in the meantime, to visit Baron Maurice Hirsch in Hungary, and had reached Vienna on 5 October with a party of friends who included Lady Randolph Churchill, Lady Lilian Wemyss, Lord Dudley, Horace Farquhar, Lord and Lady Georgiana Curzon and the Arthur Sassoons.

After laying a wreath on the Crown Prince Rudolf's tomb on the morning of 6 October, the Prince of Wales gave a luncheon party for Hirsch and the King of Greece at the Grand Hotel. When it was ended, he left with his friends and Hirsch, by special train for St Johann, near Hohenau, on the Austro-Hungarian border, while the Austrian arch-dukes gasped.

An average of ten guns killed twenty thousand partridges during the ten days which followed, and the Prince of Wales wrote [51] (19 October) to Prince George: 'This certainly beats everything on record and will quite spoil me for any shooting at home.' All birds flew high and well because the Baron, who employed several hundred beaters, had devoted an unprecedented degree of technical skill to the organization of that massacre. The Prince found his few Austrian and Hungarian fellow-guests congenial, although not aristocratic and the 'unpretentious' house 'most comfortable'.

Exhilarated and refreshed, the Prince returned (18 October) to Vienna, where he called formally upon all the resident archdukes and dined with the Emperor Francis Joseph, who took him to the opera. He stayed on his way home in Paris where he called upon President Carnot, and he braced himself to face resolutely the problem posed by his elder son. He decided to persuade the Princess, if he could, that the Duke of Clarence, whose dissipated life was beginning to cause scandal, must either marry suitably during 1891, or be despatched on a tour of South Africa, Australia and New Zealand, as a punishment and to preserve him from harm.[52]

The Prince in Trouble

1891–4

i

THE year 1891 was the unhappiest in the Prince of Wales's
life. He wrote[1] on 30 December to the Empress Frederick:
'I cannot regret that the year '91 is about to close as, during
it, I have experienced many worries and annoyancies which
ought to last me for a long time. My only happiness has been
Eddy's engagement and Georgy's recovery.' His reputation
suffered when he was publicly involved in a gaming scandal
about which too much has been written; and he had also to
face the threat of an unrelated but more serious scandal
about which almost nothing has been written, although the
facts were widely known in society and discussed for weeks
on end in every fashionable London drawing-room and club.
Some of the hysteria which the affair at Tranby Croft provoked was caused by the fear that worse might soon follow,
but the Prince behaved with courage and an entire absence
of hypocrisy or self-pity.

In the absence of a popular press, the social code continued
to allow the rich a privileged degree of latitude so long as
public scandal was avoided; but the Prince of Wales was
jealously watched. Despite the existence of a taboo on open
criticism of his actions, an undercurrent of dissatisfaction
existed, and a strait-laced comment by Lord Alington's
daughter, Winifred Sturt, while staying at Sandringham for
the first time in January 1890, is typical. Miss Sturt, who
thought that George Lewis, the solicitor, was an odd fellow-
guest, and who was amazed to find baccarat being played
into the small hours, wrote[2] to her financé, Charles Hardinge,* (23 January): 'I think it is a shocking affair for the

* Lord Hardinge of Penshurst, K.G., P.C., G.C.B., G.C.S.I.,
G.C.M.G., G.C.I.E., G.C.V.O. (1858–1944).

Royal Family to play an illegal game every night. They have a real table, and rakes, and everything like the rooms at Monte Carlo.'

Having given up dancing, the Prince liked baccarat to be played wherever he went, and he carried with him always a set of counters (in denominations varying from five shillings to ten pounds, engraved with the Prince of Wales's feathers) which were a present from Reuben Sassoon. Many young men had abandoned dancing, in consequence, for baccarat at the London balls; and it was natural that that game should be played at Tranby Croft, near Hull, where the Prince stayed for the first and last time with the shipowner, Arthur Wilson, whom he knew only slightly, on the nights of 8, 9 and 10 September 1890, during the St Leger race week.

The Prince had often stayed for Doncaster races at Brantingham Thorpe with Christopher Sykes; but 'the great Xtopher' was in trouble. He was on the verge of bankruptcy and although, after feminine pressure had been applied, the Prince contrived to arrange that sufficient funds should be made available to avert that catastrophe, his old friend was in no position to act as host.

Sykes, in those circumstances, was a guest of the Wilsons, and the party began badly when the Prince's special favourite, Lady Brooke, was prevented at the last moment by the death of an uncle coming to Tranby Croft. Much worse followed on the first evening when young Arthur Wilson, the son of the house, saw Lieutenant-Colonel Sir William Gordon-Cumming, Baronet, of the Scots Guards, cheating at baccarat.

Young Wilson alerted his friend, Berkeley Levett, who was one of Sir William's subalterns, and Levett was soon compelled to admit that his colonel was deliberately cheating. Sir William was manipulating counters, after looking at his cards, by a sleight-of-hand trick known in French casinos as *la poussette*; and, late that night, young Wilson informed his parents, who were appalled.

Next morning young Wilson told his sister's husband, Lycett Green, a master of hounds, who alerted his wife, with the result that on the following evening (when young Levett declined to play) the baronet was watched at the baccarat table by his host and hostess, as well as by their son, daughter and son-in-law, and was seen to cheat on a number of occasions. Sir William won £225 during the two evenings, mainly from the Prince of Wales who kept the bank; and Lycett Green spoke next morning to Lord Edward Somerset (a brother of the unfortunate 'Podge') who suggested that two older fellow-guests, Lord Coventry and Lieutenant-General Owen Williams, should be consulted. Coventry and Williams accepted the evidence laid before them by five witnesses and informed Gordon-Cumming of the accusation which had been made.

After denying hotly that he had cheated, Sir William made no request to be confronted by his accusers. He asked only what he should do, and begged to be allowed to discuss the matter with the Prince of Wales. The Prince, who had suspected nothing, warned his old friend, after a dreadfully constrained dinner, that denial was useless because the evidence of five persons was conclusive, but added: 'We have no desire to be unnecessarily hard on you.'

Coventry and Williams had recourse to what was, in effect, a traditional method of handling such cases with a minimum of unpleasantness. Intending to protect the Prince of Wales, they composed a brief note for Sir William's signature which read[3]: 'In consideration of the promise, made by the gentlemen whose names are subscribed, to preserve silence with reference to an accusation made in regard to my conduct at baccarat on the nights of Monday and Tuesday, 8th and 9th September, 1890, at Tranby Croft, I will on my part solemnly undertake never to play cards again as long as I live.'

The Prince made no allusion to that paper in conversation with Sir William, but Coventry and Williams threatened the baronet with exposure unless he signed without delay and left the house early next morning. The unhappy man, who protested that that would be tantamount to an admission of guilt, was informed that that was correct; but he signed, nevertheless, and withdrew after muttering something about blowing his brains out, and about the difficulty of preserving a secret known to many people.

On the advice of Coventry and Williams, the Prince of
Wales preserved that document in his archives, after adding
his signature as a witness; and the nine other men (Lord
Coventry, General Williams, Arthur Wilson, Alfred Somerset, Lord Edward Somerset, Lycett Green, young Wilson,
Berkeley Levett and Reuben Sassoon) who had played baccarat with Sir William also signed. Next day the Prince
said that he, too, would quit Tranby Croft, and he watched
the last day's racing from the Cavalry Barracks in York,
where he spent the night with the 10th Hussars, before
summoning Lord and Lady Brooke to see him off, with
Christopher Sykes, from York to Abergeldie by special train
on the evening of 12 September.

The virtual impossibility of keeping that affair secret had
been insufficiently appreciated; and the Prince did not reply
to a letter [4] (12 September) in which Gordon-Cumming
stated that the secret would be out if he were suddenly to
stop playing whist with his brother-officers, or if the Prince
of Wales were to cut him when they next met. Early in the
New Year, while staying with Maurice Hirsch at Wretham
Hall, Norfolk, in a party which included Lord Hartington,
Henry Chaplin, the Brookes, the Carringtons, Lady Randolph Churchill and Count Kinsky (a Hungarian magnate),
the Prince heard that the secret was already out and that
Gordon-Cumming intended to bring an action against his
five original accusers (the Wilsons, the Lycett Greens and
Berkeley Levett).

Before starting proceedings, Gordon-Cumming tried to resign from the Army, but the Prince of Wales and his friends
obstructed that plan. They wanted a military court to inquire privately into the charge which had been brought
against Sir William's honour as an officer and as a gentleman, and they argued that, once Sir William had been com-
demned at that secret inquiry, any subsequent action in a
civil court, where the Prince would be compelled to give evidence in public, would have been rendered virtually impossible.

With that object, Lord Coventry and General Williams
visited the Adjutant-General, Sir Redvers Buller, V.C., at

the War Office on 4 February 1891, before sending him a formal letter [5] later that day from the Carlton Club. They outlined what had happened at Tranby Croft, and asked that a full inquiry should be instituted by the military authorities forthwith.

Sir Redvers responded by rejecting Gordon-Cumming's application to go on half-pay, and by ordering him to appear before a military court of inquiry; but Sir William's solicitors were men of weight and ability. They appealed successfully to the Adjutant-General's sense of fair play and to the British tradition of 'cricket', and begged him not to prejudice a civil action which they undertook to prosecute with all possible speed.

After consulting the Judge Advocate-General, Sir Redvers Buller 'suspended' the military inquiry which he had ordered, and wrote [6] (13 February) to Sir Henry Ponsonby: 'I hear that the Prince of Wales is condemning my action ... in loud and unmeasured terms. You may have heard nothing about it, which I hope is the case, for it is not a satisfactory subject. But, in case you have, I might say that one story is often only good until another is told; and I am satisfied that I have done my duty with discretion.'

Balked by that attitude on the part of Sir Redvers Buller, Sir Francis Knollys had recourse to another plan for avoiding the full glare of publicity. Club committees acted as courts of honour at that time, but the Prince's friends overreached themselves in attempting to institute a private inquiry at the Guards' Club. Although Sir William Gordon-Cumming had resigned his rights as a member voluntarily, pending the result of his civil action, a motion that the Club's executive committee should be empowered to conduct its own inquiry was brought before a specially convened general meeting of members on 20 February. After a heated debate that motion was defeated by 78 votes to 49, and the Prince of Wales was furious.

In thanking Ponsonby for having calmed Queen Victoria, the Prince characterized [7] (22 February) the neutral attitude of Sir Redvers Buller as 'to say the least of it, most extraordinary', and he continued:

If he had acted promptly and decisively at the beginning ..
all this public scandal ... would have been avoided, and no
question of a civil action would have been thought of. ...

The decision of the Guards' Club is a terrible blow to the
Scots Guards; and I feel most deeply for the officers who have
the honour of their Regiment so much at heart. Should Cumming, by any legal quibble, win his action, I think nearly every
officer would leave the Regiment.

Ponsonby asked Knollys to make the Prince understand
that the Guards' Club could not have condemned and expelled Sir William Gordon-Cumming without prejudicing a
civil action before it had been tried; but Knollys, although a
capable and extremely loyal private secretary, suffered occasionally from blind spots, and he explained [8] (25 February)
to Ponsonby:

The great object is to put an end to the action, and to prevent the Prince of Wales from being called into the witness-
box; and the best way to have achieved that end would have
been for the Guards' Club to have turned him [Sir William]
out, and then the Marlborough and Turf could have followed
suit. There would then, in all probability, have been an end of
the whole affair, and people in that case could have talked about
the case being pre-judged as much as they liked.

Queen Victoria's letters to the Prince could not have been
more kind or understanding; and both condemned in robust
terms the action of Lord Coventry and General Williams in
advising that the Prince's signature should be added to the
paper in which Gordon-Cumming undertook to renounce
cards in perpetuity. The Queen hoped that the Prince also
would renounce baccarat at least, but he was unapproach-
able on that subject, and he refused to go to Windsor unless
his mother promised first that she would not raise it. Knollys
wrote [9] (10 April) to Ponsonby: 'The Duke of Cambridge
arrived at Sandringham, full of some messages which he
said the Queen had entrusted him with for the Prince of
Wales respecting baccarat; but not one did he give. He was
much too frightened for that. But he told me of them, and
suggested that I should tell them to His Royal Highness. It
was, however, none of my business. ...'

The trial of Gordon-Cumming's action was delayed until 1 June, and a gnawing anxiety affected the Prince of Wales's health. 'The whole thing', he informed [10] Prince George (29 March), 'has caused me the most serious annoyance and vexation, and that is one of the reasons why I thought it best not to go abroad – not knowing what might turn up.' The Princess wrote [11] (18 April) that 'Papa' was 'quite ill' from worry, and that he had been dragged into the affair 'through his good nature ... and made to suffer for trying to save ... this worthless creature' and 'vile *snob*', Cumming, whom she had always detested and who had 'behaved too abominably'.

The case was tried by the Lord Chief Justice, Lord Coleridge, on 1–9 June 1891; and it seemed to the mass of the nation as though the Prince of Wales were on trial. Subpoenaed as a witness for the plaintiff, he was in court every day except the last, and the Solicitor-General, Sir Edward Clarke, who represented Cumming, and who professed belief until his dying day in his client's innocence, went out of his way to be offensive to the Prince of Wales. He suggested in court that previous instances had been known of men who were willing 'to sacrifice themselves to support a tottering throne or prop a falling dynasty', and he claimed that Sir William was being victimized to save the honour of a Prince who encouraged habitually an illegal game; who had jumped recklessly to a wrong conclusion on bad evidence; and who had ignored deliberately article 41 of *Queen's Regulations* for the Army, which laid upon all serving officers (including Field-Marshal H.R.H. the Prince of Wales) the duty of requiring any brother-officer accused of dishonourable conduct to submit his case forthwith to his commanding officer.

'The British Jury', the Prince of Wales informed [12] the Empress Frederick (5 June), 'are composed of a peculiar class of society, and do not shine in intelligence or refinement of feeling'; and Queen Victoria wrote [13] to the Empress (8 June): 'This horrible Trial drags along, and it is a fearful humiliation to see the future King of this country dragged (and for the second time) through the dirt, just like anyone else, in a Court of Justice. I feel it is a terrible humiliation, and so do all the people. It is very painful and must do his prestige great harm. Oh! if only it is a lesson for the future! It makes me very sad.'

Lord Coleridge summed up in favour of the defendants, and the jury returned a verdict against Gordon-Cumming after an absence of less than a quarter of an hour. The baronet was dismissed (10 June) from the Army, expelled from all his clubs and socially annihilated; and the Prince of Wales wrote [14] (10 June) to Prince George: 'Thank God! – the Army and Society are now well rid of such a damned blackguard. The crowning point of his infamy is that he, this morning, married an American young lady, Miss Garner (sister to Mme de Breteuil), with money!'

Sir William, who owned nearly 40,000 acres of poor land in Scotland, lived unhappily but in dignified seclusion, collecting post-marks, until his death at a ripe age in 1930. He was guilty, predatory and mean, but the spectacle of a guest condemned upon the evidence of his hosts aroused a great wave of sympathy among the vast mass of men and women who are swayed always much more by their emotions than they are by their rational faculties. He was received, accordingly, by the Provost of Forres with an official address of welcome, a band and a popular ovation, when he brought his American bride (who had married him against the heartfelt wish and advice of every member of her distinguished family) to his home at Altyre on 13 June; and a storm of obloquy broke over the head of the Prince of Wales.

It would be difficult to exaggerate the momentary unpopularity of the Prince of Wales; and Queen Victoria informed [15] the Empress Frederick (12 June) that 'the Monarchy almost is in danger if he is lowered and despised'. She explained [16] (16 June) that 'it is not this special case – though his signing that paper was wrong (and turns out to have been contrary to Military Regulations ...), but the light which has been thrown on his habits which alarms and shocks people so much, for the example is so bad. ...'. The Kaiser had the effrontery to send Queen Victoria a letter (which has not been preserved) protesting against the impropriety of anyone holding the honorary rank of a colonel of Prussian Hussars becoming embroiled with men young enough to be his children in a gambling squabble; and with unctuous rectitude *The Times* expressed a wish (10 June) that the Prince of Wales himself would sign a pledge never again to play cards for money.

'The Press', the Prince wrote [17] (14 June) to the Empress Frederick, 'has been very severe and cruel, because they know I cannot defend myself'; and Knollys complained [18] (9 June) to Lord Salisbury's secretary, Schomberg McDonnell, that the Cabinet 'who must know what sort of man their Solicitor-General is ... ought to have taken steps to protect him [the Prince] from the public insults of one of the Law Officers of the Crown'. McDonnell replied [19] (10 June) that any attempt to restrain Clarke might have been exceedingly dangerous, but Knollys retorted [20] (11 June): 'H.R.H. remembers that, in 1869 [sic], when he was called as a witness in the Mordaunt Trial, Mr Gladstone, who was then Prime Minister, took all the *indirect* means in his power (and *successfully*) to prevent anything being brought out in the course of the Trial that could be injurious to the Prince, or the Crown.'

There had been nothing to bring out in either case except imprudence; and only pedants were interested when the Secretary for War, Edward Stanhope, admitted (15 June) in the House of Commons that the Prince of Wales had committed an error of judgement in ignoring article 41 of *Queen's Regulations* for the Army. Stanhope apologized on the Prince's behalf; but the light focused so dramatically upon an aspect of the private life of the Prince of Wales had dismayed so profoundly so many admirable and respectable people that the taboo upon public criticism of his actions was lifted for several weeks.

In an effort to restore public confidence, Queen Victoria invited the Prince of Wales to send the Archbishop of Canterbury, E. W. Benson, a letter for publication, condemning gambling as a social evil. Gladstone, as leader of the Opposition, as well as the Archbishop, endorsed enthusiastically that request, but the Prince declined absolutely to write anything which could be construed by hostile critics as hypocritical. He promised [21] Lord Cadogan, who was sent by Queen Victoria to see him (13 June), that, if the Government deemed it to be politically necessary, he would not object to the issue, in general terms, of a statement that he disapproved of gambling; but he insisted that he should be allowed to explain precisely what he meant by gambling, and it is unlikely that that explanation would have sufficed, at that moment, to allay public discontent.

The Prince equated gambling with drunkenness and professed to have a horror of both. He argued, however, that it would be as absurd to describe as gambling a harmless bet on a horse-race, or an equally harmless game of baccarat played by rich men for stakes which they could afford very comfortably, as it would be to describe as intemperance a glass or two of champagne at dinner.

Lord Salisbury was extremely diffident about offering advice, because his opinion was opposed to that of Queen Victoria; and the Prince of Wales for that reason refrained with habitual tact and good feeling from asking formally for the Prime Minister's views. He employed Lord Hartington as intermediary, and Salisbury advised [22] Hartington (16 June) that a public letter from the Prince to the Archbishop about gambling would be 'an expression of weakness' and 'a bad precedent for the future'. He continued:

I should recommend him to sit still and avoid Baccarat for six months: and, at the end of that time, write a letter to some indiscreet friend (who would publish it), saying that, at the time of the Cumming case, there had been a great deal of misunderstanding as to his views: but that the circumstances of the case had so convinced him of the evil that was liable to be caused by that game, that, since that time, he had forbidden it to be played in his presence.

On the morning of 20 June, Knollys had been on the point of starting for Lambeth Palace to see the Archbishop of Canterbury in order to discuss the possibility of arranging a satisfactory exchange of letters for publication, when the Prime Minister's emphatic advice [23] 'that anything in the nature of a public statement or correspondence would not be judicious' was delivered personally at Marlborough House by Lord Hartington. The Prince of Wales, who accepted that advice with thankfulness, asked the Archbishop to come to see him privately for an explanation and discussion of the somewhat vague issues which appeared to divide them.

The Archbishop had already refused a request, made to him by a group of great ladies, that he should remonstrate with the Prince of Wales about his private life. He conducted, however, a series of services in the chapel of Lambeth Palace which those ladies attended and which fretted the Prince because they gave some people the impression that they had been designed as a protest against the bad moral influence of the Marlborough House set.

The Princess of Wales was advised wisely by Queen Victoria not to attend those services; and the talks between the Prince and the Archbishop went well. Complete accord was unattainable, but a private exchange of letters followed; and the Prince, who found it convenient to exchange baccarat for bridge, gave clear expression [24] (13 August 1891) to his views on the subject of gambling:

... A recent trial, which no one deplores more than I do, and which I was powerless to prevent, gave occasion for the Press to make most bitter and unjust attacks upon me, knowing that I was defenceless; and I am not sure that politics was not mixed up in it. The whole matter has now died down, and I think, therefore, that it would be inopportune for me in any public manner to allude again to the painful subject which brought such a torrent of abuse upon me, not only by the Press, but by the Low Church and, especially, the Nonconformists. ...

I have a horror of gambling, and should always do my utmost to discourage others who have an inclination for it, as I consider that gambling, like intemperance, is one of the greatest curses that a country can be afflicted with.

Horse-racing may produce gambling, or it may not; but I have always looked upon it as a manly sport which is popular with Englishmen of all classes, and there is no reason why it should be looked upon as a gambling transaction. Alas! Those who gamble will gamble on anything. I have written quite openly to you, my dear Archbishop. ...

ii

Uneasiness was felt in the meantime by all members of the Marlborough House set, and by many others, as the result of a personal quarrel between the Prince of Wales and Lord Charles Beresford. Lord Charles, who had been a boon companion of the Prince for many years, had accepted the Prince's advice to resign from the Government and from the House of Commons and to resume active service in the Royal Navy in 1889, after causing gossip and scandal.

Bewitched for a time by Lady Brooke,* one of the most beautiful and interesting women of the age, Lord Charles became reconciled to his wife immediately after his resignation; but an extravagant letter of reproach addressed to Beresford by Lady Brooke fell, by accident, into the hands of Beresford's wife. Lady Charles Beresford, fearing that her husband's resolve might weaken, took that letter to the solicitor, George Lewis, and instructed him to ensure, with its aid, that its author caused no more trouble.[25]

Lady Brooke, who regretted greatly having written such a letter, appealed to the Prince of Wales to assist her in retrieving it; and the Prince, bewitched in his turn by beauty in distress, persuaded Lewis without difficulty to let him read it. He formed the view that it should be destroyed forthwith; but Lewis insisted that Lady Charles's consent was necessary, and the Prince called twice upon that lady, who told the Prince that he had no right to interfere and who refused to agree.[26]

Although as anxious as the Prince was that that compromising letter should be burned, Beresford resented the Prince's intrusion into his private affairs as hotly as he despised what he termed [27] 'the lickerish servility' of George Lewis. He failed to persuade his wife, however, to give the letter up, because she thought that she might need to use it to destroy her former rival's social position. After recovering the letter from Lewis, Lady Charles Beresford agreed finally to send it for safe-keeping to her brother-in-law,

* Frances Maynard, Countess of Warwick (1861–1938).

Lord Waterford, whom she and her husband both trusted; but the Prince of Wales showed his resentment and disapproval by ceasing to invite Lady Charles to parties at Marlborough House.

Lady Brooke, on the other hand, who was hated, naturally, by Lady Charles Beresford, was constantly with the Prince of Wales. For some years she filled the place in his life and affections which Mrs Langtry had once held; and Beresford blamed the Prince for what he described as the social boycott of his wife. He became so much incensed, in consequence, that before leaving for the Mediterranean to take command of the cruiser, *Undaunted*, he called (12 January 1890) at Marlborough House in order to have matters out with the Prince of Wales. High words passed at that interview, and Beresford, who had little control of his hot Irish temper, came within an ace of striking the Prince with his fist. He called him a blackguard and a coward, and departed after saying that he would exact reparation or revenge.[28]

While the merits of that quarrel were being canvassed eagerly for many months, the social boycott of Lady Charles Beresford grew more rigorous. She was a beauty in her own right, and sympathy was felt with her in some quarters; but the Prince's pleasure prevailed, and by the summer of 1891 Lady Charles put her London house up for sale, after informing her family and friends that she planned to live abroad in order to avoid further humiliation.[29]

In a bold effort to retrieve a deteriorating situation, Beresford, in his cabin in the *Undaunted*, composed[30] (10 July 1891) a violent letter to the Prince of Wales. The operative sentence read: 'The days of duelling are past, but there is a more just way of getting right done than can duelling, and that is – publicity.' He sent that letter to his wife with instructions to show it immediately to the Prime Minister, and to deliver it at Marlborough House on receipt of a telegram from himself.

In a very long letter[31] (22 July) to Lord Salisbury, Lady Charles Beresford, at her husband's suggestion, rehearsed every intimate detail of her husband's quarrel with the

Prince of Wales, and of her own related quarrel with Lady Brooke. She emphasized that the situation had been rendered 'still more complicated by the Prince of Wales's open disavowal of the lady (luckily for my cause)' before continuing: 'If the Prince of Wales's answer to Lord Charles is not a completely satisfactory one, Lord Charles ... announces that I am to inform you that he asks at once for leave home from his ship on "urgent private affairs", to bring the matter to *public notice* – publicity being evidently our only remedy.'

After explaining that 'no trivial reparation will do, such as an invitation to Marlborough House', and that 'the highest legal authority' had assured Lord Charles that he was in a position to precipitate and to document a scandal which, coming after that of Tranby Croft, would be 'damning to the Prince of Wales', Lady Charles Beresford asked Lord Salisbury for an immediate interview. She added that she was sure that he would recognize the need for exerting personal and official pressure upon the Prince.

Lord Salisbury, unlike Disraeli, did not relish handling matters which were so far outside the normal field of a Prime Minister's duties, but he replied most courteously that he would call and discuss the matter with Lady Charles at her convenience. He explained that he went so little into society that he doubted his ability to help, but he advised her most strongly not to send her husband's letter to the Prince of Wales.

Sir Edward Clarke, whom Lady Charles consulted professionally, gave similar advice; but before he called, the Prime Minister received a slightly hysterical warning letter from Lady Charles Beresford. It stated [32] (26 July) that her sister had 'already written out the whole story, and intends publishing; and it has already been shown, as an interesting episode in the Prince of Wales's mode of life, to several people who want to make use of the story at the next General Election for purposes of their own. ... People are beginning to ask themselves how much more evil the Prince of Wales will work in an endeavour to deteriorate Society, which is already at a low ebb.'

Although unable to allay Lady Charles Beresford's anger and jealousy, Lord Salisbury wrote [33] (10 August) a very kind and wise letter to her husband. He advised him to be mindful of certain obligations of honour, and not to break unwritten social laws, because 'there is no point that the public opinion of our class would take up more warmly'; and Beresford agreed, in consequence, that his threatening letter to the Prince of Wales should not be despatched at that time.

Lord Marcus Beresford (who managed the Prince of Wales's stud at Sandringham, and who supervised his eleven horses in training which won over four thousand pounds in small prizes during 1891) tried also to make his brother see reason; but the affair, unfortunately, had become much too widely known. Lady Charles continued to complain, and Lord Marcus was horrified to read, and to discover that other persons, less discreet, had read also a copy of the defamatory pamphlet to which his sister-in-law had referred in her letter of 26 July to Lord Salisbury.

Rumours about that unhappy business caused great distress to the Princess of Wales, who was expected back in England on 13 October 1891 after staying with her parents in Denmark. Instead of returning in those circumstances, she decided to go to Russia and to stay with her sister, the Empress, in the Crimea, without saying when she would come home. She remained at Livadia during the Silver Wedding celebrations of the Emperor and Empress, leaving the Prince of Wales to explain as best he could the reasons for her absence on 9 November 1891, on the occasion of his fiftieth birthday.

The Prince of Wales celebrated his fiftieth birthday in some physical discomfort, as well as personal mortification, at Sandringham. A fire on 1 November had damaged the house quite badly; but he received deputations and many presents, and a body of actors and theatre managers brought him an eighteen-carat gold cigar box, weighing a hundred ounces, on which his plumes and feathers were picked out in diamonds of the first water.

The dangerous illness of Prince George, who was attacked

by typhoid, brought the Princess of Wales home with all speed from the Crimea. She reached England on 22 November, and a shared and overwhelming anxiety dispelled overnight the cloud which had troubled momentarily the Prince of Wales's domestic life. Prince George was declared to be out of danger on 3 December; and, while his father turned in a mood of fury to deal with the scurrilous pamphlet about his private affairs which was rumoured to be in circulation, Lady Charles Beresford telegraphed an urgent appeal to her husband to return from the Mediterranean to protect her.

After reaching England on 17 December 1891, Lord Charles despatched [34] a fiery letter (18 December) to the Prince of Wales. He denied that any pamphlet was in circulation, but said that he had divined the existence on the Prince's part of 'such a direct intention to damage my wife' that 'I now demand an apology fom Your Royal Highness, failing which I shall not only apply for an extension of leave, but I shall no longer intervene to prevent these matters becoming public'.

That letter precipitated a crisis, and Lord Salisbury remained in constant touch for one week with Queen Victoria, the Prince of Wales and the Beresfords in an effort to secure an acceptable settlement and to avert Lord Charles's reckless threat to publish details about the Prince's private life. Knollys wrote [35] (19 December) to Schomberg McDonnell:

> I think Lord Salisbury should know that the Princess of Wales is still more angry with Beresford than even is the case with the Prince; and especially with his letter, which she describes as most disrespectful and improper.
>
> She warmly supports the Prince in everything connected with the unfortunate affair, and is anxious to do all in her power to assist him.

After four frantic days, on the last of which Beresford was on the point of summoning representatives of the Press and Telegraph Agencies to his home in Eaton Square in order to recite his story before sacrificing his career and good name and bolting overnight to France with his wife, a settlement was reached by the Prime Minister. It was based upon a formal exchange of letters (drafted by Lord Salisbury) be-

tween the Prince of Wales and Lord Charles Beresford, and
the temporary exclusion from Court of Lady Brooke. Beresford's letter demanded a formal apology from the Prince of
Wales, who spent Christmas Day in London for the first
time since childhood, and the Prince replied [36] (24 December:

Dear Lord Charles Beresford,

I regret to find from your letter of 23rd instant that circumstances have occurred which have led Lady Charles Beresford to
believe that it was my intention publicly to wound her feelings.

I have never had any such intention, and I regret that she
should have been led to conceive an erroneous impression upon
the point.

I remain
   Your truly . . .

Young Reginald Brett (Lord Esher), who was in Queen
Victoria's confidence, noted [37] that 'Lord Salisbury brought
peace – whether with much honour or not may be ques-
tioned'; but occasional typhoons were an inevitable product
of some tropical aspects of the contemporary social climate.
Although the Prince of Wales had been at fault in intruding
into the Beresfords' private affairs, Lady Charles Beresford's
complaint, that a great personage who had formerly noticed
her had ceased to do so, was undignified; and her husband,
who blustered, was not entitled to redress. He earned, nevertheless, a wide measure of involuntary and irrational admiration for the spirited stand which he had made; and his
brother, Lord Waterford, was thankful to be able to return
to Lady Brooke (24 March 1892), for consignment to the fire,
the letter which had caused so much trouble.

Lord Waterford informed [38] the Prince of Wales (26
March) that Lady Charles Beresford had requested him
'ENTIRELY of her own free will' to return that letter 'to
its author'; but the Prince replied [39] (6 April) from the South
of France, where he was accompanied for a part of the time,
that year, by the Princess:

I have no desire to advert to what occurred at the end of last
year; but I can never forget, and shall never forgive, the conduct
of your brother and his wife towards me. His base ingratitude,

after a friendship of about 20 years, has hurt me more than words can say.

You, who have so chivalrous a nature and are such a thorough gentleman in every sense of the word, will be able to form some idea of what my feelings on the subject are!

I am personally most grateful to you for all you have done. . . .

Gladstone, who became Prime Minister for the fourth and last time, to Queen Victoria's distress and alarm, in August 1892, expressed privately to his family the view that the true remedy for trouble of that kind would be the abdication of the Queen and the assumption of responsibility by the Prince of Wales. There was no prospect of that, and Queen Victoria treated her eldest son with a deep, tender and indulgent affection, while continuing to exclude him from her confidence. When, for example, the Government was being changed in 1892, Knollys informed [40] Ponsonby (15 August) 'The Prince of Wales writes to me that there is not much use his remaining on at Cowes (though he is willing to do so), as he is not of the slightest use to the Queen; that everything he says or suggests is pooh-poohed; and that his sisters and brother are much more listened to than he is. . . .'

Two of the Prince's less happy suggestions were that Lord Carrington should be sent to India as Viceroy, and that Mrs Gladstone should receive a peerage and become Mistress of the Robes; but he was more helpful in the case of Lord Rosebery. Queen Victoria authorized the Prince of Wales to approach Rosebery, who had made great difficulty about becoming Foreign Secretary, without using her name; and Rosebery informed Gladstone that the Prince's intervention had tipped the balance and that it had induced him to accept.

Immediately after his return to office, Gladstone revived [41] officially with Queen Victoria the question of the form in which reports of proceedings in the Cabinet should be communicated to the Prince of Wales. A practice had grown up over the years whereby the Prince received, at irregular intervals, edited and shortened versions of the reports of Cabinet meetings which the Prime Minister sent regularly to the Sovereign and which constituted, until 1916, the only record; and Gladstone's secretary, Sir Algernon West, wrote [42] (14 November 1892) to Sir Henry Ponsonby:

... I hope you will trust to my discretion in what I say to the Prince of Wales. My idea was to let him know generally what was going on, rather than anything else. If there was anything personal to H.M., or, unhappily, any difference in the Cabinet, I should not mention it. ...

There will be some Cabinets shortly, and I will send you a specimen of what I say, and you can compare it with what Mr Gladstone says to the Queen, and tell me if you approve.

Such information was always sent to the Prince in a red Cabinet despatch box to which he, in common with the Queen and all ministers and private secretaries, owned a key. Disraeli had presented the Prince with that key in the first instance, but it was one thing to possess a key, and another to find, inside his personal box, the information for which he thirsted; and the Prince of Wales had acquired great skill in supplementing the meagre information sent to him by means of conversations with individual ministers as occasion offered.

Foreign Office despatches and papers interested the Prince much more than did any others; but they were circulated in boxes to which he possessed no key. That deprivation had embarrassed him at times, and while quarrelling with the Kaiser during the spring of 1889 he had had to return unread some relevant papers, which Lord Salisbury had sent him in a Foreign Office box, with a request that they should be sent back in a Cabinet box: 'I am sorry', the Prince wrote [43] (9 April 1889) to Lord Salisbury, 'to have given you the trouble of sending me another box, but since a long time I have only possessed the Cabinet key.'

Lord Rosebery rectified that position in 1892 by sending the Prince the special gold key which had been made for the Prince Consort and used by him to open the Foreign office boxes. Thereafter, except when he was abroad, the Prince of Wales was kept as well-informed about Foreign Office business as Queen Victoria was, and in informal conversations with the Foreign Secretary, ambassadors and others, he supplemented documents which he read.

In the meantime, the Prince of Wales's private life continued to be troubled. His elder son, the Duke of Clarence, was so difficult and unsatisfactory that his parents were almost at their wits' ends to know what to do, and three different plans were devised.[44] The Princess of Wales wanted the Duke to remain in Ireland with his regiment, so that she could control and see him as much as possible; Queen Victoria wanted him to travel in Europe; and the Prince of Wales wanted to send him, as a punishment and precaution, to the furthest ends of the Empire.

'If you think Eddy too English,' the Prince of Wales wrote [45] (5 August 1891) to Queen Victoria, 'it is a good fault in these days and will make him much more popular. ... His remaining in the Army is simply waste of time. ... His education and future have been a matter of some considerable anxiety to us, and the difficulty of rousing him is very great. A good sensible wife with some considerable character is what he needs most, but where is she to be found?'

Sir Francis Knollys explained [46] (8 August 1891) to Lord Salisbury's private secretary:

As you are aware, the Queen strongly advocates Prince Eddy travelling in Europe, instead of visiting the Cape of Good Hope (or, rather, South Africa), New Zealand, Canada, etc.

Unfortunately, her views on *certain social* subjects are so strong, that the Prince of Wales does not like to tell her his real reason for sending Prince Eddy away, which is intended as a *punishment*, and as a means of keeping him out of harm's way; and I am afraid that neither of those objects would be attained by his simply travelling about Europe. She is therefore giving her advice in the dark.

Queen Victoria was fairly well-informed, in fact, about the life which Prince Eddy was leading, and she suggested [47] to the Prince of Wales (5 August) that although there were as many 'designing pretty women in the Colonies' as there were everywhere else, a young Prince would acquire more polish by visiting European Courts. 'A Prince ought to be cosmopolitan. What has made William what he is, is, to a great extent, owing to his never having travelled.' She added, not very hopefully, or helpfully:

You speak of his apathy and want of application. *You* disliked your lessons very much, and it was very difficult to make you apply. But you travelled a great deal, and with good people, and you profited immensely by what you saw, and by the number of interesting and clever people you got to know.

No doubt you were much more lively than Eddy. ...

After a fortnight's anxious deliberation the Princess of Wales had her way. Prince Eddy's courtship of Princess Hélène d'Orléans had been abandoned, but it was decided that he should remain all winter with his regiment, and that he should be married to Princess May of Teck during the spring. Knollys wrote [48] (19 August 1891) to Ponsonby:

I think the preliminaries are now pretty well settled, but do you suppose Princess May will make any resistance? I do not anticipate any real opposition on Prince Eddy's part if he is properly managed and is told he *must* do it – that it is for the good of the country, etc., etc.

The Prince of Wales undertook to manage his son, who was promoted to lieutenant-colonel's rank, and who proposed successfully to Princess May of Teck on 3 December 1891, while staying at Luton Hoo with the Danish Minister, C. F. de Falbe. The nation and Empire rejoiced with the Prince and Princess of Wales in the young lovers' prospect of happiness; but the Duke of Clarence retired to bed at Sandringham on 8 January 1892 with influenza and died six days later, of pneumonia.

The promotion of Prince George to the position of heir presumptive to the throne was a merciful act of providence. Prince George, who possessed a strong and exemplary character as well as a robust constitution, had early given promise of becoming the embodiment of all those domestic and public virtues which the British peoples cherish; but the untimely death of the Duke of Clarence, who had been nicknamed 'Collar and Cuffs', plunged the nation, for the moment, into gloom. His parents were drawn very closely together; the Prince of Wales sobbed at the funeral service held at Windsor on 20 January, and Queen Victoria wrote [49] (16 January) to the Empress Frederick: 'He is broken down, and poor dear Alix, though bearing up wonderfully, does nothing but cry, Bertie says.' The Prince himself had written [50] two days earlier to his mother: 'Gladly would I have given my life for his, as I put no value on mine. ... Such a tragedy has never before occurred in the annals of our family, and it is hard that poor little May should virtually become a widow before she is a wife.'

After visiting Denmark in May for the golden wedding celebrations of the King and Queen, at which the Emperor and Empress of Russia were present also, the Prince and Princess of Wales spent the summer of 1892 at Sandringham. A new wing had been added, after the fire; but the Prince of Wales became extremely restless, and Queen Victoria wrote [51] (13 June) to the Empress Frederick: 'Poor Bertie – his is not a nature made to bear sorrow, or a life without amusement and excitement – he gets bitter and irritable.'

The Prince amused himself by ordering the construction on the Clyde of a new racing cutter, *Britannia* (300 tons), which outclassed all rivals for four years. Besides accommodating her owner and a guest or two in luxury, *Britannia*, which carried a crew of 28, began her racing career in 1893 by winning 32 prizes in 43 races. On the turf, on the other hand, the Prince was much less successful, but he allowed Hirsch and Lord Marcus Beresford to move his horses from John Porter's stables at Kingslere to those of Richard Marsh at Newmarket which were more accessible from Sandringham.

When the mourning period was ended, the Prince of Wales informed [52] Prince George (5 August 1892) that 'William the Great' had been on his best behaviour at Cowes – 'not the least grand, and very quiet, most amiable in every respect'. The Prince left Cowes for Homburg, and arranged there that his son, who left the Navy to be groomed for future kingship, should be coached intensively by a professor at Heidelberg University. He instructed [53] his son (24 and 27 August) to bring out his *'whole* German uniform, with boots', and *'all'* his German orders, 'as well as the Garter', adding: 'I have ordered fresh epaulettes for you.'

After settling Prince George, the Prince travelled to Abergeldie for deerstalking, but returned to London on 9 October to meet the Duke and Duchess of Teck. He had never cared much for the Duke and Duchess, but he was utterly devoted to his surviving son, Prince George, who was created Duke of York and whom he wished to see early and happily married. Prince George had been distressed beyond measure by the death of his elder brother and was tempted by excessive diffidence for a time to regard himself as almost an interloper in the direct line of succession to the throne. His father became increasingly convinced that an engagement during the spring to Princess May of Teck would be productive of great happiness, and that one effect of such happiness would be to fortify the self-confidence of the Duke of York.

It was fortunate that a happy contemporary family precedent existed for a switch which, however natural and desirable, posed some self-evident initial difficulty. The Princess of Wales's sister, 'Minny', the Empress Marie Feodorovna of Russia, had, as Princess Marie Sophia Frederika Dagmar of Schleswig-Holstein-Sonderburg-Glucksburg, been engaged first to her husband's elder brother, the Grand Duke Nicholas, who died in 1865. More than a year later, in November 1866, she had married instead the younger brother, 'Sasha', who became the Emperor Alexander III.

Preoccupied by that delicate and important private matter, the Prince of Wales remained at Newmarket when the poet laureate, Lord Tennyson, was buried in Westminster Abbey on 12 October 1892, and his absence from the funeral excited comment. Critical chatter was unfair, for the Prince had scarcely known the famous laureate; but the contrast between his neglect of authors, and his encouragement of artists and actors, deprived the Prince of a measure of literary goodwill which he might otherwise have consolidated. Similar neglect on the part of ancient Jewish kings may have inspired some harsh judgements recorded against their names in the Old Testament; and while the young Rudyard Kipling described the Prince of Wales rudely, in America, as a corpulent voluptuary, Max Beerbohm started later to draw a long series of extraordinarily venomous caricatures.

In December 1892, the Prince of Wales accepted an invitation from Gladstone to become a member of a Royal

Commission on the Aged Poor, over which Lord Aberdare
and, later, Lord Playfair presided. The Prince was the more
delighted to serve because Lord Salisbury, in 1891, had rejected his offer to serve on a more palpably controversial
inquiry into the relations between employers and employed.
The new Royal Commission was concerned with the question of relief for persons rendered destitute by old age, and
the Prince gave up his annual visit to the South of France
to attend its meetings during the spring of 1893.

'I don't think', the Prince wrote [54] (16 March) to the
Duke of York, 'that I have been more busy in my life';
and he attended 35 out of 48 sessions during the two years
while the commission sat. He addressed many shrewd questions to witnesses; was most affable to his working-class
colleagues, Henry Broadhurst, M.P., and Joseph Arch, M.P.;
and doodled Union Jacks at odd moments with the aid of
red and blue pencils.

A majority report in March 1895 rejected any plan of
State pensions for the aged poor 'in view of the financial and
economic difficulties involved', but a minority report recommended pensions on a contributory insurance basis. Several
members signed individual recommendations and comments, and Henry Broadhurst was alone in declaring unequivocally that pensions should be awarded as of right,
without any previous contributions by beneficiaries.

The Prince of Wales was eager to see suffering relieved,
but he equated socialist remedies with revolution. He feared
the risk of damage to the organic structure of a hierarchical
society which he regarded as divinely ordained, and the unforeseen bitterness of the controversy aroused by the inquiry inhibited him from expressing or endorsing publicly
any view. He signed, therefore, a statement that he was
obliged to observe strict political neutrality; and no action
was taken to provide State pensions until Lloyd George's
Old Age Pensions Act of 1908.

Family life brought the Prince of Wales much happiness
in 1893 and 1894, and he enjoyed an ideal relationship with
his surviving son, the Duke of York: 'We ... are more like
brothers', he wrote [55] to him (25 August 1894), 'than Father

and son'; and the Duke, while retaining wholesome awe of his father, reciprocated that affection most warmly. To the great joy of the nation, he married (6 July 1893) Princess May of Teck, who gave birth to a prince (the Duke of Windsor) in June 1894.

Although the success of his racing yacht, *Britannia*, continued to be offset by failure on the turf, there were, in the Prince of Wales's stables, one or two good-looking and promising colts. All were sired by *St Simon* (owned by the Duke of Portland) out of *Perdita II* which the Prince had bought for nine hundred guineas. *St Simon* had also sired *Matchbox*, which Maurice Hirsch had bought, and which started as a 6–4 odds on favourite for the Paris Grand Prix on 17 June 1894. *Matchbox*, unhappily, was beaten at the post by a short head, and the six hundred pounds lost by the Prince of Wales on that race is the largest recorded bet which he ever placed on an individual horse for a win.

In that month, the Czarevitch (Nicholas II), who succeeded his ailing father, Alexander III, before the year was out, came to England to spend some weeks at Windsor with his fiancée, Princess Alix (Alicky) of Hesse, under the chaperonage of Queen Victoria, who was the Princess's grandmother. The Prince of Wales invited the Czarevitch, whom he thought charming but weak and unsophisticated, to spend two days (28–29 June) at Sandringham.

The Czarevitch, who had been shielded from the world, was bewildered by the company at Sandringham. It included Maurice Hirsch, who was less interested on that occasion in horses, or even in railway contracts, than he was in philanthropic plans to succour oppressed Russian Jews. The Prince of Wales had gone to Sandringham only in order to auction some of his horses; and the Czarevitch, in a letter to his mother, the Empress Marie (who was always horrified and astonished by her brother-on-law's philo-semitism) described [56] the house party as 'rather strange. Most of them were horse dealers, amongst others a Baron Hirsch! The Cousins rather enjoyed the situation and kept teasing me about it; but I tried to keep away as much as possible, and not to talk.'

13
Locust Years

Big yacht racing from 1893 to 1896, and horse racing there-after, did most to consolidate the popularity of the Prince of Wales. As Commodore of the Royal Yacht Squadron and of the Royal Thames Yacht Club, and as president of the Yacht Racing Association, he lifted the prestige of that sport to an unprecedented height. He discountenanced international rivalries and never participated in races for the America's Cup, while affording vicarious enjoyment to millions, and social opportunities to millionaires.

Loving excitement and sea breezes, the Prince sailed per-sonally as often as possible in races aboard *Britannia* in home waters as well as in the Mediterranean; and he was jealous of the reputation which he acquired as the greatest sportsman of his day and age. He achieved many successes, and, after defeating Barclay Walker's *Ailsa* and Lord Dun-raven's *Valkyrie III* in northern waters on 3 July 1895, he wrote[1] proudly to the Duke of York: 'To-day's victory indeed makes *Britannia* the first racing yacht afloat!'

Having made the sport of big yacht racing his peculiar province, the Prince of Wales was vexed when the Kaiser interfered. His nephew, whom he dubbed 'The Boss of Cowes', started to inject an element of national and per-sonal rivalry into the sport, and the annual regatta was transformed, in consequence, from a cosmopolitan social gathering into a political arena.

The Kaiser used Cowes to display the nascent might of the German Navy, and to demonstrate his country's ability to challenge England effectively at sea. His giant *Meteor II*, which was an improved edition of *Britannia* by the same designer but on a much larger scale, outclassed all racing cutters in 1896. The Prince, who had found yacht racing a drain upon his resources, lacked the means to meet that challenge, and he took, therefore, in 1897 a painful, sudden but firm decision to abandon the sport.

The Prince tried at first to induce 'Boni' de Castellane, who had married a daughter of the American multi-millionaire, Jay Gould, to take *Britannia* off his hands for ten thousand pounds; but de Castellane, who was building a miniature Trianon Palace in pink marble in the Avenue du Bois in Paris, preferred also to have his yachts constructed to his own specifications. *Britannia* was sold, accordingly, in the autumn of 1897 to the inventor of Bovril, John Lawson-Johnston; and the Prince, who bought her back for sentimental reasons as soon as he became King, never participated personally in yacht racing again.

The Princess of Wales was intensely proud of her husband's prowess in big yacht racing, and in other fields. She was inhibited, however, by deafness as well as by temperament, from sharing many of his activities, and she found increasing consolation in the society of her two unmarried younger daughters. Queen Victoria and the Empress Frederick thought that her affection was much too possessive and that both young Princesses were being deprived of any adequate chance to marry. The Queen explained[2] (6 June 1894) to the Empress that she had discussed the subject exhaustively with the Prince of Wales, who had informed her 'that Alix found them such companions that she would not encourage their marrying, and that they themselves had no inclination for it (in which I think she is mistaken as regards Maud). He said that he was "powerless", which I cannot understand. . . . It is very unfortunate.'

The Prince of Wales enjoyed spoiling his daughters, while leaving all serious aspects of their welfare entirely in the hands of his wife to whose domestic caprices he had learned to yield, although not always with a good grace. Lord Rosebery dismayed[3] the Princess of Wales by appearing to consider himself a candidate for Princess Victoria's hand, but his suit was not pressed and she died unmarried in 1935. Princess Maud, on the other hand, became engaged in October 1895 to her first cousin, Prince Charles of Denmark, who was an officer in the Danish Navy. The wedding took place very quietly in the private chapel of Buckingham Palace on 22 July 1896; and the Princess lived for another forty years. She became Queen of Norway in 1905, when her husband, who took the name of King Haakon VII, was elected* to that country's throne.

Throughout the 1890s the Marlborough House circle was galvanized by a spectacular infusion of new wealth from the gold and diamond mines of South Africa; and the presence in a house party at Sandringham (10–12 July 1895) of three of the newest millionaires (W. W. Astor, Colonel John North and J. B. Robinson) caused a gasp of surprise in London and resentment in old-fashioned quarters. The Prince, who took his name off the Travellers' Club when its members blackballed Cecil Rhodes, regarded money as the most practical and convenient social yardstick. He equated it with power which he loved to see exercised whether by Rhodes who enjoyed an annual personal income of six hundred thousand pounds or by other friends. He was delighted, for example, when his American friend, Mrs Ogden Goelet, bribed Mlle Yvette Guilbert successfully, with an unprecedented fee of six hundred pounds, to break a contract in Paris in order to sing before him at Cannes on 16 March 1894. He was so much pleased and impressed that he promised to do all in his power to make the singer's debut in London an outstanding triumph.

On 13 May, accordingly, the Prince took the Dukes of Cambridge and Connaught to a supper party which he asked the composer, Sir Arthur Sullivan, to give for Mlle Guilbert in London, and at which the Austrian ambassador, Count Deym, was so unguarded that fellow-guests were terrified lest his remarks should be overheard. He told his neighbours that the Prince was much too familiar in Paris with La Goulue, a famous dancer at the Moulin Rouge, and that on a recent occasion, when La Goulue had greeted his appearance

* See p. 426 below.

with a ringing shout of "Ullo Wales!", he had merely chuckled and ordered that all dancers and members of the orchestra should be supplied immediately with champagne.[4]

In response to an urgent appeal addressed by the Empress of Russia (Minny) to her sister, the Princess of Wales, the Prince left London (30 October) with the Princess, at only twenty-four hours'notice, for Livadia in the Crimea, where the Emperor Alexander III was lying critically ill. At the British Embassy in Vienna, the following evening, the Prince learned that the Emperor was already dead; and in ordering the Duke of York (1 and 5 November) to come immediately to St Petersburg, 'out of respect for poor dear Uncle Sasha's memory' and because 'the opportunity to see the great capital of Russia is not one to be missed', the Prince wrote[5]: 'Poor Mama is terribly upset. ... This is indeed the most trying and sad journey I have ever undertaken.'

The Prime Minister, Lord Rosebery, begged the Prince of Wales to take advantage of that unique opportunity to woo the impressionable young Emperor, Nicholas II; and the Prince and Princess reached Yalta on 4 November. The Princess went to stay with her widowed sister, whose bedroom she shared, while the Prince was allotted a separate palace overlooking the sea.

On 8 November an imperial train started to convey the Emperor Nicholas II, his fiancée, Princess Alix (Alicky) of Hesse, the Empress Marie (Minny), the Prince and Princess of Wales and the embalmed corpse of Alexander III by easy stages from Sevastopol via Moscow to St Petersburg. At St Petersburg the body was laid in state in the Cathedral of St Peter and St Paul where long services, with elaborate ceremonial, were held every day and attended punctiliously by the Prince of Wales.

Besides the Duke of York, and Prince Henry of Prussia, the Kings of Denmark, Greece, Rumania and Serbia came also to St Petersburg; and Queen Victoria was persuaded by the Prince of Wales to appoint Nicholas II to be Honorary Colonel of the Scots Greys. The Prince, in return, was made Honorary Colonel of the 27th Dragoon Regiment of Kiev on his birthday (9 November); and Lord Carrington found him trying on the uniform when he was ushered (16 November) into the Prince's apartments at the Anitchkoff Palace. Carrington, who came out with others to reinforce the Prince's suite, was astonished[6] to see 'a fat man in a huge shaggy greatcoat looking like a giant polar bear. It was the Prince of Wales!! Royalties look dreadful in ill-fitting foreign uniforms.'

'Visit Emperor and present myself in new uniform … 10.15', the Prince recorded[7] (17 November) in his diary; and remembering his failure with his German nephew six years earlier at the funeral of Frederick III, he did everything he could think of to cosset the young Czar. He was equally attentive to his niece, Princess Alix of Hesse, with whom the Czar was deeply in love; and in the intervals of sight-seeing tours, conducted for the Duke of York's benefit by the frivolous but highly intelligent Grand Duke Vladimir, who was the Czar's uncle, the Prince enjoyed long conversations about Anglo-Russian relations with the aged Foreign Minister, Nicholas Giers.

When the Prince confided doubts to Carrington about his nephew's autocratic outlook and lack of worldly sense, his friend remarked that a revolution was inevitable. The Prince retorted[8] that nothing was inevitable, but that it was necessary everywhere to move with the times, and that even in England a modern reform of the House of Lords was overdue. The Prince added that Queen Victoria hated that idea, but that he personally was 'all in favour' of it. He explained that Rosebery had convinced him of its necessity, and he suggested that early action would strengthen Rosebery's hand by preventing his Radical tail from swinging too far towards the left.

The Prince of Wales went out of his way to be kind to the King of Serbia, who was snubbed by all the Grand Dukes on account of his lack of polish; and everyone acknowledged the Prince's charm. He was regarded as much the most outstanding personality in the capital, and the Russian Press was enthusiastic in his praise. He made no complaint about the funeral service which lasted for over four hours, and

which was a severe ordeal for those who had to kiss the
dead Emperor's lips: 'As he lay uncovered in his coffin',
Carrington noted[9], 'his face looked a dreadful colour and
the smell was awful. He was not embalmed until 3 days after
death!'

'Alix', the Prince of Wales wrote[10] (16 November) to
Queen Victoria, 'is everything in the world to Minny just
now.' The Princess was always with her sister, the Dowager
Empress, who appeared to have the young Emperor under
almost complete control. She would not even permit him to
leave the Anitchkoff Palace to spend a brief honeymoon at
Tsarskoe Selo after court mourning had been suspended for
twenty-four hours on 26 November, when he married his
Hessian Princess. Writing from the Kremlin on 11 November 1894, the Prince of Wales reassured[11] Queen Victoria
that 'Nicky does everything so well and quietly, but is naturally shy and timid. ... He and Alicky are quite devoted to
one another.' He added, 'There is no doubt that the greatest
loyalty and affection for the Emperor and his family exists
among the people, but they only wish to be trusted by him;
and if Nicky is liberal in his views, and tolerant to his subjects, a more popular Ruler of this country could not possibly
exist.' There was, however, nothing liberal about the last of
the Czars, who seized an early opportunity to describe democratic ideals as senseless dreams. He may well have been
right to distrust his subjects, but the unimpaired autocracy
which he strove to maintain was hopelessly inefficient, and
that weakness proved fatal.

After their wedding the young Emperor and Empress did
not leave the Anitchkoff Palace, in which the Dowager Empress continued to live and in which the Prince and Princess
of Wales were staying. The Prince told[12] Carrington that
the newly married couple 'came down to breakfast next
morning as if nothing had happened', but that the Emperor
had marked the occasion by giving the Princess of Wales a
beautiful crystal flower, made by Fabergé, with a great
diamond at its centre, in a gold pot. The Prince often expressed admiration of that Russian court jeweller's crafts-
manship, and he and the Princess loved to give and to

receive pretty Fabergé objects at Christmas and at other times, including birthdays.

The Princess of Wales remained for two months with her sister after her husband and son had gone home; and in London on 6 December 1894 the Prince was congratulated by the Prime Minister, whom he entertained at luncheon, on 'the good and patriotic work' which he had accomplished. 'Never', Lord Rosebery wrote [13] (6 December), 'has Your Royal Highness stood so high in the national esteem as to-day, for never have you had such an opportunity. That at last has come, and has enabled you to justify the highest anticipations, and to render a signal service to your country as well as to Russia and the peace of the world.'

On that day the Empress Alix, who had started already to acquire an ascendancy over her husband, wrote [14] to Queen Victoria: 'I never can thank God enough for giving me such a husband; and his love for you touches me also so deeply, for have you not been as a mother to me since beloved Mama died?' The Czar wrote [15] (15 February 1895) equally affectionately to the Prince of Wales, and in acknowledging the gift of a gold and jewelled sword, 'with a touching inscription on the blade', he thanked his uncle for having allowed 'Aunt Alix' to stay behind with his widowed mother: 'We do all we can to help her in her misery. Good-bye, dearest Uncle Bertie. Please give my tenderest love to all. Believe me, ever your most loving nephew, Nicky.'

The young Emperor, who was an untried political factor of the utmost consequence, had spoken vaguely, but at considerable length, to his uncle about his hopes for world peace and disarmament. Russia was so backward industrially that she had most to gain by such a plan; and the Prince of Wales, who regarded all such talk as crack-brained, visionary folly, never altered the opinion which he formed about his nephew at that time: 'As regards the Czar's idea of disarmament throughout all nations,' he wrote [16] (September 1899) to Lady Warwick,* 'it is the greatest rubbish and nonsense I ever heard of. The thing is simply *impossible!*'

* Lord Brooke succeeded his father as fifth Earl of Warwick in 1893.

Although he liked his nephew better than he had liked the more formidable and much more intelligent Emperor Alexander III, he described him sadly, but invariably, as 'weak as water'.

The Foreign Office valued, nevertheless, the very happy personal relationship which had been established between the Prince of Wales and the hereditary 'autocrat of all the Russias'. It was as different as possible from the painfully strained relationship which existed between the Prince and his German nephew, who arrived at Cowes on 4 August 1895, escorted by his two latest and fastest warships, *Wörth* and *Weissenburg*.

On 6 August 1895 the Kaiser exasperated the Prince of Wales by showing greater want of tact than on any previous occasion. He celebrated the twenty-fifth anniversary of the Germany victory at Wörth, during the Franco-Prussian War, by delivering, aboard the cruiser *Wörth*, a sabre-rattling speech which was as hotly resented by the British, as it was by the French, Press because it had been made in British waters and on a purely social occasion.

Two days later (8 August), while dining with the Prince of Wales, the Kaiser, in boisterous humour, gave further personal offence. The talk turned upon negotiations which were in progress for a definition of the frontier between British India and French Indo-China; and the Emperor suggested, as a joke, that a breakdown might lead to war. Forgetting that his uncle was sensitive about the fact that he had never seen active service, the Emperor thumped him suddenly on the back, and exclaimed[17]: 'So you'll soon be off to India again, and we'll see at last what you're really good for as a soldier!'

Such troubles were trivial, but the Prince, in his fifties, could not help being a little jealous of the opportunities enjoyed by his nephews, the Kaiser and the Czar. The world hung upon their words, however commonplace or foolish, while his experience, except on nice questions of etiquette, was rarely in demand. He was interested at that moment in the problem of selecting an ambassador to succeed Sir Edward Malet in Berlin, but no one sought his opinion, and after dubbing his nephew, who had shown no wish to discuss the subject, as 'the most brilliant failure in history', he escaped thankfully (20 August) to Homburg.

The Prince wanted Field-Marshal Lord Wolseley to take the Berlin Embassy in order that the forty-five-year-old Duke of Connaught, who was Queen Victoria's favourite son, might succeed the seventy-six-year-old Duke of Cambridge as Commander-in-Chief of the British Army. But a hitch occurred after the Prince had helped to persuade the Duke of Cambridge to resign at last in November 1895, and after the Kaiser had expressed delight at the prospect of receiving Wolseley as ambassador. The Cabinet invited Wolseley to choose between Berlin and the Horse Guards, and he chose the latter without hesitation.

A career diplomatist, Sir Frank Lascelles, was appointed, accordingly, to Berlin; and Wolseley went out of his way to soothe and conciliate the Prince of Wales. One of his first actions as Commander-in-Chief was to persuade Queen Victoria to withdraw an invitation which she had extended out of pure goodness of heart to the Duke of Cambridge, to represent her at the annual ceremony of trooping the colour on the Horse Guards Parade; and the Prince of Wales was immensely gratified at being authorized (14 May 1896) to take that birthday parade on the Queen's behalf in 1896 and in all subsequent years.

Lord Salisbury, who became Prime Minister again in June 1895, was less communicative than Lord Rosebery had been, and the Prince of Wales manifested impatience in consequence. He was vexed, for example, at not being advised when his candidate for the post of British Minister in Stockholm was rejected in favour of a more senior diplomatist; but Knollys assured [18] Salisbury (29 June 1896) that 'he really only requires to have things properly explained to him, and he is then always most reasonable'.

A year later, the Prince was vexed by Lord Salisbury's refusal to send copies of despatches on the Greek problem to the Princess of Wales. The Prime Minister undertook, instead, to keep the Princess posted with the latest news, but the Prince retorted that Queen Victoria had made, and failed to keep, the same promise. The King of Greece, who was the Princess's favourite brother, had been compelled by his subjects to involve his country in a disastrous war with Turkey in an attempt to annex Crete; and the Prince of Wales wrote [19] (17 July 1897) to Salisbury: 'If only England would lead the way, and "put her foot down", Greece may yet be rescued from the terrible position in which she is now placed.'

Greece was rescued by the Great Powers, and the Prince of Wales used his influence with the Czar in an effort to secure the post of High Commissioner of Crete for Prince George of Greece. Despite German and Austrian objections, that arrangement was carried into effect; but arbitrary government by Prince George provoked an increasing measure of unrest.

The fight waged by his fat friend, King Carlos of Portugal, against bankruptcy and revolution gave the Prince of Wales intermittent concern for many years. The Portuguese dream of retrieving their financial plight by exploiting an Empire stretching across Africa, from Angola to Mozambique, conflicted with the ambitions of the British South Africa Company, of which the Prince of Wales's son-in-law, the Duke of Fife, was Vice-President. After Portuguese hopes had been blasted by a British ultimatum in 1890, King Carlos's army began to display symptoms of disaffection, and a republican movement reared its head.

Until he was assassinated in 1908, King Carlos was extraordinarily well served by his agent in London, Luis de Soveral,* whose effervescent sparkle and conversational gift captivated the Prince of Wales. Nicknamed 'The Blue Monkey', Soveral concealed discreetly his outstanding ability, and proved irresistible to many of the Prince's women friends. He played a very prominent part in Edwardian social life before and after the Prince of Wales became King; and he remained an intimate friend of King Edward, as well as Portuguese Minister in London, until the end.

* Marquis de Soveral, G.C.M.G., G.C.V.O. (1862–1922), Portuguese Foreign Minister, 1895–7 and Portuguese Minister in London, 1897–1910.

Anxious to do what he could to help King Carlos, the Prince of Wales explained at the outset that his position was most difficult: 'I have had frequent conversations with Lord Salisbury and M. de Soveral', he wrote [20] (28 February 1891) to the King, '... but you must understand that we have also a public opinion to deal with which, though better instructed, is equally exacting.' After Portuguese public opinion had caused bloody rioting in Oporto, the Prince of Wales persuaded Queen Victoria, with much difficulty, to confer the Order of the Garter upon King Carlos, whom he invited to stay at Sandringham in November 1895.

Territorial and financial negotiations between the British and Portuguese Governments were spread over many years. The German Government would have liked to buy some Portuguese colonies and was therefore closely concerned; and the Prince of Wales was torn between his enthusiasm for Cecil Rhodes and the British South Africa Company, and a well-founded fear for the stability of his friend's throne. The issue formed part of the much wider problem of the future of the South African sub-continent, where the initiative lay no longer within the direct control of the British Government.

That initiative was divided in 1895 between Cecil Rhodes, Prime Minister of the self-governing Cape Colony, and Paul Kruger, President of the Boer Republic of the Transvaal. Rhodes wanted to transform the entire sub-continent into a loyal and federated British dominion on the Canadian model: Kruger hoped to use the economic supremacy of the Transvaal to attract the whole of South Africa into a republican federation owing no allegiance to the British Crown.

Believing delay to be dangerous, and discounting German professions of support for Kruger, Rhodes attempted to organize a revolt in the Transvaal which he timed to coincide with a lightning raid on Johannesburg, led by his close friend, Leander Starr Jameson, at the head of 470 of the South Africa Company's mounted police with eight machine-guns and three pieces of artillery. Both plans miscarried, for the Transvaal conspirators failed to rise; and Jameson, who crossed the border on 30 December 1895, was surrounded and compelled to surrender near Johannesburg, on 2 January 1896.

After presiding at a conference of ministers on 3 January, the German Emperor telegraphed his congratulations to President Kruger, thereby drawing upon himself a storm of British popular abuse which might otherwise have been directed at the maladroit and reprehensible conduct of Cecil Rhodes. Lord Salisbury admitted [21] to the Prince of Wales that public opinion would have compelled Great Britain to declare war upon Germany if, as had seemed likely at one moment, marines from German East Africa had been landed at Delagoa Bay and marched thence to Pretoria as a reinforcement to Kruger.

After resigning his office as Prime Minister of Cape Colony, Rhodes came to London to face a Parliamentary Committee of Inquiry which held its first public session in Westminster Hall on 16 February 1897. He admitted that he had been 'a naughty boy'; but the Prince of Wales, who attended several sessions, linked arms as he entered the Hall on that first occasion with the Duke of Abercorn, President of the British South Africa Company, and Lord Selborne, Under-Secretary for the colonies.

The Prince, who displayed open sympathy with the misguided Jameson raiders, scolded Lord Salisbury, genially but with serious intent, for his refusal to receive Cecil Rhodes. He asked [22] the Prime Minister (4 February 1897) to send his reasons in writing to Sir Francis Knollys; he entertained Rhodes frequently himself; and he invited to Sandringham (17–19 April 1897) Sir John Willoughby, who had been released a few days earlier from prison, and who was being subjected to a damaging examination by the Parliamentary Committee of Inquiry about the part which he had played in the raid.

During the final years of his long apprenticeship, the Prince continued to protest [23] at intervals to Joseph Chamberlain, the Colonial Secretary, as well as to Lord Salisbury, that he was not being kept sufficiently well informed about the course of events. His frustration was relieved, however, by a dramatic change in his fortunes on the turf. He had

had little luck before 1896, when he started the season with thirteen horses in training, including the redoubtable *Persimmon* (by *St Simon* out of *Perdita II*); but *Persimmon* developed an abscess in the mouth which prevented his running in the Two Thousand Guineas. That race was won by Leopold de Rothschild's *St Frusquin*, which started as an odds-on favourite for the Derby (3 June 1896), run on ground as hard as iron. Odds against *Persimmon*, which had been a most difficult horse to train, were quoted at 5-1; but amid thunderous applause he won the Derby by a head from *St Frusquin*, and the Prince of Wales, after giving his annual dinner that evening at Marlborough House to the members of the Jockey Club, and after supping at midnight with Lady Dudley, went to bed at last the happiest as well as the most popular man in the kingdom.

The Prince of Wales earned £28,734 in stake money in 1896, and £15,219 in 1897, and in both years he was second on the list of winning owners. He was much less successful in 1898 and had a miserable year in 1899, but in 1900, when he won the Derby again with *Persimmon*'s brother, *Diamond Jubilee*, he earned £31,744. He sold *Diamond Jubilee*, when its racing career was ended, to an Argentine dealer for £31,500; and, taking profits on sales of horses into account, he had the satisfaction of making racing pay a very handsome dividend over the years, apart from the immense popularity and pleasure which he harvested. Between 1886, when he began, and 1910, when he died, his stallions earned £269,495 in stud fees, and his horses won £146,345 in stake money – £415,840 in all.

ii

The Prince of Wales was delighted when that brilliant young soldier, Sir Herbert Kitchener, was ordered to advance southwards from Egypt on the first stage of the conquest of the Sudan: 'I hope, as you do,' he wrote [24] (20 March 1896) to the Duke of York, 'that the Force will be large enough, as any reverses would be disastrous to our interests. The French are mad with rage with us about it; but, as we never do right in their eyes, it is useless paying any attention to their abuse.'

Convinced that British isolation was becoming increasingly dangerous, the Prince agreed with his mother that it was necessary to forget the Kaiser's telegram to President Kruger: 'From reliable sources', he informed [25] the Duke of York (20 April), 'I hear he is very sorry about that unlucky telegram, and is most desirous to be on the best terms with us – especially publicly.' The Germans were eager to exploit Anglo–French differences; and Queen Victoria had been amazed when the Prince of Wales begged her impulsively to telegraph congratulations to old Prince Bismarck on his birthday in 1895. She refused,[26] on the grounds that she had never done so before, that Bismarck was no friend of hers, or England's, and that it would have annoyed the French; but the Prince held that the gesture would have been a useful token of goodwill.

The Prince considered also that steps to end British isolation were required; and the fact that his country was without a friend in the world had been made apparent not only by the Jameson Raid but by a preposterous crisis which occurred in South America at the same time. Venezuela had laid claim, on historical grounds, to a large part of British Guiana, and while negotiations were in progress President Cleveland of the United States sent a blustering and provocative message to Congress on 17 December 1895. Pleading the Monroe Doctrine, and focusing his gaze on the next Presidential Election, he announced that he proposed to settle the Anglo-Venezuelan dispute himself and to employ force, if necessary, to impose his decision; and that vigorous twist administered to the lion's tail caused a transport of unseemly belligerent enthusiasm to convulse America.

That utterly unexpected but imminent prospect of war with the United States aroused bewilderment and horror in Great Britain; and, at the height of the crisis, the proprietor of the *New York World*, Joseph Pullitzer, cabled an invitation to the Prince of Wales to state his views. The Prince composed a perfect reply which he showed to Lord Salisbury, who reminded him that it was his constitutional duty to be silent; but the Prince felt so strongly about the wicked absurdity of an Anglo–American war that he rejected that advice and cabled (23 December 1895) to Pullitzer: 'I thank you for telegram. I earnestly trust, and cannot but believe, present crisis will be arranged in a manner satisfactory to both countries, and will be succeeded by same warm feeling of friendship which has existed between them for so many years.'

Published on Christmas Eve, that message could not possibly have done harm, and its effect was, in fact, conciliatory and helpful. The dispute was referred later to an arbitral commission composed of two Englishmen, two Americans and a neutral chairman, whose award, in October 1899, was substantially in favour of Great Britain.

No action to conclude a foreign alliance was taken by the British Government at that time; but the Prince of Wales turned his gaze upon Russia. He cut short his annual holiday at Homburg at the beginning of September 1896, to superintend personally every detail of the arrangements made for the Czar's forthcoming visit to Queen Victoria at Balmoral. While the Princess remained in Denmark, the Prince, after staying for three days with Lord Rosebery at Dalmeny, donned his Russian uniform on 22 September before driving in pouring rain to Leith, where he welcomed the Emperor and Empress who arrived by sea in a new and superb imperial yacht with their infant daughter, the Grand Duchess Olga.

To the accompaniment of torchlight processions and bonfires on the hills, the imperial guests were drawn by train to Ballater and driven thence to Balmoral, where the vigorous and buoyant Prince of Wales dragged his reluctant nephew out shooting every day. The Czar, who complained bitterly in letters to his mother about the cold, the rain and the wind, and who developed neuralgia with a swollen cheek, shot no stags and only one brace of grouse during that entire visit.

Lord Salisbury arrived at the Castle on 26 September, and the Prince of Wales was not invited to participate in the formal conversations held between the Czar, Queen Victoria and the Prime Minister. He departed, accordingly, to Newmarket on 29 September, with two senior members of his nephew's suite; and the twenty-eight-year-old Czar wrote [27] (14 October) to his mother: 'After he had left I had an easier time, because I could at least do what *I* wanted, and was not *obliged* to go out shooting every day in the cold and rain.... Granny was kinder and more amiable than ever.'

Friends considered that the Prince of Wales was beginning to look pinched and worn, but he continued to be as assiduous as ever in the discharge of public engagements. Besides attending 25 committee meetings in 1897, and race meetings on 53 separate days, he shot on 43 days, went 65 times to the theatre or opera, and undertook 56 opening ceremonies, visits of inspection, reviews and charity dinners.

Radical opinion was deeply appreciative of the charming way in which the Prince of Wales presented certificates at the Queen's Hall, Langham Place, on the evening of 5 February 1897, to scholars and exhibitioners chosen by the Technical Education Board of the newly constituted London County Council. The State had done nothing previously for technical education, and Sidney Webb informed Lord Carrington, who told [28] the Prince of Wales, that his performance at the Queen's Hall had served once more to confirm the profound loyalty and affection felt for the royal family by the entire British Socialist movement.

On account of Queen Victoria's Diamond Jubilee, the London season of 1897 was brilliant and strenuous, and the Prince of Wales was put to great trouble and even greater expense in entertaining colonial prime ministers, as well as Indian and foreign princes. The presence of so many distinguished visitors made all London balls and receptions unpleasantly crowded; and the Princess of Wales confessed [29] that she had been 'horribly bored', for that reason, at the memorable fancy-dress ball, given on 2 July by the Duchess of Devonshire, at which the Prince wore the uniform of Grand Master of The Knights Hospitaller of Malta.

A much worse crush two days earlier did more harm than the Jameson Raid had done to the reputation of the millionaire ex-Radical Secretary for the Colonies, Joseph Chamberlain. His young American third wife gave a dinner on 30 June to distinguished colonials, followed by a reception for which far too many invitations were issued and which the Prince and Princess had promised to attend. At the moment when the Prince arrived, a fight broke out between a posse of his host's footmen and a mob of idle but harmless spectators who were obstructing the entrance; and, during the scuffle, the Prince was astonished to see his daughter, Princess Maud, who had driven up immediately in front of him, being hustled on the pavement.

White with fury, the Prince of Wales helped to rescue his daughter whom he assisted, unhurt, into his own carriage; and he declined subsequently to discuss the matter. He noted [30] laconically in his diary: 'Drive to Mrs Chamberlain's evening party at Piccadilly, 11.15. Owing to dense crowd, unable to enter house, and drive home.'

The Prince of Wales went to some trouble to inaugurate a permanent memorial of the Diamond Jubilee. Hospitals were still run on a voluntary basis, and on 21 January 1897, he summoned to Marlborough House a representative committee which established a 'Prince of Wales's Hospital Fund for London'. £228,000 were subscribed before the year was out; and that Fund was from the outset a much greater success than the Imperial Institute, which the Prince had inaugurated as a memorial to the previous Jubilee, ever was. Incorporated in 1907, the Fund's capital amounted half a century later to more than eight million pounds.*

The heavy expense, which he could not avoid incurring during the Diamond Jubilee year, caused the Prince of Wales to review his financial foundations. He had lost the advice and help of Baron Hirsch, whose death, aged sixty-five, in Hungary on 21 April 1896, he had noted in his diary without using the conversational epithet 'sad'. The Prince had grown a little tired of Hirsch, whose social ambition he had forwarded and whose idealistic enthusiasms he had not

---

* Since the establishment of the National Health Service, the income has been used for a variety of special purposes, including the training of administrators, matrons, ward sisters and caterers.

always shared; but with Hirsch's executor, Ernest Cassel, who took charge of his private investments from 1897 onwards, he formed the most intimate masculine friendship of his life.

That friendship was heartfelt because it was cemented by an uncomplicated harmony of taste and opinion, as well as by mutual self-interest. Undistracted by academic or artistic curiosity, Cassel, who was aged forty-five in 1897, was a financial genius whose attitude to the society which fawned upon him was aloof and realistic. Social life to him was a means and not an end; and the roots of the very warm sympathy which he felt with King Edward VII were sunk deeply and securely into the human soil of an exceptionally imperious love of power.

Politics and society were intertwined traditionally, but financiers and merchants owed much to the countenance of the Prince of Wales. Besides the Rothschilds and Sassoons, his intimate friends, during the closing years of the nineteenth century, included Hirsch's brother-in-law, Louis Bischoffsheim; the banker and courtier, Horace Farquhar, who was made eventually an earl, but who bequeathed a dubious financial reputation; the bachelor grocer, Sir Thomas Lipton, who embarked suddenly in 1897 upon a career of philanthropy and big yacht racing; and the furniture manufacturer, Sir Blundell Maple, who dispensed a princely hospitality and who was immensely gratified by being elected to the Jockey Club in 1903.

Although less human than Hirsch, Cassel was much the most remarkable of all King Edward's financial friends. Born in Cologne in 1852 into an insignificant Jewish family, he left a commercial school when he was aged fourteen to become a clerk. Migrating to England where he was naturalized in 1880, he became London manager of the international financial house of Bischoffsheim and Goldsmidt at the age of twenty-two, at an annual salary of five thousand pounds.

Cassel was befriended by Hirsch who had married a Bischoffsheim, but hard work, unerring judgement, ruthless drive and unswerving integrity made him a multi-millionaire in his early forties. Operating independently, he used his growing prestige to push British interests, as well as his own and those of anyone who was useful to him, in the Americas, Sweden, the Far and Near East, North Africa and the British Isles.

Cassel filled the several houses which he bought or rented with a profusion of old masters and suitable treasures; and he was a generous host, although smart masculine society bored him. He joined the Jockey Club in 1908, but cared little for it, or for the Marlborough Club, much preferring the exhilarating society of the vivacious and pretty women who surrounded King Edward.

After distributing two million pounds to public charities before dying in seclusion at Bournemouth in 1921, Cassel's will was sworn at more than seven and a half millions during an acute post-war depression; but his austere personal habits, which contributed to that result, were not reflected in his attitude to decorations. He considered that he was entitled to purchase what he required, and when the Foreign Secretary, Sir Edward Grey, begged him in 1908 to oblige the State Bank of Morocco (which he had been the prime mover in founding) with an immediate loan of half a million pounds, Cassel agreed [31] on the sole condition that he should receive the Grand Cross of the Order of the Bath. Although displeased, King Edward made no difficulty; and Grey, who cared personally as little for honours as he did for the great financier, was much amused.

Cassel took readily to shooting, hunting and horse racing, but his bluntness caused offence and his success stirred envy. Enemies accused him of subsidizing the King and the King's friends; and he was so reserved that everyone, except King Edward, was amazed when he proclaimed himself a Roman Catholic while being sworn as a Privy Counsellor, within a few months of his friend's accession to the throne. After he had waved aside the hat which the Clerk of the Council, Sir Almeric Fitzroy, had retrieved thoughtfully, in the belief that a Jew was being sworn, it was disclosed that Cassel had been received into the Church of Rome by Father Cyril Forster in accordance with the dying wish of his wife, Annette Maxwell, of Darlington, a Roman Catholic by birth, whom he had greatly loved.

Many of Cassel's overseas operations were conducted with the unofficial backing of the British Government; and, in concert with Cromer and Kitchener, he left Egypt for ever in his debt. He eased the miserable lot of the peasantry by financing irrigation on an unprecedented scale, and he helped to galvanize a precarious economy into vigorous life by irrigating it with capital and by establishing a banking machinery. The magic of capitalism fascinated King Edward and kindled an imagination which mght otherwise have grown sluggish, and the intimate friendship which he formed with Cassel was happy and fortunate in every respect.

Besides Sir Ernest Cassel, another intimate friend entered the Prince of Wales's life in 1898, in succession to Lady Warwick, who turned Socialist. The Hon. Mrs George Keppel, youngest child of Admiral Sir William Edmonstone, had married a brother of Lord Albemarle; and she and her extraordinarily handsome husband, who lived permanently in London, entertained the Prince to dinner for the first time on 27 February 1898.

Alice Keppel was then aged twenty-nine; and an understanding, which arose almost overnight, was unclouded until the end of King Edward's reign. Immediately after the King's death, Lord Hardinge of Penshurst, permanent head of the Foreign Office who had just been appointed Viceroy of India, added the following note [32] to his private file:

I take this opportunity to allude to a delicate matter upon which I am in a position to speak with authority. Everybody knew of the friendship that existed between King Edward and Mrs George Keppel, which was intelligible in view of the lady's good looks, vivacity and cleverness. I used to see a great deal of Mrs Keppel at that time, and I was aware that she had knowledge of what was going on in the political world.

I would like here to pay a tribute to her wonderful discretion, and to the excellent influence which she always exercised upon the King. She never utilized her knowledge to her own advantage, or to that of her friends; and I never heard her repeat an unkind word of anybody. There were one or two occasions when the King was in disagreement with the Foreign Office, and I was able, through her, to advise the King with a view to the policy of the Government being accepted. She was very loyal to the King, and patriotic at the same time.

It would have been difficult to find any other lady who would have filled the part of friend to King Edward with the same loyalty and discretion.

That noble tribute was richly earned, and Mrs Keppel was invited to almost all the houses, except Hatfield and Welbeck, which King Edward visited. She made him happy by relieving his boredom and frustration, and Cassel looked after her investments with happy and fortunate results. She was so charming and wise that she had virtually no enemies; King Edward showed an innate delicacy by never once mentioning in her presence the name of her predecessor, Lady Warwick [33]; and Queen Alexandra, who would have preferred [34] to draw a distinction between invitations to Sandringham and invitations to Windsor, came to accept Mrs Keppel and to feel at home and at ease with her.

One other new friendship which dated from February 1898 was that of Miss (Sister) Agnes Keyser,* founder of a military officers' nursing home which she ran as matron with the help of her younger sister, Fanny, in her house at 17 Grosvenor Crescent. Known later as King Edward's Hospital for Officers, the establishment fulfilled a useful role during the Boer War and extended a special welcome to patients from the Household Cavalry and Brigade of Guards.

Miss Keyser, a beautiful and formidable woman who hated any kind of publicity, devoted her entire life and fortune to the work which she had found to do. Enjoying the friendship and support of most members of the royal family, she received financial help from many of King Edward's friends. She entertained King Edward frequently at dinner when he wanted to relax in an informal and domestic way; and King George V showed her special favour after his father's death.

---

* Miss Keyser (1852–1941) was the daughter of Charles Keyser, of Stanmore, Middlesex, who was a partner in the Stock Exchange firm of Ricardo and Keyser.

14
King at Last

THE Prince of Wales's contacts with affairs of state remained peripheral throughout the final phase of Queen Victoria's reign. He called, for example, for a better understanding with France when laying the foundation stone of a new jetty at Cannes on 10 March 1898; and he signed a British declaration of neutrality in the Spanish-American War while presiding at the age of fifty-seven for the first time in his life on the Queen's behalf, at a ten minutes' meeting of the Privy Council which had been summoned urgently on 23 April at Marlborough House.

The Prince of Wales was laid up for some weeks during the late summer of 1898 as a result of a fall while staying with Ferdinand de Rothschild at Waddesdon. He recorded[1] in his diary: 'P. of W. falls downstairs, 10.00 a.m., and fractures knee-cap'; and the doctors would not allow him to travel to Copenhagen when the Queen of Denmark died on 29 September after being nursed devotedly by the Princess of Wales.

While the Princess cruised aboard *Osborne* in the Mediterranean during the spring of 1899, the Prince wrestled boldly with a wave of anti-British sentiment in France. French opinion was extremely hostile, on account of a recent incident at Fashoda which had brought the two peoples to the brink of war immediately after Kitchener's conquest of the Sudan. In the absence of adequate promises of Russian support, French claims to sovereignty over a wide area of the Upper Nile Valley had had to be withdrawn, and the Prince of Wales found himself hissed in consequence in Paris, and cruelly caricatured. He was much happier on the Riviera where the atmosphere was more relaxed; but, while concentrating upon golf, he greatly missed his racing yacht *Britannia* which he had sold in order to economize.

That autumn, when the Princess went to spend two months in Denmark, the Prince enjoyed a month's cure at Marienbad before going to Balmoral to discuss with Queen Victoria the impending visit to England of the German Emperor. War was imminent already between Great Britain and the Boer Republics of the Transvaal and Orange Free State; and after meeting the Princess on her return from Denmark (10 October) – the day before war was declared – the Prince's diary recorded [2] the rare entry: 'P. and Pcss. dine alone, 8.15.'

The howl of execration which the Boer War excited against Great Britain throughout the world concealed much hypocrisy, for most nations would gladly have possessed themselves of the gold and diamond wealth of the Transvaal. Discounting that clamour, the British Government was inclined, nevertheless, to attach slightly more significance than it would otherwise have done to the German Emperor's eight days' visit during November; and the Prince of Wales gladly cooperated. He arranged personally every social and ceremonial detail, and agreed to overlook a ludicrous incident [3] which had occurred as recently as 3 August at Cowes.

In her owner's absence the Kaiser's yacht, *Meteor II*, had won the Queen's Cup, but the Kaiser had taken strong exception to the system of handicapping which the Prince of Wales, as Commodore of the Royal Yacht Squadron, had approved. An exuberant telegram of protest from Potsdam had been posted in the Squadron's hall, and one unlucky phrase – 'Your handicaps are perfectly appalling' – had aroused resentment and derision.

The Emperor insisted upon bringing, as his naval A.D.C., Admiral von Senden with whom the Prince of Wales was not on speaking terms, and he threatened to cancel his visit unless his uncle would promise to treat Senden as a friend. A compromise had to be arranged through the good offices of the Duchess of Devonshire, and the Prince agreed to treat the Admiral as an acquaintance at Windsor, while the Emperor undertook not to bring him to Sandringham.

Credit was due to the Emperor for defying German public opinion by coming to England at that time, and the success of the visit exceeded expectation. The Kaiser spent 25–28 November at Sandringham, where he met, amongst others, Lord Acton, the historian, and Lord Wolseley, the Commander-in-Chief; and Count (afterwards Prince) von Bülow, the German Secretary of State for Foreign Affairs, compared [4] the Prince talking politics to the Emperor, with 'a fat malicious tom-cat, playing with a shrewmouse'.

The Emperor complied cheerfully with the custom of the house, which required him to appear at breakfast and to consume porridge as well as bacon and eggs; but the Princess of Wales had difficulty in suppressing her strong prejudice against her guest. She had been amused to learn that the Emperor proposed to bring three valets and a hairdresser, and she was seen to shake with laughter and was heard [5] to exclaim, 'Ach, the fool!', when she discovered that the hairdresser had brought an assistant who curled the imperial moustache.

The Kaiser, who possessed many amiable qualities and who could be a charming companion when he chose, had been placed, by an accident of history, in a position which few men could have sustained. That position entitled him to exercise immense power, but he was irresponsible, and his mind contained no natural or built-in defences against the continuous flattery to which it was exposed. After his return home, he started to bombard the Prince of Wales as well as Queen Victoria with prancing letters and memoranda embodying a plan of campaign for the British armies in South Africa.

Those armies, at that time, were suffering a series of humiliating and utterly unexpected reverses; and on 4 February 1900, the Kaiser coolly reminded [6] his uncle that 'last year, in the cricket match of England v. Australia, the former took the latter's victory quietly, with chivalrous acknowledgment of her opponent'. The Prince of Wales replied [7] patiently (8 February):

I am unable to share your opinion, expressed in the last paragraph of your Memo, in which you liken our conflict with the Boers to our Cricket Matches with the Australians, in which the latter were victorious and we accepted our defeat.

The British Empire is now fighting for its very existence, as you know full well, and for our superiority in S. Africa. We must therefore use every effort in our power to prove victorious in the end!

Sixteen months later, after he had succeeded to the throne, King Edward found it necessary to write [8] (19 June 1901) in somewhat similar terms to his Russian nephew, the Emperor Nicholas, who had written [9] on 4 June in order to advocate peace by negotiation:

Suppose that Sweden, after spending years in the accumulation of enormous armaments, had suddenly forbidden you to move a single Regt. in Finland and, on your refusing to obey, had invaded Russia in *three* places, would you have abstained from defending yourself; and, when war had once begun, would you not have felt bound in prudence and honour to continue military operations until the enemy had submitted? . . .

We have every reason to hope that the end is not far off; and we entertain no doubt whatever that, when peace and order have been fully restored, the territories which belonged to the two Republics will enjoy in full measure the tranquillity and good government which England has never failed to assure to the populations which have come under her sway.

It was inevitable that Germany, Russia and France should consult about means of taking advantage of Great Britain's difficulties; and the French holiday plans of the Prince of Wales, as well as those of Queen Victoria, were disrupted in 1900 as a result of a spate of hostile articles and offensive caricatures in the French Press. The Prince abandoned his annual spring holiday on the Riviera, and declined to attend the opening in Paris on 15 April 1900, of an International Exhibition, although he was President of the British Section. He went instead, with the Princess, to Denmark for Easter; while Queen Victoria visited Ireland for the first time in forty years.

Leaving London for Copenhagen on 4 April 1900, the

Prince of Wales recorded [10]: 'Arrive at Brussels, 4.50. Walk about station. Just as train is leaving, 5.30, a man fires a pistol at P. of W. through open window of carriage (no harm done).' The criminal fanatic, who was grabbed and disarmed by the stationmaster after he had discharged one bullet only from a six-chambered revolver, was found, on interrogation, to be a Belgian student named Sipido who belonged to an anarchist club, although aged only fifteen.

The Prince and Princess of Wales, who behaved with exemplary self-possession, ordered the train to proceed after a few minutes pause, and in many letters to friends the Prince joked about the bad marksmanship of his would-be assassin. He asked the authorities not to punish the criminal too severely, but he was exasperated in July when a Belgian Court absolved the boy of criminal intent, on account of his youth, and ordered merely that he should be placed under police supervision until he came of age.

After skipping across the frontier into France, the boy went into hiding, and the Kaiser wrote [11] characteristically (18 July) to the Prince of Wales: 'The behaviour of the Belgians in the Sipido affair is simply outrageous, and people in Germany are at a loss to understand the meaning. Either their laws are ridiculous, or the jury are a set of d——d, bl——y scoundrels; which is the case I am unable to decide. With best love to Aunty and Cousins.'

Leaving the Princess to spend some weeks in Denmark, the Prince returned (20 April) to London and was received with thunderous and gratifying applause by cheering crowds as he drove from Charing Cross to Marlborough House. He composed that night an address of thanks to the British nation which was published in all newspapers; and he instructed [12] Knollys to ask the Prime Minister for an explanation. He said that he had received warm messages from public bodies and private persons throughout the world; that the German Emperor had taken the trouble to travel from Potsdam to Altona to wring his hand; and that the legislatures of Greece and Portugal had recorded votes of congratulation upon his escape. Why had not the British Parliament recorded its thankfulness, as it had done in

April 1870, when the Duke of Edinburgh escaped assassination at the hands of Irish gunmen in New South Wales?

Lord Salisbury explained [13] (26 April) that the matter had been discussed in Cabinet on 6 April and that precedents had been reviewed, but that a parliamentary vote of congratulations would have involved the recall, for a special sitting, of the House of Lords which had been due to be adjourned on that day: 'It was thought better not to take that course, as it was not then known that the pistol contained a bullet, which the extreme youth of the culprit rendered doubtful.'

A series of resounding victories on the turf helped to console the Prince of Wales for that treatment which he regarded as cavalier; and after winning the Grand National (£1,975) with *Ambush II* on 30 March, he won the Two Thousand Guineas (£4,700), the Newmarket Stakes (£3,425), the Derby (£5,450), the Eclipse Stakes (£9,285) and the St Leger (£5,125) with *Diamond Jubilee*. The Prince, with some of his friends including Lord Marcus Beresford, Lord Farquhar, the Leopold Rothschilds and the Arthur Sassoons, was staying with Lord Derby at Knowsley when *Ambush II* won the Grand National; and with habitual generosity he distributed five hundred pounds at once to his jockey, two hundred and fifty to the head stableman and fifty to the boy who 'did the horse'. He gave other presents to the trainer and his assistant, and Lord Rosebery described [14] the Prince as 'delirious with joy' at Newmarket on 2 May, after *Diamond Jubilee* had won the Two Thousand Guineas.

Entering his sixtieth year in November 1900, the Prince continued to respond to pleasures, great and small, as well as griefs, with the same innocent, uninhibited and even childlike intensity. Time never blunted the edge of his sensibilities, and he plunged with relish into the extra duties which fell to him in consequence of the Boer War, which he followed with breathless interest. He corresponded constantly with younger friends fighting in South Africa; and Winston Churchill, for example, wrote [15] to him (30 November 1899) from the State Schools Prison in Pretoria:

... I must add a few lines about the Boers, for I confess myself much impressed by their courtesy, courage and humanity. At the end they could easily have shot us all down, and we, by continuing our flight, showed that we had no intention of surrendering. Instead of destroying us, they galloped in amongst the fugitives – at considerable risk to themselves – and so persuaded as much as compelled us to become prisoners. ... Since my capture I have been well treated.

By such correspondence the Prince was kept extremely well informed, and he made a point of receiving officers on their return, wounded or sick, from South Africa. He listened to their impressions, inspected units of the Imperial Yeomanry, and appeared in public in 1900 on 86 occasions. In addition, he presided at 31 meetings; attended the House of Lords 9 times; shot on 45 and attended race meetings on 37 separate days; and went 48 times to the opera or theatre.

One of the Prince's engagements in 1900 was the opening on 3 March of a London County Council housing estate at Bethnal Green, where he made a speech which earned high praise because it displayed rare moral courage. He told an audience composed largely of working men that he was much embarrassed as a large-scale owner of slum property in Lambeth. Admitting that conditions were a disgrace to a Christian country, the Prince expressed regret that he was in no position to rebuild because all his property was let in small lots upon long leases.

The Prince, who dearly loved the Duke of York and who fretted unless he saw him very frequently, was punctilious in visiting Queen Victoria in her old age. He liked also to see the old Duke of Cambridge, Prince and Princess Louis of Battenberg and their children, and his daughter, the Duchess of Fife to whose children he accorded in 1905 the style of Highness which Queen Victoria had withheld, to his regret, after much argument. People he stayed with in 1900 included such old friends as Lord Derby, the Duke of Devonshire, the Arthur Sassoons at Tulchan Lodge, Invernessshire, and Lord and Lady Savile at Rufford Abbey, near Doncaster; as well as a number of more recent friends. The latter included Sir Ernest Cassel at Moulton Paddocks, Newmarket, the Hon. Mrs Ronald Greville at Reigate Priory,

Surrey, Lord Iveagh, the brewer, at Elveden, Suffolk, Mrs Willy James at West Dean Park, Sussex, Sir Edward Lawson (Lord Burnham), proprietor of *The Daily Telegraph*, at Hall Barn, Beaconsfield and Sir Edgar and Lady Helen Vincent (Lord and Lady D'Abernon) at Esher Place, Surrey.

A year or two later, Hilaire Belloc composed a ballad which had a wide circulation in manuscript, but which has been omitted from his published work, about the week-end parties given by Mrs Willy James at West Dean; and a few rollicking lines may be quoted*:

> And there it is that when the dryads ope
> Their young enchanted arms to grasp the Spring,
> There comes a coroneted envelope
> And Mrs James will entertain the King!
>
> There will be bridge and booze till after three,
> And, after that, a lot of them will grope
> Along the corridors in *robes de nuit*,
> Pyjamas, or some other kind of dope.
>
> *Envoi*
>
> Prince, Father Vaughan† may entertain the Pope,
> And you may entertain the Jews at Tring,‡
> But I will entertain the larger hope,
> That Mrs James will entertain the King!

Because he could never endure to be alone or unoccupied, members of the Prince's intimate circle continued to make it a point of honour to arrange parties for him at twenty-four hours' notice, when necessary; and the chef's art was elevated to a pitch of unprecedented perfection. The Prince, who never tired of caviare but who relished also what is called plain English fare, consumed always a plateful of roast beef and Yorkshire pudding at luncheon on Sundays as a change from richer food. His dinner seldom consisted of less than twelve courses, and he adored rich and elaborate dishes.

* I am indebted to the late Vita Sackville-West (the Hon. Lady Nicolson, C.H.) who wrote down the whole poem for me, from memory.

† The Jesuit who converted Sir Ernest Cassel.

‡ Seat of Lord Rothschild.

The Prince was especially fond of grouse, partridge or pheasant stuffed with snipe or woodcock, when the latter were stuffed also with truffles and the whole was garnished with a rich sauce; and he loved ortolans, small Egyptian birds which were cooked in brandy. Another favourite dish was *Cotelettes de bécassines à la Souvaroff*, named after a noble Russian gourmet, which consisted of snipe, boned and halved, stuffed with foie gras and forcemeat, shaped into small cutlets and grilled in a pig's caul. They were exceedingly rich in flavour, and, served on silver dishes with small slices of truffle and madeira sauce, each piece melted in the mouth.

The Princess of Wales was devoted to crayfish, cooked in chablis, while her husband insisted upon observing certain traditions about the food served on particular occasions. Pigeon pie, for example, was included always on the Ascot menu, and turtle soup and whitebait in his annual Derby dinners to members of the Jockey Club, while deer pudding appeared four times a week as a savoury at Balmoral.

The Prince regarded grilled oysters as the ideal supper dish, and they appeared always on the menu when in season, followed usually by *poulet Norwégienne*, cold quails, and quails *à la Grecque*. The Prince's prodigious appetite appalled the Princess who complained [16] to his doctors that it was 'terrible', that he ate anything and everything and that she had never seen anything like it. That appetite was reputed to be insatiable, for the Prince ate with voracious heartiness at breakfast, luncheon, tea, dinner and supper. His intense enjoyment of good food was evident to all, but he bolted it and admitted to his doctors that he could not induce himself to take the trouble to masticate.

Preferring champagne to claret or burgundy, the Prince was a moderate drinker. He cared little for port, liked a single glass of old brandy after dinner and was impatient always to join the ladies. The scale of his smoking, on the other hand, was as immoderate as that of his eating. He rationed himself strictly to one small cigar and to two cigarettes before breakfast, but he smoked thereafter a daily average of twelve enormous cigars and twenty cigarettes.

Although, as he grew older, the Prince was content in London with coffee and a boiled egg for breakfast, he ate a much heartier breakfast whenever he went racing or shooting. On such occasions he consumed poached eggs, bacon, haddock, and chicken or woodcock, which must have tested his digestion, but at Homburg or Marienbad he dieted strictly and succeeded, in some years, in losing, temporarily, an extraordinary amount of weight.

The Prince's brother, the Duke of Edinburgh, who had succeeded, by agreement, to the Dukedom of Saxe-Coburg and Gotha in 1893, died of cancer at Rosenau on 30 July 1900. The Prince of Wales left for Germany at once to attend the funeral, and he was plunged for a time, on his return, into one of those moods of black depression which dismayed his Household increasingly after he had become King. He had discovered that his sister, the Empress Frederick, was stricken with the same disease, and he had been asked to observe secrecy for as long as possible.

On 3 January 1901, the Prince travelled from Sandringham to greet Lord Roberts on his return from South Africa. He drove with Roberts in procession through cheering crowds to Buckingham Palace, and protested [17] strongly (30 December and 6 January) to the Prime Minister, and to the Secretary for War, St John Brodrick, about the meanness of the Cabinet's proposal to endow the hero's new earldom with a parliamentary money grant of only fifty thousand pounds. The Prince's views were communicated to Sir Henry Campbell-Bannerman, leader of the Liberal Opposition; and in July 1901, ignoring Radical dissentients, the House of Commons voted Roberts one hundred thousand pounds.

On 7 January, the Prince went to shoot with the Duke of Devonshire at Chatsworth, where a large house party included Mrs George Keppel and Mrs Willy James. The Duke, who sat in the Cabinet as Lord President of the Council, mentioned casually that discussions about the possibility of an Anglo-German alliance were being held; and the Prince flitted thereafter between London and Sandringham. He was ill at ease, awaiting definite news about the precarious state of the Queen's health, and, late on 18 January, he was advised to travel to Osborne early next day.

After dining that evening with Agnes Keyser, the Prince started at dawn by special train for Osborne, and was joined there by the Princess who came from Sandringham. Queen Victoria was conscious intermittently; and an uncoded telegram, which upset her Household but which was appreciated immensely by the British public, informed the Prince of Wales that the German Emperor would arrive in London at 6.15 p.m. on 20 January.

The Prince returned to London to meet his nephew, calling first at Marlborough House to change into Prussian uniform. He spent the night in London and travelled with the Kaiser to Osborne at dawn next morning.

At 12.15 that day the Prince saw the Queen who put out her arms and said 'Bertie!', and he broke down after embracing her. He saw her frequently thereafter, but she appeared always to be unconscious; and at 6.30 p.m. on 22 January 1901 the Prince of Wales became King.

'He desires me to say', Knollys wrote [18] that evening to the Duke of Devonshire, 'that he would propose to call himself Edward 7th'; and, after asking the Kaiser to take charge at Osborne, the King travelled to London next morning to attend the traditional Accession Council. It assembled at 3.30 p.m. at St James's Palace; the oath was administered by Frederick Temple, Archbishop of Canterbury; and the King set the tone of his entire reign by delivering, to an audience of about 150 people, a perfect and impromptu eight minutes' speech, based entirely upon intuition.

Because it had been assumed that the King would speak on such an occasion from a prepared text, or at least from notes, no record was taken; and the published version of that speech, which had to be reconstructed from memory, was considered less remarkable than the original. Even so, it was most impressive; and the King made a moving and brilliant reference to his father. He did not, he said, undervalue the name of Albert which he bore, but there could be only one Albert 'who by universal consent is, I think deservedly, known by the name of Albert the Good'. He intended, therefore, to be known in future as Edward, a name borne by six of his predecessors; and, without any reference to the Almighty, he asked Parliament and people for their support.

Many wondered privately whether King Edward VII was really fitted by training and temperament to wear the Crown, but *The Times* was the only newspaper which verged (23 January) upon rudeness. Echoing words used by Walter Bagehot a generation earlier, it reminded readers that the King had been 'importuned by temptation in its most seductive forms', and that he must often have prayed, 'lead us not into temptation', with 'a feeling akin to hopelessness'. His public life, it was true, had been conducted uniquely well; he had 'never failed in his duty to the throne and the nation', but 'we shall not pretend that there is nothing in his long career which those who respect and admire him would wish otherwise'.

While Queen Alexandra, in her wilful and charming way, refused to allow anyone to kiss her hand or to treat her as Queen until after the funeral on 4 February, King Edward indulged his gift for organization and love of ceremony by supervising all details. Apart from that work, his immediate problem was the continued presence under his roof of his imperial nephew. The Kaiser exasperated his ministers, as well as German public opinion, by conferring the Order of the Black Eagle impulsively upon Lord Roberts, at the height of the Boer War; and by announcing that, until Queen Victoria was buried, he was remaining in England as a bereaved member of the British royal family and not as a German Emperor.

The sentimental British public was enchanted by that attitude, and the Kaiser's bearing was so gentle and modest that King Edward believed, for a week or two, that a new chapter had been opened. 'William', he wrote [19] (1 February) to the Empress Frederick who was much too ill to come to England, 'was kindness itself and touching in his devotion, without a shade of brusquerie or unselfishness'; and he added: 'I know full well how your thoughts will be with us, and how, as my eldest sister, you will give me your blessing to fulfil my arduous and onerous duties, which I have now inherited from such a Sovereign and Mother. God bless you, dearest and beloved sister, and may He mitigate your sufferings now.'

A week later (7 February), when the funeral was over, and when all the foreign royalties had departed, King Edward wrote [20] again: 'William's touching and simple demeanour, up to the last, will never be forgotten by me or anyone. It was indeed a sincere pleasure to me to confer upon him the rank of Field-Marshal in my Army, and to invest Willy* (who is a charming young man) with the Order of the Garter.

The war in South Africa, War Office administration and the bad state of the Army's medical service engrossed King Edward's attention during the first weeks of his reign. He ordered Brodrick to consult him about all questions of policy as well as about all appointments and promotions of senior officers. He expressed pleasure at the prospect of better relations with Germany, but asked the Kaiser to discuss the project of an Anglo-German alliance with the Foreign Secretary, Lord Lansdowne.

Lansdowne and Brodrick reported [21] to Lord Salisbury the gist of their conversations with the Kaiser, who professed to be the enemy of Russia. Nicholas II was bankrupt and incompetent – 'fit only to … grow turnips' – but greedy United States financiers would lend him money to expand his empire in Asia. The German Army would be happy to protect British far-flung interests from that Russo-American threat, if the British Navy would help Germany to expand in South America. Hundreds of thousands of patriotic Germans were firmly established already in the Argentine and elsewhere; and only the preposterous Monroe Doctrine restrained Germany from assisting them to seize power: 'You keep the United States off me, and I'll keep Russia off India and Constantinople.'

The Kaiser suggested that England would be squeezed out, between Russia and America, before the middle of the century if that offer was rejected, but Lord Salisbury refused to allow the Cabinet's time to be wasted by any discussion of it.

---

* The German Crown Prince (1882–1951). His name, and that of his father, were struck off the roll of the Order in 1915.

He had never believed that an acceptable basis for an Anglo-German alliance could be found, and had resented Joseph Chamberlain's public advocacy of such a project. The Foreign Office continued to examine it until the end of the year, but the atmosphere grew more cool every month.

On 23 February 1901, King Edward left England to see his sister; and he travelled to Flushing in the new Royal Yacht *Victoria and Albert* which carried a crew of three hundred and a staff of thirty personal servants. He took ashore, however, only four servants, besides his new assistant private secretary, Frederick Ponsonby,* and the doctor, Sir Francis Laking. Serenaded at Flushing, and at several stations *en route*, by crowds singing the Boer national anthem, King Edward was met at Homburg by the German Emperor and by the British Ambassador who escorted him to Friedrichschof, where the Empress Frederick was bedridden and in terrible pain.

Prompted by King Edward, Laking tried vainly to persuade the German doctors to ease their patient's sufferings by prescribing larger and more frequent injections of morphia; and Ponsonby accepted custody of two large boxes of the Empress's correspondence. She asked him to convey them secretly to England, without the Emperor's knowledge; and, after accomplishing that task, he dismayed King George V, and exposed himself to criticism, by publishing extracts in 1928 on his personal responsibility.

Because he was superstitious, King Edward was concerned to discover that thirteen people had sat down to dinner on three consecutive evenings, but he broke into his happy, gurgling laugh upon recollecting suddenly that Princess Frederick-Charles of Hesse was expecting a baby. He returned to Marlborough House, while Buckingham Palace was being modernized, on 3 March 1901; and he dined quietly that evening with Mrs Keppel at her home in Portman Square.

King Edward's practice of dining constantly in the houses

---

* Sir Frederick Ponsonby (Lord Sysonby), G.C.B., G.C.V.O. (1867–1935), was a son of Queen Victoria's former private secretary, Sir Henry Ponsonby.

of subjects in London delighted society, and represented a complete break with royal tradition. As early as June 1821, when George IV dined with the Duke of Devonshire, Henry Hobhouse noted[22] that 'this is the first instance in modern times of the King dining with a subject in London. It had been virtually also the last; Queen Victoria never dined out; and before discussing other aspects of King Edward's mode of performing his new duties, it will be helpful to set in perspective the extraordinarily regular personal routine which he followed annually as Sovereign.

King Edward continued to spend Christmas and New Year at Sandringham, through which (as well as through Windsor and Balmoral) guests perpetually flowed. He came to London, for a night, two or three times during January; and he spent one week shooting with the Duke of Devonshire at Chatsworth or, later, with Lord Iveagh at Elveden.

King Edward moved to Buckingham Palace at the end of January in time to open Parliament in State; and throughout February he entertained guests or went out to dinner, theatre and supper parties every evening without exception. He left England punctually at the beginning of March for two months holiday in the sun. He liked to spend a week in Paris, where he enjoyed strolling incognito on the boulevards, followed by three weeks at Biarritz. He would then cruise for a month in *Victoria and Albert*. He liked best to cruise in the Mediterranean, but he loved to improvise, and sent explosive telegrams to more than one First Lord of the Admiralty who tried incautiously to induce him to state his plans in advance.

Returning to London at the beginning of May in time to preside over the Season, King Edward again dined out or entertained friends every night. He gave famous and splendid suppers in a private room behind his box at the Royal Opera House, Covent Garden; and he spent every week-end at friends' houses, at Sandringham, or in his private quarters at the Jockey Club at Newmarket.

Moving to Windsor Castle for Ascot Races in the middle of June, King Edward paid an official visit (lasting three or four days) every July to some provincial centre, before going, at the end of that month, to stay with the Duke of Richmond for Goodwood Races. He left Goodwood for Cowes to preside over the Regatta at the beginning of August, when he made the royal yacht his headquarters.

Immediately after Cowes, while Queen Alexandra went to join her sister, the Dowager Empress of Russia, in Denmark, King Edward went to Marienbad in Bohemia for a month's cure. His very comfortable suite of rooms at the Hotel Weimar were furnished each year in a different style, but he travelled more simply abroad than Queen Victoria had done. His mother had rented an entire hotel and had taken at least one hundred personal servants, besides despatching in advance a great quantity of her favourite pieces of furniture and pictures.

King Edward never attempted again to travel as lightly and informally as he had done when visiting Friedrichschof in February 1901; but he seldom took more than thirty attendants, apart from his suite. Favourite servants included a Swiss courier, Fehr; an Austrian first valet, Meidinger, who called his master with a glass of warm milk and a biscuit at 7 o'clock; and an English second valet, Hawkins, who made the King's bed and who was forbidden to turn the mattress on Fridays. Other servants included a former Prussian Grenadier, Hoepner, of gigantic height and proportions, who opened the door to visitors as first footman; and an English second footman, Wellard, who brushed the King's clothes and cleaned his shoes. Wellard had also the duty of washing, combing and feeding King Edward's long-haired, white fox-terrier Caesar, who could do no wrong.

In travelling over continental railroads, King Edward used three private coaches, built for solid comfort with easy chairs, thick-pile carpets, bathrooms and spacious cupboards, which contained no gilding, carving or showy upholstery. One coach was furnished like a club-room with Spanish leather arm-chairs, card tables, books, newspapers, drinks and cigars. Three automobiles and three chauffeurs were despatched in advance to Biarritz or Marienbad, in charge of an engineer, C. W. Stamper.

On returning from Marienbad, King Edward liked to spend

a few days at Buckingham Palace during the second week of September, before going to stay with the Saviles for Doncaster Races, and then with the Arthur Sassoons in Inverness-shire. Balmoral with its grouse and deer, remained his headquarters throughout October; and from there he attended the autumn race meetings at Newmarket, using his royal train.

The first week of November was spent at Buckingham Palace; the second at Sandringham; and the last two at Windsor. The first week of December was spent at Sandringham, and thereafter, for an entire fortnight, King Edward indulged in a round of Christmas dinner, theatre and supper parties in London to which he looked forward boyishly, and which he enjoyed thoroughly until his health started to fail.

15
King Edward's Position and Methods

FORCEFULNESS was the cardinal attribute of King
Edward, whose zest and curiosity appeared boyish in his
sixtieth year. He revived and extended the ceremonial
aspect of monarchy, while providing the nation with the
most colourful Court since that of Charles II; but he had no
relish for desk work and little experience of business.

Most sovereigns contemporary with King Edward exercised far-reaching personal and discretionary executive
powers which had dwindled, in England, to a vestigial remnant. It remained only in theory for King Edward to take
executive action of any kind except upon the advice of
ministers responsible to Parliament; and it would have been
equally open, theoretically, to a Cabinet supported by Parliament, to inaugurate a dictatorship.

If such a Cabinet had drafted a Bill providing for the
sovereign's deposition, or execution, King Edward, constitutionally, would have been obliged to sign it; but the
spirit is more important than the letter of the British Constitution. Although a wicked government would be a much
greater danger than a bad king, it is just conceivable that a
sovereign's duty to observe his coronation oath and to uphold the laws and customs of his realm might conflict some
day with his constitutional duty to accept advice tendered
by a gangster Cabinet.

Those hypothetical abstractions have no relevance to the
reign of King Edward VII; and the only occasions when
he and his successors have been required to exercise personal
executive discretion have arisen whenever the office of Prime

Minister has become vacant through death or resignation. The duty of choosing a successor devolves then upon the monarch, who is not bound to seek advice; but that freedom of choice is circumscribed by the fact that no Prime Minister would be able to form a government unless he commanded the confidence of the House of Commons, and the support of his Party in that House.

Despite those limitations, the British sovereign enjoys considerable personal influence, derived ultimately from the veneration in which the monarchy is held as the oldest of the nation's institutions. The extent and nature of that influence hinges upon personal factors; and King Edward's was employed most usefully, strongly and effectively in the field of naval reform. To Admiral Sir John Fisher,[*] First Sea Lord from 1904-10, King Edward's support was indispensable; and if it had been unavailable, or withdrawn, Lord Charles Beresford and other Service and political enemies would certainly have overthrown Fisher before his necessary naval revolution had been successfully accomplished.

In discussing King Edward, whom he knew extremely well, Sir Frederick Ponsonby recorded[1] that 'Foreign Affairs, the Army and the Navy interested him most, while internal politics and the Colonies bored him. He would rush through any question relating to the latter, but would read thoroughly every despatch from abroad, often when the subject was very dull. Any inaccuracy annoyed him: even a slip of the pen put him out.'

King Edward's personal influence, which was felt strongly also in the Army, was displayed much more conspicuously, although less effectively, in the diplomatic field. Besides receiving representatives of Foreign Powers in audience without any minister or official being present, he engaged personally while abroad in diplomatic discussions for which the Foreign Secretary assumed responsibility. That activity which remained within the bounds of constitutional propriety, was as useful to the Foreign Office as is a rich unusual

* Admiral of the Fleet Lord Fisher of Kilverstone, G.C.B., O.M., G.C.V.O. (1841–1928), First Sea Lord 1904–10 and 1914–15.

sauce to a dull dinner dish; and successive Cabinets were
happy to make use in that way of the King's geniality and
charm. Misconceptions arose abroad, however, which out-
lasted King Edward's life; and criticism was often voiced in
Radical circles at home.

King Edward's first Prime Minister, Lord Salisbury, was
too old and too much exhausted to relish the task of coach-
ing an inexperienced sovereign; and his nephew and successor, A. J. Balfour, proved uncongenial. Preferring philosophy, music and conversation to horse-racing and field
sports, Balfour had had no previous experience of a personality which rose superior to intellectual gifts by reason of
robust manhood and intuitive insight into men's motives.
While King Edward continued to relax very discreetly in the
raffish tradition of Merrie England, the Prime Minister
helped to make art, literature and abstract ideas fashionable,
with the aid of a circle of frivolous but sophisticated and
utterly unselfconscious friends.

Apart from the Duke of Devonshire and Lord Rosebery,
King Edward, at his accession, was ill-provided with friends
among statesmen, some of whom eyed him with suspicion,
and his relations with Lord Lansdowne (Foreign Secretary),
Lord Selborne (First Lord of the Admiralty) and St John
Brodrick (Secretary for War) lacked warmth. They were the
three members of Salisbury's and Balfour's Cabinets in the
work of whose departments King Edward was most interested; but no minister ever exasperated him so much as
did H. O. Arnold-Forster, who succeeded Brodrick at the
War Office in September 1903.

King Edward's relations with ministers were a constant
source of worry to Lord Knollys, who served his master with
exemplary devotion and scrupulous discretion in the office of
private secretary for forty years. A moderate Liberal,
Knollys found difficulty in separating his exceedingly conscientious view of what the sovereign's constitutional role
ought to be, from the intensely personal interest which he
took in politics. He leaned always to the view that King
Edward was in danger of being treated by ministers as a
puppet; and King Edward would have been spared much

avoidable uneasiness if Knollys could have displayed greater insight and detachment.

King Edward was unable to follow in every respect, as he wished strongly to do, the example consecrated by his mother; and two new and outstanding examples which he set were exceedingly fortunate for his subjects, his successor and himself. His attitude towards his heir, and his manner of discharging the sovereign's duties, differed very widely from those which had been in use during the previous reign.

Queen Victoria had made no attempt at any time to initiate her heir into the nature of the sovereign's duties or into the mysteries of statecraft; and King Edward, who had loved and reverenced his parents, had received from neither the sympathy and understanding which his nature craved. Upon his own son, on the other hand, he lavished both with uninhibited prodigality, and it would be hard to exaggerate the debt owed to him in consequence by King George V.

King Edward's successor was accustomed to acknowledge that debt with a touching and heartfelt sincerity, and in intimate talk about his father his voice would break occasionally and his eyes brim momentarily with tears. That extraordinarily happy relationship, unique in the annals of the royal family, merits a foremost place in any estimate of King Edward VII.

Trained for the Royal Navy and immersed in his profession, Prince George, in common with other zealous and competent officers, had been conditioned to distrust and to avoid the political world. He had embraced voluntarily a strict impersonal discipline which tended to transform him into a martinet; he had never imagined that he might be summoned to ascend the throne, and he was awed by the glittering court which revolved perpetually around his father.

The revolution caused in his life and prospects by the sudden death of the unsatisfactory elder brother whom he had loved dearly, nevertheless, and his subsequent marriage to that brother's affianced bride, exacerbated a congenital diffidence which threatened to impair Prince George's self-confidence. In some moods he was tempted to regard himself as an usurping interloper, and few of his contemporaries and friends stood in greater need of the deeply affectionate indulgence and sympathetic understanding which could, in other circumstances, have been termed spoiling.

That, had it been all, would have been remarkable only in contrast with his father's youthful lot; but, by folding the cloak of a brilliant sophisticated worldliness round the shoulders of his shy and inexperienced heir, King Edward restored completely and fortified Prince George's self-confidence, while discovering and savouring the most profound personal satisfaction of his life. Unlike Queen Victoria, he opened all official secrets to his son whom he met invariably upon a footing of equality and from whom it was a torment to him to be parted for any length of time. Their relationship resembled that of brothers, but it has to be recorded that King George, who derived incalculable benefit, found himself unable, in the relationship which he established later with his own children, to repeat that delightful pattern. It enabled King George's many admirable qualities to blossom freely in the sun and to bear fruit; it helped him to become an excellent king; and it had appeared also to dispel the last traces of an obsolete tradition of hostility between the sovereign and the heir to the throne, which had its roots in the structure of English eighteenth-century politics.

Adapting his methods to the needs of his temperament and to those of an altered economic, political and social climate, King George V did his utmost to follow his father's example. His success was impressive; and despite the catastrophe of the First World War, the change which occurred during his twenty-six years' reign in the Sovereign's manner of performing his duty was less great than that which was confirmed by the nine years' reign of King Edward VII.

Queen Victoria had turned much too sternly attentive an eye upon an excessive amount of detail. She had hated, and had neglected during her widowhood, the visible aspects of sovereignty which her son fulfilled to perfection. Appearing continuously with evident relish and inimitable *bonhomie* in public, King Edward disliked intensely the desk work upon which his mother had concentrated without thereby affecting appreciably the course of events.

Resolved inflexibly to do his duty, King Edward did not at all times receive from Lord Knollys, as King George received from Lord Stamfordham, the best advice about the form in which that duty could most usefully be discharged. The growing volume and complexity of public business had necessitated for many years an increasingly drastic measure of elimination before material was selected for submission to the Sovereign. Gladstone had been the first Prime Minister who tried, characteristically, to coordinate and systematize that process by exercising a general personal supervision over the selection of such material, and by causing it to be submitted after and not before decisions had been reached in Cabinet.

Hotly resenting that claim which she considered dictatorial, Queen Victoria informed[2] Sir Henry Ponsonby (15 April 1886) that, unlike all previous Prime Ministers, who had mostly told her '*everything* that *passed* in the Cabinet, and the different views that were entertained by the different Ministers ... Mr Gladstone never once has told her the different views of his colleagues'. She explained that Gladstone attempted instead to force her to accept Cabinet decisions on matters about which she had been 'kept completely in the dark'.

The Prince Consort, who had been described fairly as an unofficial member of every Cabinet, had made a point of inducing individual ministers to consult Queen Victoria before Cabinet decisions were reached upon questions of substance within the sphere of their departments. He had protected the Queen in that way from being brought into sudden and painful collision with her Cabinets; but the Press became so obtrusive, and some ministers were so indiscreet, that the Queen's forthright views were often too widely known.

Throughout King Edward's reign, and during the reigns of his successors, the Prime Minister has continued to share with some of his colleagues the duty of serving as the Cabinet's mouthpiece in communicating officially with the Sovereign. In certain matters and at certain times the Lord

Chancellor, the Chancellor of the Exchequer, the Foreign Secretary and the Home Secretary are accustomed to speak for the Cabinet; a direct link exists with the Service ministers; and all sovereigns have continued to discuss political questions whenever they saw fit with individual ministers as well as with the Prime Minister.

The new status, nevertheless, of the Prime Minister as the supreme coordinating authority was acknowledged officially by King Edward. The office had developed so informally that it had never figured in the table of precedence, and that anomaly was remedied in 1905. In recognition of Balfour's service in assuming supreme responsibility for the coordination of imperial defence policy, the King ordered (3 December) that all subsequent Prime Ministers should be accorded fourth place in the official table of precedence, after the Archbishop of Canterbury, the Lord Chancellor and the Archbishop of York.

Encouraged by Lord Knollys and by Lord Esher, who loved to feel that they were helping in secret to make history, King Edward worried Balfour by seeking to revive the sovereign's obsolete claim to see Cabinet papers while decisions were in process of being matured. Queen Victoria had never abandoned that claim, but 'it is impossible for us to yield in a matter of this kind', Balfour wrote [3] (27 February 1904 to his secretary, J. S. Sandars; and he did not yield.

King Edward corresponded frequently with friends in a crabbed handwriting which became almost, although never quite, as illegible as his mother's, but he made no attempt to continue the voluminous correspondence which Queen Victoria had maintained with her Prime Ministers for upwards of sixty years. Relishing all new inventions, including typewriters, he insisted that his desk should be kept clear of papers; and he often indicated merely the lines which letters should follow when he was too much rushed to dictate verbatim to a secretary.

Freedom from much paper work was an immense boon to King Edward, who relied upon intuition, spent three months annually abroad and led an exhausting social life. His vast popularity enabled him to inaugurate a new phase of representative sovereignty which greatly benefited the monarchy. His forcefulness enabled him to exert quite as much personal influence as Queen Victoria had done, but he never understood and often resented that salutary change which he initiated, nevertheless, and which his brief reign confirmed, in the sovereign's manner of performing his duties; and Lord Knollys resisted it fiercely until the last.

King Edward was fretted in consequence by the nagging thought that ministers would have sought his advice more often, upon small matters as well as upon great, if they had set a higher value upon his experience and intellect. Believing that they had set a higher value upon those of Queen Victoria, he often needed more reassurance than Knollys was capable of offering; and he wrote,[4] for example (19 August 1905) with characteristic modesty to describe to Knollys the pleasure which he had derived from the knowledge that President Theodore Roosevelt of the United States considered that he was doing his duty really well. King Edward had been talking at Marienbad to Mme Waddington, the American-born widow of a former French Ambassador in London, who had stayed recently with the President in Washington which she had not visited for thirty-eight years: 'He seems to have been very complimentary about me and said he was most anxious to make my acquaintance, as I was so different from G.[erman] E.[mperor] who always wanted his name to be before the public as arbiter of the world at large. He insisted that I did my duty, to the best of my ability, and for the good of my own country and others. Those were his very words.'

After 12 November 1907, when Sir Henry Campbell-Bannerman suffered a heart attack, King Edward had just and constant cause to complain about the nature of the reports of Cabinet meetings which he received from the Prime Minister. Knollys informed[5] Esher (29 November 1907) that Campbell-Bannerman's perfunctory reports were 'really making an absolute fool of the King; but whether he ought, constitutionally, to know *everything* that passes in the

Cabinet, I cannot say. There is no use in Ministers *liking* the King if he is treated as an absolute puppet.'

After noting spitefully [6] (1 December 1907) that 'no one can make a silk purse out of a sow's ear' and that Campbell-Bannerman was 'too old not to be incurable', Esher recorded [7] his view that 'according to the ancient usage which has prevailed for 60 years', King Edward had a right to be consulted before final decisions were reached in Cabinet upon all questions of substance. He added that 'in the interests of tradition and the Monarchy ... the practice which prevailed under the Queen should be adhered to, because the position of the Sovereign should be altogether independent of the personality of the Monarch, if the Monarchy is to stand. The King's personality is the great factor nowadays, and this is a stumbling block in the way of his successors.'

Esher used his private friendship with certain ministers to obtain information, which he transmitted to King Edward, about what passed in the Cabinet. He sought to remedy in that way what he described [8] (2 September 1905) to Knollys as 'the want of painstaking care on the part of Ministers to take full advantage of the admirable monarchical system as it was worked by Peel and Aberdeen'. With the object, furthermore, of illustrating to the world the relations which had existed half a century earlier between Queen Victoria and her ministers, Esher persuaded King Edward to allow him to edit Queen Victoria's letters for publication.

Writing [9] (28 August 1905) to Knollys about the impressions which he had derived from a preliminary study of that correspondence, Esher described 'the immense care' which individual ministers had taken in early Victorian times 'not only to keep the Sovereign informed, but to ask the Sovereign's advice upon almost every question of substance within the spheres of their different Departments'. In contrasting Edwardian with Victorian practice, he noted particularly:

(a) The remissness of the King's present advisers in not keeping His Majesty informed, and in not sending their written reasons or seeking the King's authority B E F O R E action is taken.

(b) Their carelessness (almost amounting to making it a dead letter) about the sanctity of the Privy Counsellor's oath.

Influenced by Lord Esher, Lord Knollys continued to look backward instead of forward; but it is remarkable that he made no attempt to cause formal records to be kept of King Edward's conversations with the Prime Minister, or with others. He was concerned solely and rightly with what he thought best, empirically, for his master, and he regretted [10] for that reason the publication of Queen Victoria's letters. Queen Victoria's temperament and methods had been very different from those of her successor; comparisons might have been invidious; and Knollys attributed to ministerial ignorance and carelessness the change in habits of consultation. Citing an incident in December 1899, when Lord Roberts was despatched to South Africa as Commander-in-Chief without Queen Victoria's knowledge, Knollys wrote [11] (31 August 1905) to Esher:

I don't think any Minister would dare now to act in that way to the King.

Matters having gradually fallen into this unsatisfactory state, it has not been easy for the King to put them again on a proper footing; but whenever he notices, or his attention is called to any act of neglect on the part of one of his Ministers, the latter is at once, and sharply, called to account.

But the difficulty the King has to contend with is that some Ministers settle questions ... without the King or anyone else knowing of it – I am sure without the least wish to pass him by, but through ignorance or carelessness.

Knollys believed [12] that the impaired state of Queen Victoria's health at the end of her life, and the inexperience of Sir Arthur Bigge (Lord Stamfordham), who succeeded Sir Henry Ponsonby as her private secretary in 1896, had been significant contributory factors; but that view was mistaken. No evidence exists that the Queen's ability to despatch business began to fail noticeably before the autumn of 1900; whereas evidence does exist [13] that Queen Victoria's secretary's office was managed by Bigge at least as efficiently as was that of King Edward by Knollys.

The irresistible pressure of business, which prompted

ministers to relieve King Edward of the burden of much superfluous detail, would have aroused less resentment in the King's mind if he had been better advised on that subject by Lord Knollys. Throughout his reign, nevertheless, and despite failing health, he performed all his diverse duties with exemplary conscientiousness to the perfect satisfaction of his subjects; and the forcefulness which he brought to bear upon the War Office immediately after his accession alerted the Liberal Opposition.

The Secretary of State for War appeared to be closeted almost daily in London with King Edward, who was resolved to brush aside all obstacles to speedy victory in the South African War; and Sir Henry Campbell-Bannerman sent a hint through the Government Whips to the leader of the House of Commons. Campbell-Bannerman warned Balfour that he might feel compelled to ask a question about the constitutional control of the Army if newspapers continued to report that the King was receiving Brodrick so frequently in audience.

Brodrick paid tribute in his memoirs [14] to the excellent results which flowed from the King's 'uncompromising determination' to see the Army and the War Office reformed. He noted that 'the impetus which King Edward gave to all military progress was of abiding service to this country', while complaining that 'the active intervention of a constitutional monarch in the work of government' threatened to cause difficulties.

The art of constitutional government had to be learnt by King Edward, who found it increasingly convenient to meet and talk to individual ministers upon purely social occasions. Knollys informed [15] Esher regretfully (8 September 1905) that, with the exception of the Prime Minister, the Foreign Secretary, 'and Arnold-Forster occasionally – when he forces himself upon him!', the King had almost ceased to give formal audiences to ministers.

King Edward devised instead a characteristic means of bringing his influence to bear effectively with the aid of a circle of seven highly placed, trusted and congenial friends. All had different tasks; they performed collectively for King

Edward the kind of service which the Prince Consort had performed for Queen Victoria, and the special position of Mrs George Keppel was accepted and welcomed by ministers. She was ready at all times to smooth their paths while behaving with exemplary discretion, and her Liberal political views were particularly helpful after the Liberal Party had achieved power in December 1905.

The six other members were Sir Ernest Cassel; Lord Esher, who advised on military affairs and strategy; Sir John (Lord) Fisher (of Kilverstone), Second Sea Lord from 1902–3 and First Sea Lord from 1904–10; Sir Charles (Lord) Hardinge (of Penshurst), an under-secretary in the Foreign Office from 1903–4 and permanent head of that Department from 1906–10, before he went to rule India as Viceroy; Lord Knollys; and the German-hating Portuguese Minister in London, Luis de Soveral, who was as much at home in England as he was everywhere among the cosmopolitan French-speaking society of Europe.

Although Cassel chose to remain aloof, and although Hardinge was absent in Russia as Ambassador from 1904–6, Esher, Fisher, Knollys and Soveral cultivated a close solidarity. They dined regularly together at Brooks's, and the acknowledged primacy of Lord Esher, the good-looking and outstandingly able son of a former Master of the Rolls, was based upon an extraordinary subtlety combined with great driving force. Aged forty-nine in 1901, Esher's career had been moulded by his capacity for inspiring friendship. He had been intimate since Eton with Lord Rosebery, and had been a favourite of Queen Victoria who had greatly liked his mother.

After serving (1878–85) as private secretary to Lord Hartington, and after sitting for five years as a Liberal in the House of Commons, Esher idled contentedly for ten years. In 1895, however, he was induced by Rosebery to become permanent secretary to the Office of Works, which had responsibility for the upkeep of much royal property, and which organized the Diamond Jubilee celebrations of 1897. In that capacity, Esher cultivated the Prince of Wales (Edward VII), whose friendship enabled him to exert behind

the scenes the kind of authority which he craved. Hating
the dust of the arena, he refused great appointments, including the Secretaryship of State for War in 1903 and the
Viceroyalty of India in 1908; but he accepted membership of
the Royal Commission on the South African War in 1902,
became chairman of the important War Office Reconstitution Committee in 1904, and became a permanent member
in 1905 of the Committee of Imperial Defence.

On resigning from the Office of Works in June 1902,
Esher signed what he termed [16] 'an agreement with Cassel,
carefully drawn, undertaking certain engagements, with very
large profits, in certain financial concerns for 3 years'. Sir
Ernest Cassel paid Esher five thousand pounds a year, as well
as ten per cent of the profits made by certain companies in
America and Egypt; and the King and the Prime Minister
were duly notified. That arrangement was ended in June
1904, after Esher had decided that 'I was unfitted for the
City business'; and, although he retained a few directorships,
his papers contain subsequently some acid references to
Cassel.

The sound organization of Great Britain's defences had
become the ruling passion of Esher's public life, and it
prompted him to give strong support to Fisher's naval revolution as well as to Haldane's army reforms. In both fields
he was as eager as King Edward was to make the most effective possible use of the Sovereign's pent-up forcefulness.

In that way Esher became indispensable to King Edward,
who remarked [17] one day in March 1905: 'Although you are
not exactly a public servant, yet I always think you are the
most valuable public servant I have.' In reporting delighted-
ly to his younger son, Maurice, Esher added,[18] 'and then I
kissed his hand, as I sometimes do'; and that hint at a mood
of doglike devotion was combined with an odd, sensitive,
and even feminine streak. In March 1908, for example, after
a future famous proconsul had given evidence before the
Committee of Imperial Defence, Esher confided [19] to his
journal that, besides having been admirably lucid about the
Persian Gulf, the young officer was 'such a dear to look at!'

Esher's standing at the Palace, and his public reputation,

are well illustrated by a passage [20] (11 December 1905) in the diary of King Edward's old crony, Lord Carrington (Lincolnshire). Carrington was awaiting, in Knolly's room at Buckingham Palace, a summons to kiss hands formally upon being appointed President of the Board of Agriculture, when 'the door opened and in came Esher. He certainly is an extraordinary man, and has a wonderful footing in Buckingham Palace. He seems to be able to run about it as he likes and must be a considerable nuisance to the Household. He is a clever, unscrupulous man, who might be dangerous; and he is not trusted by the general public, who look on him as an intriguer.'

Esher worked closely with Knollys, whom he sometimes visited at the Palace three or four times a day; but ministers resented his habit of prejudicing King Edward's mind before Cabinet decisions had been reached. Brodrick noted [21] that 'by the time any decision had come to the point when the Cabinet could lay it before the Sovereign, the issue had been largely pre-judged on the incomplete premises of an observer who had no official status. In other words, Esher, whether intentionally or not, had constituted himself the unofficial adviser of the Crown, and ... it would be tedious to record the endless contretemps to which this usurpation of power by an outsider gave rise.'

Esher's conversation was as beguiling as his handwriting was beautiful, and the memoranda which he composed were marvellously succinct and clear. He was adept at interesting and amusing King Edward whose restlessness worried his Household. The parties which the King loved to attend and the large meals which he consumed, the numerous cigars which he smoked and the constant journeys in which he indulged at home as well as abroad, were all symptoms of that restlessness which caused him to wage a perpetual battle against fatigue and irritability. Lacking inner resources, he depended upon external distractions, and his boredom was made manifest by an ominous drumming of his fat fingers on the table, or by an automatic tap, tap tap of one of his feet.

A few minutes with nothing to do proved a trial to King

Edward's temper, which had to find an outlet and which vented itself at times upon his friends and occasionally upon the Queen. His habitual generosity and thoughtfulness, his natural kindness and heartfelt desire to see everyone around him happy and smiling inspired deep affection; but Frederick Ponsonby recorded [22] that 'even his most intimate friends were all terrified of him', and Ponsonby's daughter, Loelia (Duchess of Westminster), added [23] that 'his angry bellow, once heard, could never be forgotten'.

King Edward's temper was vented, principally and conveniently, upon the Superintendent of his Wardrobe, H. Chandler, who was well content to serve as whipping boy. Chandler understood and was devoted to his royal master; and King Edward was convinced that incessant activity was the best and only medicine for a restlessness and irritability which had become pathological.

King Edward hated to appear to do anything in a hurry, and he liked to reserve his decision whenever he had been convinced by Lord Knollys or by anyone else that it would behove him to do something irksome. If he said that he would consider the point, it could be assumed that he would presently concede it; but he had great difficulty in restraining his impetuosity and in repressing, for example, impatient gestures if his carriage or motor was held up for a moment by traffic, or slowed down. He was extraordinarily fond of routine which he found extremely helpful; and he insisted at the start of his reign upon opening personally his daily post. Because it averaged four hundred letters he had to abandon that experiment, but he rarely postponed, and he experienced almost no temptation to postpone even for twenty-four hours, the task of dealing with the many formal documents presented in boxes for his signature.

At the start of his reign King Edward addressed himself to the task of signing 6,600 * [24] military commissions which had fallen hopelessly into arrears during the last months of Queen Victoria's life and which had been multiplied during the Boer War. He announced, furthermore, that he intended in future to sign all naval commissions as well. Naval officers

* Total outstanding on 10 April 1901.

are not commissioned by the Sovereign, as Army officers are, but by the Lord High Admiral whose office is exercised by Lords Commissioner; and, after brushing aside Admiralty protests which he described contemptuously as red tape, King Edward discovered that that self-imposed labour was really too great.

In those circumstances the King ordered that his signature should be impressed in future by a rubber stamp upon all military and naval commissions; but he insisted upon a characteristic gesture. He instructed Knollys to mark with a sheet of red blotting paper the commissions of officers with whose families the Sovereign was acquainted personally, and King Edward continued to sign those selected ones with his own hand.

As the apex of the social pyramid in an age of ostentatious luxury, extravagance and snobbery, King Edward's personal expenditure was necessarily enormous, and the arrangement of his finances brooked no delay. His former Parliamentary income lapsed at his accession; his private capital had been used up; and he had nothing left except £60,000 a year from the Duchy of Lancaster. Queen Victoria's large private fortune had been bequeathed to her younger children.

A Select Committee of the House of Commons recommended that King Edward's annual Parliamentary income should be £470,000 which was £85,000 more than Queen Victoria had received; and the King summoned an inner financial circle to his aid. He confided the administration of his finances to Sir Ernest Cassel, Lord Esher (who was made Lieutenant and Deputy Constable of Windsor Castle) and Lord Farquhar (who was made Master of the Royal Household). That triumvirate, in association with the charming Keeper of the Privy Purse, Sir Dighton Probyn, V.C., established an amortization scheme, took out life insurance policies and realized such handsome profits out of judicious investments that by 1907 King Edward was relieved of all encumbrances, and was enabled to enjoy the whole of his income during the last three years of his life.

Parliament voted additional sums for pensions, upkeep of

royal yachts and repairs to palaces; and £70,000 a year was secured to Queen Alexandra in the event of widowhood. Henry Labouchère, Keir Hardie, John Burns and the Irish Nationalists were the principal critics of those generous and satisfactory arrangements; but the third reading of the Civil List Bill, which received King Edward's assent on 2 July 1901, was carried by 370 votes against 60.

The annual income of the Duke of York, who was created Prince of Wales on his father's sixtieth birthday (9 November 1901), was made up to £90,000; and King Edward's three daughters were voted a joint annual income of £18,000. Despite Lord Salisbury's protest, King Edward insisted upon reducing the annual salaries of the political members of his Household; and he extracted a promise from the Treasury that the cost of entertaining foreign sovereigns paying State visits to England should be defrayed out of public funds.

Besides Buckingham Palace and Windsor Castle, which were maintained partly by the State, King Edward had on his hands the three great private establishments of Balmoral Castle, Sandringham and Osborne House. Queen Victoria had given all her children a share by Will in Osborne House, and had tried to ensure that it and Balmoral, which had been her favourite homes, should become official instead of private royal residences.

King Edward and Queen Alexandra had no use for Osborne House in the Isle of Wight, which had been designed at vast expense in Italian renaissance style by the Prince Consort in collaboration with Thomas Cubitt; and after failing to persuade the Prince of Wales to take the place off his hands, King Edward presented it to the nation. He overcame his strong reluctance to set aside his mother's Will, ignored shrill protests from his sisters, and formed the place partly into a Royal Naval College for cadets, and partly into a convalescent home for naval officers. He opened the college, which replaced the training ship *Britannia*, on 4 July 1903; but the pavilion, which constituted the central part of Osborne House, was preserved as a family shrine and guarded from public access.

An immense number of improvements were necessary

before Buckingham Palace and Windsor and Balmoral Castles were ready to receive King Edward; and as a boy the Duke of Windsor was given to understand[25] that the effect of his grandfather's belated entry into all three was comparable with that of a Viennese hussar bursting suddenly into an English vicarage. Aided by Esher and others, King Edward found time to inspect every detail of the overdue work of modernization, and he was awed as well as impressed by the many treasures which came to light. 'I don't know much about arrt', he would say sometimes, rolling his r's, 'but I think I know something about arrrangement'; and, without initiating suggestions, he gave quick decisions and issued clear instructions when asked.

King Edward ordered the immediate destruction or discreet removal of all statues, busts and other memorials of Queen Victoria's favourite Highland servant, John Brown; and he allowed no sentimental inhibitions to stand in his way: 'Alas!', Queen Alexandra wrote[26] to the Empress Frederick (14 May 1901), after returning to Buckingham Palace from Copenhagen, 'during my absence Bertie has had all your beloved Mother's rooms dismantled and all her precious things removed.'

King Edward also wrote frequently to his dying sister; and he told[27] her (5 June 1901):

After dear Mama, you are the one person in the world who ought not to suffer, for if anyone, from her life and virtues, is more prepared to go straight to Heaven, it is yourself. It often seems to me that it is the bad people who prosper in this world, and not the good ones.

I understand the reasons you give why your doctors do not like giving you more narcotics, but I cannot help thinking that ours would....

We have had, alas, more fighting in S. Africa and loss of life. Surprises, sudden attacks, etc. When will those wretched Boers see the folly of continuing hostilities, as we must be masters in the long run. It is only a question of time – but the expense is frightful!

As early as 23 February 1901, the King had warned[28] Lord Salisbury that a proposed increase of twopence (to one shilling and twopence) in the standard rate of income tax would 'tend to make the war unpopular'; and most of the earliest duties which he undertook had to do with the war. He told [29] the Empress Frederick (12 June) that, while distributing medals on the Horse Guards Parade that morning, he had been overwhelmed by a flood of memories of a similar ceremony, performed by their mother, which he had witnessed as a child during the Russian War in 1855.

King Edward had dismayed Lord Salisbury, three days after Queen Victoria's death, by cancelling suddenly an arrangement, made some months earlier, that the Duke and Duchess of York should visit Melbourne to inaugurate the first Parliament of the new Commonwealth of Australia on 9 May 1901. Pleading a strong reluctance to be parted so soon, and for so long, from his only son, King Edward suggested [30] (22 January) that the Duke of York should be invited instead to succeed Lord Cadogan as Viceroy of Ireland.

That counter proposal was considered (1 February) by the Cabinet, which resolved [31] that the constitutional difficulty was insuperable. A minor additional difficulty was a request from King Edward that his son's salary should be supplemented by an annual entertainment allowance of between fifteen and twenty thousand pounds; and Salisbury recorded [32] (27 January) his view that 'no Government would venture to make such a proposal to the House of Commons'.

Because he was resolved not to affront Australian sentiment, Salisbury requested Balfour, as First Lord of the Treasury and leader of the House of Commons, to draft a strong letter from 10, Downing Street. Balfour took leave to remind [33] King Edward (6 February) that he was 'no longer merely King of Great Britain and Ireland, and of a few dependencies whose whole value consisted in ministering to the wealth and security of Great Britian and Ireland. He is now the greatest constitutional bond uniting together in a single Empire communities of free men separated by half the circumference of the Globe. All the patriotic sentiment which makes such an Empire possible centres in him, or centres chiefly in him; and everything which emphasizes his personality to our kinsmen across the seas must be a gain to the Monarchy and the Empire. ...'

On receipt of that veiled rebuke from a man who sometimes made him feel uncomfortable, King Edward yielded at once, but his attitude had been less selfish and shortsighted than Salisbury and Balfour supposed. It had been dictated by excessive regard for the nervous doubts and possessive affections of Queen Alexandra whom he chivalrously shielded; and he was proud to assume a new royal title as 'King of the British Dominions beyond the Seas'.

The Duke's visit to Australia took place, accordingly, as planned; and Lord Charles Beresford, who was serving as second-in-command of the Mediterranean Fleet, and who met the Duke at Malta, attempted to improve the occasion by instilling up-to-date ideas into King Edward's mind: 'I was honoured', King Edward wrote [34] (11 April) to his son, 'by a lengthy epistle from Lord C.B., who seemed as usual much in evidence during your stay. The pith of his letter was that you should associate yourself, in each place you visit, with Trade and Commerce (!) by personal interviews with Chambers of Commerce. If this is in any way possible, I cannot say. The subject is doubtless a most important one with regard to the Mother Country, our Colonies and India.'

On 14 February 1901, King Edward opened Parliament in state. Queen Victoria had allowed that ceremony to lapse; and King Edward, who had tried often but without success to convince her of its importance, insisted that it should take place in the House of Lords, as of old. He rejected Balfour's suggestion that it should be held instead in Westminster Hall, which would have offered vastly more space.

Before reading from the throne the speech which his ministers had drafted for him King Edward declared himself a Protestant in language which provoked an immediate protest from Cardinal Vaughan on behalf of his Roman Catholic fellow-subjects. A section in the Bill of Rights, 1689, required a new sovereign, addressing Parliament for the first time, not merely to repudiate the doctrine of transubstantiation but to proclaim that 'the invocation or adoration of the Virgin Mary, or any other saint, and the Sacrifice of the Mass, as they are now used in the Church of Rome, are superstitious and idolatrous.'

The Cabinet agreed with King Edward that the terms of that declaration were not in accordance with 'public policy of the present day'; and King Edward, who was a convinced and practising Anglican, asked Lord Salisbury to have the law changed forthwith. He was anxious that his son, on succeeding to the throne, should not 'have to make such a Declaration in such crude language'; but it proved to be impossible to alter the law at that time without provoking a frothy 'No Popery' agitation. After much correspondence, King Edward accused [35] the Lord Chancellor, Lord Halsbury, of 'bungling' incompetence, but King George V was compelled at his accession to proclaim in the old form his Protestant faith. Immediately afterwards, in August 1910, Asquith succeeded in causing an Act to be passed embodying a new form of declaration which satisfied the Establishment without causing offence.

The problem of honours caused occasional friction between Lord Salisbury and King Edward who was eager, naturally, to reward men whom he liked and who had served him well. Good feeling and good sense on both sides kept such friction to a minimum; but the King did not hesitate to startle his Prime Minister by making unorthodox suggestions in many fields. He informed [36] Lord Salisbury, for example, at the beginning of March 1901, that he contemplated sending for Lord Rosebery and begging him 'in the interests of the country to resume public life and the leadership of the Opposition'. The Prime Minister replied [37] (5 March) that 'as Leader of the Government', he felt that he was 'almost the last person to express an opinion'; and he added: 'The very peculiar circumstances of the Opposition with which, in all its details, Lord Salisbury is imperfectly acquainted, would make him a bad adviser in such a matter: and he doubts whether the fact of his having been consulted might not, if it happened to become known, prejudice members of the Opposition against any course which His Majesty may see fit to favour.'

The Liberal Party was rent internally at that time; and on 8 July 1901 King Edward consulted [38] Lord Salisbury about its conduct. Sir Henry Campbell-Bannerman had publicly described Kitchener's policy of burning farms in South Africa, and of herding enemy women and children into concentration camps where large numbers died of epidemic diseases, as 'methods of barbarism'; and the King proposed to send for the Liberal leader and to 'ask him to be very careful to avoid any language which might be interpreted abroad or in South Africa as an encouragement to the Boers'.

Salisbury advised [39] King Edward that 'this would be a somewhat dangerous course to pursue' because the Opposition was divided in its attitude to the war, 'and if it became known, as it certainly would, that His Majesty had seen Sir Henry Campbell-Bannerman, it might have a bad effect'. That advice was accepted without demur; but it may be thought that Lord Knollys should have been in as good a position as the Prime Minister was to guide King Edward in such a matter.

King Edward urged his Government continuously to give 'a free hand' to Lord Kitchener, 'the man on the spot'; and his vibrant energy embarrassed Brodrick at times. Although salutary, it was founded upon intuition and not upon experience, and a number of minor points of friction culminated in a trifling incident which imposed, nevertheless, a severe temporary strain upon King Edward's relations with the Secretary of State for War.

A junior officer, after displaying the white flag in action in June 1901, had been tried by court martial in South Africa. Acquitted of cowardice, he had been convicted of an error of judgement and 'permitted' to resign his commission. Lord Roberts, as Commander-in-Chief in South Africa, had recommended that conviction and sentence for confirmation but the white flag, unfortunately, had been displayed so often without adequate cause on the British side that, when the documents reached the War Office, Lord Wolseley decided that it was his duty, as Commander-in-Chief of the British Army, to make a resounding example. With

Brodrick's consent, accordingly, he set aside the conviction and sentence of the court martial; substituted a conviction for cowardice, and ordered the officer to be cashiered.

On returning to England, the broken and disgraced young officer exercised his right of appeal through the proper channels to King Edward, who was very sensitive on the subject of the royal prerogative of mercy. The King took a more generous and probably a more commonsense view of the case than that which had been taken by Brodrick and Wolseley; and he consulted Roberts, who had returned in the meantime to replace Wolseley at the War Office.

Having endorsed the original conviction and sentence, Roberts agreed warmly and naturally with King Edward; and, in an attempt to avoid offending Brodrick and Wolseley, he asked the Adjutant-General to preside at a specially convened court of inquiry. That court recommended unanimously that the conviction and sentence for cowardice should be quashed, and that the original and more merciful conviction and sentence should be restored, but Brodrick informed King Edward that he would resign from the Government if his decision and that of Lord Wolseley were overruled.

When Brodick remained obdurate, King Edward toyed with the idea of exercising his prerogative of mercy on the advice of the Commander-in-Chief but against that of the Secretary for War. He was warned, however, by Balfour that circumstances could arise in which the Government might have to consider resignation in defence of the important principle of collective Cabinet responsibility. In those circumstances the unlucky captain was transformed into a social pariah by being convicted of cowardice and cashiered, but the King persisted and gave the ex-officer a free pardon, and a medal, four years later.

That inflated affair so exasperated King Edward that Brodrick sent him a dignified and closely argued defence of his general line of conduct as Secretary for War; and the King replied [40] (15 October 1902) very amiably from the Jockey Club:

You need never fear that I shall not always give you my heartiest support in all matters concerning the reform of the Army, which is so much wanted. But at the same time you must expect my criticisms, and they will doubtless be frequently at variance with your own views....

At all times it will give me the greatest pleasure to discuss any matters relative to the Army, in which I take the deepest interest; and though I feel that reforms in the Army are most essential as an outcome of the South African War, the War Office needs also very great reforms, so as to make it thoroughly efficient.

Nearly forty years later, Brodrick emphasized [41] that 'the one great monument of King Edward's military interest was the reform of the medical system, which he pressed forward from the first day of his reign'. Relishing the company of doctors, the King numbered several, including Sir Alfred Fripp, Sir Felix Semon and Sir Frederick Treves among his friends; and he brought his influence to bear through them upon the civilian medical schools. He begged [42] Brodrick (31 August 1901) to stop fussing about the blackballing of Army doctors at Service clubs, and to concentrate instead upon the need to improve their professional competence, because that was the root problem.

In a successful attempt to secure a better class of doctor, King Edward welcomed a higher salary scale and agreed to the assumption by doctors of military rank below that of general officer. A Royal Commission recommended a number of other useful reforms, and the efficiency and reputation of the Army Medical Service was transformed within a decade.

When the Boers surrendered at last on 31 May 1902, King Edward asked [43] Lord Salisbury (13 June) not to appoint a Royal Commission to inquire into the conduct of the war:

The Government is a strong one with a large Parliamentary majority. Why, therefore, should Ministers pledge themselves, or give way to demands from unimportant M.P.s? The proposed Inquiry will do the Army and also the Country harm in the eyes of the civilized world.

This system of 'washing our dirty linen in public' the late Queen had a horror of, and the King entirely shares the views of his beloved Mother.

Explaining that he was pledged already to the inquiry, and that he could not overrule his Cabinet, Salisbury promised [44] that 'every effort will be made to render the Inquiry innocuous, and those efforts will probably be successful'; but King Edward grumbled [45] (14 June) to Knollys that the Cabinet 'is, apparently, so powerful a body that neither I nor the Prime Minister can gainsay them'.

The incorporation into the British Empire of the two former Boer republics, with an incalculable wealth of gold, diamonds, coal and other assets, chimed happily with the arrangements made for King Edward's coronation on 26 June 1902. Many foreign royalties, Indian princes and colonial dignitaries had already reached London when rumours started to circulate that the King was unwell. He had put on so much weight that his abdominal measurement – 48 inches – equalled [46] that of his chest; and after spending a wretched night at Aldershot on 14 June he noted [47] in his diary: 'The King rather ill with severe chill. Unable to dine.'

Since his accession, King Edward's iron determination to do his duty without altering his social routine had strained his endurance to breaking point. He repulsed all suggestions that he should delegate a variety of minor matters connected, for example, with the coronation, with the structural alterations at Buckingham Palace and Windsor Castle, and with the design of new liveries for his servants. He exhausted himself by going personally into endless detail with an undiscriminating degree of enthusiasm; and Sir Francis Laking incurred a serious responsibility when he diagnosed appendicitis in mid-June. Although peritonitis developed quickly, the doctor decided that it would be wrong to alarm the King, who was exceedingly irritable and depressed, and who told [48] him: 'If this goes on, I shall give it up. I shall abdicate.'

Laking asked King Edward to keep to a milk diet and to rest in bed; and he hoped in that way to avoid the necessity for a postponement of the coronation and for an operation which was regarded as a very serious one in 1902. He was compelled, in those circumstances, deliberately to mislead the Press, which never forgave him for informing it on 15 June that King Edward was suffering only from a severe attack of lumbago.

While his temperature rose and fell at Windsor between 16 and 23 June, King Edward went to bed before dinner every evening and kept mostly to a low diet; but he was a very difficult patient. He did not attend Ascot Races, but he warned Laking and others that he intended to arrive on time with the Queen at Westminster Abbey for his coronation on 26 June, even if he were to drop dead during the long service.

King Edward returned by special train on 23 June in time for luncheon at Buckingham Palace, where he was examined during the late afternoon by Sir Francis Laking and Sir Thomas Barlow. They told [49] him that he would certainly die unless an operation was performed without delay. They added that all arrangements had been made secretly for Sir Frederick Treves to operate in a specially prepared room at Buckingham Palace on the following morning; and that the coronation would have to be postponed indefinitely.

Although racked with pain and feeling desperately ill, King Edward retorted that he could not and would not disappoint his subjects. He argued furiously with the doctors before exclaiming [50]: 'Laking, I will stand no more of this. I am suffering the most awful mental agony that any man can endure. Leave the room at once.' After Barlow had withdrawn in response to a signal from his colleague, Laking told the King that obedience in existing circumstances was impossible. Pleading his long service and his disinterested devotion, he became as gentle as a woman and extracted King Edward's consent to all that he had proposed.

King Edward asked next morning that the operation should take place at once, but Lord Lister and Sir Thomas Smith were first called into consultation. Lister was dubious and hesitant; Smith agreed emphatically with Treves, Laking and Barlow; and the operation, which was begun by Treves at 12.25 p.m., was completely successful after lasting for forty minutes. In the streets of the capital the news reverberated like a thunderclap, and a dress rehearsal of the coronation in Westminster Abbey was transformed by the presence of mind of the Bishop of London into an impromptu service of intercession. Upon emerging from the chloroform, the King's first words were, 'Where's George?', meaning the Prince of Wales; but newspapers reported that he had asked, 'Will my people ever forgive me?' He fell immediately into a healing sleep, while the Empire was convulsed by a transport of emotional loyalty and of human affection for King Edward which commanded the awed sympathy and wonder of the world.

16

France

KING EDWARD'S rapid recovery from his operation for appendicitis was regarded as almost miraculous. He conferred baronetcies upon Laking and Treves, whom he thanked for having saved his life, and when he embarked, 15 July 1902, with the Queen at Portsmouth for a convalescent cruise in *Victoria and Albert*, Lords Esher and Carrington noted[1] that he was thinner by six inches round the waist; that he looked younger and appeared far less irritable; and that he was better in mind and body than he had been for years.

A penurious poet, William Watson, who had composed an ode for the coronation, complained that its postponement had spoilt his sales. The ode contained two beautiful lines which expressed the mood of the hour and which were often quoted, to King Edward and others, by Admiral of the Fleet Lord Fisher:

> Time and the ocean and some fostering star
> In high cabal have made us what we are.

Most of the foreign guests had returned home by 9 August when the postponed coronation was held; but the enthusiasm of the crowds was uninhibited, and the ancient ritual was curtailed to avoid fatiguing King Edward. He summoned his grandchildren with a few of their friends to see him in his robes before he started for Westminster Abbey; and they were too much awed to say anything when he greeted them with the words: 'Good morning, children. Am I not a funny-looking old man?' He stood the ceremony well and looked bronzed and happy, while Queen Alexandra appeared radiant and, as always, absurdly young. The very evident sincerity of the King's deep affection for his son, whom he kissed after he had sworn allegiance, was an incident which made a deep impression.

Outside the Abbey the appearance of a large number of gilded state coaches belonging to the heads of patrician families gave pleasure and evoked applause; and the King, who left Buckingham Palace in his own superb coach at eleven o'clock, returned punctually at three-thirty in the afternoon. Inside the Abbey, in a special King's box dubbed irreverently 'the King's Loose Box', the presence of a number of King Edward's special friends, including the actress, Sarah Bernhardt dressed in white, Mrs Hartmann, Lady Kilmorey, Mrs Arthur Paget and the reigning favourite, Mrs George Keppel, excited hushed wonder and admiration; but the King had his own special memory. Asked[2] by Treves what had impressed him most, he confessed that it had been an incident which 'was not intended to be impressive, and that was the simultaneous movement of the peeresses in putting on their coronets'. King Edward explained that 'their white arms arching over their heads' had suggested, inevitably, 'a scene from a beautiful ballet'.

The retirement, immediately before the coronation, of Lord Salisbury, who had been impervious to royal criticism, encouraged King Edward to exert his forcefulness in foreign affairs. Salisbury had been Foreign Secretary as well as Prime Minister until October 1900, when he surrendered the Foreign Office to Lord Lansdowne, who did not share the Prime Minister's invincible prejudice against discarding the traditional British policy of splendid isolation.

King Edward was profoundly interested in discussions upon which Lansdowne embarked in March 1901 about the possibility of an Anglo-German alliance. During the illness of the German Ambassador, Count Hatzfeldt, they were conducted with Baron Hermann von Eckardstein, who assumed charge of the German Embassy in London and who had married the only child and heiress of Sir Blundell Maple. After expressing[3] indignation (19 April 1901) to Eckardstein at the German Emperor's description of British ministers as 'a set of unmitigated noodles', King Edward remarked that the prospect of an alliance appeared exceedingly doubtful in the existing state of public opinion in both countries.

Elaborate preparations were made for a meeting between King Edward and the Emperor William at Wilhelmshöhe on 23 August 1901; and the death on 5 August of the Empress Frederick caused the King to expedite his departure for Germany. He left on 9 August to attend his sister's funeral, and asked Lansdowne to provide, for his private information, a memorandum covering any topics which the Emperor could be expected to raise.

Lansdowne dictated at short notice a series of confidential notes which King Edward had in his pocket when his nephew greeted him at Homburg on 11 August. Because he was feeling overwrought the King was anxious to avoid all risk of controversial talk about Anglo-German differences and problems during the period of the funeral and before the formal meeting at Wilhelmshöhe on 23 August, and he purchased immunity by handing impulsively to the Emperor the notes which Lansdowne had prepared.

That accident, which annoyed Lansdowne excessively, caused little harm, because the notes contained nothing offensive to Germany. They described Kuwait, incidentally, as the projected terminus of the Transcaspian instead of the Anatolian Railway, and so gave the Emperor, and the clerks in the German Foreign Office, a chance to poke fun at British ignorance of geography.

At Wilhelmshöhe on 23 August, King Edward was attended by the British Ambassador in Berlin, Sir Frank Lascelles, but the meeting was abortive and the King returned thankfully to Homburg to complete his cure. He left on 6 September for Copenhagen, where he met his more congenial Russian nephew, the Emperor Nicholas II, while the German Foreign Office attempted to make trouble. It pretended to regard the document mishandled by King Edward on 11 August as an extraordinary communication from the British Government; and Lansdowne instructed[4] Lascelles (11 September) to notify the German Government that it had not been intended for communication to them and that 'it must be regarded as a purely informal and unofficial document'.

The new German Ambassador in London, Count Paul Metternich, was informed[5] by Lansdowne on 19 December 1901 that the state of public opinion in Great Britain and Germany precluded the possibility of an Anglo-German alliance. King Edward agreed with that decision which he did not influence in any way; and Lansdowne recorded[6] five cardinal reasons for it in an interesting memorandum (11 November).

The British Cabinet did not wish to alienate France or Russia by adhering to the Triple Alliance; or to attach the British dominions and colonies formally, as the Germans insisted, to the skirts of the Triple Alliance; or to irritate the United States by ignoring the hostile and provocative attitude which Germany had adopted towards the Monroe Doctrine. It was found to be impossible to define the circumstances in which an Anglo-German alliance could operate, without using language so vague as to deprive it of practical effect, or so rigid as to hamper unduly British freedom of action; and serious doubts were entertained about the probable attitude of Parliament.

Early in the new year, after accepting an Admiral's commission in the German Navy, King Edward twice changed his mind before despatching the Prince of Wales on a goodwill visit to Berlin; but he welcomed the Anglo-Japanese Alliance which was signed on 30 January 1902. He flung himself with relish thereafter into the task of assisting his Government to cement understandings with France and Russia, while failing to achieve cordial personal relations with his Foreign Secretary.

Sir Frederick Ponsonby, at a loss to account for the lack of genuine cordiality between King Edward and Lord Lansdowne, considered[7] that 'Lansdowne may have been a little jealous at the King being supposed to run the foreign policy of the country. ... I always had the impression that if the King ever made a false move, Lansdowne, so far from defending him, would stand and look on.' Lansdowne, in fact, was always loyal and chivalrous; but a misunderstanding during the summer of 1902 imposed a strain upon his relations with the King.

Early that year the Government had invited the Shah of Persia to visit England for political reasons, although King Edward had grumbled that the visit would be very tiresome. The Shah became equally reluctant to travel, after the Treasury and the India Office had refused to sponsor a Persian loan; but the British Minister in Teheran, Sir Arthur Hardinge (a cousin of Sir Charles), saved the day by exceeding his authority. He suggested to the Shah that he would be sure to receive the Order of the Garter; and the Shah came with that sole object.

On 18–19 June, a few days before he underwent his operation for appendicitis, King Edward warned [8] Lansdowne at Windsor that he had no intention of making the Shah a Knight of the Garter and that that Order would never again be conferred upon an infidel. Lansdowne reminded the King that the Garter had been conferred upon the Shah's father, but he had no wish to excite him at that moment, and he discussed his embarrassment with the Duke of Devonshire, who was a fellow-guest. After reminding Lansdowne that the Garter was a specifically Christian Order, the Duke expressed [9] the view (19 June) that King Edward's scruples would have to be respected; and the matter rested there until 27 July when Lansdowne re-opened the subject with King Edward who said firmly that he was unable to change his mind.

When the Shah of Persia reached London on 18 August, King Edward had resumed already the convalescent cruise which had been interrupted by the coronation with its attendant festivities and reviews. He came to Portsmouth, however, to greet the Shah, whom he entertained (20 August) to luncheon on board *Victoria and Albert*.

Most of the Shah's numerous suite were given luncheon on board *Osborne*; and Lansdowne, who lunched with King Edward and the Shah, was at his wits' end to find an acceptable means of explaining to the Persian autocrat the nature of the hitch which had occurred in regard to the Garter.

The Foreign Office wanted to detach him from Russia, but there seemed every reason to fear that he would throw himself into that country's arms after being subjected to what he would be certain to regard as a mortal and inexplicable affront.

In those circumstances, Lansdowne brought to Portsmouth a memorandum which he had dictated. It declared [10] that, after King Edward's health was fully restored, the officials of the Order of the Garter, acting through the Lord Chamberlain's Office under the authority of the Prime Minister, would revise the Statutes of the Order in a sense which would enable its specifically Christian insignia to be altered when it was conferred upon non-Christians.

After luncheon, Lansdowne asked King Edward to read and assent to that document in the presence of the Shah; and he maintained subsequently that the King had assented by twice nodding his head distinctly before laying it aside. King Edward, on the other hand, who was always scrupulously truthful, declared that he had not even glanced at the document, which he had promised to read later and to consider.

Lansdowne chose to assume, nevertheless, that his difficulty had been solved, and he promised the Shah that he would receive the Garter within a week or two, or even within a few days. The Shah retorted that he never expressed the least objection to receiving the insignia in its Christian form; that it had been conferred in that form upon his father; and that he could not understand the reason for any delay. He rejected, accordingly, a miniature of King Edward which the King offered him in a gold frame encrusted with South African diamonds; and he ordered the members of his suite to reject decorations which King Edward had expressed a wish to confer upon them after luncheon, and in regard to which he had gone to personal trouble to compile and approve a list.

In an attempt to retrieve a deteriorating situation, Lansdowne outraged the feelings of touchy officials and waspish antiquaries by ordering the Court jewellers, Messrs Harrard, to make within three days a suitable non-Christian Garter star and badge, omitting the Cross of St George; and he asked the Persian Minister in London to notify the Shah and the Persian Foreign Office that that order had been given. He wrote to explain to King Edward the reasons which had made that hasty action necessary, and to request that arrangements should be made to confer the new non-Christian insignia of the Order of the Garter, of which he enclosed coloured illustrations, upon the Shah before he left England, which he was due to do in a few days' time.

At Pembroke Dock on the morning of 24 August 1902 a tremendous explosion of royal wrath rocked *Victoria and Albert*. King Edward, who could scarcely have been touched upon a more sensitive spot, flung the box containing the Foreign Secretary's letter and painted enclosures through a porthole at the far end of his cabin. It fell into a pinnace and was retrieved by a stoker, while the King dictated a violent letter which would certainly have caused Lansdowne to resign at once if Sir Frederick Ponsonby had not ventured to tone it down: [11]

'I cannot have my hand forced' was the theme of that letter; and King Edward described[12] the Shah's insulting rejection of his miniature in diamonds, and his refusal to allow decorations to be conferred upon his suite as 'a most outrageous proceeding'. It was 'unheard of' for one sovereign to be 'dictated to by another as to what Order he should confer on him'; and, after reiterating his refusal to confer the Garter in any form upon the Shah, King Edward added:

The Shah forced himself upon the King when he knew his visit this year was most inconvenient ... and if the Shah leaves this Country in the sulks, like a spoilt child, because he cannot get what he wants, it cannot be helped.

Lord Lansdowne states that a determined effort should be made to strengthen our hold upon Persia. In this the King entirely concurs. But we should not have lost the hold which Russia now possesses if the Government of the day had kept their eyes open, and had had more competent representatives at Teheran....

The Shah left England, accordingly, boiling with indignation, and King Edward warned[13] Lansdowne by letter and telegram (27 August) that the matter was closed and could not be re-opened. He expressed contempt for a foreign policy which hinged upon the conferment of a decoration, and Lansdowne wrote [14] (28 August) to the Prime Minister: 'This is, to say the least of it, awkward. It places me in a very difficult position which I shall have, bye and bye, to ask you to consider. If the King remains obdurate there is, so far as I can see, only one way out for me, and that will be "out" in the most literal sense of the word.'

It was obvious that unless King Edward could be induced to yield, Lansdowne would be compelled to resign after breaking promises made to the Shah and to the Persian Government; and the Duke of Devonshire (Lord President of the Council) advised [15] Balfour (25 October) to stand by Lansdowne. He urged the Prime Minister to present King Edward with a choice between doing what he had been advised to do, or of finding an alternative Government; and he emphazised the need for the most absolute secrecy: 'My own impression is that if we stand by him [Lansdowne] the King will give in; but it would be much more difficult for the King to give in if all the Cabinet knew of what he may call his weakness.'

Lord Knollys, on the other hand, advised [16] King Edward that to give way would involve a display of weakness which would diminish his standing in the eyes of ministers, without altering the Shah's dislike of Great Britain and without averting, in all probability, the collapse of his tottering, antiquated and scandalous regime; and the King did not lack other support. Lord Curzon, for example, as Viceroy of India, considered [17] that it would be wrong in principle to confer the Garter upon an infidel, but the King's primary objection had become personal. He resented intensely the way in which Lansdowne had tried, by a trick as he thought, to force his hand; and he told [18] Knollys that if he gave the Garter to any non-Christian it ought to go first to the Emperor of Japan, who was much more important and, probably, more agreeable that the Shah, and who had virtually asked for it when the Anglo-Japanese Alliance was signed.

Queen Victoria's action in conferring the Garter upon previous Shahs of Persia and Sultans of Turkey weakened King Edward's case; and Balfour prudently allowed the affair to simmer while he brought pressure to bear upon Lord Knollys. When he judged the moment to be ripe, he addressed [19] (3 November 1902) a carefully-worded letter to King Edward:

... Mr Balfour is convinced that Your Majesty is here solely concerned with the not unfamiliar problem of having to deal with a public servant who, by mistake, has exceeded his instructions. The question in such cases inevitably arises, is he to be 'thrown over', or is he not...?

Lord Lansdowne, erroneously believing himself to be authorized by Your Majesty, has pledged Your Majesty to bestow the Garter upon the Shah – has indeed pledged Your Majesty repeatedly and explicitly. If he be prevented from carrying out these pledges, what will be his position?... and, if he resigned, could the matter stop there in these days of Government solidarity?

After analyzing King Edward's position, Balfour concluded that 'the disavowal of an agent can hardly get rid of the obligation into which that agent has entered, although, in entering it, he may have exceeded (not his powers) but his instructions'. He urged the King to remember that although it was 'a relatively small matter' to offend the Shah, it would be unstatesmanlike to shake British credit in Persia: 'We have a very difficult game to play there. Russia has most of the cards, yet it would be dangerous to lose the rubber. Our well-known fidelity to our engagements is one of our few trumps. We must not waste it.'

That evening (3 November) Knollys wrote [20] privately to the Prime Minister: 'My dear Balfour, You may like to know that the King will, I think, give way, but is much depressed about it all.' He informed [21] Balfour officially next day that in order to avoid trouble with Russia, the King had consented 'from patriotic motives' and 'with a high sense of duty' although 'with the greatest reluctance' to confer the Order of the Garter in its traditional Christian form upon the Shah of Persia.

Knollys listed three conditions upon which King Edward had insisted. The Garter would never again be conferred upon an infidel; no decorations would be conferred upon the members of the Shah's suite who had refused them on 20 August; and an expression of the King's displeasure would have to be conveyed officially to the British Minister in Teheran, Sir Arthur Hardinge, for the part which he had played in the affair. On Lansdowne's gentle insistence, however, King Edward agreed to waive his veto on conferring decorations upon the members of the Shah's suite; and he made no difficulty, three years later, about conferring the Garter upon the Emperor of Japan.

King Edward had been intensely and rightly interested always in titles and decorations. He was the fountain of honour, and an informal letter [22] (5 June 1905) from Balfour to Knollys confirmed an understanding which had been reached between King Edward and the Government about the way in which that fountain should operate. It was ageed that the Order of Merit (which King Edward founded in 1902 on the model of Frederick the Great's Order, *Pour le Mérite*), the Royal Victorian Chain and all grades of the Royal Victorian Order should be bestowed by the Sovereign on his personal initiative and responsibility; but that all other Orders of Chivalry including the Garter, as well as all peerages and baronetcies, should be bestowed by the Sovereign in consultation with the Prime Minister and on his advice.

King Edward distributed the five grades of the Royal Victorian Order (Knight Grand Cross, Knight Commander, Commander, and Member designated Fourth or Fifth Class) in a manner which was lavish beyond precedent, and which gave a great deal of pleasure. British honours were much the most highly prized in the world; and the charming and very evident relish with which King Edward bestowed his personal Order wherever he went enhanced his influence and popularity without impairing its prestige.

Until King Edward had mastered empirically his constitutional duties, ministers continued to be startled from time to time by what they regarded as his wilfulness. He had to be restrained,[23] for example, by Lord Salisbury from despatching chivalrously, at the height of the Boer War (23 July 1901), a telegram of condolence to President Paul Kruger of the Transvaal on the death of his wife; but the Cabinet concurred [24] when he cancelled suddenly (11 March 1902) a state visit which he had arranged to pay to Dublin. The King was furious because the Irish Nationalists had risen from their seats in the House of Commons on the previous day to cheer the news of the last Boer success in South Africa (where General Lord Methuen had been ambushed and captured); and he rejected an appeal from his old friend, Lord Cadogan, who was serving as Viceroy of Ireland and who begged him to relent.

King Edward called [25] his ministers' attention to a variety of matters, from 'the trash' which the Poet Laureate, Alfred Austin, had sent him to read in November 1901 to the weakness displayed [26] by the Home Secretary, Herbert Gladstone, in giving way (1 April 1907) to a sentimental agitation in the halfpenny Press for the reprieve of the handsome but cold-blooded murderer of the 'Universal Provider', William Whiteley. King Edward's views were always forthright and independent. He dictated a note [27] (December 1905) recommending that 'life peerages should come into existence – not only for Law Lords'; and he clashed cheerfully with Balfour over the appointment of a new Regius Professor of Modern History at Cambridge after the death of Lord Acton in September 1902.

King Edward rejected [28] Balfour's choice of the American Admiral A. T. Mahan on the ground that English historians were available; and Balfour objected [29] to King Edward's choice of John Morley, on the ground that that eminent biographer was not a historian but a Gladstonian Liberal politician 'who treats history from a point of view which is certainly not in harmony with the general sentiments of the nation'. A compromise had to be arranged, and J. B. Bury was appointed who insisted upon trying to treat history as a science.

Much the greatest part of the time which King Edward spent in reading official papers was devoted to Foreign Office despatches, but he seldom wrote upon them anything more than 'approved' or 'an interesting despatch'. He made no attempt to make any contribution of substance by adding reasoned minutes, but he encouraged all his ambassadors in the great European capitals to supplement their official despatches to the Foreign Office by writing privately and personally to him.

That additional information was supplemented again by other private correspondences; and the most vivid and entertaining letters which King Edward received regularly were written by the distinguished journalist Sir Donald Mackenzie Wallace of *The Times*. An expert on Russian affairs and a fluent Russian linguist, Wallace was liked and trusted by the Emperor Nicholas; but his name was said to conceal a Hebrew origin which could have impaired his usefulness in the Russian capital at that time. When his friend Lord Carnock was ambassador, Wallace resided for months on end at the British Embassy, and was known irreverently to the young men in the Chancery as 'Mordecai the Jew'.

King Edward was constrained reluctantly to entertain the German Emperor at Sandringham from 8–15 November 1902; and the British Press and public were icy throughout that visit, which impressed no one. Fellow-guests included Balfour, Brodrick, Joseph Chamberlain and Lansdowne; and King Edward, who was heard[30] to exclaim, 'Thank God, he's gone!' as his nephew departed, started to prepare a plan of his own. He had been eclipsed completely for years, as Prince of Wales, by the spectacular quality of the German Emperor's European progresses; he was in a position to take up that challenge at last; and in profound secrecy he arranged to undertake a grand tour of Europe during the spring of 1903.

King Edward informed Lord Lansdowne that he did not intend to be accompanied by a Cabinet Minister, and that he would take no one except Charles Hardinge, an undersecretary in the Foreign Office. Disapproving strongly of that proposed arrangement, Lansdowne decided in the end not to involve himself in a second head-on collision with King Edward; and Hardinge, who was accorded the acting rank of Minister Plenipotentiary, recorded [31] that after the King had 'insisted and refused to yield', Lansdowne's formal consent was extorted with difficulty and at the last moment. 'I need hardly say', Hardinge added demurely, 'that I was greatly pleased and astonished at my exceptional good fortune and was entirely at a loss to understand why I had been selected in this unusual and unexpected manner.'

After seeing Queen Alexandra off to Copenhagen on 30 March 1903, King Edward embarked at Portsmouth with over seventy pieces of personal luggage in *Victoria and Albert* for Lisbon, which was reached on 2 April. He complained to Hardinge that the Portuguese nobles reminded him always of 'waiters at second-rate restaurants'; but he informed [32] the Prince of Wales that he had distributed 'a good many Victorian Orders, including Grand Crosses', and that Hardinge was 'invaluable in every respect'.

Hardinge urged [33] his wife to 'read all the King's speeches as they are all my composition. He is delighted with them and never changes a single word.' And King Edward was equally delighted at having asserted successfully his independence against Lansdowne's attempted constraint. Hardinge, who exercised responsibility on behalf of Lansdowne and the Cabinet and who fell quickly into all the King's ways, did not mind in the least being ordered to parade on the first day out from Portsmouth with the six other members of the suite in full dress uniform in a rough sea. Luis de Soveral, who was the King's guest, and Commendatore Eduardo de Martino, who was King Edward's Marine Painter-in-Ordinary but really the Court Jester and a butt for the King's jokes, felt ill and uncomfortable; but both were fetched from their cabins and made to join the parade. When everyone was assembled, King Edward began his inspection and proceeded with grim relish to find something to criticize in the details of all eight uniforms without exception.

Sir Frederick Ponsonby recorded that 'what struck me most during this first State visit abroad was the fact that the King himself made all the arrangements and supervised every detail. After having been on the Viceroy's staff [in India, 1893–4] when the Military Secretary practically arranged everything and told the Viceroy what to do, I was surprised to find that the King told us what to do.' Ponsonby was surprised also to discover that some of the most significant aspects of the tour were being arranged personally by the King while it was in progress.

From 8–13 April King Edward stayed at Gibraltar where he conferred a field-marshal's baton upon the Governor, Sir George White, who was the hero of the siege of Ladysmith. In agreement with the Foreign Office and Admiralty, he had already notified President Emile Loubet of France that he would be happy to visit Paris on the way home; and that he had ordered four battleships of the British Mediterranean Fleet to leave Gibraltar on 12 April and to reach Algiers in time to salute the President on his arrival there.

Deeply appreciative of that calculated but unexpected courtesy at the time when Anglo–French relations were much troubled, Loubet telegraphed warm thanks and invited the King formally to visit Paris on his way home. Lansdowne warned the King that that visit might be dangerous, but King Edward accepted immediately and ordered his ambassador in Paris, Sir Edmund Monson, to prepare and submit a detailed programme forthwith. He informed [34] the Prince of Wales (12 April) that he had decided to arrive in Paris 'in the afternoon of May 1st as the President only returns that morning from his travels and wishes to give me an official reception and meet me at Station and take me to our Embassy where I shall stay till 4th then proceed to Cherbourg and embark in *Osborne* for Portsmouth. These are my present plans ... what Mama's are I am at present ignorant of.'

Before leaving England, King Edward had accepted [35] (10 March) the Cabinet's advice that he should not visit the Pope in Rome; and a series of telegrams [36] from Balfour on 9 April reiterated emphatically that advice. One telegram reported, nevertheless, a conversation between the Prime Minister and the Duke of Norfolk, who had argued that British Roman Catholics would feel hurt and surprised if

King Edward were to leave Rome without calling at the Vatican.

King Edward telegraphed [37] immediately to ask Balfour to consult the Cabinet a second time, while Hardinge informed [38] Lansdowne's secretary, Sir Eric Barrington, that the King hoped very much that the Cabinet would change its advice. Balfour replied [39] (12 April) that he had again consulted the Cabinet, which feared 'that ordinary Protestant prejudice might fasten on the visit and declare it part of a settled scheme to buy off Roman Catholic opposition and to secure the passage of the Irish Land Bill and the success of Your Majesty's [forthcoming] visit to Ireland. This is absurd, but the people we have to deal with are absurd also!'

Barrington, on the other hand, replied to Hardinge in a different vein. He expressed [40] Lansdowne's personal wish that the King would read between the lines of Balfour's long telegram of 12 April, and that he would, if he saw fit, arrange to pay the Pope an informal but not a State visit on his personal responsibility.

Justifiably exasperated by those equivocal tactics, King Edward dictated [41] a violent telegram to Balfour, asking for honest and positive advice without vagueness or circumlocution. Ponsonby scandalized Hardinge by toning down that telegram before it was despatched; but the acting Minister Plenipotentiary had not yet learnt fully to understand King Edward's methods.

A spate of telegrams continued to flow until King Edward reached Rome, and the Cabinet agreed reluctantly to the proposed visit. No British representative was accredited to the Vatican at that time; but the British Ambassador at the Quirinal, Sir Francis Bertie, was instructed to try to induce the ninety-three-year-old Pope Leo XIII to invite King Edward to visit him privately and without formality.

Ponsonby assured [42] Knollys (26 April) that King Edward's 'very violent wish' to see the aged Pontiff Leo arose 'mostly from curiosity', but great difficulty was experienced in inducing the Pope to take the initiative by expressing a wish to see King Edward. The German Emperor, who was also a Protestant potentate, had twice visited the Vatican without seeking to extort any prior initiative on the part of his host, and the Papal Secretary of State, Cardinal Rampolla, did his best to create the impression that the King of England had requested an audience. Balfour and King Edward were both bombarded in consequence by a very large number of telegrams of protest from Protestant societies and individuals, when the papal entourage surrendered at the last moment to an ultimatum from the Duke of Norfolk. The Duke was informed that Pope Leo would expect to derive pleasure from a private visit paid to him by King Edward.

After visiting Malta (16–21 April) King Edward cruised to Naples with an escort of eight battleships, four cruisers and eight destroyers. He insisted, nevertheless, upon landing incognito, described himself as an ordinary tourist and proceeded to explore the slums of Naples with Queen Amélie of Portugal and Mrs Cornelius Vanderbilt. Hardinge explained[43] (26 April) to his wife: 'I had to give him a lecture yesterday morning about exposing himself needlessly, and I spoke to him very seriously. He was very nice, thanked me, said that I was quite right and that he would not do it again....'

King Edward was much less pleased by a luncheon party which Lord Rosebery gave him next day at Posilippo. His host resented having been asked to entertain the King and appeared in consequence to be moody, while the food was of poor quality because all arrangements had been entrusted at the last moment to a Neapolitan caterer. Although the views from the villa were marvellous, King Edward asked Hardinge if he could imagine how any man could contrive to amuse himself for days and weeks on end in such a place alone: 'He is a strange, weird man, sir', was Hardinge's laconic reply.[44]

On 27 April King Edward was met in Rome by King Victor Emanuel III, who took him to stay at the Quirinal. King Edward, unfortunately, was feeling far from well and was therefore depressed and irritable; but the visit was a great success, and the much advertised meeting with Pope Leo XIII took place on the afternoon of 29 April. King Edward drove to the Vatican from the British Embassy in the Ambassador's carriage, after ordering the members of his suite to bow to the Pope as often as they pleased but not to kneel or kiss his ring; and he was immensely impressed by his host's alertness and tact. Cardinal Rampolla displayed umbrage by absenting himself, but the Pontiff stepped forward and shook hands most amiably with all his guests before discussing with King Edward for twenty minutes the situation in Somaliland, the boundary dispute between British Guiana and Venezuela and the state of Lord Salisbury's health.

King Edward left Rome on 30 April for Paris where he enjoyed his finest hour. His special train was joined at Dijon at ten o'clock on the morning of 1 May by Sir Edmund Monson, the British Ambassador, who showed Hardinge a copy of an address which the British Chamber of Commerce proposed to present to the King that afternoon. King Edward instructed Hardinge to compose a suitable reply, which stressed his old and happy ties with Parisians, and his heartfelt wish that 'the friendship and admiration which we all feel for the French nation and their glorious traditions may, in the near future, develop into a sentiment of the warmest affection and attachment between the peoples of the two countries. The achievement of this aim is my constant desire....'

That speech, which Hardinge had submitted to Monson, was headlined in all newspapers next day. It was described universally as having been couched in King Edward's happiest vein, and Hardinge wrote [45] proudly (3 May) to his wife: 'Everybody says that my speech, which the King read, was a huge success and has contributed very much to the warmth of our reception. I think it was not bad, but I had only an hour to write it in.'

When his train reached Paris, King Edward was welcomed by President Loubet, who drove at his side at the head of a procession of six carriages along the Champs Elysées to the British Embassy. The attitude of the crowds was respectful but cool, and occasional shouts of 'Vivent les Boers!', 'Vive Fashoda!', and even 'Vive Jeanne d'Arc!' reached King Edward's ears through the intervening screen of cavalry. As always he appeared to exude warmth and friendliness, and every movement and gesture which he made was stamped with a calculated and inimitable geniality developed to the pitch of a fine art.

That evening, after dining at the British Embassy, the King and the President attended *L'Autre Danger* at the Théâtre Français, where King Edward's reception was indifferent to the point of iciness; but during the first interval he espied Mlle Jeanne Granier standing in the foyer at the centre of a group of friends. Without hesitation, King Edward walked to greet the actress and exclaimed, after kissing her hand, 'Mademoiselle, I remember applauding you in London where you represented all the grace and spirit of France.' The ice appeared to dissolve almost visibly as that remark was repeated everywhere, and Paris buzzed with it within twenty-four hours.

On the morning of 2 May King Edward drove with the President to a review held in his honour at Vincennes; and Monson reported [46] (5 May) to Lansdowne that 'it was easy to perceive a marked increase in cordiality'. On the way to Vincennes, the King was greeted politely by some of the poorest inhabitants of Paris; and a great crowd cheered warmly for the first time when he arrived at the Hotel de Ville at eleven-forty-five. In a very brief extempore speech King Edward assured his hosts that he would never forget their beautiful city to which he had returned with the greatest pleasure and where he had always felt at home.

After entertaining many old friends to luncheon at the British Embassy, King Edward drove to a special race meeting at Longchamps; and the applause from well-dressed crowds *en route* was still comparatively restrained. At the races, the King found himself seated in a box between Mme Loubet and the wife of the Governor of Paris, and as both stolid women floundered he was most profoundly bored. Summoning Ponsonby, he exclaimed in a hoarse whisper, 'Get me out of this at once!'; and Ponsonby ran to the Jockey Club where he buttonholed Prince d'Arenberg, who despatched three members on a mission to President Loubet's box. They begged King Edward as a special favour to inspect the Club's new stand; and after excusing himself with exquisite aplomb to the President, the Governor and their ladies, King Edward left to watch one race with his friends.

The climax was reached that evening, when the King drove to a gala performance at the Opera after dining with the President at the Elysée, where 300 powdered footmen attended 130 guests. King Edward's carriage had difficulty in making its way through milling crowds which seemed to have gone mad, and which chanted continuously French variants of 'Good old Teddy!' From then on, the King was greeted everywhere with thunderous popular applause, and with incessant shouts of 'Vive Édouard!', 'Notre bon Édouard!'; and it became evident, as Monson wrote [47] (8 May) from Paris to Lansdowne, that the visit had been 'a success more complete than the most sanguine optimist could have foreseen'.

The Ambassador explained, somewhat breathlessly:

The personality of the King, and the indefatigable readiness with which he adapted himself to the overcharged programme of functions ... the re-appearance of the frequent visitor of former years, the well-known and popular Prince of Wales coming back to his old friends as King of England, returning to the capital for which he had never concealed his predilection, aroused a feeling of gratification only equalled by the satisfaction of that large body of politicians who, from motives of reason, reflection and clear comprehension of this country's interests, have always systematically favoured the 'Entente Cordiale'.

Throughout that five weeks' tour, King Edward usually discussed the day's arrangements with Hardinge at breakfast; and his methods delighted the official. 'Often', Hardinge recorded, [48] 'I had to suggest a visit which I knew would be irksome, or that he should see somebody that I knew he would not want to see ... and he would exclaim, "No, no, damned if I will do it!" But he always did it, however tiresome it might be to him, without my having to argue the point or in fact say another word. He had a very strong sense of the duties which his position entailed and he never shirked them.' On Sunday, 3 May, for example, after attending church and receiving several friends, King Edward was tired and ravenous for luncheon, which he was due to take with the Foreign Minister Théophile Delcassé, but he consented to present a medal first to an old soldier who had served in the Crimea.

In addition to the five grades of the Royal Victorian Order, King Edward always distributed on his tours abroad a large number of jewelled tie pins and sleeve links, as well as cigarette cases, in gold or silver, all of which displayed his royal cypher picked out in diamonds or in enamel. He experienced great pleasure in distributing those gifts upon a lavish scale in Paris, where his last engagement was a banquet at the Embassy, to which the French President and Cabinet and all ambassadors were invited. Everyone noticed on that occasion the extraordinary attention which King Edward paid to the German Ambassador, Prince Radolin, who was disturbed, inevitably, by the diplomatic transformation which his host had helped to hasten and implement.

After being met in London on 5 May 1903, by Queen Alexandra, the Prince of Wales and other members of the royal family, King Edward was cheered most warmly at Covent Garden, where he attended a performance of Wagner's opera, *Das Rheingold*. The audience appreciated vaguely that a significant step had been taken towards settling British differences with France; and a more authoritative appreciation of King Edward's diplomatic contribution was made by a senior clerk in the Foreign Office, Sir Eyre Crowe, in a memorandum [49] drafted on 1 January 1907 for Sir Edward Grey. Grey was so much impressed by it that he circulated the document among his principal Cabinet colleagues.

After noting that statesmen were powerless to act unless they could carry public opinion, Crowe observed that the Anglo-French agreement, signed on 8 April 1904, would have been unattainable unless a spirit of confidence in British goodwill had been created previously inside France:

It was natural to believe that such confidence could not be forced, but that it might slowly emerge by a process of gradual evolution. That it declared itself with unexpected rapidity and unmistakable emphasis was without doubt due to the initiative and tactful perseverance of the King, warmly recognized and applauded on both sides of the channel. The French nation, having come to look upon the King as personally attached to their country, saw in His Majesty's words and actions a guarantee that the adjustment of political differences might well prepare the way for bringing about a genuine and lasting friendship, to be built upon a community of interests and aspirations.

Foreign policy is an organic growth which changes continuously in response to changing national interests and aspirations; but British public opinion disliked the *entente* with France, which was still regarded crudely as the corrupt and traditional enemy. It disliked the *entente* so much that the leading members of the British Liberal Cabinet, which took office in December 1905, felt justified in concealing from most of their colleagues, as well as from Parliament and the country, the fact that conversations had been initiated between the British and French General Staffs.

Public opinion disliked equally the *entente* with Russia, because it disapproved so strongly of the Czarist tyranny that it longed for its overthrow; and the mass of the British electorate never understood clearly the reasons for either *entente*. British policy, in consequence, appeared abroad to be ambivalent, and whereas everyone knew how France, Germany and Russia would act in a crisis, no one could really forecast what Great Britain would do. Despite the *ententes*, it is unlikely that Asquith and Grey would have been able to enter the First World War against Germany on the side of France and Russia unless the violation of Belgian neutrality had provided fortuitously a compulsive moral issue exhibiting dramatically the requisite degree of emotional appeal.

After the outbreak of that war, Balfour was at pains to scotch the widespread belief that King Edward had been responsible for the *entente cordiale* with France; and he wrote [50] (11 January 1915) to ask Lansdowne to confirm his recollection that 'during the years which [*sic*] you and I were his Ministers, he never made an important suggestion of any sort on large questions of policy'. That was true, but the lamentable failure of King Edward's governments and the failure, in particular, of his Liberal governments to educate British opinion more effectively in regard to foreign policy, gave King Edward the opportunity to play a forceful and helpful role in the field of public relations.

The British Government trumpeted its foreign policy to the world with a much more squeaky and uncertain note than that which was sounded by the government of any other Great Power; but everyone understood that King Edward stood honestly and positively on the side of the *ententes* with France and Russia. For that reason he was abused more vulgarly in the German Press as the arch-enemy and encircler than was any other Englishman; whereas in France and Russia he was more trusted than were Asquith and Grey.

Although the legend that he controlled British foreign policy caused King Edward to chuckle into his beard, he was so human and yet so dignified that he appeared to speak for England when he merely greeted a chance acquaintance at Biarritz or Marienbad. Men will never be governed by their reasons alone, and King Edward's reputation for statecraft was inflated hysterically at times; but he helped to acclimatize Europe to the changing spirit of British policy, and his governments reaped quite a useful harvest from the goodwill and confidence which he inspired.

17

National Security

1903–5

KING EDWARD received the Prime Minister, A. J. Balfour, in audience at 11.30 a.m. on 8 May 1903, before attending Kempton Park Races; and at 10.30 that evening he held one of the new 'Courts', or evening parties, which he had devised personally in substitution for the 'Drawing Rooms' held by Queen Victoria during the afternoons. He received the Foreign Secretary next morning before darting off again to Kempton Park; and in splendid weather from 11–14 May he fulfilled, with Queen Alexandra, a crowded programme of engagements in Edinburgh and Glasgow.

The King and Queen, who stayed outside Edinburgh with the Duke of Buccleuch at Dalkeith Palace, brought such an outsize suite that their host and hostess moved quietly into the agent's house. King Edward found it necessary to employ every artifice which might conserve energy by inducing comfort; and a week's luggage included normally some forty suits and uniforms and twenty pairs of boots and shoes. When he stayed, for example, with Lady Savile at Rufford Abbey from 7–14 September 1903, for Doncaster Races, he brought[1] a valet, a sergeant footman and a brusher, two equerries who brought a valet apiece, two telephonists, two chauffeurs, and an Arab boy to prepare coffee in the way he liked. If shooting had been in prospect then, that staff of twelve would have been increased to sixteen by the addition of two loaders for the King and by that of at least one loader apiece for the two equerries. Had Queen Alexandra accompanied King Edward, ladies-in-waiting, a hairdresser and additional personal servants would have increased that total to twenty-two.

Chatsworth and other great houses accepted such visitations as part of the year's normal routine, and house parties of forty guests, with as many personal servants as guests chose to bring, were entertained without difficulty. Rufford Abbey, on the other hand, was a comparatively small, although a luxurious house, and the size of King Edward's entourage excited comment in a party of sixteen guests who included Mrs Keppel, Luis de Soveral and the Ronald Grevilles.

Jealousy was excited inevitably among ambitious hostesses at whose houses King Edward did not choose to stay; and the Saviles and Grevilles were known as the Civils and Grovels to some unsuccessful social aspirants. King Edward regretted his inability to avoid arousing such feelings, but he worshipped harmony and made it a cardinal social rule that no species of established institution should ever be criticized in his presence.

Unlike most contemporary magnates, including the much loved and respected Duke of Devonshire, King Edward thanked servants invariably for services rendered and prefaced orders almost invariably with 'please'. His handshake and his bow, most of his gestures and many of his words and acts had become invested with a very wide range of calculated and subtly differentiated degrees of significance; and his manner of raising his hat, for example, or the intonation of his voice, were adjusted by a sixth sense, which had become second nature, to the stature of the person whom he was addressing and to the occasion and place of meeting. It was prudent to learn the rules of that sophisticated social game which helped King Edward to keep boredom at bay, and which he played with relish and with inimitable virtuosity.

After receiving a return visit (6–9 July) from President Émile Loubet of France, King Edward and Queen Alexandra paid a state visit to Ireland (21 July–1 August). Its start had been timed to coincide with the passage through the House of Lords on 21 July of the third reading of an Irish Land Purchase Bill; and the news that that Bill had been carried by a substantial majority was hailed as a happy public omen. It was balanced, unfortunately, by a private omen which troubled the superstitious King, who noted [2] impersonally in his diary late that night at Viceregal Lodge: 'The King's faithful Irish Terrier "Jack" dies suddenly at 11 p.m.'

The Corporation of Dublin refused, by 40 votes to 37, to offer King Edward an address of welcome; but eighty-two loyal addresses were presented by other bodies, and much popular enthusiasm was shown. King Edward played his part with a gusto which helped to inspire enthusiasm, and he spent three long days inspecting hospitals and schools, reviewing troops and presenting colours, visiting Trinity and Maynooth Colleges, receiving deputations, saying polite things to Roman Catholic clergy, and eating a series of enormous meals.

The King's host, Lord Dudley, whose annual expenditure upon the social duties of his office as Viceroy exceeded his salary by £30,000, was delighted by the success of that visit; and King Edward left on 25 July to visit Belfast. He stayed with Lord Londonderry at Mountstewart before embarking in *Victoria and Albert* upon a cruise along the coast which enabled him to visit many places, including Cork; and he issued (1 August) an address of thanks to the Irish people everywhere. He assured them that his 'expectations' had been 'exceeded' and that 'for a country so attractive and a people so gifted we cherish the warmest regard'.

Balfour and Lansdowne congratulated King Edward, who was perplexed about a tariff controversy which had convulsed the nation and which threatened to split the Conservative Party. The Colonial Secretary, Joseph Chamberlain, was advocating the abandonment of free trade and the adoption of a system of preferential tariffs, designed to bind more closely together the component parts of the British Empire.

Although doubtful about the political wisdom of taxing food for the sake of consolidating the Empire, the Prime Minister wanted to use tariffs as retaliatory weapons against those set up by other nations; and a deeply divided Cabinet, which discussed those grave issues on 11 and 13 August, postponed a decision for one month. Balfour informed [3] King Edward (14 August) that he intended to secure what he termed a 'liberty of fiscal negotiation'; that a ministerial crisis would almost certainly occur in mid-September; and that he was confident of his ability to carry on the Government with the support of a majority of his colleagues in any foreseeable circumstances. He undertook to do his best 'to steer between the opposite dangers of making proposals so far-reaching in their character that the people of this country could not be expected to acquiesce in them – and, on the other hand, of ignoring, in a spirit of blind optimism, the danger signals which indicate approaching perils to our foreign and to our colonial trade'.

King Edward, who left (12 August) for Marienbad after dining with Mrs Keppel on the previous evening, was convinced that the working class would never tolerate a tax on bread. He asked [4] Balfour (18 August) to submit the entire controversy to the judgement of a Royal Commission 'consisting of the ablest men in the country and thoroughly conversant with so difficult a problem', and suggested that that 'would relieve Mr Balfour and the Cabinet of a great responsibility'; but the Prime Minister explained that any representative Royal Commission would necessarily be as profoundly divided as the country was, and incapable, therefore, of presenting a unanimous report.

The behaviour of the crowds at Marienbad was particularly bad that summer, and King Edward was followed everywhere by a mob of well-dressed persons carrying cameras which clicked incessantly. He appealed to the Emperor Francis Joseph, who despatched from Vienna a force of plain-clothes police – headed by Hans Schober, a future Chancellor of the Austrian Republic – which succeeded in restoring decorum.

King Edward discovered on that visit that Sir Henry Campbell-Bannerman, whom he had avoided in previous years as a presumed bore, was excellent company and light in hand; but his greatest pleasure was to mingle incognito with the crowds. With that object he motored to Carlsbad on

22 August, and lunched outside a famous restaurant at a table reserved in his courier's name. Exasperated at having to take his turn as an ordinary guest, King Edward's irrepressible impatience provoked recognition, and a crowd assembled at once. A band, which appeared quickly, started to play *God Save the King*, and he was forced to take refuge in his car and to jettison his plan of strolling through the streets of the town.

Similar difficulties occurred fairly frequently, and Ponsonby recorded[5] an amusing one in Paris in 1905 when King Edward tried to insist upon his incognito as Duke of Lancaster while calling at an hotel where the Empress Eugénie was staying as Comtesse de Pierrefonds. The King walked to an elevator which a prosperous looking American, who had been waiting longest, attempted to enter first, although King Edward, accustomed to being made way for by everybody, stepped forward instinctively at the same time. A violent collision resulted, but weight told, and the astonished American lost his balance and his cigar and was sent sprawling, while King Edward, who was even more profoundly astonished, was carried up to the first floor.

Leaving Marienbad on 31 August 1903, to pay a state visit to Vienna, King Edward stayed with the Emperor Francis Joseph. Each created the other a field-marshal in his army, and 'nothing', King Edward informed[6] the Prince of Wales (5 September) 'could have gone off better than my visit to Vienna. The Emperor was as usual kindness itself, and I had an excellent reception from the people who are not demonstrative but wonderfully orderly.... I went out shooting with the Emperor on Wednesday ... and killed a very fine stag with very wide horns....'

The two principal matters discussed reflect King Edward's warmth of heart. He wanted to see pressure applied to the Sultan of Turkey whose Christian subjects in Macedonia had revolted against intolerable oppression; and he was equally indignant at the conduct of King Leopold of the Belgians, who had married an Austrian archduchess. Cruelties perpetrated by Leopold against his African subjects in the Congo had outraged the conscience of Europe;

and his treatment of his daughter, Princess Stephanie, was in keeping with his bad character. Stephanie, who was the slatternly widow of King Edward's friend, the Crown Prince Rudolf, had married a Hungarian magnate, Prince Elemar Lonyay; and on account of that *mésalliance* her father had refused thereafter to have anything to do with her.

Neither matter was susceptible of easy remedy, but King Edward's nature was optimistic and he wrote [7] (30 September) to Lord Lansdowne: 'As the state of affairs in Macedonia is getting worse, would it not be possible to send some ships, as Russia did, which would have a wholesome effect?' In a long letter next day the Foreign Secretary retorted [8] that any such attempt at single-handed intervention would precipitate a crisis which would be 'inopportune as well as hazardous'; but King Edward argued [9] (2 October) that 'some naval demonstration might be made, which, without attempting to "coerce" the Sultan, might have the appearance at home that we were doing something actively (not merely in words). . . . In saying this the King believes that he is only echoing the general feeling of the country, which will become stronger and shortly get "out of hand", as was the case in 1878.'

When Lansdowne suggested that the British Government was known to be acting in the best interests of everyone concerned, King Edward retorted [10] that the British public appeared to have been excluded from its Government's confidence; and Lansdowne promised to take steps to inform and to satisfy public opinion. King Edward continued to press that subject as opportunity offered until the end of his reign; and he refused also to have anything more to do with his kinsman, King Leopold II, on account of his iniquitous misgovernment of the Belgian Congo.

Leopold's request for a personal reconciliation was transmitted to King Edward in the form of a private letter [11] (31 October 1903) from the British Minister in Brussels, Sir Edmund Phipps. Trivial personal causes of past disagreements were rehearsed by Phipps at King Leopold's request; but, in a reply which he dictated (4 November) to Lord Knollys,

King Edward stated [12] unequivocally that none was of consequence – not even that of Princess Stephanie whose faults he knew well – in comparison with the burning issue of the Congo:

The Congo question is not altogether a private matter, but is largely a political and public one, in which everybody in England has expressed a unanimous and strong opinion. In this opinion His Majesty entirely agrees with his subjects, and it certainly is not one which is favourable either to the King of the Belgians or to his Ministers. No doubt exists in the mind of the British Public and, I believe, also of the British Government, that great Cruelties have been committed in the Belgian Congo territory; and the question is so far a private one that the King of the Belgians is held in a great measure responsible for them....

The King cannot, therefore, feel attracted towards a Sovereign, whether he is a relative or not, who, he considers, has neglected his duty towards Humanity....

The King has no wish whatsoever to cause an estrangement between himself and the King of the Belgians. He remembers old days and he thinks him also very clever and extremely agreeable. But His Majesty cannot deny that he has noticed of late years certain traits in his character and disposition which, in his eyes, prevent him from being what he once believed him to be.

King Leopold made further advances before he died in 1909, but all were rejected and King Edward's plain and forceful language expressed the attitude of all classes of his subjects. On the British fiscal controversy King Edward's views were almost equally clear-cut; but the Cabinet was divided and the King returned from Vienna to face the first great ministerial crisis of his reign.

The Chancellor of the Exchequer, C. T. Ritchie, who was a convinced free-trader, broadcast [13] indiscreetly at dinner parties King Edward's view that it would be madness to tax the people's food, but doubt existed for some time as to where precisely Balfour stood. On 15 September 1903, however, the Prime Minister informed [14] King Edward that, although it would be possible to devise means of taxing food without imposing hardship upon the working class, 'the present state of public feeling' made such a policy impracticable. He explained, therefore, that he had rejected Chamberlain's plan for a preferential imperial tariff, while holding himself free to threaten foreign countries with retaliatory tariffs which would 'promote, not hinder, free trade'.

Chamberlain resigned immediately in protest against that rejection of a full-blooded protectionist policy; while Ritchie, Lord George Hamilton (Secretary for India) and Lord Balfour of Burleigh (Secretary for Scotland) resigned in protest against the Prime Minister's abandonment of the pure doctrine of free trade. The Duke of Devonshire (Lord President of the Council) resigned also, three weeks later, after a prolonged wobble and despite all that Balfour could do to dissuade him.

Although his successors would have travelled to London at such a time, King Edward acted as his mother would have done and remained at Balmoral. He authorized [15] Balfour by telegram (16 September) to publish the resignations, but cancelled [16] that authority next day on the grounds that haste was 'to be deprecated'; that Balfour would be at Balmoral over the week-end; and that 'it would not look well in the eyes of the world that a matter of such importance should be settled without my having seen the Prime Minister'.

Balfour went up to Balmoral after apologizing for his action in publishing the resignations before the King's second telegram had been laid before him, and he explained that he had always intended to steer a middle course. He expressed perfect confidence in his ability to carry on the Government, and declined respectfully King Edward's suggestion that a General Election should be held. Local Conservative associations throughout the kingdom were split at that time into rival free trade and tariff reform factions, and the subject became the principal topic of conversation over port, brandy and cigars after the ladies had retired from the dinner table. In order to avoid such discussion which he found tedious, King Edward caused [17] the men to leave the table in the continental manner at the moment when Queen Alexandra signalled to the ladies to rise, but he reverted to the traditional British practice after experimenting with the other for some weeks.

Several other controversies were damaging the Conservative cause at that time, and the most rancid arose out of the Education Act, 1902, which bored King Edward. He took a vigorous personal interest, however, in the problem of Chinese labour in the Transvaal.

A post-war shortage of amenable Kaffir labour had caused the Transvaal mine-owners to agitate for an immediate importation of cheap Asiatic labour in order to ensure the extraction of gold and diamonds with the maximum degree of promptitude and profit. With the consent of the British Government some tens of thousands of hungry coolies were shipped from China to South Africa, and a ludicrous amount of sentimental opposition was excited.

King Edward expressed [18] (15 March 1904) to the Colonial Secretary his 'great regret that so much heated opposition should have been shown to such a necessary measure as the Chinese Labour Bill', which afforded a handle to Radicals despite the economic benefits which it promoted. The young Chinese, imported without women and under indentures for a term of years, were poorly paid but stuffed with meat in order to keep them fit, and were segregated in compounds and subjected to a special but not very severe penal code. In those conditions it was tempting to argue that the dignity of labour was being insulted, and easy to imply that sodomy must flourish; and frothy denunciations of 'Chinese Slavery' delivered to unsophisticated audiences from Liberal platforms throughout the United Kingdom were often politically effective and by no means invariably hypocritical.

The disarray into which that and other controversies had plunged the Conservative Government shook public confidence in its ability to overhaul the Empire's machinery of defence with any prospect of success. The incompetence displayed by the War Office during the Boer War, and the incipient naval threat from Germany, had convinced Parliament and the nation that it was urgently necessary to lift the Navy as well as the Army to a much higher level of administrative and professional efficiency; but strong opposition was encountered from vested interests in both Services. Prolonged security had caused many officers, including most of the best liked, to regard a naval or military career as a life-long holiday, and had tempted them also, as members of an entrenched caste, to employ social influence to obstruct reform.

By throwing his vast social influence upon the side of the reformers, King Edward played a salutary role. He swayed a public opinion in which the qualitative element must be distinguished from the quantitative. Whereas, for example, the lower class felt with peculiar intensity about the cost of living, and the middle class about education, the upper class felt a special responsibility for defence and foreign affairs. On those two last subjects, during the first decade of the twentieth century, the nation as a whole was still disposed to pay a measure of snobbish deference to the views entertained by society; and the known attitude of King Edward was important politically because it influenced that of the upper class.

Queen Victoria's name had never been mentioned in the Navy Lists issued monthly by the Admiralty during her reign; but on the day of her funeral King Edward ordered that his name should appear in future at the head of that List, and that it should be followed by the names of members of his personal naval staff. He took very seriously his titular position as head of the fighting Services, but the Navy ceased during his reign to be a band of brothers in the Nelson tradition. It was split into two warring factions headed on the one side by the First Sea Lord, Sir John Fisher, whom the King loved, and on the other by the popular Commander-in-Chief of the Channel Fleet, Lord Charles Beresford, whom the King cordially detested. While that fulminating quarrel was at its height, Fisher was prevented from resigning on at least two occasions by the direct personal intervention of King Edward.

King Edward's methods were outlined succinctly by Lord Esher in August 1904, in reply to a complaint by Fisher that '5 solid hours' spent in talking to King Edward had been wasted. 'The worst of it is', Fisher wrote [19] (5 August), 'that the impression is not *lasting* with him. He can't grasp details.' Esher, who was much subtler and who knew King Edward more intimately than Fisher did at that time, explained [20] (6 August) that 'H.M. has two receptive plates in his mind', and that he had proved 'over and over again' that the first plate retained lasting impressions 'of *things*'. Esher continued:

But, and this is the essential point, if you can stamp your image on number one – which you have long since done – you can rely always on carrying your point by an appeal to 'authority' – as the Catholics would say. The King will not go into details, for his life is too full for that, but he will always say to himself, 'Jack Fisher's view is so and so, and he is sure to be right.' I don't think that you need trouble about H.M., for he will always back you.

King Edward's forcefulness had been harnessed early and effectively by Esher in pressing for a root and branch reform of the War Office. Esher criticized constantly to King Edward the alleged faults of the previous Secretary of State for War, Lord Lansdowne, of the previous Commander-in-Chief, Lord Wolseley, and of the previous Adjutant-General, Sir Evelyn Wood; and early in 1903 he became equally critical of their successors, St John Brodrick, Lord Roberts and Sir Thomas Kelly-Kenny.

Esher wanted to abolish the administrative post of Commander-in-Chief of the British Army and to replace it by an Army Council, constituted on the lines of the Board of Admiralty and containing an executive Chief of the General Staff. Brodrick opposed strongly that plan to abolish the Commander-in-Chief, and as early as 16 October 1902, King Edward, writing to Lord Esher from the Jockey Club, described [21] the War Office as 'a mutual admiration society', and the weakness of its Intelligence branch as 'one of those scandals which ought to hang Lords Lansdowne and Wolseley and Sir Evelyn Wood'.

On 5 February 1903, King Edward informed [22] Esher that he had become convinced that 'radical reform' was an 'absolute necessity' and that 'should the War Office refuse to cleanse their "Augean Stable" they must be forced to do so,

or shown up to the world'. Knollys wrote [23] on that same day
to explain that 'in H.M.'s opinion the only practical War
Office reform would be to constitute it like the Board of Admiralty'.

Besides resenting particularly Esher's continuous interference on the three big issues of the Commander-in-Chief,
control of expenditure, and the status of the military members of the proposed Army Council, Brodrick allowed himself to be worried by King Edward's occasional wilfulness in
regard to detail. It took time to convince the King that 'the
hideous khaki' would prove to be more serviceable than 'the
national red'; and after yielding against his better judgement to King Edward's request that Sir Thomas Kelly-
Kenny should succeed Sir Evelyn Wood as Adjutant-
General, Brodrick hardly knew what to make of a letter (15
October 1902) in which King Edward expressed [24] 'great surprise' at having been told that day at Newmarket by Lord
Stanley that Kelly-Kenny was 'most reactionary in his views
concerning the Army'. The King added ingenuously that
although he had discussed military matters frequently with
the general, whom he found very congenial, he had always
imagined that he was 'quite of the advanced school which
shares your views'.

Esher succeeded in making himself as much at home at
10 Downing Street and at the War Office as he did at Buckingham Palace, and he converted Balfour and Lord Roberts
as well as King Edward to his plan of War Office reform. In
August 1903 he advised [25] Brodrick to resign; and Brodrick
recorded [26] ruefully that 'to fight for the Commander-in-
Chief against the [Boer] War Commission and the King, if
Roberts himself was a convert, was useless'. Balfour was
harassed by Cabinet dissensions; Roberts was conciliated by
the prospect of greater independence as head of a Board;
and the consequence was that when the Prime Minister went
up to Balmoral to discuss the reconstruction of his Government during the third week of September 1903 Brodrick was
moved against his wish from the War Office to the India
Office.

Esher and Fisher were fellow-guests with Balfour at Balmoral, and King Edward was impressed by a memorandum which Fisher wrote. It advocated a single Department of State under a single Cabinet head, as in Austria–Hungary, which should control both the Navy and Army. Fisher argued that that plan would combine efficiency with economy, 'but to achieve this result we must be ruthless, relentless, remorseless!' He explained that 'all will be useless if you leave even one of the old gang on the job', and King Edward minuted[27]: 'An admirable paper which should be kept. What a beautifully clear hand the Admiral writes!'

Esher was urged strongly at Balmoral, by King Edward as well as by Balfour, to succeed Brodrick as Secretary for War; but he refused on grounds which he described[28] privately as 'purely selfish'. They included a hatred of responsibility, a love of backstairs intrigue, and an unwillingness to sever at that time the lucrative financial relationship into which he had entered with Sir Ernest Cassel.

Greatly annoyed by that refusal, King Edward suggested to Balfour that Esher, who had been the cause of Brodrick's removal, should be invited to reconstruct the War Office as head of an independent Committee of three. Esher stipulated that Sir John Fisher, who was at that time naval Commander-in-Chief at Portsmouth, should be one of his two colleagues, and the edge of the King's anger was blunted when Balfour undertook to consider seriously that proposition. King Edward understood Esher's character, and he became even more angry with the High Commissioner in South Africa, Lord Milner, who declined, by telegram, the King's personal request that he should accept Balfour's invitation to succeed Joseph Chamberlain as Colonial Secretary. The King informed[29] Balfour (1 October) that he had noted Milner's obstinacy 'with infinite regret' and that he would 'not forget it now, nor in the future'.

Alfred Lyttelton was appointed to succeed Joseph Chamberlain; and King Edward was constrained to accept H. O. Arnold-Forster, a nephew of Matthew Arnold, as Secretary for War. The King complained to Balfour at Balmoral that Arnold-Forster lacked polish, and that his cleverness was insufficient to compensate for the ill-feeling which his social uncouthness would arouse among senior officers of the Army; and Balfour wrote [30] suavely (30 September) that he did not 'underrate the force of the criticism urged by Your Majesty. It is undoubtedly true that Mr Forster's *manner* is not his strong point. But though he wants manner, he does not want *tact*, as is proved by the regard in which he is held in the House of Commons. ... He has immense knowledge, untiring industry and a burning zeal for reform. He not only possesses these gifts but is *known* to possess them.'

The Duke of Devonshire's belated resignation was deplored by King Edward, who consulted Balfour before arranging to appoint the Duke's successor with the maximum degree of panache while staying at Wynyard with Lord Londonderry. The King delighted his hostess by holding a Council (19 October) and by ordering that all documents connected with it should be headed 'At Our Court at Wynyard' in medieval style. He then appointed Londonderry to succeed Devonshire as President of the Council before settling down to play bridge with Mrs Keppel, the Duchess of Devonshire (who had been nicknamed 'Ponte Vecchio' in allusion to her raddled appearance and passion for bridge) and an equerry, while most of the other guests played poker.

In the meantime Balfour had accepted King Edward's suggestion that Esher should be invited to advise about a drastic reconstruction of the War Office; and Esher wrote [31] (11 October) characteristically to his younger son: 'Now I think I shall be able to carry through my scheme, whereas as Sec. of State I doubt if I should have done so. It is the old story – Power and Place are not often synonymous.' King Edward stipulated only that the War Office Reconstitution Committee should be appointed by the Prime Minister and not by the Secretary of State for War; and that an express reference to the King's approval should be included in the public announcement.

That announcement was made on 7 November 1903, in the form desired by King Edward, and Balfour wrote [32] (5 November) to Knollys: 'The King has taken so keen an interest in the formation of this Committee, of which he suggested the original idea, that I thoroughly understand his

most natural wish for some public indication of his connexion with the project.' He observed, nevertheless, that the
Monarchy could become discredited if King Edward were
allowed to become involved in controversy through expressing approval of some ministerial actions while pointedly
ignoring others.

Esher's colleagues were Admiral Sir John Fisher, and Sir
George Clarke (Lord Sydenham) who became Secretary
(1904-7) of the Committee of Imperial Defence; and the
Esher Committee presented the first two sections of its Report with extraordinary promptitude on 11 January 1904.
The first section recommended a great enlargement of the
committee of Imperial Defence (first instituted in March
1903), while the second recommended a drastic reconstruction of the War Office. The Secretary of State was to be provided with an Army Council modelled on the Board of Admiralty; the administrative office of Commander-in-Chief
was to be abolished; and a General Staff was to be formed.
An Inspector-General was to be appointed to advise about
policy, and Great Britain was to be divided into seven territorial commands, each of which would enjoy a wide measure
of financial as well as administrative independence.

King Edward, who accepted both sections on 30 January
1904, approved equally warmly (26 February) of the final section which concerned the appointments of Sir George
Clarke and others as the nucleus of a permanent secretariat
of the Committee of Imperial Defence. 'This', Esher informed [33] Knollys (28 February) 'is the keystone of the
whole structure of Army Reform'; and he added that 'a
good broadside from the King would give the *coup de grâce*
to the pessimists who are urging delay in the hope of wreck-
ing us in Parliament.'

Knollys had warned [34] Esher (23 November 1903) that he
was incapable of advising King Edward about War Office detail because 'I am not sufficiently master of the subject'; but
Esher supplied all necessary advice. At his suggestion, for
example, King Edward stressed [35] frequently the importance
of allowing the Inspector-General to advise about the scale
of the Army Estimates, although Balfour, who intended to

retain strict Treasury control, insisted [36] (29 January 1904) that any such advice must be private and unofficial.

On his own initiative King Edward induced [37] the Cabinet to renounce its limp and colourless wish to re-christen the War Office as the Army Office, and to describe the four military members of the Army Council as First Military Member, etc., instead of continuing to employ such time-honoured titles as Adjutant-General, etc. The King insisted, [38] furthermore (6 February 1904), that he should have a right to send at any time for any civil or military member of the Army Council whom he might wish personally to consult, and that 'every single paper' and 'submission' should be referred to him as heretofore.

Many senior officers were openly hostile to that report, and Lord Kitchener, the most famous active soldier of the day, dubbed [39] Esher an ignorant outsider and deplored the abolition of the office of Commander-in-Chief. As Commander-in-Chief in India he was locked at that moment in mortal combat with the Viceroy, Lord Curzon, for control of the Indian Army; and he declined presently an offer conveyed by Esher to return to England in order to become Chief of the General Staff, and as Esher put it, to 'administer the Army practically unchallenged'.

The Government's action in leaning so heavily upon Esher and his colleagues, who were dubbed 'The Dauntless Three' in the Press, was widely regarded as a symptom of weakness; and the disrepute into which ministers had fallen appeared to be emphasized by the tone of the report. The Government was criticized severely, by implication, for its past neglect of national security; and Esher noted [40] (27 October 1903) that 'Arthur Balfour will have to assert his authority in political matters. It is dangerous for the King and may be dangerous for the Monarchy to let the present state of things develop.'

Dissuaded with difficulty by Balfour from decorating Esher and his colleagues, King Edward was delighted when Esher pressed strongly for the appointment of the Duke of Connaught (who was at that time Commander-in-Chief in Ireland) as Inspector-General. The King warned [41] Esher (10

January 1904) that he felt some embarrassment 'as the Duke is his brother'; and Esher ought to have felt a much greater embarrassment. He had held out to Roberts the prospect of further employment as Inspector-General, in return for Robert's acquiescence in the great plan of reform.

Before Roberts ceased (18 February) to be Commander-in-Chief of the British Army, *The Times* espoused his claim to the Inspector-General's post; but Esher was well able to handle that situation. He induced Balfour to offer Roberts the Inspector-Generalship in a form which was intended to be unacceptable, and King Edward's help was invoked when Roberts accepted nevertheless. 'The King', Esher wrote[42] (9 February) to his son, 'was most reasonable yesterday, and told me exactly what passed between him and Lord Roberts. He was very kind but very firm in telling Lord Roberts that he ought not to accept the I.G. place, that it would be undignified, etc. From what I saw of Lord R. afterwards, I don't think that he made much impression. The little man is very tenacious. The D. of Connaught called here. ...'

The veteran Field-Marshal's tenacity could not withstand the combined pressure of the King, the Prime Minister and Lord Esher; and the denouement was related[43] racily by Esher on 11 February; 'Our torpedo has exploded and the little C.-in-C. has left the W.O. for good in a devil of a temper.' The Duke of Connaught was made Inspector-General immediately. King Edward asked Arnold-Forster to accord the Duke the special salute which had been accorded formerly to Roberts, but Arnold-Forster referred that request to the Army Council which turned it down. 'No go!' King Edward minuted[44] (6 June). 'The Secretary of State for War is as obstinate as a mule'; and the Clerk of the Privy Council, Sir Almeric Fitzroy recorded[45] (15 July) that Arnold-Forster had entered upon his task 'with the enthusiasm of the apostle and the spirit of the martyr; he suffers from a super-excitation of the nerves such as six hundred years ago produced the *stigmata* and other evidences of an overheated imagination'. The passion displayed for his subject by the new Secretary of State for War exceeded even that of Lord Esher, who warned[46] Knollys (5 November 1904) that

Arnold-Forster is becoming, as regards the King, worse than Brodrick, and opposes everything H.M. proposes'. Some of Esher's most cherished recommendations were altered drastically by Arnold-Forster, with the result, for example, that the military members of the Army Council emerged as the creatures, instead of as the equal colleagues of the Secretary of State; while Army Commanders were not entrusted with discretionary control over expenditure.

On some trifling matters, such as regimental uniforms, Arnold-Forster was habitually compliant; but he dismayed King Edward by abolishing inter-regimental polo tournaments at home, on the ground that the expense penalized officers of modest means; and he ignored King Edward's request that he should not institute an Army Journal. The King argued [47] that that publication would prove to be subversive of authority and discipline, and Arnold-Forster, who lacked the diplomatic temper, sought refuge vainly in silence.

The King (Knollys wrote [48] icily [22 October 1904] to Arnold-Foster) desires me to say that he should be much obliged to you if you would have the goodness to give directions that the proceedings of the meetings of the Army Council may be sent to him, as is always done in the case of the Defence Committee meetings.

He is a little sorry to find that he has not been in any way consulted on the questions of the best mode of promulgating decentralization, and on the General Staff Scheme....

During the late Queen's reign not a step was taken at the W.O. in connection with the Army of the slightest importance without her being informed....

Arnold-Forster failed to provide the Army with an adequate General Staff; but he sent King Edward on 22 November 1904 an important Army Order embodying the Government's proposals for decentralization. It confirmed the absolute control of the Chancellor of the Exchequer over the Army Estimates, as well as that of the Secretary of State for War over the Army Council; and King Edward, on the advice of Lord Esher, raised a large number of objections.

The King informed [49] Arnold-Forster (25 November) that he could not 'sanction the administration and discipline of the Army being in any way directed by the Treasury'; But he could obtain no satisfaction on points of substance. 'You will probably agree with me', Knollys wrote [50] (1 December) to Esher, 'that it would not be judicious for the King to press Arnold-Forster too hard, as if circumstances, owing to the way in which he is behaving, obliged him to resign, it would be unfortunate if his friends (I suppose he has *some*!) went about saying he was got rid of by the King, or to please H.M.'

Arnold-Forster had good reason to resent the continuous interference of Lord Esher, who possessed a blithe *insouciance* and an easy spirit of accommodation to circumstances which must always command respect and often success. He made a point of being charming to Arnold-Forster, whom he could not like; and he tried also to restrain King Edward's anger against the minister which blazed into open enmity during the summer of 1905.

The Conservative Government, which was tottering towards a crash, hoped to win popularity by reducing the Army Estimates; and Arnold-Forster faced a most difficult problem. After reconstructing the War Office he was required to reform the Army, and to devise a scheme which would increase efficiency on lines recommended by the Report of the Royal Commission on the South African War, while reducing expenditure in accordance with Cabinet policy.

Arnold-Forster's scheme of Army reform, which was submitted to King Edward in June, and to Parliament in July 1905, was received surprisingly well in both quarters. King Edward accepted Balfour's advice that he should endorse the minister's proposals; but he complained [51] that they were 'half measures', and he toyed [52] privately with the idea of countenancing a campaign for compulsory peace-time military training which Lord Roberts had started to conduct.

Impressed by a letter of soldierly appeal from Roberts, and by the pleas of the Keeper of the Privy Purse, Sir Dighton Probyn, who had won the Victoria Cross during the Indian Mutiny, and whose character and charm excused very occasional imprudence, King Edward argued that conscription might offset the inadequacy of Arnold-Forster's plan for the militia. Knollys remonstrated successfully with King Edward, after writing strongly to Probyn; but the Prime Minister, who deplored Roberts's campaign, made no attempt to restrain a Field-Marshal on full pay, who was also a member of the Defence Committee, from stumping the country while demanding conscription and denouncing the Government's complacency: and Balfour's evident embarrassment amused King Edward.

On 5 July 1905, King Edward was invited by Arnold-Forster to sign a Royal Warrant on the subject of Army pay, allowances and promotions. No explanation was vouchsafed, and a correspondence [53] which followed failed to convince the King that the pay and allowance of many serving officers would not be cut. For that reason King Edward declined to sign until he had succeeded, at the end of November, in extracting a written promise from the minister that no officer would suffer hardship except in some cases when duties were divided or reduced.

While that issue was being fought, King Edward was made much more angry by a display of bad manners on the part of Arnold-Forster at the end of July 1905. The minister, who was much harassed, deemed it suddenly to be necessary to report to the Public Accounts Committee of the House of Commons on the afternoon of 26 July that an Army Order, which King Edward had held up, was already in force. That Order deprived general officers holding regional commands in the United Kingdom of that discretionary control over expenditure which Esher had intended that they should possess; and King Edward refused to sign it without full discussion and more explanation.

Believing that Esher was really responsible for that trouble, Arnold-Forster caused his secretary, Arthur Loring – 'a person', Esher noted,[54] in scandalized parenthesis, 'of whom His Majesty has no cognizance whatever' – to call at Buckingham Palace on the morning of 26 July. The secretary was instructed to deliver the Army Order personally into the hands of Lord Knollys with a covering letter of explanation.

That covering letter, signed by Loring and not by Arnold-

Forster, offered an explanation which was considered wholly inadequate; and Knollys was exasperated at hearing himself advised to induce the King to sign the Army Order before luncheon. Unintimidated by Knollys's formidable manner, which he noted nevertheless, the zealous but unwise and unlucky youth prejudiced still further a career which had hitherto shown promise, by following up that letter with a telephone call. As one private secretary to another, he expressed the hope that Knollys would do his best to save the minister from the embarrassment of having to explain to the House of Commons that afternoon that a vital Army Order was being held up unreasonably by the King.

That breach of etiquette and inexcusable rudeness caused a storm in the Palace. Its casual insolence and the implied ultimatum enraged King Edward, who called Knollys and Esher into conference. He signed the Army Order immediately because he would not reject constitutional advice, however quaintly or discourteously tendered; but he despatched Esher to see the Prime Minister's secretary, J. S. Sandars; and he instructed Knollys to send a formal letter of protest to Balfour.

Sandars, who was much shocked and surprised, undertook that Arnold-Forster's ungentlemanly conduct would be considered at the next full meeting of the Cabinet. It appeared, he said,[55] to imply 'an equality between the Minister and the Sovereign which one would have imagined to be repugnant to anyone thought qualified to hold high office in this country'. Esher then returned to Buckingham Palace where he helped Knollys to draft a letter[56] which was delivered that evening to the Prime Minister at 10 Downing Street:

... Upon a matter of such importance, involving as it does a question of principle, which Lord Esher's Committee considered vital to any scheme of decentralization, the King considers that he had a right to receive an explanation by the Secretary of State for War himself. It has not been customary to make explanations to the Sovereign in the form adopted by Mr Arnold-Forster, and ... I am further desired by the King to say that it will be impossible in future for His Majesty to give his assent to proposals of this degree of importance at such very short notice, practically of a few minutes only.

The King would have wished to consult you and the Chancellor of the Exchequer upon the point raised; but the method adopted by Mr Arnold-Forster made this impossible unless the King was prepared to allow the Secretary of State to use His Majesty's name in a Parliamentary Debate, which I am sure you will agree would not have been proper or desirable.

The King regrets, in fine, not only the form but the substance of the change recommended to him, which reverses the policy deliberately adopted six months ago....

In apologizing to King Edward for an 'error of judgement', Arnold-Forster pleaded[57] (28 July) that he had been tied to the House of Commons during a day of great stress and strain and while feeling unwell; and that it had been 'represented to him that it was of the highest importance to meet the views of the Treasury and of the Public Accounts Committee before the matter was brought before the House of Commons'. That unimpressive letter was acknowledged quite kindly, but no excuse for avoidable rudeness or neglect of duty can ever be valid, and Balfour offered to ask Arnold-Forster to resign if Esher would take his place.

'I am glad,' King Edward wrote[58] (18 August) to Knollys, 'to hear that A. Balfour at last sees the necessity of getting rid of A.-F., and that Esher is willing (at last) to succeed him'; but after days of agonized hesitation Esher declined to join the moribund Cabinet. He pleaded his reluctance to cause his friend, Arthur Balfour, fresh embarrassment; and King Edward showed less concern than Lord Knollys did at the news that Arnold-Forster was reprieved. 'A greater man than he is', Knollys grumbled[59] (8 September) to Esher, 'was sent about his business: Lord Palmerston. And I believe that if the country heard that Arnold-Forster had gone, it would rather strengthen the Government than otherwise.'

18
Social Reform

1904–6

i

THE abandonment of Great Britain's policy of splendid isolation, and the growing naval threat from Germany, prompted the Government to explore carefully the factors governing Anglo-Russian relations. Russian bad faith and aggression had precipitated an outbreak of war between the Russian and Japanese Empires in February 1904; and in April King Edward tried his hand at personal diplomacy while staying at Copenhagen for three weeks.

The stiffness and provincialism of the Danish Court bored King Edward, who pretended, nevertheless, to enjoy it in order to please Queen Alexandra. He dined with the eighty-five-year-old Danish King at six-thirty every evening; played whist for low stakes instead of bridge; and 'having visited every museum, picture gallery or house of historical interest ..., was eventually reduced to visiting a farm which supplied quantities of butter to England'.[1]

In an effort to dispel the tedium of that routine, King Edward held conversations with the anglophil Russian Minister to the Danish Court, Alexander Isvolsky, who was believed to be destined shortly to succeed Count Lamsdorff as Foreign Minister at St Petersburg. Isvolsky told King Edward that the Anglo-Japanese alliance was the major obstacle in the way of an Anglo-Russian understanding, and the King replied that the British Government had tried to stop Japan from going to war, and that one British object in concluding the Anglo-Japanese alliance had been a desire to exercise restraint.

Before despatching to St Petersburg a report of that conversation, Isvolsky gave a copy to King Edward, who forwarded it to Lord Lansdowne for information. The British Foreign Secretary was startled, but his tactful pro-test has been quoted [2] deservedly as a model of diplomatic urbanity. After referring to Isvolsky's misapprehension of the King's meaning, Lansdowne's letter (18 April) to King Edward continued:

In both cases M. Isvolsky has probably imputed to Your Majesty statements in excess of Your Majesty's actual observa-tions: for, as Your Majesty will remember, your Government was careful to avoid, while the Russo-Japanese negotiations which preceded the war were in progress, putting pressure of any kind, moral or material, upon the Japanese Government for the purpose of inducing them to moderate their demands. Those demands did not seem to your Government unreasonable in themselves, and they felt that nothing could be more unfor-tunate than that Japan should be able hereafter to place upon this country the responsibility of having deprived her of an opportunity, which might never be within her reach again, of ensuring her safety as a nation.

The Anglo-Japanese Alliance, although not intended to en-courage the Japanese Government to resort to extremities, had, and was sure to have, the effect of making Japan feel that she might try conclusions with her great rival in the Far East — free from all risk of a European condition such as that which had on a previous occasion deprived her of the fruits of victory.

Lord Lansdowne has, in accordance with Your Majesty's per-mission, shown M. Isvolsky's letter to the Prime Minister, who concurs in the observations which Lord Lansdowne has ventured to offer in this letter, and, like Lord Lansdowne, feels how much Your Majesty has done to promote peace and goodwill amongst nations.

A few days earlier, on 8 April 1904, while King Edward was still at Copenhagen, a comprehensive agreement, settl-ing outstanding differences between Great Britain and France, was signed in London. Almost everything had hinged upon the British attitude to French primacy in Morocco and upon the French attitude to British primacy in Egypt; but King Edward, after creating an atmosphere ex-tremely favourable to that agreement, had had no time to pay more than a cursory attention to the detailed negotiations.

Writing, for example, from Cairo on 17 July 1903, Lord Cromer had outlined to Lord Lansdowne his view of the conditions under which a deal with France would be possible; and the concluding section of that important document had discussed a few minor points of difference outside Egypt and Morocco. King Edward minuted [3]: 'A most able and interesting letter, and I entirely agree with the views expressed in it excepting Siam'; but he had seemed on that occasion, to be straining at a gnat after swallowing the camel.

When Balfour informed the House of Commons on 14 April 1904 that Parliament would be asked to consent to certain minor cessions of colonial territory in consequence of the Anglo-French agreement, King Edward protested at once. He had no objection to the cessions proposed but, alerted by Knollys, he telegraphed [4] (15 April) to the Prime Minister: '... Constitutionally power to cede territory rests with the Crown. Should be glad to hear from you why this statement was made as feel sure you would be careful to safeguard my rights.'

Although a leading article in *The Times* that day rebuked the Prime Minister for a serious misreading of the Constitution, Balfour replied [5] (16 April) to King Edward that his 'speech was made upon the authority of the Foreign Office and Law Officers'. He promised that he would 'have whole subject further examined and result submitted to Your Majesty'; and King Edward telegraphed [6] again (16 April) to Lord Knollys from Copenhagen: 'He is always so vague that probably he is wrong, but I must insist, if he is, as a matter of principle, that he *admits* it. Better see him as soon as you get this. ...'

In conversation with Knollys, Balfour cited a precedent in 1890 when Parliament had consented to the cession of Heligoland to Germany. He admitted that Gladstone had then urged that such consent was unnecessary, but added that Salisbury and he had thought it highly desirable, that the Germans had specifically asked for it, and that the Cabinet had made up its mind to follow that precedent.

In reporting fully to King Edward, Knollys reiterated his

view that the Cabinet's proposed action was unconstitutional. He explained [7] (17 April) that even in 1890 Balfour had been 'a regular House of Commons man; and he is now more than ever pronounced in the idea that very little signifies outside that body, and that every possible question should be brought before and decided by that body. This is a dangerous doctrine which tends to diminish the proper influence and authority of the Throne and to decrease the responsibility of Ministers....'

Ministers would have been powerless to act against the wish of Parliament, or to inhibit parliamentary debate; and Balfour did well to confirm in that way the sovereign's immunity from the risk of becoming involved in controversy. Lord Knollys's advice was conscientious but unenlightened, and it caused King Edward to minute [8]: 'I entirely agree with you, and Mr Balfour has treated me with scant courtesy in every respect.'

To the Prince of Wales, King Edward described [9] (13 April) the Anglo-French agreement as 'a splendid thing. ... We have really the best of the bargain and, as regards the concessions in Morocco, if we had not made them they would have taken them; and our position in Egypt is more assured than ever!' He decided that the time had come to pay an official visit to Berlin in order, if possible, to allay German discontent; but the Emperor asked that the visit should be paid to Kiel instead, because he wanted to display the growing might of the German Navy.

The large party which King Edward brought to Kiel from 25-30 June 1904, included the Prince of Monaco as well as Lord Selborne, First Lord of the Admiralty; and all appeared to go well at the time. The King laughed at the Emperor, however, for suggesting that Russia's cause was that of Europe, and that a Japanese victory over Russia would bring the world face to face with the 'Yellow Peril'; and for eighteen months thereafter the personal relations between uncle and nephew sank to the lowest point which they ever reached.

The series of personal complaints which the Kaiser brought against King Edward during that period were much too trivial to be of interest except as symptoms of a national as well as personal *malaise*. Having enjoyed respect and independence for centuries, the English find it difficult to be more than politely interested in opinions which others may form about them; but the Germans, with their brash new Empire, and a different tradition, were highly neurotic, and William II appeared to express without a great deal of exaggeration a mood of hysteria which had gripped his country at that time.

William II complained at different times in 1904 and 1905 that King Edward had inspired attacks upon him in French and American newspapers; that he went out of his way to avoid meeting him; and that the Crown Prince had been invited to England when the Emperor ought to have been asked. King Edward tried to be tolerant, but he was impatient by nature; and he was made very angry by a new turn which his nephew gave to German foreign policy early in 1905.

Acting against his better judgement, but on the advice of his Foreign Office, William II tried to take advantage of the eclipse of Russia in her war against Japan. He hoped to demonstrate to France that German might was irresistible and that the Anglo-French *entente* was no substitute for an effective Russian alliance; and he hoped later to sweep Russia as well as France into a great continental coalition under German leadership.

Morocco was chosen as the testing ground of that policy. Apart from Abyssinia it was the last profitable country in Africa which had preserved its independence, but its antiquated Government was on the brink of collapse, and the second article of the Anglo-French agreement of 8 April 1904 had acknowledged that 'it appertains to France, more particularly as a Power whose dominions are conterminous for a great distance with those of Morocco, to preserve order in that country and to provide assistance for the purpose of all administrative, economic, financial and military reforms which it may require. ...'

While France prepared with British goodwill to assert her claims in Morocco, the Sultan of Morocco appealed to

Germany for aid. Concealing his doubts, accordingly, behind a blustering manner and a gorgeous uniform, William II landed for a few hours at Tangier on 31 March 1905, while on a Mediterranean holiday cruise in the imperial yacht *Hohenzollern*.

Addressing the local diplomatic body, the Emperor astonished the world by announcing that Germany had great and growing interests in Morocco; that he was resolved to defend those interests in a country which he regarded as independent; and that 'my visit is the recognition of this independence'. At Gibraltar next day he told Prince Louis of Battenberg that he was determined to prevent France from swallowing Morocco as she had swallowed Tunisia.

Battenberg handed full notes of that conversation to his uncle, King Edward, who was cruising also in the Mediterranean aboard *Victoria and Albert*; and King Edward forwarded them to Lansdowne from Palma in Majorca with a covering letter (15 April). In it, the King described [10] the Tangier incident as 'the most mischievous and uncalled for event which the German Emperor has ever been engaged in since he came to the Throne. It was also a political-theatrical fiasco, and if he thinks he has done himself good in the eyes of the world he is very much mistaken. He is no more nor less than a political "enfant terrible" and one can have no faith in any of his assurances. ... These annual cruises are much to be deplored, and mischief is their only object.'

The Kaiser was persuaded that mischief, which he construed as a wish to ring Germany with enemies, was also an object of King Edward's many cruises; and public opinion became dangerously inflamed in France, Germany and Great Britain. The French Foreign Minister, Théophile Delcassé, whom King Edward liked and admired, was attacked savagely in the German Press for the part which he had played in negotiating the Anglo-French *entente*, as well as for that which he had started to play in negotiating with the Sultan of Morocco for a recognition of France's special interests in that country.

The British and French Foreign Offices feared that Germany wished to obtain a port on the Atlantic coast of Morocco, and Lansdowne promised Delcassé 'all the support in our power' to frustrate that object. The Germans probably misconstrued that strictly limited pledge, for President Theodore Roosevelt, who telegraphed an offer of his services as mediator, was informed coldly by Lansdowne that 'we have not, and never had, any intention of attacking Germany; nor do we anticipate that she will be so foolish as to attack us'.

At the height of that crisis, nevertheless, Sir John Fisher as First Sea Lord wrote [11] (22 April) from the Admiralty to Lord Lansdowne:

This seems a golden opportunity for fighting the Germans in alliance with the French, so I earnestly hope you may be able to bring this about. Of course I don't pretend to be a diplomat, but it strikes me that the German Emperor will greatly injure the splendid and growing Anglo-French Entente if he is allowed to score in *any way* – even if it is only getting rid of M. Delcassé.

... All I hope is that you will send a telegram to Paris that the English and French Fleets are *one*. We could have the German Fleet, the Kiel Canal, and Schleswig-Holstein within a fortnight.

From Algiers on 23 April, King Edward took what Lansdowne termed [12] 'the very unusual step' of telegraphing through the Governor-General a personal message of encouragement to the French Foreign Minister, whom he urged very strongly to stand firm and not to resign. He repeated that advice when he met Delcassé in Paris on his way home at luncheon on 3 May with the Marquis de Breteuil; and he spoke frankly to the German Ambassador, Prince Radolin, about the dangerous situation which the Kaiser's action had precipitated.

On 3 June 1905, at the suggestion of the Germans, the Sultan of Morocco invited the interested Powers to attend a conference on his country's future. Germany accepted; France refused; and, after the others had made their acceptance conditional upon that of France, Prince Radolin notified the French Government that no improvement could be expected in Franco-German relations while Delcassé remained in charge of the French Foreign Office.

The French nation was convulsed in consequence by a transport of excitement, in the midst of which Delcassé resigned on 6 June. He was sacrificed after having pinned his hopes upon Russia which was exhausted and therefore useless as a result of a lost war against Japan, and after having disgusted his colleagues by treating them contemptuously as ciphers. His overthrow, nevertheless, in such circumstances was a most bitter humiliation to France, whose Government switched his policy immediately into reverse to the extent of agreeing to attend an international conference called at Algeciras to decide the future of Morocco.

That German diplomatic triumph plunged King Edward into one of those moods of black depression which became more frequent, although not more prolonged, as his life drew towards its close. He considered that the folly of his German nephew portended war, and that the weakness of his Russian nephew portended revolution; and he informed [13] the Prince of Wales (26 October 1905) that anarchy reigned in Russia, not the Czar. He described the Russian situation as 'simply too awful' with strikes everywhere and seething unrest: 'If only', he wrote [14] (12 January 1906) 'a constitution may be acceptable to the people now, and may Nicky remain firm and stick by his promises!'

Any threat to any facet of the monarchical principle was anathema to King Edward, whose attitude was illustrated by the inflexible opposition which he offered to his Government's wish to resume diplomatic relations with Serbia. They had been broken off after the assassination in atrocious circumstances in June 1903 of King Alexander Obrenovitch and his Queen; and the new King, Peter Karageorgevitch, who was the head of a rival family, was also the brother-in-law of the Queen of Italy. King Peter exploited that channel of approach to King Edward, who informed the Italian Ambassador in London that he intended to observe trade union rules. He belonged, he said, to a trade union – a guild of kings; he could not overlook the brutal murder of a fellow member of his craft; and he satisfied

himself that all regicide officers had been placed upon the
retired list of the Serbian Army before he consented belatedly in June 1906 to a resumption of diplomatic relations.

While the Russo–Japanese war was raging, King Edward
was restrained, by the Russians as well as by his own Government, from offering his services as mediator; and he displayed personal restraint when an incident in the North Sea
very nearly caused an outbreak of war between the British
and Russian Empires. The Russian Baltic Fleet, on its way
to the Far East, fired on a number of Hull fishing trawlers,
which it mistook idiotically for Japanese torpedo boats, off
the Dogger Bank on 21 October 1904; and a tremendous outcry arose in the British Press. 'If it were not for the loss of
life,' King Edward wrote [15] (24 October) to the Prince of
Wales, 'one would laugh at the Russians for being such
damned fools ... though one does not exactly know what
to do as "what is done is done and cannot be undone".' The
incident was submitted to the Hague Tribunal, and the
Russian Government paid £65,000 in compensation; but,
after exchanging letters with King Edward, the infatuated
Czar threw himself impulsively into the Kaiser's arms.

The Czar was angry when the British Admiralty detached
warships to shadow the Russians for a time. Sir Charles Hardinge, the British Ambassador in St Petersburg, protested
strongly to Lansdowne against that provocation; and the
Czar, obsessed by dreams of national honour, invited [16] the
Kaiser (28 October) to draft a Russo–German treaty of alliance directed against 'English and Japanese arrogance
and insolence'.

The German Government had angled for that development since the start of the Russo–Japanese war. It had
courted Russia assiduously by withdrawing troops from East
Prussia and by coaling Russian ships; and it held that the
best hope of inducing France to jettison its *entente* with
Great Britain and to adhere to a Russo–German alliance
would be to confront the French Government with that
alliance in the shape of an accomplished fact.

The Czar's ministers insisted, on the other hand, that
France should be consulted before any Russo-German

alliance was concluded. They persuaded the Czar to hold his hand until the Moroccan crisis was settled, but rumours of what was afoot reached King Edward's ears through Queen Alexandra and her sister. The Dowager Empress of Russia was anti-German and jealous of the influence which her German daughter-in-law had acquired over her son; and Esher noted [17] as early as 7 September 1904 that there could be 'no doubt in the world' about the existence of 'a secret and very intimate understanding between Germany and Russia'.

King Edward remained accordingly on tenterhooks; but, in an effort to counter German approaches to the United States, he embarked (20 February 1905) upon a desultory personal correspondence with President Theodore Roosevelt – 'Dear Mr President': 'My dear King Edward' – on the basis of 'two men with certain aims in common'. The British Ambassador in Berlin wrote [18] (24 March) to Lord Knollys: 'You tell me that the King is full of distrust of the Emperor, and this is only natural after what we know of his attempts to sow distrust of us in other nations, and more especially in America. These attempts have signally failed. ...' They failed with Roosevelt, but they succeeded temporarily with the Czar, because both Emperors dwelt in cloud-cuckoo-land; and the crowning moment of their imperial irresponsibility and folly was reached on 24 July 1905.

On 23 July the German and Russian Emperors in their yachts *Hohenzollern* and *Standart* met by appointment off Viborg in the Baltic. Both travelled as tourists unaccompanied by their Foreign Ministers, and the Kaiser reported [19] (25 July) to his Chancellor, Prince Bülow, that it had been apparent immediately that 'the Czar cherishes a feeling of deep personal anger against England and the King. He described Edward VII as the greatest "mischief-maker" and the most insincere and dangerous intriguer in the world. I could but agree with him, remarking that I had suffered from his intrigues in a very special degree during the last few years, which, more particularly after his reception at Kiel, was absolutely beyond denial. I said he had a passion for contriving plots with every Power. ...'

On the morning of 24 July the Kaiser boarded *Standart* with a draft in his pocket of a Russo–German treaty of alliance which had been pigeon-holed since the previous November. He informed Bülow that his host's 'dreamy eyes sparkled' as he read it, and that 'I sent up a fervent prayer to God that He would take our side and direct the young Ruler'. 'Should you like to sign it?', the Kaiser asked: 'Yes, I will', the Czar replied. But although Bülow and the anglophobe Count S. J. Witte (President of the Russian Committee of Ministers) expressed warm satisfaction in principle, immediate and insuperable difficulties arose.

Objecting that the treaty had been altered by the Kaiser so as to apply only to Europe, Bülow pointed out that Russia could best help Germany in a war against England by invading India. He threatened to resign unless satisfaction could be obtained on that issue, but relented on receipt of a letter [20] (11 August) which ended: '*I could not survive this. . . . For the morning after receiving your farewell visit of resignation would not find your Emperor still living.* Think of my poor wife and children! W.'

The antiquated machinery of government in Germany and Russia was unequal to the strain which it had to support; and the Czar had to be reminded by his Foreign Minister, Count Lamsdorff, that the terms of the new treaty alliance with Germany conflicted with those of the Franco–Russian treaty of alliance. One section of the new treaty required Russia to persuade France to adhere to what would virtually have constituted an anti-British continental coalition; and Lamsdorff had ascertained through secret channels that the French Government would be unlikely to agree.

In a vain attempt to keep the Czar in line, the Kaiser described [21] jubilantly to him (22 August) the state of mind of 'the "arch-intriguer and mischief-maker" in Europe, as you rightly called him', Edward VII. The Kaiser alleged that at Cowes, a fortnight earlier, their distracted uncle had said:

. . . to one of my friends, a German gentleman I sent to observe the Entente Cordiale, 'I can't find out what is going on at Bjorko! Benckendorff knows nothing, *for he always tells me everything.* Copenhagen knows nothing, and *the Emperor's mother, who always lets me know everything,* has heard nothing from her son this time. Even Lamsdorff, who is *such a nice man and who lets me know all I want to hear,* knows nothing, or at least won't tell. It is very "disagreeable"!' This shows you how very wide is the net of secret information he has cast over Europe, and over you. . . .

The German Emperor suggested that King Edward had sent the Russian Ambassador in London, Count A. K. Benckendorff, to Copenhagen to influence the Czar's mother, who was staying there, against her son's pro-German policy; but the Czar retorted very sharply that he had authorized the ambassador's journey: 'What sort of conversation went on I certainly do not know, but ... Benckendorff is a loyal subject and a real gentleman. I know that he would never lend himself to any false tricks, even if they came from "the great mischief-maker" himself.' More correspondence followed, but the Russo–German treaty of alliance died before it came nominally into force on 14 October 1905 because the Czar declared that he had signed it without appreciating its implications. Explaining that his paramount duty was to guard his country's honour and interests, he refused to admit that he was bound by its terms; and a marginal comment [22] by the Kaiser was very apt: 'The Czar is not treacherous but he is weak. Weakness is not treachery, but it fulfils all its functions.'

ii

On 15 August 1905, at Marienbad, King Edward was amazed to discover lying upon his desk a very private letter from his friend, Count Gotz von Seckendorff, formerly Marshal to the Empress Frederick. It begged King Edward, on the Kaiser's behalf, to visit Homburg between 8 and 10 September for a heart-to-heart talk and reconciliation with his nephew.

'I must say,' King Edward wrote [23] (18 August) in forwarding that letter to Knollys at Balmoral, 'I think it very impertinent of him to write and tell me what to do, as if I were a little boy of 10 years old! Please write the following to him. ...' Knollys explained [24] accordingly (23 August) to Seckendorff that the King had caused his letter to be answered in that devious way 'as it is of such a confidential nature that he does not even wish those members of his Household who are in attendance upon him at Marienbad to see it'.

After denying that he had any personal quarrel with the Emperor William, King Edward declared that a visit at that moment would excite suspicion in France, and that 'under no circumstances would he consent to run after the Emperor by going to Homburg to see him, even if it were in his power to do so. It would be undignified for him to play such a part, and it would not meet with the approval of the British Government or the British nation.' Knollys concluded:

His Majesty ... directs me to tell you that he does not know whether the Emperor retains any affection for him, but, from one or two things which he has heard recently, he should say *not*, so that it would do no good if he were to pay him a dozen visits in the year. To show, however, that he has no animus against either the Emperor or Germany, the King has invited the Crown Prince and the Crown Princess of Germany to visit Windsor in November next.

The Kaiser made a tremendous grievance of that letter. He complained bitterly but candidly to the British Ambassador (who wrote [25] privately on 13 September to King Edward) that he had wanted to be invited to Windsor himself; and Knollys replied [26] (26 September) to Sir Frank Lascelles: 'Perhaps *next year*, unless the Emperor continues to trump up imaginary grievances against the King and to intrigue, whenever he has an opportunity, against this country, a meeting might be arranged; but one this year will not be possible. ... What an impossible man he must be to deal with!'

King Edward was delighted and not in the least jealous when President Theodore Roosevelt succeeded in bringing Russian and Japanese plenipotentiaries together round a conference table at Portsmouth, New Hampshire; and he minuted [27] facetiously in June 1905 that those peace talks might with advantage be adjourned to a cooler place, 'perhaps in the Rocky Mountains!' Peace was signed at last on 5 September 1905; and King Edward, who despatched telegrams of congratulations at once to the President of the United States as well as to the Emperors of Russia and Japan, informed [28] Sir Charles Hardinge (7 September) that all three prompt replies had been 'short and not very interesting'.

Lord Lansdowne spent six weeks from 12 August to 24 September on holiday in Ireland, where he owned much property; and the Foreign Secretary's increasing indolence afforded King Edward opportunities of displaying initiative. He conferred the Order of Merit upon two victorious Japanese field-marshals, as well as upon Admiral Togo, who had sent the Russian Baltic Fleet to the bottom of the Sea of Japan at the Battle of Tsushima (27–28 May 1905); and he concerned himself with a crisis in Norway.

On 7 June 1905 the Norwegians dissolved their country's union with Sweden which had existed since 1815 under the Swedish Crown. The official British attitude was one of strict neutrality, but King Edward was determined to secure the Norwegian throne for his son-in-law, Prince Charles of Denmark. Suspecting that the Norwegians would have preferred a republic, and aware that the German Emperor cherished hopes of installing one of his younger sons upon their throne, he exerted all his influence. He implored his son-in-law not to hang back, but to display the spirit of a king; and he was immensely gratified when Prince Charles was elected King of Norway on 18 November by a majority of more than five to one in a referendum.

As King Haakon VII, Prince Charles of Denmark, with King Edward's daughter, Queen Maud, at his side, made a triumphant entry into the Norwegian capital on 25 November; and King Edward assured [29] the Prince of Wales (30 November) that 'both have golden opinions and Charles's speeches are *very* good'. He added: 'The days of our Govt. are numbered. A. Balfour has determined to resign before Christmas, which I think is unnecessary and a mistake. The formation of a new Govt. will give much trouble in many ways, and I presume that I shall have to send for Sir H. C.-B. [Henry Campbell-Bannerman].'

Writing [30] (8 December) from Crichel, where he was Lord Alington's guest, King Edward informed the Prince of Wales that Balfour had resigned on 4 December, and that Campbell-Bannerman, who had promised to form a Government, was experiencing 'many difficulties in finding the right people'. He added that 'nothing could be nicer or more courteous' than the attitude of the new Prime Minister.

Balfour resigned because the Conservative Party was split from top to bottom on the issue of imperial preference; but he planned to snatch a tactical advantage by not asking for a General Election. He plumed himself upon his success in enticing the Liberals into accepting office before Parliament was dissolved, and he hoped in that way to focus the nation's attention upon deep rifts which existed within the Liberal Party. Lord Rosebery, for example, was opposed to Irish Home Rule as well as to the Anglo-French *entente*. He had declared that he would not serve under Campbell-Bannerman; and the outlook of the Liberal Imperialists, led by H. H. Asquith, Sir Edward Grey and R. B. Haldane, was known to differ significantly from that of the great Radical mass of the Liberal Party. Many Liberals believed that Campbell-Bannerman, who was aged seventy, was physically unfit to lead the House of Commons; and King Edward knew that that was also the opinion of the celebrated Dr Ott, whom he and Campbell-Bannerman consulted annually at Marienbad.

On King Edward's behalf, Lord Knollys tried to ensure that the new Cabinet would not wear too Radical a look through being deprived of the presence of the moderate Liberals. He knew that Asquith, Grey and Haldane had agreed privately, early in September, not to accept office unless Campbell-Bannerman consented to take a peerage and to allow Asquith to lead the House of Commons. 'The only thing', Haldane wrote [31] (12 September) to Knollys, 'that could affect the decision which our conference this week brought us to, is the thought that it could in any way embarrass the King'; and Knollys retorted, naturally, that it would.

'If', Knollys wrote [32] (16 September) to Haldane, 'you and your friends refused to join the Government, H.M. would be placed in an awkward position. A Cabinet of which Sir H. C.-B. was the head, without the moderates, would, it appears to me, be disastrous both for the Country and the Party. ... Of course what the King would desire would be the presence of a restraining influence in the Cabinet, being aware that many members of it would be men holding extreme views.'

Refusing to contemplate banishment to the House of Lords, Campbell-Bannerman succeeded in cajoling all dissidents except Lord Rosebery who stood aside; and he gave Asquith a private pledge that no Irish Home Rule Bill would be introduced during the lifetime of the new Parliament if the Liberals won the General Election. He presented his list of Ministers on 10 December to King Edward, who wrote [33] (15 December) to the Prince of Wales: 'It is certainly a strong Government with considerable brain-power. Let us only hope that they will work for the good of the Country and, indeed, the Empire. Sir E. Grey will, I hope, follow in the footsteps of Lord Lansdowne in every respect. Lord Tweedmouth should make a good "Ist Lord" and takes the greatest interest in his appointment. Mr Haldane, with sound common sense and great power of organization, ought to make an excellent War Minister, which is much needed as his predecessor was hopeless.'

Other appointments were those of Asquith as Chancellor of the Exchequer; David Lloyd George as President of the Board of Trade; the King's old friend, Lord Carrington, as President of the Board of Agriculture; and a working man, John Burns, as President of the Local Government Board. Campbell-Bannerman had contemplated offering Burns the post of First Commissioner of Works, which would have involved frequent communication with King Edward on the subject of the upkeep of palaces; but Burns had been critical of royalty. 'It would be almost an insult to the King', Knollys wrote [34] (24 October) to Lord Esher, 'to propose Burns for the post of First Commissioner of Works, though of course he would make no objection to his occupying some other office. ... If he is not actually a Republican, he is very nearly one.'

Parliament was dissolved on 8 January 1906; and in an election address to his constituents John Burns angered King Edward by calling for the abolition of the House of Lords. The General Election was spread over a fortnight, but as soon as the borough results were declared King Edward wrote [35] (19 January) to the Prince of Wales: 'The Liberal or, rather, Radical wave has simply swamped the Unionists,* and whether the present Govt. will appreciate the number of Labour members elected remains to be seen.' The outcome gave 377 Liberals an absolute majority of 84 over 157 Unionists, 83 Irish Nationalists and 53 Labour members.

Former members who lost their seats included Arthur Balfour, St John Brodrick and King Edward's old friend, Henry Chaplin; and the Conservatives sustained their greatest smash since 1832. Balfour informed [36] Knollys (17 January) that 'the election of 1906 inaugurates a new era', and Knollys grumbled [37] (5 March) to Esher that 'the old idea that the House of Commons was an assemblage of "gentlemen" has quite passed away'.

Campbell-Bannerman accepted [38] without demur Esher's private explanation of the special and confidential relationship which existed between himself and the King; and Esher established immediately a new and very close relationship with John Morley, who became Secretary of State for India. He obtained frequently from Morley, on the King's behalf, information which had not been provided by the Prime Minister, and he drew Morley very close to King Edward.

Known to his colleagues as Priscilla, Morley played up to King Edward as he had once, using different methods, played up to the ageing Gladstone, and he became King Edward's favourite Liberal Minister. King Edward described [39] him to the Prince of Wales (26 January) as

* In 1886 the Liberal Party split on the issue of Irish Home Rule. The Radical Imperialists, led by Joseph Chamberlain, joined a number of patrician Whigs, led by Lord Hartington, in forming a separate Liberal Unionist Party which allied itself with the Conservative Party in 1895. From 1895, accordingly, until January 1922 (when the Irish Free State was constituted) the alliance was known officially as the Unionist Party.

'wonderfully agreeable and sensible', but he found the Prime Minister increasingly antipathetic.

Campbell-Bannerman, the rich and shrewd representative of a Scottish merchant family, was anxious to please. He laughed at all the King's jokes, told good pawky ones of his own, and was much more earthy than Balfour had been. Moreover, whereas King Edward had had sometimes to wrestle with Salisbury and Balfour to secure the inclusion of such names as that of George Lewis, the solicitor, in the exiguous biennial Honours List, that situation was now reversed; and the King found it necessary to try as best he could to curb his Prime Minister's wish to reward too large and miscellaneous a host of local supporters and subscribers to Party funds.

Despite that relaxed atmosphere, Campbell-Bannerman's incommunicativeness quickly exasperated King Edward. Starting as an exhausted old man in a hurry, he had no time to study the King's ways carefully, or to attempt to convince him that he was not trying to move too fast, and that he was not responsible personally for a drastic and sudden rise in the nation's political temperature. As early as 23 March 1906, after King Edward had left for nine weeks' holiday in the Mediterranean, Knollys wrote [40] to Esher: 'Between ourselves I don't think the King will ever like C.-B. politically. I do not believe that the latter understands him, any more than Mr G.[ladstone] understood the Queen. I have just heard from the King who says, "I hope the P.M. will not abolish the House of Lords before I return".'

King Edward appreciated that the advent to power of a Liberal Government with a huge parliamentary majority had unleashed a pent-up demand for social reform. Gladstone, Salisbury, Rosebery and Balfour had all ignored that demand, and ample evidence existed that the House of Lords intended to precipitate a class struggle by blocking Liberal Bills. No Englishman of any class would have hesitated before 1914 to exact the maximum advantage from any customary or legal privilege which he possessed; and the Peers, who had merely registered approval of Conservative measures for many years, would have been ashamed not to assert their full rights against the Liberal Government in 1906. They avowed their intentions with gaiety and confidence, and the prospect of a tremendous constitutional crisis lowered like an approaching tempest over the land.

Loathing that threat which depressed and perplexed him, King Edward's greatest need was to be made to feel that his Government appreciated his efforts to allay strife and to promote compromise and goodwill. Most Liberals, however, were thirsting to settle accounts with the Lords, and Campbell-Bannerman was insufficiently sensitive to engage King Edward's sympathy by penetrating imaginatively his doubts and fears. It is much easier to endure what cannot be cured when sympathy and understanding exist, and in seeking both attributes King Edward had to look elsewhere than to his Prime Minister.

The King's first brush with his Government occurred in December 1905, when the new Colonial Secretary, Lord Elgin, suspended the operation of the Chinese Labour Act 'pending a decision as to the grant of responsible government to the Transvaal'. Neither aspect of that altered policy was notified in advance to King Edward, who expressed [41] 'regret' through Knollys (22 December) that such a 'reversal ... of the policy of Lord Milner and Lord Selborne should have been decided upon after so short an experience of office'. Foreseeing 'grave results to South Africa', King Edward called the Minister's attention to his 'constitutional right to have all despatches of any importance, especially those initiating or relating to a change of policy, laid before him prior to its being decided upon. This "right" was always observed during Queen Victoria's reign, and likewise by the late Government since the King succeeded to the Throne.'

Lord Elgin apologized, but his policy was implemented despite fierce opposition. It was natural to fear that a premature grant of self-government would provoke trouble comparable with that which had followed Gladstone's precipitate grant to the Transvaal in August 1881 of independence under British suzerainty. Age and experience had made King Edward cautious; he exercised his constitutional right to warn; and he wrote [42] (2 March 1906) to the

Prince of Wales: 'There has been a most interesting debate this week in the H. of Lords which lasted 2 days on the future of S. Africa. ... After all the blood and treasure we have expended it would be terrible indeed if the country were handed over to the Boers.' Self-government, nevertheless, was accorded promptly to the Transvaal; the Chinese coolies were shipped home in due course; and Winston Churchill, as Under-Secretary for the Colonies, handled all that business in the Commons because Elgin, his chief, sat in the Lords.

To Lord Esher on 26 March King Edward described[43] Churchill's conduct as 'simply disgraceful'; but in long letters to King Edward, Churchill adroitly defended the Government and himself. Writing (20 August) from Marienbad by the hand of Frederick Ponsonby, the King reminded[44] Churchill that 'the Transvaal is a recently conquered country'; that 'it would be deplorable to run the risk of having another war in South Africa'; and that it was 'most desirable that we should see first how the Transvaal Constitution works' before granting self-government also to the Orange River Colony. The concluding sentence of that letter, drafted by King Edward for Ponsonby to type, ran: 'The King can well understand that the onus of all these discussions in Parliament was thrown upon your shoulders, and no doubt severe criticisms were made from both extremes; but His Majesty is glad to see that you are becoming a *reliable* Minister, and above all a serious politician, *which can only be attained by putting Country before Party.*'

King Edward always loved imparting shrewd and kindly advice, and he had had been on terms of intimate friendship with Winston Churchill's parents. For that reason he took an avuncular interest in the career of a young man whose spirit he liked and admired, but whose speeches he criticized sometimes as 'vulgar and American'; and Esher recorded[45] one such occasion in September 1909. He had been breakfasting at Buckingham Palace alone with King Edward, who started to talk about Winston Churchill:

'If it had not been for me, that young man would not have been in existence.'

Esher (much startled): 'How is that, sir?'

11. Balmoral, 29 September 1896. (*Left to right*) The Empress Alix,
Grand Duchess Olga, Emperor Nicholas II of Russia, Queen
Victoria, the Prince of Wales

The German Emperor William II (12) as Prince William of Prussia
in the uniform of the 1st Regiment of Prussian Guards, 1873 and
(13) as Emperor, 1898

14. Four Generations, 1899, the Duke of York (later King George V), Queen Victoria, the Prince of Wales (later King Edward VII) and Prince Edward of York (later Prince of Wales, King Edward VIII and Duke of Windsor)

15. Francis, 1st Viscount Knollys, G.C.B., G.C.V.O., (1837–1924)

16. The Prince of Wales (with Lord Montagu of Beaulieu) in a 12-h.p. Daimler at Highcliffe Castle, July 1899

17. Alice (Mrs George) Keppel, 1906

18. King Edward VII and Emperor William II in Berlin, February 1909

19. King Edward and Queen Alexandra at Cowes, August 1909

'The Duke and Duchess both objected to Randolph's marriage. It was entirely owing to us that they gave way.'

Early in 1907, the Legislative Assembly of the self-governing Transvaal carried, by 42 votes to 19, a motion by General Botha that the Cullinan diamond, which had been mined two years earlier and which was the largest in the world, should be presented to King Edward as a token of 'the loyalty and attachment of the people of the Transvaal to his person and throne'. King Edward was much gratified by the enlightened attitude which that generous offer disclosed, but the British Cabinet and Lord Esher took what Churchill termed 'a very unimaginative view'. It was objected that the vote had not been unanimous; that the initiative had come from the Boers, and not from British settlers; and that acceptance at a time when a loan was being negotiated might cause critical chatter.

King Edward expressed himself as being most reluctant 'to snub' the Boers, and after a prolonged hesitation and an unworthy attempt on the part of ministers to shift responsibility upon King Edward's shoulders, the Cabinet on 5 November recommended acceptance of the gift. The great diamond, which weighed about a pound and a quarter in the rough, was presented accordingly at Sandringham on his sixty-sixth birthday to King Edward, who sent it to Amsterdam to be cut. He took a close interest in that work; received the cut stones back at Sandringham on his sixty-seventh birthday, and despatched the four largest to the Tower of London for incorporation into the historic regalia of the British Crown.

Campbell-Bannerman, who had been responsible personally for the decision to grant self-government to South Africa at the earliest possible moment, was responsible also for a Trade Disputes Act which troubled King Edward in February 1906. Recent judgements in the Courts had threatened to deprive trade unions of an immunity which their funds had long enjoyed from actions for damages arising out of strikes; and Knollys informed [46] the Prime Minister (13 February) that the King 'sincerely trusts' that the new Bill 'will not include a clause allowing what he thinks is rather absurdly described as "peaceful picketing" – as if it could possibly be asserted that any form of picketing could be free from occasional acts of violence, or at any rate of constant intimidation!' Many Cabinet ministers shared that opinion, but the Prime Minister brushed all proposed safeguards aside, and a Bill, sent to the Lords, gave trade unions everything for which they had asked.

The Peers did not choose to clash with organized labour on that issue; but, after rejecting a Plural Voting Bill, they tore to shreds Augustine Birrell's Education Bill which was the most important Government measure of 1906. They precipitated in that way their first major clash – which King Edward did his utmost, unsuccessfully, to avert and compose – with the new House of Commons.

Balfour's great Education Act of 1902 (devised by an inspired official Sir Robert Morant) had abolished school boards, established local education authorities and fitted a comprehensive system of state education into the pattern of British local government. All schools included in that system were aided from public funds after 1902; and the endowed schools of the Anglican and Roman Catholic Churches were rescued from a threat of bankruptcy.

Nonconformists, on the other hand, who had hoped privately that rising costs would extinguish many Anglican and Roman Catholic schools, professed disgust at being taxed for the support of such schools. The Bible reading which played a large part in the lives of many members of the dissenting sects, and which continued to form the basis of the undenominational religious teaching given in all ex-board schools, had appeared to transform those schools into a vast Nonconformist preserve. That privileged educational position had helped to reconcile Nonconformists to the legal, social and financial privileges which Anglicans enjoyed; and, when that educational privilege was forfeited in 1902, a revolt broke out in Wales against payment of the education rate.

Lloyd George, who led that revolt, argued that in many country districts where the only school was often Anglican, although all local children were Nonconformist, an oppres-

sive Anglican monopoly had been perpetuated; and the
Liberal Government, which depended upon the Nonconformist vote, lost no time in framing a new Education Bill.
In expounding it (9 April 1906) to a House of Commons
which contained about 180 Nonconformists, the President of
the Board of Education, Augustine Birrell, proposed that no
public elementary school should be allowed to teach any
specific religious doctrine; and that religion should be
taught, ordinarily, upon undenominational lines.

Despite some contingent concessions which Birrell offered,
the bishops of the Church of England, meeting in conclave
at Lambeth, resolved to adopt an attitude of uncompromising opposition to that Bill, before returning to their dioceses
to thunder against its terms and to rouse the laity to action.
Roman Catholics were equally disgusted; and King Edward
reflected robustly the views of his bishops. He wrote,[47] for
example (14 April), to Lord Esher from Corfu, where he had
interrupted another Mediterranean cruise to spend a few
days with the King of Greece:

This new Education Bill is deplorable, and has driven the
Church of England and R. Catholics to despair. What can the
Govt. be thinking of – in excluding teaching Religion in our
schools? Do they wish to copy the French! I look with considerable alarm to the way the Prime Minister is going on, and
needless to say, he never brings anything before me – never
consults me in *any* way.

The Prime Minister had informed[48] King Edward on
30 March that the new Bill, 'while remedying the injustice
in the previous Act, ... will meet the reasonable demands of
moderate Churchmen, especially of laymen, and will at the
same time, guard as far as possible the interests of Catholic
Schools', but Knollys forwarded[49] (12 April) a letter from
the Archbishop of Canterbury, Randall Davidson, which
expressed dismay. On that letter King Edward minuted:
'The Bill is most unfair and dangerous, and, instead of
smoothing matters, will produce violent dissensions between
the Church of England and Roman Catholics on the one side,
and Non-conformists on the other. In fact a kind of political–religious warfare will ensue, which is most undesirable.'

Writing, off Stromboli (24 April), to Lord Esher, King Edward deplored [50] 'the continual mistakes which the Govt. are making and the ill-timed measures they are bringing forward'. He attributed them generously to the impaired state of Campbell-Bannerman's health; but it was a cardinal feature of Liberal strategy to bombard the Lords with as many Bills as possible at one time, in the mistaken belief that they would not dare to reject more than one per session.

When the third reading of the Education Bill was carried (30 July) by a large majority in the Commons, Balfour avowed with cool insolence that 'the real discussion must be elsewhere'. The Lords proceeded to wreck the Bill in Committee; Lloyd George asked an audience at Oxford on 1 December 'whether this country is to be governed by the King and his peers, or by the King and his people'; and Knollys wrote [51] (3 December) on King Edward's behalf to Campbell-Bannerman: 'The King sees it is useless to attempt to prevent Mr Lloyd George from attacking, as a Cabinet Minister', the House of Lords, 'though His Majesty has more than once protested to you against it. ... But His Majesty feels he has a right, and it is one on which he intends to insist, that Mr Lloyd George shall not introduce the Sovereign's name into these violent tirades of his; and he asks you, as Prime Minister, to take the necessary steps to prevent a repetition of this violation of constitutional propriety and good taste.'

After apologies and excuses had been tendered by Campbell-Bannerman and Lloyd George, King Edward explained [52] (5 December) through Knollys to the Prime Minister: 'Mr Lloyd George appears to forget that as a Cabinet Minister he cannot with propriety indulge in that freedom of speech in which, if he were a private member, he would be free to indulge; and this is His Majesty's point.' Knollys added that 'the King would not expect Ministers to refrain from criticizing the House of Lords, but he does expect them to abstain from advocating, directly or indirectly, their abolition which, coming from *his Ministers*, would place him in a false position. ...'

It was, of course, inevitable that ministers should attack the hereditary principle while the peers continued obstinately to obstruct popular social aspirations; and King Edward hated naturally those attacks. Although no danger existed that the nation would fail to distinguish clearly between the metaphysical aspect of the hereditary principle which the King represented, and its physical aspect which was represented by the House of Lords, it must be said that the peers stood apart and alone in seeking at times to confuse that issue from selfish motives.

After being advised [53] (7 November) by Campbell-Bannerman that 'a most regrettable situation' would arise unless the peers were to reverse their attitude towards the Education Bill, King Edward invited the Prime Minister and the Archbishop of Canterbury to explore the possibility of a compromise in private talks at Windsor Castle during the week-end of 17–18 November. Those talks appeared to fail, but on 21 November the Cabinet authorized their continuance and their extension to include Opposition leaders; and the account of that meeting of the Cabinet which Campbell-Bannerman sent to King Edward was so absurdly perfunctory as to be misleading. It stated merely that 'the Cabinet met to-day and was entirely engaged with arrangements of public business necessary for the conclusion of the session'.

After consulting Morley, Esher transmitted [54] (22 November) an adequate account of that Cabinet meeting to King Edward. He informed the King that the Cabinet had authorized the Prime Minister to confer with the Archbishop, and with the Opposition leaders, '*before* calling on the House of Commons to consider the Lords' amendments'. Esher explained that, at Queen Victoria's behest, Gladstone had adopted a similar expedient in 1869 before the Anglican Church in Ireland was disestablished; and he advised King Edward to summon Morley to an audience and to instruct the Archbishop to approach the Prime Minister.

After remonstrating very sharply (23 November) with Campbell-Bannerman for not keeping him properly informed, King Edward wrote [55] again (25 November) to the Prime Minister:

In view of the serious state of affairs which would arise were a conflict to take place between the House of Lords and the House of Commons on the amendments passed by the former on the Education Bill, the King feels certain that Sir Henry Campbell-Bannerman will agree with him in thinking it is most important that there should, if possible, be a compromise in respect of those amendments.

The King would, therefore, ask Sir Henry to consider whether it would not be highly desirable that Sir Henry should discuss the matter with the Archbishop of Canterbury in the hope that some *modus vivendi* on the line of mutual concessions could be found to avoid the threatened collision between the two Houses. For the King thinks it would be deplorable, from a constitutional and every point of view, were such a conflict to occur.

The King proposes to send a copy of this letter to the Archbishop, and would wish also to call Sir Henry's attention to pages 7–43 in the 2nd volume of *Archbishop Tait's Life*, when a contest was on the eve of taking place between the Houses on the Irish Church question in 1869.

Informal talks were started, accordingly, between the Government, the Opposition and the Archbishop; but the Lords' amendments had had the effect of completely reconstructing the Education Bill, and the Cabinet decided on 8 December to reject them *en bloc* aand to rely thereafter upon private negotiations aimed at persuading the Lords that it would be dangerous to provoke the Commons too far. That unprecedented and impatient step dismayed King Edward, who wrote [56] (9 December) to the Prime Minister:

The King ... confesses he does not quite see where the spirit of concession 'comes in' in the proposal of the Cabinet, and he is 'afraid, from what Sir Henry says, that the chances of a compromise are not very bright. He moreover doubts whether the adoption of so drastic and novel a measure as the rejection *en bloc* of the whole of the amendments of the House of Lords will be regarded by them as a desire on the part of the House of Commons to arrive at an amicable conclusion....

Although Liberal patience was almost exhausted, strenuous efforts to reach a compromise were made as Christmas approached; and a final conference was held in Balfour's room at the House of Commons on 18 December 1906. The

Government was represented by Asquith, Birrell and Lord Crewe (Lord President of the Council); the Opposition by Balfour, Cawdor and Lansdowne; and the Archbishop of Canterbury took the chair. But no agreement could be reached and, after the Lords had adhered (19 December) to all their amendments by 142 votes to 53, the Commons resolved next day that no further consideration should be given to them.

King Edward, who had a temperamental horror of public wrangles, and in particular of any which menaced established institutions, was dismayed that his efforts as peacemaker had failed. The Education Bill had been killed, and that action by the House of Lords convinced the Government that the Constitution would have to be amended. Before Parliament was adjourned for the Christmas recess, Campbell-Bannerman assured the House of Commons amid thunderous applause that the resources of that House, and of the Constitution, were not exhausted, and that 'a way must be found, and a way will be found, by which the will of the people, expressed through their elected representatives in this House, will be made to prevail'.

19
Naval Revolution

A MEMORABLE collaboration began on Trafalgar Day (21 October) 1904, when Admiral Sir John Fisher became First Sea Lord. By appointing Fisher, after some demur at the outset, to be his principal naval A.D.C., King Edward secured to him the privilege of direct personal access to the Sovereign, which Esher had enjoyed since 1901 as Lieutenant and Deputy Governor of Windsor Castle.

Relishing Fisher's company, as well as his fanatical resolve to secure the Empire's safety behind the strongest and most efficient navy in the world, King Edward never admitted that war with Germany was inevitable. Convinced, nevertheless, that it was, Fisher suggested[1] to King Edward, very soon after his appointment, that the growing German Fleet at Kiel should be 'Copenhagened'* by a sudden assault without the formality of a declaration of war. 'My God, Fisher, you must be mad!' was King Edward's indignant rejoinder on that first occasion, but the admiral loved to shock; and exuberant words, uttered in jest by the First Sea Lord over brandy and cigars, were repeated in British wardrooms. Wafted across what King Edward called the North Sea, and the Emperor William the German Ocean, they served to fan the ominously rising flame of German arrogance, suspicion and self-pity; and an invasion scare which convulsed Germany in November 1906 was followed, in January 1907 by a fantastic rumour that Fisher was coming, which caused panic in Kiel for two days.

* A reference to the spirited action of Admiral James Gambier, who attacked and forced the surrender of the neutral Danish Fleet at Copenhagen in August 1807.

Even before the European Conference assembled on 16 January 1906 to decide the future of Morocco in the Town Hall at Algeciras, the British Liberal Foreign Secretary, Sir Edward Grey, discovered that his Conservative predecessor had taken an important decision. At the height of the Moroccan crisis of 1905, Lord Lansdowne had authorized the very secret preparation of an Anglo-French plan of joint naval and military action for use against Germany in case of need. Discussions with the French naval attaché in London had been initiated directly by Fisher, while military discussions between the Director of Military Operations, Sir James Grierson, and the French military attaché had been conducted indirectly through the military correspondent of *The Times*, Colonel Charles Repington, who was an indiscreet and unsuitable intermediary.

Grey ordered that those talks should be continued, and that the military conversations should be conducted directly between the British and French staffs. Neither Government was committed; but, in 1930, Grey recorded [2] his regret that most of his Cabinet colleagues had been left in ignorance of what was was happening until 1912. As early as 2 February 1906 Campbell-Bannerman wrote [3] to the Lord Privy Seal, Lord Ripon, whom he consulted as an elder statesman: '... Cambon* appears satisfied. But I do not like the stress laid upon joint preparations. It comes very close to an honourable undertaking: and it will be known on both sides of the Rhine. But we must hope for the best.'

Cabinet ministers who were members also of the Committee of Imperial Defence were fully informed; and the Germans were quickly alerted. When the German Emperor told Haldane in Berlin in September 1906 that his Secret Service had heard about the talks, the British War Minister noted [4] that, after he had explained why they were inevitable, in a world constituted as it is, the Emperor had 'fully admitted that this was so, and said he had no quarrel with us for doing this'.

An element of moral commitment became somewhat

* Paul Cambon, French Ambassador in London from 1898 until 1920.

more pronounced as those talks became more intimate and detailed: but early in 1906 King Edward went out of his way to heal the personal breach with his nephew. The German Emperor received, accordingly, on his forty-seventh birthday (27 January) a charming letter [5] from his uncle:

... We are, my dear William, such old friends and near relations that I feel sure that the affectionate feelings which have always existed may continue. Most deeply do I deplore the un-called-for expressions made use of by the Press concerning our two Countries....

I am well aware how anxious you are that the Conference at Algeciras may pass off well.... I entirely share those views and feel convinced that good may accrue from it – above all that a friendly feeling may exist between Germany, France and England. Be assured that this Country has never had any aggressive feelings towards yours....

The German Emperor replied [6] (1 February) from Berlin that 'the whole letter breathed such an atmosphere of kindness and warm sympathetic friendship that it constitutes the most cherished gift among my presents'. He quoted the proverb, 'let bygones be bygones', before recalling the death of Queen Victoria – 'the silent hours when we watched and prayed at her bedside, and when the spirit of that great Sovereign-Lady passed away as she drew her last breath in my arms. I feel sure that from the home of Eternal Light she is now looking down upon us, and will rejoice when she sees our hands clasped in loyal and cordial friendship. ... I trust that in the course of this year we shall be able to meet.'

The Emperor hoped to meet King Edward at the funeral in Copenhagen of Queen Alexandra's father, King Christian IX of Denmark, who had died suddenly on 29 January; but King Edward was unable to accompany Queen Alexandra to Denmark. He explained [7] (5 February) to the Emperor that he had to open the new Liberal Parliament, and that his doctors would not allow him to travel after 'a very bad attack of bronchitis just a year ago'. He added: 'It is doubly annoy-ing for me not to have the opportunity of meeting you at

Copenhagen, but in the course of the Spring I hope we shall be able to meet somewhere during our yachting cruises.'

Although Sir Edward Grey suggested [8] (13 March 1906) that any such meeting in the Mediterranean would mortally affront French opinion if the conference at Algeciras were to fail, Knollys warned [9] Charles Hardinge (4 March) that he was encountering fearful difficulty in restraining King Edward's violent wish to arrange an early rendezvous with the German Emperor in the Mediterranean. Knollys told the King that he would 'undo much of the good which it was universally admitted he had done by bringing France and England together', if he were to insist, against the advice of his Foreign Secretary, upon arranging a meeting with the German Emperor before the result of the conference was known.

Sir Charles Hardinge, who had returned from St Petersburg to become Permanent Head of the Foreign Office, persuaded King Edward to give way; and a meeting between the sovereigns was arranged for 15 August at Cronberg, after the Pact of Algeciras was signed on 2 April 1906. The terms of that Moroccan settlement were very satisfactory because bluster and mismanagement had spoiled a good German case; and the total collapse of the German attempt to use Morocco as a means of smashing the *Entente Cordiale* as well as the Franco-Russian Alliance, prompted the British Government to initiate a direct approach to Russia. Sir Arthur Nicolson (Lord Carnock), who had been the British delegate at Algeciras, was posted accordingly as ambassador to St Petersburg, with instructions to negotiate forthwith a comprehensive Anglo-Russian understanding.

Delighted by that initiative, King Edward summoned Nicolson to visit him at Biarritz, and promised him full support in overcoming formidable obstacles. Whereas public opinion in Great Britain and France hated the Czarist autocracy, ruling circles in Russia were prejudiced against Great Britain on account of the Anglo–Japanese alliance, and against France as a godless republic which had failed to enamel its neutrality with the anticipated degree of benevolence during the recent war. The German Government had displayed conspicuous friendliness towards Russia during the Russo–Japanese War; the young Empress of Russia ensured the predominance of German influence at the Russian Court; and the Czar and his advisers were attracted much more strongly towards authoritarian Germany than they were toward the western democracies.

In those circumstances Grey suggested [10] to King Edward (13 March) that 'an interview of Your Majesty with the Emperor is likely to improve our relations and to facilitate an understanding'; but King Edward thought the time ill-judged. The Emperor Nicholas was living a completely isolated life in a country which appeared to be in grave danger of revolution; and King Edward had no wish either to forfeit prestige by courting failure, or to give unnecessary offence to Germany by paying a state visit to the Czar in St Petersburg before he paid one to the Kaiser in Berlin.

King Edward's hopes for the avoidance of revolution in Russia were pinned upon the Duma, or Parliament, which had no roots in Russian history, and which was dissolved by the Czar on 22 July. Knowing that the Czar hated and despised that body, King Edward would have felt inhibited from offering advice, and he wrote [11] (22 March) to Sir Charles Hardinge:

I honestly confess that I can see no particular object in visiting the Emperor in Russia this year. The Country is in a very unsettled state and will, I fear, not improve for some time to come. I hardly think that the Country at home would much approve of my going there for a while.

I have no wish to play the part of the German Emperor who always meddles in other people's business. What advice could I possibly give the Emperor as to the management of his Country? What right have I to do so, even if he were to listen to me, which I much doubt? Witte's object is that by my going I should enable him to float a Loan. What an extraordinary idea! and one that does not appeal to me in any way....

Sir Arthur Nicolson was convinced that King Edward was wise in avoiding Russia at that time. The autocracy, which Nicholas II regarded as a sacred trust committed to him by God, was at death grips with revolutionaries who cared nothing for liberal reforms imported from the West. They concentrated upon terrorist plots against lives of members of the imperial family, provincial governors and officials, in the hope of overthrowing the social order and of establishing upon its ruins what Nicolson termed 'a socialist republic of the most advanced type'. The Ambassador warned [12] Hardinge (29 July 1906) that odds were even that 'a general upheaval' was imminent 'which will sweep away dynasty, Government, and much else'.

King Edward consented, while at Biarritz, to the announcement (9 March) of the engagement of his niece, Princess Victoria Eugénie (Ena) of Battenberg, to the twenty-year-old King Alfonso XIII of Spain. Princess Ena was the daughter of King Edward's younger sister, Princess Beatrice; and King Alfonso, who had been rejected by Princess Patricia of Connaught, was anxious, nevertheless, to marry into the British royal family. The religious difficulty caused an outcry in both countries, and the Archbishop of Canterbury was much troubled; but King Edward agreed with his Government that the marriage was desirable politically, and the Princess was received quietly into the Roman Catholic Church on 7 March 1906, at San Sebastian.

When lunching three days later at San Sebastian with King Alfonso, King Edward arranged that the Prince of Wales should represent him at the wedding in Madrid on 31 May; and the British Protestant outcry was hushed, illogically, as a result of the ordeal endured by the bridal pair on their wedding day. A bomb hurled at their coach by an anarchist blew to pieces many spectators, soldiers and horses, and King Alfonso and Queen Ena were smeared with blood and dust. They were uninjured, however, and after climbing into another coach they courageously completed the processional drive before returning to a cheerless and unhappy family luncheon.

When King Edward left Biarritz to cruise in the Mediterranean, Sir Charles Hardinge served as minister in attendance. He recorded [13] that 'the Prime Minister and Sir E. Grey made no objection whatever, the latter being strongly in favour of the proposal, which was in great contrast to the attitude of Lord Lansdowne in 1903'. Some criticism was voiced, nevertheless, by constitutionalists and pedants, on the ground that Hardinge, although a Privy Counsellor, was a civil servant, and not a Cabinet minister; but King Edward paid no heed, and Hardinge noted [14] that Grey was much easier and less reserved than Lansdowne had been. With Grey 'I was able to discuss everything with the utmost freedom, more as two equals than as Chief and subordinate, and he allowed me the greatest liberty of action. Had it not been for the complete absence in him of any feelings of petty jealousy, my relations with the King during the following years would have been a source of difficulty between us.'

The main object of the Mediterranean cruise of 1906 was to enable King Edward and Queen Alexandra to pay a state visit to Athens, while Hardinge discussed with Greek ministers a difficult situation in Crete. King Edward planned also to talk seriously to his nephew, Prince George of Greece, who had misgoverned Crete so badly, after being installed as High Commissioner by the Great Powers, that he had to be removed later in the year; and Queen Alexandra longed to be with her brother, King George of Greece. The death in January of their father, the King of Denmark, had stirred the strong family affections which were uppermost always in Queen Alexandra's mind.

King Edward and Queen Alexandra were joined in Corfu by the Prince and Princess of Wales on their way home from India; and all four stayed from 11–16 April with the King of Greece in that charming island to which Lord Charles Beresford brought the battleship squadron of the British Mediterranean Fleet. Lord Charles was under orders from the Admiralty to escort King Edward to Athens, but on the day of his arrival at Corfu he offended the King of Greece.

King George, a modest and agreeable man, had boarded Beresford's flagship on a visit of ceremony after giving due notice, and had resented the admiral's failure to take the trouble to change into full-dress uniform before receiving him. He complained to King Edward, who ordered Hardinge to bring Beresford's insulting and slovenly conduct to the notice of the Board of Admiralty forthwith. Hardinge grumbled[15] privately that 'if it had been anybody other than Lord Charles, I doubt if the King would have taken it up'; but, much as he disliked Beresford, questions of deportment and dress were important to King Edward, who spent a high proportion of his time in public and on parade. For almost forty years before his accession, King Edward had been thankful to discover, in the field of social sovereignty, an outlet for his pent-up forcefulness; and disputes were submitted to him voluntarily, as they were submitted, in a different field, to the Hague Tribunal. Obedience to his judgements helped to invest idleness with dignity, besides affording comfort to thousands who construed pursuit of pleasure as performance of social duty.

The need, for example, to change clothes several times a day provided occupation of a kind. It gave women continual opportunities for self-expression, and bound men who served Mammon, or who merely hunted and shot, into a uniform discipline with those who served the State. To King Edward, who had been taught, as a boy, that laxity in dress would 'prove a want of self-respect and be an offence against decency, leading – as it has often done before in others – to an indifference to what is morally wrong',* any failure to maintain the highest standards became personally offensive.

A large number of good-natured stories were current about King Edward's views on clothes. 'The Princess', he once observed severely, as Prince of Wales, to a lady seated next to him at dinner, 'has taken the trouble to wear a tiara. Why haven't you?' But he was usually more subtle, and Austen Chamberlain loved to repeat an order which he had overheard King Edward give to a valet as *Victoria and Albert* approached the Scottish coast in August 1902: 'Un costume un peu plus écossais demain.' The King's evident anxiety not to make the transition from English to Scottish attire too abrupt fascinated the Postmaster-General.

Pointing once to Haldane, who arrived in a shabby soft hat at a garden party, King Edward exclaimed to the ladies who surrounded him, 'See my War Minister approach in the

* See p. 41 above.

hat which he inherited from Goethe!'; but he appreciated that some men were incorrigibly careless, like the Duke of Devonshire, or incorrigibly perverse, like Lord Rosebery. To Rosebery, who often offended and who came once to an evening party at Buckingham Palace wearing trousers instead of knee-breeches, King Edward remarked: 'I presume that you have come in the suite of the American Ambassador!'; but he rebuked a minister in the Foreign Service, who boarded *Victoria and Albert* in knee-breeches, by observing, 'trousers are always worn on board ship!'; and he had trouble occasionally with his suite. He told Frederick Ponsonby, who had proposed to accompany him in a tail-coat to a picture exhibition before luncheon: 'I thought everyone must know that a *short* jacket is always worn with a silk hat at a private view in the morning.'

Although he tried, unsuccessfully, during the 1890s to revive the fashion of wearing knee-breeches as a matter of course with evening dress, and although he fought a losing battle at the end of his life on behalf of the frock-coat, King Edward introduced innovations from time to time. He popularized the Norfolk jacket and the Tyrolean hat; and he caused his trousers to be creased sideways at intervals over a long period of years. Detesting the Panama hat, he contrived, more or less, to kill it, while setting the seal of his approval upon the grey top hat in 1905, and upon the soft felt hat in 1909; and he defied convention occasionally at Marienbad. In 1903, for example, when greeting a friend at the railway station, he caused astonishment by appearing on the platform clad in a green cap, with a pink tie and white gloves, knee-breeches, grey slippers and a brown overcoat with loud checks: 'Loyal subjects must sincerely hope', the *Tailor and Cutter* commented severely (17 September 1903), 'that His Majesty has not brought this outfit home.'

The report which King Edward caused Hardinge to send to Lord Tweedmouth about the unseemly attire worn by Lord Charles Beresford when greeting the King of Greece at Corfu coincided with another complaint, addressed [16] by Sir John Fisher to the First Lord of the Admiralty on 24 April 1906, about the insubordinate conduct of the Commander-in-Chief of the Mediterranean Fleet. After canvassing his captains on the subject of Admiralty policy, and after addressing what Fisher termed an 'improper letter to the King on the subject of naval training', Beresford had proceeded to talk at an official dinner 'in unmeasured terms of scorn' about the First Sea Lord.

That action by Beresford heralded the opening of a great schism in the Royal Navy, which transformed every fleet, squadron and warship between 1906 and 1910 into two hostile interests acknowledging allegiance to 'Jacky' Fisher or to 'Charlie' Beresford. Both men were inspired by a passionate resolve to see the Navy made ready in the shortest time to meet the German challenge victoriously; but they differed profoundly about methods.

Whereas Beresford stood, in general, for tradition and orthodoxy, Fisher proceeded to implement reforms which were so drastic as to constitute a revolution. Different critics concentrated upon different aspects of his policy; and his intimate friend, Captain R. H. Bacon, reported [17] secretly (12 and 15 April 1906) to his chief, from the battleship *Irresistible* off Corfu, about the attitude of King Edward:

Last night I dined on board the Royal Yacht, and after dinner the King sent for me . . . and asked whether the schemes could not perhaps have been launched with less friction, saying that of course he knew that the Navy was ultra-conservative and hated reforms. . . .

What is upsetting the King and the Prince of Wales so much is what they call a feeling of 'unrest' within the Service. . . .

I pressed most strongly . . . that the Service agitators were weakening the authority of the Admiralty with the country. The prestige of the Admiralty must be kept up and . . . . I think, on the whole, the visit of the King and the Prince of Wales to Corfu has been most useful in this matter, since they have heard every objection confuted, and also this has been the effect on their immediate entourage. The King and Prince of Wales were always most loyal (if such a term may be used) to you personally, and to the whole of the schemes of reform, but very much disturbed at the Service agitation headed by Lord Charles Beresford and Admiral Lambton.

Fisher would have been ousted early if he had not

accepted an unrelenting public demand for a reduction in the Naval Estimates. They had risen from 27.52 millions in 1900 to 36.89 millions in 1904; but, after proclaiming that economy is the offspring of efficiency, he contrived to reduce them to 31.42 millions in 1907 by means of a ruthless process of sacking and scrapping all redundant or obsolete personnel, units and supplies.

Concentrating at the outset upon instituting a new system of common entry for all executive officers of the Royal Navy, as well as upon the technical training of senior officers, Fisher insisted upon rapid promotion on the basis of merit instead of merely upon that of seniority. He was dubbed a socialist by King Edward when he pleaded, unsuccessfully, that education at Osborne and Dartmouth should be provided free of charge in order to widen the field of entry; but, in general, he rode roughshod over all opponents, threatening genially to turn their wives into widows and to burn their houses to the ground. As early as 28 February 1904, when he was only Commander-in-Chief at Portsmouth, Fisher wrote [18] triumphantly to Lord Knollys: 'In our recent naval revolution in regard to entry and education of officers, all the senior officers of the Navy were against us to a man! *Never were such bitter things said!* Now they all see an immense success looming in the distance, magnifying the efficiency of the Navy beyond any present conception....'

Many more bitter things were said as Fisher warmed to his task of administering to the Navy the indispensable psychological shock which a series of initial defeats had administered to the Army during the Boer War; and 'keep your hair on!' was an expression used constantly by King Edward in conversation with the First Sea Lord. He urged Fisher to curb the extravagance of his language and to stop insulting opponents; and Esher explained [19] inimitably (21 October 1906) that it was best to 'be Machiavellian, and play upon the delicate instrument of public opinion with your fingers and not with your feet, however tempting the latter may be'.

Despising many soldiers and most politicians, and pinning his hopes upon King Edward, Fisher refused to serve under any First Lord of the Admiralty with whom he felt what he termed [20] 'an incompatability of temperament and views'. He demanded a free hand and warned [21] Balfour (3 March 1905) that he would resign if Beresford's friend, Walter Long, were appointed to succeed Lord Selborne. For King Edward's information, Fisher explained [22] that day to Knollys that Sir Andrew Noble, chairman of Sir W. G. Armstrong, Whitworth and Co., had visited him on 2 March and that 'an immense combination of the greatest ship-building, armour-plate and gun-making firms in the country are willing to unite under my presidency (and practical dictatorship!), and I fancy I should have about £20,000 a year'.

Apart from his salary, Fisher was a poor man; but he was a dedicated patriot, and Balfour agreed with King Edward that it would be madness to let him go. For that reason, Lord Cawdor, whose health was precarious, became First Lord of the Admiralty when Selborne went to govern South Africa; and Fisher was rewarded by King Edward with the Order of Merit, and by the Government with promotion, by Special Order in Council, to be an additional Admiral of the Fleet.

That promotion enabled Fisher to remain on the active list, implementing his revolution, until he attained the age of seventy in January 1911; and it blasted Beresford's hopes of succeeding in January 1906 to the office of First Sea Lord when Fisher would otherwise have been due to retire on attaining the age of sixty-five. A host of admirers and supporters were convinced that Beresford would have been a much more suitable First Sea Lord than Fisher was; and Beresford's promotion, which would have crowned a remarkable career, would have consolidated also the social position of Lady Charles Beresford, which her husband's quarrel with King Edward in 1891 had jeopardized for a time.

The personality of Lord Charles Beresford, a rich and prominent patrician, was a colourful compound of charm, geniality, courage and unvarying kindliness and thoughtfulness which had caused him to be idolized by the men whom he commanded. Although not clever, he understood, like

King Edward, how to use other men's brains; and his greatest weakness was a colossal vanity, and a self-confidence inflated so absurdly that King Edward was fully justified in dubbing him a 'gas-bag'. He was a born leader, nevertheless, and as popular in the country as he was in the Navy; and Fisher found him a most formidable antagonist. The audacity which he had displayed at Alexandria in 1882 while in command of the gunboat *Condor*, as well as the struggle which he had waged later on the Navy's behalf in the House of Commons, were fresh in all men's minds throughout King Edward's reign; and as a practitioner of the arts of publicity, Beresford was in every respect Fisher's equal.

Under Cawdor, and Cawdor's Liberal successor, Tweedmouth, Fisher proceeded to implement four major reforms which were opposed at almost every step by Beresford. He formed a thoroughly efficient Reserve Fleet in which 'nucleus crews', including all essential specialists, lived and trained continuously in every component warship. Fisher found the personnel for those crews by scrapping a very large number of obsolete warships which had been kept in dock at home, like a miser's hoard, or scattered throughout the Empire to show the flag and to perform police duties; and he formed a new Home Fleet in order to ensure that three-quarters of the nation's strength in battleships could be hurled at any instant against Germany. He introduced, finally, the all big-gun type of battleship and cruiser.

King Edward was much less interested in the technical arguments, which Fisher employed in justification of those reforms, than he was fascinated by their author's personality which commanded his confidence and affection. Fisher and he shared many human tastes and traits; they had been born in the same year; and Fisher loved to recall at the end of his life instances of what he termed King Edward's 'astounding aptitude of appealing to the hearts of both High and Low'. While staying, for example, as Fisher's guest at Admiralty House, Portsmouth, in February 1904, the King took the trouble to congratulate personally his host's cook, and to invite her to stay at Buckingham Palace. Saying nothing to his host at the time, King Edward assured her that 'she would enjoy seeing how a Great State Dinner was managed'; and Fisher recorded[23] that Mrs Baker 'was absolutely the best cook I ever had. She was cheap at £100 a year. She was a remarkably lovely young woman.... The King gave her some decoration.... I can't remember what it was.'

Appreciating that a legacy of complacent torpor extending backwards for three-quarters of a century could only be destroyed with the aid of rough and crude methods, King Edward threw his full weight consistently on Fisher's side. He even allowed Fisher to prejudice him for some months during the winter of 1907–8 against the Secretary of State for War, R. B. Haldane; but Esher defended Haldane, and King Edward rejected Fisher's view that the Regular Army could safely be reduced in size.

Fisher had developed a rancid hatred of Haldane, whom he described habitually as a 'soapy Jesuit'; and he was intensely jealous as well as suspicious of the War Office. He considered that the defence of the Empire could be entrusted almost exclusively to the Navy, upon which he would have liked to see more money spent. He convinced King Edward that it would be madness to adopt the plan of the War Office for transporting the miniature British Regular Army across the Channel immediately to reinforce the French left flank in the event of war with Germany; and he wrote[24] to Lord Esher on 25 April 1912:

My beloved E., ... I fully agree with you that the schemes of the General Staff of the Army are grotesque.... You will remember a famous interview we two had with King Edward in his cabin on board the Royal Yacht – how he stamped on the idea (that then enthused the War Office mind) of England once more engaged in a great Continental War! ...

Fisher had concocted a private and ill-considered plan for treating most of the British Regular Army 'as a projectile to be fired by the Navy' on to a fourteen-mile sandy strip of the coastline of Pomerania, within ninety miles of Berlin. He postulated Russian aid in seizing a base in Schleswig-Holstein; but he refused obstinately to form a Naval General

Staff, and it was impossible therefore, to expose in detail the utter impracticability of that plan which he kept locked securely within his breast and which was treated with contempt by the Committee of Imperial Defence as well as by the War Office. On 22 October 1908 the Prime Minister reported[25] to King Edward that a meeting of the C.I.D. over which he had presided that day had resolved that, in the event of war with Germany, it would be much better to offer direct support to the left flank of the French Army than it would be to attempt a military diversion in the Baltic in cooperation with the Navy:

Their conclusion was that the idea of a diversion in the Baltic did not appear to have anything to commend it from a military point of view; and that the direct support of the French Army offered a better prospect of useful result.

In their view the presence in the field, side by side with French troops, of a British Army would infuse into the former that moral confidence which they so suddenly and completely lost in 1870.

It was agreed that Calais, Dunkirk, Havre and (if Belgium were invaded) Antwerp also should be used as bases through which five fully equipped British divisions (including one cavalry division) should be concentrated immediately near Rheims; and King Edward, who loathed that prospect, was gratified by an undertaking that inquiries would be made to see if a smaller force would do. He had no temptation to explore difficult problems of strategy, but he agreed[26] (20 December 1908) with Asquith that 'as long as Germany persists at her present rate of ship-building, we have no other alternative but to build double'; and he wrote[27] (17 March 1908) to Fisher:

It goes against the grain that we should desert the Saxon for the Celtic Races, who (the Saxon) ought to be our natural allies, but I confess that the intense jealousy of one of the former countries and races makes them unfortunately our bitterest enemies. Still, I do not despair that if we continue to 'put our foot down', as we do now, they will accept the inevitable and be friendly with us, but we must never cease keeping our 'weather eye open' across the North Sea!

Fisher's dictatorial methods and alleged system of Service espionage, the avowed favouritism which he exercised in promoting his adherents and the vindictiveness with which he pursued all who declined to swim in what came to be termed 'the Fishpond', were exploited by Beresford who exchanged the command of the Mediterranean for that of the Channel Fleet in April 1907. Lord Charles displayed a spirit of insubordination unparalleled in the history of the Royal Navy, and one of the most disgraceful of many incidents occurred at King Edward's levee at St James's Palace on 11 May 1908. Upon encountering Beresford, Fisher put out his hand; but in full view of King Edward and of a crowd of ministers and officers, Lord Charles ignored it and turned his back upon the First Sea Lord.

That story was known to every bluejacket within a week, and King Edward called his Government in private a pack of cowards for not ordering Beresford to haul down his flag. He was scrupulous, nevertheless, in exhibiting an attitude of regal impartiality, and in 1906 he conferred upon Beresford the Grand Cross of his Royal Victorian Order. He never forgot that he had a duty as Sovereign to exclude any element of personal prejudice, and in 1909 he was willing to confer a peerage upon Lord Charles. He was relieved, however, when Asquith advised him that the time was inopportune.

Beresford was bold and uninhibited in making frequent personal approaches to King Edward, whom he had helped to initiate into worldly delights during the 1860s: 'Personally', he wrote [28] (7 August 1908) after the King had been his guest while reviewing the Channel Fleet, 'I shall never forget the day, as Your Majesty's kindness and charm reminded me so clearly of those happy days gone by which can never be erased from my memory.' In his reply [29] (8 August), which began 'My dear Lord Charles Beresford' and which ended 'Very sincerely yours', King Edward expressed a hope that 'nothing may occur to prevent your continuing to hold the high and important position which you now occupy'.

That sentence conveyed a kindly warning that the Cabinet could not be expected to tolerate indefinitely the admiral's insubordinate conduct. The Admiralty had for many months been pressing the Cabinet for authority to dismiss Beresford, on the ground that the schism in the Service had become so subversive of discipline that it was dangerous to the Empire and scandalous in the eyes of the world; but when that authority was accorded at last on 16 December 1908 King Edward was less happy than he had expected to be. Knollys explained [30] (22 December) to Reginald McKenna, who had succeeded Tweedmouth, that the King 'is afraid he [Beresford] now will make a disturbance and give trouble and annoyance'.

King Edward was prescient, for Beresford's head was turned by cheering patriotic mobs which swept police cordons aside and which carried him shoulder high in London, as well as in Portsmouth where he hauled down his flag on 24 March 1909. After consulting Balfour, who was a close friend, on 26 March, the Admiral called four days later in an exhilarated mood upon Asquith at Downing Street in order to warn him that he intended to stump the country in an all-out effort to overturn the Government unless his demand was met for a public inquiry into the policy and conduct of the Board of Admiralty since the day when Fisher became First Sea Lord.

Aided by Sir Reginald Custance, an able doctrinaire who had been his second-in-command, Beresford dubbed Fisher 'our dangerous lunatic' and accused him of having neglected his duty to ensure the nation's safety. Besides castigating his scrapping policy and fanatical minor economies, as well as expressing doubts about the *Dreadnought* – 'we start at scratch with that type of ship' – Beresford brought three principal charges against the First Sea Lord. He alleged (1) that the new Home Fleet was 'a fraud upon the public and a danger to the Empire' because it was dispersed under separate commands in time of peace; (2) that a dangerous shortage of destroyers and small craft invited a sudden enemy attack upon the Channel Fleet; (3) that, in case of war, the Admiralty lacked the power to put any strategic plan immediately into execution. Another charge, which was later 'very considerably modified', alleged that Beresford had never been able to obtain from Fisher any coherent plan for the employment of the Channel Fleet on the outbreak of war.

Confronted by a growing popular agitation, Asquith appointed (19 April 1909) a sub-committee (Asquith, Crewe, Grey, Haldane and Morley) of the Committee of Imperial Defence to investigate in private the very serious accusations which Beresford had made. Fisher was so hurt and angry that he wanted to resign at once, but King Edward sent [31] him (20 April) through Ponsonby a peremptory order that he should remain at his post 'even under pressure'. 'I shall of course obey His Majesty,' Fisher wrote [32] (24 April) to Ponsonby, 'but it is almost past belief how Beresford has been pandered to.... Esher is especially invited to serve on the Committee at a personal interview by the Prime Minister and is appointed – Beresford objects, and Esher's appointment is cancelled....'

At the height of that crisis, while evidence was being heard *in camera*, there were ranged, on Fisher's side, King Edward; the Liberal Press (with reservations about dreadnoughts on account of the intensified Anglo–German naval competition which they caused); *The Times*, *The Daily Telegraph* and *The Observer*, as well as the leading Service journals; and most junior naval officers, including the ablest. Against Fisher were ranged the Prince of Wales; most of the Conservative Press, including the *Daily Express* and *Daily Mail*; Society, marshalled by Lady Londonderry; and most senior naval officers, including the best loved.

Knollys had warned [33] Esher as early as 20 September 1908, that the mind of the Prince of Wales had been 'poisoned' against Fisher; but the Prince revered his father and remained passive for a time. King Edward assured [34] his son (30 March 1909) that Beresford was suffering from 'a not unusual complaint called "a swollen head"' and that 'the interest he takes in the Navy is all bosh – it is only his form of self-advertisement'; and Fisher never forgave the Prince for starting openly to support Beresford during April. That action by the Prince of Wales was taken after a journalist, Sir George Armstrong, who was a a malignant enemy of Fisher, had revealed that the First Sea Lord had been conducting over a long period and behind Beresford's back an intimate personal correspondence with Captain R. H. Bacon, who had been one of Beresford's subordinates. Fisher had caused some of Bacon's letters to be circulated secretly among selected adherents, and he was accused in consequence of ungentlemanly espionage.

Fisher's indiscreet volubility sometimes embarrassed King Edward, who had checkmated effectively the very strong social opposition which Beresford and his ally, Lady Londonderry, had aroused against the First Sea Lord. As early as 19 April 1908 Fisher described [35] to Lord Esher a 'serious' conversation which he had had that day with King Edward who had complained 'that I was Jekyll and Hyde! *Jekyll* in being successful in my work at the Admiralty – but *Hyde* as a failure in Society! that I talked too freely and was reported to say (which of course is a lie) that the King would see me through anything! That it was bad for me and bad for him as being a Constitutional Monarch.'

When Fisher retorted that 'it could not be hid that the King had backed up the First Sea Lord against all kind of opposition', King Edward, 'having unburdened his mind', changed the subject abruptly. He 'smoked a cigar as big as a capstan bar for really a good hour afterwards, talking of everything from China to Peru'; but the facts were clear. Fisher's work and methods had provoked such intense opposition and indignation that he needed continuous active support from strong political chiefs. So weak, however, owing to extreme ill-health, were Lords Cawdor and Tweedmouth, who administered the Admiralty as First Lords successively from March 1905 until April 1908, that Fisher was compelled to rely upon King Edward for the indispensable backing which his political chiefs failed to provide.

Tweedmouth especially was incapable of making up his mind between the arguments advanced by Fisher, and the counter-arguments adduced by Beresford's 'Syndicate of Discontent'; and that mind collapsed under the strain. Unhappily for Fisher, Tweedmouth was stricken with a cerebral disease which killed him in September 1909; and the history of his tenure of office would otherwise be inexplicable. A series of incidents cost the Admiralty a great amount of prestige which it could ill afford to lose; and the First Lord forgot, for example, to declare his ownership of half the ordinary shares in Meux and Co., when that firm acquired a contract for supplying beer to the Navy.

Early in 1908 a patriotic splinter group, entitled The Imperial Maritime League, invited Lord Esher to join its Council. One of the demands of that League was the dismissal of Fisher, and Esher was so indignant that he sent a copy of his refusal letter to *The Times* which printed it on 6 February: 'There is not a man', Esher wrote, 'in Germany, from the Emperor downwards, who would not welcome the fall of Sir John Fisher.'

The German Emperor informed [36] King Edward (14 February) that he was writing privately to Lord Tweedmouth to answer Esher's aspersions, as well as to allay British uneasiness at the pace and scale of German naval shipbuilding. 'My dear William', King Edward replied [37] very curtly (16 April), '... Your writing to my First Lord of the Admiralty is "a new departure", and I do not see how he can prevent our Press from calling attention to the great increase in building of German ships of war, which necessitates our increasing our Navy also. Believe me, Your affectionate Uncle, Edward R.'

In a nine-page letter to Lord Tweedmouth, dated 16 February 1908, the Emperor William described [38] Esher's reference to himself as 'a piece of unmitigated balderdash'; and in a reference to Esher's former employment as Permanent Secretary to the Office of Works between 1895 and 1902, he asked sarcastically 'whether the supervision of the foundations and drains of the Royal Palaces is apt to qualify somebody for the judgement of Naval affairs in general'. Tweedmouth showed that undignified letter to King Edward and to Sir Edward Grey before replying privately (20 February); and that reply enclosed details, most unwisely, about the British Naval Estimates which were due to be presented to Parliament in a few days' time.

Tweedmouth would have incurred less odium if he had

channelled his reply officially through the Foreign Office. It was essential to preserve secrecy in order to avoid damage to Anglo–German relations, but the First Lord was so much flattered and excited that he gossiped in clubs and drawing-rooms and read [39] the whole of the Emperor's private letter to his host and fellow-guests while staying with Lord Roths-child at Tring. Newspapers were naturally hot upon the trail, and a leading article in *The Times* (6 March), which demanded unsuccessfully that the correspondence should be made public, rebuked the German Emperor for an under-hand and impermissible attempt to influence Admiralty policy.

The Prime Minister, Campbell-Bannerman, was on his death-bed at that time, but a special meeting of the Cabinet called on 6 March by the Chancellor of the Exchequer, H. H. Asquith, decided to take Opposition leaders into its confidence. King Edward expressed [40] his appreciation when Balfour and Lansdowne agreed that Tweedmouth's ac-tion in communicating the British Naval Estimates to the German Emperor before presenting them to Parliament should be glossed over in order to avert a stormy debate which would have exacerbated Anglo–German differences.

The Admiralty suffered, nevertheless, a further severe loss of prestige at a moment when public confidence was al-ready shaken; and King Edward was vexed with Esher for a time: 'It is a great pity', he wrote [41] (10 March 1908) to Fisher from Biarritz, 'that there has been so much fuss and publicity about G.[erman] E.[mperor]'s letter. The 1st Lord was so pleased at hearing direct from him that he told every Lady he met, and no wonder *The Times* heard of it, but its vicious article was uncalled for. . . . I return Esher's letter. He was not likely to mention the subject of G. E.'s letter as he knows that it was the outcome of his very unfortunate one! . . .'

On 7 April 1909 Hardinge had occasion to inform [42] King Edward that the German Emperor's manuscript letter to Tweedsmouth had fallen into bad hands. It was published in full in the *Morning Post* on 30 October 1914, when it could do no more harm; but in 1909 the Foreign Office was afraid that harm might result if it were sold to the Press. Prince Francis of Teck volunteered to negotiate its purchase from the lady concerned, whom he knew, and who was said to be in serious financial straits, but his offer of two hundred pounds was rejected as insulting.

When Asquith formed his Government in April 1908 Reginald McKenna succeeded Tweedmouth as First Lord of the Admiralty. King Edward informed[43] Fisher (14 April) that he had been convinced by Asquith that it was essential that the heads of great spending departments should sit in future in the Commons, and not in the Lords; and that Tweedmouth had secured 'a charming post' as Lord President of the Council. The King added: 'When I agreed to McKenna's appointment it was on condition that you kept your present post. The Prime Minister never made the *slightest* objection – on the contrary, he was most desirous that you should remain.'

One month later, Lord Tweedmouth wrote[44] a most ridiculous letter (20 May) to Lord Knollys. He asked him to notify King Edward that he had 'about 15 young unmarried nieces who would be delighted' if the King would join them in staging a little variety entertainment, 'very bright but very proper', and at 'a stand up supper' which would follow. Asquith had warned the King on the previous day that Tweedmouth's mind was 'seriously unhinged'; and King Edward minuted[45]: 'This is very sad but explains his extraordinary behaviour on so many occasions.'

It helps also to explain Fisher's urgent need of King Edward's continuous support at a most critical period in the history of the Navy, and at a time when the insidious onset of mortal illness had disabled not only the First Lord of the Admiralty but also the Prime Minister, Campbell-Bannerman, from extending to the embattled First Sea Lord the backing to which he was entitled. The Royal Navy in those circumstances provided King Edward with the greatest opportunity which he ever experienced to exert his forcefulness in the national interest, and he made the best possible use of it.

'When Your Majesty', Fisher wrote[46] (4 October 1907),

'backed up the First Sea Lord against unanimous Naval feeling against the *Dreadnought* – when she was first designed – and when Your Majesty launched her, went to sea in her, witnessed her battle practice (which surpassed all records), it just simply shut up the mouths of the revilers as effectively as those lions were kept from eating Daniel! *And they would have eaten me but for Your Majesty!*' That was not mere hyperbole; and, while the schism in the Navy lasted, Fisher had good cause to remind [47] Esher (13 September 1909) that '*without question he, the King, now largely moulds the public will!*'

King Edward was dismayed, nevertheless, by the report of the Committee which had inquired into the charges brought by Beresford against the Admiralty. Published on 12 August 1909, it vindicated Fisher in such tepid language that Beresford brazenly claimed a victory. Knollys informed [48] Fisher (19 September) that the original draft had been favourable, but that Asquith had '"watered it down" to such an extent that it amounts to a verdict in Beresford's favour', and that 'the Committee, as I have always said, were afraid of Beresford'.

Although the view formed by Lord Knollys was a little too pessimistic, Fisher's position had been so badly undermined by controversy that his resignation became inevitable. King Edward told [49] Knollys (21 August) that, if he could help it, 'Fisher shall not be kicked out, in spite of the Cabinet, the Press, and C.[harles] B.[eresford]'; but Esher and Knollys warned Fisher rightly that his position had been weakened fatally and that he ought to regard that factor as decisive. After holding out for two months, Fisher described [50] (27 October) to Esher a talk which he had had with King Edward on the previous evening: 'He is powerless against Asquith if Asquith *won't* fight. Beresford is untiring in his intrigues. The Admiralty lies quiescent like a hippopotamus in the mud!'

Fisher's task at that time had been virtually accomplished; but, in the absence of King Edward's forceful backing, it is certain that he would have been ousted much earlier. It was arranged that his resignation should take effect on 25 January 1910, which was his sixty-ninth birth-day, and in conferring a peerage upon him, King Edward wrote [51] (29 October) from Newmarket: '... Nobody deserves the thanks of your Sovereign and your Country more warmly than you do. Time will show what admirable reforms you have created in the Royal Navy, and you can afford to treat with the contempt that it deserves "those backbiters" who have endeavoured to calumniate you!' Fisher lived to fight again when war came in 1914, whereas his enemy, Beresford (upon whom a peerage was conferred in 1916) declined into a disgruntled Party hack.

'There is no doubt whatever', Winston Churchill wrote,[52] 'that Fisher was right in nine-tenths of what he fought for'; but it was well that the First Sea Lord resigned when he did. Besides disgusting the War Office by the open contempt which he expressed for it, he had stirred up a host of naval, political and social enemies; and it was essential that the Navy should enjoy a period of rest from internal strife before it was hurled against Germany. Fisher never forgave his enemies, particularly 'the Dukes and Duchesses'; and he wrote [53] at the end of his life: 'Hereditary titles are ludicrously out of date, and the sooner we sweep away all the gimcracks and gewgaws of snobbery the better.'

Although hurt in 1909 at having been made a baron when he considered that he ought to have been a viscount, Fisher's feeling for King Edward never altered. Until his death in 1920 he loved to proclaim constantly the great debt which he owed to the King and the very deep affection which he cherished for his memory. 'Dear old Fisher writes and talks too much, but "the leopard does not change its spots"', King Edward grumbled [54] (6 April 1909) to the Prince of Wales; but Fisher let all the world know that his sun had set when King Edward died. He 'conquered all hearts and annihilated all envy', he wrote [55] (14 May 1910) to Reginald McKenna. 'He wasn't clever, but he always did the right thing, which is better than brains.' A year later, after burning loyally, at Knollys's request, all the many intimate and personal letters which he had received from the King, he wrote [56] (14 February 1911) to a friend: 'How *human* he was! He could sin, "as it were with a cart-rope", and yet could be loved the more for it! What a splendour he was in the world!'

Fisher began his book, *Memories* (1919), with the words 'King Edward had faith in me'; but his love of King Edward was expressed [57] perhaps most movingly in a letter (1 August 1911) to Lord Esher:

It is curious that I can't get over the personal great blank I feel in the death of our late blessed friend, King Edward! There was something in the charm of his heart that still chains one to his memory – some magnetic touch!

'Le cœur a ses raisons que la raison ne connaît point.' Pascal was a great man to have said that.

20
Military Reform

ALTHOUGH never as close to Haldane as he was to Fisher, King Edward enjoyed his War Minister's company and was fascinated by his cleverness. Arnold-Foster's rigid plans had been conceived in advance by a mind narrowed during the preparation of a series of educational text-books for the publishing house of Cassell; but Haldane's mind, which commanded twenty-five thousand pounds a year at the Bar, was a much more powerful and subtle instrument. The minister's task was to conciliate the Radicals by reducing the Army Estimates, while making the Army more efficient.

Haldane walked that tightrope with admirable virtuosity. He reduced his Estimates from 29.81 millions in 1905 to 27.76 millions in 1907, and he kept Knollys and Esher as well as King Edward fully informed, using methods adapted to their individual tastes. He appointed Esher to be chairman of the committee which organized the Territorial Army, and he was only a little less successful than Fisher was in enlisting on his side the full weight of King Edward's social and personal influence at the time (1906–7) when it was most valuable.

Although capricious occasionally on the subject of uniforms, King Edward deprecated the choice of expensive trappings by territorial regiments, because he wished to avoid penalizing officers of slender means; and he approached broad questions of policy in a large-minded way. He wrote,[1] for example (20 March 1906), from Biarritz to Lord Esher, about the Government's proposal to reduce the Army by 20,000 men:

... I should be very sorry to be called upon to give an opinion about how many Regular Troops would be required in Ireland in time of war. In some respects it would depend on what the Irish policy of the Government of the day consisted in! ...

I am very sorry that the Defence Committee decided to leave Gibraltar in the hands of the Military Forces, as I am strongly of opinion that it would be both advantageous and economical to hand it over to the Navy, as well as Malta, and to let both be garrisoned by Royal Marines and Royal Artillery, with either a R.M. or R.A. General as Governor, and the rest in the hands of an Admiral.

What I want to see is that the garrisons of S. Africa and Egypt should be considerably strengthened – not only for political reasons, but for the sake of drill and manœuvring ground for the Army, which any competent military expert knows the importance of – and take away *all* the Line Regiments from Gibraltar and Malta, where they have no room hardly to drill one battalion.

These are my strong views and I have written the same to Knollys, begging him to give them to Haldane, and I hope you will do the same.

In conclusion, with schoolboy gusto, King Edward expressed delight at the news, just received, that a motion critical of his Government's South African policy had been carried by 170 votes against 35 in the Lords: 'This is *most* satisfactory! And a wholesome *snub* for the Govt.!'

After conciliating King Edward by sending a cavalry regiment to South Africa, and by promising to send a second if necessary, in replacement of three infantry battalions which were withdrawn, Haldane reprieved the third battalion of the Coldstream Guards. It had been threatened with disbandment on grounds of economy, but Haldane sent it to Egypt instead; and he gave great satisfaction also by sending King Edward in diary form a sparkling and highly entertaining account of a visit which he paid to Berlin at the end of August 1906 as the Emperor William's guest.

King Edward, on his outward journey to Marienbad, had met the Emperor a fortnight earlier (15 August) at Cronberg, where he avoided all political topics but humoured his nephew who boasted, not for the first or for the last time, that he had devised personally the plan of campaign which Roberts had adopted during the Boer War. Hardinge, who accompanied King Edward, discussed controversial problems with the Emperor, and with the German Foreign Minister, Heinrich von Tschirschky; and the Emperor took his uncle, after luncheon at Friedrichshof Castle, to inspect a nearby Roman fort. He described at length the way in which he had caused it to be excavated and reconstructed; and the King expressed interest and asked suitable questions.

'Many thanks', King Edward wrote [2] (24 August) to Hardinge, 'for sending me a copy of your letter to Sir E. Grey, giving such a graphic and interesting account of your conversation with the Emperor William at Friedrichshof. I showed it to Sir H. C.-Bannerman who was naturally greatly interested.' The King added that although he shared Grey's view that England would have to be represented at the forthcoming Hague Conference on disarmament and the humanization of war, he agreed with the German Emperor that such discussions were tiresome and futile.

That meeting between the sovereigns at Cronberg would have been impossible a year earlier, and King Edward hoped that the atmosphere would be improved again after Haldane's visit to Berlin. The War Minister stayed with King Edward (27–30 August) at Marienbad, on his way to the German capital; and during picnics in the surrounding woods Haldane explained in outline his entire plan of army reform.

At Marienbad King Edward played croquet at that time, as well as a little golf which was helping to spread British manners throughout the world. He wore, in warm weather, a blue jacket with white trousers (creased sometimes in front and sometimes down the sides); but he was fond also of pinstripe grey suits, and his hats were either hard grey felts or the plumed green soft local product.

When shooting, the King always wore knee-breeches with thick stockings and brown shoes; and he enjoyed most being the guest either of Prince Trauttmansdorff at Bischof Teinitz, near Pilsen, or of Prince Schonburg-Waldenburg at Glatzen Plateau. He loved motoring, and Haldane recorded [3] in his autobiography:

He proposed to me one day that we should go in plain clothes as though we were Austrians, and drive out in a motor into the country and have coffee somewhere, because, he said, Austrian coffee was always admirable, and you could tell when you had crossed the frontier into Germany, because of the badness of the coffee. The first thing he did was to make me buy an Austrian hat, so as to look more like a native. . . .

As we were passing a little roadside inn, with a wooden table in front of it, the King stopped and said, 'Here I will stand treat.' He ordered coffee for two, and then he said, 'Now I am going to pay. I shall take care to give only a small tip to the woman . . . in case she suspects who I am.' We then drove on to a place the King was very fond of – a monastery inhabited by the Abbot of Teppel – where we had a large tea, and where the King enjoyed himself with the monks very much, gossiping and making himself agreeable.

The monastery of Teppel, which owned most of Marienbad and its neighbourhood, had grown rich out of taxes which it levied upon visitors, and out of the local waters which the monks bottled and sold. The abbot, who was highly intelligent, was a friend of King Edward, for whom, on 6 September 1906, he arranged a shoot; but the luncheon which preceded it was so magnificent that the bag was miserably small. After King Edward had warned his party in jest to expect nothing except bread and water, one delectable dish succeeded another and the wines were superb. Accurate shooting became impossible, and that hospitality was requited a year later in England, when the abbot visited Windsor and was conducted personally round the Castle and St George's Chapel by King Edward, before being decorated with the K.C.V.O.

King Edward signed at Marienbad an Army Order which Haldane had brought with him. It extended to the Army, as a whole, the general staff system which had been restricted previously to the War Office; and the King promised his support for more far-reaching reforms. A few months later (1 January 1907) he signed another Order which established a new model Army consisting of one cavalry and six infantry divisions, complete with commanders and staff, and splendidly equipped 'to the last trouser button', the War Minister declared.

Although the quality of that miniature expeditionary force was unsurpassed, its size (120,000 men) aroused controversy. Most of Haldane's Cabinet colleagues thought it too large and expensive, and argued that the Navy could be trusted to defend the British Isles. They had no wish to compete with the conscript armies of the continental Powers; they were convinced that the issue of any future European war would be decided within a few weeks of its outbreak; and the First Sea Lord, Sir John Fisher, agreed most warmly with those views.

On the other hand, French and German military opinion regarded the strength of that British Army as contemptible; and the French Premier, Georges Clemenceau, came to London in an attempt to persuade ministers to increase it. There was little chance of that, and most British generals and military experts appreciated that the War Minister had done his best in the existing climate of popular democratic opinion.

Haldane did well, in those circumstances, to secure approval without great difficulty for his reorganization of the Regular Army; but his Territorial and Reserve Forces Bill caused a tremendous storm. The future of the auxiliary forces – the Militia, Yeomanry and Volunteers – stirred much deeper prejudice and concerned far more people than did that of the Regular Army; and King Edward became increasingly discontented and critical.

Starting from the premise that the task of the auxiliary forces would be to repel any raid on British shores which happened to escape Fisher's vigilance, Haldane developed that argument until he had turned it inside out. He reorganized the auxiliary forces with the object of using them to maintain and, if necessary, to expand the Regular Army, after it had been despatched across the Channel to take part in a great continental war.

The Territorial and Reserve Forces Act became law in July 1907. It merged the Yeomanry and Volunteers into a Territorial Army organized in fourteen divisions and fourteen mounted brigades, which were to be equipped as perfectly as the Regular Army. After being embodied for home defence on the outbreak of war, the Territorial Army was to be intensively trained for some months, and to be invited to volunteer for service overseas at the side of the Regular Army in case of need.

Officered by cadets from training corps at public schools, universities and rifle clubs, the Territorial Army came under command of General Officers Commanding-in-Chief at home. It was, however, recruited and in part administered by the Lords Lieutenant of Counties with the aid of county associations created especially for that purpose. Haldane told the House of Commons that those county associations could look back to Cromwell and derive traditions from the Civil War; and he rounded off his work by inducing the Colonial Prime Ministers, meeting at an Imperial Conference in London, in April 1907, to agree to the immediate institution of an Imperial General Staff.

The Militia, which was much the oldest armed force in the kingdom, worried King Edward by refusing either to be merged in the Territorial Army or to undertake to feed the Regular Army in war. Exhorted by a host of backwoodsmen, among whom the Duke of Bedford was prominent, it gloried in its intransigence and had to be reconstituted by Act of Parliament as a special reserve.

King Edward continued to trust Haldane, but the doubts which he had repressed by an act of will were summoned to the surface by Sir John Fisher, and a mood of anger invaded the King's mind during the winter of 1907-8, after reforms had been implemented. He was indefatigable, nevertheless, in holding levees for Territorial officers, and in presenting colours personally to Territorial battalions; but was apprehensive [4] that 'young men in numbers sufficient to make the experiment answer, will not be forthcoming'. On that point he needed to be reassured at frequent intervals, and he summoned his Lords Lieutenant to a meeting at Buckingham Palace on 26 October 1907.

In a perfectly phrased speech, King Edward informed his Lords Lieutenant that he had revived and enhanced the importance of their ancient office. He commended the new County Territorial Associations to them, ordered them to co-operate energetically with the Secretary of State for War, and ruled, despite advice[5] from Knollys that he was moving too fast and too far, that no one should be recommended for appointment as a deputy-lieutenant who did not possess appropriate military experience.

Knollys and Fisher deprecated all talk in the royal circle about compulsory military training, which they regarded as impossible and ridiculous; but Esher agreed with King Edward that the voluntary system was on trial. He wrote[6] (30 September 1906) to Knollys: 'As you know, I am a confirmed believer in *compulsion*, but until a final experiment has been tried to get the *youth* of the Nation ... to *volunteer* for what is called Home Defence ... and until the experiment has proved a failure, there is not much hope of getting Parliament or the country to agree to the compulsory principle.'

Lord Milner had joined Lord Roberts in advocating conscription in time of peace, and King Edward knew that that was also the private but heartfelt desire of the Commander-in-Chief of the Indian Army, Lord Kitchener, who was the ablest and most famous serving soldier of the day. The King understood, however, as clearly as Kitchener did, that that policy had no chance whatever of acceptance by a Liberal Government, or by the British electorate.

Haldane regarded Kitchener as his most formidable military critic, and was delighted, for that reason, when the Cabinet extended the Commander-in-Chief's term of service in India. Kitchener was equally reluctant to come home because he hoped to succeed Minto as Viceroy of India and was anxious not to quarrel with the Liberal Government; but his comments were scathing. Besides dubbing Esher an ignorant outsider, Kitchener condemned Haldane as an unpractical theorist, and Haldane's Territorial Army as a mob of playboys who would fail in the hour of danger and contaminate the morale of any professional force with which they were permitted to associate. He argued that the Army ought to be administered as well as commanded in peace or war by a plenipotentiary Commander-in-Chief; that the Germans in any European war would 'walk through the French line like partridges'; and that such a war would be lost unless the British could contrive to train millions of men on sound professional lines for a protracted contest which would exact a degree of sacrifice and endurance to which only the American Civil War offered a faint but inadequate foretaste.

'I hope', Esher wrote [7] (4 October 1906) to Kitchener, 'you do not mind my showing your letters to the King sometimes, and perhaps you will allow me to use my judgement in doing so.' He suggested smoothly that Haldane's experiment was more likely to fail than to succeed, 'and, in that case ... we must have a National Army on a compulsory basis'.

That doubt caused King Edward to consult Haldane's military critics frequently during the winter of 1907-8; and Roberts warned the King repeatedly that the British Regular Army was the laughing-stock of Europe, owing to its diminutive size; and that the Territorial Army would be a liability in war, owing to inadequate and defective training. Roberts complained that Haldane had thrown dust into the eyes of Parliament as well as into those of the King; and Esher noted [8] (5 December 1907) that the War Minister 'resented the presence in the King's Councils of his military enemies', and (8 December) that King Edward at Sandringham had used [9] 'very strong language about Haldane'.

Rising from the bridge-table at which he had been sitting with the Duchess of Manchester, Lord Dalmeny and Arthur Sassoon, King Edward had stalked moodily into another room, while Gottlieb's orchestra, 'like a bee in a bottle', as Ponsonby sometimes complained, played music by Offenbach and Strauss in the hall. Conversation during a brief interlude, was turned upon the Army, and King Edward exclaimed that his War Minister was 'a damned radical lawyer and a German professor', and that 'all confidence in him was gone'.

Strictures of that kind were conveyed almost overnight to the ears of Haldane, who appreciated that success had provoked an inevitable reaction. He defended himself ably;

friends rallied to his aid; and Esher was indefatigable. Esher wrote,[10] for example, very candidly (8 April 1908) to King Edward:

> Your Majesty can *never*, under the Voluntary system, have an Army on the lines of a Continental Army.
>
> Your Majesty's House of Commons will not vote more than 27 or 28 millions for the support of an Army.
>
> For this sum, only a *small* Voluntary Regular Army can be maintained.
>
> In order that the whole of this small Force ... can be free to go abroad, 3 millions are spent upon an Army of 'Volunteers'. Somebody may think of a better system, but so far no one *has worked out in detail* a better plan....
>
> Mr Haldane's critics, and possible successors in Office, have other views. They do not believe in a Regular Army at all.
>
> They think that Your Majesty should depend for defence upon the Fleet alone; that India should keep her own Army, at her own cost, with depots here, to be paid by India; that Egypt should do the same; and that a small *Expeditionary* Force of 10,000 men, and a Brigade of Guards for Your Majesty's personal use, is all the Force required.
>
> It is anticipated that this would save the country at least 10 millions. Their views have got a deep hold upon some influential politicians, newspaper writers, and some of Your Majesty's Ministers.
>
> They are the alternatives to Mr Haldane's plan. Although Viscount Esher differed upon some points of detail from Mr Haldane, and does still, he nevertheless is convinced that Mr Haldane has done more for the Regular Army than any Minister since Cardwell, and that Your Majesty will be very unfortunate when he ceases to be Your Majesty's Secretary of State.

Among ministers who wanted to pare the Army to the bone, and to spend the money so saved upon old age pensions and other social benefits, were the Chancellor of the Exchequer, David Lloyd George, and the President of the Board of Trade, Winston Churchill; and King Edward, in a momentary flow of schoolboy wit, suggested[11] (6 April 1909) to the Prince of Wales, that 'the latter's initials' – W.C. – 'are well named!' The King replied[12] to Esher's letter with equal spirit from Biarritz, by the hand of Frederick Ponsonby on 11 April 1908:

The King desires me to thank you for your letter, but to tell you that he does not agree with a great deal of what you say.

His Majesty fears that you attach too much importance to the opinions of General Officers who have no alternative but to agree with the present scheme. It would be suicidal, His Majesty says, for them to disagree, and, ... if a new Secretary of State were to be appointed to-morrow, with a totally new scheme, would they not be equally obliged to back him up, or leave?...

The King says we are the laughing-stock of Europe. In all conversations reported from abroad with reference to possible combinations of Powers, the phrase constantly occurs, 'England in her present unprepared state'; and yet His Majesty is assured that the Army is in a better state than it has ever been before.

The King says that this thirst for economy has completely overshadowed the real aim, which should be efficiency. Wholesale reductions have been made to please the extreme and noisy portion of the Party. The whole scheme has become a compromise and therefore pleases neither side. It is the outcome of the mental gymnastic of a clever lawyer.

The King has no wish to have an Army anything on the lines of a Continental Army; but to reduce our already small Army in order to create a Territorial, or Visionary, Army which does not come into existence until 6 months after the declaration of war, seems madness. In any case it would have been wiser to create the Territorial Army before reducing the Regular Army.

A violent clash which occurred inside the Cabinet on the subject of the Army Estimates in June 1908 helped to draw King Edward close to Haldane again. Lloyd George and Churchill demanded a drastic reduction; Fisher assured everyone that they were right; and Knollys, who advised King Edward to observe a strict impartiality, was accused [13] unfairly by Esher of sacrificing principle to popularity. Fisher accepted very reluctantly Knollys's sensible advice that he should not impair his friendship with King Edward by interfering; but Esher implored King Edward to support Haldane openly against Lloyd George. Prudently rejecting that advice, King Edward let Haldane know privately that he hoped that he would stand firm and not resign; and the Minister won a hard-fought battle on his own. In consolidating that success, he owed something indirectly to a series of indiscretions perpetuated by the German Emperor, but he owed nothing directly to King Edward, whose confidence he nevertheless regained.

King Edward was so much impressed by his War Minister's adroitness that he appeared thereafter to be almost eager to defer to Haldane's views. In rejecting, for example, in June 1909, a submission from the Army Council that chaplains of fractional nonconformist denominations should be attached to Welsh territorial battalions, he argued angrily that no such religious spoon-feeding was thought necessary in the Regular Army. He accepted,[14] nevertheless, without further question, Haldane's emphatic advice that Welsh recruiting would be much improved; and he admitted cheerfully at the end of the year that the Minister had been right, and that the Welsh nation had been relieved in consequence of the unjust reproach of pacifism.

While doing what he could to ensure that his fleets and armies were prepared to repel aggression, King Edward continued his attempt to serve the cause of peace by para-diplomatic activity. Upon hearing, for example, that the Russian Foreign Minister was in Paris, he wrote[15] eagerly (19 October 1906) from Scotland to Charles Hardinge: 'The great M. Isvolsky is at Paris ... I would give anything to see him, and that you and Sir E. Grey could also do so, as there are so many important matters to be discussed. ... How is this to be managed? I leave here to-morrow and shall be in town by 7.'

Hardinge informed Isvolsky by telegram at once that King Edward had returned to London in the hope that a meeting might be arranged; and the Minister's vanity was so much excited that he crossed the Channel and came to London for forty-eight hours. Hardinge noted[16] that that visit, which 'was entirely due to King Edward's initiative', and which 'helped materially to smooth the path of the negotiations then in progress for an agreement with Russia ... was just one of those many instances when King Edward's "flair" of what was right was so good and beneficial to our foreign relations'.

The progress of those negotiations fascinated King Edward, who followed in much greater detail than was usual with him the hard bargaining on Afghanistan, Persia, the Persian Gulf and Tibet. Apart from the *entente* with France, nothing pleased him so well as the successful negotiation of the *entente* with Russia; but German suspicion of his motives was unbalanced and hysterical.

After staying at Chatsworth in January 1907, King Edward took Queen Alexandra (2 February) on a week's private visit to Paris. Many years had passed since he had invited the Queen to accompany him to the French capital; and Esher noted [17] that 'her joy was the joy of a girl – she cried it from the house-tops'. Queen Alexandra had been feeling low and depressed, and her friend, Lord Carrington, recorded [18] that her spirits, which were improved by that visit, were raised again, immediately after it, when her sister, the Dowager Empress Marie Feodorovna of Russia, came to stay with her in England for the first time in thirty-four years.

The freedom, comfort and luxury of life at Buckingham Palace and Windsor Castle made a tremendous impression upon the Dowager Empress, who wrote [19] (13 March 1907) to her son, the Emperor Nicholas:

How happily we are all living together! ... We spent Sunday at Windsor. It was the 44th anniversary of Aunt Alex's wedding! We went by car.... After lunch we went over the Castle – I have no words to describe *how magnificent* it all is. Aunt Alex's rooms are remarkably beautiful and cosy – I must say, they are the same here, at Buckingham Palace. Everything is so tastefully and artistically arranged – it makes one's mouth water to see all this magnificence! ...

I do wish you, too, could come over here a little, to breathe another air.... How *good* for you that would be! I myself feel as if I were a different person – and *twenty years* younger!'

In Paris, before that visit, King Edward and Queen Alexandra, calling themselves Duke and Duchess of Lancaster, took over the British Embassy where Sir Francis Bertie, who had intended to move to a hotel, was immobilized by influenza; and the Queen was thrilled at being taken for the first time in her life to lunch and dine in the public rooms of restaurants. It was considered necessary, in 1907, to prevent such unusual relaxations from being reported in newspapers; and the eagerness to cooperate, which editors displayed, would have been inconceivable ten years later.

Lord Northcliffe wrote,[20] for example (2 June 1908), from the offices of the *Daily Mail* to Lord Knollys:

The editors of newspapers are really very glad to receive any hint as to what or what not to publish. Sometimes, when His Majesty is at Marienbad or Biarritz, we shall be very glad to be told what to print, and what to omit.

The King has become such an immense personality in England that, as you may have noticed, the space devoted to the movements of Royalty has quintupled since His Majesty came to the Throne, and our difficulties have increased in proportion.

King Edward's freedom to enjoy a reasonable private life, which depended upon the observance of a species of taboo by the Press, necessitated also the exercise of great restraint upon his part and upon that of members of his Household. That restraint was normally displayed, but Lord Carrington noted [21] (3 February 1907) in his diary an occasion which tried the Press hard when several members of the royal household involved themselves carelessly in a City scandal:

A Siberian gold-mining company * has been formed by some Jew speculators. Francis Knollys, Lord Stanley, Lord Howe, Sir West Ridgeway and others accepted directorships, and the shares were rushed up to £16. They have gone down with a rattle, and Horace Farquhar [Master of the Royal Household] is said to have netted £70,000. He is supposed to have secured all those names, and the papers are open-mouthed at this scandal. It is deplorable that the King's private secretary and the Queen's Lord Chamberlain should have been 'let in' and mixed up in an affair like this.

King Edward enjoyed a flutter on the Stock Exchange as much as he enjoyed a stroll along the Paris boulevards, and into shops, with the Queen upon his arm; and the German

* Siberian Proprietary Mines Ltd. was registered on 8 August 1905 with Lord Knollys and Lord Stanley as two of its directors. It acquired two subsidiaries with more directors; and after the shares had bounced up and down, critical comment appeared in *The Times* (12 and 31 January 1907) as well as in other newspapers.

Press was often uninhibited in reading fantastic motives into his activities. He lunched during that excursion to Paris with the French President, and entertained the Premier and many friends in the social and official worlds; and he was accused, in consequence, of harbouring Machiavellian designs. That German Press campaign became even more offensive when the King, after leaving England again on 4 March for Biarritz, embarked (6 April) at Toulon with the Queen on another Mediterranean cruise.

While travelling abroad King Edward never ceased to attend to a great variety of business. From Biarritz, for example, on 8 March 1907, he warned [22] the Prime Minister that in raising the Nile barrage Sir Ernest Cassel proposed to submerge the Temple of Philae, and that 'all antiquaries would regret the loss of this beautiful relic of Egyptian history'. He continued to grumble to Esher and Knollys about the ministers' failure to consult and write to him more frequently, and he expressed [23] disgust to Knollys (12 March 1907) at the woolly tone of an article advocating disarmament which the Prime Minister had contributed to the first issue of The Nation, as well as at the Prime Minister's action in 'backing up the Woman's Franchise Bill'. Describing both actions as 'so unnecessary, and latter so undignified', he added, 'I suppose he will support the Channel Tunnel Bill next week!'

King Edward was especially vexed at not being kept informed about the proceedings of a Cabinet committee which was considering the problem of the House of Lords; and Knollys warned [24] Campbell-Bannerman (23 March) that the King insisted upon being consulted before any recommendations 'of grave constitutional character' were adopted. Whenever he wanted to complain King Edward much preferred to write through Knollys, but he wrote [25] personally (29 March) to Campbell-Bannerman when the Cabinet made up its mind to oppose the Channel Tunnel Bill:

I rejoice to see that you 'put your foot down' regarding the Channel Tunnel, when the matter was put forward in the House of Commons. I only wish you could have done the same regarding Female Suffrage. The conduct of the so-called 'Suffragettes'

has really been so outrageous, and does their cause (for which
I have no sympathy) much harm.

Before leaving Biarritz, King Edward refused an invitation
to pay a state visit to King Alfonso of Spain in Madrid. The
place was reported to be swarming with anarchists, and the
reputation of the Spanish police was poor; but a meeting
was arranged at Cartagena, where King Edward arrived on
8 April, escorted impressively by the entire British Mediterranean Fleet. 'Alfonso', King Edward informed [26] the Prince
of Wales (10 April), 'has created me a Captain-General in
his Army, and I wore the uniform at dinner last night. He
appeared as a 16th Lancer, which suited him very well.' But
the main object of that visit was political, and Hardinge,
who again accompanied King Edward as Minister in Attendance, scored an important diplomatic success.

By means of a secret exchange of notes, England, France
and Spain guaranteed each other's possessions throughout
the Mediterranean area; and every effort was made to prevent news of that transaction from reaching the jealous ears
of the German Foreign Office. The Germans, nevertheless,
discovered quickly what had happened, and that rebuff to
territorial aspirations which they cherished in that area
exacerbated opinion in Berlin.

From Cartagena King Edward and Queen Alexandra
visited Malta before cruising to South Italy and Sicily; and
the Mediterranean Fleet again provided an escort when
they met the King and Queen of Italy at Gaeta. That occasion was purely social and immensely enjoyable; but the
German Emperor denounced his uncle as a satanic encircler bent upon ringing Germany with enemies, and that
neurotic attitude was reflected in the German Press.

King Edward informed [27] the Prince of Wales (25 April)
that 'the damned nonsense' broadcast in the German Press
'does not hurt *me*'; but he caused Ponsonby to write [28] that
day to Hardinge, who had returned to London, in order to
ask that a formal protest should be made to the German
Ambassador, Count Metternich, 'at the comments in the
German papers on this cruise. With the exception of the
visit to Cartagena, which was a return visit, this cruise has

been entirely a private one, for pleasure. Yet, in Germany, they have imputed to His Majesty the most sinister motives, and accused him of deep-laid plots against Germany.' Sir Edward Grey was strongly averse from making any formal protest, and the Ambassador was, in any case, on leave. Hardinge was authorized, however, to say a private word to the German Chargé d'Affaires whose statement, that 'the German Press has gone mad and seems hardly accountable for its actions', was formally recorded.[29]

On the journey home through Paris at the beginning of May, Ponsonby noted[30] a characteristic incident. King Edward derived great pleasure always from a lavish distribution of the many presents which he carried with him, but was much too impatient sometimes to remember their relative values, and was liable to become exasperated if any kind of hitch occurred. All the gold cigarette cases, with or without the royal cypher in diamonds, had been given away at Biarritz and at Cartagena, in Malta, South Italy and Sicily; and King Edward wanted to present something in Paris to a racehorse owner who had shown him his stables. He sent a servant, accordingly, to ask Ponsonby to write a suitable letter enclosing a silver cigarette case with the royal cypher in enamel.

Because he considered that so shoddy a gift would harm King Edward's reputation, Ponsonby ordered the servant to return the silver case to store. It might have pleased a detective or a station-master, but it appeared unsuitable for a rich racehorse owner; and Ponsonby instructed the servant to inform the King that a gold case would be despatched from London.

King Edward stalked soon afterwards into Ponsonby's room; 'and I saw at once that he was really very angry and was trying to control himself. Slowly and deliberately he put his hat, gloves and stick on the table, and then said quietly, "Did you send me a message that the cigarette case I had chosen was not good enough?" I trembled inwardly, but replied in the affirmative'; and King Edward proceeded to abuse Ponsonby 'in a voice that shook the whole hotel'. That 'flood of oratory, delivered in a deafening tone', reduced the secretary 'to a state of speechless terror', and he only made matters worse by trying to excuse himself. 'I thought', Ponsonby recorded, 'His Majesty would have a fit, but suddenly he calmed down', and after dictating to some- one else, a charming letter to the racehorse owner, he ordered that it and the silver case should be despatched forthwith, and then departed, 'slamming the door'.

That evening, the King showed Ponsonby a fulsome letter of thanks, exclaiming: 'This shows what damned nonsense you talked!' Ponsonby retorted stupidly that it would have been difficult for any recipient to have written anything else; and King Edward's anger blazed anew. Normally, after losing his temper, he did his utmost to make amends, but he did not do so on that occasion and nearly two years passed before Ponsonby made up his mind that King Edward had really agreed with him, and that pride had pre- vented him from saying so. Light appeared to dawn in February 1909, in Berlin, when the King, prostrated by a chill, was unable to attend to anything. 'I must leave the presents entirely to you', King Edward remarked to Pon- sonby on that occasion, 'and I know that you will do every- thing perfectly – and not give anything shoddy, like I did in Paris.'

In June 1907, King Edward encountered renewed difficulty in connection with the Order of the Garter; but he emerged victorious from a minor tussle with his Government. The King of Siam visited London in the full expectation of re- ceiving it, but he was an intelligent autocrat with a feline sense of humour and was sincerely anxious that the matter should be forgotten when King Edward refused to confer it upon the Sovereign of a country which had not then attained its present importance. Some Siamese ministers were reported, nevertheless, to be afraid that they might be decapitated for having misled their Sovereign; the British Foreign Office, which had not been guiltless, was most anxious to avoid unpleasantness; and Hardinge, who recorded [31] that 'it was an awkward affair altogether', left Grey to press the matter upon King Edward. The Cabinet yielded reluctantly to an opposition which appeared adamantine; and the King won an additional victory in a dispute with the Treasury about the broad principle of meeting expenses of foreign royal visits.

It had been agreed, at the start of the reign, that the State should defray any expense incurred by King Edward in entertaining foreign sovereigns, but the Treasury had expected that a distinction would be drawn between visits which possessed a political importance and visits which were purely private. Writing [32] (1 April 1907) to Knollys, after previous correspondence, the Joint Permanent Secretary to the Treasury, Sir Edward Hamilton, asked that Knollys or Probyn should notify every future visit to the Chancellor of the Exchequer, who would 'refer officially to the Secretary of State for Foreign Affairs'.

King Edward regarded all visits by foreign sovereigns as state visits, and he stoutly refused to budge. Knollys wrote [33] accordingly (3 April) to Sir Edward Hamilton:

As I understand it, the Secretary of State for Foreign Affairs would decide what visits were of 'political importance' and what not, and the Treasury would only pay for the former.

His Majesty, however, has his own views respecting the importance, from a political point of view, of visits of Foreign Sovereigns to this country, which might not coincide with those of the Secretary of State. . . .

If the proposal in question were, therefore, to be carried into effect, there might be constant conflicts between the King on one side, and the Treasury and Foreign Office on the other. . . .

Gladstone had once proclaimed [34] (at Edinburgh on 29 November 1874) that 'it is the mark of a chicken-hearted Chancellor when he shrinks from upholding economy in detail. . . . He is not worth his salt if he is not ready to save what are meant by candle-ends and cheese-parings.' When King Edward threatened, however, on his return from the Mediterranean, to send immediately for the Prime Minister and to 'tell him that he will not stand such an attempted evasion by the Treasury of what was agreed upon in 1901, that particular attempt at cheese-paring economy was dropped.

After visiting Wales, where he made an official tour wholly by car for the first time, King Edward crossed the Irish Chan-

nel (10 July 1907) to visit an International Exhibition at
Dublin. He attended Leopardstown Races on the day of his
arrival, and was exceedingly angry at being informed by the
Viceroy, Lord Aberdeen, with whom he stayed, that the
Crown Jewels of the Order of St Patrick had been stolen a
month earlier from Dublin Castle. That loss had only been
discovered a day or two before, and the mystery which veiled
it was never pierced. King Edward insisted that Ulster King-
at-Arms, Sir Arthur Vicars, who was responsible for the safe
custody of the jewels should be suspended from office while
an inquiry was held in public; but, although rumour insisted
that the robber was highly placed, the jewels were never
recovered. After being described officially as negligent,
Vicars was dismissed, while his three assistants were permitted to resign; and King Edward, who remained profoundly dissatisfied, was thankful that worse scandal had
been avoided.

Taking advantage of a complete cessation of the virulent
German Press campaign, King Edward invited the Emperor
William to spend five days at Windsor during November;
and the Emperor, in accepting, asked that the King, on his
way to Marienbad, should meet him at the Palace of Wilhelmshöhe, near Cassel. On that occasion (14 August), despite an exhausting and flamboyant military display, the
Emperor was so gay, modest and charming that King
Edward expressed [35] (21 August) to the Prince of Wales his
intense relief and delight. All political talk was barred in the
presence of both sovereigns, but the King asked the Emperor
to stay for a week instead of five days at Windsor; and Sir
Charles Hardinge had a satisfactory exchange of views with
the Imperial Chancellor, Prince Bülow.

Leaving Cassel late on 14 August by train, using the beautifully appointed private coaches in which he always travelled on the Continent, King Edward was met next morning at Gmunden by the old Austrian Emperor, Francis
Joseph, and by what he termed a mob of archdukes and
archduchesses. He was escorted to Ischl, an agreeable spa in
the mountains, where Hardinge discussed every subject of
possible controversy with the Austrian Foreign Minister,

Baron von Aehrenthal, before reporting [36] (21 August) about both meetings to Sir Edward Grey:

> Although the King was outwardly on the best of terms with the German Emperor, and laughed and joked with him, I could not help noticing that there was no real intimacy between them. ...
>
> On the other hand, the relations between the King and the Emperor of Austria appeared to me to be of the most friendly and intimate character. They seemed to delight in each other's company and were practically inseparable. ...

Grey congratulated King Edward upon the results of both meetings which had afforded opportunities for an exchange of views; and he was pleased when the King invited Clemenceau to meet him immediately afterwards at Marienbad. Hardinge assured [37] King Edward that that well-advised action 'has given great satisfaction in France, and has allayed any susceptibilities or suspicions to which the French are too prone'; and King Edward replied [38] (30 August) that he wished Hardinge to know that 'the idea emanated from my fertile brain!!!'

While completing his cure, King Edward attended, on 29 August, a play entitled *Die Hölle* (*The Underworld*), which the theatre at Marienbad had advertised as a melodrama. It was, however, an uninspired variety show in rather poor taste, and the King left, soon after the beginning of the second act, because he was bored. Newspapers headlined that incident, and King Edward was amazed to receive sackfuls of letters from England, expressing loyal gratitude for the stand which he was alleged to have taken in the cause of morality. The Bishop of Ripon (Boyd-Carpenter), who often preached before the royal family, sent a flowery letter on behalf of the whole body of the Church of England, and Ponsonby asked what reply should be sent. King Edward who felt that at Marienbad, if anywhere, he had a right to be a man among men exclaimed [39]: 'Tell the truth, of course. I have no wish to pose as a protector of morals, especially abroad.'

On 31 August, after lunching with Sir John Fisher and taking tea with Count Benckendorff, the well-liked Russian

Ambassador in London, King Edward was informed by telegram that the Anglo-Russian Convention had been signed that day in St Petersburg by Sir Arthur Nicolson and by Alexander Isvolsky, the Russian Foreign Minister. That agreement, to which King Edward and the Emperor Nicholas affixed their signatures three weeks later, had been under discussion for four years and in process of detailed negotiations for one; and it was, as Hardinge recorded [40] 'the triumph of King Edward's policy of which the Anglo-French *entente* was the first step'.

During the course of those difficult negotiations King Edward had protested several times that, although Persia was split into spheres of influence between the high contracting Powers, the predominant British interest in the Persian Gulf was insufficiently stressed. Isvolsky was afraid of a clash with Germany in that area on the issue of the projected Berlin-Baghdad railroad, but Hardinge assured the King that the mere existence of a treaty was of greater importance than its actual content. He recorded [41] that although 'its terms might have been more advantageous to England in certain respects, it served its purpose and maintained peace and friendly relations between England and Russian for ten years, That was the aim in view....'

King Edward, who was immensely pleased, and who telegraphed warm congratulations to his Government and to Sir Arthur Nicolson, had already telegraphed some days earlier to invite Isvolsky to come to Marienbad. He informed Hardinge that Isvolsky had accepted, and Hardinge replied [42] (1 September) that 'that audience will complete the chain of interviews of last month, which I feel confident will be productive of good results', and that King Edward would be well-advised to lavish flattery upon the Minister, 'as Isvolsky is essentially a vain man'.

On 5 September – the day before he left Marienbad for England – King Edward entertained Isvolsky to luncheon, and dictated a note [43] of the interview. He avoided the subject of the Persian Gulf, but extracted an admission that the two previous Czars had been unable to restrain ambitious generals and officials from continuously extending

Russian boundaries in Central Asia, and that the British had had good cause for suspicion. On the subject of Afghanistan, Isvolsky said that 'it would be hard for anybody to realize the difficulties with which he had had to contend from the reactionary party and, to a certain extent, from the military party'; but that the military party had lost influence because Russia could not face another war.

After lauding Isvolsky for his service to the cause of peace, King Edward told the Minister that all future difficulties would be solved easily, 'in a spirit of give and take, now that the ice was so effectually broken'. With that note in his pocket, he returned rejoicing to Buckingham Palace on the evening of 7 September, and was up next morning in time to take exercise at seven-thirty in the garden before entertaining Sir Charles Hardinge, two hours later, to a hearty breakfast.

21
Russia

KING EDWARD was not expected to visit the great variety of factories and institutions which have claimed so much of his successors' time, but he appeared very much more frequently in public than Queen Victoria had ever done. He delighted his subjects, became constantly more popular, and made a point of spending three or four days once a year, during July, in some pullulating industrial centre. On those occasions he liked to stay in a congenial house party with a neighbouring territorial magnate, while inaugurating universities, docks, bridges or hospitals; and he relished the pleasure which he gave by conferring knighthoods in public upon mayors.

London hospitals were King Edward's chosen field of charitable work, and he used a gift of two hundred thousand pounds from Sir Ernest Cassel, in 1901, to found a sanatorium for tuberculosis. Wishing to help patients of the lower middle class, he specified clergymen, clerks, governesses, 'persons skilled in art', schoolteachers and young officers constrained to live upon their pay; but he was disgusted by the incompetence displayed by the committee. Mistakes caused anger and frustration to invade the King's mind and to destroy almost the whole of his interest before he performed the opening ceremony at Midhurst on 13 June 1906.

On the other hand, King Edward continued to take pride in the progress of King Edward's Hospital Fund, which he had started as Prince of Wales in 1897; and its annual income was increased from about fifty thousand to nearly one hundred and sixty thousand pounds during his reign: 'My greatest ambition', the King wrote [1] (23 October 1908) to Sir

Frederick Treves, 'is not to quit this world till a real cure for cancer has been found, and I feel convinced that radium will be the means of doing so!' He suffered[2] in 1906 from an ulcer, which was believed at first to be malignant, between his right eye and the root of his nose; but it was cured by radium in 1907, and for that reason he induced Lord Iveagh and Sir Ernest Cassell to found a Radium Institute in London, on the lines of the one in Paris.

The agonizing death's from cancer of the Empress Frederick, and of her husband, the gentle Emperor whom he had really loved, preyed upon King Edward's mind; and the contrast between what was and what might have been, tormented him whenever he had to meet their son. Preparations for the Emperor William's State visit, which was due on 11 November 1907, had been supervised in detail by King Edward, who was astonished to receive on 31 October at Newmarket a most extraordinary telegram. It announced[3] that his nephew was feeling tired and weak after 'bronchitis and acute cough effect of a virulent attack of influenza', and that he had decided not to come after all.

Sir Edward Grey suggested that a hint, conveyed through the Foreign Office, that an escort of German battleships would be inconvenient at Portsmouth, had caused that diplomatic illness; but no one could be sure. Prince Bülow thought that the impending trial of Count Philip Eulenburg for homosexual offences had caused Eulenburg's friend, the Emperor, to dread a cool reception. Whatever the reason, bad feeling would have resulted if that visit had been cancelled at the last moment, and the strongest possible pressure was applied to the Emperor by King Edward and the British Government, as well as by the German Foreign Office.

The visitors, accordingly, disembarked as planned from the imperial yacht *Hohenzollern* at Portsmouth on 11 November. They were drawn immediately by special train to Windsor; and when 180 guests were entertained to a banquet in St George's Hall on the following evening, King Edward could not resist a mischievous reference to his nephew's illness. 'For a long time', he declared, in proposing the healths of the Emperor and Empress, 'we have looked forward to this visit, and were dismayed at hearing recently that it could not take place, owing to indisposition. We are delighted, nevertheless, to see both your Imperial Majesties looking now in splendid health, which we must hope that your stay, however brief, in our country will further benefit'

King Edward declined absolutely to discuss politics with the Emperor or with any of his German guests. He left that business to his ministers, who reported fully to him; and he toyed with the idea of causing Haldane, who played a very helpful part, to be lifted from the War Office and despatched to Berlin as ambassador in place of Sir Frank Lascelles, who was reputed to be incapable of expressing disagreement with the Emperor, and who was due to retire during the autumn of 1908.

On 13 November the Emperor visited London and drove in procession to a luncheon at Guildhall. On being presented by the Lord Mayor with an address in a gold casket, he declared amid thunderous applause that 'blood is thicker than water'; and the enthusiasm of the crowds which lined the streets was uninhibited. King Edward had personally organized shoots, massed choirs, theatrical performances and banquets for the entertaining of his guests; and on 16 November, when the Emperor drove again to London, Esher recorded [4]:

The Banquet last night was said by the Germans to be finer than any spectacular display of the kind they had even seen. . . .

It is the juxtaposition of medievalism and the 20th century – the Castle itself, the lines of Beefeaters in their gorgeous dresses, and the luxury of gold plate, flowers and diamonds which impresses them.

Our King makes a better show than William II. He has more graciousness and dignity. . . .

The German Emperor failed to impress British ministers. He wasted much of the first of two long talks with Grey by declaiming wildly against the Jews; and, in discussing the projected Berlin-Baghdad railroad during the second, he displayed little real grasp of the issues involved. The Empress returned to Germany after a week's stay at Windsor, but the Emperor caused dismay by insisting upon remaining privately in England for another month. Fears were entertained that by perpetrating some fresh indiscretion he would nullify all the goodwill which had been generated; and as early as 1 September King Edward expressed[5] relief to Hardinge that a proposed visit by his nephew to Lord Lonsdale at Lowther Castle had been abandoned.

Highcliffe, near Bournemouth, was rented instead from Colonel E. J. Montagu-Stuart-Wortley, who had served with Kitchener in the Sudan and who became the Emperor's guest. Accounts of the fantastic imperial table-talk at Bournemouth reached London clubs and drawing-rooms; but nothing appeared in the Press until 28 October 1908, when the *Daily Telegraph* printed, in the guise of an interview, with Wortley's help and the Emperor's full approval, a report which caused amazement throughout the world.

Like George IV, who persuaded himself in old age that he had charged at the head of his regiment, the 10th Hussars, at Waterloo, the Emperor William appeared to suffer from a fixed delusion about the Boer War. He had corresponded with his grandmother and uncle in 1899 and 1900 about the best method of conducting the campaign, and had convinced himself that Lord Roberts had adopted his so-called strategic plan. He had bored and perplexed King Edward by referring to that plan on several occasions, and Esher recorded[6] (31 October 1908) that the King had ordered him to disinter everything which could be found relating to it in the archives at Windsor. When he showed the result to King Edward three days later, after typing it himself, both agreed that it could only be described as 'farcical' and 'almost childish'; and a reply by Haldane to a question about the Emperor's plan in the House of Commons evoked gusts of derisive laughter.

Besides claiming much of the credit for the British conquest of the Boer republics, the Emperor told Wortley at Bournemouth that the English were 'mad as March hares' in not acknowledging him to be their best friend. He alleged that he had sacrificed the political interests of Germany on the altar of his English family affections by vetoing proposals for an anti-British continental coalition at the start of the Boer War; that he alone was capable of holding in check the anti-British sentiments of a majority of his subjects; and that he was cruelly misunderstood. That irresponsible chatter did his reputation incalculable harm because it appeared to confirm suspicions that he was unbalanced at times; and he forfeited so much prestige at home that the German military and naval chiefs did not even hesitate before taking control automatically during the supreme crisis of July–August, 1914.

From the Jockey Club, on 30 October 1908, the King informed Hardinge [7] that even 'light-hearted and non-serious racing and society men' had been profoundly impressed by the egregious folly of the German Emperor; and that 'of all the political gaffes which H.I.M. has made, this is the greatest'. Another followed, however, after barely a fortnight's delay, when the Emperor, in an effort to appease German opinion, gave an interview to W. B. Hale of the *New York World*.

The Emperor told Hale that King Edward was personally corrupt, that his Court was rotten, that his country was heading for disaster, and that an Anglo-German war was inevitable; and although, under strong pressure from the German Foreign Office, the *New York World* apologized publicly for that report, which it had had every right to print, the mischief was done and King Edward was most deeply affronted. Despite a letter from Count Paul Metternich, the German ambassador in London, enclosing the Emperor's categorical written repudiation of the remarks attributed to him, King Edward wrote [8] (25 November 1908) to Lord Knollys, from Castle Rising where he was shooting with Lord Farquhar:

My dear Francis,
    After your leaving with me Count Metternich's letter, with the German Emperor's emphatic denial, I have, I presume, nothing more to do than to accept it. I am, however, convinced in my mind that the words attributed to the G.E. by Mr Hale are perfectly correct. I know the E. *hates* me, and never loses an opportunity of saying so (behind my back) whilst I have always been civil and nice to him.
    As regards my visit to Berlin, there is no hurry to settle

anything at present. The Foreign Office, to gain their own object, will not care a pin what humiliation I have to put up with. ...

King Edward's staff deplored the effect of that painful incident upon his health. It caused another fit of profound depression, after an earlier one into which he had been plunged as a result of the assassination (1 February 1908) of King Carlos of Portugal and the Crown Prince; and King Edward's doctors begged him in consequence to double the length of his normal stay at Biarritz.

King Edward's first thought, after the Portuguese assassinations, had been to secure the position of the boy-King Manuel, who did not dare to leave his palace in Lisbon even to take the necessary oath before the Cortes. Luis Soveral, the Portuguese Minister in London, implored the Foreign Office to send a British fleet to Lisbon to prevent revolution; and, in endorsing that request, King Edward told [9] Hardinge (10 March) that British residents and commercial interests were entitled to protection. He added [10] (24 March) that 'we cannot allow a state of anarchy to exist', and that in consequence 'we ought to have ships ready at a moment's notice to proceed to Lisbon, tho' naturally we have no desire to interfere in their normal internal affairs, unless they become of an alarming nature!'

The Foreign Office replied that, by precipitating civil war, such action might imperil the lives and interests which it was intended to protect; and King Edward, who accepted that advice with good temper, was disgusted when Soveral showed a tendency to sulk. After the assassination of King Carlos, João Franco, the dictator of Portugal, fled to Italy overnight; and King Edward told Soveral, who had been on excellent terms with the fallen dictator, that it was his duty to declare his loyalty to the boy-King and to the new government forthwith. He warned Soveral that he would forfeit all respect otherwise, and he informed [11] Hardinge (31 March) that he hoped to save the Minister from degenerating into a mere 'London *flaneur* – a position which, *entre nous*, is, I think, not distasteful to him!'

King Manuel kept his crown until October 1910, when a republic was established and he fled to England; and King

Edward, who did his best to inject courage into the weak young ruler, displayed his own forcefulness in a dramatic manner. Ignoring militant Protestant protests, he ordered a sovereign's escort of cavalry to attend him (8 February 1908) on a drive through London to St James's Roman Catholic Church, Spanish Place, where he was present with the Queen during the celebration of a Requiem Mass for the murdered King. A few rude newspapers commented that even James II had hesitated before attending Mass in State; but King Edward attended a Church of England memorial service also, in St Paul's Cathedral next day.

King Edward was greatly worried at that time by the state of the Prime Minister's health. Campbell-Bannerman embarrassed all his colleagues by refusing to recognize that his illness was mortal and that he ought to resign; but during a half-hour's talk at the Prime Minister's bedside in Downing Street on 4 March, King Edward said that it would be inconvenient to him personally if there were any talk or even thought of resignation until he had returned from abroad early in May.

After discussing the position with Asquith, who was deputizing for the Prime Minister, King Edward left on 5 March for a six weeks' holiday at Biarritz. Asquith promised that, if anything happened to Campbell-Bannerman, he would come out immediately to Biarritz. He added that he would make no changes in the Cabinet, and that he would continue to serve for a time as Chancellor of the Exchequer after kissing hands formally as Prime Minister.

King Edward was still sufficiently annoyed at that time with Haldane to ask that he should be moved from the War Office, but Asquith demurred and Haldane was restored presently to favour. Asquith decided, nevertheless, on reflection, that Tweedmouth would have to be moved from the Admiralty, and that some other immediate changes would be desirable; and Knollys complained [12] (22 March) to Esher that, in those circumstances, 'it would be a little difficult for all the people affected ... to go to Biarritz. ... I doubt, too, whether, except in very calm weather, a ship could lie off Biarritz, and then what could be done?'

Campbell-Bannerman died on 22 April 1908, after resigning a fortnight earlier; and Knollys, who had remained, as always, in England, was greatly troubled by King Edward's attitude, because it appeared selfish:

I wrote to him, [Knollys informed [13] Asquith on 30 March] as I told you I should, to recommend that he should come home towards the middle of April for the necessary Privy Council and kissing of hands; and I pointed out to him that it would not look at all well that these ceremonies should take place at Paris, which is so near to England, or that Ministers should troop over there for the necessary formalities.

He does not, however, like the idea of returning to London previous to his departure for his Northern visits. When you see him, I hope you will urge upon him as strongly as possible the propriety of his coming back.

I am *sure* he ought to return, and I have gone as far, and perhaps further, in what I have said to him than I am entitled to go.

But of course he will attach far more weight to your opinion on this subject, speaking as Prime Minister, than to mine.

On 2 April Knollys wrote again [14] to warn King Edward that he would place himself 'in a false position' if he were to attempt to press Asquith to delay the reconstruction of his Cabinet; and at Biarritz on 8 April, King Edward promised [15] Asquith that he would return to England on 16 April in time to hold a Privy Council that evening. He had arranged to leave on 20 April for Denmark, Norway and Sweden; and Hardinge advised [16] him (30 March) to allow his visit to Stockholm to be described as official, and to ignore the strict protocol which required the King of Sweden to visit England first. Hardinge added that in that case the Treasury would be obliged to foot the bill, and King Edward retorted [17] (2 April) that no doubt about that had ever existed and that 'of course, Treasury, as usual, will have to "pay the piper".'

Asquith reached Biarritz on 7 April and kissed hands as Prime Minister next morning. King Edward, who noted [18] that the Prime Minister had looked 'very tired' on arrival, accepted Lloyd George as Chancellor of the Exchequer, Reginald McKenna as First Lord of the Admiralty, Lord

Crewe as Colonial Secretary, and Winston Churchill and Walter Runciman as Presidents respectively of the Boards of Trade and Education, with seats in the Cabinet.

The inconvenience caused to the House of Commons by Asquith's journey to Biarritz, and to ministers by King Edward's delay in returning home, provoked widespread criticism; and it was evident that a mistake had been made. King Edward refused to plead ill-health, and some newspapers accused him for the first time in his reign of a dereliction of duty. He was so popular that the affair blew over quickly, and the House of Commons preserved a loyal silence; but *The Times* printed a venomous leading article (8 April) which the King hotly resented. After instituting inquiries, he discovered that it had been written by Colonel Repington, military correspondent of *The Times*, who nursed a personal grudge. Repington has been compelled to resign his commission in 1902 as a result of some discreditable divorce proceedings, and he knew that King Edward had rejected a plea by Roberts and a submission by Haldane that such an able man ought to be reinstated.

'Please bring with you on our journey', King Edward wrote [19] (7 April) to Hardinge, 'all the information you possess regarding the North Sea Treaties with the 3 Scandinavian Kingdoms, as our memory will require to be much refreshed on the subject!'; but King Gustavus V of Sweden was King Edward's principal target. Anglo-Swedish relations had been badly strained for three years, since Norway's assertion of her independence of the Swedish crown; and a great State banquet in Stockholm on 26 April 1908, when a record number of 250 guests were entertained, helped to restore cordiality.

That visit to the three Northern capitals was enjoyable and successful; and within twenty-four hours of his return (4 May) to Buckingham Palace, King Edward received Asquith in audience and agreed to pay a State visit to the Russian Emperor in June. Hardinge informed [20] the King (7 May) that Asquith and Grey were convinced that that visit 'will be productive of great good'; and he continued:

The visit will be considered an official one; but, in the event of questions in Parliament, stress will be laid on the personal character of the visit, and on the relationship between Your Majesty and the Emperor of Russia. ...

It is very important that this matter should be kept as secret as possible, and as long as possible; but I very much fear that now the Cabinet know of Your Majesty's project, it will be impossible to maintain secrecy. ... The sole object in keeping the matter quiet, is to avoid questions from the extreme members in the House of Commons.

Such questions were inevitable on the occasion of the only visit ever paid by a British sovereign to Russia; and rumours about a Russian alliance, and a Russian loan, filled the air almost at once. Grey found it expedient, therefore, to make a formal announcement in the House of Commons on 27 May, while the French president, Armand Fallières, was in London on a State visit, but staying, as the head of a republic, at the French Embassy and not at Buckingham Palace.

Grey informed the House of Commons that the King in his yacht would meet the Emperor of Russia in his yacht off Reval (which has been renamed Tallin) in the Baltic, and that no new treaty was contemplated; but many British Radicals and Socialists were enraged. Their hatred of the czarist autocracy was understandable, and Ramsay MacDonald, who sat for Leicester, described the Russian Emperor (in a newspaper article) as a 'common murderer'.

A debate on King Edward's forthcoming excursion was staged, accordingly, in the House of Commons on 4 June; and a motion critical of the Government's action in authorizing it was defeated by 225 votes against 59. Efforts were made to spare the feelings of the King, who was accused, nevertheless, by Keir Hardie, the leader of the Labour Party, of condoning atrocities; and although the Speaker ruled that comment out of order, King Edward's anger blazed. He was so incensed by the tone of the debate that he visited his displeasure immediately upon three members of the House.

King Edward had announced his intention of inviting all members of Parliament to a garden party at Windsor Castle on 20 June; but he commanded unwisely that two Socialists, Victor Grayson and Keir Hardie, who had spoken and voted against his Russian journey, as well as the Liberal member for Stirling, Arthur Ponsonby* (a brother of Frederick), who had merely voted against it, should be omitted from the list of invitations. He was especially vexed with Ponsonby, who had been secretary to Campbell-Bannerman, because he considered that a son of Queen Victoria's old friend and secretary, Sir Henry Ponsonby, ought to have been more discreet.

For that reason King Edward signified, after the garden party had taken place, that Grayson and Keir Hardie had purged their offence and would be invited on future occasions, but that Ponsonby would be excluded from Court until an apology had been tendered; and the bronchial trouble which helped to inspire that arbitrary action imparted an autocratic flavour to other royal social decrees that summer. Some people felt, for example, that King Edward had been disturbed unreasonably when Countess Torby, whom he liked, and who was the morganatic wife of the Grand Duke Michael of Russia, seated herself on the Duchesses' bench at a Court Ball; and others considered that he had been a little severe with the Marlboroughs who were in process of separating. Some strict Victorian conventions dissolved in the sunshine radiated by King Edward, who instructed Knollys, nevertheless, to ask [21] Winston Churchill (1 June 1908), who was acting as the Marlboroughs' mouthpiece, to notify the Duke and Duchess regretfully that they 'Should not come to any dinner, or evening party, or private entertainment at which either of Their Majesties are expected to be present'.

While the Liberal Chief Whip intervened [22] on behalf of Arthur Ponsonby, the Parliamentary Labour Party resolved that the King's action in the cases of Grayson and Keir Hardie had been tantamount to an unconstitutional attempt to influence the course of debates in the House of Commons, and the matter was accorded wide publicity in the Press. Keir Hardie stated [23] that he would attend no royal functions in future, but Frederick Ponsonby succeeded with difficulty in extracting from his brother a letter of explanation

* Lord Ponsonby of Shulbrede (1871–1946).

and apology which King Edward accepted. The King then declared [24] (2 July) that the incident was closed, and Ponsonby attended (10 July) a Court Ball; but many officious letters – some appreciative, and some critical – continued for a time to swell King Edward's post-bag.

Before leaving on 5 June to meet the Emperor of Russia, King Edward received (3 June) a memorandum from Lord Rothschild about the persecution of Russian Jews, and another from Sir Ernest Cassel about the flotation of a Russian loan. Both documents troubled Hardinge, who expressed satisfaction when Knollys, in thanking Rothschild (3 June) for a personal letter which he and his two brothers had written to the King, observed [25] that 'it would not be constitutionally right or proper' for the King to raise the Jewish question, which 'is, moreover, one of considerable political importance', with the Emperor Nicholas, or with Russian ministers, except with the full concurrence of Sir Charles Hardinge and Sir Arthur Nicolson:

I hope also [Hardinge wrote [26] on 4 June to Knollys] the King will not show to the Emperor, Cassel's memorandum about a loan which he wants to get into his hands. It is a great abuse by Cassel of the King's friendliness towards him, to ask His Majesty to mix himself up in any way in a financial transaction of which the King and his Government know nothing. . . .

It amuses me to see how the Jews, though hating the Russian Government, are always ready to give them money if they themselves can 'make a bit'!

Great capitalists exerted a very strong political influence which was regarded almost everywhere as natural and useful at that period; and Esher noted [27] that Hardinge's cautious reaction to Rothschild's letter about the Jews denoted a regrettable retreat from the forthright tradition of Lord Palmerston. Esher agreed with Hardinge in condemning Cassel's cold-blooded approach; but he was warned [28] by Knollys that King Edward, who sympathized warmly with persecuted Russian Jews, would be happy also to assist and to oblige Cassel if he had the chance.

On 13 June, Hardinge reported [29] to Knollys:

I enclose to you the Rothschilds' letter which, I am glad to say, was not presented or shown to anybody. The King, how-ever, seemed so anxious that the matter should be mentioned to somebody, that Nicolson and I decided that he might raise the question of Jews in a general conversation with the Russian Minister on the internal affairs of Russia. This he did, without alluding especially to the Rothschilds, and it went off all right.

I did what I could to discourage the King from making any mention of Cassel's loan; but I rather fancy that the King did ask the Emperor to receive Cassel if he goes to Russia, and emphasized the fact of his being a Privy Counsellor. ...

Prodded strongly by King Edward, Sir Arthur Nicolson reluctantly asked the Russian Prime Minister, Stolypin, whether or not action would be taken to remove Jewish dis-abilities and to discourage pogroms. Stolypin, who was mur-dered by a Jew in September 1911, in a theatre at Kiev be-fore the eyes of the Emperor and Empress, replied that legislation was contemplated 'for the amelioration of the lot of the Jews in Russia'; and Hardinge informed [30] Roths-child (13 June) that 'in view of M. Stolypin's assurance, the King did not consider it desirable that anything further should be said on the subject at present, until at least it is seen whether the intentions of the Prime Minister are car-ried into effect'.

Annoyed by the virtual suppression of the carefully drafted memorandum which he and his brothers had signed, Rothschild retorted [31] that, having little confidence in Stolypin's assurances, he was disinclined to express a satis-faction which he could not feel; but it was apparent that, whereas Rothschild's motive had been purely humanitarian, Cassel's had been unashamedly self-interested. Bülow re-corded [32] that the German Emperor, who had heard about Cassel's scheme, had described King Edward as nothing but 'a jobber in stocks and shares' who counted upon netting a 'colossal' personal profit out of any Russian loan; and Hard-inge was on tenterhooks lest the King's visit to Tallin should be associated in the public mind with an attempt, as he put it,[33] 'to rig the market and make a Russian loan possible in London'.

After dining with Sir Ernest Cassel on 4 June, King

Edward embarked next day in *Victoria and Albert* for Tallin,
He was accompanied by the Queen and by Princess Victoria; and, in addition to Sir Arthur Nicolson, Count Benckendorff, Sir Charles Hardinge, Admiral Sir John Fisher and
General Sir John French, his large suite included, as always,
his Marine Painter-in-Ordinary, the Chevalier Eduardo de
Martino. Knollys held that a Cabinet minister ought to have
accompanied the King, but King Edward complained that
the presence of such a minister would have made him feel
like a prisoner handcuffed to a warder while conversing with
his relatives through a grille. Hardinge served, accordingly,
as minister in attendance and, despite criticism in Parliament and the Press, the Cabinet made no objection.

Greeted, as he approached the Kiel Canal, by Prince
Henry of Prussia and by almost the entire German Navy,
and cheered continuously as he steamed through the canal
by masses of cavalry which lined both banks in gorgeous
uniforms, King Edward, wearing the uniform of the Kiev
Dragoons, anchored off Tallin in splendid weather on the
morning of 9 June 1908. He was greeted by the whole of the
Russian imperial family, in their yachts, *Standart* and *Polar
Star*; by the ministers, Stolypin and Isvolsky; and by the
exiguous remnant of the Russian Imperial Navy which had
survived the Battle of Tsushima.

That meeting at Tallin lasted for only two days, and
neither Sovereign went ashore; but banquets were held, and
balls, and King Edward, briefed always at the last moment,
participated with relish in several diplomatic conversations.
The delight which the royalties took in each other's company was apparent to all, and the Emperor was gay and at
his ease; but the shy, highly strung and unsociable Empress,
who adored and who was adored by her family, was observed on one occasion sitting apart, alone and in tears.

Little progress was made at Tallin towards extending to
Europe the recent Anglo-Russian understanding about
Asiatic problems, but popular emotion in both countries
was focused upon the goals towards which German policy
had compelled both Governments to turn their eyes. The
Emperor said that he was far happier with King Edward at

Tallin than he had been with the German Emperor at Swinemunde in August, 1907, when he had never known from one moment to another 'what might be unexpectedly sprung upon him'; and the results of the historic meeting at Tallin were summarized[34] by Sir Harold Nicolson in his account of his father, Arthur Nicolson (Lord Carnock):

> King Edward .. did not patronize the Tsar: he treated him as a highly successful nephew. ... Stolypin and Isvolsky were also reassured by the circumstance that no awkward questions had been asked, that their British visitors had shown infinite discretion. The Tsar had returned from Bjorkoe and Swinemunde frightened and humiliated: he returned from Reval [Tallin] flattered and reassured. The greatest diplomatic victories are gained by doing nothing: and King Edward, although too superficial to be a statesman, was a supreme diplomatist.

The Germans had cause in those circumstances to be apprehensive of the effect upon the Emperor and his advisers of King Edward's personality and tact, and the diplomatic sky was darkened by a thundercloud of lowering German suspicion and alarm. Attacks directed in consequence against King Edward in the Austrian as well as in the German Press attained such a pitch of unprecedented ferocity that Sir Edward Grey felt impelled reluctantly to make representations to both Governments.

International feeling was already so much inflamed in June 1908 that the British Cabinet considered it necessary to remonstrate with King Edward for the only action which he took at Tallin on his personal initiative. He created the Emperor an Admiral of the Fleet without prior reference to the First Lord of the Admiralty; and Fisher reported[35] (12 June) to Reginald McKenna that 'the Emperor is simply like a child in his delight'. King Edward told his nephew that he would find a naval uniform more useful than that of the Scots Greys, which he already possessed, because he was more likely to meet British warships in future than he was to encounter British troops; and Knollys wrote[36] (15 June) to Asquith immediately after the King had returned home:

> I had an opportunity of speaking to the King this morning about the Admiral of the Fleet incident. I mentioned how much

disturbed you and Grey had been. ... I also mentioned that Mr McKenna was much 'put out'.

Nothing could have been 'nicer' or more friendly than he was, and he took it extremely well.

He has now desired me to write to you and say ... the idea suddenly struck him ... that he was totally unaware of the constitutional point ... and that he regretted he had, without knowing it, acted irregularly.

I mentioned to him the awkward position in which you and Grey would have been placed had questions been put in the House of Commons, and I added that nothing could have been 'nicer' than you both were in connection with the occurrence. ...

P.S. The King deplores the attitude taken up by Mr Asquith on the Women's Suffrage Bill.

That spirited postscript was characteristic of King Edward, who was just sufficiently annoyed to reject [37] Asquith's suggestion that he should confer the Order of the Garter upon Sir Edward Grey. He appointed Lord Northampton instead to fill a vacancy which had arisen; but he offered Grey the Grand Cross of the Royal Victorian Order at Newmarket in October. 'Grey has refused', Esher noted [38] (23 October), 'as he was sure to do, and the King is *dreadfully* hurt. No one knows this, except Francis [Knollys] and me ....'

ii

Cassel and his friend, Albert Ballin, the Director-General of the Hamburg-Amerika Line, who was sometimes described as the Emperor William's Court Jew, discussed means that spring (1908) of drawing King and Kaiser closer together, and of putting an end, if possible, to the dangerous and expensive Anglo–German competition in naval armaments. Cassel and others accordingly approached King Edward, who consulted Asquith and Grey before arranging to meet the German and Austrian Emperors again at Cronberg and at Ischl on his way to Marienbad; and the British Government, which had been unable to devise any plan of its own for relaxing tension and for reducing the burden of armaments, welcomed that initiative.

In those circumstances, Grey provided King Edward with two memoranda about the naval building programme, for use when he met the German Emperor: 'This', Hardinge recorded,[39] 'was really a very interesting innovation, since for the first time in history the British Government briefed the King to act as their spokesman in an interview with the Head of a Foreign State, and it serves as an indisputable proof of the confidence they felt in the wisdom and tact of the Sovereign in dealing with such matters. It was arranged that I should accompany His Majesty as Minister in Attendance.'

Although the Emperor was delighted that his uncle had consented, for once, to discuss politics with him, King Edward was less happy. One of Grey's memoranda gave much fuller details than the other did about naval expenditure, and Grey's laconic note [40] – 'The King will decide which he thinks most suitable for the Emperor to see' – annoyed King Edward. He minuted [41] (6 August): 'This is, I believe, the first occasion on which the Sovereign has received instructions from his Government!'; but he was on edge, and thunder sounded, as always, in the distance when King and Kaiser met.

Grey was sorry to hear from Knollys that his carefully drafted memoranda had not been received more warmly; and he warned [42] Knollys (8 August) that the German Emperor, 'who is so sensitive about anything which may be construed as an attempt to influence German Naval expenditure', might be even more seriously upset. He asked, therefore, that King Edward should carefully prepare the ground before presenting or discussing either document, 'but I make my suggestion with great hesitation and deference, for I feel that this is a personal matter between the King and the Emperor in which the King's own knowledge and judgement of the Emperor's disposition is much superior to that of any of us'. He added that the Emperor ought not to mind hearing from the King 'a plain statement of our point of view ... after the statement of the German position voluntarily put forward in his own letter to Lord Tweedmouth'.

At Friedrischof Castle, on the morning of 11 August 1908,

King Edward and the Emperor William were closeted alone for three hours. No record exists of that conversation, but the King told [43] Hardinge immediately before luncheon that the Emperor had agreed to receive Sir Edward Goschen as ambassador in place of Sir Frank Lascelles, and that every conceivable topic had been discussed, except those of naval estimates and armaments. The King explained that he had mentioned, at one point, that he had in his pocket a document which his Government had given him about naval affairs, but that, as the Emperor 'neither asked to see it, nor to know its contents', he had made no attempt to force a discussion which his nephew seemed anxious to avoid.

It was left, accordingly, to Hardinge to grasp the nettle in two discursive conversations with the Emperor after luncheon and after dinner; and the report which he drafted drew high praise from King Edward as well as from Grey:

It is admirably drawn up and most interesting [King Edward wrote [44] on 25 August from Marienbad]. To me it is a marvel that you have so retentive a memory. . . .

It is a mercy that we have you as Under-Secretary at the Foreign Office, and that Lloyd George and Winston Churchill do not occupy that position! I cannot conceive how the Prime Minister allows them ever to make speeches on Foreign Affairs, concerning which they know nothing. . . .

Grey wrote [45] (23 August) to Hardinge:

You had to take a big fence in broaching the Navy question to the Emperor, but it would never have done to let him discuss relations between England and Germany without bringing this in. . . .

As the matter was not mentioned by the King, an exceptional responsibility fell upon you. I have purposely not made much of this in the Cabinet Paper, as it will only raise the question that, however well things have gone hitherto, there is so much responsibility to be faced at these interviews that a Cabinet Minister ought to be present. . . .

Hardinge expressed warm approval of Grey's action in making drastic excisions from his report before circulating it to other Cabinet ministers. He emphasized [46] (25 August) that it had been prepared 'for you alone, to whom I am wholly responsible'; and he added: 'I regard my position in these circumstances as that of a special ambassador who profits by the favourable conditions of a royal visit to carry out the instructions entrusted to him by the Secretary of State.'

After a charming visit to Ischl, where he persuaded the Emperor Francis Joseph of Austria to ride for the first time in an automobile, King Edward went to Marienbad for his usual cure. He invited Clemenceau and Isvolsky to visit him, and complained hotly to both, and to other friends, about the way in which recent speeches by Lloyd George and Winston Churchill were embarrassing the foreign policy of Sir Edward Grey. He said that Lloyd George, who had never been abroad before, had been laying down the law on foreign policy in Carlsbad and Berlin; and he informed Hardinge [47] (29 August) that Clemenceau, than whom *'no* man is a better judge'*, had been amazed 'by the *crass ignorance* which L. George displayed concerning foreign politics'.

Churchill was awaiting, as eagerly as any man, the 'People's Budget' which Lloyd George was planning to introduce in April 1909 in order to wage 'Implacable war' upon poverty and squalor. The Liberal Government was determined to inaugurate a new era of expanding social services and benefits; and Lloyd George and Churchill, who seized the leadership of that campaign, encouraged the public to hope that a substantial part of the cost could be met by reducing expenditure upon armaments.

Foreign policy was dragged for that reason into the forefront of the debate, and King Edward was scandalized when methods of reaching an understanding with Germany on the naval problem were canvassed by Churchill in speeches at home, and by Lloyd George during interviews which he gave while studying in Berlin the Prussian system of social insurance. The King considered that no one except the Prime Minister and the Foreign Secretary was qualified to make official pronouncements about foreign policy; and he was plunged for a time into another fit of depression.

King Edward refused [48] nevertheless, after much reflection, to send Asquith a very strong letter about Lloyd

George and Churchill which Knollys had drafted for his signature. He preferred to speak to the Prime Minister at Balmoral at the end of September; and Knollys, whose health was poor throughout that month, offered bad advice. Through excess of zeal he judged both ministers too harshly, going so far as to suggest [49] (29 August) that 'they don't behave like gentlemen, are disloyal to their colleagues and spend most of their time in unprincipled intrigue'; and (10 September) that 'the very idea' of Churchill's acting 'from conviction or principle ... is enough to make anyone laugh'.

King Edward took a more generous view, while remaining depressed and anxious. He appreciated that new forces were bursting the crust of the old social and political order, but was delighted when Esher and Mrs Keppel helped to convince [50] him that Lloyd George was an imperialist at heart. A friendship which sprang up between Mrs Keppel and Lloyd George was useful to King Edward, who spoke [51] kindly also (26 September) to Esher about Churchill. He said that Churchill was even younger in spirit than he was in years; that he might 'change very much', as Lord Randolph had changed; and that he liked Mrs Churchill immensely.

King Edward was jerked out of his depressed mood during the first week of October by a major European crisis which carried a grave threat of war. The provinces of Bosnia and Herzogovina, which form part of the modern Yugoslavia, had been administered and virtually possessed by Austria for thirty years. They remained nominally, however, under Turkish suzerainty until 6 October 1908, when they were annexed, formally and without warning, to the dying Hapsburg Empire by the brash and ambitious Austrian Foreign Minister, Baron Aehrenthal,* who had served as ambassador in St Petersburg and who gambled upon Rus-

* Aloys von Aehrenthal was the grandson of a rich Jewish merchant in Prague who was created a baron after marrying a noblewoman. Aehrenthal's father married into the highest Austrian aristocracy, and Aehrenthal himself married the daughter of an illustrious Hungarian house. Patrician and charming in manner, he was created a count before dying of cancer at the height of his reputation and to the distress of the Emperor Francis Joseph in 1912.

sia's unwillingness to risk revolution by accepting that challenge at that time.

South-east Europe was convulsed for six months by that arbitrary and unilateral breach of the Treaty of Berlin, signed in 1878; and the root question was whether Russia would, or would not, intervene actively in a conflict between Austria-Hungary and the little Serbian kingdom which demanded compensation. Many difficult ancillary problems arose, and throughout a prolonged crisis, which frayed the nerves of statesmen, King Edward fervently supported his Government's efforts to maintain peace and to adjust differences between the Great Powers which made warlike moves as they supported the rival claims of Balkan peoples whose vital interests were placed in jeopardy.

Count Albert Mensdorff, the idle but charming Austrian Ambassador, had a very hot reception from King Edward when he delivered at Balmoral before dinner on 5 October a personal letter from the Emperor Francis Joseph. The Emperor stated that Serbian irredentism had rendered annexation imperative, and King Edward vented his fury upon the unlucky Ambassador, who was thankful to escape to London. The King told the Ambassador that the plot must have been fully hatched before his visit to Ischl on 12–13 August, that the Emperor had dropped no hint of it and that Aehrenthal had been guilty of cynical perfidy. Lord Redesdale, who was a fellow-guest at Balmoral, recorded[52] that 'no one who was there can forget how terribly he was upset. Never did I see him so moved.'

Returning to Buckingham Palace late on Saturday, 10 October, King Edward gave separate audiences to Grey, Asquith and the Russian Foreign Minister, Alexander Isvolsky,* next day. He gave a dinner also on 11 October for Isvolsky who had been in Paris when the crisis broke, negotiating about the right of free passage through the

---

* Alexander Isvolsky, an ambitious snob of undistinguished origin, who made a great but supremely happy marriage, became Russian Ambassador in Paris from 1910 until the Russian Revolution. He lived thereafter upon an allowance from the French Government, but died on the Riviera in 1919.

Dardanelles. Appreciating that the Anglo-Russian Convention was insufficiently popular to consolidate his social and political position in St Petersburg, and to secure him the title of count, Isvolsky sought a diplomatic victory in the Dardanelles. The Straits had been closed to vessels of war by the Treaties of Paris, London and Berlin of 1856, 1871 and 1878; and a Russian fleet had been bottled up, in consequence, in the Black Sea.

In negotiating for the annulment of those treaty provisions, Isvolsky ignored a change in the climate of Russian public opinion which had occurred since he was a boy. He had lived so much abroad that he failed to understand that his countrymen had become less eager to seize Constantinople and to revive the Byzantine Empire, than they were to rescue the Slav peoples of the Balkan peninsula from the encroaching tide of Teutonic domination; but he had made a much more crass specific blunder. Until he came to London and saw King Edward and Sir Edward Grey, he had not paused to analyze the different interpretations which his demand for the freedom of the Straits could support. Whereas he asked in London that Russian warships should have a right of egress from the Black Sea in peace or war, and that ingress should be barred at all times to the warships of other nations, all the evidence suggests that in previous discussions with Austrian statesmen, the Russian Foreign Minister had been less precise.

Isvolsky had met Aehrenthal on 15–16 September while staying with Count Berchtold, the Austro-Hungarian Ambassador to Russia, at Berchtold's castle of Bucklau in Moravia, and the mystery surrounding what happened there fascinated King Edward during the last year of his life. That mystery has never been entirely elucidated, but it is certain that Isvolsky committed himself inadvertently to Aehrenthal to an extent which he never dared to disclose to his own Government, or to the Governments of Great Britain and France, and that Aehrenthal was tempted subsequently to take ruthless and unscrupulous advantage of Isvolsky's personal embarrassment.

It may be assumed [53] that Isvolsky at Buchlau consented

unconditionally to the annexation by Austria of Bosnia and
Herzogovina in return for a conditional promise by Aehrenthal to support the Russian claim to the freedom of the
Dardanelles when the concurrence of the other signatory
Powers had been secured. It may be assumed also that, after
that annexation had been proclaimed, it dawned upon
Isvolsky that the Czar and the Russian Government would
never consent to construe the freedom of the Straits to imply
a right of ingress to the Black Sea by the warships of any
foreign power which might be at war with Russia, and which
might, for example, be under orders to bombard Odessa.

In those circumstances, Isvolsky regaled King Edward and
the British Government in London with a most extraordinary story in an attempt to protect himself. The Russian
Foreign Minister accused the Austrian Foreign Minister,
with hysterical and startling suddenness and after a three
weeks' delay, of an act of the blackest treachery; and he
became, thereafter, Aehrenthal's most bitter personal
enemy. Isvolsky convinced King Edward for a time, and he
succeeded also, for a few days, in convincing Grey, Hardinge
and the British Foreign Office, that he had been duped by
the arrogant 'half-Jew', Aehrenthal, whom King Edward
described [54] (28 March 1909) to Hardinge as 'nearly the Devil
Incarnate'; and that he had never consented to consider
even the bare possibility of the formal annexation by Austria of the two Serbo-Croat provinces, except as part of a
general settlement of the problems of South-East Europe at
some indefinite future date.

Isvolsky's hair was scorched, even in London, by the blast
of rage which arose in Russia against his action in selling
Serbia by permitting himself to be duped; and he implored
King Edward and British ministers to come to his rescue.
Throwing dignity to the winds, he pleaded the leading part
which he had played in preparing the recent Anglo-Russian
Convention, and while Hardinge wrote [55] to Nicolson that
'we must do our best to support him, such as he is', King
Edward wrote [56] (13 October 1908) to Asquith:

... With respect to the more important point, that of the
Dardanelles, the King is afraid that, unless some hope is given

to Russia that England and the other Powers might grant the national aspirations of Russia on this question, M. Isvolsky will return to his country a discredited man, and will have to resign, and it is impossible to say who his successor might be.

The King feels that after the Russian Convention with England of a year ago, we are bound, if we wish to retain her friendship, to give way on this important point. He hopes the Cabinet are looking at this question from a European and International point of view and not merely a domestic one.

The Cabinet's view was more parochial but also more cautious than that of King Edward. It agreed in principle that the Straits ought to be opened, while bitterly disappointing Isvolsky by resolving that the moment was inopportune for raising that complicated issue with the Turkish Government. The Cabinet agreed at the same time to support Russia's demand for an international conference on the problems of south-east Europe; but the Austrian and German Governments opposed that plan.

King Edward was kept fully informed of all developments throughout that crisis, and on a letter from Hardinge, which he received at the Jockey Club, he minuted [57] as early as 15 October:

Please thank Hardinge for his interesting letter and all the information it contains.

All Sir E. Grey's memos and despatches (in this box) are perhaps the most interesting I have ever seen: and I congratulate him on having come to a successful issue in his arguments and conversation with M. Isvolsky, which have been of the most delicate and difficult nature.

Isvolsky's success in those 'arguments and conversation' had fallen short of his needs and desires; and it was arranged therefore that King Edward should write to the Emperor of Russia, recommending the unhappy Foreign Minister to the mercy of his master: 'My dear Nicky', King Edward wrote [58] (27 October) to the Czar, '... You know how anxious I am for the most friendly relations between Russia and England, not only in Asia but also in Europe; and I feel confident that, through your M. Isvolsky, these hopes will be realized.' King Edward added that he had met Isvolsky many times and that he had 'on each occasion been more and more impressed by his ability – and I must say that he pleased me very much'; and in forwarding that letter to Sir Arthur Nicolson, with instructions to deliver it personally into the hands of the Czar, he wrote [59] (27 October): 'I have endeavoured in this letter to sing to the utmost my praises of M. Isvolsky, and the great personal regard I entertain towards him.'

King Edward's intervention was successful; Isvolsky was not dismissed, as he richly deserved to be; and the Emperor of Russia, who resented Aehrenthal's alleged liaison with a Grand Duchess, as well as his social popularity in St Petersburg, thanked [60] his 'dear Uncle Bertie' (18 November) for extending personal help and kindness to Isvolsky, before summarizing Russian policy in three significant paragraphs:

I am really happy that since our two countries have come to several agreements in Asia, the want of arriving at still closer understanding upon other political questions is steadily gaining ground.

Of course you know that Russia needs peace, more than any other country at the present moment.

I am aware of the danger that arises in the Balkans especially from the uneasiness in Austria and the fermentation in Serbia; but I will do everything, and am already doing all in my power, to calm the heated spirits there, and in my country.

'We are certainly living in critical times,' King Edward wrote [61] (5 November) to Hardinge, 'but yet I hope that peace may be maintained – but only because Europe is *afraid* to go to war.' It was evident that Russia, at any rate, was mortally afraid, and that Germany was resolved to exploit that fear; but King Edward accepted with the utmost repugnance his Government's advice that he should pay a State visit to Berlin early in the New Year, and before going to Biarritz, in order to try to offset the bad effect in Germany of his recent visit to the Emperor of Russia.

Grey asked [62] Sir Francis Bertie, the British Ambassador in Paris (7 January 1909), to let it be known that 'if the visit had not taken place, it would have been a cause of offence and made all politics more difficult. For that reason I am glad it is arranged, but otherwise I do not expect much good from it. To please the Emperor does not carry so much weight in Germany as it did.' Because he was well aware of that, King Edward departed with the Queen for Berlin on 8 February 1909 in no amiable or optimistic mood. He was fussy and difficult, but was in poor health and aching to get to Biarritz and into the sun. Feeling had become so strong that he should be accompanied by a Cabinet minister on what proved to be the last State visit which he paid to any foreign crowned head that the Colonial Secretary, Lord Crewe, was made to serve as minister in attendance; but Sir Charles Hardinge travelled as usual in King Edward's large suite, which also included Admiral Sir Day Bosanquet and Field-Marshal Lord Grenfell, representing the Navy and Army.

The most successful episode during three days crowded with engagements was a visit paid by King Edward on the morning of 10 February to the Berlin Rathaus, where many virulent anti-British merchants and manufacturers were captivated by his charm and tact. But an alarming incident occurred after a luncheon at the British Embassy. King Edward, wearing a tight-fitting Prussian uniform and smoking an immense cigar, was chatting to the elegant and beautiful Princess Daisy of Pless when he collapsed in a choking fit and fainted. His doctor, Sir James Reid, was fetched immediately from another room, and everyone was asked to withdraw; but the King recovered as soon as Queen Alexandra had unfastened his collar. A quarter of an hour later the guests were invited to return; and Sir James, who had been instructed by King Edward, appeared to treat that incident in a casual manner. He told Hardinge that it was a bronchial symptom and in no sense dangerous, but Hardinge wrote at once to Knollys in order to express fears for the King and doubts about the doctor.

Thereafter, King Edward's programme was somewhat modified, but the weather was vile and his suite were thankful when he returned safely to Buckingham Palace on 13 February, and dined alone with the Queen at nine o'clock. A new tendency to fall asleep suddenly at luncheon and at dinner, as well as at the opera, alarmed the Household;

King Edward looked worn out; and he wheezed and grunted most painfully whenever he had to climb stairs.

The German Emperor told [63] King Edward in strict confidence during that visit that he was tired of his Chancellor, Bülow, whom he distrusted and intended soon to dismiss; and the King was not surprised. He continued, however, to be worried intensely by the boastful support which Germany extended to her Austrian ally. Hardinge reassured [64] him (26 March) by promising that the British Government would do its utmost, if necessary, to induce or to compel Serbia to accept any conceivable Austrian ultimatum:

It is, in reality, a case of '*reculer pour mieux sauter*', and I think it will be worth doing. We are fairly confident that Russia and France will agree with us in this course, which will have the advantage of showing the whole world that we are ready to stretch a great many points in order to secure European peace. ... Unfortunately, with us the conviction has been growing stronger day by day that the Austrian Government are determined upon war ...'

King Edward replied [65] on 28 March from Biarritz:

It is sad to see the difficulties we have to contend with. ...

It is strange that ever since my visit to Berlin the German Government have done *nothing* but thwart and annoy us in every way ... but Grey has worked with the greatest caution and determination. If we can only ensure peace it is worth giving way, as long as we can do so with honour and dignity.

After complaining that their friend, Mensdorff, the Austro-Hungarian Ambassador in London, spent all his time attending house parties and race meetings – although 'he does not know a horse from a cow!' – King Edward continued:

Unless the military party at Vienna is too strong, I hope that war with Servia may yet be avoided, for, as you say, Austria will obtain nothing from attacking Servia. We must, however, act in accordance with Russia, France and, if possible, Italy, as it would not do if these countries were detached from us.

We may safely look upon Germany as our bitterest foe, as she hardly attempts to conceal it.

Russia was not prepared to go to war with Austria-Hungary on behalf of Serbia at that time, and on 31 March Hardinge informed[66] King Edward that the crisis was ended at last:

There is no doubt, however, that the result of the conflict which has been going on for the past six months will be of a lasting character and will not tend to the consolidation of peace. There can be little doubt that the Servians will deeply resent the humiliation which they have suffered at the hands of Austria, while the Russians will never be able to forget the fact that Germany and Austria availed themselves of the moment of Russia's weakness to harass her in a humiliating and hectoring manner.

I cannot help thinking that the success of the mailed fist policy of Germany will cost her dear in the end. If the Russians have an eye to the future, they will lose no time in making good the defects in their military system and in preparing for the conflict which must inevitably follow if Germany intends to pursue the policy of military domination in Europe.

My only fear is that if a poor creature like Isvolsky remains in office, he may yield once more, quite unnecessarily, to German dictation! ... There is no doubt whatever that his capitulation to the German Ambassador at St Petersburg was absolutely unnecessary. Had he given a reply similar to that which we gave to Metternich, the Germans would not have had sufficient reason for issuing an ultimatum to Russia.

In informing[67] Hardinge (2 April) that he found Russia's abject surrender hard to understand, King Edward invited comment upon the mystery of Isvolsky's personal entanglement and deadly feud with Aehrenthal; and Hardinge replied[68] (7 April 1909):

There is no doubt whatever that Aehrenthal has in his pocket a paper in which Isvolsky has thoroughly compromised himself, and had promised to recognize the annexation of Bosnia, provided that Austria would agree to the opening of the Dardanelles.

He is terrified lest Aehrenthal shall some day publish this document; and it is the threat of publication which has made him cave in in such an ignominious manner to the Germans. ... He is a very unscrupulous and unreliable man.

On 7 April King Edward thanked [69] Asquith for having reported (31 March) the Cabinet's decision to levy the unprecedented sum of fifteen million pounds by new taxation in the forthcoming budget. The money was needed to pay for battleships, and for old age pensions; the standard rate of income tax was increased to one shilling and twopence in the pound; and a super-tax was imposed upon large incomes. King Edward was informed that an income of eighteen thousands pounds a year, for example, would be taxed at the rate of one shilling and sevenpence in the pound; and he inquired whether, 'in framing the Budget, the Cabinet took into consideration the possible (but the King hopes improbable) event of a European War? The income tax, which has always been regarded as a war tax, now stands so high, for unearned incomes over a certain amount, that any great increase would have a most disastrous effect on land generally, especially if the war lasted for a considerable time.'

22

The People's Budget

KING EDWARD's hopes for the preservation of peace in
Europe, and for the avoidance of social disturbance in the
British Isles, were based upon the maintenance of the *status
quo*; and his perplexity and discomfort increased propor-
tionately to his growing awareness that drastic and early
changes were inevitable. Abroad, the Turkish and Austro-
Hungarian Empires were in process of disintegration; and
at home, Liberal ministers were resolved to satisfy a pent-
up demand for social reform. Because he was convinced that
his Government intended to go further and faster than the
majority of his subjects desired, King Edward was as much
on edge with Asquith and Grey by the start of 1909, as he
was with Lloyd George and Winston Churchill.

Until that time the electors had displayed remarkably
little resentment of the continuous rejection and emascula-
tion of Liberal Bills by the House of Lords. Almost everything which could be achieved with the consent of the
Upper House had been accomplished by the end of 1908;
and the Cabinet was threatened with disruption on the issue
of naval armaments. The existence of the peers' absolute
veto precluded the possibility of progress on such major
aspects of Liberal policy as education, the liquor trade, Irish
home rule, Anglican Church disestablishment in Wales and
taxation of the unearned increment on land values; but
Asquith's appeal to his Party (11 December 1908) 'to treat
the veto of the House of Lords as the dominating issue in
politics' elicited small popular response.

For that reason the Prime Minister's appeal did not worry
King Edward, who told[1] Esher that Asquith was 'deficient

in manners but in nothing else'. He was dismayed, however, by the way in which the situation was transformed as the result of the rejection by the peers of Lloyd George's 'People's Budget'. Despite inflammatory speeches, public opinion had remained extraordinarily deferential towards the House of Lords before that event, but after it every road which had appeared to be blocked was re-opened to reformist traffic, and the Government was scarcely able to credit its good fortune.

The high rate of new taxation which Lloyd George sought to impose was caused partly by a navy scare which swept the country after a public disclosure of the accelerated scale of actual and potential German ship building. Reginald McKenna and the Sea Lords upset Treasury calculations by demanding six instead of four new dreadnought battleships in the 1909 programme; and, while Lloyd George and Churchill argued that four would suffice, the Opposition called insistently for eight. 'We want eight, and we won't wait!' became a popular refrain; and rancid debates in Parliament reflected a bitter struggle with the Cabinet.

In expressing [2] through Ponsonby a fervent hope to Fisher (22 March 1909) that 'eight dreadnoughts will be forthcoming', King Edward asked 'who is it who is to blame for letting Germany get ahead of us?' He complained that he had not been kept properly informed, and stated that he was 'much annoyed, because he was naturally quite unaware of the fact while he was at Berlin last month, and in ignorance of what would have been most important and useful for him to know'. There was room for argument about the pace of German shipbuilding, but Grey pleased [3] King Edward by threatening to resign unless eight new battleships were provided; and Asquith contrived adroitly to provide them, and to hold his Cabinet together. Most Liberals and all Radicals insisted, thereafter, that if money could be found for a great new fleet of battleships, it could and should be found also for the Party's full programme of social benefits; and a land tax, which provoked the House of Lords to revolt, was included, accordingly, in the Budget.

King Edward had departed in the meantime (5 March) for

a six-weeks' holiday at Biarritz, before embarking on another Mediterranean cruise. He travelled comfortably, as always, with his cherished crocodile dressing-case, which contained his diary, personal jewellery, a few photographs and a miniature of the Queen; and with a tattered silk dressing-gown which he refused obstinately to replace. He never tolerated ostentation, and Charles Hardinge had occasion to describe[4] the King's mode of travel as far less luxurious than that adopted by Lloyd George after the end of the First World War while travelling about Europe as Prime Minister, and with ladies in his train, to conferences at spas and watering places.

King Edward's habits were accepted as the criterion of sophisticated European elegance before the lights went out in 1914. His custom, for example, of greeting male acquaintances, including servants off duty, by lifting his hat right off his head, in England as well as abroad, was widely appreciated; and he fought a losing battle in defence of his right to stroll in public in England, as he did at Biarritz and at Marienbad, without being mobbed. Because the air at Brighton suited him, he liked, when he could escape from London, to spend an occasional few days incognito with the Arthur Sassoons at 8 King's Gardens in December, January, or February during the last three years of his life; and the Brighton police had strict instructions to guard his privacy. The Press behaved well, and he walked along the sea-front, as the Prince Regent had done a century earlier, unmolested by reporters with cameras; but the populace became unmanageable, and the struggle had to be abandoned after an incident on 9 February 1910.

Muffled in a great fur coat and feeling far from well, King Edward left his car to read the newspapers in the sun on Worthing pier. He dozed for a time while the news spread rapidly and a huge crowd gathered. Alerted by an equerry, the chief constable arrived, at the head of a posse of police, with the intention of clearing the pier; but the crowd had swelled to such proportions that it was possible only with great difficulty to clear a path through which King Edward regained his car, before departing to

the accompaniment of round upon round of loyal but untimely applause.

All King Edward's cars were painted a rich claret-colour
and he enjoyed choosing new ones. He loved also to be
driven fast, and was proud of having exceeded sixty miles
an hour on the Brighton road as early as 1906. He hated to
see any car in front of his, and would often urge his chauffeurs to pursue and to overtake; and his gestures were normally as vehement as his actions were brisk. He even spoke
rapidly in a voice which smoking and a distinct German
burr rendered preternaturally gruff; and his restlessness
was fantastic in a sick man aged nearly seventy.

Devoted to children and adored by his own, as well as by
his grandchildren, King Edward's mere presence generated
an atmosphere which was described habitually as electric
and which was most exhilarating. He wanted everyone
around him to be happy and, although faultlessly attired,
he encouraged friends' children to race slices of hot buttered
toast for pennies along the stripes of his trousers, with the
buttered side downwards, and to call him 'Kingy' in the
privacy of their parents' homes.

No trait in King Edward's nature was more attractive than
the pellucid simplicity which enabled him to relax without
abating one jot of his dignity; and that quality was exhi-
bited conspicuously in Scotland. Following Queen Victoria's
example, he allowed considerable licence to the stalkies, who
were empowered to place the rifles when deer were driven,[5]
instead of being stalked, because he was short of wind at
the end of his life. On one such occasion Arthur Sassoon,
while accompanying the King and the Prince of Wales in
King Edward's car, was astonished by the peremptory tone
which the head stalkie adopted: 'You stop where you
are!', the rude but loyal democrat exclaimed, addressing
King Edward who had looked inquiringly. 'But you get
out here', he added, pointing a finger at the Prince of
Wales.

Despite gusts of impatience and irritation which everyone,
except only the Prince of Wales, had cause to fear at times,
King Edward retained the heart of a schoolboy until the

end; and his energy appeared to wax and not to wane as his health deteriorated. He was always first on the ice with his skates when the upper lake froze at Sandringham, and he continued to organize games of ice-hockey, keeping goal, nominally, for his side.

When pleased, a purring 'Yes, yes yes!', uttered in a tone of infinite complacency, was King Edward's characteristic expression; and when displeased, unless he lost his temper, he generally assumed an air of martyrdom. If an order had been misinterpreted, he would repeat it with a literal and exaggerated precision, as though addressing a young child, but he sometimes spoiled the effect by bursting unexpectedly into hearty laughter at himself.

King Edward's happy, gurgling, infectious laughter was seldom repressed, except to spare somebody's feelings; but he was delighted privately when quite eminent men lost their heads occasionally and behaved with the rigidity of corpses upon being ushered into his formidable presence. Marvellously easy and charming when he chose, as he almost invariably did, it amused him occasionally, when he felt mischievous or out of sorts, to be stiff and difficult with prigs or bores. His sense of the ludicrous was exceedingly keen, and on 31 March 1909, for example, he was seen to rock with laughter almost all the way from the French frontier to San Sebastian while motoring from Biarritz to take luncheon with the King of Spain. The road was lined with troops who saluted or waved continuously, but were so undisciplined that they often failed to stand to attention or to remove cigarettes from their mouths. It was a disgraceful and extraordinary exhibition, but King Edward contrived to preserve a straight face when he thanked King Alfonso for that soldierly reception upon reaching the summer palace of Miramar.

Although feeling far from well at Biarritz in the spring of 1909, King Edward attended punctually to his boxes which contained many distasteful papers about the Morley-Minto reforms in India. Disapproving of his Government's new policy of admitting natives to a share in the government of India, King Edward concentrated upon opposing the ap-

pointment of Hindu lawyer, Satyendra Prassano Sinha,* to
membership of the Viceroy of India's Council. Most Tories,
including two vigorous ex-Viceroys, Lords Landsdowne and
Curzon, agreed warmly with King Edward, who wrote with
perfect good temper to Lord Morley, the Secretary of State,
as well as to Lord Minto, the Viceroy of India.

In pressing Sinha's appointment upon King Edward as 'an
act of high policy' which the Cabinet had endorsed unanimously, Morley explained[6] (10 March) that it was almost
as necessary as it was also expedient 'for the contentment
of Your Majesty's Indian dominions'. In reply, King Edward
wrote[7] (12 March):

> The King regrets that he cannot change his views on this
> subject, and has thought it over quite as much as Lord Morley
> has. He remains, however, of opinion that the proposed step is
> fraught with the greatest danger to the maintenance of the
> Indian Empire under British rule. ...
> As Lord Morley as well as the Viceroy recommend a Mr
> Sinha, the King has no other alternative but to agree to his ap-
> pointment to the Viceroy's Council, and can only hope that he
> may turn out trustworthy and efficient.

In thanking King Edward, Morley recalled[8] (17 March)
'the famous promise of Queen Victoria in 1858 – a promise
never forgotten in India – that race and colour should constitute no bar ...'; but King Edward[9] (20 March): 'This is
the answer to my letter! Why he should bring in the name
of Queen Victoria, I cannot see; nor how it bears on the
question. I myself do not think she would have approved of
the new departure. I have had to sign the objectionable
paper.'

During correspondence with Minto, King Edward characterized[10] Sinha's appointment as 'the thin end of the wedge'
(21 May), after admitting[11] (22 March) that he held 'very
strong and possibly old-fashioned views on the subject,
which my son, who has so recently been in India, entirely
shares'. He explained (22 March):

* Lord Sinha of Raipur, P.C., K.C.S.I., (1864–1928), became later
a member of the Imperial War Cabinet, and of the Judicial Committee of the Privy Council.

The Indian Princes, who are ready to be governed by the Viceroy and his Council, would greatly object to a Native, who would be very inferior in caste to themselves, taking part in the Government of the country. However clever the Native might be, and however loyal you and your Council might consider him to be, you never could be certain that he might not prove to be a very dangerous element in your Councils, and impart information to his Countrymen which it would be very undesirable should go further than your Council chamber. ...

The growing unrest in India prompted King Edward to press for the appointment of Lord Kitchener as Viceroy, when the time came for Minto to retire; but Morley was extremely reluctant to appoint a soldier. He recommended King Edward's friend, Sir Charles Hardinge, and was deeply disappointed when the King retorted that Hardinge, as an expert diplomatist, ought to 'stick to his last'. After the assassination in London by an Indian student, on 1 July 1909, of Morley's Political A.D.C., Sir William Wyllie, King Edward reiterated that a firm military hand was needed, and he minuted[12] (1 July): 'The sooner those Indian students are sent back to their own country, the better. They fall into bad hands, and return to India anarchists and socialists.' Morley admitted that Kitchener's appointment might have to be considered seriously, if the Indian situation deteriorated; but he would not promise more, and the matter was left in abeyance while friends of the rival candidates intrigued.

Sinha, who became a forceful member of the Viceroy's Council, was eager to resign in September 1909, because his wife disliked Simla. He complained that he was not given enough responsibility,[13] but was persuaded to postpone his resignation for some months, to the dismay of King Edward who wrote[14] (10 September) to Esher while under the impression that it would be effective immediately: 'So the Native Member resigns his seat in the Viceroy's Council! Do try and induce Morley not to be so obstinate by appointing another Native. He knows how strong my views are on the subject, and so does Minto; but they don't care what I say, nor does any member of my precious (!) Govt.'

Leaving Biarritz on 15 April for Paris, King Edward met Queen Alexandra, who had been suffering from a mild attack of pleurisy, and escorted her and Princess Victoria to Genoa by special train. His sister-in-law, the Dowager Empress of Russia, who had been staying at Buckingham Palace, travelled also to Genoa by another route from Paris in a Russian imperial train, before embarking with the King and Queen for Sicily in *Victoria and Albert*.

A military revolt in Turkey threatened to mar the harmony of that cruise. On visiting Malta on 21 April, King Edward had expected to be met by the Mediterranean Fleet; but that fleet had been ordered, a few hours before his arrival, to quit Malta in order to make a demonstration off the southern ports of Asia Minor. Startled by that sudden decision, King Edward dictated a series of explosive telegrams asking why he had not been consulted and informed; and McKenna explained that the uncertain movements of *Victoria and Albert* had increased the difficulty of notifying the Sovereign at that instant when the Cabinet took its urgent decision. In accepting the Minister's explanation, King Edward retorted [15] (24 April) that 'on a cruise like this, any sort of cut-and-dried programme is tiresome. The whole point of yachting is to be able to go where you like and when you like.' He nursed his grievance for a short time, while notifying [16] Hardinge (25 April) that the Dowager Empress of Russia was 'very properly' urging her son to retain the unfortunate Isvolsky in office; and that an abortive attempt had been made to arrange a meeting at Syracuse with the German Emperor, who was cruising also in the Mediterranean, and whose delay in dismissing Prince Bülow had puzzled the King.

King Edward was distressed at Malta by a personal disagreement with the Duke of Connaught, who had been established in the Palace at Valetta since the Summer of 1907 as High Commissioner and Commander-in-Chief of all British garrisons in and bordering the Mediterranean. King Edward had pressed [17] that appointment very strongly indeed upon his reluctant brother, in the belief that it would prove to be a step in 'the military federation of the Empire by a process of gradual development'. Some 800 officers and 20,000 men had come under command of the Duke, who had annoyed King Edward from the outset by complaining that the plan was academic and ill-conceived.

The Duke informed King Edward at Malta that the experiment had been proved to be a failure, and that the Mediterranean Command, which was a source of inefficiency in peace, would be a positive danger in war. He added that his position was equivalent to that of a fifth wheel on a coach, and that he proposed, accordingly, to resign and to come home.[18]

King Edward, who had always been proud of his brother's professional prowess, was committed warmly to Haldane's view which was directly opposed to that of the Duke of Connaught. Unkind words, which were not meant to be taken seriously, were written and spoken on both sides, and a personal element was injected into that dispute. King Edward argued that his brother had taken so much home leave that the experiment had not been given a fair chance; and the Duke and Duchess replied that their personal popularity in England had inspired King Edward's wish that they should continue to reside abroad.[19]

On 15 July 1909, King Edward wrote [20] to Asquith who had seen the Duke of Connaught on the previous day:

... The King regrets very much to learn that the Duke persists in wishing to be relieved of his duties. ...

The Duke of Connaught must now consider his military career at an end, and if he does not intend returning to Malta he should resign his appointment at once, and not wait until October, as he suggests.

The King is much annoyed at his Brother's persistent obstinacy.

In response to a direct personal appeal from King Edward, the Commander-in-Chief in India, Lord Kitchener, accepted the Mediterranean Command with extreme repugnance. He shared the Duke of Connaught's opinion that Haldane had blundered, and King Edward came round presently to that view. Only eight days before he died he released Kitchener from his personal promise to take up the

Mediterranean Command; assured him that it was 'a damned rotten billet' [21]; and tried vainly almost with his last breath to make amends by begging Asquith and Morley to send Kitchener back to India as Viceroy.

King Edward's sunny nature was so generous and affectionate that he was most anxious to make amends also to the Duke of Connaught for the abrupt termination of his military career. In the first flush of anger, he refused [22] to see his brother, and minuted [23] (15 July) that all thought of sending him to govern Canada must be abandoned; but as early as 8 September he implored [24] Haldane to allow the Duke to continue to serve as President of the War Office Selection Board. King Edward pleaded his past support of the War Minister's great reforms, as well as the fact that 'his brother was the only brother left and the late Queen's favourite son'; but the Commons had already been told that the Duke's appointment had been ended, and Haldane said that he would resign, if overruled. Convinced by Asquith and Haldane, after much argument and correspondence, that it was impossible to retain on the Selection Board an officer who had ceased to be actively employed, King Edward's mind reverted to Canada; and two years later, but at the earliest opportunity, the Duke of Connaught proceeded [25] to Ottawa as Governor-General.

Before King Edward returned on 8 May to England, the intense and even priggish scrutiny to which his words were subjected was illustrated in a private letter [26] (30 April) to Hardinge from the British Ambassador in Italy, Sir Rennell Rodd. The Ambassador reported that while entertaining the King and Queen of Italy to dinner off Naples on the previous evening, King Edward had made unexpectedly a speech in which he alluded to an Anglo-Italian alliance. 'It is unfortunate', Hardinge minuted [27] to Grey, 'that the King should have spoken of an alliance which does not exist. Fortunately it did not get into the Press'; and Grey alerted the Prime Minister by minuting, [28] 'It has been a lucky escape. Asquith minuted [29] 'Tactless'; but no harm was done, and King Edward reported [30] that King Victor Emanuel and his Foreign Minister, Tommaso Tittoni, had

displayed a morbid anxiety to stand well with Germany because they were hypnotized by German might.

Although friends noticed his drawn appearance with concern at the start of the London season, King Edward's health
improved for a time after an unparalleled personal and
popular triumph on Epsom Downs on 26 May 1909, which
was the birthday of the Princess of Wales. King Edward's
horse *Minoru*, ridden by Herbert Jones at odds of 4–1, carried the royal colours of purple, scarlet and gold to victory
by half a head in the Derby Stakes; and a surge of elemental
joy went out to greet the Sovereign whose ample frame and
genial face embodied every human quality which his
countrymen understood best and loved.

Tens of thousands of people sang 'God Save the King' and
cheered again and again. They indulged a delirious abandon
which relieves very occasionally the reserve to which most
Englishmen become habituated; and even the stolid police-
men who moved mechanically to surround the King when
he left the royal box to lead in his horse, threw care to the
winds, waved helmets in the air, and joined jockeys, peers,
shopkeepers and touts in yelling, 'Good old Teddy! Teddy
boy! Hurrah! Hurrah!'

King Edward had won the Derby twice before as Prince
of Wales, but he attained apotheosis on that third occasion.
He gave his annual dinner that evening to members of the
Jockey Club at Buckingham Palace; went on to Lady Farquhar's ball in Grosvenor Square, where he played bridge until
dawn; and tumbled into bed as birds were singing in his
garden, the happiest man in the world.

When the King attended Epsom Races again, on the day
after his victory, a lout yelled: 'Now, King. You've won the
Derby. Go back home and dissolve this bloody Parliament.'[31] King Edward laughed heartily because he was
disgusted with his Government and dismayed by a sudden
and unprecedented rise in the nation's political temperature.

The 'People's Budget', presented to the House of Commons on 29 April 1909, had aroused passionate Unionist resentment. Lloyd George's Celtic eloquence transmuted
every new and increased tax into 'flags and symbols in a

ringing debate'[32] between luxury and squalor; but Asquith held [33] rightly that the land taxes had done most to 'set the heather on fire'. They included provision for a complete valuation of all land in Great Britain, as well as for the payment, whenever land changed hands, of a duty of twenty per cent of any increase in its value which could not be attributed to its owner's efforts.

Those land taxes were not implemented as planned, but as Radicals continued to croon their music hall refrain, 'The land belongs to the people!', land values sank in inverse proportion to the mounting fears of its owners. Rival leagues were formed to attack and to defend the Budget, and in that campaign of platform oratory, which raged throughout the kingdom, the Unionists appeared to come off badly.

At countless 'budget protest' meetings, composed mainly of business men, over which the Dukes of Northumberland, Rutland or Westminster often presided, Unionists accused the Liberals of planning a social revolution; and Lloyd George, Winston Churchill and others retorted by spattering rich men everywhere with ridicule. Radical denunciations of efforts made by an exiguous class of predatory capitalists to strangle social reform drew no distinction between self-made plutocrats and hereditary territorial magnates.

Starting with Lord Rothschild, who had exposed himself stupidly, Lloyd George quickly focused his insults upon 'the Dukes' whom he described as 'the first of the litter', and whom he selected as the most convenient symbol of the obstructive power of the House of Lords, which constituted his principal target. While castigating selfish property owners at Limehouse on 30 July, the Chancellor of the Exchequer observed that 'a fully-equipped Duke cost as much to keep up as two dreadnoughts', and that he was less easy to scrap.

The Opposition was offended by such language, and King Edward, who had complained frequently on other occasions, spoke strongly to Asquith at Cowes on 2 August. He wondered [34] whether it was his duty to write a letter for the

Prime Minister to read in the Cabinet; and Knollys wrote [35] (1 August) to Lord Crewe:

The King thinks he ought to protest in the most vigorous terms against one of his Ministers making such a speech and putting himself almost on a level with Grayson – one full of false statements, of Socialism in its most insidious form and of virulent abuse against one particular class, which can only have the effect of setting 'class' against 'class', and of stirring up the worst passions of its audience.

It is hardly necessary, perhaps, to allude to its gross vulgarity.

The King cannot understand how Asquith can tacitly allow certain of his colleagues to make speeches that would not have been tolerated by any Prime Minister until within the last few years, which H.M. regards as being in the highest degree improper, and which he almost looks upon as being an insult to the Sovereign when delivered by one of his confidential servants.

I have purposely not marked my letter 'confidential'.

Excuses tendered by Asquith and Crewe were dubbed [36] 'pitiful' by King Edward, who directed [37] Knollys (3 August) to express regret to Crewe that his 'relations with some of the members of the present Cabinet should be increasingly the reverse of harmonious'. Knollys complained [38] on that day to Esher that 'the present Ministers are really hopeless as regards the King', and that relations had become 'impossible almost'; but a dignified and temperate letter [39] (5 August) from Lloyd George was well received at Cowes by King Edward.

The Chancellor of the Exchequer explained that he had been goaded beyond endurance by the violence of his opponents; and it was true that some Tory Speeches had been extremely unfair and unwise. Knollys informed [40] Esher (25 October) that King Edward deplored the immense harm caused by 'foolish and *mean* speeches and sayings' of 'great landowners and capitalists'; and the King replied [41] kindly to Lloyd George, on 8 August. While regretting all attempts 'to inflame the passions of the working and lower orders against people who happen to be owners of property', King Edward gave the Chancellor of the Exchequer 'every credit for the patience and perfect temper which he has shown, under provocation, during debates on the Budget'. 'Perhaps you may think the King's answer too moderate,' Knollys wrote [42] (23 August) to Esher, 'but it would not, in my opinion, be dignified for him to write too strongly, especially to a man like L. George.'

Against a background of British naval display, King Edward had the satisfaction of receiving at Cowes from 2-5 August an official return visit from the Emperor and Empress of Russia. They came in their yacht *Standart* with the ministers, Stolypin and Isvolsky, and with the Czarevitch, who was King Edward's godson and an extraordinarily pretty child, and were warmly acclaimed despite frantic Labour and Radical protests. Talks conducted at sea between British and Russian statesmen and diplomatists were very cordial although intrinsically unimportant; but the unhappy aftermath of the Bosnian crisis deprived King Edward of the pleasure of paying what had given promise of becoming an annual visit to the aged Emperor of Austria at Ischl during August. The King had written reproachfully to the Emperor about the annexation, and had rejected Grey's subsequent advice that he should congratulate Aehrenthal upon being made a count. Aehrenthal retaliated by insisting that no informal meeting should be arranged between the Sovereigns until King Edward had made amends by formally requesting one.

Pique and protocol precluded any such request, and King Edward returned (4 September) from Marienbad improved in health but without having seen the Emperor Francis Joseph. He went at once to stay with the Saviles at Rufford Abbey for Doncaster Races, and after describing [43] (8 September) in a letter to the Prince of Wales how thoroughly he had enjoyed, as always, his three weeks' cure in Bohemia, he added happily: 'I have crossed the Channel 6 times this year!'

Immediately after King Edward's return from Bohemia, it began to appear more probable every day that the House of Lords would precipitate a most grave and unprecedented constitutional crisis by rejecting the Finance Bill which embodied the Budget. Parliament remained in almost continuous session throughout the summer and autumn, and the Finance Bill was passed by the Commons on the night of 4–5 November; but worry caused by the nagging prospect of its rejection by the Lords dismayed King Edward and made him irritable and overwrought. It appeared certain that the Liberal Government would accept that challenge, and that it would seek to curb the power and perhaps also to dilute or alter the hereditary character of the Upper House; and Lord Knollys feared that the passions engendered by such an open quarrel upon class lines might impair the prestige of the throne.

The aristocracy had remained dominant throughout the nineteenth century in Great Britain because the existence of vast hereditary concentrations of property in private hands had bewitched public opinion. Those background concentrations buttressed a social order which endowed many men who were not individually rich, but who belonged to patrician families and who might have been insignificant otherwise, with artificial importance. Well endowed mentally as well as physically, they often transmuted into second nature the qualities popularly attributed to them; and that metamorphosis made them, upon the whole, much the best material available in public life.

King Edward's need for amusement, and the influence exerted by the professions, universities and public schools, were two among many factors which tended to mitigate exclusiveness and to foster the assimilation of most forms of reputable achievement or outstanding ability; and the middle and lower classes were fairly content. They enjoyed being represented by men who observed a uniform patrician code, and who used evidence of a willingness to observe it as a criterion of suitability for any species of public employment.

Constitutional convention entitled the House of Lords, which was the citadel of that patrician social order, to reject outright, but not to amend, Money Bills. The Lords had often rejected Money Bills imposing, increasing, reducing or removing customs and excise duties after, as well as before, the Reform Act, 1832; but more than two centuries had passed since they had rejected a Budget.

The right of the Lords to reject a Budget appeared, accordingly, to be as obsolete as was the right of the sovereign to veto legislation; but before 1861 the Budget included only those permanent taxes which the Commons renewed annually as a matter of routine. Whenever it was desired to alter any such tax in order to balance the Budget, or for any other reason, a special Act had to be passed.

Although such special Bills were never rejected by the Lords if the Budget was directly affected, room often existed for argument about the precise definition of direct and indirect effects, as well as about the degree of priority which ought to be accorded to the social aspect of measures which came up from the Commons in the guise of Money Bills. In 1860, for example, the Lords rejected a Liberal Bill which provided for the repeal of the excise duty on paper; and the reasons adduced were that the Budget was only affected indirectly, and that it was socially undesirable to penalize established organs of public opinion by removing a useful curb upon the activities of a cheap and nasty popular Press.

Thereafter, in order to circumvent the Lords, every tax without exception was incorporated by the Commons in the annual Finance Bill; and that novel system was resented by the Lords as a species of chicanery. But because it was still influenced by the fright which it had suffered during the quasi-revolutionary agitation of the 1820s, '30s and early '40s, the House of Lords never dared, before 1909, to reject such a Bill, even when Sir William Harcourt inaugurated in 1894 a radical attempt to redistribute the national income by means of death duties.

The morale and prestige of the House of Lords burned much more brightly at the start of the twentieth century than they had done fifty years earlier. Not a dog had barked, for example, from John O'Groats to Land's End, when the Lords threw out Gladstone's second Irish Home Rule Bill by an overwhelming majority on 8 September 1893; and the ripple of restrained hand-clapping with which an awed and respectful crowd greeted the peers as they climbed into their carriages after the division helped to induce a complacency which turned to arrogance and led to nemesis in 1911.

After the great Liberal triumph of 1906, the House of Lords continued for a time to behave with a measure of circumspection. It was most careful to avoid antagonizing the trade unions and working class, and for that reason it allowed the Trade Disputes Act, the Workmen's Compensation Act and the Eight Hours Act to pass quietly into law; but it fortified its morale and even enhanced its prestige by rejecting many other Liberal measures, including the Education Bill of 1906 and the Licensing Bill of 1908. Always on tenterhooks lest the peers should overplay their hand, King Edward deplored the rejection of the Licensing Bill; but the disgust felt by Liberal leaders at the deferential apathy manifested in the constituencies by the mass of the electorate lent a touch of unreality and hysteria to the cry, 'Peers against People', which was raised continuously upon public platforms by Lloyd George, Winston Churchill and others.

That apathy, and the gnawing fear that frustrated Liberalism might be engulfed presently in a swelling tide of Socialism, caused some Liberal leaders to attempt deliberately to provoke the Lords, by means of taunts and ridicule, into rejecting the Finance Bill of 1909. That Bill embodied no ordinary Budget, for with the aid of a little rhetoric and imagination the land taxes alone could be construed as implying a threat of social revolution, while other taxes could be depicted as wholly destructive of the revenue motive for an imperial tariff, and as postponing indefinitely, in consequence, all prospect of the ultimate triumph of the Unionist policy of tariff reform.

On the evidence of by-election results, the political tide was flowing strongly in the Unionists' favour; but a legacy of internal differences on the fiscal issue weakened the quality of the leadership which Lansdowne and Balfour offered. Both took strongly into account the demagogic influence exerted upon the Unionist rank and file by Lord Northcliffe, who controlled *The Times* as well as the *Daily Mail*, and who urged the Lords to give tariff reform a fair chance by rejecting the Budget and forcing a dissolution.

'The order of battle was now fairly set for a campaign of class warfare', wrote [44] a diehard backwoodsman Tory master of hounds, Lord Willoughby de Broke, in a most attractive volume of memoirs which constitutes a valuable contribution to social history: 'I offered myself as a recruit, and tried to learn my job.' Lord Willoughby discovered quickly that whereas London audiences asked merely to be amused, 'a provincial audience in the home counties nearly always contained enough high and dry Tories to warrant the success of an appeal to the crusted tradition of the Constitution in Church and State, not forgetting to mention Lord Roberts and the National Service League'. The 'most difficult audiences were to be found in some of the large manufacturing towns of the Midlands. There was usually a strong Jacobin, little England, class-conscious element which gave voice to a noisy and implacable hostility that was wellnigh impenetrable.'

The inhabitants of Lancashire provided Lord Willoughby with his most profitable audiences. 'They were exacting without being difficult, critical without being hostile, and ... they would take to a speaker who knew his subject as a pack of foxhounds takes to a huntsman who knows his job. It was an honour to talk to them. ... Many of these good people, moreover, sprang from families who had lived in Lancashire for generations; they were proud of their ancestors and were by no means averse from hearing about the hereditary principle.'

Class warfare, such as it was, can rarely have been conducted on such civilized lines, and Karl Marx would have been disappointed and contemptuous. The peers, who were still worshipped in the countryside, and often also in the cities, as tutelary idols, were about to make the bad mistake of stepping off their pedestals and of exposing themselves, like Homeric gods, to mundane hazards. They would have to be taught a lesson, but most people trusted that light punishment only would be inflicted; and it was in that climate of opinion that King Edward, who was concerned naturally about the hereditary principle, resolved to mediate between Lords and Commons.

In an admirable memorandum (8 October) prepared for King Edward on a single sheet of notepaper, Esher summarized[45] the precedents. The two latest were Queen Victoria's interventions when the Lords and Commons had reached deadlock over the Irish Church Bill in 1869, and over the Reform and Redistribution Bills in 1884. On both occasions the Prime Minister, Gladstone, had admitted 'that the constitutional intervention of the Queen had prevented the conflict between the two Houses'; but in 1909 the Government's contention that the House of Lords was exceeding its powers in rejecting a Budget introduced an entirely novel factor.

Haldane and McKenna, who were at Balmoral at the end of September, 1909, and who found Leander Starr Jameson of the famous 'Raid' among their fellow-guests, advised King Edward that the rejection by the Lords of the Finance Bill would be unconstitutional. They said that it would cause such inconvenience that legislation would be needed to define and curb the powers of the Upper House.

Lord Cawdor, on the other hand, a diehard Tory leader who arrived on 3 October at Balmoral, advised King Edward that the Lords had a constitutional duty to afford the electorate an opportunity to pronounce its views upon what was, in reality, an important piece of social legislation masquerading as a Finance Bill. Cawdor added that that object could best be achieved if the Lords were to reject the Budget without discussion, because the Government would feel obliged to request a dissolution and to appeal to the country at a General Election.

The course indicated by Cawdor was that to which the Unionist leaders had virtually already resigned themselves; and Knollys wrote[46] (28 September) to Esher: 'I am filled with dismay at what you tell me ... about the decision arrived at by Lansdowne and Balfour regarding the Budget. They appear totally to ignore the effect it will probably have on the Crown, and the position the King will be placed in. ...' After detailing the apprehensions which he entertained on King Edward's behalf, Knollys concluded that it

was vital that the House of Lords should be induced some-
how to pass the Budget: 'I fear that in politics, at the present
day, even the most high-minded politician must not only
consider what is right, but must also take into account what
is expedient.'

That was also the opinion of King Edward, who consulted
the Prime Minister on 6 October at Balmoral. Asquith
noted [47] that the King had asked:

... whether I thought he was well within constitutional lines
in taking upon himself to give advice to and, if necessary, put
pressure upon the Tory leaders at this juncture.

I replied that I thought what he was doing, and proposing to
do, perfectly correct from a constitutional point of view; and
that the nearest analogy was the situation and action of William IV at the time of the Reform Bill. In both cases the country was threatened with a revolution at the hands of the House
of Lords.

He said that, in that case, he would not hesitate to see both
Balfour and Lansdowne on his return to London.

He went on to say that they might naturally ask what, if they
persuaded the Lords to pass the Budget, they were to get in
return. It had occurred to him that the best answer would be:
'An appeal to the country – such as you say you want – only
after, and not before the final decision on the Budget.' In other
words, a dissolution and general election in January.

What had I to say to this? Should I approve his holding such
language to them?

Asquith did not consider that that bribe would attract the
Tories, who must calculate that they would benefit from
delay while passion cooled. A General Election immediately
after the Lords 'had climbed down and given in' would be
bad for the Tories, and difficult for the Liberals to justify
to the country at a moment when Parliament had run only
half its term. Accepting that argument, King Edward summoned Balfour and Lansdowne to Buckingham Palace at
noon on 12 October, and invited them to persuade the Lords
to pass the Budget. No inducement was offered; they were
stiff and uncommunicative [48]; and 'I doubt', King Edward
wrote [49] next day from the Jockey Club to Lord Esher,
'whether any result of importance will accrue from my

conversation with them, or that they have decided on any particular policy yet.'

Balfour and Lansdowne felt extremely uncomfortable because their followers were forcing their hands; and Lord Onslow privately informed [50] his friend Lord Carrington (President of the Board of Agriculture) that a meeting of Tory peers on 28 September had recommended that the Budget should be thrown out. No final decision was possible until the mass of backwoodsmen peers reached London for the critical debate; but Unionist M.Ps were almost unanimous in urging the Lords to reject the Budget as a fraud, and in warning them that the Upper House would be despised for ever if it tamely surrendered.

The Finance Bill was rejected by the House of Lords on 30 November 1909 by a majority of 350 votes against 75 after a six days' debate. Knollys had been strongly tempted to vote with the minority; and he informed [51] Esher (8 November) that McKenna agreed with him 'in thinking it would not be a bad thing if it *were* supposed (for it *can* only be a supposition) that the King is opposed to the rejection of the Budget'. Knollys was eager to prevent what he termed 'a disaster happening to the Constitution and, incidentally, to the Monarchy'; but King Edward very properly restrained his secretary from voting. He continued to deplore privately the suicidal folly which the peers had displayed, but Knollys confessed [52] (11 December) to Esher that King Edward had been annoyed 'at being credited with having endeavoured to avert the action of the House of Lords'.

The rejection of the Budget, which menaced the nation with financial chaos, necessitated an immediate General Election, and King Edward dissolved Parliament on 3 December 1909. The House of Commons had resolved on the previous day that the action of the House of Lords was 'a breach of the Constitution and a usurpation of the rights of the Commons'; and King Edward informed [53] thirty house guests at Sandringham that he had never spent a more miserable day. He had a tooth extracted during the afternoon by his dentist, who came from London with Lord Crewe and Lord Wolverhampton, and who was made to dine and to stay the night; and when asked at dinner whether gas had been used, King Edward replied characteristically, 'Oh dear no! I can bear pain.'

On that day (2 December), Knollys received from Lord Esher a letter [54] recounting a very secret conversation with Haldane about the Cabinet's plans. Ministers were considering whether to advise King Edward to transfer permanently into the hands of the Prime Minister of the day the Sovereign's prerogative of creating peers; or whether to frame a Bill curbing the powers of the House of Lords after obtaining from King Edward a pledge, which would be made public before the General Election, that the Sovereign would create a sufficient number of Liberal peers to ensure its passage through the House of Lords. In informing [55] Esher (2 December) that he had decided not to show that letter to King Edward, 'at any rate for the present', Knollys explained that 'it would be a mistake to set him still more against his Ministers', but he characterized both proposals as 'outrageous' and added that the former 'would tend to weaken the Monarchy so considerably that it would be better that the King should abdicate than agree to it'.

The former proposal, which had only been advanced tentatively in the hope that it might spare King Edward's feelings, was discarded quickly by ministers; but the second could have been foreseen, and Knollys's explosive reaction was unhelpful. Much room existed for negotiation about the timing of any pledge by King Edward to create peers, and about the form in which it might be given; and in the absence of some such pledge, or the threat of it, the constitutional crisis would have been insoluble if the Liberals were to win the General Election and if the House of Lords were to remain obdurate.

It is true that King Edward was exceedingly sensitive about anything which touched his prerogative even remotely, and that he had declined, for example, in June to surrender the Lord Chamberlain's right to censor plays. 'The question', Knollys explained [56] (4 July) to Asquith, 'involves a point of his Prerogative, as both the Lord Chamberlain and the Reader of Plays are in his Household'; but on the great constitutional issue King Edward stood in need of more balanced advice than that which he received from Lord Knollys. Until King Edward died, his secretary remained convinced, or almost convinced, that it would be better for the King to abdicate than to give a pledge to create enough peers to ensure the passage of a Parliament Bill; and a feeling of helplessness engendered in consequence caused King Edward to relieve his feelings by discussing the subject of abdication with intimate friends from time to time during the winter of 1909–10.

That talk was not intended to be taken seriously, and it was not so regarded by those to whom it was addressed. It was a symptom of sickness and depression, for King Edward's nature was unyielding, happy and brave. A month before the King's death, Knollys wrote (17 April 1910) to Esher: 'I know ... that however much Sovereigns may threaten to abdicate, they rarely, more than Ministers, carry their threat into execution. In this respect they are like people who say they are going to commit suicide.'

23

The Lords

1910

i

'I MYSELF', Lord Knollys wrote [1] to the Prime Minister's secretary, Vaughan Nash, on 31 October 1909, 'do not see how the House of Lords can go on as at present constituted'; and King Edward had believed for many years that a moderate reform might be desirable. Whereas, however, it appeared to the Government that the problem was insoluble unless King Edward would consent in case of need to create several hundred Liberal peers pledged to pass an Act limiting drastically and in perpetuity the legislative powers of the Upper House, it appeared to Lord Knollys that that revolutionary expedient would impair, perhaps fatally, the prestige of the monarchy.

King Edward agreed with Lord Knollys that such a wholesale creation of peers would be equivalent to the destruction of the House of Lords, and that such destruction would entail the forced enlistment of the Crown in political controversy on the Liberal side. The Unionist Party was an alliance formed to resist Irish Home Rule; no Home Rule Bill could be passed while the Unionists continued to control the Upper House; and Unionist leaders professed to be outraged by the bare suggestion that the Sovereign would be justified constitutionally in accepting advice that he should open the road to Home Rule by destroying the power of the House of Lords.

The House of Lords had been abolished for a decade, together with the monarchy, by a republican and regicide government in 1649; but the only actual precedent for a creation of peers to ensure the passage of a particular measure was that of 1712, when Queen Anne created twelve

Tory peers to outvote opposition to the indispensable Treaty of Utrecht. In 1832, moreover, William IV gave a contingent promise, which he was not required to implement, to create eighty Whig peers, if necessary, to secure the passage of the Reform Bill.

Although the House of Lords would have been destroyed a second time by revolution if it had failed to pass the Reform Act of 1832, its rejection of the 'People's Budget' in 1909 stirred no comparable popular discontent. Lord Lansdowne had allayed the urgency of the crisis by pledging the Lords to pass the Budget unamended and without delay if the Liberals won the General Election; but the Liberals had accepted their opponents' challenge, and Asquith issued a dignified declaration of war on 10 December 1909.

In opening his Party's General Election campaign in a speech at the Albert Hall in London, the Prime Minister demanded for the Commons absolute control over finance, as well as the effective limitation of the legislative powers of the Lords: 'We shall not assume office', he declared, 'and we shall not hold office, unless we can secure the safeguards which experience has shown us to be necessary for the legislative utility and honour of the Party of progress.'

While shooting in Cheshire with the Duke of Westminster, King Edward decided to play for time by stretching his constitutional role. Appreciating that if the Liberals won the General Election he would be invited to create, or to threaten to create, several hundred Liberal peers in order to ensure the passage through the House of Lords of Bills implementing the Government's policy, he despatched Lord Knollys to inform[2] the Prime Minister's secretary at 10 Downing Street on 15 December that he would not feel justified in accepting such advice until a second General Election had been held.

Knollys explained to Nash that King Edward regarded 'the policy of the Government as tantamount to the destruction of the House of Lords', and that he considered that the country had a right to be consulted at a General Election about the specific means which Government proposed to employ in order to effect that object. He added that the

King's objection to a wholesale creation of peers would be 'considerably diminished' if all could be life peers, but Nash retorted that 'would involve legislation to which the House of Lords might object'.

Knollys then asked that alternative means of coercing the House of Lords should be considered, such as withholding a writ of summons from all peers who would not pledge themselves to vote with the Government, but that and other possibilities were discarded later, after being explored by lawyers. Knollys insisted that King Edward's stipulation about a second General Election was intended at that time for the Prime Minister's ear alone, and Asquith attempted loyally to adjust his plans and to manage his Party in accordance with the Sovereign's wish.

Because he needed to find an outlet for a growing dislike of his Government, King Edward, after becoming reconciled with Haldane, started to vent his discontent upon the head of the Home Secretary, Herbert Gladstone. As the youngest son of Queen Victoria's Prime Minister, Gladstone owed his position more to birth than to ability; he was the weakest member of the Cabinet, and he greatly vexed King Edward by giving permission in September 1908 for Roman Catholic priests in vestments, led by the papal legate, Cardinal Vanutelli, to carry the Host in procession through the streets of London. Planned as the culminating moment of a Eucharistic Congress, that procession was advertised tactlessly as an act of reparation for the Reformation, and a flood of Protestant protests flowed into Buckingham Palace as well as into Whitehall.

King Edward's admiration for stately ceremonial, the charming curiosity which caused him to visit Lourdes and the tolerance which he invariably displayed, had given rise to unfounded rumours that he cherished leanings towards the Church of Rome. He begged Gladstone to veto that procession in order to avert a breach of the peace; but the Home Secretary, who was on holiday in Scotland, made no response. His supine inactivity left the public to infer that King Edward wanted the procession to take place; and the King alerted the Prime Minister. Asquith asked Lord Ripon, who was the only Roman Catholic member of the Cabinet, to approach the Archbishop of Westminster, Cardinal Bourne, at the last moment; and, after persuading the Archbishop with difficulty to eliminate the Host and the priests' vestments, Ripon resigned his office of Lord Privy Seal. He did so ostensibly on grounds of health, but actually because he resented the task laid upon him; and King Edward rebuked Gladstone for muddle, lack of foresight and inertia.

In rebuking Gladstone a year later for appointing two women, Lady Frances Balfour and Mrs H. J. Tennant, to serve as members of a Royal Commission on Divorce, King Edward was on weaker ground. He had approved previously of the principle of appointing women to serve on Royal Commissions, but he warned[3] the Home Secretary (10 September 1909) that divorce was a subject 'which cannot be discussed openly and in all its aspects with any delicacy or even decency before ladies'. In giving his consent with extreme repugnance he informed[4] Asquith (15 September) that he regarded the two appointments as 'the thin edge of suffragetism, and feels sure that its adherents and supporters will get stronger and more persistent in their demands when they see the principle, on which they base their claims, partially recognized'.

Appreciating that Gladstone was an indifferent Home Secretary, Asquith seized a chance to drop him honourably from the Government. He asked King Edward to appoint him to be the first Governor-General of the Union of South Africa; and the King fought hard, with mixed feelings, against that suggestion. He had described the Union of South Africa Act as premature when he signed it on 20 September 1909; but he argued that a new Dominion was entitled to expect someone more competent than Herbert Gladstone as its first Governor-General. The Home Secretary bore, nevertheless, a famous Liberal name, and when the matter became urgent, Knollys laid before King Edward a memorandum[5] (20 October) which stated that responsible opinion in South Africa was unanimously in favour of Gladstone's appointment. 'The King', Knollys wrote[6] next day to the Prime Minister's secretary, 'in answer to my memorandum, says that if the Prime Minister cannot find a better Governor-General, he supposes he must approve of the appointment, but that he thinks it a very bad one'.

Because his health worsened that winter, King Edward decided to stay at Brighton as the guest of the Arthur Sassoons when the General Election, which was spread over a fortnight, began on 14 January 1910. His diary recorded [7] on that day: 'In the morning, walk on beach at Shoreham – in the afternoon, motor to Worthing and walk on promenade'; he was low and depressed, and the anxiety which gnawed him as he strolled on the sea front with Mrs George Keppel, Mrs Willy James or Mrs Arthur Sassoon was caused by the pledge about safeguards which Asquith had given to his Party on 10 December.

Talk in King Edward's intimate circle revolved round the problem of what it behoved the sovereign to do if the Liberals won the General Election, and if Asquith then asked for what came to be known as advance guarantees. Many Liberals assumed that King Edward had promised already to create several hundred Liberal peers if necessary; and some foolish Unionists seemed disposed to blame the King for having already favoured their opponents in that way.

Believing [8] that a Liberal victory was probable, King Edward toyed [9] in moments of deepest gloom with the fear that backwoodsmen Tory peers might repudiate Lord Lansdowne's pledge to pass the Budget. In that event it was obvious that an immediate wholesale manufacture of Liberal peers would have been imperative in order to avert financial chaos; but in all other circumstances it appeared reasonable to hope that the Prime Minister would accept a delay in settling accounts with the House of Lords. Hoping that it would be possible to arrange a suitable compromise, King Edward appreciated that the secret stipulation which he had made about a second General Election would, unless challenged, necessitate an early public repudiation by Asquith of the pledge which he had given publicly at the Albert Hall; and he waited, accordingly, on tenterhooks while seeking to ascertain the views of the Unionist leaders.

In a letter [10] (29 December 1909) to Lord Esher, Lord Knollys explained that *under no circumstances* could it ever be right for a promise by King Edward to create peers to be made public at the time when a Bill was introduced to reform the House of Lords. In such an event 'it would look as if the King had delivered himself body and soul into the hands of the extreme left'. Although a second General Election would now be necessary before any Bill could be introduced to destroy the House of Lords, 'for that is what it really amounts to', Knollys begged Esher to consult Balfour urgently and as a precautionary measure on the King's behalf. King Edward wished to know whether, if he refused a request by Asquith to create peers, and if Asquith resigned in consequence, 'Balfour would consent to form a Government. If the King understood beforehand that he would do, it would strengthen his hands enormously.'

In reply to the obvious argument that a Liberal majority in the Commons would outvote Balfour immediately, Knollys added [11] (8 January): 'Even if the King knows beforehand that Balfour would decline to form a Government, I think he (the King) ought to send for him, as he could then present a better front and could say, "Well! what can I do? The Liberals won't remain in office and the Conservatives refuse it. I have, therefore, no possible option but to give way."'

Esher recorded [12] (9 January) that although the leader of the Opposition had refused to say whether or not he would be willing or able to form a Government before the General Election results were known, Balfour 'could not believe that it was really intended to ask the King for a promise to create Peers *before* a Bill was introduced dealing with the H. of L. He was amazed at the impudence of the thing. He has no shadow of doubt that the K. ought not under any circumstances to agree ... it would be a breach of the King's duty, if not of his coronation oath, to pledge himself to create Peers to pass a Bill which he has never seen.' There might, Balfour conceded, 'be some justification' for asking King Edward 'to use his prerogative powers to pass a Bill which had already received assent of an overwhelming majority of the H. of C.'; but there could be 'NONE for asking him to promise to use it for the purpose of passing ultimately, through the H. of L., a Bill which the H. of C. has not even seen'.

Balfour promised that he would be willing, if Asquith resigned, 'to state in Parliament the dilemma in which Ministers had placed the King, and Mr Balfour feels confident that the King would be supported by the country'. He added that 'whatever risk may be run by the Sovereign in refusing such a request as it is assumed Asquith will make next month, there would be greater risk in acceding to it'.

King Edward's dearest wish was to avoid forfeiting prestige and popularity by becoming involved in a controversy which the country as a whole continued to regard with comparative and extraordinary detachment. Despite fervent Radical efforts, the mass of the electorate treated the problem of the House of Lords and even the fate of the Finance Bill as remote topics; and it was open therefore to statesmen on both sides to conduct a fulminating but academic debate. They argued in terms of constitutional precedent and of an unwritten patrician code, while leaving platform orators to acquire experience and to provide audiences throughout the kingdom with stimulus and entertainment.

275 Liberals; 273 Unionists; 82 Irish Nationalists; and 40 Labour Members were returned at the General Election of January 1910. The Liberals lost 104 seats; the majority of 86 which they had secured over all other Parties in 1906 was transformed into a minority of 120; and the majority of 220 which they had secured over the Unionists alone in 1906 was reduced to a beggarly 2. But, despite that bitter disappointment, Asquith could count upon Irish and Socialist support in dealing with the House of Lords and in according Home Rule in Ireland. Although the attitude of the Irish towards the Budget hinged partly upon the rate of the whisky duty, Asquith concluded that Balfour would be incapable of forming a Government on the basis of a House of Commons so constituted and disposed; and the Cabinet decided, accordingly, that it was its duty to remain in office.

On 24 January 1910, Esher wrote [13] from Windsor Castle

to Balfour: 'The recent elections have caused great relief here.... There can be no question, with this lowered majority dependent upon the Irish, of Asquith trying to "bully" the King.' Asquith had no such intention, but the Archbishop of Canterbury, Randall Davidson, who was also at the castle, advised King Edward to reject any demand for guarantees, and offered to mediate between the Parties.

The need for mediation became greater as the prospect of irreconcilable deadlock increased. Liberals argued that they could never hope to govern the country effectually until the House of Lords, which was incorrigibly Tory by nature, had been stripped of its usurped control over finance, and of its predominance over other legislation. They held that Asquith had a duty to offer and that King Edward had a duty to accept constitutional advice that the Royal Prerogative should be used, if necessary, to ensure the passage of an Act of Parliament restricting drastically the powers of the Upper House.

Unionists retorted that a revolutionary expedient, which might be justified as the extreme medicine of the Constitution, could not be its daily bread, and that the crisis of 1910 was being artificially sustained. The country was bored and indifferent as well as evenly divided; the Prime Minister was not entitled to tender hysterical advice; and, as Lansdowne had pledged the Lords to pass the Budget, no crisis necessitating urgency in dealing with the Upper House could reasonably be held to exist.

Stripped of ancillary matter, that was the nub of an argument which showed a constant tendency to descend from austere constitutional heights into the attractive but forbidden garden of King Edward's personal predicament. The man in the street could not resist the temptation to discuss what King Edward might do in this or that contingency, but statesmen were most anxious to spare him embarrassment or distress, and Asquith's conduct was chivalrous. He contrived, nevertheless, to annoy King Edward by refusing a command to visit Windsor at the end of January, because he wanted to snatch a brief rest in the South of France.

At Windsor, accordingly, on 30 January, King Edward

expounded to the Colonial Secretary and Lord Privy Seal, Lord Crewe, a plan for redressing the ill-effects of the inequality of Party representation in the House of Lords. He suggested [14] tentatively that every existing peer should retain his right to sit and speak, but that the right to vote should be restricted to one hundred peers, of whom fifty should be nominated by the leaders of each of the two main Parties. King Edward expressed his hope that such a select body would learn to insist upon compromise amendments, bearing always in mind the need to avoid collisions with the Commons; but Crewe replied that Party leaders would be tempted to appoint nonentities who could be trusted to vote on strict Party lines, and that eminent non-Party men – the Archbishop of Canterbury, for example, or Lord Rosebery – could scarcely hope to be nominated.

King Edward had formed that plan on his personal initiative, without consulting Lord Knollys who was anxious that the Sovereign's strict constitutional neutrality should not be prejudiced by direct intervention at that time. During the General Election campaign some Radicals had suggested that King Edward sympathized with the principle of Irish Home Rule, and a diehard Tory leader, Walter Long, wrote stupidly to ask Knollys for authority to contradict that rumour. After refusing, very properly, Knollys wrote [15] (10 January) to Esher: 'Of course the King is not a Home Ruler; but, all the same, I cannot think it would be judicious, or even right, that this should be publicly announced. Otherwise people might be asking about his views on all sorts of subjects.'

The sky darkened quickly and ominously before King Edward opened the new Parliament in State with Queen Alexandra on 21 February. Whereas Asquith's most urgent problem was the re-introduction of the ill-starred Finance Bill, the Irish Nationalists, upon whose support he had to depend, were much more interested in the problem of the House of Lords. They wanted to destroy the Lords' veto at once in order to prepare the way for a Home Rule Bill; and their leader, William Redmond, threatened to order his followers to vote with the Unionists against the Budget in the

House of Commons unless Asquith promised that a Bill dealing with the veto of the House of Lords would be forced through Parliament that year.

The Irish Nationalists shared the Tory outlook on tariff reform. Abominating also the increased excise duty which the Budget imposed on whisky, they would gladly have followed their leader into the Opposition lobby against the Finance Bill, but Asquith refused to surrender to Irish intimidation. He went to Brighton on 10 February to see King Edward, who was again lodging with the Sassoons; and the King informed [16] Knollys (12 February) that the Prime Minister had been 'reasonable and amiable' but that the Government found itself 'in a very "tight place"'.

Besides obtaining approval for certain Cabinet changes, Asquith told King Edward that the Government did not consider that it would be fair at that time to ask for any guarantee about the creation of peers. He explained that the Finance Bill took priority over all else; that it was menaced by an unnatural Unionist-Irish combination in the Commons; and that it was conceivable, therefore, that it might never reach the Lords which were pledged to pass it unamended. Asquith suggested that King Edward, in those circumstances, might feel inclined to put out a 'feeler' to Balfour, in order to ascertain whether the Unionists really considered it to be necessary to oppose the Budget in the Commons; and King Edward undertook to do that.

Esher begged [17] Knollys vainly to cause systematic records of such important conversations to be kept; but the Cabinet met on the morning of 11 February and Asquith confirmed [18] immediately in writing what he had said about guarantees: 'His Majesty's Ministers do not propose to advise or request any exercise of the Royal Prerogative in existing circumstances, or until they have submitted their plan to Parliament. If, in their judgement, it should become their duty to tender any such advice, they would do so when – and not before – the actual necessity may arise.'

Before returning to Buckingham Palace, King Edward instructed Knollys to sound Balfour's secretary, John Sandars, about Unionist intentions when the Finance Bill was reintroduced into the House of Commons. Knollys invited Sandars, accordingly, to visit him at Buckingham Palace on the morning of 14 February; and, when that conference was ended, Sandars was taken by arrangement to see King Edward for a few casual moments before luncheon.

King Edward wrote [19] on 15 February to Asquith: 'My dear Prime Minister, I had hoped that the result of the "feeler" I threw out yesterday might have been of a nature which would have minimized the difficult position in which the Government now finds itself, but from what I can gather I find that the Opposition will probably vote against the Government on the Budget, in consequence of the attitude which they took up in Parliament and at the elections in regard to the salient points of that measure.' Asquith replied [20] at once that although the Unionists could not rely with any degree of certainty upon the support of the Irish Nationalists in a renewed attack upon the Budget in the Commons, 'such a combination is undoubtedly a contingency which must be regarded as within the range of possibility'.

On 21 February 1910, a few hours after King Edward opened Parliament, Asquith made a remarkable speech. Moved by loyalty and chivalry he qualified, to a point which was too close to repudiation to be tenable, the celebrated pledge about guarantees which he had given to his Party on 10 December. He informed the House of Commons on 21 February that he had neither requested nor received such guarantees; that it was 'the duty of responsible politicians in this country, as long as possible and as far as possible, to keep the name of the Sovereign and the Prerogatives of the Crown outside the domain of Party politics'; and that he would act only in the public interest. He continued: 'But to ask, in advance, for a blank authority, for an indefinite exercise of the Royal Prerogative, in regard to a measure which has never been submitted to, or approved by, the House of Commons, is a request which, in my judgement, no constitutional statesman can properly make, and it is a concession which the Sovereign cannot be expected to grant.'

That statement, which gratified King Edward before his departure for Biarritz, disgusted Irish Nationalists and Labour Members. It also disappointed a large number of Liberals who accused their leader of being too quixotic, and who asked how many more General Elections they could expect to have to fight before settling their Party's account with the House of Lords. Asquith had to manoeuvre with some adroitness to conciliate his Cabinet and to retain his hold on the House of Commons; and, while preoccupied with those problems, he was accused by King Edward, who was made irritable by failing health, of being secretive.

ii

Doctors had been urging King Edward to hasten his departure for Biarritz; but he only agreed on 1 March to leave England on 6 March after Asquith had assured him categorically that no immediate crisis impended which would require his presence at home. His diary during that final week was crowded with engagements, and he continued to be forceful and forthright. He reminded Asquith, for example, that no meeting of the Committee of Imperial Defence had been held for eight months, and urged him to summon one forthwith; he begged Morley to forget Hardinge and to appoint Kitchener to succeed Minto as Viceroy of India; and he praised Winston Churchill for the 'very interesting and instructive reports' of the debates in the House of Commons which he summarized daily, as Home Secretary, for the Sovereign's information.

On the evening before he went abroad, King Edward gave the last of a series of dinners which he had instituted recently at the Palace for men of distinction in various fields. A number of senior civil servants were invited on that occasion, and King Edward was seen to do full justice to turtle soup, salmon steak, grilled chicken, saddle of mutton, several snipe stuffed with foie gras, asparagus, a fruit dish, an enormous iced concoction and a savoury. He left next day for Paris, where he caught a chill on 7 March while witnessing Edmond Rostand's play, *Chantecler*, at the Théâtre de la Porte

St Martin; and he wrote[21] (16 March) to the Prince of Wales:

> I was dreadfully disappointed with *Chantecler* at Paris. I never saw anything so stupid and childish and more like a Pantomime! The heat at the Theatre was awful and I contrived to get a chill with a threatening of bronchitis. ...
>
> The schemes of the financial matters worked out by the Govt. are very clever and intricate; and I am not sure that they have not stolen a successful march on the Unionists

After reaching Biarritz by special train on 9 March, King Edward collapsed and was confined to his rooms at the Hotel du Palais by Sir James Reid. He refused to remain in bed, but received only a very few visitors, who included Soveral and Mrs Keppel; and although he insisted upon going out on 21 March, Sir Arthur Davidson informed[22] Esher (22 March) that no business had been transacted for a fortnight.

Towards the end of March, King Edward felt better and was urged by Queen Alexandra to leave 'that horrid Biarritz' and to join her on 14 April at Genoa, where she was due to embark on a Mediterranean cruise in the new royal yacht *Alexandra*. King Edward explained[23] (12 April) to the Prince of Wales that that was:

> ... quite out of the question, as it might be necessary at any moment for me to return (and I can do so under 24 hours at any time) should the Govt. resign, dissolve, or commit any act which entails my presence at home.
>
> Their ways get worse and worse, and our great Empire is now being ruled by Messrs Redmond and O'Brien * (in their different ways), aided and abetted by Messrs Asquith, L. George and W. Churchill! The other Ministers who really know better (Crewe, Grey and Haldane) quickly agree to anything.

King Edward, while ill, had been kept informed by Asquith of the Government's resolve to ensure the passage through all its parliamentary stages of the Finance Bill of 1909 before both Houses rose for the Easter Recess, and of its

---

* William O'Brien led a group of seven independent Irish Nationalist Members of Parliament who hoped to attain their goal by means of 'Conference Conciliation and Consultation'. Those hopes were blasted in 1918 by the rise of Sinn Fein.

resolve also to introduce a Parliament Bill into the Commons. The Parliament Bill was prefaced by a statement that, whereas it was intended 'to substitute for the House of Lords a Second Chamber constituted on a popular instead of hereditary basis', that change could not be brought immediately into effect; and it was provided in the meantime:

1. that the House of Lords should be disqualified from rejecting or amending bills which had been certified as Money Bills by the Speaker of the House of Commons;

2. that any Bill passed by the Commons which had been rejected by the Lords in three successive sessions, after being sent up to the Lords at least one month before the end of each session, should become law, on the Royal Assent being declared, when two years had elapsed between the date on which it had been introduced into Parliament and the date on which it had passed its third reading in the Commons;

3. that the duration of future Parliaments should be reduced from seven to five years.

That Bill was introduced on 14 April 1910, following a series of resolutions which had been adopted previously by consistent majorities of over one hundred votes. It caused the Government no anxiety in the Commons where, on the other hand, the Finance Bill was gravely menaced by an odd but invincible combination between the Unionists and the Irish Nationalists. For that reason Asquith wrote [24] (13 April) a long explanatory letter warning King Edward that he must be prepared at any moment to receive his Government's resignation; but he telegraphed [25] on the same day that it would be unnecessary for the King to be back in London before 19 April.

After explaining that he would resign immediately if his Government were defeated in the Commons on the previous year's belated Budget, Asquith stated that it was impossible to see how any other Government possessing a parliamentary majority could be formed: 'A crisis of an unexampled and most embarrassing kind would, therefore, arise', and another General Election, 'after an interval of barely three months', would almost certainly be necessary:

It is an acute sense of those public disadvantages and dangers, and not any desire to prolong their own official life which, under existing conditions, is far from being a bed of roses, that has induced Your Majesty's Minister to authorize the Chancellor of the Exchequer to interchange views on the subject of the Budget with the leaders of the two sections of the Nationalist Party. From the first both were made clearly to understand that the Chancellor had no authority to offer concessions or to make bargains....

The Irish Nationalists had offered to vote with the Government on the Budget if the increased duty on whisky was eliminated, but 'after full consideration ... Your Majesty's advisers are strongly and unanimously of opinion that to purchase the Irish vote by such a concession would be a discreditable transaction which they could not defend'. It was not necessary for Asquith to explain that his Nonconformist supporters would never have forgiven him; but, after stating that that Irish demand had been rejected, the Prime Minister observed that no recourse remained except to bid for the Irish vote by threatening publicly and at once to invoke the use of the Royal Prerogative to ensure the passage of the Parliament Bill through the House of Lords.

Asquith had tried hard to spare King Edward's feelings by holding that weapon of advance guarantees in reserve. The Commons had now expressed approval of the detailed terms of a specific Bill, and Asquith's letter continued:

The Cabinet had further under consideration the course which they ought to take (apart from any question of the Budget) in the event, which is now imminent, of the Resolutions in regard to the relations between the two Houses being carried by the Commons and rejected or laid aside by the Lords.

They came to the conclusion that, in that event, it would be their duty at once to tender advice to the Crown as to the necessary steps – whether by exercising the Royal Prerogative, or by a Referendum *ad hoc*, or otherwise – to be taken to ensure that their policy, approved by the House of Commons by large majorities, should be given statutory effect in this Parliament.

If they found that they were not in a position to accomplish that object, they would then either resign office, or advise a dissolution of Parliament. But in no case would they feel able to advise a dissolution except under such conditions as would secure that, in the new Parliament, the judgement of the people as expressed at the Elections would be carried into law.

The Cabinet were all of opinion that, as far as possible, the name of the Crown should be kept out of the arena of Party politics.

Asquith's reference to the unprecedented expedient of a referendum proves the lengths to which he was prepared to consider going in an effort to discover an alternative means of solving the constitutional deadlock. He informed the House of Commons on 14 April that 'if the Lords fail to accept our policy ... we shall feel it our duty immediately to tender such advice to the Crown as to the steps which will have to be taken if that policy is to receive statutory effect in this Parliament'. That reference to 'this Parliament' committed the Government unequivocally again to the position which Asquith had taken on 10 December, but which he had qualified on 21 February; and it ran counter to King Edward's stipulation about the need for a second General Election. In a veiled reference to the possibility of a referendum, Asquith added that he could not state what 'the precise terms' of his advice to the Crown would be; but grave doubts were entertained about the propriety of a referendum, and King Edward was faced again with the imminent prospect of being asked for a guarantee to swamp the House of Lords by creating several hundred Liberal peers.

Asquith purchased for the Budget in that way the indispensable support of the Irish Nationalists; and as a responsible democratic statesman he could not have acted otherwise. King Edward, inevitably, was cruelly depressed; Balfour accused the Prime Minister of having bartered and betrayed the dignity of his high office; and the fury of Lord Knollys was almost hysterical.

In reply to Asquith's letter of 13 April, King Edward asked[26] curtly (16 April) for a telegram informing him of the result of the next critical division on the Budget in the Commons, 'so that he can make his plans accordingly'; and in that division the Government was successful on 18 April. On the previous day Knollys, who had remained, as always, in England, wrote [27] to inform Esher that Asquith was about:

> to commit the greatest outrage on the King which has ever been committed since England became a Constitutional Monarchy; and, if I were the King, I would, should the Elections be in favour of the Radicals, rather abdicate than agree to it. ...
> I am very glad that Balfour thinks it a good thing that the King should remain away for the present, but I fear that is not the view taken generally of his absence. I understand you to say that if the King appealed to Balfour on the 'creation' business, he would not hesitate to respond by accepting office.

On the initiative of Lord Knollys, who asked [28] for 'some assistance in unravelling the tangle in which he found himself involved', Balfour conferred with Esher, Knollys and the Archbishop of Canterbury at Lambeth Palace at three o'clock on the afternoon of 27 April 1910. Esher summarized [29] the arguments used and the conclusions reached; and the published version omitted a significant and characteristic observation by Balfour. As he started to dissect King Edward's predicament, the leader of the Opposition remarked,[30] with visible relish, 'If we look at it as we should look at pieces on a chess-board, disregarding the flesh and blood characteristics....'; but that degree of detachment was unattainable.

Balfour assumed that 'the time was not far distant when the King would be asked either to create 500 Peers for the purpose of passing the "Veto" Bill through the present Parliament, or to grant a dissolution coupled with a promise to create peers in the event of a Liberal majority being returned after the Election'. In undertaking that the Unionist Party would be willing to advance to King Edward's aid in either contingency, Balfour agreed [31] with the Archbishop that, 'in view of the weakness of the present mandate', King Edward could safely reject advice from Asquith that peers should be created in order to force a Parliament Bill through the Upper House of the existing Parliament.

On the other hand, Balfour considered that 'the future of the Monarchy itself might depend' upon 'the substance and form' of the reply addressed to Asquith, if King Edward decided to reject his Government's request for a dissolution coupled with advance guarantees. The Archbishop observed that the task of drafting that letter of refusal in such a way as to exclude all appearance of political bias would be almost insuperably difficult; but Balfour was convinced that, by taking trouble, it would be possible to frame 'a satisfactory document' which 'would add much lustre to the position of the Sovereign'.

Esher's view [32] that the Sovereign retained a clear constitutional right to reject advice which ministers tendered, if he could find other ministers to carry on the Government, was obsolete and unhelpful in 1910; and Knollys remained doubtful after as well as before that Lambeth conference. He might have advised King Edward to adopt the bold and rash expedient of rejecting Asquith's constitutional advice; but after death had deprived him of the comfortable support of his old master's immense prestige, he urged King Edward's untried successor to adopt, at the ultimate moment, the opposite course.

At Lambeth on 27 April 1910, it was arranged that Balfour should form a Unionist Government if the Liberal Government were to resign in either of the two contingencies envisaged. Balfour explained that he would ask for a dissolution at once, and that he would appeal to the country at a General Election; and it was agreed that there was no objection to the King proposing a compromise if any reasonable basis could be found.

After warning Esher that no compromise appeared to be possible 'in view of the relations between the Government and the Irish', Balfour also warned Knollys that Asquith had discarded the idea of a referendum, which had attracted King Edward as a possible means of avoiding the question of advance guarantees. Knollys started, accordingly, to urge Hardinge to induce Grey to revive that idea in the Cabinet, and Hardinge reported [33] regretfully (3 May) that the Foreign Secretary was 'a broken reed to lean on'. Hardinge suggested that King Edward should speak privately to Grey, who was 'very impressionable', in his most forceful manner; but that forcefulness was exhausted at last.

The conference at Lambeth ended only a few minutes before King Edward returned from Biarritz to Buckingham Palace at a quarter to six on 27 April. Although exceedingly tired, he insisted upon dressing at once before attending the opera, and upon approving a large number of audiences which had been arranged. He received Asquith in audience on 28 April, and Lord Kitchener and Lord Morley on the following day; and he tried hard to persuade Morley to send Kitchener to rule India with a strong hand.

After attending *Siegfried* at Covent Garden on Friday, 29 April, King Edward went next morning to Sandringham, where an east wind sprang up after luncheon on Sunday and pierced him as he inspected his home farm and pedigree stock. Coughing and wheezing, he returned on Monday, 2 May, to Buckingham Palace, in time to dine quietly with Miss Keyser in Grosvenor Crescent; and on 4 May the unique last entry in the impersonal diary, which he had kept at his father's behest in his own hand since boyhood read [34]: 'The King dines alone.' Alerted in Corfu, Queen Alexandra reached London on the evening of 5 May, but King Edward failed for once to greet her at the station. Exclaiming frequently, 'I must fight this!', he had continued to give formal audiences throughout the day – the last to the Agent-General for Queensland, Major T. B. Robinson – but his colour and physical weakness struck fear into all hearts, except his own; and a medical bulletin, signed that evening by Laking and others, announced that he had bronchitis, and that his condition caused 'some anxiety'.

Dressing early on Friday, 6 May, King Edward rejected indignantly the informal clothes which his valets had laid out. He called for a frock-coat before receiving Lord Knollys, who found him very feeble in voice but not in mind. He lit a large cigar when he received Sir Ernest Cassel at noon, and collapsed,[35] after taking a light luncheon in his bedroom, while playing with two pet canaries in a cage by an open window. Nurses raised him to his feet and supported him to an armchair; Princess Victoria fetched the Queen; but a series of heart attacks followed and King Edward fought for breath.

Five doctors abandoned hope after a brief examination; morphia was administered to deaden pain, and the Archbishop of Canterbury was summoned. King Edward, who displayed exemplary courage during intervals of consciousness, was visited by relays of friends who called to inquire at the Palace throughout the afternoon, and who were taken to see him, by Queen Alexandra's order, if they so wished and had known him well. Mrs Keppel and others said goodbye to him as he sat hunched in his armchair, resisting, even when seemingly unconscious, attempts to assist him on to his bed; and he was informed by the Prince of Wales during a lucid interval soon after five o'clock that his horse *Witch of the Air* had won the Spring Two-Year-Old Plate at Kempton Park by half a length.

'I am very glad', King Edward replied, before lapsing soon afterwards into a coma; and it became evident at about 11.30 p.m. that the end was at hand. He was lifted then on to his bed, while the Prince of Wales fetched the Archbishop from the room in which he had been waiting for some hours. And at 11.45 p.m. on Friday, 6 May 1910, King Edward VII died quite peacefully in his sixty-ninth year. The Archbishop said a brief prayer and spoke a few words of comfort; and King George V wrote [36] simply in his diary: 'I have lost my best friend and the best of fathers. I never had a word with him in my life. I am heartbroken and overwhelmed with grief.'

About a quarter of a million people filed silently through Westminster Hall where the body lay in State from 17–19 May upon a catafalque beside which the Emperor William came to pray; and vast crowds watched the funeral procession through the streets of London to Paddington Station in splendid weather on 20 May. Immediately behind the gun-carriage, which bore the coffin, walked King Edward's disconsolate fox-terrier Caesar, in charge of a Highland servant, followed by the German Emperor and eight kings.

Besides King George V and the Emperor William II, the funeral was attended by the Kings of Belgium, Bulgaria, Denmark, Greece, Norway, Portugal and Spain; by many princes and princesses including the Archduke Francis

Ferdinand of Austria-Hungary and other heirs to thrones; and by Queen Alexandra's sister, the Dowager Empress Marie Feodorovna of Russia, and ex-President Theodore Roosevelt of the United States. King Edward was buried in the vault beneath St George's Chapel at Windsor; and, after King George had led his mother gently away, luncheon was served at the Castle to twelve hundred distinguished mourners in the Waterloo Chamber and in St George's Hall.

A Party truce was called immediately in the constitutional controversy,* out of respect for King Edward's memory and out of sympathy with his untried heir; and it was even argued that worry had caused the untimely death of a much-loved sovereign. That partisan suggestion was, of course, untrue; and, in historical perspective, King Edward's death in 1910 may not even appear in fact to have been untimely. Cherishing warmly until the last the traditional values of an older Merrie England which had its roots in the countryside, he was increasingly perplexed when confronted by evidence of the changing values of a population which contained in 1914 only eight per cent who continued to work upon the land.

Despite the pygmy appearance which the Edwardian social conscience presents to the trained eye of captious critics in a later age, King Edward was a thoroughly conscientious sovereign who made pleasure his servant and not his master after his accession to the throne. His private life, which was not free from what moralists could term blemishes, included an ideal relationship with his heir; and the dignity of his public life, his immense popularity and charm, and the zest, punctuality and panache with which he performed his duty forcefully and faithfully until the day on which he died, enhanced the prestige of the monarchy. The journey upon which he embarked in boyhood towards the bourne of his future subjects' approbation may be compared with a voyage to the Antipodes. Safe havens were attainable from opposite directions; parents and tutors pointed one way but he found another; and he arrived.

* The outcome of that controversy is related with certain other matters, in the appendix.

Appendix

1910–13

IMMEDIATELY after King Edward's death, King George V's private secretary, Sir Arthur Bigge (Lord Stamfordham), suggested with characteristic high-mindedness that Lord Knollys should serve as joint private secretary while Party leaders strove to settle privately the constitutional crisis, in order to avoid causing embarrassment to an inexperienced sovereign. Lord Stamfordham appreciated the profound respect which King George felt for the wisdom of King Edward's old friends and servants, and Lord Knollys was entrusted with special responsibility for handling political questions; but that arrangement worked badly.

A constitutional conference, which followed King Edward's death, broke down on 10 November 1910 after twenty-one sittings behind closed doors, and a General Election during December left the previous state of the Parties in the House of Commons almost unchanged. Before that election, Asquith coupled his request for a dissolution of Parliament with a request that King George should give the Cabinet a secret pledge to create enough Liberal peers to ensure the passage of the Parliament Bill through the House of Lords, if the Liberals were returned to power.

Asquith explained [1] to King George that he was bound by the statement which he had made in the Commons on 14 April, and that he would resign if his request were rejected; but Lord Stamfordham advised King George not to grant a dissolution on those terms. He argued that the Cabinet ought to trust the King to act rightly at the right time; that Asquith's resignation should be accepted; and that Balfour should be invited to form a Unionist Government which would have had to appeal to the country at once.

Lord Knollys argued, on the other hand, that confidence in the political impartiality of the throne would be shaken severely if a dissolution which had been refused to a Liberal Prime Minister were granted to a Tory one a few days later. He advised King George to accede to Asquith's demand, and he assured him that King Edward would have accepted that advice.

On that issue, before his death, King Edward had been in no position to guide his heir, because he had not made up his mind what he would do. Had King Edward lived, it is virtually certain that he would have been content to be guided by Lord Knollys; and it is possible that Lord Knollys's advice would have accorded with that tendered to King George by Lord Stamfordham. The new Sovereign, however, had not had time to acquire the prestige which his father had enjoyed, and Knollys changed[2] his mind at the last moment, after a conversation with Mr Asquith and Lord Crewe on 15 November 1910. To the great and enduring regret of Lord Stamfordham, King George accepted on 16 November the arguments adduced by Lord Knollys, and Asquith was granted accordingly on that day a dissolution coupled with a secret contingent guarantee about a wholesale creation of Liberal peers.

That guarantee, disclosed at a time and in a manner chosen by the Government after the Liberals had won the General Election, sufficed by a narrow margin to ensure the passage of the Parliament Bill through the House of Lords. King George resented especially the secrecy in which the transaction had been wrapped, and he formed the view that on 16 November 1910 Lord Knollys had failed to disclose vital information about the attitude of the Unionist Party in general, and about the willingness of Mr Balfour in particular to form a Unionist Government.

When the Irish Home Rule controversy was at its height three years later, Lord Esher recorded[3] at Windsor on 18 November 1913:

The King talked very excitedly to me yesterday for 1½ hours, still overweighed by the idea that, if he had refused the guarantees in November 1910, all present troubles would have been

obviated. That is by no means so clear. But what *is* clear, beyond all question, is the suppression (accidental, I think) of
vital information by F.[rancis] K.[nollys] of what the Opposition thought in 1910 of the general situation, of what the King
ought to do. F.K. is old – and he was under the recent agitation of the death of his old master. Anyhow he did *not* give the
King the information which was due to him.

Looking backwards, with the advantage of hindsight, it is
fair to suggest that the advice tendered by Lord Knollys in
very difficult circumstances was more prudent and, in all
probability, more expedient than that which Lord Stamfordham had offered; but the Unionist leaders thought
otherwise. Party feeling ran so high between 1910 and 1914
that it was difficult even for the Sovereign to form a view
untinged by prejudice; and, after that unhappy affair, King
George gave the whole of his confidence to Lord Stamfordham. Lord Knollys became jealous in consequence, and so
resentful of the attitude of the Opposition leaders that he
would scarcely speak to them. After discussing [4] that position with King George, Lord Esher urged [5] his old friend in
a long and tactful letter (19 January 1913) to retire with a
good grace; and Lord Knollys informed [6] the King accordingly (14 February) that he appreciated the need to depart
without delay. He added: 'It is necessary, however, that I
should first look over, sort and, when advisable, destroy the
great mass of letters and papers of all descriptions which
accumulated at Marlborough House, and which have since
accumulated at Buckingham Palace – in fact from the year
1863 to the present day.'

King Edward's Will had directed [7] that all his private and
personal correspondences, including especially those with
Queen Alexandra and with Queen Victoria, should be destroyed; and Lord Esher, who assisted Lord Knollys in that
part of the task which could be accomplished within the
Royal Archives, was amazed by the lack of system which he
found. 'No papers', he wrote, [8] 'were ever in more dire confusion'; and it is clear that only a limited amount of sifting
was attempted, and that a vast number were burned.

That lamentable combustion signalled the climax of a

period of incendiary activity which started when Queen Victoria's diary passed in 1901 into the hands of her youngest child, Princess Beatrice. In fulfilment of a charge [9] laid upon her by her mother, the Princess transcribed passages from that invaluable historical and personal record into a series of blue copybooks; and she destroyed Queen Victoria's manuscript by fire as she went along. That process of transcription and destruction, which was spread over a great number of years, distressed King George V and Queen Mary who were powerless to intervene; but no one could dispute Queen Victoria's absolute right to leave such directions as she thought proper about the disposal of her most intimate papers.

About the method of that transcription and the extent of that destruction, a limited amount of evidence exists. It is possible, for example, to collate certain passages quoted by Sir Theodore Martin from the original diary, which he used while writing the Prince Consort's biography under Queen Victoria's personal supervision, with the Princess's subsequent transcriptions in the Windsor copy-books. It can be stated that Princess Beatrice felt constrained not merely to destroy, without transcribing, substantial portions of her mother's diary, but also to alter substantially a great many other portions which she did transcribe; and it must be added that posterity has suffered in consequence an incalculable and irreparable loss.

In December 1906, Lord Esher noted [10] that a correspondence between Queen Victoria and Lord Granville, as well as many letters about Lady Flora Hastings, had been burned by King Edward's command. A worse act of what must be termed vandalism occurred in the following year when Esher discovered, as a result of editing Queen Victoria's letters, that the Queen's correspondence with Disraeli, as well as other confidential papers, were in the custody of Lord Rothschild as a trustee of the Hughenden property.

At King Edward's request that material was despatched from New Court to Windsor Castle, where all private letters from the Queen about her family – Esher described [11] them (16 November 1907) as 'very private' – and almost all letters written to Disraeli by King Edward as Prince of Wales were burned. Letters from Queen Victoria to Disraeli on political subjects were returned to Lord Rothschild, after other material from the same collection, including correspondence about Princess Frederick's marriage and letters addressed to Disraeli by other members of the royal family, had been destroyed. As late as 26 January 1913 Esher noted [12] that King George V had ordered on that day the destruction of a mass of material relating to George IV in the royal archives.

From his office at Buckingham Palace on 17 March 1913 Lord Knollys wrote [13] laconically to King George V: 'Sir, I have finished the papers and am vacating my room here today.' He had been constrained to burn a substantial part of the social record of the nineteenth century, including much material which a biographer of King Edward VII would have wished to consult; and one deplorable later loss must also be recorded. Queen Alexandra died intestate [14] on 20 November 1925; but her wish that all her papers should be burned after her death was executed [15] with scrupulous fidelity by Lord Knollys's sister, the Hon. Charlotte Knollys,* who had served the Queen as a Woman of the Bedchamber from 1870, and as confidante and intimate friend.

* Rumour had often insisted that Miss Knollys, who was accorded the rank of a baron's daughter by Royal Warrant in 1901, and who died unmarried in April 1930, would wed General the Rt. Hon. Sir Dighton Probyn, V.C., G.C.B., G.C.S.I., G.C.V.O. (Keeper of the Privy Purse to King Edward VII and thereafter Comptroller to Queen Alexandra), a widower since 1900, who died in June 1924.

Lord Knollys, G.C.B., G.C.V.O., K.C.M.G., I.S.O., who was made a baron in 1902, a privy counsellor in 1910 and a viscount in 1911, died in August 1924.

Reference Notes

'R.A.' is the abbreviation for the Royal Archives at Windsor Castle. '*Letters*' is the abbreviation for *The Letters of Queen Victoria*, 1st Series edited by A. C. Benson and Viscount Esher, 2nd and 3rd Series edited by George Earle Buckle.

CHAPTER ONE: EDUCATIONAL EXPERIMENT

1 R.A., Queen Victoria's diary
2 L. B. Namier, *Personalities and Powers*, 19
3 Manuscript diary of F. W. Gibbs, tutor to the Prince of Wales, in the possession of Mrs M. H. Prance
4 Sir Theodore Martin, *Life of the Prince Consort*, I, 314
5 *Letters* 1st Series, I, 449
6 Martin, *Life of the Prince Consort*, I, 316
7 Ibid., 75
8 R.A., M.12/14
9 *Letters*, 1st Series, II, 49
10 The Duke of Windsor, *A King's Story*, 216
11 R.A., M.12/14
12 R.A., M.12/46
13 *Letters*, 1st Series, I, 458
14 R.A., M.12/44
15 R.A., M.14/45
16 R.A., M.14/24
17, 18 R.A., Queen Victoria's diary
19 Copy of report in the Gibbs Papers
20 Gibbs's diary
21 R.A., M.15/8
22–4 Gibbs's diary
25 Copy in the Gibbs Papers
26 R.A., M.12/40
27–30 Gibbs's diary
31 Copy in the Gibbs Papers
32 Lincolnshire Papers
33, 34 Gibbs's diary
35 Viscount Esher, *The Influence of King Edward*, 30
36, 37 Gibbs's diary
38 R.A. Add. U/32

39 *The Greville Memoirs*, edited by Lytton Strachey and Roger Fulford, VII, 305–6
40 R.A., T.1/183
41 R.A., Prince of Wales's diary
42 Copy in the Gibbs Papers
43 *The Greville Memoirs*, VII, 156–8
44 Arthur Ponsonby, *Henry Ponsonby*, 85
45 R.A., Queen Victoria's diary
46 *The Greville Memoirs*, VII, 388–9
47, 48 R.A., Y.176
49 R.A., Z.141/19
50 A. Ponsonby, *Henry Ponsonby*, 26
51 Hawarden MSS
52 R.A., Z.126
53 R.A., Prince of Wales's diary

CHAPTER TWO: THE NEW LAND

1 Esher, *The Influence of King Edward*, 10
2, 3 R.A., Queen Victoria's diary
4 Martin, *Life of the Prince Consort*, IV, 206–7
5 Esher, *The Influence of King Edward*, 16–22
6 E. C. Corti, *The English Empress*, 45
7 R.A., Prince of Wales's diary
8 R.A., Add. U/32
9 R.A., Z.141/36; and Esher, *The Influence of King Edward*, 13–15
10 *The Greville Memoirs*, VII, 383
11 Esher, *Journals and Letters*, II, 368
12 R.A., Add. U/32
13 Corti, *The English Empress*, 50
14 R.A., Add. U/32
15 Corti *The English Empress*, 50–51
16 R.A., Add. U/32
17 Corti, *The English Empress*, 50–51
18 R.A., Z.461/92
19 Corti, *The English Empress*, 54
20 R.A., Prince of Wales's diary
21 Martin, *Life of the Prince Consort*, IV, 485–6
22 R.A., Add. U/32
23 R.A., T.2/88
24 Esher, *The Influence of King Edward*, 26
25 Gibbs's Papers
26 Esher, *The Influence of King Edward*, 27–30
27 R.A., Z.141/61
28 R.A., T. 3/2
29 Corti, *The English Empress*, 59

30 ibid., 61
31 Martin, *Life of the Prince Consort*, V, 87
32 R.A., Z.467/42
33, 34 R.A., T.3/57
35 R.A., Z.172/17
36 R.A., Queen Victoria's diary
37 Martin, *Life of the Prince Consort*, V, 191
38 Corti, *The English Empress*, 63

CHAPTER THREE: ROMANCE

1 R.A., Z.446/13
2 R.A., Z.446/14 and 15
3 R.A., Add. MSS. A.3/38
4 R.A., Add. MSS. A.3/40
5 R.A., Add. MSS. A.3/144
6 R.A., Z.141/81
7 R.A., Z.141/82
8 Corti, *The English Empress*, 67
9 ibid., 68
10 R.A., Z.446/38
11 R.A., Queen Victoria's diary
12 R.A., T. 3/94
13 R.A., Add. MSS. A.3/59
14 R.A., Add. MSS. A.3/64
15 R.A., T.3/89
16 R.A., Add. MSS. A.3/64
17 R.A., Add. MSS. A.3/125
18 R.A., Z.412/87
19 R.A., Z.12/16
20 R.A., Queen Victoria's diary
21 Corti, *The English Empress*, 72
22 R.A., Z.141/91
23 R.A., Z.141/92
24 R.A., Queen Victoria's diary
25, 26 R.A., Z.141/94
27 R.A., Z.141/95
28–30 R.A., Queen Victoria's diary
31 Corti, *The English Empress*, 72
32 R.A., Add. MSS. U/32
33, 34 R.A., Add. MSS. U/16
35 Lincolnshire Papers; Cadogan Papers
36 R.A., Add. MSS. U/32
37 R.A., cf. *Letters*, 2nd Series, I, 14 (where the printed entry
   has been garbled)
38 R.A., Queen Victoria's diary
39 Lincolnshire Papers

40 Hector Bolitho, *Queen Victoria the Widow and her Son*, 11–14
41 R. E. Prothero and C. G. Bradley, *Life and Correspondence of Dean Stanley*, II, 82
42 R.A., Prince of Wales's diary
43 R.A., Z.446/83
44 Esher, *The Influence of King Edward*, 35–6
45–7 R.A., Queen Victoria's diary
48 R.A., Add. MSS. U/32
49 Paget Papers
50 *Letters*, 2nd Series, I, 41–2
51 R.A., Z.447/22
52 R.A., Z447/23
53 R.A., Z.447/27
54, 55 *Letters*, 2nd Series, I, 43
56 R.A., Z.463/67
57 R.A., Queen Victoria's diary

CHAPTER FOUR: SOCIAL SOVEREIGNTY

1 R.A., Z.463/83
2–4 Paget Papers
5 Corti, *The English Empress*, 97
6 R.A., Queen Victoria's diary
7 Paget Papers
8 ibid.
9 Corti, *The English Empress*, 98
10 R.A., B.20/7
11 Paget Papers
12 R.A., ACC. 372a
13 *Letters*, 2nd Series, I, 72
14 A. L. Kennedy, *My Dear Duchess*, 213–14
15 R.A., Queen Victoria's diary
16 L. B. Namier, *England in the Age of the American Revolution*, 15
17 R.A., Z.448/130
18 Lord Percy of Newcastle, *Some Memories*, 18–22
19–22 R.A., Add. MSS. U/32
23 R.A., Z.448/185
24 R.A., Z.448/186
25 R.A., Queen Victoria's diary: 31 March 1866
26 Corti, *The English Empress*, 164
27 R.A., Add. MSS. U/32
28 *Letters*, 2nd Series, I, 64
29 G. M. Young, *Portrait of an Age*, 187
30 R.A., Z.449/2

CHAPTER FIVE: AN UNEMPLOYED YOUTH

1 R.A., Queen Victoria's diary
2 *Letters*, 2nd Series, I, 64
3 R.A., B.20/101
4 Gibbs's Papers
5 R.A., Prince of Wales's diary
6 R.A., L.25/51
7 Lincolnshire Papers
8 R.A., Z.448/11
9 R.A., F.448/17
10 R.A., I.91/28
11, 12 R.A., T.4/42
13 *Letters*, 2nd Series, I, 194
14 R.A.. I.198/158
15 R.A., I.198/159
16 *Letters*, 2nd Series, I, 175–6
17 R.A., J.36/137
18 R.A., I.36/140
19 R.A., I.36/142
20 R.A., I.36/141
21 R.A., Queen Victoria's diary
22 R.A., Z.447/118
23 R.A., Z.447/121
24 R.A., Queen Victoria's diary
25 R.A., Z.448/54
26 R.A., T.4/45a
27 R.A., C.14/81
28 R.A., Z.448/73
29, 30 R.A., Add. MSS. U/32
31 Sir Stanley Lee, *King Edward VII*, I, 256
32–6 R.A., Add. MSS. U/32
37 R.A., T.4/84
38 R.A., Z.448/119
39–42 R.A., ACC.372a
43 R.A., Prince of Wales's diary
44 R.A., ACC.372a
45 Lincolnshire Papers
46 R.A., ACC.372a
47 *Eighteen Years on Sandringham Estate*, by 'The Lady Farmer' (Mrs George Cresswell), 67–8
48 R.A., Z.449/65
49 R.A., Add. MSS. A.3/145
50 R.A., Add. MSS. A.3/137
51 *Letters*, 2nd Series, II, 19–20
52 R.A., Z.449/100

53 Lee, *King Edward VII*, I, 269
54 R.A., Z.448/134
55-7 R.A., Acc. 372a
58 R.A., Add. MSS. A.3/93
59 R.A., Z.448/180
60 R.A., ACC.372a
61 Lincolnshire Papers
62 R.A., ACC.372a
63 R.A., Add. MSS. A.3/96
64-7 R.A., ACC.372a

CHAPTER SIX: A PROPOSED EMPLOYMENT

1 Lincolnshire Papers
2 R.A., ACC.372a
3 *Letters*, 2nd Series, II, 512-13
4 R.A., Acc.372a
5 R.A., Add. MSS. A.3/1108
6 R.A., T.5/13
7 R.A., Z.449/27
8 R.A., Add. MSS. A.3/117
9 R.A., Add. MSS. A.3/128
10 R.A., Queen Victoria's diary
11 R.A., Add. MSS. A.3/131
12 Corti, *The English Empress*, 165
13 R.A., Z.449/39
14 R.A., Add. MSS. A.3/121
15 R.A., Add. MSS. A.3/123
16 R.A., Add. MSS. A.3/125
17 R.A., Add. MSS. A.3/125
18 R.A., Add. MSS. A.3/124
19 R.A., Add. MSS. A.3/131
20 R.A., Add. MSS. A.3/132
21 R.A., Z.449/51
22 R.A., Add. MSS. A.3/135
23 R.A., ACC.372a
24 Christopher Sykes, *Four Studies in Loyalty*
25 R.A., Add. MSS. A.3/151
26 Lincolnshire Papers
27 R.A., Z.449/67
28 R.A., F.499/66
29 R.A., Z.449/70
30 R.A., Z.449/74
31 R.A., Z.449/80
32 R.A., Z.449/90
33 R.A., Z.449/86
34 Lincolnshire Papers

35 R.A., Z.449/94
36 R.A., Z.449/106
37 R.A., F.449/112
38 Chatsworth Papers
39 *The Political Correspondence of Mr Gladstone and Lord Granville, 1868–1876*, ed. Agatha Ram, I, 131
40 ibid., 160
41 ibid, 161
42 ibid., 170–72
43 A. Ponsonby, *Henry Ponsonby*, 252
44 R.A., Z.449/140
45 R.A., T.5/43
46 *The Glandstone–Granville Correspondence 1868–1876*, II, 261
47 R.A., Queen Victoria's diary
48 *The Gladstone–Granville Correspondence 1868–1876*, II, 291
49 Philip Magnus, *Gladstone*, 209
50, 51 ibid., 210
52 R.A., T.5/76
53 R.A., T.5/80
54 A. Ponsonby, *Henry Ponsonby*, 102
55 Philip Guedalla, *The Queen and Mr Gladstone*, I, 340
56 R.A., Add. MSS. U/32
57 Magnus, *Gladstone*, 211

CHAPTER SEVEN: INDIA

1 R.A., T.5/104
2 Guedalla, *The Queen and Mr Gladstone*, I, 315–8
3 R.A., Z.459/35
4 Guedalla, *The Queen and Mr Gladstone*, I, 359–61
5 Magnus, *Gladstone*, 216
6 *The Gladstone–Granville Correspondence 1868–1876*, II, 335–6
7 Guedalla, *The Queen and Mr Gladstone*, I, 361–6
8 lbid., 368–9
9 Magnus, *Gladstone*, 215
10 Guedalla, *The Queen and Mr Gladstone*, I, 374–9
11 ibid., 379
12 *The Gladstone–Granville Correspondence 1868–1876*, II, 343
13 Chatsworth Papers
14 Magnus, *Gladstone*, 216
15 R.A., Z.459/48
16 R.A., Z.459/62
17 Guedalla, *The Queen and Mr Gladstone*, I, 383
18 ibid., 385
19 A. Ponsonby, *Henry Ponsonby*, 103
20 R.A., T.6/115
21 Harold Nicolson, *King George V*, 61–3

22 R. Rhodes James, *Rosebery*, 57
23 *The Gladstone–Granville Correspondence 1868–1876*, II, 375
24 Chatsworth Papers
25 R.A., Add. MSS. U/32
26 *The Gladstone–Granville Correspondence 1868–1876*, II, 437
27 ibid., 422
28 R.A., Acc. 372.A
29 R.A., Z.450/124
30 R.A., T.5/131
31 R.A., Z.450/126
32, 33 Salisbury Papers
34 *The Letters of Disraeli to Lady Bradford and Lady Chesterfield*, ed. Marquis of Zetland, I, 292
35 R.A., T.6/39
36 R.A., T.6/18
37 R.A., T.6/22
38 Hardinge Papers (private)
39 Lincolnshire Papers
40 Lee, *King Edward VII*, I, 399
41 R.A., Z.468/98
42 R.A., Geo. V, AA.13/5
43 R.A., Z.469/63
44 R.A., Geo. V, AA.13/13 and Geo. V, AA.13/14
45 R.A., Prince of Wales's diary
46 Lincolnshire Papers
47 R.A., Z.469/42
48 R.A., Z.469/67

CHAPTER EIGHT: A PERSONAL QUARREL

1 R.A., Add. MSS. A.12/345
2, 3 R.A., Add. MSS. A.12/302–4
4 R.A., Add. MSS. A.12/302
5 Chatsworth Papers
6 Lincolnshire Papers and R.A., Add. MSS. A.12/302
7 R.A., S.31/36
8 R.A., Add. MSS. A.12/305–6
9 R.A., Add. MSS. A.12/302
10 R.A., T.6/82
11 R.A., Z.469/73
12 R.A., T.6/88
13 Lincolnshire Papers
14 R.A., Add. MSS. A.12/309
15 R.A., S.31/50–1
16 R.A., S.31/57
17 R.A., Add. MSS. A.12/356
18 R.A., T.6/102

19 R.A., S.31/52
20 R.A., Geo. V, AA.15/52
21 R.A., T.6/112
22 Lady Gwendolen Cecil, *Life of Lord Salisbury*, II, 95
23 R.A., T.6/129
24 *Letters*, 2nd Series, II, 559
25 R.A., Z.452/100
26, 27 R.A., Add. MSS. U/32
28 *The Diary of Lady Frederick Cavendish*, ed. John Bailey, II, 235
29 *Letters*, 2nd Series, II, 580
30, 31 R.A , T.7/31
32 R.A., T.7/34
33 Salisbury Papers
34, 35 R.A., T.7/109
36 R.A., Z.453/9
37 R.A., Z.453/11–15
38 The Rev. J. N. Dalton, *The Cruise of the Bacchante*, 1886

CHAPTER NINE: EGYPT

1 *Letters of Disraeli to Lady Bradford and Lady Chesterfield*, ed. Zetland, II, 246
2 R.A., Z.453/44
3 R.A., Geo. V, AA.13/63
4 *Letters of Disraeli to Lady Bradford and Lady Chesterfield*, ed. Zetland, II, 245–6
5 R.A., Prince of Wales's diary
6 R.A., Geo. V, AA.13/58
7 R.A., T.7/56
8 R.A., T.7/57
9 R.A., Z.453/79
10 Chatsworth Papers
11 A. Ponsonby, *Henry Ponsonby*, 108
12 R.A., T.7/112
13 A. Ponsonby, *Henry Ponsonby*, 184
14 R.A., T.8/6
15 R.A., Add. MSS. A.12/526
16 Magnus, *Gladstone*, 305–6
17 S. Gwynn and G. M. Tuckwell, *Life of Sir Charles Dilke*, I, 329
18, 19 ibid., I, 414
20 ibid., I, 501
21 Roy Jenkins, *Sir Charles Dilke*, 144
22 R.A., Z. 473/34
23, 24 R.A., Z.453/96
25 R.A., Z.453/121

26 R.A., Prince of Wales's diary
27 R.A., H.44/9
28 R.A., Z.454/140
29 R.A., Geo. V, AA.14/3
30 Lincolnshire Papers
31 R.A., T.8/62
32 R.A., T.8/63
33 R.A., T.8/80
34, 35 Lee, *King Edward VII*, I, 460
36 R.A., Z.162/7
37 R.A., Prince of Wales's diary
38 R.A., Z.474/63
39 R.A., Z.173/4
40 R.A., Z.173/5
41 R.A., Z.173/15
42 R.A., Z.173/18
43 R.A., Z.173/19
44 Lincolnshire Papers
45 R.A., Geo. V. AA.14/54
46 Lincolnshire Papers
47 *Henry Broadhurst, M.P.: Told by Himself*, 1901, 148–53

CHAPTER TEN: GERMANY

1 Marquess of Crewe, *Lord Rosebery*, I, 204
2, 3 Lincolnshire Papers
4 R.A., T.8/149
5 R.A., T.8/160
6 *The Holstein Papers*, ed. M. Rich and M. H. Fisher, II (Diaries), 145
7 R.A., Add. MSS. U/32
8 *The Holstein Papers*, ed. Rich and Fisher, II (Diaries), 144
9 E. C. Corti, *Alexander von Battenberg*, 125
10 ibid., 126
11 ibid., 151–6; and *The Holstein Papers*, ed. Rich and Fisher, II (Diaries), 172
12, 13 R.A., Z.455/4
14 R.A., T.8/159
15 R.A., T.9/5
16 R.A., T.9/10
17 R.A., T.9/13
18 R.A., Geo. V, AA.15/21
19 R.A., Z.455/17
20 R.A., Geo. V, AA.19
21 R.A., Z.455/20
22 R.A., Z.455/22

23 R.A., Z.455/26
24 R.A., Geo. V, AA.15/34
25 *The Holstein Papers*, ed. Rich and Fisher, II (Diaries), 254
26 R.A., Geo. V, AA.15/38
27, 28 *The Holstein Papers*, ed. Rich and Fisher, II (Diaries), 254
29 ibid., 222–3
30 R.A., T.9/59
31 R.A., T.9/61
32 R.A., T.9/62
33 R.A., Geo. V, AA.15/41
34 R.A., Geo. V, AA.15/46
35 Lincolnshire Papers
36 R.A., Geo. V, AA.17/9
37 Lincolnshire Papers
38 R.A., Geo. V, AA 16/23
39 R.A., Z.162/10
40 R.A., Geo. V, AA.16/43
41 R.A., Geo. V, AA.16/44
42 R.A., Geo. V, AA.16/47
43 *The Holstein Papers*, ed. Rich and Fisher, III (Correspondence),
    219
44 Lincolnshire Papers
45 R.A., Geo. V, AA.17/14
46 *Letters*, 3rd Series, I, 374
47 ibid., I, 417
48 *The Holstein Papers*, ed. Rich and Fisher, II (Diaries), 195
49 R.A., Geo. V, AA.17/24
50 *Letters*, 3rd Series, I, 419

CHAPTER ELEVEN: WILLIAM THE GREAT

1 Lincolnshire Papers
2 R.A., Z.228/5
3 R.A., Z.228/10
4 R.A., Z.228/11–14
5 R.A., Z.280/304
6, 7 R.A., Z.281/2
8 R.A., Z.281/19
9 R.A., Z.281/2
10 R.A., Z.281/5
11 R.A., Z.280/65
12 R.A., Geo. V, AA.17/41
13, 14 R.A., Geo. V, AA.17/42
15 *Letters*, 3rd Series, I, 438–40
16 Gwendolen Cecil, *Life of Lord Salisbury*, IV, 113 and 367
17 *Letters*, 3rd Series, I, 440–41

18 R.A., Z.281–34
19 R.A., Z.281/36–7
20 R.A., Z.281/48
21 R.A., Z.281/49
22 R.A., Add. MSS. A.4/9
23 R.A., Add. MSS. A.4/11
24 R.A., T.9/161
25 R.A., Z.280/74–5
26 R.A., T.9/158
27 R.A., Add. MSS. A.4/14
28, 29 Salisbury Papers
30 R.A., Add. MSS. A.4/29
31 Acland Papers
32 R.A., Z.280/53
33 Salisbury Papers
34 Lincolnshire Papers
35 R.A., Geo. V, AA.18/6
36 R.A., Z.456/105
37 Sir Rennell Rodd, *Social and Diplomatic Memories*, I, 190
38 R.A., Z.456/105
39 R.A., Z.456/160
40 Lord Rendel, *Personal Papers*, 138–9
41, 42 Salisbury Papers
43 Carl Lonyay, *Rudolf – The Tragedy of Mayerling*, 177
44 R.A., Add. MSS. A.12/1793
45 R.A., Geo. V, AA.18/26
46 R.A., Z.475/3
47 Salisbury Papers
48 R.A., Add. MSS. A.12/1714
49 R.A., Geo. V, AA.18/32
50 R.A., Geo. V, AA.18/38
51 R.A., Geo. V, AA.18/33
52 Salisbury Papers

CHAPTER TWELVE: THE PRINCE IN TROUBLE

1 R.A., Add. MSS. A.4/45
2 Hardinge Papers
3 R.A., Y.182/7
4 R.A., Y.182/27
5 R.A., Y.182/6
6 R.A., Y.182/5
7 R.A., Add. MSS. A.12/1752
8 R.A., Add. MSS. A.12/1755
9 R.A., Y.182/21
10 R.A., Geo. V, AA.18/55

11 R.A., Geo. V, AA.31/17
12 R.A., Add. MSS. A.4/31
13 R.A., Add. MSS. U.32
14 R.A., Geo. V, AA.19/10
15, 16 R.A., Add. MSS. U.32
17 R.A., Add. MSS. A.4/32
18–20 Salisbury Papers
21 Cadogan Papers
22, 23 Chatsworth Papers
24 E. F. Benson, *As We Were*, 218–19
25–36 Salisbury Papers
37 Esher Papers
38, 39 Salisbury Papers
40 R.A., Add. MSS. A.12/1910
41 *Letters*, 3rd Series, II, 178
42 ibid., 180–81
43 Salisbury Papers
44 R.A., Add. MSS. A.12/1797
45 R.A., Z.475/18
46 Salisbury Papers
47 R.A., Z.475/19
48 R.A., Add. MSS. A.12/1797
49 R.A., Add. MSS. U.32
50 R.A., Z.95/5
51 R.A. Add. MSS. U.32
52 R.A., Geo. V, AA.19/31
53 R.A., Geo. V, AA.19/35 and 36
54 R.A., Geo. V, AA.19/45; Geo. V, AA. 19/54
55 R.A., Geo. V, AA.20/36
56 *The Letters of the Czar Nicholas II and the Empress Marie*, ed. E. J. King, 84

CHAPTER THIRTEEN: LOCUST YEARS

1 R.A., Geo. V, AA.20/54
2 R.A., Add. MSS. U.32
3 Esher Papers
4 Yvette Guilbert, *Chanson de ma Vie*, 218–24
5 R.A., Geo. V, AA.20/42 and 43
6 Lincolnshire Papers
7 R.A., Prince of Wales's Diary
8, 9 Lincolnshire Papers
10 R.A., Z.274/50
11 R.A., Z.499/111
12 Lincolnshire Papers
13 Crewe, *Lord Rosebery*, II, 474

14 R.A., Z.274/57

15 R.A., T.10/41

16 Frances, Countess of Warwick, *Life's Ebb and Flow*, 118

17 Baron von Eckardstein, *Ten Years at the Court of St James's*, 56

18–23 Salisbury Papers

24 R.A., Geo. V, AA.20/69

25 R.A., Geo. V, AA.20/73

26 R.A., Add. MSS. U.32 (Queen Victoria to Empress Frederick, 3 April, 1895)

27 *The Letters of the Czar Nicholas II and the Empress Marie*, ed. King, 119–20

28, 29 Lincolnshire Papers

30 R.A., Prince of Wales's diary

31 Lord Hardinge of Penshurst, *Old Diplomacy*, 164–5

32 Hardinge Papers (private)

33, 34 Esher Papers

CHAPTER FOURTEEN: KING AT LAST

1, 2 R.A., Prince of Wales's diary

3 Eckardstein, *Ten Years at the Court of St James's*, 120

4 Prince von Bülow, *Memoirs*, trans F. A. Voigt, II, 339

5 Lincolnshire Papers

6, 7 Lee, *King Edward VII*, I, 756–9

8 R.A., W.42/16

9 R.A., W.42/11

10 R.A., Prince of Wales's diary

11 R.A., T.10/120

12, 13 Salisbury Papers

14 Lincolnshire Papers

15 R.A., W.60/16

16 Manuscript account by Sir Frederick Treves of the operation which he performed in 1902 upon King Edward VII. (Library of the Royal College of Surgeons)

17 Salisbury Papers

18 Chatsworth Papers

19 R.A., Add. MSS. A.4/198

20 R.A., Add. MSS. A.4/199

21 Lord Newton, *Lord Lansdowne – A Biography*, 198; and Earl of Midleton, *Records and Reactions 1856–1939*, 174–6

22 *The Diary of Henry Hobhouse*, ed. A. Aspinall, 68

CHAPTER FIFTEEN: KING EDWARD'S
POSITION AND METHODS

1 Sir Frederick Ponsonby, *Recollections of Three Reigns*, 275

2 A. Ponsonby, *Henry Ponsonby*, 195

3 Kenneth Young, *Arthur James Balfour*, 227

4 R.A., W.46/252a

5, 6 Esher Papers

7 Esher, *Journals and Letters*, II, 265

8 ibid, 107

9 ibid., 104

10–12 Esher Papers

13 F. Ponsonby, *Recollections of Three Reigns*, 102

14 Midleton, *Records and Reactions 1856–1939*, 159–71

15 Esher Papers

16 Esher, *Journals and Letters*, II, 230

17, 18 ibid., 149

19 Esher Papers

20 Lincolnshire Papers

21 Midleton, *Records and Reactions 1856–1939*, 149–50

22 F. Ponsonby, *Recollections of Three Reigns*, 275

23 Loelia, Duchess of Westminster, *Grace and Favour*, 32

24 R.A., W.22/1

25 The Duke of Windsor, *A King's Story*, 95–6

26 R.A., Vic. Add. MSS. A.4/213

27 R.A., Vic. Add. MSS. A.4/217

28 Salisbury Papers

29 R.A., Vic. Add. MSS. A.4/218

30 Salisbury Papers

31 R.A., R.22/4

32 Salisbury Papers

33 Nicolson, *King George V*, 67

34 R.A., Geo. V, AA.22/61

35–9 Salisbury Papers

40 R.A., X.40/33

41 Midleton, *Records and Reactions 1856–1939*, 163

42 R.A., X.40/6

43 R.A., R.22/96

44 R.A., R.22/97

45 R.A., R.22/98

46 Manuscript account by Sir Frederick Treves of the operation which he performed in 1902 upon King Edward VII. (Library of the Royal College of Surgeons)

47 R.A., King Edward VII's diary

48–50 Manuscript account by Sir Frederick Treves of the operation which he performed in 1902 upon King Edward VII. (Library of the Royal College of Surgeons)

CHAPTER SIXTEEN: FRANCE

1 Esher, *Journals and Letters*, I, 339; and Lincolnshire Papers

2 Manuscript account by Sir Frederick Treves of the operation

which he performed in 1902 upon King Edward VII. (Library of the Royal College of Surgeons)

3 Eckardstein, *Ten Years at the Court of St James's*, 216–17
4 *British Documents on the Origins of the War*, ed. G. P. Gooch and H. Temperley, II, 92
5 ibid., 83
6 ibid., 77
7 F. Ponsonby, *Recollections of Three Reigns*, 128
8 R.A., W.42/87
9 R.A., W.42/88
10 R.A., W.42/96
11 F. Ponsonby, *Recollections of Three Reigns*, 146–7
12 R.A., W.42/104
13 R.A., W.42/107
14 R.A., W.42/107
15 R.A., W.42/145
16 Esher Papers; and R.A., R.22/126
17 Earl of Ronaldshay, *The Life of Lord Curzon*, II, 306
18 Esher Papers
19 R.A., R.23/8
20 R.A., R.23/8a
21 R.A., R.23/10
22 R.A., R.26/34
23 Salisbury Papers
24 R.A., R.22/73
25 Lee, *King Edward VII*, II, 42
26 ibid., 53
27 R.A., R.26/98
28 R.A., R.22/117
29 R.A., R.22/121
30 Eckardstein, *Ten Years at the Court of St James's*, 245
31 Hardinge of Penshurst, *Old Diplomacy*, 85
32 R.A., Geo. V, AA.23/38
33 Hardinge Papers (private)
34 R.A., Geo. V, AA.23/38
35 R.A., R.23/55
36 R.A., W.43/65–77 and Hardinge Papers
37–40 Hardinge Papers
41 F. Ponsonby, *Recollections of Three Reigns*, 162–5
42 R.A., W.43/78
43–45 Hardinge Papers (private)
46 *British Documents on the Origins of the War*, ed. Gooch and Temperley, II, 762–3
47 ibid., VI, 767
48 Hardinge of Penshurst, *Old Diplomacy*, 96–7
49 *British Documents on the Origins of the War*, ed. Gooch and Temperley, III, 398
50 Newton, *Lord Lansdowne*, 293

CHAPTER SEVENTEEN: NATIONAL SECURITY

1 Viscount Mersey, *Journals and Memories*, 158
2 R.A., King Edward VII's diary
3 R.A., R.23/79
4 R.A., R.23/82
5 F. Ponsonby, *Recollections of Three Reigns*, 218
6 R.A., Geo. V, AA.23/46
7 R.A., W.43/130
8 R.A., W.43/131
9 R.A.. W.43/132
10 R.A., W.43/35
11 R.A., W.43/144
12 R.A., W.43/145
13 Esher, *Journals and Letters*, II, 1–2
14 R.A., R.23/84
15 R.A., R.23/86
16 R.A., R.23/92
17 Lincolnshire Papers
18 Lee, *King Edward VII*, II, 180
19 A. J. Marder, *Fear God and Dread Nought*, I, 323
20 ibid., 324
21–23 Esher Papers
24 R.A., X.40/33
25 Midleton, *Records and Reactions 1856–1939*, 149
26 ibid., 156–7
27 Esher Papers
28 Esher, *Journals and Letters*, II, 14
29 R.A., R.23/100
30 R.A., R.23/99
31 Esher, *Journals and Letters*, II, 27
32 R.A., R.24/17
33, 34 Esher Papers
35 R.A., W.25/129; and Esher Papers
36 R.A., R.24/58
37 R.A., R.24/57
38 R.A., W.39/30
39 Philip Magnus, *Kitchener*, 228
40 Esher, *Journals and Letters*, II, 30
41 Esher Papers
42 Esher, *Journals and Letters*, II, 42
43 ibid., 44
44 R.A., W.25/98
45 Sir Almeric Fitzroy, *Memoirs*, I, 212
46 Esher Papers
47 R.A., W.25/100

48 R.A., W.25/112
49 R.A., W.25/129
50 Esher Papers
51 R.A., W.39/82
52 Esher Papers
53 R.A., W.26/73–7
54 R.A., W.39/85
55 R.A., W.39/86
56 Esher Papers; and R.A., W.26/74
57 R.A., W.26/77
58, 59 Esher Papers

CHAPTER EIGHTEEN: SOCIAL REFORM

1 F. Ponsonby, *Recollections of Three Reigns*, 186
2 Newton, *Lord Lansdowne*, 308–9
3 *British Documents on the Origins of the War*, ed. Gooch and Temperley, II, 301
4 R.A., W.44/86.a
5 R.A., W.44/87
6 R.A., W.44/88
7, 8 R.A., W.44/92
9 R.A., Geo. V, AA.23/56
10 Lee, *King Edward VII*, II, 340
11 Marder, *Fear God and Dread Nought*, II, 55
12 Newton, *Lord Lansdowne*, 342
13 R.A., Geo. V, AA.24/24
14 R.A., Geo. V, AA24/37
15 R.A., Geo. V, AA.24/1
16 *The Kaiser's Letters to the Tsar*, 138
17 Esher, *Journals and Letters*, II, 62
18 R.A., W.45/146
19 *Letters of Prince von Bülow*, ed. and trans. by F. Whyte, 152–8
20 ibid., 173; and *Memoirs of Prince von Bülow*, trans. F. A. Voigt, III, 130–44
21 *The Kaiser's Letters to the Tsar*, 198–201
22 *Die Grosse Politik der Europäischen Kabinette*, 23A, 161
23 R.A., W.46/252
24 R.A., W.46/285
25 R.A., W.47/205
26 R.A., W.47/315
27 *British Documents on the Origins of the War*, ed. Gooch and Temperley, II, 92
28 Hardinge Papers
29 R.A., Geo. V, AA.24/29

30 R.A., Geo. V, AA.24/30
31 Sir Frederick Maurice, *Haldane* (1927), 147–51
32 ibid., 152
33 R.A., Geo. V, AA.24/31
34 Esher Papers
35 R.A., Geo. V, AA.24/36
36 R.A., W.64/73
37, 38 Esher Papers
39 R.A., Geo. V, AA.24/37
40 Esher Papers
41 R.A., W.7/35
42 R.A., Geo. V, AA.24/42
43 Esher Papers
44 R.A., W.7/53
45 Esher Papers
46 R.A., R.27/21
47 Esher Papers
48 R.A., R.27/46
49 R.A., W.64/99
50 Esher Papers
51 J.A. Spender, *The Life of Sir Henry Campbell-Bannerman*,
        II, 314
52 ibid., 316
53 R.A., R.27/96
54 Esher, *Journals and Letters*, II, 203–4
55 Spender, *The Life of Sir Henry Campbell-Bannerman*, II, 302
56 ibid., 301

CHAPTER NINETEEN: NAVAL REVOLUTION

 1 A. J. Marder, *From the Dreadnought to Scapa Flow*, I, 113
 2 Viscount Grey of Falloden, *Twenty-Five Years*, I, 99
 3 Spender, *The Life of Sir Henry Campbell-Bannerman*, II, 257
 4 R. B. Haldane, *An Autobiography*, 191
 5, 6 Lee, *King Edward VII*, II, 525–6
 7 ibid., II, 527
 8 R.A., W.48/84.a
 9 Hardinge Papers
10 R.A., W.48/84a
11 R.A., W.48/97
12 Harold Nicolson, *Lord Carnock*, 223
13 Hardinge of Penshurst, *Old Diplomacy* 124
14 ibid., 122
15 ibid.. 124
16 Marder, *Fear God and Dread Nought*, II, 79–80
17 ibid., 72–7
18 ibid., 301–2

19 Esher, *Journals and Letters*, II, 199
20–22 Marder, *Fear God and Dread Nought*, II, 53
23 Lord *Fisher, Records*, 25
24 Marder, *Fear God and Dread Nought*, II, 454
25 R.A., W.41/83
26 R.A., R.29/72
27 Marder, *Fear God and Dread Nought*, II, 170
28 R.R., W.59/47
29 R.A., W.59/49
30 Marder, *From the Dreadnought to Scapa Flow*, I, 104
31, 32 Marder, *Fear God and Dread Nought*, II, 247
33 Esher Papers
34 R.A., Geo. V, AA.25/52
35 Marder, *Fear God and Dread Nought*, II, 174
36–38 Lee, *King Edward VII*, II, 605–6
39 Lincolnshire Papers
40 Hardinge Papers
41 Marder, *Fear God and Dread Nought*, II, 168; and R.A.
42 Hardinge Papers
43 R.A., Vic. Add. MSS. U.38/10
44 R.A., R.29/16
45 R.A., R.29/15a
46 Marder, *Fear God and Dread Nought*, II, 141
47 ibid., 264
48 ibid., 267
49 Esher Papers
50 Marder, *Fear God and Dread Nought*, II, 174
51 ibid., 275
52 Winston S. Churchill, *The World Crisis*, abridged and revised (1931), 65
53 Fisher, *Records*, 73
54 R.A., Geo. V, AA.25/53
55 Marder, *Fear God and Dread Nought*, II, 325
56 ibid., 42
57 ibid., 380

CHAPTER TWENTY: MILITARY REFORM

1 Esher Papers
2 Hardinge Papers
3 Haldane, *An Autobiography*, 208
4–6 Esher Papers
7 Esher, *Journals and Letters*, II, 189–91
8 ibid., 267
9 Esher Papers
10 Esher, *Journals and Letters*, II, 302–3
11 R.A., Geo. V, 25/53

12–14 Esher Papers
15 Hardinge Papers
16 Hardinge of Penshurst, *Old Diplomacy*, 133
17 Esher Papers
18 Lincolnshire Papers
19 *The Letters of the Csar Nicholas II and the Empress Marie*, ed. King, 222
20 R.A., W.66/25
21 Lincolnshire Papers
22 R.A., R.28/23
23 R.A., R.28/27
24 R.A., R.28/30
25 Lee, *King Edward VII*, II, 468
26 R.A., Geo. V, AA.25/11
27 R.A., Geo. V, AA.25/14
28 Hardinge Papers
29 Hardinge of Penshurst, *Old Diplomacy*, 139
30 F. Ponsonby, *Recollections of Three Reigns*, 220–21
31 Hardinge Papers
32, 33 Lee, *King Edward VII*, 29–30
34 Magnus, *Gladstone*, 149
35 R.A., Geo. V, AA.25/18
36 *British Documents on the Origins of the War*, ed. Gooch and Temperley, VI, 46
37, 38 Hardinge Papers
39 F. Ponsonby, *Recollections of Three Reigns*, 241
40, 41 Hardinge of Penshurst, *Old Diplomacy*, 146
42, 43 Hardinge Papers

CHAPTER TWENTY-ONE: RUSSIA

1 Lee, *King Edward VII*, II, 404
2 Manuscript account by Sir Frederick Treves of the operation which he performed in 1902 upon King Edward VII. (Library of the Royal College of Surgeons)
3 R.A., W.52/47
4 Esher, *Journals and Letters*, II, 255
5 Hardinge Papers
6 Esher Papers
7 Hardinge Papers
8 R.A., W.53/37
9–11 Hardinge Papers
12 Esher Papers
13 Crewe Papers
14 R.A., W.71/26
15 Crewe Papers
16, 17 Hardinge Papers

18 R.A., Geo. V, AA.25/35
19, 20 Hardinge Papers
21 R.A., W.66/23
22, 23 Asquith Papers
24 R.A., W.66/39
25, 26 Hardinge Papers
27, 28 Esher Papers
29–31 Hardinge Papers
32 *Memoirs of Prince von Bülow*, trans. F. A. Voigt, III, 309
33 Hardinge Papers
34 Nicolson, *Lord Carnock*, 274–5
35 Marder, *Fear God and Dread Nought*, II, 181
36 Asquith Papers
37, 38 Esher Papers
39 Hardinge of Penshurst, *Old Diplomacy*, 158
40, 41 Hardinge Papers
42 R.A., W.54/5
43–7 Hardinge Papers
48–51 Esher Papers
52 Lord Redesdale, *Memories*, I, 178
53 Nicolson, *Lord Carnock*, 262–314
54 Hardinge Papers
55 Nicolson, *Lord Carnock*, 282
56 Asquith Papers
57 Hardinge Papers and R.A., W.54/111
58 Hardinge Papers
59 *British Documents on the Origins of the War*, ed. Gooch and
    Temperley, V, 468
60, 61 Hardinge Papers
62 *British Documents on the Origin of the War*, ed. Gooch and
    Temperley, VII, 227
63–8 Hardinge Papers
69 Asquith Papers

CHAPTER TWENTY-TWO: THE PEOPLE'S BUDGET

1 Esher Papers
2 R.A., X.5/17
3 Hardinge Papers
4 Hardinge of Penshurst, *Old Diplomacy*, 264–5
5 A. E. T. Watson, *King Edward VII as a Sportsman*, 124
6 R.A., W.5/66
7 R.A., W.5/68
8 Lee, *King Edward VII*, II, 386–8
9 R.A., W.5/70
10, 11 Lee, *King Edward VII*, II, 386–8
12 R.A., R.30/36

13, 14 Esher Papers
15 Lee, *King Edward VII*, II, 689
16 Hardinge Papers
17 R.A., W.31/26: (Kitchener to Haldane, 5 August 1909)
18 R.A., W.31/43
19 Esher Papers
20 Asquith Papers and R.A., R.30/41
21 Magnus, *Kitchener*, 248
22 Esher Papers
23 Asquith Papers
24 Esher Papers
25 R.A., Vic. Add. MSS A.15/8988 (H. H. Asquith wrote on 5 March 1910 to offer the appointment to the Duke of Connaught, who accepted it)
26–30 Hardinge Papers
31 Almeric Fitzroy, *Memoirs*, I, 379
32 J. A. Spender and Cyril Asquith, *Life of Lord Oxford and Asquith*, I, 255
33 Earl of Oxford and Asquith, *Fifty Years of Parliament*, II, 69
34, 35 Crewe Papers
36 Esher Papers
37 Crewe Papers
38 Esher Papers
39 Frank Owen, *Tempestuous Journey*, 180–82
40 Esher Papers
41 Owen, *Tempestuous Journey*, 180–82
42 Esher Papers
43 R.A., Geo. V, AA.25/36
44 Lord Willoughby de Broke, *The Passing Years*, 251–3
45 Esher, *Journals and Letters*, II, 413
46 Esher Papers
47 Spender and Asquith, *Life of Lord Oxford and Asquith*, I, 257–8
48 Lincolnshire Papers
49 Esher Papers
50 Lincolnshire Papers
51, 52 Esher Papers
53 Lord Knutsford, *In Black and White*, 245
54 Esher, *Journals and Letters*, II, 423–5
55 Esher Papers
56 Asquith Papers

CHAPTER TWENTY-THREE: THE LORDS

1 Asquith Papers
2 Spender and Asquith, *Life of Lord Oxford and Asquith*, I, 261–2

3 R.A., R.39/75
4-6 Asquith Papers
7 R.A., King Edward VII's diary
8-11 Esher Papers
12 Esher, *Journals and Letters*, II, 435–6
13 ibid., 440
14 Lee, *King Edward VII*, II, 695–7; James Pope-Hennessy, *Lord Crewe*, 77–9
15 Esher Papers
16 Lee, *King Edward VII*, II, 698
17 Esher Papers
18 Spender and Asquith, *Life of Lord Oxford and Asquith*, I, 273
19 Lee, *King Edward VII*, II, 699
20 Asquith Papers
21 R.A., Geo. V, AA.25/70
22 Esher Papers
23 R.A., Geo. V, AA.25/74
24 R.A., X11/28
25 R.A., R.30/12
26 R.A., X.11/29
27 Esher Papers
28 Esher, *Journals and Letters*, II, 457
29 ibid., 456–9
30, 31 Esher Papers
32 Lee, *King Edward VII*, II, 713
33 Hardinge Papers
34 R.A., King Edward's VII's diary
35 Esher Papers
36 John Gore, *King George V – A Personal Memoir*, 237

APPENDIX

1 Esher Papers, (*Journal:* 19 November 1910)
2 Nicolson, *King George V*, 133–9
3–6 Esher Papers
7 Official information
8 Esher Papers
9 Official information
10 Esher Papers
11 Esher, *Journals and Letters*, II, 256
12, 13 Esher Papers
14 Official information
15 Sir Edward Cadogan, *Before the Deluge*, 120

Index

A selection of books published by Penguin is listed on the following pages.

For a complete list of books available from Penguin in the United States, write to Dept. DG, Penguin Books, 299 Murray Hill Parkway, East Rutherford, New Jersey 07073.

For a complete list of books available from Penguin in Canada, write to Penguin Books Canada Limited, 2801 John Street, Markham, Ontario L3R 1B4.

Four by Thomas Hardy

JUDE THE OBSCURE
Edited and introduced by C. H. Sisson

Jude Fawley, whose long search for an education is thwarted by poverty, appears to find fulfillment with the modern, emancipated, and high-principled Sue Bridehead. When tragedy strikes, however, it is Sue who proves unequal to the challenge. *Jude the Obscure* is Thomas Hardy's final and most outspoken novel – a devastating revelation of his ever-deepening pessimism.

THE MAYOR OF CASTERBRIDGE
Edited and introduced by Martin Seymour-Smith

Michael Henchard is a strong and selfish man determined to overcome fate, yet he is finally defeated by the selfishness that is the very basis of his strength. This intricately plotted novel is Hardy's most powerful statement of the idea that 'character is destiny'.

THE RETURN OF THE NATIVE
Edited and introduced by George Woodcock

Against the gigantic, menacing background of Egdon Heath, which represents the impersonal, inexorable forces of nature, are enacted the stories of Clym Yeobright, the returning 'native', and Eustacia Vye, who cries out: 'I was capable of much; but I have been injured and blighted and crushed by things beyond my control.'

UNDER THE GREENWOOD TREE
Edited and introduced by David Wright

At once nostalgic and delicately ironic, *Under the Greenwood Tree* is a rustic romance, a vivid recreation of village life without the somber undertones of Hardy's later work.

Also:

FAR FROM THE MADDING CROWD
TESS OF THE D'URBERVILLES

THE DUCHESS OF JERMYN STREET
Daphne Fielding

Here is the story of Rosa Lewis, the remarkable real-life heroine of the Masterpiece Theatre television production *The Duchess of Duke Street*. Outspoken, high-spirited, delightfully madcap, and one of the most entertaining women of her time, the 'duchess' began her career as a kitchen maid and ended it as owner of the venerable Cavendish Hotel, which she ran according to principles uniquely her own. A culinary genius, she met – and was loved by – a long succession of famous (or sometimes infamous) people, among them the Countess of Paris, Lady Randolph Churchill, the Kaiser, King Edward VII, and most of the Edwardian and Georgian fast set, whose wild pranks she encouraged and often initiated. She even appeared as a character in Evelyn Waugh's celebrated 1920s novel *Vile Bodies*, but only Daphne Fielding, who knew her intimately, could tell her surprising true story. 'Mrs Fielding has given us a remarkable picture of Rosa Lewis – certainly frank, but always affectionate and understanding and (the true test of this kind of biography) leaving a vivid impression on the minds of those who never knew her' – *Times Literary Supplement* (London). 'The first full, true portrait of a warm-hearted, comic, and totally original woman' – Evelyn Waugh.

HERMIT OF PEKING
The Hidden Life of Sir Edmund Backhouse
Hugh Trevor-Roper

Hermit of Peking is one of the most remarkable pieces of literary detection of recent years. It all began when Hugh Trevor-Roper acquired the voluminous memoirs of Sir Edmund Backhouse, up till then known only as a distinguished Chinese scholar who had lived quietly in Peking until his death in 1944. The memoirs depicted a very different person – a man who said that he had been 'intimate' with many notables, from Lord Rosebery to Paul Verlaine, and whose lovers had included the Dowager Empress of China. In fact, the memoirs were so fantastic that Trevor-Roper felt obliged to discover all he could about the man who had written them – and what he reveals here is the story of one of the most outrageous forgers, confidence tricksters, and eccentrics of the century.

THE LIFE OF NOEL COWARD
Cole Lesley

This 'life of Noel Coward' is told, as no one else could know it or tell it, by his secretary, friend, collaborator, companion, and confidant of nearly forty years. Here is the precocious child performer touring the music-halls, the aspiring young playwright-actor, the author of huge successes like *This Year of Grace*, *Bitter Sweet*, and *Conversation Piece* (and of some equally huge failures), and, above all, the friend of Beatrice Lillie, Alfred Lunt and Lynn Fontanne, Laurence Olivier, Vivien Leigh, Nancy Mitford, Marlene Dietrich, Cecil Beaton, Somerset Maugham, Winston Churchill, George Bernard Shaw, and the royal family, to mention only a few among many, many others. Loyal beyond measure, serious about his craft, hilarious, and extremely hardworking, Coward appears in these pages in all his minor selfishnesses and major generosities – a connoisseur of living, surrounded by people instantly aware that the moments they spent with him would count among the most delectable of their lives.

THE GLITTERING PRIZES
Frederic Raphael

This witty and sardonic novel is based on the much acclaimed television series of the same name. From their student years at Cambridge in the 1950s to the onset of middle
age two decades later, a small and talented group of men
and women pursue 'the glittering prizes' that success in an
acquisitive society can offer. Although they achieve varying
degrees of material wealth and spiritual poverty, none of
them can ever forget those heady, golden days at Cambridge
spent unravelling the knots of friendship and in exploratory
sex and badinage. 'There are many stories here, and in all
aspects of writing, this book goes beyond simple entertainment' – *Publishers Weekly*.

THE ENCHANTED PLACES
Christopher Milne

Millions of readers throughout the world have grown up
with the stories and verses of A. A. Milne, have envied Christopher Robin in his enchanted world, laughed at Pooh – a
bear of very little brain – and worried about Piglet and his
problems. What was it like, however, to be the small boy
with the long hair, the smock, and the Wellington boots? At
the age of fifty-four Christopher Milne has recalled his early
childhood, remembering 'the enchanted places' where he
used to play in Sussex. The Hundred Acre Wood, Galleon's
Lap, and Poohsticks Bridge not only existed in the stories
and poems but also were part of the real world surrounding
the Milne home at Cotchford Farm. With deftness and
artistry, Milne has drawn a memorable portrait of his father
and an evocative reconstruction of a happy childhood in
London and Sussex. It is a story told with humour and
modesty.

DEAR ME

Peter Ustinov

'Dear me!' says Peter Ustinov as he traces the history of his ancestry, a mad tale of revolutions, dangerous border crossings, suitcases stuffed with money, and wild coincidences; recalls his ambivalent relations with his father, a journalist and spy; relives the vicissitudes of his career in the theatre; and, indeed, recreates all the ups and downs of a life story so rich in droll and colorful anecdotes that even Ustinov could not have invented it. Primarily known as an actor, having made his debut as a pig in a school play, he has in his fifty-odd years also been a film and opera director, playwright, novelist, producer, and short-story writer, as well as one of the world's most brilliant conversationalists. This last talent is shown to perfection in these scintillating memoirs, which, incidentally, include delightfully witty verbal portraits of Laurence Olivier, Edith Evans, John Gielgud, Ralph Richardson, Charles Laughton, and David Niven, among many others. Said William Cole in the *Saturday Review:* 'The trick has always been to write as easily as you talk. Peter Ustinov does just that, and he's the grandest monopolistic talker I've ever stood in a circle around, spellbound. Now here's his autobiography, *Dear Me,* and it's one of those books you hate to get up from and can't wait to get back to.'